THE INSIDERS' GUIDE® TO

THE POCONO MOUNTAINS

THE INSIDERS'[1]® GUIDE TO

THE POCONO MOUNTAINS

by
Brian Hineline
&
Leona Adamo Maxwell

The Insiders' Guides Inc.

Co-published and marketed by:
Pocono Record
511 Lenox St.
Stroudsburg, PA 18360
(717)421-3000

Co-published and distributed by:
The Insiders' Guides Inc.
The Waterfront • Suite 12
P.O. Box 2057
Manteo, NC 27954
(919) 473-6100

•

FIRST EDITION
1st printing

•

Copyright ©1996
by Pocono Record

•

Printed in the United States
of America

•

Publications from The Insiders' Guides®
series are available at special
discounts for bulk purchases for sales
promotions, premiums or fundraisings.
Special editions, including personalized
covers, can be created in large
quantities for special needs. For more
information, please write to The
Insiders' Guides Inc., P.O. Box 2057,
Manteo, NC 27954 or call
(919) 473-6100 x 233.

ISBN 0-57380-013-9

Pocono Record

President & Publisher
Carolynn Allen-Evans

New Media Ventures Manager
Jinx M. Perszyk

Sales Executives
Peg Cowden

Graphic Artist
Roger Ort

The Insiders' Guides Inc.

Publisher/Editor-in-Chief
Beth P. Storie

President/General Manager
Michael McOwen

Affiliate Sales and Training Director
Rosanne Cheeseman

Partner Services Director
Giles MacMillan

Sales and Marketing Director
Julie Ross

Creative Services Director
Mike Lay

Online Services Director
David Haynes

Managing Editor
Theresa Shea Chavez

Fulfillment Director
Gina Twiford

Project Editor
Dan DeGregory

Project Artist
Stephanie Myers

Pocono Record
"Your Good Morning Newspaper"

511 Lenox Street
Stroudsburg, PA 18360
Telephone (717) 421-3000
Fax (717) 424-2056

CAROLYNN ALLEN-EVANS
Publisher

Allow me to extend a warm welcome to you from a very special place, the Poconos and beautiful Northeastern Pennsylvania.

We who live in this wonderful part of the country carry about us a considerable pride, a pride which we are always pleased to share with others who visit with us or who plan to join us as permanent residents.

You are reading the first edition of a fact-filled guidebook, written by local writers who have brought a distinct insiders look at what we have to offer. We believe this to be the most complete, informative and interesting guide to this area. We're confident you'll enjoy perusing its pages.

A unique feature of this book is that it contains informative advertising from some of the finest businesses the Poconos have to offer.

The Insiders' Guide® to the Pocono Mountains has been in preparation stages for over one year. It has been a monumental undertaking. The Pocono Record, the region's daily newspaper, is pleased to bring this book to you, working in partnership with Insiders' Guides Inc.

Enjoy!

Carolynn Allen Evans

Preface

Welcome to the Poconos and Northeastern Pennsylvania! We have so much to share with you about what and who make up this beautiful region in this first edition of *The Insiders Guide® to the Pocono Mountains*.

We know you probably have some notion of what you'll find here. Honeymooners and couples are sure they'll find romantic hideaways with heart-shape tubs and Jacuzzis — and they will; skiers know they'll find snow all winter long because of area ski resorts' snowmaking capabilities — and they will. But, for those of you who have only heard a little about those opportunities and might have other interests, we have much more to show you!

First, let's clarify where you'll find the Poconos. A garage mechanic confided that people are always stopping at his station in Stroudsburg to ask "How do I get to the Poconos? Where are they?" Well, the Poconos are all around you as soon as you cross the Delaware River from New Jersey to Pennsylvania, whether at Stroudsburg, Portland or Milford. If you're coming from the south, the Poconos are all around you as soon as you get off Pa. Highway 33 in Saylorsburg or the Northeast Extension of the Pennsylvania Turnpike in Lehighton or Blakeslee. If you're coming from the west, you're in the Poconos as soon as you reach Blakeslee on Interstate 80. And if you're coming from the north on Interstate 84, once you cross the Delaware River from Port Jervis, New York, to Matamoras, Pennsylvania, you're in the Poconos. You'll know you're here when you look in any direction and see rolling mountains and reaching peaks; you'll be going up and down hills on curvy roads whatever direction you travel; and you'll sense a calming influence as you drive past the streams, ponds, lakes and rivers that criss-cross the beautiful landscape.

In this country place, there's a great deal more to do than ski and luxuriate in private tubs for two. If you love the outdoors, check out our chapters on Parks; Recreation; In, On and Around the Water; Fishing and Hunting; Golf; Our Natural World; and Winter Sports. We have horseback riding, swimming, whitewater rafting, canoeing, snowboarding, ice skating, fishing and virtually any other conceivable outdoor activity you can imagine — and some you probably haven't imagined. Golfers can play here at a different course every day for a week and still not play them all. Anglers can fish for weeks and never tap all of the hidden hotspots. If you like to camp, the national and state parks provide tremendous opportunities, as do all the private campgrounds here.

If you are artistically inclined, our Arts and Culture and Annual Events chapters highlight art galleries, music festivals, craft festivals, stage performances, concerts and more for your artistic pleasure.

If you like to shop, you'll find our Shopping chapter full of great places to spend some time — and money. We have outlets, antiques shops, craft stores, collectibles shops, Christmas shops, even a special teddy bear shop! Many festivals noted in the Annual Events and Festivals chapter offer some shopping opportunities in the way of crafts and arts — not to mention fun-filled activities. And Poconos wineries are great places to try and buy new wines for your collection.

If you are a history buff, you will find that this area of our nation is full of remnants and recollections from days gone by. In our Arts and Culture, History, Attractions and Native Americans chapters, you will find many places to satisfy your penchant for the past. Annual events and festivals sometimes are tied into historical themes as are daytrips and attractions, so check out those chapters too.

If you have the kids, we have lots for you to consider. The chapters on Kidstuff, Childcare, Camps and Education are great resources to help young people discover the Poconos.

Wondering what we eat here? Great food! Our Restaurants and Nightlife chapters present a fine selection of places where you can discover just how good eating in the Poconos can be. Our Shopping chapter also points out some fun, quick eateries where you can stop while you shop.

If an evening's entertainment is what you seek, we have that too. The Nightlife chapter lists many fun places to spend your late-night hours. Arts and Culture also offers nighttime entertainment opportunities in the way of plays, performances and art exhibits.

We know that once you visit us, you probably will want to move here; so, we've included the Real Estate chapter to help you find your dream home in the Poconos. If you want to retire here, our Retirement chapter will be a great source of information.

Don't worry if you get sick while you're here. Our Healthcare chapter will point you in the right direction for your medical needs.

And speaking of direction, didn't we start off by telling you the most asked question — Where are the Poconos? Well, our Getting Around chapter tells you how to navigate the country roads and get to all the wonderful places we have written about. We aren't a city; we are the country; and the way to get around is on the backroads. Let loose and enjoy discovering that all these routes intermingle; you can completely circle the Poconos by traveling only the country roads — an exciting prospect if you have some time.

History indicates the first settlers who came here knew this was the place they wanted to stay — where the mountains meet the rivers; the valleys spread out amid lakes, ponds and steams; the fields present a constantly beautiful array of wildflowers; and all roads lead somewhere beautiful.

Welcome! We're glad you've come.

FYI

Unless otherwise noted, the area code for all phone numbers in this guide is 717.

About the Authors

Brian Hineline, a lifelong resident of Northeastern Pennsylvania, has visited much of the United States, only to return to this region's unique combination of scenic beauty, diverse cultural opportunities and proximity to big-city excitement.

After high school, Brian attended East Stroudsburg University, arriving as an undeclared major striving to avoid full-time employment. Through the encouragement of several professors, he became an English and speech communication major and graduated with a degree in both in 1990.

While attending ESU, Brian edited the student newspaper, *Stroud Courier*, and wrote articles for *The Easton Express*, now *The Express-Times*.

Quickly realizing he did not want a career of covering school board debates and cat ordinance disputes, Brian abandoned newspapers and began editing *Pocono World Magazine*, a glossy regional publication that was as ambitious as it was short-lived.

Brian still saw a need for a general-interest magazine devoted to Northeastern Pennsylvania and founded *Mountainsides* in 1992. It was well-received, if not overly profitable. Publication continued until financial pressures forced Brian to accept a job editing *Country Wagon Journal* in New Jersey.

A desire to end a lengthy daily commute brought Brian back to Northeastern Pennsylvania to handle production responsibilities for *The Pike County Courier*, the Milford-based newspaper where he still works.

Throughout this time, he has published hundreds of articles and photographs; co-authored a video documenting the history of Monroe County, Pennsylvania; received a few literary awards; and volunteered as a public relations assistant for the United States Equestrian Team.

Although much of Brian's writing is region-themed, he also specializes in music and concert reviews and celebrity interviews. He has photographed or reviewed more than 100 concerts and interviewed both rising stars and living legends.

Brian's hobbies include collecting vending machines and regional memorabilia and participating in sports in which the advantage goes to tall guys with long arms.

Leona Adamo Maxwell moved to the Poconos in 1986 with her husband, teenage daughter and two toddler sons. Their objective was to find the good life in the country. Having lived here for 10 years, she believes they found it. The air, the views and the mix of country and town provide her family with a great place to live and grow and her with the perfect spot to pursue her freelance writing and editing career. To Leona, the Poconos is country enough for quiet concentration and personal growth opportunities and town enough for daily visits from overnight express companies bringing work from around the United States.

A favorite Poconos bonus is the opportunity to work outside on her deck in beautiful weather while her children play in the yard below. Another is the peaceful beauty that surrounds her as she drives to assignments in her job as freelance editor for the *Pocono Record* publication *Dignity* — a monthly magazine for seniors who are "fifty-plus and anything but retiring." Coming to the Poconos also gave her the opportunity to begin her career at Northampton Community College as an adjunct professor of English, to devote time to her own writing (she has completed her first novel, *Strange Gods*, and is looking for a publisher), and to eventually give up a two-hour commute to New Jersey where she was an editorial consultant to AT&T for 10 years, managing projects in all areas of documentation.

The Poconos is also town enough. Her town's location ensures Leona overnight access to the rest of the nation as she edits books for several major college textbook companies, including Prentice-Hall, Allyn and Bacon, Macmillan and Simon & Schuster. And it's town enough to provide the artistic, intellectual and educational environment that nurtures writers and other artists.

Leona really dislikes biographical sketches because she feels they tend to make authors sound stodgy, and Leona is not stodgy — a truth to which her husband, children, students and friends will testify. She'd rather people knew that she loves discussing literature and theology and their place in the development of our sense of self; or, that she adores meeting all the wonderful 50-plus people she interviews for *Dignity*. She'd also like them to know that she finds teaching incredibly stimulating because there are so many people with whom to exchange ideas and so much joy in watching students grow and discover their potential; she finds editing textbooks exhilarating — the constant interaction with authors who are writing tomorrow's information today is a daily learning high. And what she really wants readers to know is that she is so thankful her husband, Jim, convinced her to leave New Jersey and come to the Poconos; that it is a joy to talk to him every night over after-dinner coffee; that her daughter Jessica is a truly delightful, intelligent woman; and that her two sons — Miles and Joshua — make her laugh all the time and are part of the sunshine in the Poconos!

Acknowledgments

Brian . . .

Growing up in the Poconos, I always thought someone should write a book about all there is to see and do here. Now, I think I know why no one ever did. It's a lot of work. Trying to include every unique, entertaining and enlightening aspect of our sprawling, largely rural region is a pretty overwhelming task. However, I believe we did a fine job.

Of course, all of this information could not be compiled without all kinds of help. I want to thank everyone who answered a few questions, offered suggestions or mailed some much-needed data. Trying to name every public relations person, government employee, business owner and longtime resident whose thoughts are included would be impossible. I hope my sincere appreciation and this book are thanks enough.

I must especially thank my single-greatest source of research on this project — Kristine Petersen at the Pocono Mountains Vacation Bureau. Try as I did, I was unable to make an information request she was unable to fulfill. Her timely attention to my numerous pleas for insight was instrumental in the completion of this book.

The hospitality I encountered throughout my writing is best symbolized by the members of the Country Inns of the Poconos. They went beyond familiarizing me with their businesses; they made me a welcome guest and showed off their properties with deserved pride. Do yourself a favor and visit one, or more, while in the Poconos.

I think everyone involved in the creation of this book would agree that it was more work than we ever expected. The *Pocono Record's* Jinx Perszyk, our project leader, did a wonderful job of juggling all of the business of publishing a book. Her infectious enthusiasm provided necessary reassurance that all this effort would be worthwhile. Peg Cowden zealously faced the daunting task of selling ads for a new publication. The timely updates of their activities made the writing much easier. Dan DeGregory, our editor, provided valuable comments that made sure we did not overlook questions we should have been asking. He made the book more user-friendly and reminded us not to assume our readers had prior knowledge of the region. Without his insight, support and reassurance, this book would not have been written.

Working with Leona Maxwell was a pleasure. I still do not know how she juggled all of her other responsibilities to find time to do such a good job. Her combination of humor and professionalism made our meetings fun. Whenever I needed to complain to someone about having to travel all day and write all night, she was there.

The following is a random list of people, places and things that in some way helped me and that I want to thank: my friends for their encouragement and ideas; Saturn for getting me there; Teddy's for the diversion; New York City for being so close yet far enough away; singers Jim Roberti and Diane Paquee for the Tuesday nights and Wednesday nights respectively; Skip for her countless hours of help; Video USA for the patience; *The Pike County Courier* for the flexibility; Danielle for smiling at all the right times; Alexander for his promising future; Vic Chestnutt for writing thoughtful songs; Big Head Todd & the Monsters for the music; WZZO for playing Billy Squier; and all the magazines and books that I read either to get ideas or to get away from the Poconos for awhile.

Most importantly, I want to dedicate this effort to the folks who made it possible — my parents, Howard and Loretta Hineline, and Vala Wiesenberg. Without them I would not be writing and probably would not have lived my entire life in the Poconos. They taught me not to take beauty for granted, even when it surrounds you every day.

Leona . . .

When you undertake a project of this size, you know you'll need to ask for help. Luckily, many people are willing to give it. In this section, I would like to thank some of those fine folks in this region and in my family that have helped me provide you with the best and the brightest in the Poconos.

You ask a lot of questions, and many people give you answers; some go way beyond giving answers and provide a great deal of help. To the following people I'd like to say "Thanks": Janet Mishkin, director of the Monroe County Historical Association; Susan Stillo-Wilkins, music teacher, FADS founder and friend; Karen Clarkson, home-school mother and friend; Julia Saeger, friend and childcare provider; Laura Goss, Monroe County Arts Council director; Debbie Kobelski, Promised Land Park Service contact; Kristine Petersen, Poconos Mountains Vacation Bureau resource; Rev. William Cohea, director of Columcille; Don Wild Eagle, Grey Bear and Pat Running Bear, Natives of the Western World and now friends; Laura Thomas and Barbara Loeffler from the Laurel Arts Festival and Mauch Chunk Historical Society; Patty Fretz, Monroe County Area Agency on Aging supervisor; Tina Sebring, fellow funnel-cake maker; Mrs. Hineline, my co-writer Brian's mother who was a wonderful support; all those delightful folks who gave snacks to my kids and spent time with them when we visited their establishments, including Nanda and Ron from the Sheradin House, Dale, Mark and MaryAnn from the Tobias House and Mrs. Von Dran from Bischwinds; and all the rest of you, thanks.

You also need support within your organization when you undertake a task like this one. Thankfully, it was there. Jinx Perszyk, our project leader, has been the glue and the inspiration that held us together. Every Monday morning she cheered us on to greater and greater heights and helped find a way through the forest, without losing sight of the trees. Our sales team, Peg Cowden was tremendous help in getting us up-to-the-minute information on what was going on in the sales field. Our editor Dan DeGregory was what every writer hopes her editor will be: supporting, guiding, helping and focusing. Only if you have been an editor can you realize the tremendous amount of work he had to do in helping us through our first edition of this book. And of course, my co-writer Brian Hineline was a Godsend. He knows everybody and everything. He always had a piece of information that brought sunshine through the clouds that sometimes appeared on my writing horizon. His calm way and gentle help were truly supportive while doing this book. Thanks to the team — all of you.

And of, course, you know who needs to be thanked the most. Those who lived in the house with me while I ran hither and yon, researching new places, revisiting old places and meeting deadlines: my husband, Jim; my daughter Jessica; and my two travel-weary sons, Miles and Joshua. Jim, thanks for cooking, cleaning, babysitting, managing and helping with the millions of things that needed to be done that I couldn't do. Jess, Miles and Josh, thanks for sitting, waiting, watching, driving, listening and taking notes as we drove along these country roads. Thanks is a small word, but it's what I mean. Thanks.

How To Use This Book

This book is designed to be your owner's manual to the Poconos. Whether your time in our region is measured in days or years, you will find all you need to know to visit or reside in one of the most desirable areas in the northeastern United States.

Do not feel daunted by the hundreds of pages. This is a guide not a novel. You do not need to read it cover to cover in one sitting. Our book is intended to be used every day — strap it to your bike, throw it in the back of the car, read it in your hotel room, put it in your backpack, take it in your canoe. Use it and abuse it as you see fit.

Each chapter exists independently. Need a good Japanese restaurant? Just fly past the History and Accommodations chapters, and you can find one in the Restaurants chapter. Want to know how Pike County got its name (it has nothing to do with fish)? Turn back to the History chapter. We hope you will start by reading a chapter that suits your initial interest, and then turn to other parts of the book as time permits. Even if you are not specifically interested in real estate, we bet you will still find some useful or surprising knowledge. The content is designed to inform those unfamiliar with the Poconos and supplement the knowledge of long-time residents.

Newcomers to the Poconos might want to begin with the History, Overview or Real Estate chapters to familiarize themselves with the towns and lifestyles of the different parts of the region.

You will notice that many businesses appear more than once. For example, a resort with a terrific golf course will be discussed in both the Accommodations and Golf chapters.

We have decided to arrange each chapter's content by seven geographic regions: Delaware Water Gap, Stroudsburg/East Stroudsburg, Mount Pocono Area, West End, Milford Area, Lake Wallenpaupack Area and Slate Belt. We thought these would be more easily located than county designations. So, if you are looking for things to see or do in your specific part of the Poconos, simply turn to the relevant chapter and visit the corresponding geographic subsection.

While we have spent many months of driving, talking and reading to create our interpretation of everything you need to know about the Poconos, we might have overlooked or omitted some worthwhile spot you discover. If you know something you believe should be included in future editions of this book, please write to us at the subsequent address. This region continues to grow rapidly; keeping up with all the changes is tough. Even Insiders do not know everything. One of us, a lifelong resident of the Poconos, will admit that several research missions were extended by getting lost on the backroads in search of some mythical shortcut. If you have a compliment, criticism or complaint regarding our book, please write:

Insiders' Guides Inc.
P.O. Box 2057
Manteo, North Carolina 27954

The Poconos Region

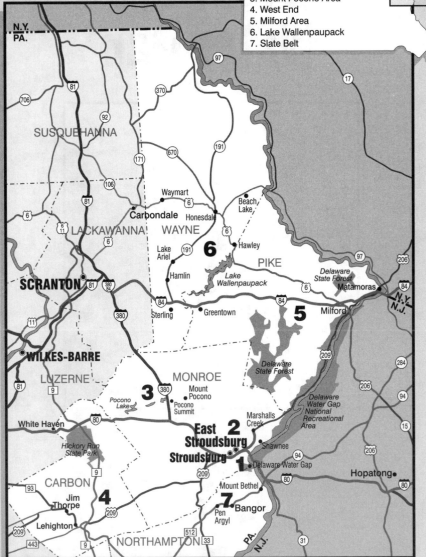

N.Y.
PA.

SUSQUEHANNA

Waymart

Carbondale Honesdale

Beach Lake

LACKAWANNA WAYNE

Lake Ariel

Hawley

SCRANTON PIKE

Hamlin

Lake Wallenpaupack

Delaware State Forest

Matamoras

N.Y. N.J.

WILKES-BARRE

Sterling Greentown

Milford

LUZERNE

MONROE

Delaware State Forest

White Haven

Pocono Lake

Mount Pocono

Pocono Summit

Marshalls Creek

Delaware Water Gap National Recreational Area

Hickory Run State Park

East Stroudsburg

Stroudsburg

Shawnee

Delaware Water Gap

Hopatong

CARBON

Jim Thorpe

Mount Bethel

Lehighton

Pen Argyl

Bangor

NORTHAMPTON

PA.
N.J.

Delaware
Water Gap

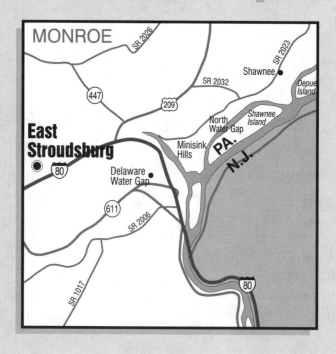

Stroudsburg
East Stroudsburg

Mount Pocono Area

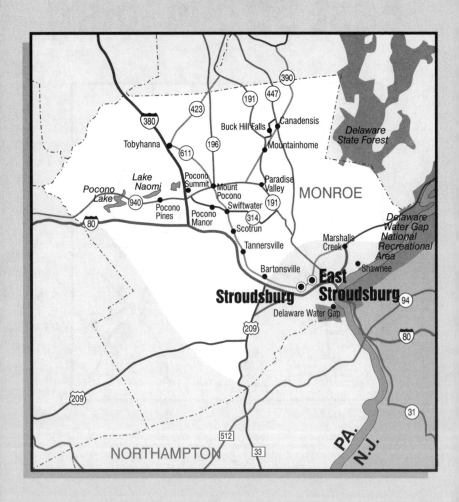

Delaware State Forest

390

191 447

423

380

Buck Hill Falls · Canadensis

Tobyhanna

611

196

Mountainhome

Lake Naomi

Pocono Summit

Paradise Valley

MONROE

Pocono Lake

940

Pocono Pines

Mount Pocono

Swiftwater

191

Delaware Water Gap National Recreational Area

80

Pocono Manor

314

Scotrun

Tannersville

Marshalls Creek

Bartonsville

East Stroudsburg

Shawnee

Stroudsburg

94

Delaware Water Gap

209

80

209

31

512

33

NORTHAMPTON

PA.

N.J.

West End

Milford
Area

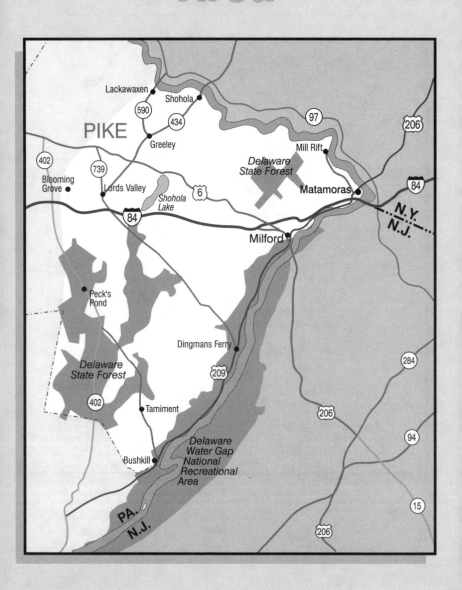

Lake Wallenpaupack
Area

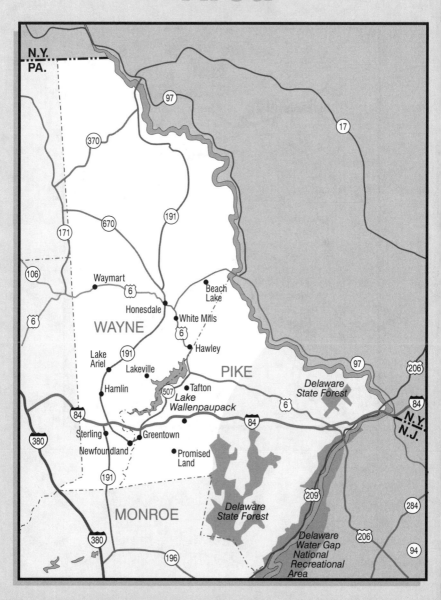

Slate Belt

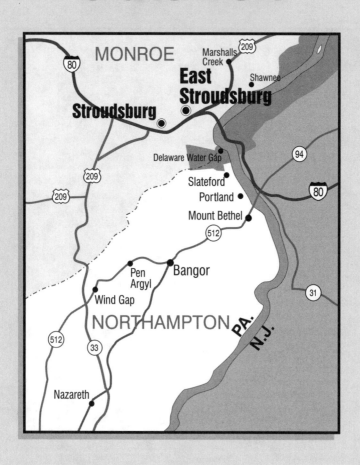

Table of Contents

Directory of Maps

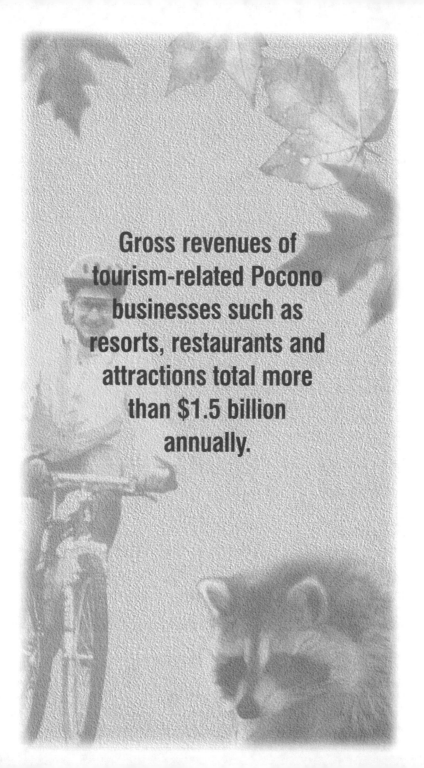

Gross revenues of
tourism-related Pocono
businesses such as
resorts, restaurants and
attractions total more
than $1.5 billion
annually.

Overview

Writing *The Insiders' Guide®* to the *Pocono Mountains* creates a number of challenges. First of all, the Pocono Mountains are a vaguely defined land mass. No two residents will give the exact same answer when asked where the region begins and ends.

For our purposes, we have covered all the area typically regarded as the Poconos and surrounding communities. For easy recognition, each chapter is divided geographically into subregions and identified by towns rather than counties.

To the north, the Pocono Mountains region ends around Honesdale in Wayne County. From there it continues eastward through all of Pike County (the "Milford Area" subsection throughout this book) to the Delaware River, the eastern border for the state of Pennsylvania. Continuing south, we enter Monroe County, the heart of the Pocono Mountain area. Delaware Water Gap, Stroudsburg/East Stroudsburg, the Mount Pocono area and a small portion of the West End (also geographic subsections) are in Monroe County. South of Monroe County, in Northampton County, is the Slate Belt (Bangor, Pen Argyl, Roseto, Wind Gap, etc.), and to the west of Monroe are Jim Thorpe and surrounding communities in Carbon County (part of the West End subsection).

This represents a total of more than 2,500 square miles — twice the size of the state of Rhode Island.

However, you won't find any metropolitan areas per se. Stroudsburg and East Stroudsburg are cities, albeit more like towns compared to New York City to the east, Philadelphia to the south and even Scranton to the north. The Poconos region is sprawling and largely rural. Many back roads were navigated to find that great restaurant "nestled in the woods in the heart of the Poconos" (read: in the middle of nowhere). East Stroudsburg has the largest population: approximately 9,800.

Other towns and their number of permanent residents include: Stroudsburg, 6,100; Honesdale, 5,000; Jim Thorpe, 5,000; Lehighton, 5,900; Mount Pocono, 2,000; Wind Gap, 2,700; Hawley, 1,200; Delaware Water Gap, 775; and Milford, 1,300.

Even though the Poconos have no metropolises to call their own, many are a short drive away. Approximate distances to some from the mythical "heart of the Poconos," a vaguely defined spot generally regarded to be in the Stroudsburg are: New York City, 75 miles; Philadelphia, 85 miles; Scranton, 41 miles; Allentown, 45 miles; Harrisburg, 125 miles; Hartford, 175 miles; and Baltimore, 180 miles.

Proximity to major population centers combined with the natural beauty here are responsible for our No. 1 industry — tourism. The Poconos are the leading tourist destination in the state of Pennsylvania. Gross revenues of related Pocono businesses, such as resorts, restaurants and attractions, total more than $1.5 billion annually. More than 18,000 people are employed by tourism-based businesses. And roughly 80 percent of the resorts in the entire state are here.

The organization responsible for promoting the area's merits as a tourist destination is the Pocono Mountains Vacation Bureau (see the "Visitor Resources" section at chapter's end for a list of vacation bureau locations and phone numbers). It receives more than $1.4 million annually in matching funds (the largest single amount awarded in Pennsylvania) from the state's $12.5 million budget. The bureau is a valuable resource for vacation planning. It operates 10 visitors centers and a toll-free information line. Staff members provide brochures, answer questions and assist with reservations. Call (800) 762-6667 to request literature, which you'll receive by mail.

Throughout the 20th century, the Poconos area has depended on vacationers for its survival. Prior to that, mining, lumbering, ice harvesting, farming and tanning were the main money-makers. However, progress (darn that modern refrigeration anyhow) doomed many of these ventures. Today, a number of factories producing such varied goods as brushes, medicines, huge blenders, cosmetics, hardware and clothing are scattered throughout the Poconos, as are industrial parks, such as the eight-company Pocono Mountains Industrial Park near the intersection of interstates 80 and 380. Compared with the dollars generated by tourists, however, their impact is relatively minor.

The lack of commercial growth can be explained by the lack of available property, particularly in Pike County. Most commercial zones flank major highways. The main thoroughfare in Pike County, U.S. Highway 209, is largely controlled by the National Park Service as part of the Delaware Water Gap National Recreation Area, thus eliminating its commercial potential.

Until the mid-1990s, there were no fast-food restaurants and only one large supermarket in Pike County. Today, they abound, including five along U.S. 209 from Milford to Matamoras, outside the recreation area.

Although industrial growth is limited, residential growth has been phenomenal. Pike and Monroe counties have ranked first and second in Pennsylvania in population growth throughout the 1980s and '90s. Monroe County's population increased 124 percent, from 42,727 to 95,709, from 1970 to 1990, compared to a 147 percent increase between 1870 and 1970. Pike County's growth rate during the last two decades was 135 percent, increasing from 11,745 to 27,600 residents.

These numbers are impressive, but they are compounded when the number of second-home owners are included. In 1990, the Pike County Planning Commission reported that 60 percent of the homes in the county were second homes. In the southern part of the county, closer to Interstate 80, the numbers jumped to approximately 80 percent. The 1990 Pike County population of 27,600 would inflate to nearly 80,000 if seasonal residents were included. The same year, roughly 50 percent of all seasonal residents who responded to a 1990 Pike County Planning Commission survey stated they planned to sell their primary homes in order to live here. Pike County's permanent population has increased dramatically in the 1990s, as many of these second-home owners have chosen to retire or raise their families here and became full-time residents.

The entire Pocono Mountains region is faced with the problem of handling two distinct population groups with different concerns. The general profile is as follows: Second-home owners usually are more affluent than regional primary-home owners. They care more about the environment than the job opportunities, according to the 1990 Pike County second-home owners' survey. The respondents were asked to prioritize their concerns, and commercial growth received 2.4 percent of the votes as most important, job opportunities were cited by 6 percent of respondents and environmental protection received 29 percent of the tally.

In Pike County, 60 percent of second-home owners make more than $50,000 per year compared to roughly 17 percent of the year-round residents, the majority of whom earn less than $30,000. Affordable housing for families with lower incomes has become a problem. A 1988 state-wide report ranked Pike County's average housing cost of $105,027 as fifth-highest out of 67 counties, right behind four counties surrounding Philadelphia — Chester, Bucks, Delaware and Montgomery.

The popularity of the Poconos as a second-home spot created the demand for planned residential developments. One of the oldest and largest is Hemlock Farms in Pike County, which began in 1963. These communities provide the amenities that people coming from suburbs of major metropolitan areas expect, such as swimming pools, clubhouses and, often, private security forces .

Along with second-home owners, other Pocono residents who earn their livings elsewhere are commuters. Monroe County is the preferred commuter residence, due to the ease of access to major highways such as interstates 80, 81, 84 and 380. Many people drive one to two hours each way to work in New Jersey or New York City. They reap the dual benefits of higher-paying jobs available in those areas and the scenery, safety and lifestyle here.

THE POCONO MOUNTAINS

Get Away To It All.

For all the ways to obtain a FREE Poconos Vacation Guide,
brochures and information see reverse side.

Pennsylvania
Memories last a lifetime.™

Pocono Mountains Vacation Bureau, Inc.
1004 Main Street, Box 55I, Stroudsburg, PA 18360

Planning a visit to the Pocono Mountains?

The Pocono Mountains Vacation Bureau, Inc., the official Pennsylvania convention and visitors bureau for the area, can provide all the information you need for a fabulous trip.

CALL US:

1-800-POCONOS* and
*(1-800-762-6667) — Free Brochures and Lodging Information

(717) 421-5565 — Fall Foliage/Ski Conditions (in season)

(717) 424-6050 — Immediate Information

(717) 722-9199 — Group Information

FAX US:
(717) 476-8959

VISIT OUR WEB SITE:
http://www.poconos.org

E-MAIL US:
pocomts@poconos.org

WRITE US:
Pocono Mountains Vacation Bureau, Inc.
1004 Main Street, Box 551, Stroudsburg, PA 18360

Photo: Pocono Mountains Vacation Bureau, Inc.

Sailing is popular on Pocono Lakes.

Other parts of the Poconos have significant commuter populations. Some Slate Belt, West End and Carbon County residents work in the Lehigh Valley near Allentown, Bethlehem or Easton. Northern Carbon County, near the Monroe County border, is also a prime second-home area. A few people living in rural northern Wayne County are known to drive to work in New York State and even Connecticut. However, most commuters from Wayne work in the Scranton/Wilkes-Barre area.

Ironically, in the 19th century, people came to the Poconos for work rather than scenery. The region probably would not be the vacation magnet it is today if not for the strength of its early industries.

Most of the original trees were cleared for farms that produced goods for outside markets. Lumber companies floated trees down the Delaware River to build ships in Philadelphia. Canadensis, near Mount Pocono, got its name from the giant hemlocks (*Tsuga canadensis*) prized by the lumber and tanning industries. Tanneries used tannic acid from the bark of the trees to process animal hides into leather. In winter, many farmers earned money harvesting ice (sold as far away as New York City) on the large lakes in the Poconos, many of which were built by the ice industry. Bluestone from the Shohola area of Pike County was used to construct buildings in Manhattan. Coal traveled by canal boat, and later by rail, through the region to surrounding cities. The train tracks constructed for these operations later were used to transport vacationers. Inns built to accommodate men rafting lumber on the river became some of the first resort hotels. Farmers took in summer boarders to supplement their incomes at what could be called early bed and breakfast inns.

This transition to tourism was encouraged by the decline of the original industries. Ice harvesting, lumbering, milling and mining were no longer needed by the modernizing cities. Instead, we were asked to give the city folks something they did not have — natural beauty. Fortunately, the infrastructure created for the obsolete industries provided a means for getting the vacationers here and giving them places to stay and things to do.

The history of the Poconos is more thoroughly covered in our History chapter. The following community overviews are designed to give you an idea of what to expect today in each area of the Poconos.

Delaware Water Gap

Originally, Delaware Water Gap was the vacation destination of choice in the Poconos because trains went there directly and the scenery was magnificent. The town's proximity to New York City and Philadelphia made it one of the leading vacation spots in the country during the early 20th century.

However, Delaware Water Gap has made a transformation unique in the Poconos. It has gone from major tourist attraction to quiet community. First, expanded rail service, then the invention of the automobile and the related road system made other areas of the Pocono Mountains accessible to vacationers. People on their way to resorts and attractions in more commercialized areas such as Stroudsburg/East Stroudsburg and Mount Pocono now just pass through the famed natural wonder that gave Delaware Water Gap its name. In 1994, according to the Delaware Water Gap Joint Toll Bridge Commission, 15,080,939 vehicles used Interstate 80 through the Delaware Water Gap.

The town's old wooden hotels have burned down or were converted to other uses. The magnificent train station has been abandoned. Ironically, it is falling apart underneath a toll bridge for the interstate that made it obsolete.

Delaware Water Gap is known today as a haven for artists, who draw inspiration from the scenery, the Victorian architecture, the small-town community spirit and the rich history. Commuters also look for property near the town because of the easy access to I-80. Fewer than 1,000 people live here.

The Main Street business district is dominated by craft shops and boutiques. Local artists display their works at the Antoine Dutot Schoolhouse gallery. Internationally recognized jazz musicians live in the area and perform at Deerhead Inn. Artists, performers and chefs come together each year in early September for the Delaware Water Gap Celebration of the Arts, held on Main Street across from Deerhead Inn (see our Annual Events chapter for more information).

Nature lovers sometimes visit the town while hiking the Appalachian Trail or spending a day in the Delaware Water Gap National Recreation Area. Currently the 11th most-visited park in the National Park System, the recreation area hosted a record total of 4,833,659 people in 1994.

Tourism in this region moved up the Delaware River to Shawnee-on-Delaware. Shawnee Inn has expanded its ski and golf resort to include Shawnee Place (a children's play area), timesharing units and vacation rental townhouses.

Stroudsburg/ East Stroudsburg

The seat of Monroe County, Stroudsburg was settled in 1730, when a log house was built at what is now the intersection of Ninth and Main streets. The first home in East Stroudsburg was built in 1737 on property now occupied by Pocono Medical Center.

Stroudsburg and East Stroudsburg are two of the larger towns in the Poconos. The estimated 1994 population totals are 9,801 for East Stroudsburg and 6,113 for Stroudsburg.

In addition to Pocono Medical Center (see our Healthcare chapter), East Stroudsburg is also home to East Stroudsburg University, one of the 14 universities in the Pennsylvania State System of Higher Education. Approximately 4,600 undergraduate and 900 graduate students are enrolled in more than 60 degree programs. (See our Education chapter for information.)

Crystal Street, East Stroudsburg's main

INSIDERS' TIP

There are no Pocono Mountains! Don't let this fact stop you from visiting, but by strict geological definition even the region's highest peak (Big Pocono — 2,131 feet above sea level) does not qualify as a mountain. The Poconos region is actually a large plateau averaging 2,000 feet above sea level. The lowest point is the Delaware River, which is at sea level.

The Poconos is still the honeymoon capital of the East.

business district, is slowly seeing a return of commercial activity following a devastating fire in 1996. The former train station, built in 1856, is now home of a popular local restaurant, The Dansbury Depot. East Stroudsburg was once known as Dansbury, in honor of founder Daniel Brodhead, until the railroad arrived, and the name was changed to better identify that the station also served Stroudsburg.

Main Street in Stroudsburg is an ideal traditional business area — a long, tree-lined street sprinkled with a mix of shops selling essentials such as food and medicine, and boutiques offering fine clothing, handcrafted jewelry and assorted gift items. Near Main Street, on Ann Street, is an extensive complex of outlet stores. If you prefer to shop at malls, Stroud Mall is on Ninth Street. (See our Shopping chapter for more information.)

Mount Pocono Area

Many of the Poconos' largest resorts and employers are in this region northwest of Stroudsburg. Mt. Airy Lodge, Caesars Brookdale on the Lake, Cove Haven, Stricklands and The Summit are just a few of the couples-oriented getaways. In 1963, the fabled heart-shaped bathtub was invented by Morris Wilkins at Cove Haven. Later came the 7-foot Champagne Towers whirlpool baths that took romance to another level. The Poconos have been a leading honeymoon destination for decades, primarily because of the resorts near Mount Pocono.

For those who like their romantic activity a little more subdued, dozens of country inns and bed and breakfasts are in the area. The finest in European elegance is provided at

Skytop Lodge in Skytop. (See our Accommodations chapter for more information.)

Other than resorts, leading employers include Tobyhanna Army Depot (Tobyhanna), Weiler Brush Company, Inc. (Cresco), Connaught Laboratories, Inc. (Swiftwater) and the eight companies with a total of over 500 workers at the Pocono Mountains Industrial Park in Mount Pocono. The Pocono Mountain School District serves approximately 9,000 students and provides many education-related jobs. Another significant employer is Crossings Factory Stores in Tannersville.

Mount Pocono, with a population of 2,010, has fast-food restaurants and shopping malls. Nearby towns such as Mountainhome, Cresco, Canadensis and Paradise Valley have inviting antique and specialty shops. They are all accessible by taking a scenic drive along Pa. Highway 191.

West End

Southwest of Stroudsburg, the view along U.S. Highway 209 has changed dramatically. Housing developments have sprouted on farmlands; small businesses line the road; traffic clogs the stretch near Brodheadsville, particularly on weekends.

Continuing south on U.S. 209, you turn off to Palmerton or arrive in Lehighton and Jim Thorpe, the seat of Carbon County. The first two towns are close-knit communities with few tourist activities. However, Jim Thorpe, with its trendy shops, has made a remarkable transition into a travel destination along the order of New Hope, Pennsylvania.

You will be amazed at the sudden change in scenery as you travel down through a winding valley along the Lehigh River to Jim Thorpe, a miniature European enclave known as the "Switzerland of America." Bus tours arrive regularly in the summer. Scenery lovers, mountain bikers and hikers, white-water rafters, shoppers and railroading buffs all will want to spend time in Jim Thorpe.

Milford Area

Milford, the county seat of Pike County, indirectly owes its name to an early industry. The area was called Wells' Ferry, after a grist-mill owned by the Wells brothers, during the Revolutionary War. But people living below the mill crossed the Delaware River by fording a creek, thus the name Mill-ford or Milford.

Milford's most famous resident was Gifford Pinchot. In 1905 he became the first chief of the Forest Service established by President Theodore Roosevelt. Pinchot was elected governor of Pennsylvania in 1923 and 1931. In 1963 President John F. Kennedy visited Milford to dedicate Grey Towers, Pinchot's estate, as the Pinchot Institute for Conservation Studies. Less than two months later, Kennedy was assassinated. Grey Towers is open to the public for tours of the mansion and surrounding grounds.

Today's Milford is a Victorian town with numerous antique and gift shops. Outdoorsmen enjoy the plentiful state game lands and excellent fishing.

Pike County is the fastest-growing county in Pennsylvania. One-third of the population of the United States lives within a six-hour drive. Four interstates are easily accessible.

Though the location would seem ideal for commercial growth, industry is not a major factor in the Pike County economy. Of a total land area of 350,000 acres, more than 140,000 acres of county land are designated as state forests and game lands. This protects the environment but also limits opportunities for large corporate projects. Leading employers are the state and county government, Delaware Valley and Wallenpaupack school districts, Woodloch Pines and Tamiment resorts, Best Western at Hunt's Landing, Wal-Mart and Kmart. Commuting to jobs in New Jersey and New York City is convenient via Interstate 84 or the Metro-North Commuter Railroad, which stops in nearby Port Jervis, New York.

Lake Wallenpaupack Area

Wayne County's major towns all take their names from the coal mining and canal industries. Honesdale, the county seat, is named in honor of Philip Hone, first president of the Delaware & Hudson Canal Company. With a population of 4,972, it is considered the only urban area in this rural county.

Hawley, population 1,244, was named for Irad Hawley, first president of the Pennsylvania Coal Company. Waymart was derived from that town's former use as a place to stockpile coal and weigh it — a "weigh mart" — before transport to Honesdale. The transport of coal from the mines in Lackawanna County through Wayne County to New York City was responsible for creating the significant towns here.

Of course, the region's economy is no longer based upon coal transportation. The leading employers are Wayne Memorial Hospital, the state government, school districts, Moore Business Forms and Goodquality Sewing in Honesdale and Caesers Cove Haven Resort in Lakeville. More than 700 small farms are operated in Wayne County, mostly in the northern areas.

Perhaps the best-known business is *Highlights for Children* magazine. Founded in Honedale in 1946, this monthly magazine's circulation of more than 3 million is the largest of any national periodical for children. Offices are at 803 Church Street.

Tourism was not a major factor in this area before construction of Lake Wallenpaupack was completed in 1926. Built for hydroelectric power by Pennsylvania Power & Light Company, the lake became a major recreation destination.

As the northern-most part of the Poconos, this region is also the coldest. In winter, the average temperature is 25 degrees with a record low of 27 below zero. Average snowfall is 57 inches, and there is at least 1 inch of snow on the ground on an average of 52 days.

Slate Belt

Often considered part of the Lehigh Valley rather than the Poconos, the Slate Belt shares few characteristics with the rest of the regions in our guide. Tourism is not the dominant source of revenue. Most residents of Bangor, Pen Argyl, Roseto, Wind Gap and other communities are employed by small industries and businesses. Others commute to jobs in the Lehigh Valley.

Only Wind Gap, which is strategically situated at the intersection of Pa. Highway 512 and Pa. Highway 33, has seen significant commercial growth. Strip malls, fast-food restaurants and department stores are plentiful.

While still in operation on a greatly reduced scale, the slate industry is no longer the economic force it once was.

Visitor Resources

Staff at the following Pocono Mountains Vacation Bureau information centers can assist visitors to the region with referrals, reservations and any travel-related questions. Brochures also are available.

Center locations include Delaware Water Gap, Exit 53 off I-80, 476-0167; Marshalls Creek, Exit 52 off I-80 to U.S. 209 N., 223-0266; Tannersville, Exit 45 off I-80 at Pa. 715, 629-1730; White Haven, Pa. 940 and Northeast Extension of the Pa. Turnpike (also Exit 42 off I-80), 443-8429; Hickory Run, I-80 E. between exits 39 and 40, 443-8626; on I-84 E. and W. (both directions) between exits 6 and 7, 857-0747 and 857-0791 respectively; Hawley, U.S. 6, 226-2141; and Crescent Lake, I-80 E. between the I-380 interchange and Exit 44.

By the turn of the century, approximately 500,000 people were visiting the Pocono area annually.

History

Much of the land in what is now the Poconos was acquired from Native Americans in the Walking Purchase of 1737. William Penn signed a treaty with the Minisink Indians to acquire all the land from the Delaware River to as far north as a man could walk in three days. After Penn's death, his sons arranged for the agreement to be completed. Their representative covered 86 miles, ending near where Tannersville is today.

The Minisinks claimed the settlers cheated them by having their man run part of the way, greatly increasing the amount of land they received. In retaliation, several massacres of settlers took place in the 1750s, and Benjamin Franklin ordered a string of forts built along the frontier — in Bushkill, Shawnee, Stroudsburg and Kresgeville

Gen. John Sullivan's expedition against the Iroquois Indians came through the Poconos region in 1779. Brinker's Mill in Sciota was the storehouse and advance post for the troops. On the second day of the march, they camped near Tannersville (named after an early industry, tanning) at Learned's Tavern, the last house on the frontier. Their path roughly followed what is today Pa. Highway 940 and Pa. 611, which are still referred to as Sullivan Trail.

Of the four counties that make up the bulk of the Poconos, Wayne was first to be formed. The county came to be on March 21, 1798, cut from Northampton County. Wayne County was named in honor of Gen. Anthony Wayne.

Honesdale, named for canal operation owner Philip Hone, was established in 1826 as the western terminus for Hone's Delaware & Hudson Canal Company. Coal was brought to Honesdale by gravity railroad from mines in the Lackawanna Valley for transport by canal boat to New York. These boats then traveled 108 miles to the Hudson River. In both 1855 and 1856 more than a million tons of coal passed through Honesdale. Each canal boat could carry approximately 130 tons of coal.

Pike County was established on March 26, 1814, from land in Wayne County. Its name comes from Col. Zebulon Pike, a hero of the War of 1812 who later discovered Pike's Peak. One of the earliest means of crossing the Delaware River was via a ferry built in 1735 near what is now Dingmans Ferry. The privately owned bridge linking New Jersey and Pennsylvania at Dingmans Ferry is at the site of the original connector. People have crossed the river at this point by either bridge or ferry for more than 260 years. At least eight other ferries operated on the Delaware between Delaware Water Gap and Port Jervis, New York. All were replaced by bridges by the early 1900s.

Originally part of Pike and Northampton counties, Monroe County was formed on April 1, 1836, and named for President James Monroe. However, settlers arrived as early as 1727. Nicholas Depuy built a home near Shawnee that year.

Col. Jacob Stroud founded the town of Stroudsburg in 1799. A home he built for his son in 1795 at Ninth and Main streets has been restored and is operated as a museum by the Monroe County Historical Association. East Stroudsburg began as Dansbury (hence the name Dansbury Depot, the former train station turned restaurant) in 1738 when Daniel Brodhead founded the town.

Northampton and Monroe counties contributed the land for Carbon County on March 13, 1843. The name comes from carbon, the basic element of the area's rich anthracite coal deposits. Jim Thorpe was originally two towns, Mauch Chunk and East Mauch Chunk, until the communities merged in 1954 and were renamed in honor of the famed athlete, who is buried there.

Since the Civil War, residents of the Pocono Mountains have been dependent on outside populations as income sources. Most early industries catered to the folks in the surrounding big cities. Then, as tourism became more popular, many of the people in the region made their livings serving those who visited.

Each area of the Poconos region — Delaware Water Gap, the Stroudsburgs, Mount Pocono, the West End and Jim Thorpe, Milford, the Honesdale/Lake Wallenpaupack area and the Slate Belt — is discussed here, with emphasis on events of the past 100 years. Our desire is to show some of the significant and/or unusual moments that influenced the area. The region's Native American presence is related in our Native Americans chapter.

One dramatic natural disaster affected the entire Pocono Mountains region and deserves special mention. In August 1955, a severe flood caused mass destruction. More than 200 people died (80 in Monroe County alone), businesses and homes were destroyed and bridges were washed away.

The foundation for the flood was created when Hurricane Connie brought the Poconos 12 inches of rain on August 13. The storm was greeted as a welcome relief from a summer drought. When more rain began to fall on the night of August 18, few residents were concerned. Weather forecasters predicted only showers, but Hurricane Diane dumped another 13 inches of rain on the already-saturated ground.

The Brodhead Creek rushed over its banks by the morning of August 19. Water rushed through Canadensis and Analomink, where 38 people were killed at Camp Davis. All bridges leading to East Stroudsburg were washed away, cutting off the town and the hospital. Thirty-two people died in homes in the Lincoln Avenue "flats" area now occupied by the Pocono Plaza and Wal-Mart. People were being evacuated from attic windows into rowboats.

The worst flood in the history of the Poconos destroyed 42 highway bridges, 17 railroad bridges, most water mains and telephone lines; electric power was cut. More than 20,000 homes were lost. Only five out of a total of 400 resorts were ruined by the flood. However, the publicity generated by the disaster dropped occupancy rates from 96 percent to 20 percent immediately after the storm. An estimated 8,500 people lost their jobs due to the flood. Damages in Monroe County totaled $28.5 million. Pike County received $5.3 million in damages and Wayne County, $3.3 million. The flood was less devastating in Wayne County because that area had experienced a similar disaster in 1942 and constructed dikes and other flood-prevention measures.

Rebuilding efforts emphasized flood control for the future. Most longtime residents have stories to share about how they lived through this tragedy.

Partly as a result of this flood but also as a source of recreation and hydroelectric power, the controversial Tocks Island Dam project was proposed in 1962. The plan called for constructing a dam on the Delaware River north of Shawnee, Pennsylvania, and creating a large lake stretching to Milford. The government purchased thousands of acres of land on both the Pennsylvania and New Jersey sides of the river from Shawnee-on-Delaware to Milford and forced residents, many of whom were farmers, to relocate. Many people left the region, but those who stayed have bitter attitudes regarding the dam proposal. Once-thriving small towns, such as Bushkill, lost their business districts to the government and have never recovered economically. Resorts, farms and boarding houses were purchased and demolished. The dam never was constructed, and the land eventually became the Delaware Water Gap National Recreation Area in 1965.

Delaware Water Gap

The original hub of Poconos vacations was created by Antoine Dutot who purchased the land for the town around 1793. At this time it was named Dutotsburg.

Mauch Chunk, the original name of the current town of Jim Thorpe, was the Indian phrase for Bear Mountain. Indians believed the humped ridge across the Lehigh River from the town resembled a sleeping bear.

VISIT THE HISTORIC VILLAGE OF DELAWARE WATER GAP

"THE POCONOS START HERE"

Great Entertainment, Memorable Scenery, Activities For All

DINING

American Cookery
717 420-0481

Brownie's
717 424-1154

Deer Head Inn
717 424-2000

Trails End Cafe & Catering Co.
717 421-1928

Water Gap Diner
717 476-0132

Water Gap Country Club
717 476-0300

LODGING

Glenwood Hotel & Resort Motel
717 476-0010

Ramada Inn
717 476-0000

Shady Acres Campground
717 897-6230

Shepard House Bed & Breakfast
717 424-9779

Water Gap Country Club
717 476-0300

CHURCH/MUSIC

Presbyterian Church of the
Mountain – 717 476-0345

SHOPPING

The Christmas Factory
717 421-3607

The Gap Mini Mart
717 476-3180

Village Farmer & Bakery
717 476-0075

ACTIVITIES

Antoine Dutot School & Museum
1 – 5 pm, Saturday & Sunday
Memorial thru Columbus Day

Celebration of the Arts Jazz
Festival – week-end following
Labor Day – 717 424-2210

Pack Shack Outdoor Adventure
717 424-8533 • 800 424-0955

The Studio
717 421-2426

Water Gap Country Club Golf
717 476-0300

Water Gap Driving Range &
Club Repair Center
717 476-0130

Water Gap Trolley Sight Seeing
Tours – 717 476-0010

SERVICES

W.T. Conway Insurance Financial
Services – 717 421-6664

C. Solliday Piano Service
717 420-9588

For Brochure Call Chamber of Commerce
717 420-9588
PA Route 611, Exit 53 off of Interstate 80

Early access to the town was provided by a ferry and a wagon road along the Delaware River.

The first vacationers arrived in 1820 and stayed in the private homes of residents. By 1829, Dutot began constructing a small hotel called the Kittatinny, which opened in 1833. It was expanded and by 1884 could accommodate 275 guests. The Resort Point overlook is on the hotel's site (parts of the old foundation are visible). Visitors who park there today see the same panoramic view of the gap and the river that attracted guests more than 100 years ago. The only major changes are the addition of the highway and toll bridge.

Like its rival farther up the mountain, the similarly sized Water Gap House, the Kittatinny eventually burned — the fate of many original hotels in the Poconos. Owners never considered the dangers of building large wooden structures in areas with poor access to running water.

By the turn of the century, approximately 500,000 people were visiting Delaware Water Gap, Pennsylvania, and the Pocono area annually. There were more than 20 places for them to stay within the borough.

At the heart of the downtown was Hauser's, a large souvenir store; the Central House, today home to the Deer Head Inn's outstanding live jazz concerts; and Castle Inn, which became the headquarters for renowned band leader Fred Waring's publishing enterprises.

The Castle Inn's finest hour occurred August 20, 1912, when John Philip Sousa's band performed for a crowd of 875. The main concert hall of the inn since has burned. A new open-air stage has been erected, which is the site of the town's annual jazz festival. World-famous jazz performers, such as Phil Woods and Urbie Green, live in the village and enjoy playing with other local musicians and students at the early-September show.

President Theodore Roosevelt arrived in Delaware Water Gap August 2, 1910, and stayed at Water Gap House. Many tour guides published at that time regarded the Water Gap as one of the country's 15 scenic marvels.

The Delaware, Lackawanna and Western railroad station was the point of arrival for most tourists. Built in 1853, the station was once the scene of constant activity — hundreds regularly arrived and departed. Today, it sits rotting below the Delaware Water Gap Toll Bridge, a symbolic victim of the popularity of the automobile.

Early recreational activities included burro rides, scenic walks, golf, boating on nearby Lake Lenape, steamer boat rides on the Delaware and swimming in the river. Soon a large wooden pier was installed. Tourists also could take a trolley to Stroudsburg and East Stroudsburg.

Delaware Water Gap's cozy charm remains intact. The town's main street still is bordered by some of the architecturally impressive buildings from its glory days. Folks with healthy imaginations have no trouble picturing the excitement that once filled this now-quiet street.

Stroudsburg/ East Stroudsburg

The county seat of Monroe County, Stroudsburg was founded by Jacob Stroud who laid out the town in 1799. The house he built on Main Street for his son John is known as Stroud Mansion, the headquarters of the Monroe County Historical Association.

One of the earliest hotels was the Stroudsburg House, 700 Main Street, which was built in 1833. A hotel has occupied that corner ever since. After modernizing the facade in 1971, the owners of the former Penn Stroud Hotel reopened as the Penn Stroud Hilton. The hotel became the Best Western Pocono Inn in 1981.

Another early, large Main Street hotel was the Indian Queen. The first automobile to visit the Poconos stopped there August 23, 1899. Mellon Bank has assumed its spot in the business district. A portion of the Indian Queen still stands next door.

Stroudsburg possesses a beautiful traditional main thoroughfare filled with boutiques, eateries, nightclubs, banks and retail stores.

Stagecoach routes were scattered throughout the Poconos in the late 1800s. The fare from Brodheadsville to Stroudsburg was 35 cents in 1889. Gone since 1928, trolleys and streetcars once commuted regularly between Stroudsburg and East Stroudsburg. In 1870 passenger cars were pulled by mules through Stroudsburg. A steam engine was used from 1892 to 1902. After that, electric cars traveled through Stroudsburg, East Stroudsburg and Delaware Water Gap. During the 1920s, Crystal Street in East Stroudsburg was crowded with streetcars, trolleys and automobiles. Trolleys were discontinued in 1928 because the increased automobile traffic made them dangerous, and the tracks were removed by 1930.

Rail travelers arrived in East Stroudsburg at the Delaware, Lackawanna and Western station, built in 1856. This significant structure was restored and opened to the public as The Dansbury Depot Restaurant (see our Restaurants chapter for information).

Train service peaked in 1900 with the arrival of the legendary *Phoebe Snow*, "the finest passenger transportation vehicle in the world," according to service advertising. Its comfortable sleeping cars and lavish dining and lounge cars were well-publicized. D. L. & W. advertising also pictured a woman dressed in white to show how clean anthracite coal burned in the locomotives.

Fronting the station, Crystal Street businesses thrived, and several hotels were successful. One, the Lackawanna Hotel, still operates as a bar and coffee shop with small apartments on the upper floors.

A coal station and turntable for locomotives were located on Stokes Avenue in East Stroudsburg until 1950. As winter sports became popular, a special "ski train" was added on weekends in the 1930s and the stations in East Stroudsburg and Cresco were jammed with tourists carrying skis. The D. L. & W. merged with the Erie Railroad in 1960 and became known as the Erie Lackawanna Railroad. Passenger rail service ended on January 5, 1970, and freight trains ran far less often.

The local railroad with the most colorful history was the Delaware Valley Railroad. It puffed along from the East Stroudsburg station to Bushkill, following roughly the course of the present U.S. Highway 209. Due to the lack of a turntable, the train, known locally as "the Dink," ran backward to Bushkill and forward to East Stroudsburg.

From 1901 to 1938, the DV carried everything from tourists and school children to such staples as coal, ice, grain and produce. Without the DV, many children in rural areas would not have had the opportunity for an education beyond grade school, because no transportation was provided for them to reach the high school in town. The availability of a train helped develop more of the river region for tourists and summer camps. Vacationers could arrive at the station in East Stroudsburg and board the DV to take them to resorts along the river. They no longer were required to stay close to East Stroudsburg and Delaware Water Gap

Ironically, one of the DVR's last missions was hauling concrete to build U.S. 209, the highway that made the Dink obsolete.

Early industries in the Stroudsburgs — breweries, glass factories, silk mills, a cigar factory, a duck farm, a shoe peg factory, tanneries and brick factories — catered to the leisure needs of folks in New York and Philadelphia. A portion of East Stroudsburg was, and is, known as Bricktown because most of its buildings are constructed of bricks made by the Zacharias family still in business at Zacharias Pond near N. Courtland Street. When in operation, the tannery near the train station in East Stroudsburg filled the air with the less-than-pleasant aroma of animal hides floating in huge vats of water.

Of special importance are Pocono Medical Center and East Stroudsburg University; their histories are discussed in our Healthcare and Education chapters, respectively.

Stroudsburg retains much of its elegant past. The houses along Sarah, Thomas and Scott streets are mansions of remarkable architectural diversity displaying styles from Victorian to Gothic. Main Street has not changed drastically during this century. Some of its buildings still contain evidence of the Underground Railroad, which was used to shuttle slaves to the North during the Civil War.

Another historical footnote concerns J. Summerfield Staples. This Stroudsburg resident was chosen by lottery to be President Abraham Lincoln's official representative soldier during the Civil War. Staples is buried in the cemetery on Lower Main Street where a monument explains his noteworthy if not spectacular place in Civil War history. Staples never actually fought.

Mount Pocono Area

More than the Stroudsburgs, the Mount Pocono region became the playground for the rich. As Delaware Water Gap became overcrowded and passenger rail service to Cresco north of Mount Pocono exploded, the mountain area became the new popular spot in the

The Switchback Railroad: America's First Roller Coaster

Josiah White, founder of the Lehigh Coal & Navigation Company, designed and invented many devices for the operation of his canal and mines. As his business prospered during the 1820s, White needed a more efficient system to transport his coal

from the mines in Summit Hill to the Lehigh River and the canal docks at Mauch Chunk, now Jim Thorpe.

White's solution became his most fabled enterprise — the Switchback Railroad. It was the first coal railroad in the United States, and many people consider it to be the first and longest roller coaster ever built.

The 9-mile Gravity Road was completed in April 1827. Ten wagons, each carrying 1.5 tons of coal, traveled down Summit Hill powered entirely by gravity. A brake attached to a cable was the only means of control. Mules pulled the empty cars back up the hill then rode down with the coal in a car of their own. With the mules' help, the trip up Summit Hill took three hours; the gravity-assisted descent lasted 35 minutes.

The Industrial Revolution of the 19th century increased the demand for coal, especially in New York City and Philadelphia, so White looked to increase the productivity of his railroad.

In the 1840s, the old track was expanded to become a continuous 18-mile figure eight, thus allowing empty cars to travel back to the mines while, simultaneously, full ones descended to the canal.

Two inclined planes, at Mount Jefferson and Mount Pisgah, were used to transport the cars up the sides of the mountains. Stationary steam engines at the top of each plane supplied power. Cars were pushed uphill by a "safety car," which was attached to a steam engine by bands of Swedish steel. The rest of the trip, approximately 17 miles, was powered by gravity. The entire journey took about an hour and 20 minutes.

This wild, scenic ride began to catch the eyes of tourists. Soon, all afternoon trips were reserved for passengers (coal was hauled in the morning). Locals used the Switchback as a means of commuting between Mauch Chunk and Summit Hill. The return trip became legendary for its remarkable views and fast pace, with speeds exceeding 50 miles per hour.

By the mid-1870s, major railroads began to service the mines; the Switchback became exclusively a tourist attraction. Rail excursions from nearby cities were scheduled to coincide with its operating hours. Among the highlights of the trip were the trestle spanning the ravine at Mount Pisgah, the views from the cliffs and summits, the entrance to the Hacklebernie Mines, and the Indian Stairway, reportedly built by Indians as a means of crossing the mountains.

The Switchback became the second leading tourist destination in America, behind only Niagara Falls. It attracted 75,000 people annually, each of whom paid $1 for the ride. On holidays and other occasions, trains departed every six minutes.

Noteworthy riders included Thomas Edison, who marveled at the technological wonder and pronounced that he would not change any part of its operation. Another visitor fashioned an amusement park ride after the Switchback — the roller coaster. Tourism soon competed with coal as the region's primary industry.

The Switchback prospered until ridership steadily declined during the 1920s. The popularity of the automobile hastened the ride's demise, and the Great Depression sealed its fate. The last car ran October 31, 1933. On September 2, 1937, the entire operation was sold as scrap for $18,000. The metal eventually ended up in Japan, which was improving its military preparedness.

Restoration efforts were discussed occasionally over the next few decades, but none materialized. In 1986, however, the Switchback Gravity Railroad Foundation was formed. Studies have concluded that complete restoration is feasible and environmentally safe. (Currently, most of the old track beds are used as hiking and cross-country skiing trails.) This nonprofit organization is raising funds to bring back this amazing part of history for future generations of tourists to enjoy.

Poconos. The resorts here were first-class, particularly The Inn at Buck Hill, Pocono Manor and Skytop.

Built near Buck Hill Falls, The Inn at Buck Hill boasted the Poconos' first golf course, which opened in 1904. It also first introduced the region to such winter sports as skiing and tobogganing. Because it was founded by Quakers, no drinking was allowed on the premises. The inn has closed, but its main building still stands. Many residents live in magnificent cottages on the grounds.

Equally elegant, Pocono Manor also offered recreational opportunities early in the resort history of the Poconos. The manor is still open; it's discussed in detail in our Accommodations chapter.

Also thriving today is the legendary Skytop, an opulent hotel of European-style sophistication. Perched on top of a mountain overlooking much of the region, the five-story stone hotel boasts large porches and an observation deck to maximize the view.

Skytop brought hotel entertainment to new levels. In addition to the expected golf course, toboggan slide, skating and skiing, guests enjoyed such activities as winter carnivals, rodeo shows, dog shows, polo matches, boxing matches and hunting parties. Guests could ice-skate while being pulled across the lake by tractors or ski with the assistance of an airplane. Called "ski joring," this daring skiing adventure involved guests being pulled across the snow by the Skytop Auto Gyro. Ski cycling, skiing behind a motorcycle, also was popular. During the 1930s, commuters in a hurry could be flown from New York to Skytop by the lodge's private plane.

There was never a need to leave the main building. Everyday necessities such as a barber, hair dresser, drugstore, laundry, grocery, health staff, post office, photographer, tailor, stenographer and boot black were provided. There was even a separate building to house servants, if they had traveled with guests who planned an extended stay.

Naturally, all accommodations were not this lavish. More typical hotels catered to weekend tourists and the early honeymoon trade.

Fishing hotels, such as the Henryville House, opened to accommodate the many sportsmen who discovered the outstanding fly-fishing in the mountain streams. First opened in 1836, the Henryville House hosted such celebrities as Annie Oakley, John L. Sullivan, Lily Langtry and Buffalo Bill Cody. Presidents Grover Cleveland, Benjamin Harrison, Calvin Coolidge and Teddy Roosevelt also signed the guest register. Civil War hero Gen. Phillip Sheridan was so impressed by the surroundings that he dubbed the area "Paradise Valley," a name that has stuck to this day.

The major industries all catered to the city populations. Lumbering, farming and ice harvesting all thrived because of rail service to large markets.

Much of the timber used as supports (to hold up the roofs of the tunnels after anthracite was removed) in the coal mining areas came from around Mount Pocono. Farmers grew produce and locals picked huckleberries and wintergreen that were shipped to New York and Philadelphia.

During winter, ice harvesting became a source of income for the region's farmers. The huge lakes the glaciers left behind, along with those created by loggers who had dammed streams to make log-holding areas, produced a bounty of ice that was transported on rail lines built for the coal industry. Workers earned 30¢ per hour and worked 10-hour days while constantly battling frostbite and the risk of falling into icy water. They handled blocks of ice weighing approximately 300 pounds. This ice was stored in enormous buildings roughly 50 feet wide, 50 feet high and nearly 300 feet long. Sawdust and hay provided insulation.

This industry peaked in the early 20th century when more than a million tons of ice were harvested annually. During a typical summer, more than 100 railroad cars filled with ice left the Poconos each day.

As refrigeration in private homes became more common in the 1930s, the ice industry declined. Many of the ice houses burned or simply collapsed and rotted away. The only evidence of their existence are foundations that are visible near most of the lakes throughout the mountains.

Of lesser importance, albeit noteworthy, the Mount Pocono area was popular for growing Christmas trees and decorative rhododendrons, which also were shipped to the cities.

Still a significant employer in the region, Tobyhanna Army Depot has a long history. It was first used by the Army as a training ground for troops and artillery in the summer of 1913. During World War I, ambulance and tank personnel were prepared for combat here. From 1935 to 1937 it was a Civilian Conservation Corps camp accommodating 400 men. They planted trees and performed many government construction projects in a national project to provide work during tough economic times.

INSIDERS' TIPS

During the winter of 1951, Les Paul and Mary Ford vacationed near Stroudsburg. While there, Paul designed his famous Gibson Les Paul Standard guitar, and the couple recorded many songs, including "Bye Bye Blues" and "Take Me in Your Arms and Hold Me."

When the United States entered World War II, the depot was used by the Air Service Command. Gliders assembled and packaged here were used in the Normandy invasion in 1944. Near the end of the war, the depot became a camp for German prisoners of war. Since the 1950s Tobyhanna Army Depot has stockpiled, repaired and distributed communications equipment.

West End

The southern part of the Poconos differs greatly from other regions because of its lack of a significant tourist industry. This was farming country full of flat land and good soil.

There was no big draw for outsiders, other than Saylors Lake, which hosted all the famous Big Bands in its pavilion and provided swimming, boating and fishing facilities. Today, the Beltsville Dam provides outdoor recreational activities.

Driving along U.S. Highway 209 south from Stroudsburg, tourists will see a greatly changed West End, as the western portion of Monroe County is known locally. Housing developments occupy former farmland because farmers saw their land become more valuable than the crops they could raise on it. Strip malls line either side of the road through Kresgeville and Brodheadsville. Few residents speak the Pennsylvania Dutch that once was more popular than English in this area.

Continuing farther south on U.S. 209, you'll find Pa. 248 to Palmerton and the Lehigh Gap. Like the Delaware Water Gap, the Lehigh Gap was created by a river (this time the Lehigh River) cutting through a weak spot in a rock formation. Ostensibly as beautiful as the more famous gap, it should be an equal draw for scenery-lovers. However, the New Jersey Zinc Company chose to build its factory near Palmerton rather than in Delaware Water Gap, creating an unfortunate eyesore in an otherwise attractive natural setting.

Begun in 1898, the West Plant of the New Jersey Zinc Company was heralded as a welcome boost for the local economy. Palmerton's namesake, Steven Squires Palmer, was the original president. Demand for the company's oxides and sulfuric acid was so great that a second factory, called the East Plant, was completed in Palmerton in 1912.

World War I created more business. New Jersey Zinc Company's entire output during the hostilities contributed to the manufacture of arms and ammunition.

Even after the war, the factory employed 3,000 men and was the largest manufacturer of zinc products in the world.

The downside was the poisonous sulfur-dioxide smog these factories emitted into the air. As a result, more than 10,000 acres of vegetation were killed during the company's 82-year production history. Today, the barren landscape surrounding the East and West plants resembles war-torn countryside more than a tourist area.

The factory closed in 1980, and efforts have begun to reclaim the hillsides. Green patches are visible again on Lehigh Gap, but there is still much work to be done. Most of the mountainsides are still barren, and fertilizing and replanting will take years to bring the valley back to anything resembling its former natural beauty.

Farther up the Lehigh River, a former industrial town has successfully embraced the transition to tourism. The former Mauch Chunk, renamed Jim Thorpe in 1954 when the town became the final resting place of the famed Native American athlete, more resembles a European hamlet than a typical Poconos town. In fact, one of its early tourism campaigns dubbed it the "Switzerland of America."

Travelers descending winding U.S. Hwy. 209 along the Lehigh River are suddenly greeted by a pocket of Victorian mansions, narrow, steep streets and tightly packed stone row houses. You almost get the feeling that time passed over the surrounding mountains and forgot about the little village.

The town was developed in the mid-19th century to accommodate the nearby mining industry. Coal was hauled from the mines to Mauch Chunk where it was placed on canal boats — and later, trains — for transport to cities.

Millionaire Asa Packer, founder and president of the Lehigh Valley Railroad, owned the mining operation as well and used the fabled Switchback Railroad (see this chapter's related closeup) to move his coal to Mauch Chunk.

Packer's mansion, an ornate Victorian home built in 1868, is open to tourists and well worth a visit. In addition to his industrial exploits, Packer, a colorful character, founded Lehigh University and ran for U.S. president in 1868.

An opera house was built in 1881. It still hosts performances and art exhibitions.

Race Street, developed in 1849, got its name from the race (channel) of water that cascades down the hill below the pavement to the Lehigh River. Along this street, Asa Packer built 16 stone row houses as homes for the artisans and engineers he hired to work on his various enterprises. These buildings are now occupied by an assortment of boutiques and art galleries.

At the end of Race Street, the gothic-style St. Mark's Church boasts a unique combination of interior features such as a wrought-iron elevator, Tiffany windows, a baptismal font with gas standards and a tile floor made in England. It is open to the public for tours. See our Attractions chapter for details.

The entire town and much of the Pocono Mountains region can be seen from the top of Flagstaff Mountain, a former tourist attraction that's still accessible to the public.

Lovers of the supernatural should visit the Carbon County Jail. Built in 1871, it's set into the mountainside and resembles a fortress. On one of the jail's walls is a hand print. Popular local legend states that the print was made by a man about to be hanged who maintained his innocence. He claimed the print would remain as a symbol of his unjust execution. Every time it has been painted over, it has reappeared — even after a complete replastering and repainting.

Milford Area

Like other resort communities during the early 20th century, Milford, Pike County's seat, parlayed its location and scenic beauty into a profitable enterprise. Large hotels employed many of the townspeople. Other residents provided laundry services and such staples as eggs, milk, butter and produce. As in much of the rest of the Poconos, most of Milford's lavish old hotels are long gone. Prior to the invention of the automobile, most people vacationed for long periods — often an entire summer. The advent of the automobile offered the temptation to see more places in the same period of time.

One of Milford's early resorts hosted D.W. Griffith, film director of the famous *Birth of a Nation* (1915). Prior to its filming, Griffith arrived at the Sawkill House in 1912 to shoot the films *The Informer* and *A Feud in the Kentucky Hills* (even then, the movie industry fudged locations to save money).

Among the 60 people accompanying Griffith were actresses Mary Pickford and Dorothy and Lillian Gish. Griffith was quoted at the time lauding the Milford area as "one of the greatest locations I have ever visited for the making of moving pictures . . . the entire troupe is in ecstasies over the beautiful natural scenery."

The primary industry in the Milford area was bluestone mining. The bluestone quarried here was shipped to Boston, New York City, Philadelphia, Trenton, Scranton and Wilkes-Barre. Many of the sidewalks, building blocks, hitching posts and cemetery markers in those cities were built with stone from Pond Eddy and Parker's Glen.

Although the quarries near Parker's Glen alone once employed nearly 1,000 men in 1887, the industry died before the start of the 20th century when cheaper, more easily transported building materials such as concrete were developed. In Milford, the Tom Quick Monument, Grey Towers and Forest Hall are made of bluestone.

The Tom Quick Monument commemorates a man known as "The Indian Slayer" or "The Avenger of the Delaware." After Quick's father, the first white settler in Milford, was killed by Indians in 1756, Quick made it his mission

A beautiful Pocono sunset ...

to avenge the death — hence his nickname. Quick's bones were placed in the cornerstone of the monument.

Historians are split on whether Quick Jr., the first white child born within present-day Milford, was a hero or a villian. While the rest of the Quick family settled into society, he carried on his one-man vendetta, killing a reported 99 Indians. Robert Ripley in "Ripley's Believe It or Not" claims that Quick died of smallpox; and, still bitter over his actions, Indians dug up his grave and contracted the disease.

Grey Towers is the estate of legendary conservationist and two-term Pennsylvania governor Gifford Pinchot. The lavish home and grounds are maintained by the United States Forest Service and are open to the public.

On his property, Pinchot established the first successful forestry school in the United States, The Yale School of Forestry. An earlier venture at Cornell began in 1898 and failed by 1903. The previously mentioned Forest Hall, which still stands today at the corner of Broad and Harford streets, housed the classrooms and today houses several shops. The medallions on its side are likenesses of artist-sculptor Bernard Palissey, 19th century tree expert Andre Michaux and soldier-statesmen Lafayette.

On September 24, 1963, President John F. Kennedy visited Milford to dedicate Grey Towers as the Pinchot Institute for Conservation Studies.

Another historic attraction, Rohman's Inn, in Shohola, is one of the truly unique inns of the Poconos. Rohman's Inn has hosted Gloria Swanson, Charles Lindbergh, Jean Harlow, Bette Davis, Babe Ruth and Paul Newman. During the Civil War, the inn temporarily became a hospital in 1864 when a trainload of Confederate prisoners crashed nearby. Some of these men escaped and settled in the area. In the 1940s, a four-lane bowling alley was installed on the second floor. Although still in operation, it's not automated, so expect to set your own pins. Rohman's still has the 19th-century wooden barstools that pull down from the bar.

Western novelist Zane Grey dined regularly at Rohman's while living in nearby Lackawaxen from 1905 to 1918. His home is maintained as the Zane Grey Museum and contains many original manuscripts and memorabilia. (See our Attractions chapter for more information.)

One access to Lackawaxen is the Roebling Aqueduct, designed by John Roebling who patterned the Brooklyn Bridge after what he learned in Lackawaxen. Originally built in 1848 and 1849 for the canal industry, the bridge now carries cars across the Lackawaxen River, making it the country's oldest suspension bridge still in service.

Lake Wallenpaupack Area

Honesdale was created as a direct result of the Delaware & Hudson Canal's presence. The company's 108-mile canal flowed from Kingston, New York, to Honesdale, Pennsylvania. Coal from the anthracite mines near Scranton traveled by rail to Honesdale where it then was loaded onto the canal boats. More than 900 tons of coal were delivered to Honesdale each day. In the 19th century, Honesdale was an industrial hub of activity. In fact, the town is named for Philip Hone, the first president of the canal company.

Washington Irving, author of *Rip Van Winkle* and *The Legend of Sleepy Hollow*, traveled with Hone on the canal in 1841. Irving visited Honesdale on this trip and admired a nearby mountainside, which became known as Irving Cliff as a result of his casual interest. More than 150 years later, its name remains.

In 1884, a magnificent hotel was built on the cliff; it never opened. Financial setbacks caused the completed building to remain idle. New owners had prepared for a grand opening on June 22, 1889, but a fire on May 28 of that year — possibly caused by someone who lost money on the venture — slowly destroyed the building. The town's water hoses could not carry water up the 300-foot cliff. Salvaging what they could, firefighters moved furniture as the fire burned methodically. The only financial benefit the people of Honesdale ever received from the Irving Cliff Hotel (which according to newspaper accounts might have been the grandest hotel ever in northeastern Pennsylvania) were the doors, beds, desks, chandeliers, linens and silverware carried out during the fire. Instead of greeting hundreds of money-spending tourists, the residents were left with trinkets from an enterprise that could have made the town a major early resort.

Both Honesdale and nearby Hawley contain many wonderful Victorian homes, the style of choice of those towns' wealthy industrialists. On the outskirts of Hawley is The Castle, the largest bluestone structure in the United States (see our Shopping chapter). In former lives, this building was a silk mill, a glass cutting factory and an electric power plant. It currently houses an antique/reproductions shop.

The area changed dramatically when Pennsylvania Power & Light Company (PP&L) constructed a hydroelectric power plant and dam on Wallenpaupack Creek. As a result, Lake Wallenpaupack was born.

Around 1924, the company purchased 12,000 acres of land at the going rate of $20 per acre. Much of this land comprised the town of Wilsonville, named for James Wilson, a signer of the Declaration of Independence. Wilsonville was the Wayne County seat; Honesdale is today. Contrary to popular local rumor, no intact houses exist at the bottom of the lake, according to PP&L.

The dam is up to 70 feet high, 1,280 feet long and includes a huge pipe to control the flow of water from the dam to the power plant 3.5 miles away.

The 5,700-acre Lake Wallenpaupack offers extensive recreational opportunities both on and around it (see our In, On and Around the Water chapter for details). Tourists have embraced Lake Wallenpaupack, and it has become an essential part of the local economy.

Railroad buffs should plan a visit to the Wayne County Historical Society's museum in Honesdale to see *Stourbridge Lion* (see our Attractions chapter), a replica of the first locomotive ever run on a commercial track in the United States. It made its first (and only) trip from Honesdale on August 8, 1829. The original engine is housed in the Smithsonian Institution in Washington, D.C.

Slate Belt

The name tells the story. No other part of our region has relied upon a particular industry as strongly as the Bangor, Pen Argyl, Roseto and Wind Gap areas have depended on slate production.

The geological gods graced the Slate Belt with a seemingly endless supply of this useful stone. Pool players should know that no other place in the United States produces billiard-quality slate. Other uses for slate include chalkboards, curbs, roofing and burial vaults.

Slate quarries are still in operation in this area, and their past and present efforts are apparent. Mountains of scrap slate, called "slag," litter the region. Huge holes from past quarrying efforts fill with water and become deceptively inviting swimming holes. They should be avoided. Their depth is impossible to gauge, and many people have drowned in them.

Bangor, named after a Welsh mining town, was the longtime center of activity in the area. Farms and mills dominated the landscape until slate was discovered in 1831. The borough of Bangor alone had 11 quarries by 1877. Its slate was more highly regarded than that of Pen Argyl. By age 14, most boys and girls quit school to work with their fathers in the quarries.

Around 1880 a railroad line was constructed so slate could be shipped anywhere in the country. At their peak in the 1890s, Bangor quarries produced two-fifths of the country's roofing slate. In 1914, half the slate sold in the United States came from the Slate Belt.

After World War I, less expensive shingles were made using asphalt and asbestos, and individual school slates in classrooms became obsolete. Slate production declined with the lack of demand, effectively ending the boom years in the Slate Belt.

Orchards and blouse factories are all that remain of the once significant farming and milling operations. One of the largest companies in the Slate Belt is Grand Central Sanitation, Inc., a landfill that serves much of Northeastern Pennsylvania and the Lehigh Valley. Small businesses have been the core of the local economy for the last few decades. Many residents commute to jobs in the Lehigh Valley.

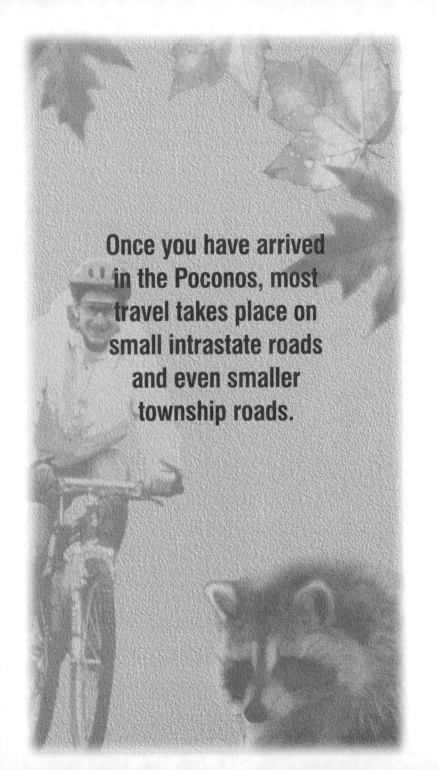

Once you have arrived in the Poconos, most travel takes place on small intrastate roads and even smaller township roads.

Getting Here, Getting Around

The Poconos region is bounded by major interstate highways that bring you to its northern, central and southern sections. The major interstates that get you to, and in most cases through, the Poconos are: Interstate 80, from either the east or the west; Interstate 84 from the east and west; Interstate 81 from the northeast and southwest; Interstate 78 from southeast or southwest; and Interstate 95 from the north and the south. (Interstates 80 and 84 are discussed in the subsequent "By Auto" section.)

Interstates 81, 78 and 95 never actually enter the Poconos but get you to the outskirts — and to appropriate feeder highways. I-81 skirts the Poconos west of the Blakeslee area.

Interstate 78 parallels I-80 but remains south of the Poconos, traversing the Allentown area. If you come into this area of the Poconos on I-78, you will have to take either Pa. Highway 33 N. to the Stroudsburg area, or the Northeast Extension of the Pennsylvania Turnpike (now I-476) to the Lehighton or Blakeslee area.

Interstate 95 doesn't enter the Poconos either, but if you are traveling it through Philadelphia, look for I-476 W. and take it to the Northeast Extension of the Pennsylvania Turnpike. Proceed on the Northeast Extension to Allentown area, Lehighton or Blakeslee.

Once you have arrived in the Poconos, most travel takes place on small intrastate roads and even smaller township roads.

The only substantial public transit system is **MC Transit**, 424-9500, which serves Monroe County. The route schedule is very complex, but in general it runs between Mount Pocono, Stroudsburg and Brodheadsville. **Shared Ride** is a senior-citizens transportation service also operated by MC Transit; call to schedule a ride (see Retirement for more on this option).

Taxis are not a major mode of transportation in this area. Stroudsburg is served by **WGM Transportation**, 421-6068; the Mount Pocono area, by **Road Runner Taxi**, 839-1881; and Milford, by **Tri-State Taxi**, 296-8294. Yes, options are scarce, so having a car here is very important. If you want to rent a limousine, however, you can rent one at **Pocono Limousine Taxi**, 839-2112, in Swiftwater.

Taxis also are not how folks generally get to their Poconos destination from surrounding airports; rental cars are the best option. If you want to rent a car when you arrive, or have it waiting, call ahead for a reservation (see our "By Plane" section for phone numbers of rental companies that serve the airport where you'll be arriving). If you are flying into the area and are staying at a major resort, the resort will send a limousine or van to pick you up.

By Auto

Most travel is by car, so knowing your way

around the roads is of value. Speaking of roads, they can be dangerous. Conditions affecting travel are snow, ice and fog. Obviously, snow and ice are issues in the winter, but they can create problems as early as November and as late as April.

Main roads are plowed quickly and covered with cinders, but these highways are undulating and winding. Driving uphill in the snow requires caution because of the slippery conditions created by the snow on an incline plane. It is very easy to slide off the road if you accelerate too quickly as you go uphill or downhill. If the snow is heavy, try to pull off into a rest area or parking lot. Do not stop on the side of the road; drivers often are blinded by the snow and can't always see the lanes, so the shoulder of the road is not a safe place in snow (or fog).

There are also concerns with the ice. We have "black ice." That's ice that looks like a wet spot on the road. Whenever the temperature is near freezing, treat all "wet" spots as if they were ice and tread slowly. If you are heading into higher elevations, be aware that the town you are leaving may be warmer than your destination; so even if ice isn't a problem when you depart, it may become one en route. Bridges — we have lots of them that traverse creeks, streams and drain pipes — ice over quickly when the temperature plummets. So drive carefully across bridges when the temperature might be dropping, especially at dusk.

Fog also might influence driving conditions at higher elevations. Again, if you are heading toward an area of higher elevation, the air might be cooler; fog will develop with a quick change in temperature, especially as warmer air rising from the valleys intermixes with colder mountain air, forming condensed water vapor. This is especially true on secondary roads such as Pa. highways 940 and 314, and it also profoundly affects travel on the interstates. During the winter months, always check road con-

ditions before you travel. Drive slowly, turn on your low beams and use extra caution.

This section provides a primer on the major primary and secondary roads in the Pocono region. Maps are still your best bet, but asking locals usually works too.

> ## FYI
> Unless otherwise noted, the area code for all phone numbers in this guide is 717.

Interstates and U.S. Highways

I-84

You would be on Interstate 84 if you're coming from the east, northeast or northwest. I-84 comes into the Poconos in the northern areas at Matamoras and west of Lake Wallenpaupack, and is a gateway to the Milford and Newfoundland areas. Quite a few residents use I-84 to commute to jobs in Waterbury and Danbury, Connecticut. Exit 11 will take you to U.S. Highway 209 where you can travel southward toward Marshalls Creek, Stroudsburg and down to Lehighton and Jim Thorpe.

You can also take I-84's Exit 9 near Lords Valley, which leads to Pa. Highway 739 and Dingmans Ferry. Exit 8 will take you to Pa. 402, which leads north through Delaware State Forest to U.S. Highway 6 and the Lake Wallenpaupack area or south to Resica Falls, Marshalls Creek and East Stroudsburg. Exits 5 and 6 lead to Pa. Highway 191, which in turn leads to Newfoundland, Buck Hill, Canadensis and ultimately to Pa. Highway 447. All these roads eventually come out near Stroudsburg and its environs.

I-80

I-80 goes right through the center of the Poconos — the areas surrounding Delaware Water Gap, Stroudsburg and East Stroudsburg, Mount Pocono and Marshalls Creek. It provides immediate access to interstates 380 and 81 and eventually links with Interstate 84. It also provides access to

INSIDERS' TIPS

Some interstate highways allow a 65 mph speed limit; most highways in the Poconos don't, including Pennsylvania's state highways. Please observe area speed limits carefully.

U.S. 209, which parallels the Delaware River from Delaware Water Gap north and travels through the Delaware Water Gap National Recreation Area, and Pa. highways 611, 115, 940, 903 and 33.

U.S. 209

This highway runs from Milford south to Jim Thorpe and Lehighton. It passes a lot of towns on the way and is traversed by Interstate 80. It is also part of the Delaware Water Gap National Recreation Area. At points north of Marshalls Creek and Bushkill you'll pass farms, meadows and woods and catch glimpses of the Delaware River. In summer, it's congested between Stroudsburg and Marshalls Creek because of the Pocono Flea Market/Antique Bazaar, Bushkill Falls and other area attractions. You can avoid it by taking Pa. highways to 191 and 402 to some northern areas. You can also get off U.S. 209 at Fernwood in Bushkill at River Road, which parallels U.S. 209 and leads to the town of Delaware Water Gap. U.S. 209 joins I-80 near East Stroudsburg. U.S. Highway 209 Business connects Marshalls Creek and Sciota; so, if you prefer, you can travel through the Stroudsburgs and small villages instead of zipping along an interstate.

Secondary Roads

Pa. Highway 611

This road takes you from Tobyhanna, in the northwest, past Mount Pocono toward Philadelphia to the south. It follows the Delaware River from Easton to the Poconos, essentially parallel to Pa. Highway 33 (although "parallel" doesn't exactly describe the winding course it takes along the river, past farms and through Delaware Water Gap). At Delaware Water Gap, Pa. 611 heads away from the Delaware River, through Stroudsburg and then northwest to Mount Pocono and the Tobyhanna area.

Pa. Highway 903

This road can be reached from Interstate 80 or Pa. Highway 940 via Pa. 1155. It leads to Jim Thorpe and is a lovely road that takes you through nice country across a ridge that was part of the infamous Walking Purchase (see our Native Americans chapter). From this road you can see forest to the west and valleys and lower mountains that fill the range from this point to the Delaware Water Gap. Pa. 903 is also the access road for Big Boulder Ski Area and Split Rock Resort.

Photo: Pocono Mountains Vacation Bureau, Inc.

Air tours are available at several Pocono air fields.

Dingmans Bridge

Close-up

One of the delights of the Poconos is the bridge at Dingmans (the official spelling from Colonial days) Ferry. This small two-lane bridge is made from sections of a railroad trestle that traversed the Susquehanna River before the turn of the century. It was originally the crossing point of a ferry operated by Andrew Dingman, who claimed the spot in 1735 as part of a land grant from William Penn. The ferry was in Lenape land and provided an escape route during occasional Indian raids. The bridge is owned by Dingman's descendants and others who bought into the Dingmans Choice & Delaware Bridge Company in 1836. The company's name is derived from the local legend that Andrew Dingman declared his land by the Delaware River, saying, "This is my choice."

The bridge has existed in various incarnations since 1836 and is owned by the same originating families, though members now live all over the United States. Every year in October, however, they come together for a board meeting.

The bridge has been the subject of a Charles Kuralt special. In April 1996, it was the subject of a Japanese news show. It remains one of the few privately owned bridges in the country.

Turn east off U.S. Highway 209 in Dingmans Ferry to reach the bridge. Suddenly, you'll find yourself in another setting — almost another time. The bridge exudes a charming otherworldly quality. Bridge keepers walk out to your car to collect the 75¢ toll

Photo: Leona Adamo Maxwell

The Dingmans Bridge spans the Delaware River and two centuries of service.

(it's been the same amount for as long as we can remember), talk about the weather or the bridge, and if they get to know you, inquire as to how you and your children are doing. The toll collectors also are great sources of bridge history.

It is a treat to just cross the bridge and come back. Stop at the recreation area on the Pennsylvania side of the river; it's a great place to enjoy the view of the bridge, walk in the water, have a picnic and allow your children some space to run.

(Thanks to Elsie Bensley for providing information about Dingmans Ferry. The 77-year-old bridge manager has served in that role for more than 21 years — part of that time with her now-deceased husband, Carl.)

Pa. Highway 715

This highway begins in Brodheadsville where you can pick up Pa. Highway 115 to the Pocono International Raceway. From Brodheadsville north, Pa. 715 leads to Inter-

state 80 and the Stroudsburg connecting road (Pa. 611 in Tannersville); or you can cross Pa. 611, continue through Henryville and connect with Pa. Highway 447 to Canadensis.

From Pa. 715 in Brodheadsville, you can

also take U.S. 209 north to Stroudsburg or south to Lehighton and Jim Thorpe.

Pa. Highway 33

Pa. Highway 33 is your connecting route to the Lehigh Valley area, including Lehigh Valley International Airport. It connects you to U.S. Highway 22/Interstate 78 to the south in the Bethlehem/Easton area. Heading north through the Slate Belt to the heart of the Poconos, Pa. 33 connects with U.S. Highway 209 (north-south), Interstate 80 and Pa. Highway 611 (north-south).

Pa. Highway 191

Pa. Highway 191 cuts across the Poconos from Honesdale to Newfoundland and through East Stroudsburg and Stroudsburg, crossing Pa. 611 in Stroudsburg and heading over Bangor Mountain to Bangor. This highway takes you all over the Poconos from north to south, dovetailing with Pa. 390, in Mountainhome, for a spell.

By Plane

The major area airports are outside the main Pocono region. The two closest international airports are Lehigh Valley International Airport and Wilkes-Barre/Scranton International Airport. The Lehigh Valley International Airport is in the Allentown-Bethlehem-Easton area, which is south of the Pocono region but only an hour's drive from its heart; the Wilkes-Barre/Scranton International Airport is in Avoca, which is west of the Poconos (also about an hour's drive from most of the main Pocono destinations). Newark (N.J.) International Airport is about a 1½-hour drive east of the Poconos; while some folks drive to the Poconos from Newark (via I-80), most arrange connecting flights to the Lehigh Valley or Wilkes-Barre/Scranton airports.

The two small municipal airports are Pocono Mountains Municipal Airport and Stroudsburg-Pocono Airpark. Many of the larger resorts will arrange to pick you up from and deliver you to area airports.

More than 40 flights depart daily from **Lehigh Valley International Airport**, (610) 266-6000, to more than 12 cities, with connecting flights to nearly every U.S. and many

international locations. This airport is serviced by: **USAir**, (800) 354-9822, and **USAir Express**, (800) 428-4253; **United/United Express**, (800) 241-6522; **Delta**, (800) 221-1212; **Northwest and Mesaba/Northwest Airlink**, (800) 225-2525; **Continental Express**, (800) 525-0280; **COMAIR – The Delta Connection**, (800) 354-9822; and **Air Ontario**, (800) 776-3000. When you land, you can take a cab or a bus right outside the baggage area; but if you are heading for the Poconos, your best bet is a rental car. Agencies include **Avis**, (800) 831-2847; **Hertz**, (800) 654-3131; and **National**, (800) 328-4567.

Wilkes-Barre/Scranton International Airport, 457-3445, is a regional airport that provides direct jet/commuter service to major East Coast cities. You can fly to or from more than 350 cities. The Fixed Base Operator (FBO) is **Tech Aviation Services**, 457-3400. The major airlines that service this airport are: **Delta**, (800) 221-1212; **USAir/USAir Express**, (800) 428-4322; and **United Express**, (800) 241-6522. To get to the Poconos once you land, you'll need to rent a car or take a cab. Arrange airport pickups with the individual car rental companies: **Avis**, (800) 831-2847; **Hertz**, (800) 654-3131; **Budget**, (800) 527-0700; and **National**, (800) 328-4567

Pocono Mountains Municipal Airport, 839-6080, is managed by **Moyer Aviation Inc.**, Pa. Highway 611, Mount Pocono. Services provided include tie-downs, fueling, maintenance, storage and sales and service. Rental cars can be arranged through **Thrifty Rental**, 676-3366, or **Northern Car Rental**, 839-2215.

Another small airport is the **Stroudsburg-Pocono Airpark** in East Stroudsburg off U.S. Highway 209 Bus. Tie-downs are available here, and pilots can even camp under the planes. However, this airport is primarily a tourist attraction for sightseeing flights and daytrips. Call 421-9036 for flight information. (See our Attractions chapter for details.)

Bus Lines

You can get to the Poconos by **Greyhound** or **Martz Trailways** buses. They come into the region from New York and Scranton. For bus information, call Greyhound, 421-4451, or Martz Trailways, 421-3040.

Many Poconos resorts become family traditions after awhile; generation after generation have come to regard them as summer vacation homes.

Accommodations

The Poconos are a vacation wonderland. As such, business proprietors try to meet the needs of many types of vacationers. In this chapter we point out our top resorts, family fun places, couples/honeymoon spots and motels and motor inns. Close-ups spotlight housekeeping cottage retreats, camping facilities and timesharing options. We have included bed and breakfasts and country inns in a separate chapter, for those who are so inclined.

Accommodations presented here cover a wide range of price and design, ensuring there are some to suit every budget and every taste. If you see a place that isn't mentioned here, check it out for yourself; we might not have found it yet!

Before we journey 'round the mountains, let's get some business concerns out of the way.

• Major credit cards generally are accepted — we note any exceptions. If you wish to know about a specific credit card's acceptability, contact individual establishments that interest you.

• Pets are usually not allowed; however, this is not etched in stone, so we note if an establishment will accept your pets.

• As a general rule, smoking is only permitted in designated smoking areas.

• Handicapped-accessibility is a consideration for some people, and most establishments comply with the Americans With Disabilities Act. We suggest, however, that you check with establishments that interest you for information about their facilities and restrictions.

• Most of the accommodations in this section have convention and conference facilities. Even the top-of-the-line resorts do a great deal of business catering special events, and most have meeting rooms, separate convention facilities and dedicated staffs. If you're planning a group meeting of any size, contact any of the resorts, hotels and motels in our area for available opportunities.

• A final word about price: Because of the range of options, pricing varies; some rates are for the week, some rates are for the night; many spots offer packages that include midweek discounts as weekend bonuses. When possible, we have included price codes for each category (as we did in Bed and Breakfasts and Country Inns) that reflect the type of pricing used. Don't forget the 6 percent sales tax in Pennsylvania that is not included in the quoted rates. Some places add a gratuity to the bill; we note that where applicable.

Resorts

On Top of Our World

Each of the following top resorts are different. All offer terrific amenities for the whole family, just for you or a couple, even an entire convention; yet they range in overall personality from formal to casual. Many Poconos resorts become family traditions after awhile; generation after generation have come to regard them as summer vacation homes. Since most of these resorts are reserved for at least a weekend — and all have packages, room and cottage types and meal plans — we mention in the individual entries what you can expect to pay at each of the resorts "at the top."

Mount Pocono Area

Skytop Lodge
Pa. Hwy. 390 W., Skytop • 595-7401

This elegant resort was built in the 1920s as a members-only hunting and fishing lodge; it was designed and built to be a top-notch accommodation at the top of the world. Drive toward it along a winding country road that leads to the sudden view of a grand, stone bridge over an enormous, beautiful lake; continue up the driveway to what seems to be an incredible English country estate. It certainly does seem like one of the most luxurious spots at the top of the world.

The circular drive in front of the grand, stone portico entrance (where you are met by stately, jacket-clad bellhops) is surrounded by beautiful gardens and expansive lawns. From the wooden rocking chairs on the beautiful South Porch, you can see the Delaware Water Gap. From any room in the European-style grand lodge, Skytop's more than 5,000 acres spread out before you across meadows, down mountains, into woods, along streams, beneath waterfalls and around a lake. The land encompasses a beginners ski slope, cross-country skiing trails, an 18-hole championship golf course, pro-caliber tennis courts, an outdoor pool, a bathing beach on the sparkling lake, jogging and hiking trails and a weather-protected ice-skating rink. The grounds also include lovely guest cottages and a convention center. The lodge is the centerpiece of the private community of astonishing summer homes built around it as part of the original plans.

Skytop is the choice for an elegant, Old World-style weekend getaway, a midweek escape or a week-long family vacation. Guests dress up — men wear sport jackets, ladies don appropriate attire (no shorts, bathing suits, tank tops or jeans) — for dinner in the distinguished dining room; casual attire is fine for breakfast and lunch. Floor-to-ceiling windows look out over the south lawn and provide a backdrop of foliage and views in every season that only nature could design. Waiters (many of them) attend to your every need, serving and pampering you at every meal.

The main lobby of the lodge intensifies the feeling of luxury with its huge fireplace, Oriental rugs, wingback chairs and lovely seating groups. Pickled pine beams rib the ceilings and form the huge columns in the grand ballroom-size entrance. More floor-to-ceiling windows look out on the South Porch and beyond. Afternoon tea or morning coffee can be enjoyed on the South Porch.

In summer, abundant activities for the entire family are included in your stay: Sunday evening concerts on the South Porch; miniature golf; archery; movies; dancing; bridge; hiking; nighttime deer watches; stargazing; relaxing in the sauna, whirlpool, kiddie pool, indoor or outdoor pool; lake swimming in July and August; table tennis; and picnicking. An expanded health club with treadmills and stair-step machines and Marcy gym stations are part of the fitness facilities. There's even massage for deep-down relaxation. Special activities at a modest charge: tennis, $7 per hour per person; golf (see our Golf chapter), the base rate of $60 includes cart and greens fees, but there are always specials; mountain biking, $6.50 per hour; boating (kayaking, rowboating and canoeing) for $5 per hour; and summer day camp for children (mid-June to Labor Day), $18 per day. Fishing is available but you must have a valid fishing license and your own equipment. There are miles of hiking trails to see beautiful mountain vistas, ancient forests, sparkling lakes, cascading waterfalls and other beauties of nature. Trails take you close to native fauna, such as minks, bobcats, black bears, coyotes, river otters and more than 175 kinds of birds. Naturalist John Serrao leads nature walks, and the *Skytop Trail Guide* and other publications explain trail characteristics and delights in great detail.

In winter, downhill skiing (lessons are available on site for beginners) at Alpine, Big Boulder, Camelback, Jack Frost and Shawnee is just a 30- to 45-minute drive away (see our Winter Sports chapter). Cross-country skiing and ice skating in a weather-protected rink round out activities.

Accommodations in the lodge itself include double rooms, minisuites and VIP suites. And cottages are within walking distance of the lodge. One set of cottages adjoins the fairway — perfect for golfers; the other set adjoins a children's playground — perfect for families.

Skytop, like many of the resorts in the Poconos, is redecorating and has recently renovated a number of rooms to reflect the cozy comfort of an accessorized sitting room rather than simply a room in a hotel. A nice feature is adjoining rooms for children — separate yet convenient. Suites and a new four-

FYI

Unless otherwise noted, the area code for all phone numbers in this guide is 717.

bedroom cottage have been added to the list of accommodations.

There are many ways to enjoy Skytop. You can come to experience a theme weekend (how about a Dickens Christmas Weekend, a Country Weekend or a Father/Daughter Weekend); enjoy a romantic getaway; appreciate an Autumn Nature Weekend or a Golf Getaway package for unlimited golf on the 18-hole course (see our Golf chapter); play tennis all weekend; or take in a Broadway-caliber play at Pocono Playhouse or Shawnee Playhouse.

Rates at this retreat vary based on type of accommodation and length of stay. In addition to what we've mentioned, there are family plans, senior-citizen plans, bed and breakfast packages, midweek packages, even conference packages for groups and family reunions. The basic parameters of each money-saving option are available upon request.

High-end weekend rates, which include meals on the American Plan, are $275 per person per night, double occupancy in a full-bed lodge room; $320 for a king or queen cottage; and $390 for a VIP suite. The family plan allows children 16 and younger to stay in their parents' room for $20 per child per night. Children occupying their own room pay half during the week or receive a $100 discount for holidays and weekends. A 15 percent service charge is added to your bill in lieu of gratuities for regular lodge services.

If you are looking for an elegant place at the "top of the world," you should treat yourself to a stay at Skytop.

Pocono Manor Inn and Golf Resort
Pa. Hwy. 314 W., Pocono Manor
• 839-7111, (800) 233-8150

This comfortable, welcoming historic Quaker retreat (built in 1902) has been nominated and proclaimed eligible for the National Register of Historic Places. The gracious summer cottages are part of its historic charm. It has evolved from a 65-room summer retreat into a beautiful inn with 255 guest rooms, 14 meeting rooms, eight banquet facilities and a main dining room (seating capacity 550) with a breathtaking view of the surrounding mountains. In 1966 the inn and its accompanying 3,000 acres were bought by the late Samuel Ireland, owner of the Ireland Coffee Company; the property is still owned by the family today.

There is a friendly, family atmosphere you feel as soon as you walk into the blue- and cream-colored tranquility of the main lobby. Here, as well as in other sitting rooms throughout, you'll find fireplaces that blaze all winter long. A nice touch is the ever-present coffee table in the main lobby, with fresh java for guests any time of day.

Winter or summer you'll find little nooks, indoors and out, where you can relax and take afternoon tea. The quiet charm of the inn's Quaker heritage has been infused with the warmth of relaxed country comfort. The Irelands have almost completely renovated and refurbished this historic inn. The main public areas have been re-carpeted and redecorated in wonderful combinations of green, burgundy and taupe; the rooms have been redecorated with historically representative yet modernly functional decor. The custom, hand-carved wood furniture is from the local Bethlehem Furniture company; the dining room features solid cherry, comb-back chairs made by the famous Duckloe Furniture Company (see Shopping).

Entertainment amenities include color TVs and in-room movies. There are about 190 rooms in the main lodge, all of which have lovely views of the surrounding mountains, and some from which you can see the Delaware Water Gap. Across from the front entrance (beautifully restructured in stone) are about 60 rooms in the Adams and Manor Hall buildings, which guests access by a covered walkway. These rooms surround the lovely outdoor swimming pool, where in summer guests enjoy a lunch of hot dogs and hamburgers cooked by the chef on the large stone grill. Also with access to the outdoor grill, the delightful Fireside Lodge hosts private events of up to 150 people.

For indoor eating, the light and airy main dining room overlooks the mountains and woods of Pocono Manor. Outdoors, beneath this dining room, is a large barbecue area for summer events.

Renovated and updated amenities include indoor and outdoor pools and a kiddie pool, saunas, indoor (additional charge) and outdoor tennis courts, racquetball courts (addi-

Accommodations

tional charge), a 13-station Nautilus fitness center and two 18-hole championship golf courses (see our Golf chapter). On-site activities include horseback riding (additional charge) on the beautiful trails that grace the 3,000 acres of wooded grounds, hay rides (additional charge), dancing and playing games in the game room. Trap shooting (additional charge) is a popular old-fashioned activity here. For less strenuous pursuits, The Old Lamplighter Lounge features live music, a library with a pool table and large screen TV and movies on weekends.

The same amenities are available for children, as is a supervised camp for kids ages 5 to 12 (every day during the summer until Labor Day and Friday through Sunday the rest of the year). There's also a fine tennis program open to the general public.

Winter activities include cross-country skiing and snowmobiling (additional charge), ice-skating at a delightful outdoor rink nestled at the base of the main lodge and sledding on a special hill maintained with snow-making equipment. Ski packages are available in conjunction with Camelback Ski Area, just a 5-minute drive away (see Winter Sports). These "bed and breakfast" packages, midweek or weekend, include a hearty mountain breakfast, deluxe room, free lift ticket, complimentary hors d'oeuvres from 6 to 7 PM and access to all Pocono Manor amenities previously mentioned. One interesting ski-package option includes a lift ticket at Camelback or free equipment rental for the 40 miles of cross-country ski trails. You can mix and match these freebies, taking a lift ticket one day and cross-country ski equipment rental the next, if you'd like.

Theme weekends include the Irish Extravaganza or Chocolate Lovers Weekend. And there is always some type of entertainment, such as the Big Band sounds of Spencer and Nancy Reed.

There are plenty of facilities for groups, organizations, conventions, seminars, family reunions and such. If you are planning a wedding, we suggest you look at the Heritage Room and the Terrace Ballroom. Both have lovely views of the surrounding mountains and grounds of Pocono Manor, and both are beautifully decorated; each also adjoins a lounge

area (tea can be served here in winter) that can be used as a private reception area.

Standard high-season room rates are $90 per couple per night, excluding meals. For a standard room plus meals on the modified American Plan, the rate is $198 per couple. Children younger than 8 stay for $15 per night; children 8 and older stay for $50 per night. Packages are available, and if you are interested in staying for a week, midweek, convention or any type of weekend, be sure to ask about special discounts.

If you haven't been to Pocono Manor since it's been renovated, take a look. If you've never been there, you can see it at its best and brightest.

Split Rock Resort & Conference
Pa. Hwy. 903, Lake Harmony • 722-9111, (800) 255-7625

This resort was once a hunting and camping retreat for executives of the Lehigh Coal and Navigation Company; it was developed by company president Robert V. White in 1941. The original lodge was surrounded by five private cottages. When it became apparent its location and beauty would sustain expansion into a ski resort, White began one in 1946. Split Rock, thereafter, became a favorite weekend retreat. And it was the first mountain in Pennsylvania to try snowmaking (see related Close-up in our Winter Sports chapter).

Today, after passing through other owners and surviving a devastating fire, Split Rock is a premier family resort. Its grounds are between Big Boulder and Jack Frost ski areas (see Winter Sports) and include an 18-hole golf course, a lake for swimming and boating and several types of accommodations including rooms in the lodge, suites in the Galleria complex, slopeside suites for skiers, cottages near the lake or villas near the golf course. This is an energetic, casual, activities-oriented resort.

When you enter the complex through the private toll road, you are on your way to the ultramodern Galleria complex. There is the excellent Galleria restaurant, a movie theater, The Pit Lounge and the Galleria Night Club with entertainment almost nightly. There's also a fitness center and sports complex (indoor tennis and racquetball courts) and an indoor

pool. The Galleria complex is close to the on-site, family-size ski area too.

After you have passed Galleria and looked at the lovely, casual vacation homes (A-frames and lodges, both with lots of decks), you'll wind around the homes toward the lodge. As you head toward the lodge, you'll pass Westwood Villas (behind which is the golf course), and farther on, the ski lodge, mini golf course, outdoor tennis courts and out-door pool. The lake, swimming lagoon and boat dock are the backdrop for the main lodge. Its amenities include the Heri-tage Dining Room, overlooking Lake Harmony, for indoor, cozy, fireside dining in winter and al-fresco dining on the deck in summer; and the SRO lounge. For quick eats at Split Rock, there's the Coffee Shop and the Old Fashioned Ice Cream Parlour in Galleria, and Harmony Pizza Shop in the lodge area.

There's always something happening here: music festivals such as the Pocono Blues Fes-tival, Pocono Country Music Festival and Pocono American Roots Music Festival; food-related events such as the Great Tastes of Pennsylvania Wine and Food Festival and Great Brews of America Classic Beer Festival; and other activities. The resort is near Pocono Raceway, which makes it a great place for race fans to stay. The town of Jim Thorpe is nearby if you are interested in enhancing your vacation with a cultural turn in a museum or art gallery or at the Laurel Arts Festival.

Family fun is a focus, with children's camp and full-time, daytime and evening activity programs for children 3 and older. Family ac-tivities also include the 18-hole championship miniature golf course, softball, bumper boats, archery and much more. Swimming is avail-able indoors (in the main lodge and in Galle-ria) and outdoors as well as from the sand beach in the lagoon on the lake. For the times you'd rather be on the water than in it, you can go boating; cruise your own sailboat, paddleboat or rowboat or take a ride on a pontoon boat for an additional charge. You can water-ski here too.

Other outdoor amenities include volleyball, croquet, badminton, shuffleboard, boccie ball, a children's playground and hiking and biking

trails. Indoor facilities include an eight-lane bowling alley, a video game room, billiards and Ping-Pong tables. Indoor fitness options are enhanced by whirlpools and a massage center. There's also a salon to keep you hair in shape.

In winter, enjoy skiing at the family-size ski area with lodge. Eight slopes are served by a chair lift and a T-bar. Sledding is available as well as ice skating and snowboarding.

Split Rock can accommo-date groups of five to 1,500 for conferences, trade shows, meetings and other group events. Staff members are pleased to assist in planning your event and attending to de-tails while it's in progress. Costs depend on the type of accommodations and the length of stay.

If you and your family or group are looking for an energetic, activity-filled vacation, Split Rock in the western Poconos is a good op-tion. Rates range from $135 to $275 per couple per night with meals on the Modified Ameri-can Plan. Children ages 5 to 15 are $39 per night (MAP); kids 16 and older or an extra person in a room are $49 (MAP). Children younger than 5 are free, but meals are not included.

Lake Wallenpaupack Area

Woodloch Pines Resort Inc.
Pa. Hwy. 590, Hawley • 685-7121, (800) 572-6658

This resort has been recognized three times by *Better Homes & Gardens* as one of the top family resorts in America, and it has become a family tradition for many. Woodloch Pines is a first-class winter and summer playland. From its highly rated golf course (see our Golf chapter) to its Broadway-style theme shows, this resort provides a first-rate informal family funfest and a variety of accommodation options.

Woodloch Pines surrounds an enormous crystal-clear mountain lake that offers boating (sailboats, rowboats, paddleboats, scenic boat rides), swimming, water skiing, fishing (li-censes are sold at Woodloch; bring your own equipment) and, in winter, ice skating and ice

fishing. A beautiful outdoor pool stretches alongside the lake, increasing the feeling of "water, water everywhere."

Each month, staff arrange different activities and package options designed with the entire family in mind. With few exceptions, nearly all resort activities and amenities are included in your family's stay as well as three meals a day (two meals are an option as is bed and breakfast at some times of the year). Holiday specials include Thanksgiving and Christmas midweek, miniweek and weekend options. There are winter weekend specials for school holidays as well as St. Patrick's Day and winter getaways. Spring and summer feature full-fledged week-long fun fests, with entertainment, tournaments and events focused on families doing fun things both together and apart (kids camps and activities). Fall events celebrate the change of season and include Halloween festivities. Children's activities such as arts and crafts are available winter or summer, and special facilities for the young ones include a children's playground, climbing wall,

kiddie pool, kiddie cars, toddler room, video game rooms and a miniature golf course.

Other general activities include aquanastics (water gymnastics), badminton, basketball, bingo, boccie ball, bicycling, bumper cars, IROC go-carts, cooking classes, exercise classes, horseshoes, shuffleboard, karaoke, line dancing, nature trails, scavenger hunts, trap shooting (extra charge), Ping-Pong, racquetball (extra charge), tennis and lawn bowling. Additional on-site winter options are snowmobiling and snow tubing. You'll also find a rifle range and a shooting gallery.

Accommodations include an impressive array of comfortable and homey rooms, suites and houses — decorated in rustic, country decor or country-refined. Basic rooms with a private bath, two double beds and color TV are available in lodges near the lovely woods that surround Woodloch. Larger rooms with separate areas for family privacy also are near the lodges, and some overlook the lake. Rooms adjoining the main lodge — all with private balconies — afford lovely views of the lake and are suitable for families or couples.

Photo: Pocono Mountains Vacation Bureau, Inc.

Skytop Lodge in the Poconos.

Suites, attached to the indoor swimming pool complex, feature varying degrees of luxury and are set up for extended families — at least two bedrooms, full baths and TVs. Homes are available about 2 miles from the main facilities. Prices vary considerably here, depending on the accommodation, season, time of the week and any package options you might be participating in.

Overall, the low end for rooms is $260 per person (double occupancy) for a summer weekend (winter weekends are less expensive; holiday summer weekends are more expensive); the high is $332. For a week in summer, rates range from $895 per person to $1,080. Children staying with two adults for a week range from $200 to $535 (age increments are 3 to 6, 7 to 12 and 13 to 19; kids younger than 3 stay free). Weekend children's rates with the same parameters are $65 to $168.

Many packages are available here, so be sure to look at the elaborate brochure that spells out what's available week by week, weekend by weekend, all year long. All rates include access to all resort amenities except for the previously noted few that require an additional fee. All meals are included in your stay unless a two-meal option is chosen. Excellent country cooking — a choice of appetizers, two entrees, desserts and, on special weekends, a spectacular smorgasbord — is served family-style, all-you-can-eat.

Nearby activities include cross-country skiing, downhill skiing at Jack Frost or Big Boulder (about an hour's drive) and all the goings-on in the Hawley area (see the "Lake Wallenpaupack Area" section of Arts and Culture, Shopping, Attractions and Daytrips).

Down By The River

Two of our resorts are famous for their proximity to the Delaware River and the Delaware Water Gap.

Delaware Water Gap

Shawnee Inn Resort
River Rd. Shawnee-on-Delaware
• 421-1500, (800) SHAWNEE

The Shawnee Inn was once owned by Fred Waring, famed conductor of the Pennsylvanians, owner of Shawnee Press and inventor of the Waring Blender. It is an impressive turn-of-the-century, grande dame — a historic site — with lawns meandering to the water's edge, lovely gardens, hiking trails, horse stables and riding trails, a regulation golf course (see Golf), on-site ski slopes (see Winter Sports), a lake (with ice skating in winter, weather permitting), a miniature golf course and a fitness center with Jacuzzi, whirlpool and sauna.

Activities here include fishing on the lake and in the river (licenses and equipment required), boating (see In, On and Around the Water for rental information), hiking, bicycling, roller skating, golf, miniature golf, swimming (indoors and outdoors) and just relaxing down by the river.

Rooms are at the inn itself. Breakfast, dinner and most amenities are included in your room rate. Skiers often prefer accommodations closer to the ski area, and lodging is available within walking distance to the Mountain at Shawnee Valley in two- and three-bedroom townhomes and châteaus with fireplaces and kitchens; some even have whirlpools. Shawnee Village, a short shuttle ride away form the Mountain, is a complex of villas with fireplaces, kitchens and room enough to sleep six.

Rates at Shawnee Village and Shawnee Valley during peak ski season range from $835 to $870 per couple per week; $460 to $465, off-peak. Shawnee Inn rooms are approximately $75 per night per person, including breakfast and dinner. Shawnee also can accommodate group meetings or conferences; call for details.

Glenwood Hotel & Resort Motel
Main St. (Pa. Hwy. 611 S.), Delaware Water Gap• 476-0010, (800) 822-2054, (800) 833-3050

Glenwood, in Delaware Water Gap, is walking-distance to all the happenings in town and down by the river. It is a throwback from the resort's heyday at the beginning of the century. The Watergap Trolley, part of the ambiance here, takes visitors on a tour of the area and historic points of interest from the time of the Native Americans and early settlers through the period when the resort industry flourished.

The Glenwood has a fun golf course, boccie courts, indoor and outdoor pools, fitness facilities (whirlpool, sauna, gym, exercise equipment), an archery range, miniature golf, indoor and outdoor Ping-Pong and shuffleboard, horseshoe and quoits pitches, tennis courts, an indoor playroom, trout fishing on the property (license required; see our Fishing and Hunting chapter), a restaurant and nightclub and cocktail lounge. Many of the activities here relate to the amenities: tennis matches, boccie contests, dance lessons, golf tournaments (for beginners too), field games, shuffleboard and archery contests as well as guest talent shows and all kinds of break-the-ice parties. Casual clothing is fine for breakfast (no tank tops for ladies, please); dinner requires appropriate attire for ladies (no tank tops or shorts) and gentlemen (jackets on Thursdays and Saturdays).

Four types of accommodations are available: main lodge rooms, glenside cabanas (park at your door), courtside cabanas and motel rooms (park at your door). All rooms have color TVs, private baths, telephones and refrigerators. Motel rooms have twin beds; courtside cabanas have king-size beds; glenside cabanas have king size-beds and two-person whirlpools; main lodge rooms with double beds and tile showers are convenient to the lobby, dining room, game room and nightclub.

Rates at Glenwood are based on double occupancy per person, per night and include three meals a day. The weekend high is $99; low is $84. A full week's high rate is $628, and the low is $526. Rates depend on which accommodation you are in. The Glenside cabanas are the most expensive; the Courtside cabanas and motel rooms are the lower priced; and the lodge rooms are the least-expensive rooms. Discounts and packages are available, so be sure to inquire when you call.

Up and Down the Mountains

The Poconos have resorts to suit every taste. Are you in the mood for the quiet, lakeside beauty of Tamiment or the joint-is-jumping atmosphere of Fernwood? How about the country casual family environment of Hillside Lodge or the nonstop family activities of Daniels? Do you care for the hilltop casualness and family focus of Mountain Laurel or the keep-them-moving-all-the-time atmosphere of Mount Airy? And then there's the pleasure of a place at the base of Camelback like the gracious Chateau or the relaxation of

a place near the award-winning golf course of Mountain Manor.

Stroudsburg/East Stroudsburg

Hillside Inn
Frutchey Dr., East Stroudsburg • 223-8238

This resort holds the distinction of being the first and only resort in the Poconos owned by an African American family. It opened to cater to the black community when no hotels in the Poconos did. While that clearly is no longer the case, Hillside Inn still prospers with guests of all races that come to enjoy this newly renovated 30-room, modern resort. The hotel currently is owned and operated by Retired Judge Albert Murray Sr. (the original owner) and his wife, Odetta.

Amenities include an indoor exercise room, game room, swimming pool with hot spa and live entertainment that draws locals from all around. Hillside features the best in classical, jazz, gospel and dance music. (The Sunday gospel programs are a real treat.) Outdoor activities include tennis, golf (practice course), basketball, volleyball, softball, shuffleboard, Ping-Pong, horseshoes, hiking, walking and jogging. Fishing is available in the private lake; no license is required for guests.

Rooms feature either king, queen or double beds, and all contain wall-to-wall carpeting, color TVs, telephones, private baths and air-conditioning. Larger rooms also have sitting areas with sofas. Rates for a room with two double beds range from $156 to $195 per person, double occupancy, for a weekend stay. Included in the rate is a Friday-night welcoming buffet plus breakfast and dinner Saturday and Sunday. Children ages 1 to 3 stay for a quarter of the adult rate; kids ages 4 to 11 stay for half the adult rate. Rates vary by time of year; considerable discounts are available on midweek stays (Sunday to Friday).

The on-site dining room specializes in Southern, Caribbean and traditional American cuisine. The motto of this lovely hillside resort is "Old-fashioned warmth, good food and personal service."

Hillside is a high-water mark in the Poconos for its ground-breaking past. The inn is close to Delaware Water Gap National Recreation Area as well as golf courses in Shawnee, Dela-

YOUR TICKET TO FUN IN THE POCONOS

Ticket No 722-9111	Price FUN FOR ALL AGES	Price FUN FOR ALL AGES
Split Rock Resort Lake Harmony, PA email: srinfo@prolog.net http//www.splitrockresort.com		Open to the Public Year Round ! TEL: 717-722-9111 FAX: 717-722-8831

- **Health Club & Spa:**
  Memberships Available
  (Ext.514)
- **Tennis Courts** (Ext. 673)
- **8 Bowling Lanes** (Ext. 504)
- **Championship Golf Course:**
  Driving Range & Putting
  Green(Ext. 774)
- **18 Hole Championship
  Mini-Golf Course:**
  7th hardest on the East Coast
  (Ext. 671)

- **First Run Movie Theater**
  (Ext.871)
- **Restaurants:
  The Heritage Restaurant**
  (Ext.756) &
  The Galleria Restaurant
  (Ext.835)
  Call for Reservations
- **Conference Center:**
  Facilities can accommodate
  from 5 to 1500 people.
  (Ext. 805)

ware Water Gap, Marshalls Creek and Analomink — seven courses in all within a 20-minute drive). It is also near Shawnee and Alpine Mountain ski areas (about 20 minutes) and about a half-hour drive from Camelback.

Mountain Manor Inn & Golf Club
**Off Pa. Hwy. 402, Marshalls Creek
• 223-8098**

Mountain Manor is another Pocono establishment that attracts families year after year. The cozy 450-acre resort is owned and operated by the Scott family. There are lovely hiking trails that lead you along streams, over bridges and through the woods. The main lodge has a white-columned central entrance that leads to the lobby, gift shop and dining room; some of the guest rooms at this country resort are in the wings of the building.

Golf is the main activity here; there are four, nine-hole regulation courses (36 holes of unlimited play for guests) and two nine-hole executive courses. (See our Golf chapter for more information on the award-winning golf club.) The Scott's estate and inn also feature indoor and outdoor tennis; indoor and outdoor swimming; indoor ice skating in winter (see Winter Sports) and roller (or in-line) skating in summer; a fitness center with Nautilus equipment; a game room with video games and pool table; and an indoor gym for basketball, tennis and volleyball. Winter activities also include sledding and cross-country skiing on the grounds.

Stays at Mountain Manor include dinner and breakfast, hayrides in season and a full schedule of daily activities, such as line-dancing classes, unlimited golf, horseshoes, softball, weenie roasts and more. Breakfast and dinner are served in the dining room; or you can enjoy lunch specials and dinners (five nights a week) in The Club. There is a snack shop on the golf course too.

Mountain Manor offers packages based on golf, weather, themes, sports, holidays, shopping or nothing at all. The shopping package is great for those who want to take advantage of all the retail opportunities in the Mount Pocono area (see our Shopping chapter for details). Another neat option is the "stay-over" package — an additional night and breakfast at no extra cost (see Mountain Manor's brochure).

Accommodations are available in duplex units and motel units — Creekside, East Wing, West Wing and Golf Club — with private baths and cable TVs. Duplex accommodations include two floors, a living room with fireplace and fold-out couch, a kitchenette and a bedroom. Motel units include two double beds, cheery decor, a separate dressing room, a refrigerator and balconies overlooking the golf course. Rates include Modified American Plan meals and are based on per person, double occupancy. Children ages 4 to 11 staying in same room as adults pay $26 each per night; ages 12 to 17, $48. High rates for adults in the motel units are $69 per weekend; the duplex units are $95 per weekend. Midweek and package rates are lower. Mountain Manor's brochure is extensive, listing all variables; call to obtain a copy.

This resort is only a half-mile from U.S. 209 in Marshalls Creek. Peruse other chapters to learn about other fun things to see and do in and around the Mount Pocono area.

Mount Pocono Area

Caesars Brookdale
Pa. Hwy. 611, Scotrun • 839-8843, (800) 233-4141

Caesars Brookdale is one of four famed Caesars resorts in the Poconos, yet while the others cater to couples only, Brookdale has facilities for families too. Brookdale is surrounded by woods on a 260-acre estate on the corridor between Stroudsburg and Mount Pocono. It includes a trout-stocked lake as well as lovely hiking and bicycling trails. The atmosphere is rustic, relaxed and comfortable. Couples enjoy the heart-shape tubs and champagne towers (7½-foot-tall, champagne glass-shape whirlpools) big enough for two.

But the whole family can take part in activities such as indoor roller skating, outdoor ice skating, tennis, racquetball, indoor and outdoor miniature golf, billiards, archery, indoor and outdoor swimming; exercising at the health club and spa; and playing outdoor basketball, volleyball and softball. On the lake, enjoy kayaks, paddle boats and sailboats.

The Caesars group has an option called the Key Around Club, which offers guests free use of facilities at the other Caesars resorts. With the Key Around Club from Brookdale, you can cross-country ski at Pocono Palace (see the subsequent "Couples/Honeymoon Rereats" section), toboggan at Cove Haven, play indoor racquetball at Paradise Stream and Cove Haven, golf at Pocono Palace, use the golf driving ranges at Pocono Palace and Cove Haven and water-ski at Pocono Palace and Cove Haven. Brookdale is also only minutes away from Camelback ski area and about a 30-minute drive from Alpine Mountain and Shawnee Mountain, if skiing is your interest.

Top-name entertainers come to the resort's nightclub, The Applause, throughout the year; past performers include David Brenner and the late George Burns. Many famous prize fighters work out at Caesars too, such as Sugar Ray Leonard and Lennox Lewis; the public is invited to watch training sessions for a fee. Two full-course meals are part of your accommodations package; for honeymooners there is a champagne breakfast in bed. The setting at Brookdale is lovely; the country-casual resort was once owned by the prestigious Wilkins family (well-known Poconos real estate magnates and hoteliers).

Rates are per couple and include two meals daily and free use of all facilities plus Key Around Club options. They are based on a minimum of two nights and three days but you can add to the base package in daily increments up to seven nights and eight days. Rates for a suite in the main lodge or for one of the mountain villas range from $430 for two nights up to $1,260 for seven nights. The rates go up based on additional in-room amenities, such as pools and spas. The most expensive are the Roman Towers, luxurious two-story accommodations including a downstairs living room with fireplace and cathedral ceiling, a dining area, a private heart-shaped pool and a loft area with bedroom. The bedroom contains a round bed with a starlight ceiling. The Roman Tower also includes a health spa with Jacuzzi, sauna and the Champagne Tower whirlpool, which you reach from the loft level. Rates are $720 for two nights and $2,240 for seven nights. At Brookdale, children older than 12 are $55 daily; children 12 and younger are

FREE VACATION PLANNING KIT

FILL OUT THE COUPON OR CALL 800-POCONOS (800-762-6667) AND RECEIVE YOUR FREE POCONO MOUNTAINS VACATION PLANNING KIT.

Name_____

Address_____

City_____ State_____ Zip_____

Telephone Number_____

IS THIS FOR A _____Family _____Couple _____Single

WHAT TYPE OF LODGING ARE YOU INTERESTED IN?
_____Bed & Breakfast _____Resort Lodging
_____Motel/Motor Lodge _____Resort w/Meals
_____Villa/Home Rental _____Campground
_____Midweek Packages _____Pets Accepted
_____Housekeeping Cottage _____Country Inn

_____Other_____

One international raceway
Thirteen ski areas
Four Victorian towns
One-hundred-and-one factory outlets
One-hundred-seventy river miles
Fourteen waterfalls
Thirty-five golf courses
Two-hundred-eighty places to stay
Thirteen rafting tours
Hundred-fifty lakes
Nine state parks

FREE

THE POCONOS
Get Away To It All.

WHAT TYPE OF ACTIVITIES ARE YOU INTERESTED IN?
___Auto Racing ___Biking ___Canoeing/Rafting
___Fishing ___Horseback Riding ___Historical Sites
___Golf ___Nature Guide ___Lake on/nearby
___Events ___Fall Foliage ___Antiques/Flea Markets
___Hiking ___Museums ___Boating/Rentals/Rides
___Restaurants ___Playhouse/Theatre ___War Games/Paint Ball
___Tennis ___Train Rides ___Skiing/Winter Sports
___Attractions ___Shopping ___Summer Water Sports
___Spring/Summer Activities ___Fall/Winter Activities

___Other_____

WHEN ARE YOU PLANNING YOUR TRIP?

Month_____ Year_____

THE POCONOS

Pennsylvania
Memories last a lifetime.™

PLACE PROPER
POSTAGE HERE
Post Office will
not deliver
unless proper
postage used

POCONO MOUNTAINS VACATION BUREAU
1004 MAIN STREET, BOX 551
STROUDSBURG, PA 18360-1695

Enjoy magnificent scenery while biking through the Pocono Mountains.

$40 daily; and infants are free. Consult your travel agent to arrange fly-in packages via USAir.

The Chateau at Camelback
300 Camelback Rd., Tannersville
• 629-5900

The Chateau is at the base of Camelback Ski Area, which makes it a great choice for skiers who want to be as close as possible to the slopes but in a hotel rather than a townhouse or condominium. This hotel looks like a French château set among mountains and nestled against its own little lake. One side of The Chateau is all glass, affording views of the mountains in four-season splendor from the lounge, main lobby, indoor swimming pool, Jacuzzi and dining room. The outdoor pool and surrounding gardens, gazebo and multi-level sun decks also have mountain views. The pond is perfect for boating and fishing. You can play tennis, volleyball and shuffle-

Timesharing and Vacation-home Rentals

Timesharing offers vacationers the opportunity to own a share of a two- or three-bedroom townhouse-style property. Typically, you purchase a $1/52$nd interest in a home, owning a fraction of the house and grounds. This entitles you to stay at the house for the same one-week period every year. The rest of the time, other people stay there.

With a timeshare, your vacation accommodations already are arranged each year. You enjoy the benefits of owning a second home in the country without the worries of year-round maintenance and bills. All repairs, upkeep and renovations are handled by the company that operates the facility. In addition, you have access to a wide range of amenities, such as pools, fitness centers, recreation centers, golf courses and tennis courts. Planned activities are arranged throughout each day — everything from scavenger hunts and hikes to bingo or skiing outings.

Most homes sleep eight to 10 people and have a full living room, bathroom, kitchen and whirlpool/spa.

Theoretically, you may trade the week you purchase for the same period of time at one of several hundred timeshare resorts throughout the world.

Also, you have the opportunity to rent your share to others, loan it to friends, sell it and even pass it on to your heirs.

Timesharing, or "deeded fractional vacation ownership" as those in the business call it, has increased in popularity 700 percent in the last 16 years, currently boasting more than 675,000 "members."

In the Poconos, the two major timesharing resorts are The Villas at Tree Tops and Fairway and Shawnee VillaShare.

The Villas at Tree Tops and Fairway are off U.S. Highway 209 south of Bushkill. This company is a subsidiary of Resorts USA Inc., which is part of The Rank Organization. The same company also owns the Fernwood Resort, less than a mile away. For additional information, call 588-9451.

Shawnee VillaShare, is on River Road near Shawnee-on-Delaware. It is part of the Shawnee Inn resort complex. For information or to schedule tours, call 424-1300.

At each facility, property owners are allowed to use the amenities at the corresponding resort.

Separate from timesharing, the two resorts also offer vacation home rentals.

Fairway Villas' two-bedroom accommodations sleep six and include access to Fernwood's entertainment, activities and recreational opportunities. A trolley shuttles guests throughout the grounds. Activities are scheduled each day from early morning to around midnight. Of course, participation is optional.

Rates range from $610 (for seven nights) to $830, depending on the season. Summer and winter rates are higher than in fall and spring. Two- and three-night packages are available as well. They range from $270 for two nights mid-week during fall and spring to $390 for a weekend in the summer or winter. Holidays cost $100 to $200 more. This does not include tax and a refundable $200 security deposit. No pets are allowed.

For information or reservations, call (800) 343-8676.

Shawnee's Northslope, Valley View and Shawnee Villas townhomes and chateaus range from $1,020 for one week in winter at a three-bedroom unit at Northslope to $485 for a week in winter at an efficiency-style rental. A security deposit is required. Rentals include free or discounted ski lift tickets and twilight golf passes. Guests may also use the amenities of Shawnee Inn, Shawnee Place Play & Water Park, Shawnee Mountain Ski Area and Shawnee Racquet & Fitness Club.

For information and reservations, call (800) 742-9633 Ext. 8970.

Many Poconos residents rent their homes on a weekly or monthly basis, particularly in private communities and near recreation areas such as Lake Wallenpaupack. These are discussed in our Real Estate chapter. Consult a local real estate agent for rates and availability in the region you desire.

---

board; hike in the woods; dance in the lounge to some of the best DJs and bands in the Poconos; hang out in the game room; tone-up in the exercise room; join an aerobics class; or treat yourself to a massage.

The rooms are large and comfortable with two double beds, and all have wonderful views. Poolside rooms have balconies overlooking the pool and pond with Camelback as the backdrop. Rates per person for a weekend stay range from $90 to $150; midweek rates range from $50 to $90. Conferences, conventions and groups are welcome. And weddings outside by the pool or in the poolside, Ledges or Mountainview dining rooms are truly lovely. This hotel is up the mountain from Crossings Factory Stores (see our Shopping chapter) — a great option if some in your group want to shop while others ski.

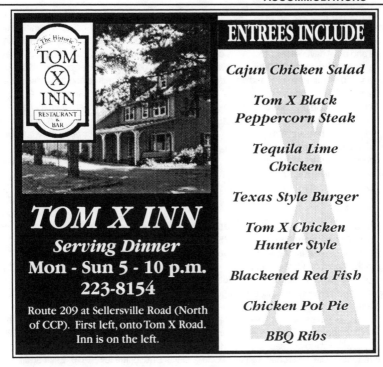
Mount Airy Lodge
Off Pa. Hwy. 611 or 447, Mount Pocono • 839-8811, (800) 441-4410

Mount Airy Lodge is in the midst of things in the Stroudsburg-Mount Pocono corridor. Action — all the time, all year long — is what happens here. The program sheets in the lobby are full of nonstop fun activities for kids, young and old. The resort spreads out to include a 35-acre lake, an 18-hole golf course, 21 indoor and outdoor tennis courts, two Olympic-size pools (one indoor, one outdoor), racquetball courts, a game room, sports palace (basketball, Ping-Pong, soccer, archery), a health club (with sauna and steam room), restaurants, cafes, dining rooms, show rooms (with big-name performers), club rooms and a disco.

There are supervised activities — swimming, tennis and outdoor nature walks to name a few — for the children all summer long and in ski season. In winter, kids and adults enjoy downhill skiing on seven slopes, snowboarding, cross-country skiing, snowmobiling, indoor ice skating and much more (see Winter Sports). In summer, guests can sail or water-ski on the lake; take out a bumper boat, rowboat or canoe; fish or scuba dive (additional charge). Or, around the lake, you can ride a horse, hike or bicycle. Skeet shooting, archery and indoor roller skating are also part of the available activities. The fitness center even offers massages for deep muscle relaxation.

There are many types of accommodations at Mount Airy because it also includes Pocono Gardens Lodge and Stricklands Mountain Inn and Cottages. Wherever you stay, your rate includes two full-course meals (breakfast and dinner) daily and access to all facilities and activities at Mount Airy Lodge. A few activities require an additional charge (golf, scuba diving and skiing), but everything else is included in your room rate. In the Mount Airy Lodge a standard room is $150 per couple for a weekend night or $875 for seven nights and eight days; a champagne suite is $270 for a weekend night or $1,750 for seven nights and eight days (there are many levels in between). In Pocono Gardens Lodge a villa is $150 for a weekend night and $875 for seven nights and eight days; a top-of-the-line Nestlewood chalet is $275 a weekend night or $1,785 for seven nights and eight days. At the Stricklands complex a standard room is $150 for a weekend night and $875 for seven nights and eight days; the Camelot Suite with private pool is $275 a weekend night and $1,785 for seven nights and eight days. There are also conference and banquet facilities. Couples-only packages and options also are available and include sunken tubs or private pools, heart-shape tubs, Jacuzzis and more.

FYI

Unless otherwise noted, the area code for all phone numbers in this guide is 717.

Daniels Top-O-The-Poconos Resort
Pa. Hwy. 447 N., Canadensis • 595-7531

Being at Daniels is like spending Christmas in the home of a large family. There are children everywhere, lots of activity, lots of laughing and carrying-on, and events going on all the time. This place is for families — the boisterous, let's-have-a-good-time kind. The facilities include three outdoor pools, an indoor pool with hot tub and sauna, softball field, full-size lighted basketball court, lighted boccie courts, three tennis courts, an archery range, playgrounds, a video game room and more than 80 beautiful country acres to walk, hike, take hayrides or cross-country ski in winter. There are oodles of family-oriented activities all summer. And on winter weekends before Christmas, Daniels allows guests to cut their own trees for free from the resort's property to take home for the holidays. Other activities include a karaoke sing-along for folks arriving on Saturdays, talent nights, tournaments in all the sports, arts and crafts, nature walks, rafting trips, bingo, live show bands and more.

Food is excellent and plentiful; guests are served a hearty breakfast each morning and a full-course dinner each night. Breakfast includes eggs or omelettes; homefries; bacon or sausage; pancakes, French toast or waffles; and hot or cold cereal. Lunch is available at the snack bar, although most guests say

they're usually too full from breakfast to eat lunch. Dinner might be baked Virginia ham, sweet and sour chicken, roast beef with gravy, chicken cordon bleu or Chinese pepper steak, each with potatoes and vegetables.

Daniels is a family place that folks come back to year after year. Some kids from returning families see each other year after year and even say their off-to-college good-byes here. It is a comfortable, unassuming place.

Accommodations include inn rooms, poolside cottages and the Hilltop Lodge and Cottages. Hilltop's accommodations have a separate outdoor pool and play area a quarter-mile from the inn, so having your own transportation is a good idea if you're staying there. Rates depend on the number of persons per family, but for our purposes we assume two adults and children younger than 15 for a week-long (Saturday to Saturday) stay. (Note: Bring your own towels.) For a party of two with two children younger than 15, the high rate is $620; the low rate, $575. For six in a family, the high rate is $1,050; the low, $910. Each additional adult in a room is $175.

Daniels advertises the cheapest rates in the Poconos; call for a brochure to survey specific options. Daniels also offers weekend getaway packages and special rates for groups, including reunions. Daniels is near many Poconos delights (see the "Mount Pocono Area" section of Shopping, Winter Sports, Attractions and Arts and Culture chapters). If you want a break from the scheduled activities here, daily or hourly excursions are viable options.

Hillside Lodge Resort Motel and Cottages
Pa. Hwy. 390, Canadensis • 595-7551, (800) 666-4455

Hillside is a quiet, cozy family resort of suites and cottages in the mountains near Canadensis. Innkeepers Dave and Sandy Kline emphasize family and plan activities to suit your entire clan.

Note the on-site whitetail deer ranch as you drive onto the property. And be sure to check out the calender of weekly events. Nature walks with naturalist Dr. Tom Laduke, volleyball, horseshoes, boccie ball, minigolf and swimming in the outdoor pool are available for families to enjoy together or apart. Nightly entertainment includes karaoke, bonfires, marshmallow roasts, dancing and games. A whitewater rafting adventure is planned each week for adults and children 6 and older. A summer camp is available for children ages 6 to 12; participants sign up on a daily ($15) or weekly ($65) basis plus a $25 registration fee.

Meals are served in the colorful dining room, with a private table for each family or group. Those who wish to dine without children can sit on the enclosed porch.

Accommodations include large, spacious suites or cottages, some with fireplaces and some with sunken heart-shape tubs. The cottages have refrigerators and separate living rooms and bedrooms. Suites and cottages are decorated with matching drapes and quilts or spreads that complement the wall-to-wall carpeting.

Rates include breakfast and dinner (children's menu is available) daily and are based on double occupancy. Options include daily and weekend rates and weekly rates for July and August. Weekend packages offered throughout the year include theme events and discounted rates. There are ski packages,

mystery weekend packages, fall foliage weekends, Halloween party weekends, a Mother's Day special (mom stays free), Christmas week (kids stay free), midwinter packages (kids stay free) and others; be sure to inquire when making a reservation. In June, Hillside Lodge offers an outdoor adventure minivacation for five nights and six days at a reduced rate.

The daily base room rate is $138 per person; for a suite, $170; and for the most extravagant cottage with king-size bed, fireplace and heart-shaped tub, $180. Weekly rates run $890, $1,070 and $1,135 respectively. Children's rates begin at $15 daily for ages 1 to 5 and range up to $37 daily for ages 13 to 17; weekly rates are $95 to $235 respectively. Children younger than 1 stay free. There are discounts for seniors, military personnel and clergy, and some midweek rates excluding meals are as low as $65 per couple. Since this resort is near Alpine Mountain and Camelback, and only a quick swoosh to Shawnee, it is an attractive option in winter for folks who spend all day on the slopes.

Tamiment
Resort & Conference Center
Bushkill Falls Rd., Tamiment • 588-6652, (800) 233-8105

Tamiment, a four-season resort, surrounds a beautiful mountain lake, which you'll surely notice as you drive in toward the main lodge. From the lakefront, the beauty of rolling hills, woods and the Robert Trent Jones-designed 18-hole golf course (see Golf) makes you feel like you're being cradled by nature. Amenities here include eight lighted outdoor tennis courts and three indoor courts, indoor and outdoor basketball, volleyball, indoor racquetball and miniature golf. Fitness amenities include a full fitness room with state-of-the-art equipment, Jacuzzi, steam room and sauna. Swim in the enormous lakeside pool or lovely indoor pool. The spectacular spring-fed lake offers boating and fishing. Tamiment's 2,200 acres provide ample room to ride horses, hike; or in winter, weather permitting, go cross-country skiing, snowmobiling or sledding.

Breakfast and dinner are served in the formal dining room overlooking the lake. Lunch is available at Par 4 (on-site cafe) or at the poolside snack bar. There is a nightclub here for your big-show entertainment. Recreation programs for adults and children take place all day long. There are also meeting rooms and facilities large enough to hold the most demanding convention, corporate meeting or family reunion. Golf outings are popular too. The staff is ready to help plan group activities such as meals and team-building programs.

Accommodations include guest rooms and suites, ranging from standard to deluxe. They are available in the Tamiment House Hotel or Golf Clubhouse. All are carpeted, color-coordinated, climate-controlled and equipped with private baths, color TVs and telephones. Tamiment is a casual lakeside retreat right up the road from Bushkill Falls and midway between Stroudsburg and Milford, off U.S. Highway 209. Rates are $127 per person per night for double occupancy on the Modified American Plan. Children ages 5 to 12 are $7.50 per night (MAP); kids 13 and older are $44 per night if staying in the same room (MAP). Winter rates are less, and fall golf specials are available.

Fernwood Resort and Country Club
U.S. Hwy. 209 Bushkill • 588-9500,
(800) 233-8103

Did you say you like action and want to feel in the middle of things? Did you say a vacation for you not only means mountains and trees, but also mountains and trees in the middle of action? Well, Fernwood is action.

Fernwood's 600 acres flank U.S. Highway 209, which separates this resort's skiing areas and snowmobiling trails from the lodges. But it's this separation that gives Fernwood that right-in-the-middle-of-things feel. Everywhere

Campgrounds

For a vacation that is both affordable and scenic, you can't beat a stay at a campground.

Your outing can be as primitave or modern as you desire. Facilities range from a simple tent site in a state park with no water or electric hookups to a spot in a commercial campground boasting full hookups and a variety of recreational opportunities.

When considering camping in the Poconos, decide on your priorities. Do you want

to be near a certain town, attraction or region? Do you want privacy or interaction with other campers? Do you want to "rough it" in the woods or be closer to civilization? Are you looking to hunt, fish, boat or just get away from it all?

Nearly every campground in the Poconos provides showers, picnic areas, laundry facilities, bathrooms and dumping stations.

The most desirable campsites are large and wooded. Many people also want to be close to a lake or river. Some campgrounds charge an extra $3 to $5 for their prime sites.

The full-service facilities include such amenities as swimming pools, recreational pavilions, planned activities and outdoor sports (horseshoes, tennis, volleyball, basketball and softball).

A campsite without water and electric costs $15 to $25 per night for two people. Weekday rates are cheaper than weekends. You can add $3 to $5 for hookups. Additional family members generally are charged an extra $2 to $5 each. Cable television and air-conditioning hookups, when available, cost around $2 to $3 each. Guests of campers who visit for the day usually are charged a fee around $3, which entitles them to use the campground's amenities. Seasonal rates and camper storage are offered frequently.

To ensure a site, call ahead for reservations. This is especially a concern during the summer when most of the campgrounds do big business every weekend. If you want to camp on a holiday weekend, reserve your site at least a month ahead of time.

In addition to the commercial operations discussed here, you may also camp in most Poconos state parks. See our Parks and In, On and Around the Water chapters for information on these facilities.

The following is a list of some of the region's campgrounds that provide better-than-average amenities and sites.

If you want to be on the **Delaware River**, try River Beach Campsites, U.S. Highway 209, Milford, 296-7421 or (800) 356-2852. This campground is owned by Kittatinny Canoes and offers special rates and choice sites for those who want to camp and canoe or raft on the river. Two people can camp and hit the water for around $70.

Another good campground on the Delaware River is Dingmans Campground, U.S. Highway 209, Dingmans Ferry, 828-2266. It is along the river within the Delaware Water Gap National Recreation Area, making it ideal for anyone who wants to hike, hunt, fish or swim.

In **Stroudsburg/East Stroudsburg** try: Cranberry Run Campground, Hallet Road, Analomink, 421-1462 or (800) 233-8240; Fox Wood Family Campground, Mt. Nebo Road, East Stroudsburg, 421-1424; Mountain Vista Campground, Taylor Drive, East Stroudsburg, 223-0111; Delaware Water Gap KOA, Hollow Road, East Stroudsburg, 223-8000; and Otter Lake Camp-Resort, 4805 Marshalls Creek Road, East Stroudsburg, 223-0123 or (800) 345-1369.

In the **Mount Pocono area** try: Fern Ridge Campground, Exit 43 off of Interstate 80, Blakeslee, 646-2267 or 800-468-2442; Mount Pocono Campground, Pa. Route 196, Mount Pocono, 839-7573; Four Seasons Campground, Babbling Brook Road, Scotrun, 629-2504; and Hemlock Campground & Cottages, 362 Hemlock Drive, Tobyhanna, 894-4388.

In the **West End** try: Otto's Camping Resort & RV Center, 1500 Rock Street, Lehighton, (610) 377-5313; Jim Thorpe Camping Resort, Lentz Trail, Jim Thorpe, 325-2644; and Don Laine Campground, 790 57 Drive, Palmerton, (610) 381-3381.

In the **Milford area** try: Ken's Woods Campground, Bushkill (follow signs from U.S. Highway 209), 588-6381.

In the **Lake Wallenpaupack area** try: PP&L Lake Wallenpaupack Camping, U.S. Highway 6 and Pa. Highway 590 W., Lake Wallenpaupack, 226-3702; Rainbow Mountain Family Campground, Pa. Highway 670, Honesdale, 253-0424; Cherry Ridge Campground, Camp Road, Honesdale, 488-6654; and Keen Lake Camp-Cottage Resort, Keen Lake Road, Waymart, 488-6161 or (800) 443-0412

In the **Slate Belt** try: Sandy Acres Campgrounds, Turkey Ridge Road, Portland, 897-6230.

Call the campgrounds for information on amenities, current rates and reservations. Also, contact the Pocono Mountain Vacation Bureau, 421-5791 or (800) 762-6667, and request a free copy of its brochure on campgrounds and its *Poconos Vacation Guide,* which also contains information on campgrounds.

you look, people are on their way to activities — and there you are on "main street" in the mountains! There are restaurants and bars that offer full dinners (Astor Room, Tom X Inn and Weathervanes); Las Vegas-style entertainment (Astor Room); lounges with karaoke or dancing (Weathervanes); a '50s-style snack bar (Hollywood Diner); and banquet and conference facilities for meetings, parties and weddings.

Winter activities such as snowmobiling, skiing and sledding abound (see our Winter Sports chapter for details), but summer, spring and fall are activity-filled too. Fernwood's grounds are great for biking and hiking and include a private lake for fishing or paddleboating. Golfing options include an 18-hole championship course or a nine-hole course. You can swim indoors or outdoors, then take advantage of the sauna and whirlpool. Tennis anyone? Indoor and outdoor courts are available. The Recreation Center rounds out the complement of amenities, with a state-of-the-art fitness center, Nautilus workout equipment, an on-call masseuse, a great video arcade, miniature golf, Ping-Pong, billiards and indoor volleyball.

Kids activities for ages 4 to 12 are available two sessions a day. Depending on the season, there are games, contests and all kinds of planned group activities. Get the schedule at the front desk. (Ski equipment rentals and some activities, such as snowmobiling, require an additional fee; ski lift tickets and most activities are free.)

Accommodations range from standard to deluxe and include guest rooms, parlor rooms, suites and deluxe suites. Choose from rooms in the main hotel, in the wings or in lodges a short walk away. Parlor suites have Jacuzzis and living room/bedroom combinations. Dream suites have heart-shape Jacuzzis; round, mirrored king-size beds; private saunas; and electric fireplaces. The deluxe dream

suite is more luxurious and spacious with a sitting and lounging area. There are also economy rooms with just the basics for those who only intend to sleep in their rooms. Rates depend on the type of room and length of stay but include breakfast, dinner and all amenities except those noted as carrying an additional charge. Rates range from $59 per person, double occupancy, to $117. There is an additional 15 percent gratuity added as well as sales tax. Children 6 and younger stay free; kids ages 7 to 12 are $15 per night, and folks ages 13 to 17 are $20 per night.

Pocmont Resort
Bushkill Falls Rd., Bushkill • 588-6671, (800) 762-6668

Pocmont is undergoing a major renovation following a devastating fire in spring 1996. At press time a great deal of the renovation was complete, and plenty of activities were ready and waiting for guests. The health club has floor-to-ceiling windows that look out to the outdoor pool. The indoor pool is close to the sauna, whirlpool and steam rooms. You can get a body massage too. Of course, there's a game room, coffee shop and lounge with large-screen TV.

Activities abound: tennis, boat rides on the lake, archery, shuffleboard and volleyball. We did mention the Olympic-size outdoor pool, didn't we? Entertainment happens in the Pocono Star Room; dancing too. Dinner is served in two lovely dining rooms. In winter you can ride the resort's snowmobiles or walk its miles of trails; summer walks are a delight too.

Accommodations are in suites, with luxuries including Jacuzzis, hydromassage whirlpool, king-size beds, and in some cases, fireplaces or terraced balconies. There are also standard rooms in the hotel plus cottages, some with king-size beds and separate living rooms.

Autumn beauty.

Rates depend on the type of accommodation, but average about $65 per person per night, double occupancy and include a continental breakfast.

This resort is just up the road from Bushkill Falls, off U.S. Highway 209. It is convenient to attractions, shopping, arts and cultural events anywhere within a 30-minute drive along the U.S. 209 corridor from Milford to Stroudsburg and Shawnee-on-Delaware too.

The Mountain Laurel Resort & Golf Club
Off I-80 Exit 42, White Haven • 443-8411, (800) 458-5921

This resort is in the western Poconos. It is a relaxed getaway with a focus on "Leav[ing] the kids with us." The facilities include indoor and outdoor swimming pools, four lighted tennis courts, a sauna (a masseuse is available too), golf and nature trails for hiking and walking, a miniature golf course and, in winter, sledding trails. Skiing is available nearby at Jack Frost and Big Boulder.

The big news here, however, is the highly acclaimed children's program. People come again and again just for the great care their children get in this experiential, noncompetitive environment. There is a one-time camp cost for guests on the meal program, whether the kids stay for the weekend or the week in the summer season, or for the weekend in winter. The fee of $12 pays for the "Kidtraks" T-shirt. Along with children's activities, there is the special dinner program at Treetops restaurant. The kids eat here (in their T-shirts, of course) and receive a special Kidtraks menu, table settings and other niceties. They are taught the art of formal dining, including ordering from the menu and practicing other helpful meal manners. And while the kids are enjoying their meal — and they really do — parents are free to enjoy a special dinner for two. The toddlers (3 and younger) are in an experiential program that includes close supervision, exercise, crafts, petting-zoo time, birthday parties and other fun, age-appropriate activities. The toddler program costs $10

Housekeeping Cottages

Imagine yourself in a wooden cottage sitting on a quiet country brook. Trees, birds and the sounds of nature surround you. Although there are plenty of recreational activities on the grounds of your accommodations, you can not think of a reason to leave your cottage. Best of all, you do not have to — it has a full kitchen, bath and fireplace. This is life in one of the Poconos' housekeeping cottages.

Many folks stay at a cozy housekeeping cottage for either a romantic getaway in the woods or an affordable way to take the entire family to the Poconos and reduce the costs of food and rooms.

Most housekeeping-cottage resorts offer fewer than 10 units, so reservations are a good idea. Usually you may rent cottages with one, two or three bedrooms.

A couple staying on the weekend can expect to pay around $90 per night for a one-bedroom cottage. Mid-week rates are around $65.

When choosing a housekeeping cottage, consider the location you desire. Do you want to be in the woods away from everyone or near popular attractions? If you are bringing the whole family, you might want to check on the available amenities to make sure the kids will be entertained.

The following are some of the housekeeping cottages in the Poconos. Call them for reservations, availability, current rates and, in some instances, detailed directions (some are tricky to find, so call ahead and ask). Some are only open in the spring and summer, so make sure your cottage of choice is open when you want to vacation. For listings of individual amenities, contact the Pocono Mountains Vacation Bureau, 421-5791 or (800) 762-6667, for a copy of the *Poconos Vacation Guide*.

In the **Delaware Water Gap** area, try Minisink Acres, River Road, Minisink Hills, 421-4447.

In **Stroudsburg/East Stroudsburg** try: Countryside Housekeeping Cottages, Bartonsville Avenue, Stroudsburg, 629-2131; Echo Valley Cottages, Lower Lakeview Drive, East Stroudsburg, 223-0662; Kovarick's Housekeeping & Motel, 1328 Dreher Avenue, Stroudsburg, 421-6842; Rimrock Country Cottages, 425 Rimrock Drive, Stroudsburg, 629-2360 or (800) 441-2193; and Willow Run Housekeeping Cottages, Pa. Highway 715, Stroudsburg, 629-0752.

In the **Mount Pocono area** try: Alvin's Log Cabins, Henryville, 629-0667; Fiabane Housekeeping Cottages, Beartown Road, Canadensis, 595-2770; Leisure Lake, Swiftwater, 839-0529; Mountain Springs Lake Resort, Mountain Springs Drive, Reeders, 629-0251; Naomi Village, Pa. Highway 390 N., Mountainhome, 595-6069 or (800) 33NAOMI; and Martinville Streamside Cottages, Pa. Highway 390 N., Canadensis, 595-2489.

In the **Milford area** try: Shohola Falls Inn, Shohola, 296-7396; Bilmar Cottages, Greentown, 857-0811; Pine Crest Lodge, Pa. Highway 507, Greentown, 857-1136; and Sylvania Tree Farm, Lackawaxen, 685-7001.

In the **Lake Wallenpaupack area** try: Wyler Lake & Cottages, Hawley, 226-3360; NemanieVillage Inc., Hawley, 226-4518; Loch Highlands Cottages, Paupack, 857-0529; Bunnell's Pond Resort, 587 Cliff Road, Honesdale, 253-2655; and Martins Lakefront Cottages, Fairview Lake and Lake Wallenpaupack, Hawley, 226-9621.

per day; there is a 5-to-1 ratio of certified life-guard counselors to kids. Other activities for kids include hayrides, "mousercize," basketball, pool games, nature hikes, relay races, arts and crafts and story time.

The weekend rate for a double-occupancy room ranges from $84 to $94 for two nights and two meals. The nightly children's rate for kids 12 and younger is $5 for one child per adult in a room (two adults can bring two children for this rate); children older than 12 pay $32 for the weekend. This resort allows you to combine on-site activities with the myriad attractions in Jim Thorpe.

Couples/ Honeymoon Retreats

Stroudsburg/East Stroudsburg

Caesars Pocono Palace
U.S. Hwy. 209, Marshalls Creek
• 588-6692, (800) 233-4141

Pocono Palace offers a country club setting with the amenities of a Caesars couples resort. It has a nine-hole golf course and specializes in sports activities. It's also part of the Caesars Key Around Club. Pocono Palace is set back off U.S. 209 and is surrounded by woods, so it's secluded yet close to the corridor between Stroudsburg and Milford. Water skiing is a favorite activity here. Or you can go boating by rowboat, kayak or paddle boat; fish; or hike or bike the lovely wooded grounds. There are heart-shape tubs and champagne towers, cottages and other room and suite options.

Amenities here and through the Key Around Club include indoor roller skating, outdoor ice skating, tennis, racquetball, indoor and outdoor miniature golf, billiards, archery, indoor pools and outdoor pools, a health club and spa and outdoor basketball, volleyball and softball. You can cross-country ski at Pocono Palace, toboggan at Cove Haven, play indoor racquetball at Paradise Stream and Cove Haven, use the golf driving ranges here and at Cove Haven and water-ski here and at Cove Haven.

Pocono Palace's nightclub often features Las Vegas headliners. Two full-course meals daily are part of your package. And honey-mooners can enjoy a champagne breakfast in bed. If you're coming from afar, inquire about USAir packages.

Rates are based on a two nights-three days minimum stay plus aforementioned meals. You can add extra days and nights to extend your stay to as many as seven nights and eight days. Key Around Club privileges apply. In the Club Lodge, expect to pay $390 per couple for a room and $430 for a suite for a minimum stay; for seven nights, rooms are $1,120 and suites $1,260. In-room pools and spas will add to the rate. The most expensive accommodations, the Roman Towers, cost $720 for two nights and $2,240 for seven nights. Discounts are available for seniors 60 and older; ask about additional options.

Penn Hills Resort
Pa. Hwy. 447 N., Analomink • 421-6464, (800) 233-8240

This is one of the well-known honeymoon or couples resorts in the Poconos. It has all the amenities of a first-class resort and all the romantic touches of a couples retreat. The resort is adjacent to Evergreen Park in Analomink — part of the resort's facilities — and offers golf in summer and cross-country skiing (weather permitting) in winter on ungroomed trails. There is a beginner ski slope for guests who want to give *schussing* (skiing) a try. A year-round ice-skating rink is another sports option. Tennis, swimming in the indoor pool and wedding bells-shape outdoor pool, paddleboating on the lake and picnicking by the lake are some fun things to do. Shuffle-board, Ping-Pong, video games, archery, miniature golf and fitness activities on the Fitness Par Course are other options. Entertainers perform in the patio bar or cocktail lounge, and strolling violinists in the dining room keep the evenings as lively as the days.

Accommodations include the Penthouse Towers at the base of the mountain, with inlaid heart-shape whirlpool baths, relaxing European saunas, round beds, log-burning fireplaces, refrigerators and color TVs. This is the most expensive option, with a low of $460 per couple per weekend including meals, candlelight champagne dinner and all amenities; for a week, $1,265. There are also villas and suites with the same basic amenities, and rates per couple

Photo: Pocono Mountains Vacation Bureau, Inc.

Pocono resorts feature heart-shape everything for honeymooners.

range from $240 to $460 for two nights, all inclusive; for a week, $640 to $1,265. There are always specials, and they are worth asking about when you call for reservation information.

Analomink is near major Poconos byways, including Pa. highways 191, 715, 390 and 940. See our Getting Around, Shopping, Attractions and Winter Sports (Penn Hills is close to Alpine Mountain) chapters for details about places to go and things to see and do . . . if you decide to leave your heart-shape tub.

Mount Pocono Area

Birchwood
3400 Birchwood Dr., Tannersville
• 629-0222, (800) 233-8177

This lovely couples resort is off Cherry Lane Road, actually between Analomink and Tannersville. Set in the woods, Birchwood resembles a little village. Activities here include fishing and boating (canoes, paddleboats and pontoon rides) on the lovely lake at the entrance and ice skating in winter, weather permitting. There are two pools, indoor and outdoor tennis, a games room, a gymnasium, boccie, archery, putting greens, a golf driving range, miniature golf, bowling, roller skating, shuffleboard, horseshoes, nature walks, hay rides and other fun things to do — all are free. For an additional charge, there's trap shooting, a rifle range and billiards.

Accommodations are in townhouses, chalets, a manor house and mansion, and budget suites and rooms in multi-room houses. Among the room choices, amenities include log-burning fireplaces, balconies, steambaths, Jacuzzi tubs for two, queen-size canopy beds, refrigerators, color TVs and separate living rooms.

Rates range from $165 to $200 per night per couple to $500 per night per couple, depending on room type. The price includes two meals a day and is based on a two-day minimum stay.

The Red Baron restaurant is a well-known component of this quiet country resort.

Caesars Paradise Stream
Pa. Hwy. 940, Mount Pocono • 839-8881, (800) 233-4141

Paradise Stream is another of the famed Caesars resorts in the Poconos for couples only. The winding stream and bridges that weave through this property make it a romantic spot for couples to wander. Its prime central location is notable: Mount Pocono to the west, Stroudsburg to the east, Tannersville to the south and Cresco and Canadensis to the north. That means it's close to Alpine Mountain, Shawnee Mountain and Camelback. It is also part of the Caesars Key Around Club, and other Caesars resorts are easily accessible from here.

The atmosphere and accommodations are not only relaxed and comfortable, but also exciting, with classic towers, villas and champagne towers. Amenities available here and through the Key Around Club include indoor roller skating, outdoor ice skating, tennis, racquetball, indoor and outdoor miniature golf, billiards, archery, indoor and outdoor pools, a health club and spa and outdoor basketball, volleyball and softball. On the lake here as well as at Cove Haven and Brookdale you'll find kayaks, paddle boats and sailboats. With the Key Around Club you can cross-country ski at Pocono Palace, toboggan at Cove Haven, play indoor racquetball at Paradise Stream and Cove Haven, golf at Pocono Palace, use the golf driving ranges at Pocono Palace and Cove Haven and waterski at Pocono Palace and Cove Haven.

Entertainment is always available at the resort's Red Apple Lounge. Las Vegas-type stars such as George Carlin make appearances throughout the year. Two full-course meals are part of your package here, and a champagne breakfast in bed is available for honeymooners. USAir packages are coordinated through Caesars resorts for guests coming from a distance.

Rates are per couple, with two meals and free use of all facilities including Key Around Club options. They are based on a minimum stay of two nights and three days; you can add up to five individual days and nights to extend your stay. A lakeside villa rate ranges from $470 for two nights to $1,365 for seven nights. The rates increase with additional in-room options such as pools and spas. The champagne towers, the most expensive option, range from $640 for two nights to $1,995 for seven nights. Seniors 60 and older are eligible for discounts; be sure to ask about other discount options as well.

The Summit Vacation Resort
Pa. Hwy. 715, Tannersville • 629-0203, (800) 233-8250

This luxurious couples resort is right off I-80 at Exit 46 in Tannersville. It has three levels in the main building, where three meals a day are served as well as nightly hors d'oeuvres and midnight snacks. Late risers can have breakfast delivered to their rooms.

The rooms surround the main building in villas and penthouse suites. Options include in-room pools, heart-shape whirlpool baths, sunken Roman tubs, heart-shaped Jacuzzis, private saunas, fireplaces, outdoor decks, private garden patios and balconies, sitting areas, mirrored walls and ceilings, and king-size beds of all manner (heart-shape, hexagonal, round, canopied and mirrored, to name a handful).

Outdoor activities abound, whatever the season, including paddleboating, swimming, tennis, volleyball, miniature golf, archery, a rifle range, boccie, badminton, horseshoes and bicycling. In winter, enjoy toboggans and snowmobiles. All activities and equipment is free.

Indoors you'll find a pool, whirlpool spa, fitness center, steam bath, Swedish sauna, tanning beds, miniature golf, shuffleboard, tennis, a golf driving range, volleyball, basketball, ice skating, roller skating and Ping Pong.

There's Scheherazade Nightclub and Kismet Cocktail Lounge for live entertainment, a coffee shop for a quick break and a gift shop for browsing or souvenir hunting.

A two-day stay, including three meals a day and all amenities, costs between $299 and $445 per couple, depending on the type of accommodation.

Lake Wallenpaupack Area

Caesars Cove Haven
Pa. Hwy. 590, Lakeville • 226-2101, (800) 233-4141

Cove Haven, between Hawley and Milford, is the farthest north of the Caesars resorts. It's a top-notch facility on the shores of Lake Wallenpaupack, with the lake as its focal point and woods all around. The lake provides the ultimate in fishing and boating opportunities, including water-skiing and speed boating. The lovely wooded grounds feature trails for hiking and biking, and in winter, spots for snowmobiling and tobogganing. The atmosphere is casual.

You'll find many activities for couples. Of course, there are heart-shape tubs and champagne towers in some rooms. Amenities here and through the "Key Around Club" include indoor roller skating; outdoor ice skating; tennis; racquetball; indoor and outdoor miniature golf; billiards; archery; indoor pools and outdoor pool; a health club and spa; and outdoor basketball, volleyball and softball. With the "Key Around Club," you can kayak and row on the smaller lake at Brookdale; cross-country ski at Pocono Palace; play indoor racquetball at Paradise Stream as well as at Cove Haven; golf at Pocono Palace; use the golf driving ranges at Pocono Palace and here at Cove Haven; and water-ski at Pocono Palace.

Big-name entertainment, such as David Brenner and George Carlin, is featured in the nightclub; ask about the performers scheduled to appear. Packages include two full-course meals, and for honeymooners, a champagne breakfast in bed. Caesars coordinates packages with USAir that include air transportation for guests coming from a distance.

Rates are per couple with two meals and free use of all facilities here and at other Pocono Caesars resorts, through Key Around Club, are based on a minimum of two nights and three days, adding a day and a night up to a maximum seven nights and eight days. Rates increase depending on in-room options, such as pools and spas. A room in the Harbourette, adjacent to the spa, costs $390 for two nights and $1,120 for seven nights. The most expensive digs, the Champagne Towers, are $640 for two nights and $1,995 for seven nights. Always ask about special programs; for instance, seniors 60 and older are eligible for a discount rate.

Motels/Motor Inns

The following rates apply for a double-occupancy room during peak season. Unless otherwise specified, basic in-room amenities apply (standard bath, telephone, TV, heat/air-conditioning unit and handicapped-accessibility). Expect that you're paying for a place to spend the night, close to all the great Poconos opportunities we discuss in other chapters such as Shopping; Winter Sports; In, On and Around the Water; Daytrips; Attractions; and Arts and Culture. Any extra charge for children is noted.

Price-code Key	
$50 or less	$
$51 to $95	$$
$96 to $130	$$$
$131 and more	$$$$

Delaware Water Gap

Ramada Inn
$$-$$$ • 101 Broad St., Delaware Water Gap • 476-0000, (800) 228-4897

This chain motel features 104 deluxe rooms with free HBO and indoor and outdoor pools. It is right off I-80 Exit 51. This Ramada is walking distance to all Delaware Water Gap opportunities, including shopping, live entertainment (the Deer Head Inn is a must-stop for jazz lovers; see Nightlife), eateries and cultural events, such as the Delaware Water Gap Celebration of the Arts and art shows at the Dutot Museum (see Arts and Culture for details). Children 18 and younger stay free.

Stroudsburg/
East Stroudsburg

Best Western Pocono Inn
$$ • 700 Main St., Stroudsburg • 421-2200, 421-2201

This Best Western is in the heart of Stroudsburg, so you can walk to anything happening on Main or Lower Main streets (see Arts and Culture and Shopping for some ideas). There are 90 large rooms, each with two double beds. Amenities include a lovely indoor pool with whirlpool spa on the side, and a game room. There are three places to eat here: Cafe Pocono, for a casual breakfast,

Photo: Pocono Mountains Vacation Bureau, Inc.

This couple enjoys life by the pool at a Pocono resort.

lunch or supper; the Chop House, for steak and seafood; and the Country Pheasant, an elegant country inn-type dining room. Children 16 and younger staying with adults are free.

Budget Motel
$$ • I-80, Exit 51, East Stroudsburg • 424-5451, (800) 233-8144

Insiders talk about this place for its great food. Everyone comes to eat at the on-site J.R.'s Green Scene restaurant, even if they aren't staying here. The lovely greenhouse dining room overlooks the Stroudsburgs and features a menu with delicious contemporary American cuisine.

All 115 rooms have controlled heating and air-conditioning and color cable TVs. Rooms have two double beds or king-size beds. Budget Motel is convenient to Poconos shopping, winter sports, watersports and attractions.

Plaza Hotel
$$ • 1220 W. Main St., Stroudsburg • 424-1930, (800) 777-5453

This lovely motel, owned by CNN Hotels Inc., is on W. Main, close to Exit 48 of I-80. There are 133 rooms, including outer views, poolside rooms and suites. The indoor pool with tropical motif includes the poolside Gazebo bar. Saunas, miniature golf and an arcade room complete the general amenities here. You'll also find meeting rooms for small groups. Evergreens Restaurant overlooks the tropical courtyard, and entertainment is featured nightly (except Sunday) at Whispers.

This hotel is close to I-80, Pa. Highway 611, U.S. Highway 209 and Pa. Highway 191, so nearby shopping, watersports and cultural opportunities abound. Children 18 and younger stay for free with parents.

Shannon Inn
$$ • U.S. Hwy. 209, East Stroudsburg • 424-1951

This motel is right off I-80's Exit 52. It has 120 newly redecorated guest rooms with cable TVs, an indoor pool with a tropical motif and complimentary continental breakfast. On Fridays and Saturdays the Shannon Pub features Irish entertainment. Children 12 and younger stay free in their parents' room. Call for group rates.

Mount Pocono Area

Harmony Lake Shore Inn
$$ • Pa. Hwy. 903, Lake Harmony • 722-0522

This little motel offers only basic in-room amenities but is right on Lake Harmony. Boating, fishing and swimming are available at the lake. In winter there's ice skating (weather permitting) and snowmobiling. Children are $5 extra.

Take Exit 35 from the Northeast Extension (Pa. Turnpike) or Exit 42 from I-80 and proceed east on Pa. 940 to its junction with Pa. Highway 115.

Holiday Inn – Bartonsville
$$-$$$ • Pa. Hwy. 611, Bartonsville • 424-6100

This lovely Holiday Inn is easily accessible off Exit 46B on I-80. It has a lovely tropical indoor pool as well as a lounge, disco, restaurant and game room to complement its 152 rooms with standard or king-size beds and TVs with free Showtime. Children 12 and younger stay free with parents.Banquet facilities are available.

Lazy Rock Lodge
$$ • Pa. Hwy. 191, Cresco • 595-2165

This rustic stop has four motel units and three cabins. The cabins have fireplaces; one sleeps up to six, with two bedrooms and a living room. All accommodations have showers in private baths. There is cable TV is every room, and a full breakfast is served every morning in the on-site cafe. Lunch and dinner are also served, and the menu choices include American and Mexican food; the cafe is open to the public.

This lodge is in Paradise Valley in a very quiet, lovely location that suits its fenced-in outdoor pool. It is right next door to the Crescent Lodge (see our Bed and Breakfasts and Country Inns and Restaurants chapters).

Penn's Woods Motel & Cottages
$-$$ • Pa. Hwy. 611, Tannersville • 629-0131

This motel has 12 rooms and two cottages, a trout pond in back (guests can fish without a license, so bring your pole or rent one at the motel) and an outdoor pool. In winter, ski packages are available in conjunction with Camelback, Big Boulder, Jack Frost and Alpine. Options include single- and double-occupancy rooms. Some larger rooms have Jacuzzis; cottages have kitchenettes.

Penn's Woods is just 1.5 miles from Crossings Factory Outlets.

Pocono Ramada Inn
$$-$$$ • Pa. Hwy. 940, Lake Harmony • 443-8471

This Ramada is close to Lake Harmony and, in winter, good skiing at Big Boulder or Jack Frost. The 139 rooms include standard units (some with king-size beds) and suites. Rooms have two double beds and color TVs.

Amenities include an indoor pool, saunas, an indoor sun deck with sun lamps and a putting green. The pool is snowman-shape! Children 18 and younger stay free with their parents.

There are two restaurants at the inn, a coffee shop for breakfast and a main restaurant for lunch and dinner.

Super 8 Motel/Pocono Fountain
$$ • Pa. Hwy. 611 S., Mount Pocono • 839-7728

Right on Pa. 611, this 40-room motel has an outdoor pool, rooms with Jacuzzis, waterbeds and king-size beds, free HBO and large rooms for families. Children 12 and younger stay in their parents' room free. This Super 8 has truck parking and is a short drive to Camelback.

Village Court
$$-$$$ • Pa. Hwy. 390, Canadensis • 595-7888

This village motel is right in the heart of

Canadensis and within walking distance to all its shops and restaurants. There are 12 motel rooms and four cottages. The cottages are beside the privately owned lake and have decks, two bedrooms, living rooms with fireplaces and kitchens with all amenities. The motel rooms have eating areas, two double beds, refrigerators and coffee makers. Each room is decorated differently with country casual furnishings.

Paddleboats and rowboats are available for guests as part of the room rate. Around the outdoor pool you'll find picnic tables and barbecue grills.

Cottage prices are based upon four people, with $10 per night for each additional person. Children 12 and younger are free.

West End

The Country Place Motel
$$ • Pa. Hwy. 903, Jim Thorpe • 325-2214

This quaint, country motel has 12 rooms and one efficiency, each with color TV and basic cable. The large rooms are decorated with country antiques and old-fashioned country schemes of plaids and flowers. The rooms all have full baths and double beds.

The Country Place was in the process of remodeling as this book went to press and expects to offer more options by spring 1997.

Children 7 and younger are free if staying in the room with parents. Each additional adult is $15; children, $7.50. Maximum occupancy per room is four people.

From April to October a free continental breakfast is available.

This spot is about a mile from the Jim Thorpe Mausoleum, burial place of the legendary Jim Thorpe, and about 15 miles from the twin ski and recreational areas of Jack Frost and Big Boulder; it's also near the Pocono International Raceway (see the Close-up in Attractions).

Milford Area

Best Western Inn at Hunt's Landing
$$ • 900 U.S. Hwys. 6 and 209, Matamoras • 491-2400

This is a truly super motel. It has wonderful views of the mountains and the Delaware River from its Hunt's Landing location on the Delaware River. The 108 guest rooms include kings, suites and doubles, some with Jacuzzis. Each room has two vanity sinks in separate rooms, and a color cable TV with HBO. Meals are served in the gracious Evergreen Restaurant overlooking the grounds. Annie's Café on site offers after-dinner cocktails and dancing.

Malibu Ranch
Seventh St., Milford • 296-7281

This dude ranch has rodeos and other special horse events throughout the year. You can stay here overnight or make a daytrip just for the rodeos. A day at the rodeo costs $40 per person, including lunch and all events. If you want to participate in the rodeo, the entry fee is $5 per competition.

Malibu Ranch has unlimited horseback riding, swimming, fishing and boating. Horseback riding is available hourly; take an all-day trail ride or an overnight pack trip. Other outdoor activities include whitewater rafting nearby on the Delaware River, tennis and shooting at the rifle range. The ranch provides guns for kids and adults who know how to shoot. There is also an indoor pool and sauna.

Accommodations are in the main hotel, which has suites as well as double rooms (all rooms have double beds), chalets and cabins. The cost based on a weekend stay is $165 per adult and half that rate for children ages 6 through 12; kids 5 and younger are free (see Kidstuff for additional information). The rate includes three meals a day and all scheduled activities.

Lake Wallenpaupack Area

Comfort Inn
$-$$ • Pa. Hwy. 191, Lake Ariel • 689-4148, (800) 523-4426

This is the only chain hotel in the lake region. It is a great stop for parents taking their children to one of the area's camps and generally is booked heavily on summer weekends for this reason. The 124 rooms include doubles or kings (some with Jacuzzis) with satellite TVs. There is a suite with a whirlpool and wet bar. Meals are available at the Twin Rocks Restau-

rant nearby. Cocktails are served in the Prince Edward Island Lounge. An excellent complementary continental breakfast is included in your room rate. Children 18 and younger stay free with parents. General amenities include an exercise room with a sauna and Jacuzzi.

Pocono Pines Motor Inn
$-$$ • Pa. Hwy. 507, at Lake Wallenpaupack, Tafton • 226-2772

This lovely motel is right across from Lake Wallenpaupack and has boats and docks at the lake for guests. Twelve rooms and six cottages (with kitchens and fireplaces) are available; cottages are not available in winter. A playground is available for children, and barbecue pits and picnic tables are scattered about for guests to use. The game room is also a fun hangout for kids, and movies are shown nightly. Lawn games such as shuffleboard and badminton are available too. Children 12 and younger stay free

Slate Belt

Travel Inn of Wind Gap
$$ • Pa. Hwys. 33 and 512 (Bath exit), Wind Gap • (610) 863-4146

There are 35 modern rooms in this close-by-the-highway motel. One room has a king-size bed, one has a queen, one has a waterbed and one room has three beds. There is a color TV (free HBO and Cinemax) and a direct-dial phone in each room.

Children 10 and younger are free in the room with parents. Children ages 12 to 16 are $5 per night.

There are restaurants nearby along Pa. Highway 512.

Wind Gap is in the Slate Belt but is close to Blue Mountain Ski Area (see Winter Sports) and Pocono International Raceway (see Attractions).

THE MOUNTAIN VILLAGES OF CENTRAL POCONOS

Most bed and breakfasts offer a quiet place to sit and converse or enjoy an evening relaxing after an activities-filled day in the Poconos.

Bed and Breakfasts and Country Inns

Bed and breakfasts and country inns have operated in the Poconos for years. Some are restored summer homes from the height of the summer "resorts" boom during the Victorian era in the 1800s; others are farmhouses that have been lovingly restored and decorated to reflect the cozy, homey atmosphere of days gone by on a Pennsylvania farm; some are restored townhouses in the center of once-prosperous mining towns; and still others are elegantly appointed inns with all the modern conveniences of a grand hotel in a quaint, stylish setting.

In this area, bed and breakfasts usually are smaller facilities, generally restored townhouses, farmhouses or summer places that offer rooms — some with private baths, some with shared baths — tastefully decorated in cozy, period decor or exquisite antiques. (Of course, "usually" doesn't mean "always," as the grandeur of Bischwind proves.) A morning meal complements the stay, ranging from a simple continental breakfast to a hearty farmhouse repast with eggs, muffins or pastries and homemade specialties of the house. Most bed and breakfasts offer a quiet place to sit and converse or enjoy an evening relaxing after an activities-filled day in the Poconos. Very few, however, offer on-site activities such as pools, tennis courts and the like. Places that do offer such amenities are noted. What a bed and breakfast inn does offer is charming ambiance, proximity to things

to see and do and a feeling of home away from home — complete with fresh coffee in the morning that you don't have to make yourself.

A country inn is a larger establishment that usually includes bigger rooms with private baths, often sumptuously decorated to reflect an era or style. Some offer fireplaces and/or Jacuzzis; others, suites; and some have extended facilities in cottages outside the main lodge. To be considered an inn by the Independent Innkeepers Association, dinner must be served and the owners must be in residence. Breakfast can be chosen as an option with the room, and most accommodations also have highly regarded restaurants on the premises touted by inn guests as well as diners who come just for excellent cuisine. There are usually some other amenities, such as a pool, game room, tennis courts or a great room for relaxing in front of a fireplace after a day of cross-country or downhill skiing or vigorous antiquing. Country inns, unlike bed and breakfast establishments, are more along the scale of small, grand hotels of the past, when a hotel was an enclosed environment offering a menu of options on-site as well as serving as a homebase for guests who preferred browsing and wandering.

Whatever your needs or tastes, you are sure to find a bed and breakfast inn or country inn that suits your temperament and pocketbook somewhere in the beautiful, mountainous countryside or towns of the Poconos region. With the wealth of attractions, sports activities (winter and summer), shopping opportunities, public parks, scenic areas and arts and cultural happenings, wherever you stay and whatever its menu of on-site activities, you will find that your choice is convenient to those particular pleasures of the Poconos that beckon to you.

Before we take a journey through the towns and hamlets to review the enticing array of inns, let's get some matters of business out of the way:

• Credit cards are generally accepted — exceptions will be noted. If you wish to know about a specific credit card's acceptability, check with an establishment about its policies.

• Pets usually are not allowed. However, this is not etched in stone, so we note if an establishment does accept pets.

• Many establishments don't accept children younger than a certain age; and others, not at all. We note the policies where guidelines are explicit; call to verify age acceptability if it is a concern.

• As a general rule, smoking is not permitted; some establishments allow smoking on verandahs or porches; and a small few allow smoking in a designated area. If smoking is a concern for you, contact the accommodations that interest you about their policies.

• Handicapped-accessibility is a consideration for some people. Since some of these establishments are very old, they might not be appropriate for some individuals' needs. We suggest you inquire in advance about handicapped-accessibility if you or someone in your party has special needs.

Costs for bed and breakfasts and country inns vary widely and can depend upon type of accommodation, length of stay and amenities. Reservations for these establishments are usually a good idea. Most are filled during the ski season, summer season and general holiday seasons (Thanksgiving, Christmas, Easter, Presidents Weekend). Reservations always require a deposit, which is credited toward your bill. If canceling is necessary, deposits are gen-

FYI

Unless otherwise noted, the area code for all phone numbers in this guide is 717.

erally refunded with enough advance notice. Check with the individual establishments for their reservations and deposit policies.

The following key is a general guideline of average rate you would pay per room per night (double occupancy) during peak season; prices are subject to change.

Price-code Key	
$50 or less	$
$51 to $95	$$
$96 to $130	$$$
$131 and more	$$$$

Delaware Water Gap

Eagle Rock Lodge
$$ • River Rd., Shawnee-on-Delaware • 421-2139, (516) 248-4963

This property appears on deeds as far back as the late 1700s. It is in the lovely town of Shawnee-on-Delaware, one of the earliest settlements in the area (see our History, Native Americans and Worship chapters). The main dining room has a low ceiling, representative of farmhouses of the early 1800s. This farmhouse has wide-plank floors, and a very intricate wooden room divider separates the foyer and a sitting area. There is also a game room. The stairway to the second floor is narrow and steep, indicative of Colonial architecture. The house has been augmented bit by bit, and it has a rambling, homey feel. The seven rooms (one has a private bath; others share the large, country-inspired baths) are cozy and tastefully decorated with period furnishing, such as pineapple finials, double beds and marble-topped dressers. The entire house is decorated in blue and white. Some rooms have exquisite views of the Delaware River and New Jersey's Kittatinny Mountains.

The house is alongside the road — again, indicative of its very early origins. It has a large, screened porch on two sides (also decorated in blue and white) overlooking a lawn that meanders down to the Delaware River. You can swim in the river, accessed from the little beach at the foot of the lawn, right below the shuffle-

board and bench area. The property cuddles up to the Delaware and provides more than 10 acres to wander, including paths along the shore. Eagle Rock Lodge is within walking distance of Shawnee Playhouse, Mimi's Streamside Cafe and Delaware Water Gap National Recreation Area.

In summer, breakfast is served by the owners, Jim and Jane, on the lovely porch with river breezes and views; in winter, it is served in the dining room. Breakfast is a full country meal befitting a farmhouse. It includes homemade blueberry muffins and pancakes, coffee and fresh fruit juice. The house specialty is Eagle Eggs; ask Jim to explain what they are able to create with a poached egg!

Jim and Jane have hosted folks on their 10.5 acre haven on the Delaware since 1982; families are encouraged; and they gladly host groups for reunions.

The Shepard House
$$, no credit cards • 108 Shepard Ave., Delaware Water Gap • 424-9779

This bed and breakfast inn was built in the early 1900s as a boarding house. It was called "The Fair View House" because of the beautiful valley view from its location at the top of the town of Delaware Water Gap. The Trabulsi family, which also owned the Wolf Hollow Golf Course (now the Delaware Water Gap Country Club), bought it in 1919. They added what remains a lovely feature of the house — a wraparound verandah. They also added a third floor and kept the house as a summer retreat until 1986, when it was sold. The present owners — innkeepers Jean, John and Bob Shepard — bought it in 1990 to fulfill their dream. Today, that dream includes a lovingly restored, Country Victorian guest house in the heart of historic Delaware Water Gap. (See our History, Arts and Culture and Annual Events chapters for related information about Delaware Water Gap).

The beautiful verandah is a relaxing, romantic spot, colorfully accented with flowering plants and furnished with rockers and an old-fashioned wicker porch swing for two. Catch the breezes as you read, look at the surrounding mountains, watch for the deer and hummingbirds or just relax. You also can pack a lunch to munch on in the picnic area.

The double-occupancy rooms are accented with beautiful antiques, lace curtains and special accents of color and design to enhance your experience. The house is fully air-conditioned, and guests can relax in the private living room with a large color TV.

Shepard House is just off the Appalachian Trail, a short walk to all the Delaware Water Gap events and activities, even the pool at Shaw Park (see our In, On and Around the Water chapter). And during the winter holiday season, the Shepards enthusiastically deck the halls.

Breakfast and afternoon tea are served daily. Fresh-ground and brewed coffee, fresh-squeezed juice and homemade muffins start your breakfast. Appetizers and a home-cooked special complement your morning meal. Afternoon tea is served with a selection of sweet treats and other refreshments.

Children 10 and older are welcome.

Stroudsburg/ East Stroudsburg

The Inn at Meadowbrook
$$ • Cherry Lane Rd., East Stroudsburg • 629-0296, (800) 441-7619

This inn is a refurbished 1867 farmhouse that was once part of a horse farm. And an air of horse-country gentry establishes this inn's mark of excellence. The white fencing surrounding the grounds, house, stables, rings and tack shop reinforces Meadowbrook's genteel character. Inside, the country-gentleman aura is intensified by the dark green walls of the dining room with its white Palladian arches, French doors, built-in bookcases and gracious fireplace. The tack shop and stables, grazing horses and the bridge over the creek that leads to the pond (a lovely place to ice-skate in winter, so don't forget your skates) graciously encourage you to step back into another era.

If you don't feel like dining out after a full day of antiques-hunting or skiing (Camelback is a five-minute drive; Alpine Mountain, 10 minutes), relax and enjoy the fine dining that is also a mark of Meadowbrook's excellence.

Meadowbrook is a delightful choice for small, elegant weddings. Another complement to its venue is its relationship with Pocono Country Carriages (see our Winter Sports and Recreation chapters). Horse-drawn carriage or sleigh rides in luxurious antique coaches and sleighs are a romantic interlude that your hosts, Bob and Kathy Overman, will be glad to arrange for you.

Children 12 and older are welcome at Meadowbrook.

Stroudsmoor Country Inn
$-$$$ • Pa. Hwy. 191 and Stroudsmoor Rd., Stroudsburg • 421-6431/6962

This country inn's main building, built in sections during the 1840s and 1880s, houses 14 of the 30 guest units. Two of the main rooms are suites, and there are two more suites in the Highlander cottage across Marketplace Commons, a green resembling the commons of a country village. On the other side of the commons, directly across from the inn, you'll find 14 cottages with private baths and color TVs. The main building's lobby, filled with lovely antiques, has wainscoted walls and a fieldstone fireplace.

The inn is situated on its own 150-acre mountain overlooking Stroudsburg. The views are spectacular and take in the panorama of the Pocono Mountains. Part of the inn's charm is its family tradition; it's been operated for 10 years by the Pirone family — mother, father, daughters, sons-in-law and grandchildren.

Guests awaken to a hearty country breakfast, and they are welcome to partake in any of the celebrations that have become part of the Pirone family tradition — Italian festivals, Oktoberfest celebrations, scarecrow-stuffing contests and pumpkin festivals, Thanksgiving feasts, country crafts fairs, Christmas tree-lighting celebrations and a large antiques fair in

May. The events, the quaint shops, the outdoor swimming pool, delightful indoor natatorium (with Victorian Iron furnishings, twinkling chandelier and whirlpool spa) and the highly acclaimed on-site restaurant, The Stroudsmoor, which offers an Italian feast every Friday, all make staying here a wonderful experience.

Rooms in the inn are cozy and decorated with period antiques. All have air-conditioning, private baths and color TVs. The cottages have the same amenities, complemented with country-style curtains and wallcoverings plus semiprivate porches.

Bed and breakfast lodging includes a four-course breakfast each day. On Sundays a champagne brunch is served.

Mount Pocono Area

Brookview Manor B&B Inn
$$$ • Pa. Hwy. 191, Canadensis • 595-2451

This Victorian home was built in 1911. The huge wraparound porch and stone-and-clapboard siding are reminders of the heyday of summer homes in the Poconos. "Romantic" is the feeling innkeeper Maryanne Buckley has created here. The downstairs main rooms are painted in rich, deep shades of green and plum. The floors are highly polished hardwood, graced with contrasting area rugs. In the main sitting room, a white painted fireplace with inset bookshelves and benches provides a lovely backdrop to the dramatic look of the rounded corner window area where a piano sits surrounded by the beauty of the woods looking in past the porch outside. Just off this lovely, warm room is a smaller sitting room decorated for the hunt in plums and green plaids with woodsy-scene borders. Afternoon refreshments — part of the amenities at Brookview — can be enjoyed here.

Dining areas also are accessed from the central parlor. The dining rooms are exquisite. Rich burgundy walls set off by white lace curtains and white trim make the center room a jewel. To its right is a lovely enclosed sun porch with curtains and cheery decorations. To the left is a raised formal dining area, set for dinner beneath a bank of windows with transoms of stained glass in oak leaf and acorn patterns

— truly delightful. Brass, etched-glass and crystal lighting fixtures throughout the house are original, including the chandeliers in the dining room and wall sconces in each guest room and in the hallway.

There are 10 rooms, including those in the carriage house across the lawn from the main house. All rooms have private baths, and each is furnished with beautiful antiques. The Fireplace Room, as elegant as any in this lovely home, has a fireplace and a dramatic four-poster bed covered with a crocheted lace coverlet over pink. The suite has a separate sun porch sitting room with a carved-wood daybed and a huge bedroom. The bed is queen-size, and the bathroom is made even more beautiful by its stained-glass windows.

Maryanne Buckley is a gourmet cook, so breakfast here is always a special treat. Fresh-baked muffins, homemade cranberry and blueberry nutbreads, fresh fruit, French toast, special breakfast casseroles and melon topped with fresh jewels of fruit fit for a crown are some of the offerings. Breakfast can be served in your room by request if you and your partner want a romantic morning alone. Afternoon refreshments, including more delicious homebaked specialties, are served in the sitting room, on the porch or anywhere else you'd like to enjoy it. In nice weather, the little patio across from the house is an ideal spot to spend a relaxing afternoon under the trees that tower over the gracious lawns here.

There is quite a bit of property to roam here; for a real treat, cross the road toward the brook and follow the path (about a mile) to a secluded waterfall. Maryanne will be glad to direct you there and any other spot you're interested in seeing.

Crescent Lodge
$$- $$$$ • Pa. Hwys. 191 and 940, Paradise Valley • 595-7486, (800) 392-9400

This beautiful and gracious country inn is at once elegant and homey. It has been owned by members of the Dunlop family for almost 50 years. Accommodations include rooms in the main inn and private cottages on the grounds. Meals are served in the elegant dining room, including breakfast. The grounds contain a heated outdoor pool, tennis court and hiking trails. The lodge is central to all towns and attractions accessed by Pa. 191 in Paradise Valley.

Options include private rooms with double or queen-size beds, deluxe rooms with canopy bed or a suite with living room. All cottages have private sun decks and vary by layout and amenities (Jacuzzis, fireplaces, canopy beds). And a private cottage, set off a pathway leading to the lodge's facilities, includes a country kitchen, a TV with VCR and a sunken Jacuzzi.

All accommodations are beautifully decorated with matching draperies, lace, floral patterns, warm pastels, wall-to-wall carpeting and much more.

The Crescent Lodge is in a delightful, elegant country setting. The grounds are lovely, expansive and inviting. The restaurant itself is highly acclaimed, and folks come just for dinner.

Dreamy Acres
$$ • Pa. Hwy. 447 and Seese Hill Rd., Canadensis • 595-7115

This little hideaway is across a bridge that traverses the creek running through Dreamy Acres. Bill and Esther Pickett have owned this old-time bed and breakfast for 39 years — "before there were bed and breakfasts," as Mrs. Pickett tells it.

The main house has two guest rooms with a shared bath, and the adjacent lodge has four rooms, two with private baths and two with a shared bath. The decor in each is contemporary. The lodge has a main living room for all lodge guests and a screened porch with traditional green chairs. From May until October only, a continental breakfast — juice, coffee, sweet rolls and muffins — is served in the dining room of the main house. Rooms are available all year, however. Families return to Dreamy Acres generation after generation with their children.

Farmhouse Bed & Breakfast
$$-$$$ • Grange Rd., Mount Pocono • 839-0796

This farmhouse has been in the Asure family since Jack Asure was a child. He and his wife, Donna, have renovated the homestead and made it into a unique group of four suites and a caretaker's cottage.

There are two comfortable furnished suites in the main house — the Parlour Suite and the Master Suite. Each has a private bath, queen-size bed, refrigerator, color TV with VCR and private telephone. Each also has a fireplace for winter and air-conditioning for summer. Each suite is uniquely decorated and has its own special feel. A wall of library shelves in the Parlour Suite adds a homey touch. Each room has one or two pieces of antique furniture that seem to perfectly fill their spots. A marble-topped East Lake bureau, a four-poster, a country-primitive desk — all add touches of time to well-maintained modern suites. Each suite has its own entrance from the lovely, screened, slate porch that guests are free to enjoy.

A short distance from the main house is the cozy and romantic Caretaker's Cottage. This welcoming suite is in the renovated ice-house of the original 1850 homestead. Downstairs is a lovely sitting room with fireplace. Upstairs is the adorable bedroom with a big, comfy four-poster bed and a private bath, all decorated in warm, pastel country prints. This is a romantic spot to spend a weekend.

Also on the 6.5-acre property are two more suites — the Sundown and Sunup. Both have all the same amenities as the Master and Parlour but in a completely modern setting. The rooms are large and delightfully decorated. Donna Asure has stenciled and sponge-painted the rooms in cheerful colors and designs that are at once country-casual and cozy. These two suites adjoin, perfect for two couples who want to spend a weekend together but apart. Each suite has a separate entrance and fireplace. The Sunup has a kitchen for those who wish eat in and an extra bedroom with a daybed — a plus for two adults traveling together but sleeping separately. A deck runs the full length of the lodging; it looks out over the rustic beauty of the Farmhouse's wooded property.

And what about breakfast you ask? Well,

Donna and Jack love to cook, so they are always experimenting with new ideas. One of their favorite pastimes is developing new recipes for French toast. Donna notes that if you stayed for a week, you would never have the exact same breakfast twice! There are always fresh-baked, homemade muffins and a new omelette adventure, a breakfast meat, fresh juice and probably French toast. They have also developed a wonderful recipe for stuffed French toast — with raspberry and cream cheese filling. What more could you ask? Well, Donna even brings homemade cookies to your room for your snacking enjoyment.

Breakfast is served at a large, family-size table in the dining room, which overlooks the property through floor to ceiling windows that encompass one whole wall. The chef's delightful kitchen overlooks the dining area and the Asure sitting room, joined by a huge fireplace. This homey area is full of great kitchen antiques. An old enamel stove, grinders, boxes and lots of oak are just some of the items that catch your eye.

While weekend reservations are the norm, you are welcome to stay longer if you wish. Business travelers might find this stop a welcome home away from home, especially with the private phones and an extra room to work in. The Farmhouse is convenient to most business locations in the Poconos. Also, it is quite close to attractions such as Memorytown (on the same road), Alpine Mountain, Camelback, Crossings Factory Outlets and just about anywhere else you need to reach in the central Poconos surrounding Stroudsburg.

The Asures will be happy to direct you to the best places for what you need, some good spots for dinner (see Restaurants) and what cultural events might be happening in the region.

Children are welcome in some suites with daybeds. Smoking is not allowed.

From Pa. Highway 611 N. or 940 W., turn on Grange Road in Paradise Valley (east of

Mount Pocono). Follow Grange Road to the Farmhouse Bed & Breakfast.

Frog Town Inn
$$ • Pa. Hwy. 390, Canadensis • 595-6282

This inn has been a stopover for travelers since the 1890s. Stan and Carol Zimmer bought it in 1994 and have restored it. The Zimmers have developed a fine reputation for serving elegant "French Country" meals, and Frog Town Inn is becoming a well-respected dining spot in the Poconos.

All 10 guest rooms have private bath and are decorated with beautiful antiques. Five suites have couches and sitting areas. All rooms have color TVs. Each room or suite is decorated differently: one has a four-poster bed, one has a brass bed and another has an antique maple bed; some have marble-top dressers or side tables; and all have different colors schemes.

The inn has a cozy pub, open to the general public, with a fireplace and a TV for relaxing after a rough day of Poconos shopping, skiing, hiking, swimming or just enjoying the views. The restaurant also is open to the public.

A full breakfast is prepared daily for guests by Stan Zimmer. It generally consists of pancakes or French toast, a fresh-made omelette full of goodies such as shittake mushrooms, bacon or sausage, fresh muffins and popovers, fresh fruit and juice.

The Merry Inn
$$ • Pa. Hwy. 390, Canadensis • 595-2011, (800) 858-4182

This cozy home away from home is run by innkeeper Meredyth Huggard. It has six rooms — four rooms share two baths, and two rooms have private baths; all rooms have color TVs. The decor is a mix of country-casual plaids and florals with Victorian accents. The large rooms are complemented by two outdoor decks, one of which has a Jacuzzi overlooking the woods. There are two large common areas used as lounges and sitting areas.

Children are welcome here, since Huggard herself has a little 3-year-old who helps keep the atmosphere homey.

A full breakfast is served every morning. It always includes a choice of three or four main

choices with bacon or sausage and home-fried potatoes. Choices include omelettes, pancakes with apples, French toast stuffed with raspberries and cream cheese, orange French toast or eggs any style.

Overlook Inn
$$ • Dutch Hill Rd., Canadensis • 595-7519

There are 18 quaint rooms in this sprawling inn, set off the road in the woods. The spot is perfect for wildlife watching. It is also close to all the major Mount Pocono area attractions (see our Attractions chapter).

Overlook Inn has a lounge and an on-site restaurant that serves breakfast and lunch. The inn is open year round; in summer it opens an outdoor pool for guests.

Pine Knob Inn
$$$-$$$$ • Pa. Hwy. 447, Canadensis • 595-2532

This inn dates from the Civil War period. There are 18 rooms, all with private baths and uniquely decorated with antiques; each room has its own character, though all are informal and cozy. The circular driveway leads to an expansive porch surrounding two sides of this comfortable country place. Two gazebos grace the lawns, and a white picket fence surrounds some of the flower-filled gardens.

A swimming pool and an array of lawn games are available for relaxation and recreation. Brodhead Creek runs by, and fishing is allowed with a valid Pennsylvania license.

Innkeepers John and Cheryl Garman pride themselves on their excellent food, so overnight accommodations can also include a five-course gourmet dinner of continental cuisine.

This inn is in the heart of the Poconos on Pa. 447, which leads into just about every other country road, so enjoy your stay and enjoy exploring the Poconos from this spot.

White Cloud Inn
$$ • Pa. Hwy. 447, Newfoundland • 676-3162, (800) 820-0320

This country inn is in a 100-year-old farmhouse and a reconstructed barn. There are 18 rooms furnished in modest, country-casual style. Some rooms have private baths, others share. No two rooms are decorated alike, though the emphasis is on simplicity. There is

a dining room in the farmhouse that also houses the well-known White Cloud vegetarian restaurant. A full, vegetarian natural-food breakfast is served as part of your stay. Breakfast includes homemade oatmeal, pancakes, omelettes, muffins, granola and fresh fruit. Lunch and dinner are also available here from the vegetarian-only menu.

A beautiful stone building, appropriately called the "stone house," comprises one of the gathering rooms. There are also a library, chapel and other gathering rooms — one in the farmhouse and another in the barn building.

The property encompasses more than 50 acres. A hiking trail traverses the grounds, offering an exhilarating outdoor experience. Or, guests can enjoy a match on the tennis court.

No smoking is allowed here, but you can bring your pets. There are facilities here for small groups of up to 30 people.

West End

Alpine Inn
$$, no credit cards • 80 Broadway, Jim Thorpe • 325-9484

This bed and breakfast inn is in a row house on Broadway in the center of Jim Thorpe. The owners are in the process of restoring this turn-of-the-century spot that has seven guest rooms and can accommodate up to 15 people.

Ceilings are high and decorated with molding indicative of the Victorian era in which it was built. This is a relatively new bed and breakfast and is accumulating many antiques and dressings commonly found at other bed and breakfasts.

There are nice touches throughout, such as a floor-to-ceiling handbuilt cupboard in the large dining room and the original louvered doors that close in front of the actual bedroom doors (a nice touch for the summer, which allows airflow and maintains privacy). A continental breakfast including fruit, cold cereal and fresh-baked muffins is served in the dining room or al fresco on the terraced patio that climbs up the backyard mountain and cradles many of the lovely townhomes on this street.

The owners are in the process of remodeling a room on the third floor as a play room for children. They are very comfortable with children, and kids are welcome, as are pets.

Inn at Jim Thorpe
$$-$$$$ • 24 Broadway, Jim Thorpe • 325-2599

This inn is in the heart of Jim Thorpe. The exterior bespeaks Victorian elegance, with wrought-iron porch railings and balconies. According to legend, many greats have passed through here — Gen. Ulysses S. Grant, President William Howard Taft, Buffalo Bill Cody, Thomas Edison and John D. Rockefeller.

The Inn's rooms are elegantly furnished in

Victorian manner. Lace abounds, as do ornate wooden headboards and period antiques. There are private baths in each room, with pedestal sinks and marble floors. The rooms have air-conditioning, cable TV and telephones. The suite for special occasions has a fireplace, Jacuzzi, king-size bed, kitchen, TV and VCR. The decor is absolutely elegant.

A continental breakfast is served, with large selections of fresh muffins, pastries and cereals to accompany your morning coffee and juice. The Emerald Pub is part of the inn and is a wonderful place for elegant, Victorian-appointed dining.

The Inn is central to all that is happening in and around Jim Thorpe.

Children younger than 5 stay free.

Sheradin's 1860 House

**$$$ • Pa. Hwy. 715, Brodheadsville
• 992-1219, (800) 992-1860**

Sheradin's 1860 House is a restored farmhouse originally constructed between 1835 and 1860. The Sheridan ancestors lived in it until very recently. The oldest living member of the family, Emma Rinehart, advised Ron and Nanda Sheradin while the Sheridan's restored this cozy home.

The polished wooden floors are original, as are the molding and trim in the main areas. All rooms are decorated in white or tan, which offsets the richly colored bedding and linens throughout. There are two sitting areas downstairs. The library has a beautiful white baby grand piano as a focal point. The comfortable sitting room opposite the library leads to a pristinely appointed dining room where separate tables for each guest room stand out in dark green elegance.

There are three cozy suites in the main house plus the separate Garden Suite (private entrance, small kitchen and sitting room with fireplace and trundle bed), which adjoins the deck of this lovely farmhouse. Green, yellow and florals create a botanical feel in this large suite; its cozy bedroom features white wicker accents and a queen-size bed. The large adjoining bathroom is painted in rose and mauve tones.

The Huntington is a vibrant combination of burgundy and beige, reflecting the "hunt" era of the 1800s. The queen-size country high-rise bed is made of English bird's-eye maple and contributes to the country charm of this room. The Victoria is furnished in Queen Anne elegance, complemented with cream- and peach-color walls and linens. The queen-size canopy bed is surrounded by an original handcarved memoir desk and armoire. A separate sitting area and porcelain Queen Anne sink complete this room. The Port Charleston Suite has a nautical theme featuring navy and white colors. This room is named for the port where the first settler of this farm dropped anchor during his emigration from Germany in the 1800s. The dark furnishings are reminiscent of a sea captain's state room and include the original steamer trunk from that journey of more than a century ago. There is a cozy wood-burning jack stove in the room that keeps the chill away on winter nights. The lovely sitting room adjoining Port Charleston Suite has a sofa bed and is separated from the suite by glass doors.

The rooms have lots of special touches. All rooms have private baths that contain remarkable showers. Showers, you say? In the main house the shower heads are Old World ceiling dowser showers. Ron searched all over for these delightful accessories. Each room has a sink separate from the bathroom — traditional European layout — and each sink area is set off as a little oasis, allowing two people to ready themselves at the same time. Ceiling fans, fresh flowers in your room and beds with mattresses of the highest quality are meant to assure a good night's sleep. A sweet pillow treat welcomes you to bed, and breakfast awaits you in the morning. A truly delightful touch is a journal in each room; guests are encouraged to write their thoughts and memories (some of the grandchildren of the original owners have stayed here) for others to read.

Nanda loves to cook, and if dietary needs are a concern, you can communicate them to her when you make your reservations. The breakfast menu always includes fresh-baked muffins and treats as well as fruit and juices and specialties of the house including time-honored tastes from the 1800s and Tex-Mex recipes hailing from her home base of Texas.

Ron has spared no attention to detail in his restoration of this charming farmhouse. Outside is an adorable wading pool with miniature dock, boathouse and hammock. There are acres to wander and enjoy. Sheridan's 1860 House is centrally located between Tannersville and Brodheadsville, barely a 15-minute drive to Camelback and 30 minutes to Blue Mountain ski areas.

Tobias House
$, no credit cards • Gilbert Rd., Gilbert • 681-4854

The Tobias house is a bed and breakfast home. What this means is that you are invited to spend your time outside your private bedroom with the family members. Breakfast is served in a large country kitchen that the Thomas family and grandmother Mariellen Duval share with you. They also share their TV room, sitting areas, spacious 3-acre lawns, access to the trout brook that runs behind the property (you can buy a fishing license at the corner store) and all the amenities, including the hammock that hangs in the shade between two towering trees near this 1830 farmhouse. As a grandmother and full-time manager of the property, Mariellen Duval says staying here is like "coming to visit your grandmother."

The home originally was a farm, then became a stagecoach stop for a while. The cozy rooms have stenciled walls and washstands and little amenities that enhance the country-home flavor. Antiques are tucked here and there. The fireplace in the sitting area is large and inviting, and the entire place feels like home. The 6-inch-thick oak walls are astonishing. The rooms share a communal shower, and some have private half-baths.

Breakfast is prepared by Mariellen and her son-in-law Mark Thomas, who is known for his breakfast special "strata"— a fascinating concoction including layers of sausage, mushrooms, asparagus and eggs — that you must request. Other natural, homey breakfast treats include homemade muffins, waffles, strawberry yogurt, pancakes, baked apples with granola and so on.

The grounds are delightful. Fruit trees, hammocks and old-fashioned gardens all add to the country feel of this place. Mark and Dale Thomas have children, so yours are welcome. There is a large playroom stocked with games and toys and all kinds of fun things for kids, and all are for your children's use.

This fun home is near Blue Mountain Ski Area and on the way to Jim Thorpe. The area is full of Moravian history, and Tobias house is close to the Gnaden Huetten settlement (see Native Americans) destroyed in the Pennsylvania Indian Wars. The house itself is named for Tobias, a Native American converted by the early Moravians in the 1750s. So while you stay here, walk down to the Moravian cemetery and check out the local history.

Tiffany's Grand Victoria
$$ • 218 Center St., Jim Thorpe • 325-8260

This bed and breakfast is a short walk from the main street area of Jim Thorpe in a lovely, quiet, tree-lined neighborhood. There is turn-of-the century elegance everywhere — three fireplaces, a mahogany-beam ceiling, a romantic grape arbor and an expansive verandah. The home was built in 1846 and eventually became the home of Judge Laird Barber and his wife; he was the presiding judge in the infamous Molly Maguire trials (see our Overview chapter).

The five rooms here are decorated in 1930s style, reminiscent of "grandma's house." Owners Bob and Rita Hydro added a swimming pool for guests to enjoy — a nice complement. There is air-conditioning for summertime comfort, color TV in every room and a fireplace to read beside in winter.

Breakfast is a departure from the norm. Guests receive a voucher for a free morning meal at the nearby Sunset Diner.

Children older than 12 are welcome at Tiffany's.

Victoria Ann's Bed and Breakfast
$$, no credit cards • 68 Broadway, Jim Thorpe • 325-8107

This little row-house bed and breakfast is in the heart of Jim Thorpe on Broadway. It is full of Victorian niceties and antiques. The eight rooms are decorated in Victorian decor; some have king-size beds, some doubles, and all rooms have Victorian-style curtains, bureaus, side tables and porcelain. Three of the rooms open out onto the second story verandah on the side of the house and overlook the visually appealing gardens. The verandah extends the length of the house, and guests are invited to have friends over to enjoy refreshments al-fresco. This bed and breakfast is colorful, lacy and flowery, with high ceilings, polished floors, nooks and crannies and art all over the place. Classical music fills the air in the sitting room.

A full breakfast is served daily in the dining room. Hostess Louise Ogilvie is a cabaret singer who can serve up not only a lovely song, but also a delightful breakfast of fresh fruit, melon or grapefruit, cereal with bananas, hot porridge with white raisins, a choice of scrambled eggs with mushrooms or blueberry pancakes, and either bacon or ham.

Milford Area

Black Walnut Country Inn
$$-$$$ • Firetower Rd., Milford • 296-6322, (800) 866-9870

Innkeepers Charles and Kathleen Mentken delight in pointing out the niceties of the Black Walnut Country Inn and Restaurant. There's the fireplace mantel (a gift from Gov. Pinchot), lovely antique brass beds and other antique furnishings and paintings artistic guests have created and sent back as reminders of their wonderful stay at this "way off the beaten track" inn. Elizabeth Taylor and Malcolm Forbes have stayed at Black Walnut, and many playwrights and theater-types come here to enjoy the solitude, especially in winter. One New York playwriting couple used the inn one weekend and spread their script all over the empty room floors as they continued their creative frenzy. Moments like those make the Black Walnut fun.

The Mentkens are children of owner Stewart Schneider, an amiable New Yorker who owns the house across the road. The inn has 12 rooms — four with full baths, four with half- baths and four with no private baths (there is a shared bath on each floor). Some rooms have TVs. All rooms are decorated with simple antiques. Victorian bureaus and side tables accent the flowered wallpaper, comforters and curtains.

Other fun things besides the cozy, antiques-filled rooms are on the grounds. There are paddle boats on the pond and a swimming dock to race to and sun on. You can enjoy the animals in the petting zoo; swing in a hammock; hike (or cross-country ski in winter) the 160 acres of woods and trails; relax in the hot tub; or play a game of pool. And the pond is stocked for catch-and-release fishing.

The excellent, gourmet Black Walnut Inn Restaurant also is part of this establishment. Its dining room is full of glass and looks out over the grounds. Breakfast, served buffet-style, includes a variety of fruits, baked goods, juices, eggs, sausage, bacon and other morning treats.

Pine Hill Farm Bed & Breakfast
Pine Hill Farm Rd., Milford • 296-7395

This 1800s hillside country farm is wonderful for adults seeking a quiet, well-mannered weekend getaway. The delightful farm is perched above the Delaware River north of the village of Milford, seemingly miles away, yet quite close to the town and all of its attractions, including antiques dealers, museums and retail shops (see our Arts and Culture, Attractions and Shopping chapters for details).

Pine Hill Farm is owned by Bob and Lynn Patton. It is the result of Lynn's search for the farm her grandfather used to tell her about in days gone by — a farm that belonged to his uncle. Eight years ago, in a drawer of an old secretary bookcase in the house, she found an old real estate magazine and a map, showing the location of the farm. It was for sale — and so the story goes. She and her husband took a break from the world of Madison Avenue and headed west to restore and renovate this spectacular 268-acre farm into a genteel and elegant bed and breakfast inn.

As with so many restored bed and breakfasts, continued beauty comes from the commitment and artistry of the owners. The same is true of the Pattons. They have tastefully redecorated the three guest rooms in the Main

Photo: Pocono Mountains Vacation Bureau, Inc.

The Poconos features many beautiful waterfalls, both large and small.

House, each with queen-size bed, private bath and air-conditioning. The Carriage House is a charming work of country elegance. There are beamed ceilings in the two suites, each with queen-size beds, private baths and spacious living rooms. Antiques abound in the cottage suites, and the bathrooms are tastefully appointed with antique sideboards and elegant curtains and wallpaper. The decor is country elegant. The adorable cottage has a lovely porch and separate entrances for each suite. The second-floor suite has a daybed in the sitting room to accommodate an extra adult traveler. The entrance to the porch and to the suites is appointed with little antique novel-

ties. In fact the little corner closet below the steps leading to the Main House rooms is full of antique general store trappings, boxes and tins that have graced many an ad or commercial shoot.

The expansive dining room is the site for winter candlelight breakfasts beside a warm, cozy fire. This room has some truly exciting antiques. On one wall is an almost-floor-to-ceiling antique apothecary cabinet, full of drawers and doors with all kinds of neat knobs that make it fascinating to just look at. On the opposite wall is a very special Bergen County Dutch Kas (or case). Its style was only made in Bergen County, New Jersey, and is known for its boxy grandeur. In summer, breakfast is served on the lovely slate verandah that overlooks the hills and woods of Pine Hill and affords views beyond to the Delaware River. A full country breakfast of eggs, pancakes, breakfast meat, cereal and muffins is served between 8:30 and 9 AM to accommodate guests' daytrips.

Reservations are required. The Pattons are committed to your comfort and enjoyment, which includes knowing who you are and what your needs are before you arrive. This is a wonderfully gracious spot for adults to enjoy.

To reach Pine Hill Farm Bed & Breakfast, take U.S. 209 north from Milford to Cummins Road. Follow Cummins Road to Pine Hill Farm Road, then proceed to this establishment.

Roebling Inn On The Delaware
$$ • Scenic Dr., Lackawaxen • 685-7900

The Roebling Inn, a quaint yet stately Greek Revival home, was office and home to Judge Thomas J. Ridgway, superintendent and tallyman for the Delaware and Hudson Canal Company. The home has been fully restored by innkeepers Jo Ann and Donald Jahn, and it is now eligible for the National Register of Historic Places. Lovely little gardens and paths lead to the various doorways around this white clapboard, shuttered jewel. One of the joys of this inn is its location on the Lackawaxen River. It is directly across the street from the river (actually, it's barely a street — rather, a little road — but one that also leads two doors down to the Zane Grey Museum), and its lawn area extends to the river's edge. On the riverside is a dock from which you can go boating. The front porch, complete with comfy chairs, overlooks the Lackawaxen as well.

The cozy rooms are furnished with country antiques and accessorized with cheerful matching comforters and curtains. One lovely room has a delightful raised sitting area with daybed. Each room has a private bath, airconditioning, great beds (mostly queen-size) and cable TV. (Donald feels that while he and Jo Ann have kept this lovely home historically accurate for the sake of its place in history, guests should have a decision about watching TV in privacy in the evening.) There is also a private sitting room for guests. The breakfast room is decorated in cheery white and

floral prints, and delicate white sheers grace the stately windows. The tables are set for two or four, and diners at each table are treated to a peaceful view of the river.

Both JoAnn and Donald enjoy entertaining guests. That includes providing a hearty, cold breakfast buffet table, with homemade fruit cobbler, your choice of cereal and fruit. They add to this tasty spread their own special turn at eggs and bacon, hearty omelettes or hot, steamy pancakes and coffee. Donald was originally a restaurateur and country club manager, and he has focused all of his expertise on this little gem of an inn by the riverside.

In addition to the rooms at the inn, there is an adjacent one-bedroom cottage for two to four guests and a three-bedroom plush contemporary cottage with fireplace, a few miles from the inn that accommodates two to six guests; call about rates for each.

The Jahns' have lived here more than 10 years, so they are knowledgeable about local history and special places (hidden waterfalls for a quiet picnic) that they enjoy pointing out to guests. They'll also point out the many places to walk, play tennis, swim, canoe, fish and sightsee (ask about the Roebling Aqueduct). Walking along the Lackawaxen River on a quiet road en route to places of interest transports you to another time, surrounded by charm and peacefulness.

Some notes of interest: Personal checks are accepted; smoking is permitted in public rooms and porch areas; children are welcome; and the inn usually closes for a month in the winter.

This place is perhaps trickier than most for first-time visitors to find. From Milford take U.S. Highway 6 to Pa. Highway 434. Go 2 miles and bear left on Pa. Highway 590 W. Go 4 miles and turn right on Scenic Drive. Roebling Inn is on the left. If you are coming from the Port Jervis, New York, area, take U.S. 6 W. to N.Y. Highway 97 N. to the Roebling Bridge. Cross the bridge and turn right at the stop sign onto Scenic Drive; the inn is on the left.

Pegasus Bed & Breakfast
$$ • Woodtown Rd., Shohola • 296-4017

This home in Shohola was built in 1923 as a country inn. While it has been modernized, it retains the charm it was originally designed to afford its guests. The wraparound porch, formal dining room and immense living room complement its rustic natural setting.

This inn has one suite with private bath, two rooms with private baths across the hall, and six with a shared bath between the two floors of guest rooms. Each room is furnished with an iron bed and antique dressers and are wallpapered in cozy floral patterns. Many of the guests are Europeans who, according to the innkeeper, seem to enjoy Pegasus' casual hominess.

The third floor features a shared kitchen equipped with microwave and refrigerator for guests who wish to cook for themselves. A VCR and 146-movie library are available as well as a stereo and player piano. This country-casual, old-fashioned inn offers a continental breakfast or a full breakfast including fresh-squeezed orange juice plus eggs from the innkeeper's own chickens, waffles, pancakes or French toast — the items change everyday.

Children are not only allowed but also welcome here — for no extra charge. The game room is full of games and toys for them; the film library features Disney classics; and a volleyball net, basketball hoop on the garage and a rope swing in a big tree summon young recreation enthusiasts.

Groups come here for family reunions, old-fashioned weddings and to find comfy accommodations while visiting friends and family during the holidays.

Lake Wallenpaupack Area

Academy Street Bed & Breakfast
$$ • 528 Academy St., Hawley • 226-3430, (609) 395-8590 (in winter)

Seven large, air-conditioned rooms make up this delightfully restored Victorian in the middle of Hawley, just five minutes from Lake Wallenpaupack. Four rooms have private baths, and three share a central bath. Each room is decorated differently in a Victorian motif. There is the wicker room, furnished entirely in antique wicker, and the four-poster room, featuring a queen-size four-poster bed. All rooms have floral wallpaper with coordinated or matching coverlets. The dining room — the setting for breakfast — has a lovely fireplace, as do the sitting and main rooms. The lovely porches with antique seating arrangements overlook the carefully planted and maintained Victorian gardens.

A full gourmet breakfast is made daily by owner Judith Lazan and her husband, Sheldon. Amaretto French toast, omelettes, soufflés, eggs Benedict, fresh fruit, muffins and other delicious items await you. More delights are served at high tea each afternoon.

This establishment is open from Memorial Day to Columbus Day.

Bischwind
$$$$ • One Coach Rd., Bear Creek • 472-3820

This Bavarian manor is breathtaking in its Old World splendor. The original home was built in 1886 by Albert Lewis, an industry magnate and contemporary of industrial magnate Asa Packer. The home has hosted Presidents Theodore Roosevelt and William Howard Taft and famed aeronautical engineer Igor Sikorsky. The estate is set among tiered gardens of baronial grandeur that lead from a magnificent slate terrace that graces two sides of this miniature castle.

The entrance hall features polished wood, Oriental rugs and marvelous antiques from here and abroad. Off this hall is a cozy fireplace with comfortable seating for those who wish to warm up after a winter outing. Leading from the hall is the Bridal Salon, a truly spectacular room with Louis XIV furnishings amid pink, blue and white valances, drapings and carpets. A bank of leaded-glass windows graced with white lace comprises one wall of this delightfully airy salon. Under the windows are wide, comfortable window seats that face the center of the room or the 100-year-old, white Steinway piano. The crystal chandelier crowns this breathtaking room, which is used for weddings or other grand occasions of up to 50 guests.

Opposite this salon is the Presidential Dining Room, with Tiffany transoms in the windows that top the French doors and windows opening onto the terrace. The opposite wall of the dining room has a fireplace with a leaded-glass window above that presents a view of the fenced grounds and woods of the entrance side of this wondrous home. The fireplace flues form arms around the fireplace and windows.

Impressive suites available here feature fireplaces, living rooms, private baths and antiques. Four-posters, marble tops, armoires and black lacquer add to the opulence. The Bridal Suite has a library, chaise, leather wing-backed chairs and a library table adorned with an enormous Christmas cactus; the headboard of the queen-size bed travels toward the ceiling in a design seemingly afforded only royalty. Laces and beautiful hangings add a soft touch. This is a truly romantic and elegant place to start a new life or renew old vows.

Breakfast at Bischwind is a five-course brunch that includes filet mignon or poached salmon, fruit juice, cheese omelettes, fresh fruit compote, Bischwind or dilled potatoes and a choice of desserts accompanied by fresh coffee and non-alcoholic champagne. Arriving guests are treated to fresh fruit and cheese in their rooms.

This estate is the home of the Von Drans, who have spent their lifetime restoring it to the splendor it exhibits today. The romantic elegance of Bischwind is intensified by the presence of Mrs. Von Dran, a very delightful woman. If you have the opportunity, ask her to recite her excellent mock-Elizabethan poetry, full of wit and intelligence and enhanced by her almost professional delivery.

Adults only are allowed to stay at this Old World estate. Weddings are splendid here; and exclusivity is the keyword for executive meetings away from the office, catered with exceptional delicacies and elegance.

Blue Berry Mountain Inn
$$-$$$ • Thomas Rd., Blakeslee
• 646-7144, (800) 315-BLUE

This gracious country inn takes you by surprise as you come upon it on a winding dirt road that branches off Pa. 115 outside Blakeslee. Its salmon-color exterior and white trim immediately attract you. Expansive verandahs jut off into interesting architectural angles and accent this at-once modern and colonial Caribbean-style structure.

Built in 1994, the inn is filled with antiques that date back more than a century. There are five rooms (all have queen-size beds) and one master suite. All rooms are beautifully accented with a potpourri of antiques including walnut tea carts, wing-back chairs and a piano. The Violet room has furniture brought from Italy by inkeeper Grace Hydrusko's grandmother's great-grandmother. There are two sitting rooms for guests, a great room with a wonderful stone fireplace and a library. You'll also find an indoor pool, outdoor spa, game room and a shared kitchen for guests. There is a lake on the property for fishing (no license required, but bring your own equipment) and canoeing.

Saturday breakfast includes French Toast, pancakes and waffles with bacon, or eggs and homefries. On Sunday, a breakfast buffet of crepes, quiches and other goodies is served. Special dietary needs can be accommodated with advance notice.

Business travelers can take advantage of fax service and telephones as well as corporate account options.

The French Manor
$$$$ • Huckleberry Rd., South Sterling
• 646-3244, (800) 523-8200

This inn is owned by the same family that owns the Sterling Inn (see subsequent entry). This French château is made of stone and lumber from the woods on-site at Huckleberry Mountain. You'll find six guest rooms and three suites, four of which are in the newly renovated Carriage House. This château was built in 1932 and has been a retreat for Joseph Hirschhorn and Samuel Kress of Kress Department Stores. It is modeled after Hirshhorn's French manor in the south of France and is full of unique European touches that make outstanding elegance the keynote of this château.

The roof of The French Manor is made of imported Spanish slate; the interior and great hall are cypress. Romanesque architecture dominates; vaulted ceilings in the dining room, a huge stone fireplace and grand arches complete the picture.

The grounds contain an indoor swimming pool, Jacuzzi, tennis court and nine-hole putting course. There's also a private lake for swimming, boating, fishing and ice skating; a nature trail — marked and maintained — that leads to a waterfall; and cross-country skiing trails. This is truly a magnificent retreat.

The meals feature European cuisine, sumptuously prepared and elegantly served. The inn is owned and operated by Ron and Mary Kay Logan, who maintain it as a getaway for the discriminating guest.

The Settlers Inn at Bingham Park
$$-$$$ • 4 Main Ave., Hawley
• 226-2993, (800) 833-8527

The Settlers Inn in Hawley is European-inspired in the style of a Tudor manor. There are 18 rooms full of antiques and decorated with wicker and soft, quilted, matching comforters and drapes. All rooms are air-conditioned and have private baths and telephones.

The dining room looks out over the lovely grounds that nestle in the lake region of our Poconos. A hearty country breakfast featuring the abundant foods of the area is your morning delight here. The restaurant at The Settlers Inn is well-known for its wonderful presentation of fresh local vegetables, fruits and herbs; and its menu is responsive to the seasons. Guests need not look elsewhere for their eating pleasure after breakfast; lunch and dinner are served here too.

Adjoining the inn is a gift shop and gardener's spot, the Potting Shed.

This is a lovely spot to stay as you enjoy the bounty of the lake area (see In, On and Around the Water).

The Sterling Inn
$$$-$$$$ • Pa. Hwy. 191, South Sterling
• 676-3311, (800) 523-8200

This inn is owned and operated by Ron and Mary Kay Logan, who also own the French Manor. The Sterling, the first of the Logan's inns, exudes relaxed country charm.

You'll find 26 rooms in the main inn and 28 additional accommodations scattered about the grounds in cottages and the lodge. Four cottages have one- and two-bedroom suites, fireplaces and country decor (plaids, ginghams and ruffles). Two larger cottages each house four suites, each with fireplace. The lodge has two sections, with 12 and seven guest rooms respectively, and two parlors, one with a fireplace and one with a TV for all guests.

The amenities include an indoor pool and spa; a lake for swimming, boating, fishing and ice skating (in winter); acres of trails for hiking and cross-country skiing (in winter). You'll also find tennis courts, shuffleboard, volleyball and a nine-hole putting course. Enjoy a picnic along the creek that flows nearby or at any of the other great little areas that surround you.

Breakfast, lunch and dinner are served in the Hearthstone Dining Room. All meals include hearty country fare, and gourmet picnics can be prepared for your afternoon jaunt into the woods.

Many restaurants grow their own herbs and buy produce from local farmers.

Restaurants

In talking with chefs to prepare this chapter, we discovered one consistent theme: People in the Poconos expect large portions for their meals. Most restaurants offer just that — hearty servings of traditional steak, chicken, veal and seafood dishes.

There is more exotic fare. It can be found in the more populated areas such as the Stroudsburgs, Milford, Jim Thorpe, Hawley and Honesdale.

Many of the better restaurants grow their own herbs and buy produce from local farmers. Some even use meats from within the region. The Settlers Inn in Hawley is particularly noteworthy for its creative use of homegrown products.

The vast area included as the Poconos made it more logical to group restaurants by region, not by type of food served. We did not want you to read about a fantastic German restaurant only to be demoralized to discover it is more than two hours away. And there really are not enough ethnic eateries to warrant organization by type of cuisine.

In addition to the following restaurants, keep in mind that the resorts, hotels and country inns profiled in other chapters usually serve food to the general public.

If you want a quick meal that will be familiar, the Poconos has pockets of fast food restaurants. Like birds, these places tend to migrate together, making them easy to find.

Areas that contain strips of popular fast food places (at least six each) include Pa. Highway 611, north of Stroudsburg toward the Stroud Mall; Pa. Highway 940, west of Mount Pocono; U.S. Highway 209 in Brodheadsville (West End); U.S. Highway 6, west of Milford; U.S. 6, 2 miles east of Honesdale (Lake Wallenpaupack area); and Pa. Highway 512, Wind Gap (Slate Belt).

Diners are discussed in this chapter's Closeup.

Other neat local options: Church groups and fire departments regularly sponsor lunches, dinners and breakfasts as fund-raisers. The food is almost always homemade and reasonably priced. In summer, check out the fairs and carnivals for very good snacks and meals.

Within each restaurant write-up you will notice a dollar-sign guide. This figure is based on dinner for two without drinks, desserts or a tip. We tend to estimate on the high end so you will not be shocked when you arrive. The dollar signs represent the following price ranges:

Price-code Key	
$	less than $15
$$	$15 to $25
$$$	$26 to $40
$$$$	more than $40

Unless noted, all restaurants accept major credit cards and serve alcohol. Most places accommodate both smokers and nonsmokers, but call to make sure if you are particularly concerned.

Reservations generally are a good idea, especially at the more expensive restaurants. We let you know when reservations are required or strongly recommended.

Many good eateries are not included because of space and time considerations. We try to focus on restaurants in varied price ranges that have earned a favorable local reputation. That does not mean a place not mentioned should necessarily be avoided.

Delaware Water Gap

American Cookery
$$ • Pa. Hwy. 611, Delaware Water Gap
• 420-0481

Diners are greeted by an inviting fireplace and a small bookstore upon entering American Cookery. These accessories help make a very large dining room feel like home. The menu includes seafood, steaks, chicken and turkey. Favorites for hearty eaters are the all-you-can-eat baby back ribs and the drunken filet (charbroiled filet mignon covered with sauteed mushrooms and served with a Jack Daniels brown sauce). The restaurant has a separate bar area. Dinner is served daily; lunch, on Saturday and Sunday only.

Brownies
$$ • Main St., Delaware Water Gap • 424-1154

Brownies is a popular gathering place for locals, and you're certain to overhear dozens of conversations. It's an informal place — no need to dress up or leave the kids at home. The operation is owned by highly regarded caterers, and the food is very good. Burgers (8 ounces of grilled beef served on a kaiser roll), Mexican items, sandwiches and salads served in an edible bowl are among the lighter menu items. Folks with larger dinner appetites might want to tackle a strip steak, stuffed filet of flounder or pasta primavera, a house favorite. Bands perform on Friday and Saturday nights. The bar serves approximately 40 different bottled beers. Lunch and dinner are served daily.

Deer Head Inn
$$$ • Main St., Delaware Water Gap • 424-2000

As mentioned in our Nightlife chapter, the Deer Head is *the* place for live jazz in the Poconos. However, you can complete your evening with a great dinner to accompany the music. Dinner is served Tuesday through Sunday. The regular menu is rather standard — steaks, crab cakes, chili, sandwiches and burgers. However, residents flock here for the specials, served Thursday through Sunday. These could include whitefish du jour in parchment with basil butter, vegetable tofu or chicken paprikash.

The Gallery
$$ • 760 Broad St., Delaware Water Gap • 424-5565

Mediterranean and Southwestern motifs along with the work of local artists create a sophisticated, cafe atmosphere at The Gallery. The menu is dominated by vegetarian dishes such as meatless ravioli and spanokopita (spinach pie). Soybean burgers, lentil walnut loaf and chickpea burgers are among the more exotic fare. More conventional items, such as burritos, pastas, salmon steak, roast fresh turkey and chicken breast saute are included for less adventurous diners. When the growing season permits, most of the produce used is from the restaurant's own garden. Dinner only is served daily.

Saen
$$ • Shawnee Sq., Shawnee-on-Delaware • 476-4911

Thai cuisine combines common seasonings such as garlic, ginger, basil and mint with less familiar items — lemon grass, tamarind, kaffir lime leaves and galanga. It can be as spicy as Indian food or as mild as Chinese. Curries, Thai salads and meat dishes (no lamb) are popular entrees. A favorite appetizer is satay, marinated chicken skewers grilled and served with a peanut sauce and cucumber salad. The peanut sauce, a house speciality, is delicious. The restaurant is small (13 tables) and contains an appropriately Oriental decor that is tastefully elegant. Lunch and dinner are served Tuesday through Sunday. Saen is closed on Mondays.

The Streamside Cafe
$ • River Rd., Shawnee-on-Delaware • 424-6455

An informal bar atmosphere, good food and reasonable prices make for an enjoyable evening here. The burgers are outstanding; try the Shawnee cheeseburger, the Worthington (with bacon and melted cheese) or the Hollow Road (with sauteed onion, green pepper and melted cheese). Seating on the outdoor deck is available when weather permits. Streamside has an outstanding reputation with area residents, and its location (adjacent to Shawnee Inn's entrance) attracts vacationers. Lunch and dinner are served daily.

Trails End Cafe
$$$ • Main St., Delaware Water Gap • 421-1928

Dinner is served only on Friday evenings

FYI
Unless otherwise noted, the area code for all phone numbers in this guide is 717.

Dining Out

at Trails End. Several specials along with staples such as sea scallops, shrimp Marsala and zuppa de pesce (assorted seafood poached in white wine with marinara over pasta) are served. Menu items are balanced between unusual combinations and the more familiar. Breakfast and lunch are served Wednesday through Saturday, and brunch is served on Sunday. For breakfast, try the homemade granola or house specialities such as Napoli eggs or a breakfast burrito. Pasta, sandwiches, salads and pizzas made with Trails End's own sauce on plain or whole wheat crust are featured for lunch. The dining room is informal. Smoking is not permitted.

Water Gap Diner
$ • 55 Broad St., Delaware Water Gap • 476-0132

American, Greek and Italian foods supplement the traditional diner fare. All the pies, breads and other baked goods are made in the diner. Look for daily lunch specials. Water Gap serves some of the best soups in the Poconos. Breakfast, lunch and dinner are served daily. On Fridays and Saturdays, the Water Gap Diner is open 24 hours.

Wolf Hollow Restaurant at Water Gap Country Club
$$$ • Mountain Rd., Delaware Water Gap • 476-0300

This country club's dining room serves lunch daily and dinner Tuesday through Sunday. Dinners include sauteed breast of chicken Santa Fe, shrimp and scallops Mediterranean, grilled swordfish and rack of lamb. An outstanding appetizer is the smoked trout mousse. The expected dress is "casual but proper." Reservations are requested for dinner. Wolf Hollow closes each year around Thanksgiving and reopens in early April.

Stroudsburg/ East Stroudsburg

Angelo's Oyster House
$$ • 100 Park Ave., Stroudsburg • 424-2624

Since oyster is part of the name, you can bet seafood is a draw here. Salmon with

béarnaise sauce, red snapper with a basilico (pesto) sauce, shrimp fra diavolo and shrimp scampi are specialties. Veal also is a treat here, served scaloppini, piccata and marsala. Another treat is the paella, the Spanish seafood and rice dish that you usually have to travel to New York City to find.

Meals are served in a dining room with white linen tablecloths and a subdued color scheme of beige and white.

Bamboo House
$$ • U.S. Hwy. 209 Bus., East Stroudsburg • 424-2460

This traditional Chinese restaurant has a variety of Szechuan, Hunan, Cantonese and traditional Chinese favorites. It also offers an American selection of steaks for those in your party who are not inclined to Chinese, and a children's menu that is more American in choices, including hamburgers. It has two dining rooms decorated in an Oriental motif.

Dinner is served seven days a week, and lunch is offered Wednesday through Sunday.

Beaver House
$$$ • 1000 N. Ninth St. (Pa. Hwy. 611), Stroudsburg • 421-1020

This restaurant is an old-timer — more than 35 years at this location. It has nine dining rooms, including the very colorful Terrace Room with pink flowers, tile floors and lots of plants. Live Maine lobster and fresh seafood of other varieties (including entrees or entree additions of king crab legs and claws) are part of what makes this restaurant a winner in this area. Another terrific choice is the king-size prime rib.

The Beaver House is open every day for lunch and dinner, and the restaurant serves from an à la carte menu between those two meals.

The Big A Restaurant
$$ • U.S. Hwy. 209 S., Marshalls Creek • 223-8314

The Big A steak is what draws people to this little restaurant in Marshalls Creek. It's intimate and cozy with the feel of a neighborhood tavern. They grill the steaks right there in the dining room behind a semi-circular counter, across from the salad bar. There's a

children's menu. Imagine haute cuisine menu items such as escargot and baked brie at such a quaint spot! There is a different special every night; Friday is famous for the barbecued baby back ribs!

Reservations are a good idea on weekends because the Big A is small and fills up fast. Lunch and dinner are served daily.

Brandli's Pizza, Pasta & Vino
$$$ • 6A Foxmoor Village (U.S. Hwy. 209), Marshalls Creek • 223-1600

Great Italian appetizers, wonderful vegetable creations and traditional Italian favorites make dinner here very exciting to the tastebuds. If you don't want a big meal, the pizza (stuffed or topping-laden), calzone and stromboli make excellent, less expensive choices. The atmosphere is simple, light and airy. Lattice dividers separate the casual pizzeria side from the more formal two restaurant side rooms with country decor; either way you'll find a basically relaxing place to stop to eat.

There is also an outdoor cafe area for al fresco dining in summer. Brandli's is open every day year round for lunch and dinner.

China Buffet
$$ • 24 Eagle's Glen Mall (U.S. Hwy. 209 Bus.), East Stroudsburg • 476-7658

This is a great place if you love all kinds of Chinese food and want some of everything. The buffet is served every day at lunch and dinner, and there is also a dinner menu. The food is constantly replenished, so it is always hot and fresh. Szechuan, Hunan and Cantonese dishes such as General Tso chicken, shrimp and green beans (delicious -- lots of fresh garlic), sweet and sour pork, dumplings, chicken and broccoli and wonton soup, and standbys such as egg foo young and fried rice, are at the buffet and on the menu. There is a reduced price for children.

The Dansbury Depot
$$$ • 50 Crystal St., East Stroudsburg • 476-0500

This depot was built as a railroad station and freight house in 1864 and saw many changes while serving as an important stop for those heading to summer camp in the mountains or coming for vacation. It also served as a canteen for servicemen stationed at Tobyhanna Army Depot during World War II. Today The Dansbury Depot is one of the most popular restaurants in the area. The restaurant's railside windows offer a view out over the tracks that once were humming with activity. It is a bright and cheerful place.

Be careful when you order because they put the most wonderful breads on the table — the lemon poppyseed bread is famous — and it's tough to keep from filling up on them. (They are for sale as you leave, if you want to continue the experience at home.) There are lots of specials, such as twin lobsters stuffed with crabmeat, surf and turf or The Mailbag, a classic American combination of barbecued baby back ribs, barbecued chicken breast and Angus strip steak.

Dinner is served after 4 PM, Monday through Saturday and all day Sunday. On Monday through Saturday, lunch is also served. An à la carte menu and an Express Train menu for folks in a hurry are choices on those days as well.

Everybody's Cafe III
$$ • 905 Main St., Stroudsburg • 424-0896

This lovely restaurant is in a beautifully appointed, restored Victorian house on Upper Main Street. The decor is rich and warm-looking with deep greens, cane-backed chairs and Victorian print wallpapers in each of the intimate dining rooms, centered around fireplaces with blackboards above announcing the specials of the day. Outdoor dining on the front porch is a treat for those who love to enjoy the fresh air as they dine elegantly.

There is a very exciting vegetarian menu here as well as some tempting continental items. There are some great tastes in "pocket" foods: pitas, baguettes, gyros, tapas and so on. Dessert tortes are also quite tempting.

It's closed Monday but open for lunch and dinner the rest of the week.

Gibson's Seafood Grille
$$-$$$$ • U.S. Hwy. 209 N. Bus., East Stroudsburg • 420-8898

This restaurant, as its name implies, is famous for its seafood. King crab legs are a special item that folks love. Other seafood greats are scallops and shrimp scampi. Large steaks and chicken cordon bleu are great choices for the landlubber. The atmosphere is very casual, and the decor exudes relaxation and comfort. There are some tables in the bar area, but the restaurant is the draw, especially for the seafood.

Gibson's is open every day for lunch and dinner; reservations are necessary for dinner Friday and Saturday.

Historic Tom X Inn
$$ • Tom X Rd. (off U.S. Hwy. 209), Marshalls Creek • 223-8154

Continental cuisine is served at this historic inn in Marshalls Creek, a favorite spot for Delmonico and peppercorn steaks. Seafood specials include scallops au gratin and shrimp scampi with lots of lemon, garlic and dry sherry. Chicken dishes and casseroles are on the menu as well as hamburgers (also on the kids menu).

Tom X Inn is rustic, with lots of wood and plants and windows, some of which overlook the stream that runs past the property.

Tom X Inn is closed Monday.

J.R.'s Green Scene
$$ • Budget Motel, at Exit 51 off I-80, East Stroudsburg • 424-5451

Insiders love this place. It has a great, 35-item salad bar, terrific Friday night specials (lasagna is a big favorite), fresh baked breads and lots of good choices. There is even a vegetarian section on the menu. The seafood sampler is a bountiful combination of lobster tail, sea scallops, large shrimp, clams and fillet of fish, all broiled with butter, white wine and paprika. J.R.'s also claims no one beats their stuffed sole, engorged with real crabmeat and topped with a whole sea scallop and shrimp.

The dining room is decorated in green, pink and gray, with a glassed-in porch room overlooking I-80. There is a light, airy feeling here. Three different seating areas are decorated with pink tablecloths and napkins.

J.R.'s is open every day for breakfast and dinner year round. The children's menu is reasonably priced.

FYI
Unless otherwise noted, the area code for all phone numbers in this guide is 717.

INSIDERS' TIPS

Check the local newspapers for advertisements on nightly restaurant specials and discount coupons.

Gracie's Place
$$ • 395 N. Courtland St., East Stroudsburg • 421-5514

Tucked away on a largely residential street, Gracie's is the ultimate Insider hangout. The food draws rave reviews. Choose from entrees such as chicken Francaise, pasta primavera or prime rib. In good weather, you can enjoy your meal at the cute bistro tables on the front porch. Lunch and dinner are served daily except Sunday. (See our Nightlife chapter for information about Gracie's after hours.)

Marita's Cantina
$$ • 745 Main St., Stroudsburg • 424-8355

This is a terrific little spot for Mexican food. The decor is fun with painted chests, ponchos on the walls, brightly painted tables and chairs. The portions are very large, so you can enjoy the fun of sharing with a friend and still have plenty for yourself. All the favorites are here: soft and hard tacos, chili, chimichangas, burritos, fajitas, Southwest shrimp and more. Some of this stuff you may have not even heard of. There are always tortilla chips on the table to dip in a very tangy salsa. And, of course, nachos and quesadillas for appetizers.

Marita's is open daily for lunch and dinner.

Mollie's
$$ • 622 Main St., Stroudsburg • 476-4616

Mollie's is a legend in this area. Mollie started her restaurant during the Depression, across the bridge in East Stroudsburg. It was a place where no one left hungry, whether they had money or not. Mollie knew what everyone wanted, and lunch boxes were brought in each morning and filled with food while folks sipped coffee.

Today Mollie's is a lovely restaurant on Main Street. Uncovered brick walls; clean (Mollie's hallmark), polished hardwood floors; and a bright, airy dining area all make this one of the most popular stops for locals. Light lunches, gourmet treats and satisfying desserts fill the menu. There are daily specials posted on the blackboard as you walk in.

Concern for others is still a Mollie's tradition. The restaurant supplies food for Meals-on-Wheels and for the guests at The Comfort of Home Adult Day Care Center (see our Retirement chapter).

Northeastern Pizzeria & Video
$$ • The Village Shopping Center • U.S. Hwy. 209, Marshalls Creek • 223-7534

This place puts a new twist on "spending the night in." If you don't want to go out for dinner, you can enjoy pizza, subs or a good Italian entree — plus a video — without setting foot outside your door. Northeastern Pizza & Video will deliver your order to your home, resort room or vacation retreat anywhere from Bushkill to Shawnee-on-Delaware, along Pa. 402 or U.S. 209, for a $1.50 delivery charge.

Specialties include white pizza, vegetable pizza, Chicago deep-dish pizza, Chicago supreme pizza and 9-inch personal pan pizza with your choice of toppings. Hot subs include meatball, sausage and sausage with peppers and onions -- all can be made parmigiana. Cold subs are great too. If you crave mussels, calamari, shrimp scampi, veal or eggplant — delivered, mind you — this is a good place to call. You can eat at the restaurant (there are a few tables), but delivery is Northeastern's specialty. Not a bad idea after a full day of skiing, shopping, sightseeing, hiking, swimming, skating . . .

Peppe's Ristorante

$$$ • Eagle Valley Mall, Pa Hwy. 447 N., East Stroudsburg • 421-4460

Fine Italian and American cuisine are served here in a very earthy setting with brick walls, arches and bistro-style tables. All dishes are homemade and very tasty, lightly seasoned and delicately flavored. The homemade pasta, espresso and cappuccino are specialties as well as their lasagna and seafood dishes such as lobster tails, shrimp scampi, filet of sole and linguine with clam sauce.

This restaurant is open for lunch Monday through Friday and dinner Monday through Sunday.

Petrizzo's Italian-American Restaurant

$$$ • U.S. Hwy. 209 S. (next to Fernwood), Bushkill • 588-6414

Homemade Italian lasagna, pasta and specialty dishes share the menu with great American ribs, steaks and chops. Pizza and daily specials round out the menu. This casual eatery has a full bar with beer on tap and a good selection of wines.

It's open daily for lunch and dinner.

Pocono Pub

$ • Pa. Hwy. 611 (across from Holiday Inn), Bartonsville • 421-2187

A fun little family restaurant and tavern, Pocono Pub serves all the expected pub sandwiches and appetizers. Burgers, Philly steak sandwiches, pizza and chili are some of the favorites. Full dinner entrees from fried chicken to New York strip steak are also available. The kids menu is very, very reasonable. Pocono Pub is open every day. Visit Sunday afternoons in fall to watch pro football on the pub's TVs; other entertainment usually happens weekend evenings.

Pocono Happy Days

$ • U.S. Hwy. 209 Bus., East Stroudsburg • 420-9866

So you just want a good old hamburger, fries and a shake like the old days. And maybe some good old be-bop music. Well, you're in luck at this old-fashioned diner complete with 1950s jukebox, old-fashioned hamburgers, Texas Tommy, milkshakes, homemade waffles, hard ice cream and sundaes like you enjoyed when you were a kid. And if you missed it when you were a kid, here's your chance to make up for it.

This restaurant is open seven days for breakfast, lunch and dinner.

Red Rooster

$$-$$$ • Pa. Hwys. 715 and 314, Henryville • 629-9598

The atmosphere here is exciting: The colors are bright; the lights are low but sparkly; the different room settings add intimacy; and the Native American artifacts add mystery. And all the food here is cooked from scratch, so enjoy the time you spend waiting for your "classic American fare." For starters you can have Lazy Lobster (lobster meat in garlic sauce) or beer-batter mushrooms with horseradish sauce. If your appetite is up to the task, a vegetable, fruit and cheese tray plus drinks is complimentary with dinner selections. There are meatless dishes, stir-fry veggies over linguine or pasta Provencale with tomatoes, mushrooms, peppers, garlic and herbs over linguine. Other entrees include steaks, veal and several chicken dishes including Sante Fe (a Southwestern-style treat with cheese), stir-fry vegetables and scampi. If you like seafood, try a Seafood Fiesta — a plate of shrimp, clams, scallops, langostinos and more. Sandwiches are available too. The kids menu features burgers and chicken tenders.

Red Rooster is open for dinner Tuesday through Saturday, and early-bird specials are available between 5 and 6:30 PM Tuesday through Friday.

Ribs & More

$$$ • Pa. Hwy. 611, Bartonsville
• 421-7444

Barbecued beef ribs and baby back ribs are obviously the specialty at this sports-oriented restaurant. You can have your ribs alone or with chicken or shrimp. You can have them Cajun style. . . . Babe Ruth style . . . Joe Louis style. Even Andre the Giant style! There also are lots of other good things to eat; many named after sports heroes such as the Mickey Mantle burgers, Jim Thorpe burgers, Charles Barkley burgers. . . . You get the picture. There's also a salad bar, early bird and lunch specials and a Pee Wee League menu for the kids.

You can eat at Ribs & More any day for lunch or dinner. An express lunch is available for those in a hurry.

Sarah Street Grill

$$ • 550 Quaker Alley, Stroudsburg
• 424-9120

The menu is quite varied at this lovely spot in Stroudsburg. It's back-street location makes it quiet and accessible from Sarah Street and Quaker Alley. There are two rooms inside to eat in and two great bars — one to sit at and one to stand at. The outside, second-floor dining deck is settled in the trees and makes for a great spot for lunch, dinner or drinks and a snack.

Delmonico steaks — big Delmonico steaks — are the specialty. Other items include sand-

wiches, pastas (with GIANT meatballs), chicken, scampi with asparagus and vegetarian meals such as artichoke and mushroom pesto with penne pasta.

Check it out. Sarah Street Grill is open every day for lunch, dinner or in-betweens. See our Nightlife chapter for more on the two bars here. There are seven TVs to watch sports.

Shannon Inn & Pub

$$$ • U.S. Hwy. 209 and Pa. Hwy. 447,
East Stroudsburg • 424-1591,
(800) 424-8052

Seafood stuffed ravioli, Chicken O'Brien, Tequila Shrimp, shepherd's pie, pasta primavera — do these dishes sound Irish? OK, maybe just a couple of them, but they are all good, and they are served at the Shannon Pub. There's also snacking pub fare, such as fajitas and chicken fingers, nachos, authentic Buffalo wings and potato skins (now we're talking Irish!).

Shannon Inn & Pub is open for dinner every day. On Friday and Saturday, the green in 'em really does come out with authentic Irish entertainment and Irish food specialties.

Steak & Rib Inn

$$$ • U.S. Hwy. 209 N., East Stroudsburg
• 588-9466

Can you believe a 32-ounce Porterhouse steak? Well they have them here as well as steaks cut to order. Want more choices? Try the delicious pasta dishes and ocean-fresh seafood.

Steak & Rib Inn is open all day and features a special sandwich menu as well as a children's menu, so everybody can enjoy. Also check out "the bullpen," where you'll find six beers on tap as well as bottled imports and domestics. The environment is casual and cozy — a place for two or a whole family.

Willow tree Inn
$$$ • 601 Ann St., Stroudsburg • 476-0211

What a lovely place to eat lunch or dinner, or as owner George K. Nunn puts it, "pass the time of day, be it in the parlor, the lounge, the restaurant or the southyard veranda beneath the shade of the tree." This beautiful restaurant is in another restored Victorian house in Stroudsburg, right on McMichaels Creek. From the front, you see a lovely house. When you walk in, you see a cute parlor and bar area. Then in the dining room is a spectacular view of a giant willow tree by the creek, as seen through a wall of floor-to-ceiling windows. The dining room has two levels, both of which face the tree. Outside is the veranda, beneath the tree, for screened-in dining.

Just sitting here is a joy, but the food is top-quality gourmet fare. Cheese tortellini Alfredo, seafood creole, sole Française, chicken Katharine, veal Française or marsala, tournedos au poivre and salmon fillet are just some of the menu items that will tempt you. Desserts are daily specials. The Willow Tree Inn is open every day for lunch, dinner and in-between.

Wine Press Inn
$$$ • Pa. Hwy. 611 (Star Route), Bartonsville • 629-4302

This intimate dining inn has three seating areas, all intimate and cozy, and a bar area where brick and wood accents create a rustic yet casual feel. It also has a fine menu of American and Italian specialties. The house salad is so good, you could make a meal of it. But you'll also want to sample the excellent Italian and seafood specialties that make up the bill of fare. For an entree consider baked stuffed shrimp or shrimp scampi; Italian-style crab cakes made with lump crab meat and served

with a pesto alfredo sauce and raw tomatoes; or scrod oreganata. Veal cutlet sorrentino has prosciutto, eggplant and cheese in a tomato sauce. Try a rack of veal Valdostana for a real mouthful, or the old Italian favorite — osso bucco. For dessert try the delicious tiramisu.

The Wine Press Inn is open every day for dinner.

Mount Pocono Area

Baileys Grille & Steakhouse
$$ • Pa. Hwy. 611, Mount Pocono • 839-9678

The Ultimate Onion, Jamaican jerk wings, mesquite-grilled shrimp, pesto cheese bread, baby back ribs and pan-fried crab cakes are just a few of the menu items at Baileys. Plus you can find out what grouper fingers are. This place sells hundreds of the popular steak and seafood combinations every week.

This bar/restaurant provides a fun, informal setting for casual meals. Lunch and dinner are served daily.

The Bloomin' Onion
$ • Pa. Hwys. 390 and 191, Cresco • 595-6315

This tiny spot (20 seats inside or on a lovely porch) is a local favorite for breakfast and lunch. Any of the egg dishes for breakfast are tasty; lunch selections include sandwiches and chili. Almost everything is made from scratch, a rare thing at such a reasonably priced restaurant. The restaurant's namesake dish is outstanding.

The Bloomin' Onion serves breakfast and lunch every day except Tuesday.

Britannia Country Inn & Restaurant
$$ • off Pa. Hwy. 314, Swiftwater • 839-7243

British and American cuisine — beef Wellington, steak Diane and bangers and mash — are featured for dinner Wednesday through Saturday at this inn. The best choice on Wednesday is fish and chips with peas and a bottle of English beer. The full menu is served Thrusday through Saturday. A piano player performs on Friday and Saturday nights.

Cameltop
$$ • Camelback Rd., Tannersville • 629-1661

This lodge at the summit of Camelback Mountain serves lunch from spring to fall every day. The mountainside deck provides a panoramic view of most of the Pocono Mountain area. The atmosphere is definitely casual. You may either drive to the top of the mountain or park at the bottom and take the ski area's chairlift. Sandwiches and snacks are served cafeteria-style.

Cappuccino Ristorante
$$ • Pa. Hwy. 191, Cresco • 595-2833

Italian entrees such as shrimp Francaise, boneless chicken Cacciatore, baked lasagna and assorted pasta and veal entrees are served in this restaurant's dining room; though not overly formal, it's appropriate for an affordable but romantic dinner. Best of all, meals include the well-stocked antipasto and spinach bar (also available as an entree). Dinners also include a large bowl of fresh fruit and a loaf of fresh-baked bread.

Dinner is served daily; reservations are suggested on weekends.

Christine's Reeders Inn
$$$ • Pa. Hwy. 715, Reeders • 629-1210

This former train stop has been serving the public since the turn of the century. In the past, the building has been used for square dancing and, in 1958, was the first Chinese restaurant in the Poconos. Today traditional dishes and Southern favorites are served. A popular side order is Hoppin' John Rice, a Southern dish served for good luck in the New Year. This mix of black-eyed peas, rice and sliced sausage is available year round at Christine's. Dinner is served daily.

Crescent Lodge
$$$-$$$$ • Pa. Hwy. 191, Paradise Valley • 595-7486

A favorite in the region, Crescent Lodge serves more than 20 different entrees in a country inn atmosphere. The marinade of fresh vegetables served with each meal is delicious. House specialities include New York sirloin steak, roast crisp Long Island duckling and Châteaubriand boquetiere beef tenderloin for two. The appetizers are worth a try too — lobster ravioli, smoked Pennsylvania trout, Southern-style alligator and wild mushroom blend. Dinner is served daily, and reservations are suggested.

The Edelweiss
$$ • Pa. Hwy. 940, Pocono Lake • 646-3938

If you can't make a trip to Germany, this authentic Old World restaurant provides a convincing re-creation of a German dining experience. Generous portions of food emphasize the Black Forest region: wiener, jaeger or paprika rahm schnitzel; veal Edelweiss; and sauerbraten. You'll also find American dishes such as steak and seafoods. Waitresses complete the theme by wearing traditional dirndels. A lighter menu is served in summer. The most popular dessert is hot Austrian apple strudel. Lunch and dinner are served daily. The restaurant hosts a variety of festivals, including food and music, from February to July and a huge Octoberfest in early September. Adjacent to the restaurant is a pastry shop and a gift shop filled with beer steins, cuckoo clocks, nutcrackers, smokers and Christmas decorations.

Fanucci's
$$$ • Pa. Hwy. 611, Swiftwater • 839-7097

You can not miss the giant wooden barrel at the entrance to Fanucci's. Once inside, you will find an elegant dining room with a fireplace — an ideal setting for enjoying northern and southern Italian cuisine. Try the veal con melangane, a cutlet baked with layers of eggplant and mozzarella cheese topped with tomato sauce, or pork chops pizzaiola, simmered in marinara sauce, sweet peppers and mushrooms. Pasta dishes are made with both homemade and imported pasta. Fish, chicken, veal and steak entrees round out the menu.

Fanucci's is open for dinner daily. Look for early dinner specials.

The Forks at Buck Hill
$$$ • Pa. Hwy. 390, Mountainhome • 595-7335

Large portraits of unindentified ancestors and the assorted antiques remind patrons that this building has a history dating back to 1878. The wooden tables, the understated green and red decor and country crafts provide an elegant complement to an already beautiful building. Meals include pastas, chicken, seafood, veal and steaks. Consider the cheese ravioli in a sun-dried tomato sauce, chicken stir-fry, lemon sole, salmon bearnaise and pork chops pizzaiola. In addition to the main dining area, there is a separate lounge and an outdoor deck.

The restaurant serves lunch and dinner daily.

Frog Town Inn
$$$ • Pa. Hwy. 390, Canadensis
• 595-6282

Residents of nearby Buck Hill Falls have made this a popular spot for dinner Wednesday through Sunday. The inn, bearing the former name of Canadensis, has frog-theme items stragecially placed within its elegant yet country-style decor. Off to one side of the dining room is a romantic, isolated table surrounded by books in a small library room — perfect for intimate conversations. You might encounter such entrees as rack of lamb persille, roast duckling, Cornish hen, poached salmon filet, New York strip steak or roquefort and penne pasta. Be sure to try an appetizer of house-smoked salmon, baked brie orgalantine of duck (boneless duck stuffed with rabbit, herbs, figs and lemon zest and served with a black currant sauce).

Hampton Court Inn
$$$ • Pa. Hwy. 940 E., Mount Pocono
• 839-2119

The steaks are cut and trimmed in-house at Hampton Court. This gives some indication of the care that goes into preparing every meal. No artifical preservatives or flavor enhancers are used, and very little salt is added. Regulars know they can special-order varations of menu items. Grilling is done over lava rocks because of concerns regarding the healthiness of charcoal cooking. Entrees include lamb, seafood, veal and an excellent roast duckling served with Hampton Court Inn's own Grand Marnier cranberry sauce.

The three dining rooms are small, so reservations are a good idea. Dinner only is served every day except Tuesday.

Heritage Inn at Memorytown
$$ • Grange Rd., Mount Pocono
• 839-1680

Traditional Pennsylvania recipes are used to prepare the family-style meals. The fresh-made breads, soups and desserts are very good. The restaurant is open for dinner only Wednesday through Saturday. Fridays feature an all-you-can-eat buffet consisting of several entrees and plenty of side dishes. The restaurant is in Memorytown, a complex of shops including a popular spot for live country music, Memorytown Tavern by the Lake.

Homestead Inn
$$-$$$ • Sand Spring Dr., Cresco
• 595-3171

Andrew Wyeth prints and a fireplace set an appropriate early American atmosphere in which to enjoy London broil, rack of lamb in pesto sauce, Maryland-style crab cakes, grilled swordfish, roasted pork tenderloin, scallops chardonnay, medallions of veal piccata and baked Norwegian salmon. The wine selection is exceptional. Dinner is available daily.

Inn at Meadowbrook
$$$ • Cherry Lane Rd., Tannersville
• 629-0296

Using many locally grown products, Meadowbrook creates some interesting luncheon and dinner offerings. For lunch, choose from a soup sampler; whole-wheat crust pizza with smoked chicken, red onion and three cheeses; grilled mango chicken salad; poached salmon with buttermilk-dill sauce over white bean salad; angel hair pasta tossed lightly with garlic green pesto and asparagus tips; or an organic spinach salad with shrimp and a warm bacon dressing and garlic. House specialities for dinner are chicken and shrimp Milano, veal valdastana, chicken Oscar and cioppino (shrimp, scallops and clams stewed

INSIDERS' TIPS

Many of our restaurants are in rather isolated areas. Be sure to allow ample driving time when considering reservation times.

Photo: Pocono Mountains Vacation Bureau, Inc.

Fine restaurants abound in the Poconos.

in a spicy tomato broth served over linguine). While the decor is unpretentious, the dining room and its view of the surrounding countryside provide an appropriately romantic atmosphere. Lunch is served Wednesday through Saturday; dinner, Monday through Saturday.

Murphy's Loft
$$ • Pa. Hwy. 115, Blakeslee • 646-2813

Lunch and dinner are served daily. Breakfast is available on Saturday and Sunday. In addition to the restaurant, you may dine or have drinks on the deck or at the outdoor bar overlooking a waterfall, garden and in-ground heated pool. Live entertainment is featured on the deck on Saturdays. Menu items include steaks, seafood, veal, burgers, steamers and pizza. Billed as a Pocono tradition, Murphy's serves an 18-ounce T-bone steak for less than $10.

Pagoda
$$ • Pa. Hwy. 611, Scotrun • 629-0250

Dr. Austin Kutschler, the author of an encyclopedia of Chinese food and cooking, called Pagoda's dishes "the finest Chinese food in the Poconos." For atmosphere, there are waterfalls, walk-through gardens and a 30-foot-long saltwater aquarium. Health-conscious patrons can order dietary or vegetarian dishes. Lunch and dinner are served daily. A separate, 80-seat room is reserved for nonsmokers.

Pines Cafe
**$$ • Pa. Hwy. 940, Pocono Pines
• 646-1313**

Lunch and dinner are served every day at Pines Cafe. Both a restaurant menu and a light-fare tavern menu are available. Highlights on the tavern menu include appetizers such as potato skins, Cajun wings, calamari and steamers along with sandwiches, soups and salads.

For dinner, try the house specialities, including filet au poivre, a 10-ounce cut with cracked peppercorn, or veal Saltimbocca. Poultry, veal, seafood and pasta entrees also are offered.

An outdoor deck overlooks Lake Naomi. Musicians perform on Saturdays and Sundays.

Pine Knob Inn
$$$ • Pa. Hwy. 447, Canadensis • 595-2532

This lovely country inn serves dinner Friday through Sunday. The gourmet dining in the Brodhead Room includes such specialties as lobster à la Brodhead, Michael's trout and scallops, prime rib of beef, blackened tuna steak and chicken Pine Knob (sauteed chicken breast in a Romano cheese sauce with prosciutto, snow peas and melted provolone). Regular menu items are more familiar: stuffed flounder, filet mignon, chicken Française, New York strip steak and fettuccine Alfredo.

The inn's long history dates back to 1847 when it was built as a house for tannery owner Dr. Gilbert Palen. He was responsible for renaming the town (nee Frogtown and later Coveville) Canadensis after *tsuga canadensis*, the botanical name for the hemlock trees so prevalent in the area. The house began accepting guests in 1886.

Pocono Mountain Travel Center Mega Buffet
$ • Pa. Hwy. 611, Bartonsville • 421-1770

A lot of food at a very affordable price is the attraction at the Mega Buffet. A salad bar, soup bar, Mexican dishes, an Italian bar, homemade baked goods, carved meats and a dessert bar are offered. The buffet is available for dinner every day.

Pump House Inn
$$$ • Skytop Rd., Canadensis • 595-7501

Sophisticated country dining is on the bill at the Pump House Inn. A traditional menu dominated by steak, seafood and chicken dishes is served for dinner Tuesday through Sunday. The restaurant is closed Mondays.

Robert Christians
$$-$$$ • Pa. Hwy. 940, Blakeslee • 646-0433

Serving lunch and dinner daily, Robert Christians is known for its established specials: Mondays, all-you-can-eat baby back ribs; Tuesdays, Delmonico steak; Wednesdays, all-you-can-eat shrimp; Thursdays, the seafood combo or prime rib; and Sundays, roast turkey or ham steak. The regular menu includes steak, seafood and pasta selections.

Smuggler's Cove
$$ • Pa. Hwy. 611, Tannersville • 629-2277

Seafood dinners are served in the main dining area. The Castaways Lounge offers burgers, wings, fajitas and seafood — available until midnight. Try the coconut shrimp, tortellini with feta and spinach sauce or the mussels Neapolitan. Captain Crab, a seafood store just behind Smuggler's Cove, sells fresh crabs and other nautical delights. The restaurant and lounge are open for lunch and dinner every day. Reservations are appreciated.

Tannersville Inn
$$ • Pa. Hwy. 611, Tannersville • 629-3131

Tannersville Inn serves reasonably priced steaks and seafood. For late-night appetites, a bar menu, featuring pork ribs, scallops in garlic butter, broiled swordfish tips and an assortment of sandwiches, salads and chicken dishes, is served until 1:30 AM. The restaurant menu has fancier seafood meals such as lobster tail and shrimp stuffed with crabmeat plus plenty of steak, chicken and pasta offerings. The inn began serving the public as a stagecoach stop in 1825 and has become a popular local gathering spot.

Lunch and dinner are available daily. Bands perform Friday, Saturday and Sunday nights.

Tokyo Tea House
$$-$$$ • Pa. Hwy. 940, Pocono Summit • 839-8880

Thought you couldn't get sushi or sake at the top of the Pocono Mountains? Guess again. If the thought of eating uncooked fish intimidates you, this restaurant also serves steaks, vegetarian specials and other seafood offerings as alternatives to its Japanese specialities. Tokyo Tea House serves lunch and dinner Wednesday through Monday.

Diners

If you are hungry at 3 AM, what do you do? If you want breakfast at 8 PM, who are you going to call? A Poconos diner, that's who.

Many residents swear by their beloved diners. For example, the Snydersville Diner's baked goods are worshipped. Every Sunday, the line to enter stretches out the door and through the parking lot.

Diners have a lot of things going for them: great prices, diverse menus and plenty of local color. They are gathering places where workers, families and couples can comfortably share meals without worrying about dress codes or social status.

Most diners look roughly the same — boxy, weathered, perhaps even arrogantly shabby (a compliment for a diner). You enter and are greeted by a counter for those who just want to sit down to a quick meal or a cup of coffee. Behind the counter, just out of reach but within eyesight, are the baked goods. Booths line the walls, and tables are placed wherever there is room.

The following list highlights some of the more popular diners in the Poconos. Some are open 24 hours and serve breakfast all the time. Call up the diner in your area for information on hours and menu availability.

Delaware Water Gap
Water Gap Diner, 555 Broad St., Delaware Water Gap, 476-0132.

Stroudsburg/East Stroudsburg
Arlington Diner, 834 N. Ninth St., Stroudsburg, 421-2329; **Besecker's Diner**, 1427 N. Fifth St., Stroudsburg, 421-6193; **209 Diner & Restaurant**, U.S. Hwy. 209, Marshalls Creek; and **Key City Diner**, 1947 W. Main St., Stroudsburg, 421-5903.

Mount Pocono Area
Pioneer Diner, 508 Belmont Ave., Mount Pocono, 839-7620; **Blakeslee Diner**, Pa. Hwy. 115, Blakeslee, 646-2800; **Billy's Pocono Diner**, Pa. Hwy. 611, Tannersville, 629-1450; and **Mountainhome Diner**, Pa. Hwy. 390, Mountainhome, 595-2523.

West End
Sunrise Diner Inc., 3 Hazard Sq., Jim Thorpe, 325-4093; **Snydersville Diner**, U.S. Hwy. 209 Bus., Snydersville, 992-4003; **Chestnuthill Diner**, U.S. Hwy. 209, Brodheadsville, 992-3222; **Meadowbrook Diner**, U.S. Hwy. 209, Brodheadsville, 992-5205; and **Effort Diner**, Pa. Hwy. 115, Effort, 610-681-4212.

Milford Area
Milford Diner, U.S. Hwys. 6 and 209, Milford, 296-7033.

Lake Wallenpaupack Area
Hamlin Diner, Pa. Hwy. 590, Hamlin, 689-0424; **Hawley Diner**, 302 Main Ave., Hawley, 226-0523; and **Towne House Diner**, 920 Main St., Honesdale, 253-1311.

Slate Belt
New Portland Diner, Pa. Hwy. 611, Portland, 897-5600; and **Mt. Bethel Diner**, Pa. Hwy. 611, Mt. Bethel, 897-6409.

Van Gilder's Jubilee Restaurant

$$ • Pa. Hwy. 940, Pocono Pines
• 646-2377

Van Gilder's strives to make sure no one leaves hungry, and to that end this restaurant has been "expanding waistlines since 1968." Breakfast platters such as the Pocono Sampler and the Country Boy Breakfast are local legends. The Pocono Sampler, as described on the menu, begins with an appetizer, then the chef serves what is described as his creation. The menu proclaims: "You have to be hungry for this one. It is a little bit of everything on the menu. Don't ask questions." More conventional, the Country Boy Breakfast features two stacks of pancakes, scrambled eggs, bacon and sausage.

Breakfast, lunch and dinner are served daily. The on-site Pub in the Pines, open every evening, serves tavern food including six flavors of chicken wings.

Woody's Country House

$$ • Pa. Hwy. 115, Blakeslee • 646-9932

Mediterranean cuisine, with some Mexican thrown in, is served for lunch and dinner every day except Tuesday. There is an outdoor deck, and the restaurant serves until 1 AM. Specials, such as 15¢ wings, are offered nightly.

Zum Jagermeister

$$ • Pa. Hwy. 390, Mountainhome
• 588-9978

The decor has just a slight German flair, but the dinner menu and bar selections are strictly Bavarian. Look for bratwurst, knockwurst, kassler rippchen, schinken steak, wienerschnitzel, schweinschnitzel, jagerschnitzel and rahmschnitzel. Do not pass up the delicious side dishes — sauerkraut, potato salad, cucumber salad and spatzle. Six German beers are served on tap, and another nine are available by the bottle.

Lunch and dinner are served Wednesday through Sunday.

West End

Black Bread Cafe & Catering Co.

$$$ • 47 Race St., Jim Thorpe • 325-8957

A Victorian home in the middle of one of the most interesting shopping areas in Jim Thorpe, Black Bread Cafe describes itself as providing "artful and intimate dining." The entrees are certainly diverse, including salmon puttenesca, rabbit with baby lima beans, honey-roasted half duckling and Key lime chicken. This cafe is well worth seeking out if you enjoy a romantic — and unique — meal. Black Bread Cafe serves lunch and dinner Thursday through Monday.

FYI
Unless otherwise noted, the area code for all phone numbers in this guide is 717.

Blue Heron Grille

$$ • Lake Shore Dr., Lake Harmony
• 722-9898

This chef-owned/operated restaurant is on Big Boulder Lake and features lake views from the dining room. Steaks, chops, seafood, veal, pasta, salads, burgers and pizza are served. After dinner, go to the on-site Cellar Night Club for live music, dancing and bar games.

Caruso's

$$ • 99 E. Bridge St. (Pa. Hwy. 443 and U.S. Hwy. 209), Lehighton • (610) 377-5666

An informal restaurant serving lunch and dinner daily, Caruso's features standard Italian pasta, chicken and veal entrees. The pizza is very popular too. The wine list is surprisingly good for such a casual restaurant.

Close Quarters Bar/Restaurant

$$ • Lake Shore Dr., Lake Harmony
• 722-8127

This place has been a favorite spot for more than 20 years for fans of casual dining in a bar atmosphere. Close Quarters specializes in Italian entrees including veal, steaks, fresh fish, red and white pizzas and strombolis.

Dinner is served daily.

DeMelos
$$ • 304 Delaware Ave., Palmerton • (610) 862-5454

Known for its famous tacos, DeMelos also serves very good steaks, seafood and pasta. The cuisine is Italian-American, and the prices are reasonable. This restaurant's interior resembles a well-dressed pizza parlor.

Lunch and dinner are available every day.

The Emerald Restaurant
$$$ • 24 Broadway, Jim Thorpe • 325-8995

In the beautifully restored The Inn at Jim Thorpe, built in the 1840s, this restaurant offers the finest in Irish-American and Continental cuisine. The Victorian dining room has a tin ceiling and paintings of old Mauch Chunk, the former name of Jim Thorpe. The combination of Irish hospitality and Victorian romance is unbeatable. Try the Irish offerings such as shepherd's pie, bubble and squeak (roast turkey, ham and vegetables with homemade mashed potato topping), chicken pot pie or Dublin-style fish and chips. After dinner, visit Molly Maguire's Pub where the true spirit of Ireland really kicks in.

Dinner is served daily.

Frank's Schoolhouse Tavern
$$ • 4740 Long Run Rd., Lehighton • (610) 377-5745

We bet students in the late 1800s would never have expected their schoolhouse to become home of terrific chicken wings and spare ribs. The original building has been expanded to accommodate this successful business. Lunch and dinner are served daily except on Sunday, when no one goes to school.

The Hamilton
$$ • Hamilton South Rd., between Sciota and Saylorsburg • 992-9108

Hardwood floors, spacious seating, quilts, assorted crafts and antiques provide an informal yet gracious setting for diners at The Hamilton. Beef, veal, pork, chicken and seafood entrees are offered. The liver is a local favorite. Those less hungry can try a sandwich or a personal pizza. Serving dinner daily, The Hamilton is strictly nonsmoking.

Hotel Switzerland
$$ • 5 Hazard Sq., Jim Thorpe • 325-4563

Another Jim Thorpe landmark, the Hotel Switzerland has been serving guests since 1830. Cold sandwiches named for local attractions, hot sandwiches and traditional steak and chicken dinners are featured. The bar gets into the local names as well, with its Lehigh Rafter (vodka, rum, sour mix, melon liqueur and pineapple juice) and Pocono Snow Blower (coffee, brandy, Kahlua and whipped cream).

The Inn of William Stoddard
$$$ • Stage Coach Rd., Stemlersville • (610) 377-3878

This historic inn predates the Civil War. You can picture folks relaxing on the large porches and socializing as they have for well more than 100 years. It is a casual gathering place that combines nostalgia with such specialities as quail, pork satay, frog legs and Alaskan king crab. The inn is open Wednesday through Sunday for dinner only. Reservations are appreciated but not required.

King Arthur Dining Room
$$$ • U.S. Hwy. 209 Bus., Sciota • 992-4969

The English theme decor is carried over to such menu items as brook trout Sir Galahad. Steak, lobster and veal also are featured. Save room for a dessert such as baked Alaska meringue, three flavors of ice cream and cake flambé at your table. Lunch and dinner are served daily.

The Library at Hideaway Hills Golf Club
$$$ • Hideaway Hills Rd. (off U.S. Hwy. 209), Kresgeville • (610) 681-6000

The rolling hills of the golf course provide a majestic view while enjoying dinner at The Library. The pastas, especially the cheese ravioli marinara, are excellent. Also worth considering are the steak, chicken and seafood offerings. Lobster Fradiavolo, a 9-ounce tail in marinara sauce with clams and shrimp over linguine, will tempt any seafood fan. It is a highlight of The Long Course, the main dinner menu. Less hungry folks should stick to The Short Course — pastas and appetizers. This elegant restaurant is open for dinner Thursday through Sunday.

Platz's Restaurant
$$ • 101 Harrity Rd., Lehighton • (610) 377-1819

This restaurant/bar resembles an overgrown rec room. Old books, pictures of unidentified ancestors, old sports equipment, signs and other random knickknacks fill every available space. The atmosphere is casual, stressing fun over formality. Sandwiches, seafood, pasta and steaks are included on a menu packed with familiar favorites. Dinner is served daily. Reservations are recommended on weekends, as the combination of residents and daytrippers from nearby Beltzville State Park often make for standing-room only.

Riedmiller's on the Lake
$$ • Hamilton South Rd., Saylorsburg • 992-7018

Overlooking Saylors Lake, Riedmiller's speciality is prime rib of beef au jus. Steaks, turkey, chicken and seafood dominate a menu that complements the sportsman's decor. An imposing presence at the restaurant entrance is a mounted 1,150-pound world-record class grizzly bear killed by Xavier Riedmiller in Alaska in 1970. Riedmiller's is open for dinner every day except Tuesday.

Stone Bar Inn
$$$ • U.S. Hwy. 209 Bus., Snydersville • 992-6634

A country tavern with fireside dining, intimate booths and namesake stone bar, this restaurant serves classic American cuisine such as prime Angus beef, rack of lamb and native game such as venison, moose and buffalo. The chef smokes his own trout and makes the sausage and ice cream himself. The appetizers, including grilled quail with roasted peppers vinaigrette and clams posilipo, are worth a taste. The Stone Bar Inn is open for dinner every day except Monday.

Trainer's Inn
$$$ • 845 Interchange Rd., Lehighton • (610) 377-4550

A hearty 24-ounce Delmonico steak is the big gun on Trainer's menu. Pasta, chicken, pork and veal also are offered. Trainer's is especially proud of its chicken wings. Another favorite light item is Buffalo shrimp, prepared Cajun-style and covered in the wings sauce. Burgers and cheesesteaks are good as well. Lunch and dinner are served daily. Look for daily specials.

Ye Olde Saylors Inne
$$ • Pa. Hwy. 115, Saylorsburg • 992-5200

Area residents consider this restaurant one of the true bargains in the Poconos. Large portions of familiar American dishes such as ham, steaks, chicken and fish are served in a friendly, family atmosphere. You will not find any exotic specials or pretentious decor, just simple, good food served in large dining rooms decorated with crafts created by local artists. Dress casual and arrive hungry.

Dinner is served Wednesday through Saturday.

Milford Area

Apple Valley Restaurant
$$ • 101 Pine Acres, Milford • 296-6831

Apple Valley serves classic American favorites in large portions at reasonable prices. Lasagna, barbecued ribs, steaks, burgers, Chicago-style pizza and assorted chicken and pasta dishes are all available. The restaurant serves lunch and dinner daily.

Alley Oops Pub, a nightclub at Apple Valley, features bands or comedians on weekends and daily appetizer specials (see our Nightlife chapter). The restaurant and pub are part of the Apple Valley Village complex of gift shops.

Black Walnut Inn
$$$ • Fire Tower Rd., Milford • 296-6322

Everything offered at the restaurant of this country inn is prepared by hand when ordered, which explains the 15-minute interval between reservations. The chef has extensive training in French restaurants in both France and Manhattan.

Complimentary hors d'oeurves, which change daily, are served first. Entrees change frequently — some reappear in another form; others disappear forever. If available, try the Long Island duckling served over a dark-amber shallot marmalade and flanked by cabbage and carrot shreds. The staff gladly explains any unfamiliar menu items.

The restaurant sits atop a mountain and is surrounded by woods and a lake. Assorted wildlife such as ducks and deer wander the grounds. Dinner is served daily, but call for reservations and hours, especially in winter when weather can force the restaurant to close.

Cliff Park Inn

$$$ • Cliff Park Dr., Milford • 296-6491

The original inn was built as a farmhouse in 1820 by George Buchanan. Around 1913 the family converted the farmland into a nine-hole golf course. The antiques used to decorate are mostly family heirlooms; portraits of ancestors dominate the parlor.

The family atmosphere prevails in the dining room, with its large wooden tables, lace and decorative antique glassware. On the menu, you will find unusual offerings such as terrine of lemon sole wrapped in spinach and stuffed quail napped with truffle sauce. For the health conscious, the chefs offer a no-butter, no-salt dinner. After dinner, relax on the porch overlooking the golf course, sit by the fire or talk over drinks.

The inn serves breakfast, lunch and dinner daily for both guests and the general public. Children are welcome, but the atmosphere is relaxed yet formal, particularly at dinner.

Dimmick Inn Steak House

$$$ • 101 E. Harford St., Milford
• 296-4021

The Dimmick has been entertaining guests since 1855. Original owner Frances Dimmick was one of the most colorful women in Pike County history. She was an accomplished violinist, horsewoman, flycaster and markswoman who preferred to wear men's clothing (unheard of in the late 19th century).

The building anchors the southern end of the town; its large porches offer a view of much of downtown Milford. The inn's green and white interior and hardwood floors present an atmosphere of elegance without stuffiness. The menu includes a number of dishes made with buffalo meat, which is lower in cholesterol, fat and sodium than beef, turkey or chicken. Buffalo steaks, burgers and hot dogs are available for take-out to be prepared at home as well.

Not only is the serving staff friendly, they maintain a sense of humor as well. On your birthday, you can be serenaded by the Dimmick Inn Marching Kazoo Band. On the third floor of the building, the art of renowned local painter Joe Splendora is displayed.

Lunch and dinner are served daily.

Flo-Jean Restaurant

$$$ • U.S. Hwys. 6 and 209, Port Jervis, N.Y. • (914) 856-6600

Don't let the New York address fool you. This restaurant is just one short, free bridge away from being in Pennsylvania. For that trip you will be treated to a spectacular view of the Delaware River as the Flo-Jean is as close to it as you can get without a boat.

The Flo-Jean's history can be traced to Western writer and Lackawaxen resident Zane Grey, who took a friend on a fishing trip to the area. The man and his wife opened the original El Patio Flo-Jean Tea Shoppe in 1929.

The main dining room is decorated with Victorian-era clothes and dolls in ornate carriages. Pink tablecloths and white lace fill the room. You will find dinners such as baked scrod, lobster, filet mignon with mushroom caps and roast turkey with "secret stuffing," the same recipe since 1929. In summer, an outdoor deck is open for drinks and light fare.

Below this room is the Toll House Pub & Grill. The name is derived from the building's original use for fare collection to cross the bridge that traverses the Delaware River. A sign detailing the cost of passage still hangs here. People paid 2¢ to cross, except when going to church on Sunday. This room offers lower-priced fare in a more masculine setting. A wood-burning stove keeps you warm no matter how cold the wind off the river gets. The food here consists of steaks, burgers and sandwiches.

The main dining room is open Wednesday through Sunday for dinner. The Toll House serves lunch and dinner daily.

The Inn at the Edge of the Forest
$$$ • U.S. 209 N., Milford • 296-7177

The cuisine at this intimate, casual restaurant is traditional continental. It is rather secluded, north of Milford in a wooded area just off U.S. 209.

Meals begin with a complimentary plate of Swiss cheese and ham plus a silk rose for female guests. Those with appetites for well-prepared red meats will enjoy the filet mignon supreme, which comes wrapped with bacon and stuffed with bleu cheese and chives. Lamb, seafood and chicken also are featured prominently on the menu. For dessert, try the pineapple mousse tart.

The restaurant is open Wednesday through Sunday for dinner only.

Landmark Restaurant & Lounge
$$ • 1012 Pennsylvania Ave., Matamoras • 491-2004

This recent addition to the region's restaurant scene stresses large portions in an unpretentious atmosphere. Chicken, steak, veal, seafood and pasta dominate a menu that presents all the expected standards. The wood-burning brick-oven pizza is particularly good.

Lunch, a menu filled mostly with sandwiches, and dinner are served daily.

Le Gorille
$$$, no credit cards • Twin Lakes Rd., Shohola • 296-8094

As the name implies, primate memorabilia dominates the decor. The menu for the day is written on a blackboard; there is no set list of entrees. The owners prepare the food, purchase the produce locally and smoke the meat in their own smokehouse. In the spirit of environmental goodwill, they even compost leftovers, a practice which sometimes draws a black bear to entertain guests. Two meals you might encounter are grilled shell steak marinated with beer and fried shallots, or roast grouper with horseradish crust and parsley sauce.

Le Gorille is open for dinner only Wednesday to Sunday from April through December. From January through March, the restaurant is open only Fridays, Saturdays and Sundays. Reservations are recommended as the dining room accommodates fewer than 40.

Mill Rift Inn
$$ • Mill Rift • 491-2946

In a town so small that street addresses are not necessary (residents all know each other, and outsiders will be able to see the entire hamlet from their cars), folks are fortunate that the only restaurant in the area is a very good one. The inn has a bar, a stage for live music on weekends and a small dining room. The dinner menu, available only on Friday and Saturday nights, includes a vegetarian burrito, Sheepshead Bay calamari, chicken piccatta, steaks and burgers. The pizza is fresh, homemade and excellent, especially if you like garlic.

The inn's tavern menu is available for lunch and dinner Monday through Saturday. It features more burgers, sandwiches, pizza and standards such as shrimp or chicken in a basket. Memorabilia fans will enjoy looking at the old area photos and artifacts that adorn the walls.

Tom Quick Inn
$$$ • 411 Broad St., Milford • 296-6514

This inn, recently restored to its Victorian grandeur following a fire, is named for the local folk hero who in the 1750s avenged his father's death at the hands of the Delaware Indians, hence the nickname "The Indian Slayer." The Quick family lived about a half-mile north of the inn.

The cuisine is a combination of American and continental. Seafood, poultry, beef and veal are well-represented. Lunch and dinner are served daily. On Sundays, breakfast and brunch are offered.

At the back of the building, the Back Door Saloon offers burgers, sandwiches, pizzas and appetizers for dinner and late-night snacking in a sports bar atmosphere. (See our Nightlife chapter for more information.)

Water Wheel Cafe & Bakery
$ • 150 Water St., Milford • 296-2383

In a 1996 article about the Poconos, *The Washington Post* labeled the Water Wheel "the most perfect luncheon spot in all the Poconos." Certainly the food and atmosphere are outstanding.

The Water Wheel is in The Upper Mill, a complex of shops in a restored gristmill over-

Photo: Pocono Mountains Vacation Bureau, Inc.

Diners in the Poconos can find gastronomic options from the mild to the wild.

looking the Sawkill Creek. The sandwiches are local legends. Favorites include melted open-faced brie with Granny Smith apples and toasted almonds on Swiss health bread, and prosciutto, goat cheese, roasted peppers and sundried tomatoes on Italian bread. Several vegetarian dishes are offered.

Lunch is the main event, but breakfast is also served. Dinner is available only on Friday and Saturday, and reservations are necessary due to limited seating. Alcohol is not served, but you may bring your own.

Lake Wallenpaupack Area

A.J.'s Fireplace
$ • Pa. Hwy. 507, Tafton • 226-2701

The fireplace in the name sits outside the building. It is a relic from an earlier structure. The bar and restaurant inside are handy for folks in a hurry who need a plain old good meal. Burgers, sandwiches, appetizers and

pizza are offered for lunch and dinner every day. The dinner menu adds a few more entrees such as steaks and chicken. The restaurant stays open until 2 AM, so it is great for late-night stops. Take-out service is available.

The Alpine
$$$ • U.S. Hwy. 6, Honesdale • 253-5899

Lovers of German foods need to visit The Alpine. In addition to the restaurant, there is a gift shop and butcher shop. Deli cases are filled with homemade wursts, fresh sausage and cut-to-order beef, veal and pork. The bakery offers everything from apple strudel to assorted European tortes. Gift items such as beer steins, crystal crafts and even German newspapers, magazines and compact discs are on sale.

Lunch and dinner are prepared daily in the restaurant. The cuisine, decor, music and dress of the waitresses is straight out of the beer garden. Throughout the year, The Alpine hosts festivals and outdoor barbecues at their own pit. The biggest is an Octoberfest held in the middle of August. Call for information on the dates of other activities.

Blueberry Hill Restaurant
$$ • Pa. Hwy. 191, South Sterling • 676-3550

Tucked among an unassuming assortment of gift shops and an unfinished-furniture store, this restaurant offers a surprisingly diverse menu. Entrees include charbroiled swordfish steak marinated in lime and olive oil, and salmon fillet baked with dill butter and splashed with cognac in parchment paper. The room's cozy, homey decor invites casual conversation and attire. Save room for dessert; baked goods are homemade.

Lunch — mostly sandwiches and salads — and dinner are served daily. A Sunday brunch is offered.

Cordaro Restaurant & Lounge
$ • 186 Grandview Ave., Honesdale • 253-3713

For more than 40 years, the Cordaro family has served food in Honesdale. In the 1950s, Phil Cordaro began providing coffee and doughnuts to the workers constructing Honesdale High School. Since the coffee often arrived too cold to drink, Phil started to deliver it in stainless-steel containers. So began the "coffee run," a staple in Honesdale ever since. Phil purchased a customized truck to take food and beverages to gas stations and construction sites around town.

In 1961 the family gave up the coffee run and the old restaurant to move to this location. The dining room and C.C. Lounge nightclub were added in 1981.

Breakfast, lunch and dinner are available daily. The menu offers sandwiches, seafood, pasta, salads and burgers. A discounted menu is provided for seniors older than 55.

Erhardt's Lakeside Restaurant
$$ • Pa. Hwy. 507, Hawley • 226-2124

The Erhardt family has been in the restaurant business for more than 50 years. Several generations work at the restaurant that overlooks Lake Wallenpaupack. The atmosphere is casual, allowing couples and families to enjoy the view and have fun.

Lunch favorites include a selection of "sloppies," named for the notoriously messy Oscar Madison, Fat Albert and John Madden. The size and sauces make neat eating impossible.

Erhardt's is open daily for lunch and dinner. A breakfast buffet is served on Sundays. Take-out service is available. For those who arrive by boat, slips are provided. In July and August, the Upper Deck serves bar food such as wings, steamers, hot dogs and hoagies.

Falls Port Inn & Restaurant
$$$ • Main Ave. and Church St., Hawley • 226-2600

For a short period, Hawley was called Falls Port because of its waterfalls. The inn that bears the old name was built in 1902 by Baron von Eckelberg and has been completely restored. The dining rooms contain antiques, cut glass, brass fixtures and other Victorian accessories. The owners refer to the atmosphere as "affordable elegance."

Steaks and seafood are staples of the dinner menu. The pasta is made fresh daily out of semolina flour. Desserts are homemade. Like dinner, lunch is served daily. That menu offers a variety of salads, soups and sandwiches. Sunday brunch is available.

The inn also rents 12 guest rooms for overnight accommodations.

The French Manor
$$$$ • Huckleberry Mountain, South Sterling • 676-3244

This elegant French restaurant was constructed as a private retreat in 1932. It is modeled after the original owner's estate in France. German and Italian masons were brought in to construct the stone château, using stone and lumber from the surrounding mountains. Many children of these workers still live in the region. The manor boasts an imported Spanish slate roof, cypress interior and a dining room with a Romanesque arched entranceway, thick-beamed ceiling and a massive stone fireplace. See our Bed and Breakfasts and Country Inns chapter for more information on overnight accommodations.)

The lunch and dinner menus offer strictly fine French entrees. Lamb, quail, chicken, veal, beef and pork are available. Sole and salmon are served to those who prefer seafood. Typical of the hors d'oeuvres is lobster and prawn quenelle afloat in a pool of classic sherried shellfish tomato cream sauce. Meals are served daily, and there is a Sunday brunch.

Hazzard's Raintree Restaurant
$$ • Pa. Hwy. 191, South Sterling • 676-5090

The Hazzard family menu appeals both to health-conscious folks and serious, quantity-conscious eaters who enjoy a casual atmosphere. The Kitchen Sink of Fresh Vegetables sauteed over linguine and salmon stew with artichokes and pink peppercorns in a rice bowl are ideal for those who watch their diets. Big appetites with less regard for cholesterol and fat can tackle the assortment of steaks and barbecued chicken or pork. Biggest of all is a mammoth 64-ounce filet nicknamed The Challenger. Only one person has ever finished it and gotten it for free. Desserts, such as the sticky bu cake, are made from scratch.

A large yard and a pond filled with ducks are outside the restaurant. On your way in, try not to wake the two cats who stand guard at the front door. Lunch, dinner and Sunday brunch are served every day. Reservations are suggested.

Hotel Wayne
$$ • 1202 Main St., Honesdale • 253-3290

This historic hotel has been serving meals since 1827. Overlooking the Lackawaxen River, the old hotel is slightly worn but still majestic.

Lovers of old buildings will appreciate the stone work and decor. The menu is rather standard fare, featuring steaks, ribs, seafood and spaghetti. Other sandwiches and platters are of the bar food variety. A tasty appetizer is the house speciality, crabmeat-stuffed mushrooms. Dinner and lunch are available daily. Lunches are very affordable, easily falling under our $15-for-two range.

And, yes, the building still is a working ho-

tel. Twenty rooms with private baths provide overnight accommodations.

The Inn at Peck's Pond
$$ • Pa. Hwy. 402, Peck's Pond • 775-7336

The deer heads and mounted fish on the walls give a good indication of both the menu and atmosphere. This is a restaurant for outdoor enthusiasts. Seafood, steaks and pasta in large servings are presented in a dining room that overlooks Peck's Pond. Most of the tables have a view of the water and surrounding woods.

In the adjoining bar, anglers gather to swap stories and exaggerate memories. The restaurant and bar are popular with residents of nearby private communities such as Hemlock Farms. The restaurant is closed Wednesdays. Lunch and dinner are offered every other day plus breakfast on Sunday.

Inn at Woodloch Pines
$$$$ • Off Pa. Hwy. 590, Hawley • 685-2661

The entire Woodloch operation is top shelf, offering friendly elegance in every phase of the resort complex. The meals available to the general public at the restaurant are no exception.

The Mountain Laurel Dining Room serves a complete meal package including appetizer, entree, dessert, salad, vegetable, potato of the evening, bread and nonalcoholic beverages for a set price. Featured entrees are strip steak, filet mignon, veal marsala, stuffed fillet of sole, scallops florentine, pasta primavera, chicken cordon bleu, roast duckling and shrimp scampi. A nightly family-style meal is also offered, where the food is served on platters and everyone helps themselves.

Dinner is served daily. After the meal, you can have drinks in the Oak Bar Lounge.

Jack Trainor's Restaurant and Lounge
$$$ • Terrace St., Honesdale • 253-3733

Trainor's offers casual dining in a fun at-

INSIDERS' TIPS

Allen House in Honesdale was the first concrete building in Pennsylvania. It was built in 1857 at the corner of Ninth and Church streets.

mosphere. The menu contains numerous beef, veal, chicken and seafood entrees. Specialities include New Zealand rack of lamb and Triple Parms (veal, chicken and shrimp parmigianas).

Dinner and lunch are served daily. The lunch menu has an appealing assortment of salads and sandwiches. A menu of lighter entrees, including pastas, and burgers is available for both lunch and dinner. Imported coffees and desserts such as peanut butter pie are an ideal way to end the meal.

Journey's End Restaurant & Inn
$$ • Pa. Hwy. 739, Lords Valley • 775-0805

Steaks and seafood are the main attractions. Lunch and dinner are served daily. The bar menu of appetizers and other light fare is served throughout the day. For those in need of overnight lodging, the inn has rooms with private baths.

Journey's End is just off Interstate 84 at Exit 9. Reservations for dinner are suggested.

Lakeside Resort
$$$ • Pa. Hwy. 507, Lake Wallenpaupack • 857-0234

Large windows allow patrons to see much Lake Wallenpaupack's waters over the trees. Available dinner entrees include chicken, prime rib, salmon and a Cajun sirloin with bayou peppers and onions. Sandwiches, salads and a few appetizers round out a relatively small menu.

The food is very good, but most people come for the outstanding view. The Lakeside is open for lunch and dinner daily.

Lange's
$$$ • 108 Welwood Ave., Hawley • 226-2390

Lange's was once the Eddy Hotel, one of the first hotels in Hawley. Their menu combines typical American favorites with international offerings.

On the more worldly side are veal fromage

marinara, angel poulet coq au vin, jaegerschnitzel and roast canard a la Chasseur. Steaks and seafood are offered for those who prefer more familiar fare.

Although there is no need to get out the Sunday best, the atmosphere leans toward elegant. The restaurant is open every day for lunch and dinner.

The Main Street Beanery
$$$ • 1139 Main St., Honesdale • 253-5740

The price guide indication here only reflects the cost of dinners, which are served in an outdoor dining area on Friday and Saturday nights only. On those evenings a chef from the Culinary Institute of America prepares such delicacies as poached salmon.

Lunch is served daily in a coffeehouse atmosphere. The walls of the Beanery are decorated with old pictures of downtown Honesdale. Particularly striking are ones of the flood of 1902. Sandwiches and quiches are named in honor of noteworthy locals of the past, such as Mad Anthony Wayne, a brigader general who served under George Washington. Wayne County was named in his honor. The Thomas Galvin roast pepper turkey is named for a man who owned a turkey farm on nearby Irving Cliff. On May 28, 1889 a fire destroyed the entire operation. A wealthy guest of Galvin's lost a large Russian diamond that night that is rumored to still be on the cliff. Abriam Winston is honored with the chicken sandwich for being fined in 1845 for free-ranging his chickens through the downtown streets.

Exotic coffees, teas and espresso are available. You may bring your own spirits; the establishment does not serve alcohol.

Overboards Restaurant
$$$ • Pa. Hwy. 507, Greentown • 857-0254

At first glance, Overboards looks like just another bar/restaurant operation. It does not appear to be the type of place where you would expect to dine on Cajun-style mako shark or house-cut scallopini of veal marsala in a rich demi-glace.

The dining room is very small and often is filled with locals who regularly dine on the steak and seafood offerings. Lunch and dinner are served daily. The lunch menu is more conventional, mostly soups, sandwiches, burgers and cheesesteaks.

Paupack Hills Golf and Country Club

$$$ • Yacht Club Dr. (off Pa. Hwy. 507), Greentown • 857-0251

Although on the grounds of a private country club, the restaurant is open to the public. The view of the golf course and surrounding woods would make anyone want to leave the table and hit the links. Proper attire is required. Patrons do not need to wear jackets and ties, but wearing jeans and a T-shirt will likely leave you hungry. Dress for casual, leaning toward elegant, dining.

On the menu's high end, the twin lobster tails and rack of New Zealand lamb are excellent. Less costly and also tasty is the penne rigati, an old-world macaroni served with Neapolitan meat balls. Lunch is served daily; dinner, Wednesday through Sunday.

The Restaurant at the Old Mill Stream

$$$ • 120 Falls Ave., Hawley • 226-1480

Atmosphere and unique food combine to create a memorable experience at the Old Mill Stream. The main dining room is housed in the old stone walls of the original mill. The building was constructed in 1890 of native bluestone, and the restaurant is in the old turbine room. Two decks, one enclosed with screens, extend from the main building into the gorge. On the open-air back deck, guests sit among remains of old stone foundations and enjoy the waterfall that cascades behind them. The water makes just enough noise to be noticed without overpowering conversation as it makes its way through the large, jagged boulders.

The menu changes regularly but typically features such fare as sea scallops with saffron, Thai red curry shrimp, escargot, pork chops with apple cider sauce and Yucatan-style burrito grande. The outdoor grill deck menu is à la carte; the indoor dining room menu favors entrees of a more sophisticated nature.

In spring and summer, dinner is served nightly. During fall it's typically open only Friday, Saturday and Sunday. Call to confirm dates of operation, to make reservations and to find out the winter schedule. Bad weather may force the restaurant to close at various times.

The Settlers Inn at Bingham Park

$$$ • 4 Main Ave., Hawley • 226-2993

The Settlers Inn's atmosphere of inviting elegance begins when you enter the lovely Tudor mansion. The large bluestone fireplace near The Tavern calls out for people to gather around it and chat. Stone patios and elaborate gardens decorate the outside. Gothic cathedral chairs and candles accent the dining room.

The owners have researched the culturally diverse early settlers of the Poconos and patterned the cuisine after theirs. As a result, you will find some Scandinavian, African and Native American dishes on the menu. Whenever possible, Pennsylvania products are served, and this includes wines, beers, mushrooms and cheeses. Herbs are grown out back; the meats are smoked in-house. Maple syrup, meats and fish are purchased from local farms and hatcheries. All breads and baked goods are prepared in the inn kitchen.

Since most of the entrees use local products, the menu changes with each season. A personal favorite is hickory-smoked pork chops cured with garlic, thyme and shallot, served with beans baked with maple syrup and garlic-sauteed kale, arugula and bok choy.

The restaurant is so popular in the Poconos it keeps a mailing list to inform regulars of upcoming menu additions and special events with special menus. The Settlers' Victorian Christmas dinners sell out annually; people often make reservations months in advance.

Lunch and dinner are served daily. The dining room and guest rooms at the inn are strictly nonsmoking. Reservations are recommended. (See our Bed and Breakfasts and Country Inns chapter for more information on accommodations.)

The Spirit of Paupack at Tanglewood Lodge Marina
$$$$ • Pa. Hwy. 507, Lake Wallenpaupack • 226-6266

For romantic elegance on the high seas in the Poconos, the options are rather limited. However, one company does offer an excellent meal served away from land.

Operating approximately from Memorial Day to Labor Day, weather permitting, the *Spirit of Paupack* provides a 2½-hour dinner cruise around Lake Wallenpaupack. Cruises depart twice each evening on Wednesday, Friday and Saturday. Entree choices are prime rib of beef au jus or stuffed chicken breast. Dessert and soft drinks are included. Reservations are required, and boarding takes place 30 minutes before departure. Call for hours and schedule updates.

The boat contains two fully enclosed decks. The captain provides commentary on the sights and local history. Day cruises without meals are offered Wednesday through Sunday in the afternoon.

Slate Belt

Ackerman's Restaurant
$$ • 147 N. Broadway, Wind Gap • (610) 863-5194

Ackerman's is popular with local families; many folks in the Slate Belt eat here more than once a week. The unpretentious building might easily be overlooked if you did not know about the great food inside. Don't worry about dressing up. Just bring an appetite — the portions of seafood, steaks, chicken, pasta and veal are large.

Open for dinner Tuesday through Sunday, Ackerman's offers nightly specials that are even less than the indicated price guide.

Galley Restaurant
$$$ • 6615 Sullivan Tr., Wind Gap • (610) 863-7585

The large mast overlooking Pa. Hwy. 33 not only serves as a beacon for the Galley, but it also re-enforces the nautical theme of the landscaping, decor and menu.

Business people from throughout the Slate Belt flock here for lunch, taking advantage of the classy atmosphere and reasonable prices. The main dining room boasts a high, arched wooden ceiling with thick beams and brass accents. Bringing in seafood from California, Florida, Alaska, Rhode Island, Massachusetts, the Chesapeake Bay region, South Africa and South America allows the Galley to present an exceptional variety of surf-type fare for a restaurant so far from the ocean.

The Galley is open daily for lunch and dinner.

J&R's Smokehouse
$$ • 1420 Jacobsburg Rd., Wind Gap • (610) 863-6162

At J & R's, patrons can enjoy Mexican and barbecued foods without feeling self-conscious if they cover themselves in sauce in the process. Many dishes are somewhat spicy, such as the Cajun-blackened seafood and the chicken El Paso. The lunch menu has sandwiches and burgers for lighter appetites. The atmosphere is very casual; there is no need to get dressed up or worry about bringing the kids.

Lunch and dinner are offered daily, and there is a breakfast buffet on Sunday.

Mama Lucia's Trattoria
$$ • Pa. Hwy. 191, Bangor • (610) 588-7677

Traditional Italian food served in a family atmosphere brings local residents to Mama Lucia's. Sitting down to enjoy homemade lasagna and pastas, you feel more like a guest of the hosts than a mere patron. Eggplant lovers should try the Melanzana Al Forno — fried eggplant topped with pomodoro sauce and mozzarella cheese.

Mama Lucia's serves lunch and dinner every day except Sunday. Reservations are strongly recommended.

Valley View Inn & Restaurant
$$ • 794 Sunrise Blvd., Mount Bethel • 897-6969

Locals, former residents and return visitors may remember the Valley View by its former name, Charlemagne. Little has changed — the chef and the European cuisine are still the same, and the decor still favors the look of a Bavarian restaurant. Beef selections such as barbecued baby-back ribs

flavored with honey and hickory, and pork chop braised in dark beer and honey are still on the menu.

The restaurant is surrounded by apple orchards, corn fields and a large pond. Dinner is served on Friday and Saturday. A buffet is featured throughout the day on Sundays.

Wah Shing Restaurant
$ • 141 Blue Valley Dr., Bangor
• (610) 588-8300

Creating a convincing Oriental atmosphere amid heaps of discarded slate is a challenge. Wah Shing's ornate, tiled exterior does a fine job. The dining room and bar are equally well-themed. The Chinese menu includes all the seafood, rice, pork and combination platters expected. Lunch and dinner are available daily, as are take-out and delivery.

There is plenty of nighttime entertainment around, but many consider the Poconos the land of romance, so you do not need to go out *every* night.

Nightlife

After leaving the Hard Rock Cafe of Henryville, turn right for the Paradise Valley Planet Hollywood. In nearby Cresco, visit the Club Extreme, a five-story dance club/theme park that attracts thousands of partyers every weekend.

Of course, none of these places exist. Do not come to the Poconos expecting trendy dance halls or fancy theme eateries owned by sports stars and actors. Our nightlife is much less exotic. We prefer small bars and clubs with a good band over large, decadent discos. There are no entertainment districts where you can park and experience a number of places in one night. The possible exception to this statement is the small cluster of bars on and around Main Street in Stroudsburg. Most locals choose one destination for the evening and stay there. Since some driving is always involved, usually over winding back roads, it's best to let a designated driver navigate the countryside late at night.

This chapter is separated into two sections; one covers resort lounges and their nighttime activities, and the other highlights the remaining assortment of dance-and-mingle clubs and bars. Emphasis has been placed on venues that are unique in some way, be it atmosphere, entertainment or crowd. In addition to the places included, there are hundreds of corner bars that provide inexpensive drinks and free local color in the many towns in the Poconos. Also, many restaurants have separate barrooms and lounges and occasionally some entertainment. These are discussed in our Restaurants chapter because serving meals, rather than drinks, is their primary appeal.

Alternatives for nighttime entertainment are circuses, carnivals and bingo games sponsored by area fire departments, night skiing and bowling. But remember, many consider the Poconos the land of romance, so you do not need to go out every night.

Nearby Live Music Venues

While this introduction might have given you the impression that there is nothing to do in the Poconos once the lights are turned down, fear not. Live music is everywhere. Not at big concert halls where you and the performers are barely in the same room, but in tiny clubs where you can buy a good act a drink and chat awhile. Most bars that host bands on weekends have a cover charge, usually less than $5 per person. The closeup in this chapter mentions some of the well-known musicians, but there are hundreds of others as well. Nationally known bands can be heard within a one-hour drive of the Poconos. During summer, **Montage Mountain Performing Arts Center**, Interstate 81 at Exit 51 in Scranton (see our Daytrips chapter), hosts a concert series that usually begins in early June. Last year Sting, The Allman Brothers Band, Bob Seger, Rod Stewart and Ozzy Osbourne were just a few of the acts who visited this lovely outdoor arena. The stage is set at the bottom of a ski slope on top of a mountain overlooking the Wyoming Valley. Concertgoers may either purchase reserved seats at the base of the mountain or bring a blanket and choose a spot on the slope to relax under the stars. For current schedule information, call 969-7669. Tickets are available at the box office or through TicketMaster outlets. To charge by phone, call 693-4100 or (215) 336-2000.

To our south, touring bands often visit Allentown to perform at the **Allentown Fairgrounds** that hosts outdoor shows usually in late summer and early fall. During the Allentown Fair at the beginning of September, there is a show every night for one week. Most are country-and-western themed. For schedule information, call (610) 433-7541. Tickets may be purchased at the box office or TicketMaster outlets or by calling (215) 336-2000.

On the campus of Lehigh University in Bethlehem, **Stabler Arena** is used mainly as a basketball court, but some very well-known bands perform there as well. Years ago, Billy Joel played a show there as a gesture to the fans he immortalized in his song "Allentown." More recently, Hootie and the Blowfish spent the day at amusement mecca Dorney Park before spending the night performing at Stabler. A few moments from that day were included in a video the band released in 1995. Concerts are held throughout the year. Call (610) 867-8202 to see which concerts are scheduled. To purchase tickets, contact either the box office or TicketMaster outlets or call (215) 336-2000.

Also in Bethlehem, a folk music club named **Godfrey Daniels**, 7 E. Fourth Street, attracts big names — Christine Lavin, former Bethlehem resident John Gorka, Bill Morrissey and John Renbourne to name a few — for a very small room. For ticket and schedule information, call (610) 867-2390.

Living blues legends and the best young prospects regularly visit just east of the Poconos across the Delaware River. The **Stanhope House** on Main and High streets in Stanhope, New Jersey, has just the well-worn roadhouse character to create the best atmosphere for folks such as Johnny "Clyde" Copeland, Clarence "Gatemouth" Brown and Lonnie Mack plus good local bands such as Mike Dugan and the Blues Mission. Call (201) 347-0458 for its current schedule. Also good for established blues acts is **The Sterling Hotel**, 343 Hamilton Street in Allentown, whose narrow exterior is deceptive. This room has one of the longest bars in the country.

In Easton, located along the Lehigh River approximately 45 minutes from the Poconos, the majestic **State Theatre**, 453 Northampton Street, has been fully restored to resemble the ornate palace it was in the 1920s. In addition to lavish stage productions, the theatre hosts big-name comedians such as Steven Wright, Bobby Collins, Carol Burnett and Carrot Top; singers such as Julio Iglesias and Anne

Murray; and jazz, classical and international ensembles. The box office phone number is (610) 252-3132 and the 24-hour credit card line to charge tickets is (610) 821-4732.

Of similar beauty is the **F.M. Kirby Center for the Performing Arts** at 71 Public Square in Wilkes-Barre. In addition to concerts by The Northeastern Pennsylvania Philharmonic and dance and theater performances, world-famous musicians sometimes appear. For complete schedule information, call 826-1100.

FYI

Unless otherwise noted, the area code for all phone numbers in this guide is 717.

Movies

If you want to catch a movie instead of a band, we have plenty of theater options. Call the phone numbers listed to see what is playing and for showtimes. For catching the latest blockbusters, try one of these multi-screen operations: **Stroud Theatres**, Stroud Mall, Pa. 611, Stroudsburg, 421-5700, with seven screens; **Foxmoor Cinemas**, Foxmoor Outlet Complex, U.S. Highway 209, Marshalls Creek, 223-7775, with five screens; and **Mahoning Valley Cinema**, Carbon Plaza Mall, Pa. Highway 443, Lehighton, (610) 377-8626, with eight screens.

A few theaters show movies that have been around for a while at reduced rates. In Wind Gap, the **Gap Theatre**, Pa. Highway 512, (610) 863-9828, offers all seats for all shows at $3. The **Milford Theater**, Fourth and Catherine streets, Milford, 296-9941, charges the same price.

While many drive-in theaters have become flea markets, a few still thrive in the Poconos and to our south in the Lehigh Valley. Within our region are: The **Mahoning Drive In**, Lehighton, (610) 386-9907; **Tri-State Theatres**, U.S. highways 6 and 209, Matamoras, 491-5000, which also has an indoor cinema,; and **Maple Drive-In Theatre**, U.S. Highway 6, Honesdale, 253-2800.

Pocono Cinema & Coffee Shop, 88 S. Courtland Street, East Stroudsburg, 421-3456, offers foreign films and arthouse hits that are overlooked by the bigger theaters. The atmosphere is much classier than the typical shopping mall cinema.

Bars and Nightclubs

Delaware Water Gap

Deer Head Inn
Main St. • 424-2000

The Deer Head is the heart of a thriving jazz community in the Poconos. Legends Phil Woods, Bob Dorough (of "Schoolhouse Rock" fame) and Urbie Green live in the area and occasionally perform here. However, the inn has earned its reputation for booking quality acts for more than 40 years, so even the local artists who are unfamiliar to you are well worth seeing. Lately, the club also has been attracting big-names who usually appear only in Manhattan. Late-night jam sessions are common. Come early and have dinner; the food is fantastic. In early September, the Celebration of the Arts jazz festival is held across the street from the Deer Head. (See our Annual Events chapter for a complete description.) The rest of the year, just look for the old deer head sign on the large, white Victorian and enjoy the best jazz west of Manhattan.

Brownies Casual Eatery in the Gap
Main and Oak Sts. • 424-1154

Owned by well-regarded local caterers, Brownies is a local favorite for lunch and dinner. The entire menu, including the popular steamed clams, is served until closing. Live music, typically country, rock or blues, is featured on Friday and Saturday nights. Local favorites Mike Dugan and the Blues Mission perform here often.

Minisink Hotel
River Rd., Minisink Hills • 421-9787

Don't let the rustic decor deter you from visiting the Minisink. It's a great Insiders' hangout with old-fashioned charm. A refreshing change of pace from homogeneous bars, the Minisink wears its scars of aging with pride. Games are limited to a pool table — with purple felt — and a dartboard — with steel darts instead of those trendy new plastic ones most bars have. But people come to the Minisink to talk and eat. The food, particularly the pizza, is delicious; and best of all, it's served until the bar closes. Locals love the place and so do guests and skiers of nearby Shawnee Mountain — once they discover it.

Stroudsburg/ East Stroudsburg

The Hoop
745 Main St., Stroudsburg • 424-1950

One of the largest nightclubs in the Poconos, The Hoop is an easily recognized fixture of nightlife in downtown Stroudsburg.

Let Them Entertain You

On any given night in the Poconos, talented local artists perform original music. As in all the other arts, the quality and diversity of our local musicians is well above average for a predominantly rural region. Many claim the scenery and lifestyle inspires them. They persevere, often playing in a crowded bar in front of the dart board. Others perform in more traditional settings such as intimate nightclubs.

Occasionally one of the big fish in our small pond swims to larger waters and national acclaim. Former "Saturday Night Live" bandleader and guitarist for Bob Dylan, Stroudsburg native G.E. Smith began his musical career in a lounge band working the resort circuit. His successor at SNL, George Young, also lived in Stroudsburg.

Although from just outside the Poconos in Selinsgrove, the Badlees were regulars at Stroudsburg's The Hoop until being signed by A&M Records and achieving national success with their *River Songs* CD. Chances are you have heard one of their hits such as "Fear of Falling" or "Angeline Is Coming Home." When not touring the country, the band often returns to The Hoop or larger clubs in the Allentown or Scranton area.

Toby Costa and M.J. Law played in high school bands, impressing classmates with enthusiastic covers of songs by The Kinks and The Clash. That led to the creation of Solution a.d., which currently includes Kevin Leggieri and Mike Hoover. After a few years of gigs in local clubs and at East Stroudsburg University, they created a large enough following to break into the Philadelphia and New York scenes and become the opening act for scores of nationally known bands. In 1995 guitarist Chad Taylor, of the multi-platinum band Live (York, Pennsylvania's native sons), produced a recording for Solution a.d. The following year, Tag/Atlantic Records released *Happily Ever After*, also produced by Taylor. MTV aired the video for the song "Fearless"; radio stations across the country added the single to their rotations; and suddenly the whole coun-

Photo: Brian Hineline

Singer/songwriter Diane Paquee hosts a popular open-mic night at the Sarah Street Grill in Stroudsburg.

try knew "our" alternative band. Luckily they are not too famous to forget about the Poconos; look for them at The Hoop.

Cesar Diaz's unassuming nature hides his talents as a guitarist. He has worked with Stevie Ray Vaughn, Eric Clapton and Bob Dylan as a guitar technician. For a while, he was in Dylan's touring band. When the world celebrated the fabled songwriter at a 30th anniversary concert at New York's Madison Square Garden, Diaz was on stage with him. (Coincidently, the music director for that monumental event was G.E. Smith.) Diaz owns a company in East Stroudsburg that designs amplifiers for many major rock bands including Live, Collective Soul and Solution a.d. He has a habit of visiting area open-mic nights, particularly at Stroudsburg's Sarah Street Grill on Wednesdays and Front Row on Thursdays. For no cover charge, you can listen to an amazing musician play some of the several hundred songs he learned during his time with Dylan.

The Pocono Mountains are filled with folks who deserve more than regional acclaim. Probably the hardest working man in the local music scene is Jim Roberti. Fortunately he also is one of the most talented. Nearly every night, he entertains large crowds with a mix of originals and covers ranging from Elvis Presley to Elvis Costello. Check the individual club descriptions for information on when to hear Roberti.

Building on a solid base of traditional folk music, guitarist/pianist Renard Cohen adds essentially every other style of popular music to both his own songs and those made famous by others, such as his reggae-flavored rendition of "Brown-Eyed Girl." He is an engaging performer with plenty of personality and colorful stories. The best place to see him is at Sarah Street Grill on the Wednesday open-mic night or at one of his solo shows there.

Fans of bluegrass music will enjoy The Lost Ramblers. Local legends The Cramer Brothers are the best bet for country music. However, the McWilliams Brothers are always fun too. Gumbo Combo plays great Cajun music, and George Wesley & The Irietations are a wonderful reggae group. Mike Dugan and the Blues Mission are a blues band worth hearing. In the loosely defined alternative rock genre, Dresden has the most musical and lyrical ability. They are equally enjoyable unplugged at open-mic nights or fully amplified at their club shows. In the resort lounges, King Henry & the Showmen have the reputation as one of the most versatile and entertaining dance bands.

Talented jazz performers are plentiful. You cannot go wrong by checking the schedule of the Deer Head Inn in Delaware Water Gap. Cover bands playing classic or modern alternative rock hits are the staple of many area live music venues. Some of the most enjoyable bands are Martian Tom, Mint, Shotgun, Honey Buzzards and Psycho Bettie.

Local musicians are an important element of the cultural environment of the Poconos. No amount of time spent here would be complete without giving them a chance to entertain you. For dates and times for live music, buy the Friday or Saturday *Pocono Record* or the local newspaper in your part of the Poconos.

The complex consists of a 1950s-style diner and an old Victorian mansion that have been forged together. On the first floor, live bands, mostly modern rock, perform. Club Vogue, a city-style dance club, fills the second floor. Also, there is a small game room on the third floor and an outdoor deck. The Hoop, is openMonday and Wednesday through Saturday, and draws a mix of vacationers, locals, and college students from nearby East Stroudsburg University. Club regulars particularly enjoy Wednesday nights, when there are drink specials, cheap chicken wings, Jim Roberti on stage, and no cover charge.

Front Row Sports Bar and Grille
Main and Seventh Sts., Stroudsburg
• 421-2200

Other than a few old *Sports Illustrated* covers framed on the walls and ESPN on the many televisions, calling the Front Row a sports bar is misleading. True, there are pool tables, a dartboard and assorted other games. But the main reason people come here is to mingle. Monday is disco night. Thursday is open-mic night, and a disc jockey usually entertains on the weekends, although sometimes a band is booked. Conveniently, the pizza parlor next door has a window for service in the bar.

Flood's
732 Main St., Stroudsburg • 424-5743

Exotic-beer lovers will appreciate the selection at Flood's. With 25 beers on tap and more than 100 bottled beers available, there is something for every taste. If you are hungry, the burgers and chicken wings are very good. On Monday nights Jim Roberti performs.

Sarah Street Grille
N. Fifth and Sarah Sts., Stroudsburg • 424-9120

Sarah Street provides good intimate, coffeehouse-style atmosphere in which to enjoy acoustic music. The Wednesday open-mic night hosted by Diane Paquee attracts many of the region's best artists. On Thursday through Saturday, look for The Lost Ramblers and Renard Cohen. The bar has a great beer selection, served in frosted pilsner glasses, and very good food. You can start your evening here with dinner in the restaurant and then step into the bar for some music and a nightcap.

Teddy's Tavern
Second St., Stroudsburg • 424-6578

With all the ambiance of a fraternity house basement, Teddy's is a popular social spot for ESU students. Locals often visit during the day for lunch or dinner. While there are no tablecloths, or windows for that matter, the food is very good and the portions are intimidating. The bar is packed every Tuesday for singer/songwriter Jim Roberti.

Gracie's Place
395 N. Courtland St., East Stroudsburg • 421-5514

Tucked away on a largely residential street, Gracie's is the ultimate Insider hangout. Folks in East Stroudsburg rave about the food. Weekend entertainment includes jazz, blues and comedy. Look for good piano players such as Jesse Green. Tuesday nights Gracie's presents an enjoyable cabaret atmosphere with a combination of comedians and musicians.

FYI
Unless otherwise noted, the area code for all phone numbers in this guide is 717.

Smokin' Joe's
425 N. Courtland St., East Stroudsburg • 420-1551

Locals and some East Stroudsburg University students have discovered the food and drink specials at Smokin' Joe's. On Monday nights during football season, hamburgers are 50¢ and it's only $3.50 for all the chicken wings you can eat — the current individual record is 60. On Wednesday nights every drink in the bar is $1.50 between 10 PM and midnight. Happy hour is Monday through Friday from 5 to 7 PM. Wings cost 15 cents each, draft beers are $1 and mixed drinks are $1.50. A disc jockey or solo performer provides entertainment on weekends. A pool table, dartboard and a few arcade games are available. When the weather is warm enough, try your luck in the horseshoe pits behind the building. This cozy bar has earned a reputation for good, affordable food (the chicken sandwiches are outstanding) and friendly service.

Rudy's Tavern
90 Washington St., East Stroudsburg • 476-9604

Rudy's is the local gathering place for friendly socializing. It is the one bar in East Stroudsburg you can visit any time and be assured of good conversation. The crowd is dominated by older residents, but college students and vacationers coming from dinner at

INSIDERS' TIPS

The Friday Weekend section of the *Pocono Record* is a great source for current entertainment schedules.

the nearby Dansbury Depot add to an interesting mix of people. Other than a pinball machine or video game, there is no entertainment. Rudy's St. Patrick's Day parties have been local institutions for years.

Sports Extra Bar and Restaurant
Jay Park, U.S. Hwy. 209, Marshalls Creek • 223-9817

Centrally located in a booming part of the Poconos, Sports Extra draws crowds on weekends for dance music at the large downstairs dance floor. Upstairs is sports-themed, with plenty of games and large-screen televisions.

Mount Pocono Area

The Abbey at Swiftwater Inn
Pa. Hwy. 611, Swiftwater • 839-7206

For a bar in a mammoth old inn, The Abbey is remarkably small. On weekends the room is packed for live bands. If you do not get a seat, expect to stand along one of the walls. The lucky few snag one of the handful of tables in front of the band. You have to walk through the stage area, around the band's equipment and up a couple of steps, to play pool. But the cramped quarters only add to the festive atmosphere. The Abbey is popular with area residents, employees of Connaught Laboratories (right across the highway) and guests of nearby resorts who are out for a night of local entertainment. The Swiftwater Inn has been serving guests since 1778 and is on the National Register of Historic Places.

The Thirsty Camel Bar & Grille
Sullivan Tr., Tannersville • 620-1844

Proximity to the Crossings Factory Outlets and Camelback Ski Area make this a favorite watering hole with vacationers. The Thirsty Camel is roomy, with games religated to a

second floor that overlooks some tables and the bar. Exposed beams and an unfinished ceiling combined with assorted sports paraphernalia create a rec-room-type atmosphere. You get the sensation of being in a friend's basement. Sandwiches and bar snacks are sold. For $2 or less, you can nibble on pistachios, cashews, or beef jerky, all of which are sold by the quarter-pound.

Barley Creek Brewing Company
Sullivan Tr. and Camelback Rd., Tannersville • 629-9399

Housed in an 1880s farmhouse, this micro-brewery has developed a loyal following in only one year. Some of the more popular ales crafted at this English brewhouse are Renovator Stout, a very dark brown, bold stout, and Brown Antler Ale, an American-style brown ale that is slightly sweet and has a deep chocolate color. The spacious lounge books live music Wednesday through Saturday, typically country, folk and bluegrass. The popular Lost Ramblers frequently perform here. In addition to being open-mic night, Wednesdays feature Bike-and-Brew. Beginning in spring, cyclists travel the nearby bike trails and return to Barley Creek for drink specials and snacks. Free tours of the brewery are given during the week. High ceilings, polished beams and white walls create a sophisticated, city-style atmosphere. The stainless steel brewing tanks, visible behind the bar, reinforce the notion that you are drinking a unique product. Steaks, shepherd's pie, a great knockwurst and beer kraut plus assorted sandwiches, salads and munchies will take care of your appetite. Due to Pennsylvnia law, the only alcohol the brewery is allowed to serve is their own ales and lagers. Don't worry, they have a beer for all tastes. The decor, food, music and beer are all outstanding, making this a must-visit gathering place if you are in the area.

Memorytown Tavern
Grange Rd., Mount Pocono • 839-1680

Part of a complex of shops, this tavern features live country-and-western music on Fridays and Saturdays. Look for The Cramer Brothers playing here. The decor might remind you of what would happen if there were an explosion in your grandparents' attic. Funhouse mirrors and a vintage scale at the entrance give a hint of the surprises inside. In the bar, the walls are covered with patches, license plates and helmets from fire departments. Shotguns, a sleigh, a canoe, a large drum, mounted fish, mounted animal heads of species unknown and vintage tools fill every available inch of wall and ceiling space. You will enjoy sitting at a table and trying to identify the odd accessories that surround you — or at least making up uses for them. More than 100 beers from around the world are served, and the view of the lake is beautiful.

Pocono Pub
Pa. Hwy. 611, Bartonsville • 421-2187

Across the street from the Holiday Inn, the Pocono Pub draws residents and hotel guests for the live music. It's a large, recently remodeled bar with surprisingly good acoustics. You'll be lucky to get a seat if local favorite Gumbo Combo is playing its Louisiana-flavored music.

The Inn at Tannersville
Pa. Hwy. 611, Tannersville • 629-3131

On Fridays, the inn hosts Murder Mystery Dinner Theatre. The script for the production was written especially for the event by longtime *Ellery Queen* magazine author Jerroild Hontz. Musically, the eclectic bookings cover a variety of genres: blues or bluegrass on Fridays; rock or country and western on Saturdays; and Dixieland, complete with Mardi Gras costumes and Cajun food, on Sundays. Reservations are required for the dinner theater.

Murphy's Loft
Pa. Hwy. 115, Blakeslee • 646-2813

Murphy's offers a beautiful atmosphere in which to sip a drink at the end of a busy day. The outdoor bar overlooks a waterfall, gardens and in-ground heated pool. The deck has live entertainment on Saturdays. Every Thursday, the restaurant has a special that is a Pocono legend — an 18 oz.-T-bone steak for $9.95.

Tudor Inn
Pa. Hwys. 115 and 903, Blakeslee • 646-3300

The Tudor Inn advertises having the "largest dance club on the mountain." Whether it is or not, there is plenty of room to dance every weekend. While there, try the Tex-Mex dishes and drinks, which are particularly good.

West End

West End Elations Teen Club
Regency Plaza, U.S. Hwy. 209, Brodheadsville • 992-0150

Teenagers 13 through 20 looking for a dance-club atmosphere come here. Parents will be glad to know that Elations provides a safe environment. Security guards monitor the activity both in and outside the club. Snacks, sodas and nonalcoholic drinks are served.

Flagstaff Restaurant & Ballroom
Flagstaff Rd., Jim Thorpe • (610) 325-4554

Once a tourist attraction, Flagstaff has been converted into a large nightclub featuring live bands and disc jockeys. Classic and modern rock bands playing original music and covers are booked. Before you leave, be sure to enjoy the view from the mountain top; it's one of the prettiest in the Poconos.

Shenanigans
Off Pa. Hwy. 903, Lake Harmony • 722-1100

The club's two dance-floor areas feature nearly every type of danceable music: disco, classic rock, blues, Top-40, you name it. Best of all, Shenanigan's is open every day, and there is never a cover charge. Friday and Saturday feature karaoke. Baby Boomers, a dance club within Shenanigans, is open Thursday through Saturday. A pool party with crabs, clams and live music takes place on the deck Saturdays and Sundays.

Photo: Pocono Mountains Vacation Bureau, Inc.

Dining, dancing and entertainment abound at Pocono resorts.

Joey Dee's Night Club
Big Bear Center, Pa. Hwy. 903, Albrightsville
• 722-8255

Conveniently located between Lake Harmony and Jim Thorpe, Joey Dee's has a large dance floor and a game room. Pool is free on Tuesdays. The kitchen stays open until 1:30 AM on Friday and Saturday to satisfy post-dancing appetites.

The Cellar Night Club
Lake Shore Dr., Lake Harmony • 722-9898

The club strikes a good balance between bar games and live entertainment. The music on Fridays and Saturdays is usually blues or country/rock. The club is beneath a very good restaurant, The Blue Heron Grille.

Milford Area

Back Door Saloon
411 Broad St., Milford • 296-6514

Behind the Tom Quick Inn, this sports bar is much larger than it appears from the outside. Games include air hockey, pool, pinball and darts. Being close to the courthouse, the place fills up on Fridays when attorneys and government workers unwind after a long week.

Alley Oops Pub
Apple Valley Village, U.S. Hwy. 6, Milford • 296-6831

This is the place for live entertainment in Pike County on Fridays and Saturdays. Always popular are comedy nights when you can enjoy three comedians for less than $10. Solo musicians are featured, including Jim Roberti, Tom Davis and Tom Riccobono. Look for fun food specials such as 10¢ wings, taco night, steamers and pan pizzas.

Garris' Log Cabin
Bushkill Falls Rd., Bushkill • 588-6398

This local institution serves good food and has a disc jockey who plays mostly oldies on Wednesdays, Fridays and Sundays. Sometimes there is a band, but it has to be small because space is limited. The Log Cabin is a favorite of employees of the area resorts. The bar even has several drink specials for them on Wednesday nights.

Inn at Peck's Pond
Pa. Hwy. 402, Peck's Pond • 775-7336

"Pond" is a misleading name for the substantial body of water on which the Inn sits. The Inn is frequented by second-home owners who have cabins in the area and fishermen who swap stories. Bands take the stage on Fridays and Saturdays.

Lake Wallenpaupack Area

CW Steakhouse & Dance Club
Cherrywood Park Complex, Pa. Hwy. 196, Sterling • 676-9930, (800) 624-1369

CW's is the country-style roadhouse of the Poconos. Dance to live country music on weekends, when free line-dancing lessons are available. In case you are not a country fan, there is another dance floor below the main one

which offers alternative rock, disco and an interesting selection of imported club music.

Slate Belt

Slateford Inn
Slateford Rd., Slateford • 897-5149

Just off Pa. 611 between Delaware Water Gap and Portland, Slateford is one of the smallest towns in the Poconos. Whenever the Delaware River decides to broaden its horizons, most of the town ends up under water. It has one street, and at the northern end sits the Slateford Inn. Bands perform here on weekends. Popular music includes blues, oldies, rock and country. The large bar area has plenty of room for dancing and socializing. Pool tables and arcade games are available, but most people come to the Slateford to talk or listen to music. The clientele is mostly town residents; Slateford is off the beaten tourist path.

Blue Valley Lounge
Pa. Hwys. 33 and 512, Wind Gap • (610) 863-7067

The lounge is part of Blue Valley Lanes, so you can bowl a few games first, grab a drink then take part in karaoke every Friday and Saturday.

Resort Nightlife

Resort entertainment takes many forms in the Poconos. Nearly every type of accommodation has at least a cocktail lounge. The larger resorts usually have floor shows on weekends. Some book well-known comedians and music acts. Tickets for these shows often may be purchased by non-guests, or you can stay at the resort and receive complimentary tickets for the show with your room package.

The four Caesars resorts (Cove Haven, Paradise Stream, Pocono Palace and Brookdale) are famous for hosting comedians such as Jay Leno, Dennis Miller, Elayne Boosler and Howie Mandel. Oldies acts are

Photo: Pocono Mountains Vacation Bureau, Inc.

A candlelight dinner is the perfect way to cap off a fun-filled day of activity.

popular at all the Pocono resorts; some devote entire weekends to them. In addition to big names, most places have local bands playing dance music in their lounges. These always are open to the public, frequently without cover charge. If you prefer a more romantic evening of slow dancing, we have plenty of places for you as well. Many acts work at several resorts throughout the week, so there is a great deal of entertainment overlap. The following section presents an overview of resorts with cocktail-lounge entertainment. More detail on the resort facilities may be found in our Accommodations chapter. All the places mentioned are open to the public.

Delaware Water Gap

Glenwood Hotel
Main St. (at the traffic light) • 476-0010

Yes, the town is so small that directions like this can be given. The hotel's Mr. B's Lounge has music, dancing and live entertainment on Fridays and Saturdays. Wednesdays are devoted to Big Band music with the Fred Bevan Showband.

Continental Gourmet Restaurant & Sports Bar
Broad St., Delaware Water Gap • 420-1770

At the Ramada Inn, this gathering place

has a well-designed bar area, allowing for minglers and those who want a private booth. The expected token sports pictures are on the walls, but don't expect a lot of gaming diversions. A large television screen is provided, and the menu is dominated by salads and sandwiches. Karaoke is featured on Saturdays.

Stroudsburg/ East Stroudsburg

Hillside Inn
Frutchey Dr., off U.S. Hwy. 209, Marshalls Creek • 223-8238

The club's name, The Walnut Room, originates from a large walnut tree that fell in the old outdoor swimming pool and was used to build the bar. Disco dancing with a disc jockey is featured in the Walnut Room on Friday nights. Live music, often jazz, fills the club on Saturdays.

Plaza Hotel
1220 W. Main St., Stroudsburg • 424-1930

Whispers lounge always has dance music on weekends and oldies on Thursdays. The lounge has a large dance floor, a square-shaped bar in the middle of the room and plenty of tables and booths for those looking for privacy.

Shannon Inn & Pub
U.S. Hwy. 209, East Stroudsburg
• 424-1951

The Shannon is a favorite for dinners and late-night snacks. The burgers and chicken wings are considered by some to be the best in town. Irish music is featured regularly. This is the first bar you will see after taking Exit 52 off Interstate 80 to travel through the Poconos on Highway 209 North. Keep it in mind as a possible stop for a break after a long drive.

Mount Pocono Area

Crescent Lodge
Pa. Hwy. 191, Cresco • 595-7486

Every Saturday evening, this award-winning country inn features Mark Sobol at the piano in the lounge, performing everything from classical and jazz music to show tunes. The lounge is closed Monday and Tuesday.

Penn Hills Resort
Pa. Hwys. 447 and 191, Analomink
• 421-6464

Dance bands entertain in Reflections nightclub, along with magicians, comedians and vocalists. Call for a schedule and reservations. Events are held nightly and begin at 8 PM with no cover or minimum drink charge.

The Chateau at Camelback
Camelback Rd., Tannersville • 629-1661

Locals flock to the after-work party held here on Fridays from 5:30 to 7:30 PM. The Legends Nightclub overlooks a pool and boasts three outdoor decks with great views of the surrounding mountains and lake. The entertainment at night is more diverse than many Pocono resorts, ranging from classic rock with bands such as Higher Ground to singer Gloria Kaye.

Caesars Brookdale on the Lake
Pa. Hwy. 611, Scotrun • 839-8843

One of four Caesars resorts in the Poconos, Brookdale features nightly entertainment in its Rolls Royce Lounge. Comedians and bands perform in the Applause Night Club. Shows begin at 9 PM weekdays, 9:30 PM Friday and Saturday and 8:30 PM Sunday. Try a special drink called the Caesars Passion Potion and keep the glass. There is plenty of room for dancing. Away from the dance floor, another bar area has a large-screen television.

The Caesars resorts regularly book nationally known comedians and oldies music acts. Tickets are included with room packages or may be purchased for $20 to $35 each, depending on the show.

The other Caesars resorts have similar lounges and clubs with dance music and live entertainment nightly. They are: **Caesars Paradise Stream**, Pa. Highway 940, Mount Pocono, 839-8881; **Caesars Cove Haven**, Pa. Highway 590, Lakeville (near Lake Wallenpaupack), 226-4506; and **Caesars Pocono Palace**, U.S. Highway 209, Echo Lake (near Bushkill), 588-6692.

Mount Airy Lodge
Pa. Hwy. 611, Mount Pocono • 839-8811

Dancing and intimate snuggling are the attraction in the Celebrity Room. The room is dark except for the dance floor. Disc jockeys usually provide the entertainment, but well-known performers are scheduled occasionally. Mixed drinks are offered at reduced prices during happy hour at 5 PM.

West End

Mountian Laurel Resort
Pa. Hwy. 534, White Haven • 443-8411

On weekends look for one of the best lounge bands in the Poconos, King Henry & the Showmen. Singer Lynn Harris, who performs Mondays through Wednesdays also is entertaining.

INSIDERS' TIPS

Many Poconos nightspots participate in a designated-driver program that allows that person to drink sodas for free. Ask your bartender for details.

The Resort at Split Rock
Lake Drive, Lake Harmony • 722-9111

The Rock Bar has a disc jockey playing alternative and dance music every weekend. Live bands are also booked on Saturdays. The DJ spins on Thursday and karaoke takes over on Wednesday. Open daily, weather permitting, the Lakeside Patio Bar provides a romantic outdoor atmosphere overlooking Lake Harmony.

Milford Area

Fernwood
U.S. Hwy. 209, Bushkill • 588-9500 Ext. 4145

Dance music is performed live every night in the Weathervanes Lounge. Often there is also a comedian or audience-participation contest. For dinner and a floor show on Friday or Saturday nights, go to the Astor Room, named for the chandeliers from the famed Astor Hotel that hang overhead. The resort regularly hosts professional boxing, occasionally televised on ESPN, and professional wrestling.

Lake Wallenpaupack Area

Comfort Inn
Exit 5 off I-84, Hamlin/Newfoundland • 689-4148, (800) 523-4426

Friday nights are good times to visit the Comfort Inn's lounge. Local singer/songwriters such as Ted Satterthwaite and Ron Sanders perform from 9 PM to midnight.

Each Main Street in the Poconos has a character all its own, reflecting the spirit of the community.

Shopping

For some people, shopping is a major activity while on vacation. For Insiders, it's part of our daily routine. Whatever your reason for shopping, you'll find plenty of choices here. In this chapter we will focus on some of the specialties that make shopping in the Poconos fun. As you might have noticed, we cover a large geographic area in this book, so we'll focus on a few selections from the noted specialties and mention some of the highlights of our "Main Streets." However, shopping here is an experience you can have every time you venture out on our roads.

As we noted in our Getting Around chapter, the Poconos region is comprised of primarily country roads. To get from one place to another, you must travel a distance on at least one of these picturesque Pennsylvania byways — interstates and four-laners are only peripherally involved in our town-to-town travel. That means you constantly — almost every other mile — come upon a delightful shop that you will cause you to blurt out, "Hey Hon, there! Stop there! I want to see what they have." Most of the shops we have noted are on a secondary Pennsylvania highway, such as 940, 611 or 191; these establishments are not alone. As you head toward one, you're sure to find 10 more shops along the way. So enjoy your tour of the Poconos; check out our Getting Around chapter to see where you'll end up; and experience the fun of discovering a special shop.

Of course, if you want to shop, you need money. In case you run out, there are plenty of banks around; or if you are shopping for loans, CDs or IRAs, you'll certainly find a bank to help you out. Three top area banks with offices all around the region are PNC Bank, Mellon Bank and Nazareth National Bank. PNC is almost nationwide and has locations in every major area of the Poconos and on many of the routes we point out to you here and in our Getting Around chapter. For information

about locations, call (800) 443-2347; you can even access your PNC accounts and do your checkbook balancing through this customer-service response line. Mellon Bank has established full-service banking offices in the Insalaco's food markets in Mount Pocono and East Stroudsburg (East Stroudsburg Savings Association has a branch in the Tannersville Insalaco's). These banks are not only full-service but also open on Sundays in these locations. The central number for Mellon is (800) 245-4920. The Nazareth National Bank has branches in Stroudsburg and Brodheadsville. In 1997 it will open an office in East Stroudsburg in the long-awaited Wal-Mart store that will be opening concurrently. Its central number is (800) 996-2062.

Most stores accept major credit cards, and many stores are equipped with systems that accept your ATM card for purchases. Some merchants take local checks from customers with enough identification (driver's license and credit card); in the very large complexes, some stores are more willing to accept an out-of-state check. Crossings Factory Store and Foxmoor have ATMs on-site, so you can get cash if you need it. ATMs also are available at virtually every bank in the Poconos, and you'll find banks along every Pocono road.

Outlets and Malls

The Poconos are replete with outlet complexes, some small and some large; this area also has stand-alone outlet stores, the Stroud Mall and many minimalls. In this section we highlight representative stores in outlet complexes, independent outlets and notable malls and minimalls. Some points of note before we jump into a shopping frenzy: First, store hours change depending on the day and season; we have included a main number for each outlet complex, so you can call ahead to verify hours before you go to shop. Second, please note that retail outlet stores come and go (another good reason to call ahead), so hurry up and shop — so many stores, so little time!

Stroudsburg/ East Stroudsburg

Foxmoor Village Outlet Center
U.S. Hwy. 209 N., Marshalls Creek • 223-8706

Foxmoor is designed like a small village; there is even a little bridge to cross the stream that runs through the site. All paths lead inward to a central gazebo with benches, shrubbery, bright flowers in season and a view of all directions in which your husband or wife might have wandered in search of a special store. You can sit here and let the children play or eat an ice-cream cone and enjoy the view — it's even nice in winter! The Foxmoor Cinemas are also here; so, dad and the kids can see a movie while mom takes her time contemplating the bargains and making the big-money decisions — one pair of Bugle Boy jeans or two?

Speaking of which, the Bugle Boy Outlet is a major draw here, with serious bargains and sales happening daily. For additional clothing options, check out the Swimwear Outlet (bathing suits and coverups for women and girls of all sizes from toddler to plus), Capacity Outlet and Bon Worth, both of which have large selections of clothing for all occasions in sizes from petite to XXL. You'll also find Ducks Unlimited Sportswear, a nature designs shop with sportswear for college students as well as quality casual everyday wear. (A third of this manufacturer's net profits go to support wetlands conservation.)

Other Foxmoor shopping stops represent an interesting mix of merchants. Crafts enthusiasts can choose from Phyllis' Craft Supplies and Phyllis' Needlecraft. Sneakers Unlimited has a fine selection of name-brand shoes including Fila, Nike, Reebok and Adidas; it also stocks sportswear from Nike, Reebok and Fila. Book hounds can while away the day at Book Warehouse. And the Libbey Glass outlet has glassware for every possible purpose — mugs and assorted drinking glasses, bowls, plates and vases.

Oh, and you can eat here too. Brandli's Pizzeria and Italian Restaurant has terrific stuffed pizza. Or pick up a bagful of zeppoles here to munch on at the gazebo while you wait for your kids to come out of the movie. You can also treat yourself at the Bagel King to a complete breakfast (if you are an early shopper) or a bagel sandwich for lunch or a good old bagel and cream cheese for any time.

This shopping oasis is open everyday except Christmas, New Year's and Thanksgiving.

FYI

Unless otherwise noted, the area code for all phone numbers in this guide is 717.

Odd-Lot Outlet
U.S. Hwy. 209, Marshalls Creek • 223-1844

This shop is aptly named; it has thousands of items including hard-to-find home catalog items (more than 20,000) that they buy from mail-order catalog companies and fund-raising houses. These items can't be sold in stores simply because they aren't in gift boxes or otherwise appropriately packaged; Odd-Lot sells them for less than half the catalog price (and without shipping and handling charges).

Odd-Lot is the largest seller of Pocono souvenirs, T-shirts (prices range from $1.99 to $4.88 for a good-quality souvenir T), key chains, mugs, salt and pepper shakers and so on. The big draw here is the free gift bar from which every customer that enters can choose a free gift (yes, even if you have 10 kids, every one gets a gift). Items include combs, small brass ornaments, children's toys, holiday items and corkboards.

This store is open every day (except major holidays) and has new merchandise all the time.

Passion Jewelry
U.S. Hwy. 209 Bus., Marshalls Creek • 223-8996

Custom-made silver and gold (14k and 18k) jewelry are the specialty here at 30 percent to 60 percent savings. Besides custom designs there is an extensive ready-made collection designed and made by the store owner.

Stroudsburg's Downtown

Staff can mount or reset diamonds or stones of any type and do repairs while you wait.

This shop has a factory in New York, so whatever is selling well in Manhattan is immediately shipped and sold here too — at discounted prices. The Christmas sale features items for up to 60 percent off the original (already discounted) prices.

This store is open every day of the week. Take Exit 52 from I-80.

Pocono Outlet Complex
S. Ninth and Ann Sts., Stroudsburg • 421-7470

This group of outlets is centered around the American Ribbon Store, which is housed in a historic textile mill (the textiles industry was once strong in this region). There are new stores opening up all the time, so we focus on some that have become draws over the years.

American Ribbon is loaded with ribbons for every need and an extensive selection of supplies for making bridal favors, decorations and other wedding novelties. The sister store is American Ribbon Fabric, with fabric and needlework supplies as well as foam, batting and other necessities for the serious seamstress or upholsterer — all in one well-stocked location.

The Ann Street Book Exchange is a great find for voracious readers. Ask about the Book Exchange Club that offers you sizable discounts on purchases based on your exchanged used books.

The International Boutique features exotic clothing from Europe and India. Crompton's Menswear is a find for the men in the family not only for the large selection of quality clothing, but also for the separate sections for Big and Tall men and husky boys. Be sure to check out the back room for specials.

Beer drinkers and wine tasters should check out On Tap Systems (for beer dispensing needs) or the Wine Shop of Franklin Hill Vineyards to taste and buy some *vino*. Cards, Wrap & More has your other party needs covered.

Pocono Linen Outlet has all you need to keep your beds well made. Printer Plus has a great supply of printers and other computer needs — you even can refill your ink cartridges here to save money. The Potting Shed has a huge selection of silk flowers, foliage, house plants and dried flowers.

Another notable shop is the Senior Craft Store, operated by senior citizens who make all the crafts sold here. It was started with the help and support of the Monroe County Area Agency on Aging (see our Retirement chapter) as a way to help seniors maintain economic independence. (Senior crafters are welcome to inquire about selling their wares here too.)

If you need sustenance to keep up your shopping energy, nourish yourself at Kandy Corner (confections), Cakes 'N Trim (homemade cakes and party favors), the Backstreet Eatery (sandwiches and deli items), Gary's Meat Market (old-fashioned butcher shop), Keyco Warehouse (bulk discount food) or Big Al's (Cajun and soul food groceries).

This complex is open every day except Christmas, New Year's and Thanksgiving.

Stroud Mall
N. Ninth St., Stroudsburg • 424-2770

This mall is anchored by major department stores Sears, JCPenney and The Bon-Ton. You'll find 65 specialty shops and smaller stores representing national, regional and local merchants. All shops are on one level; the second-floor is occupied by Sears, which introduced the area's first escalator when it opened three years ago. Wall-to-Wall Sound is here, dress shops, Payless Shoes and This End Up furniture. One cute aspect of this mall is the little carts throughout selling items such as candles, fragrances, T-shirts and dried flowers; at Christmastime the number of carts increases dramatically. The big draw for kids is Willie T. Haus, which has a blacklight room and sells shirts, incense, patches — lots of patches — and all those specialty items that kids love to buy with their never-ending discretionary income.

You'll also find Waldenbooks and Kay-Bee Toy and Hobby Shop here.

If you need a place to sit (other than the many benches that line the center of the mall), you can relax and grab a bite to eat at the Pavilion Food Court, a fast-food oasis including McDonald's, Boardwalk Fries, American Cookie and Sbarro's.

Stroud Mall has a central information desk

where wheelchairs are available for free for those who need them; strollers are available for rent. A multiplex movie theater is at each end of the mall.

Mount Pocono Area

Crossings Factory Stores
Pa. Hwy. 611, Tannersville • 629-4650

By far the largest and most impressive outlet entity is Crossings Factory Stores, in Tannersville, immediately off Exit 45 of I-80. This beautiful complex of seven buildings, including a loft area, is literally at the crossroads of I-80 and Pa. highways 611 and 715 and easily is reached by any highway that feeds I-80. There are approximately 90 stores here. The following list of names will give you a sense of the types and quality available; there is no particular order or weight to the list: Etienne Aigner, J. Crew, Pfaltzgraff, Oneida, Aileene, Champion Hanes, Bass, Maidenform, London Fog apparel, Liz Claiborne, Anne Klein, Napier, Corning Revere, Carole Little, Geoffrey Beene, Mikasa, Toy Liquidators, Osh Kosh B'Gosh, Levi's, Carter's, Nordic Track, Big Dog, Perry Ellis, Izod, Van Heusen, Nine West shoes, Book Cellar, Stone Mountain Handbags, Designer Fragrances, the Ribbon Outlet, Reebok athletic footwear and a great deal more.

Shopping here at Christmas is an adventure; the sales are incredible (but try to come early in the day because the parking lots fill up fast). You can pick up wonderful stocking stuffers; unique gift items (silver, brass, afghans, table linens, framed art, clever toys and puzzles) from all over the world; and T-shirts, caps and trendy clothing.

If you need to replenish your strength to continue shopping the multi-leveled smorgasbord of designer and famous-brand shops, stop at the food court at the end of Building B. Just Desserts can sustain you with velvety chocolate concoctions, creamy rich cheesecakes or, if you need to justify the indulgence by touting the protein value of your dessert, nut-encrusted or nut-filled delicacies. Or indulge in Sbarro's wonderful pizza and Italian delicacies served cafeteria-style; old-fashioned deli sandwiches at Mr. Deli; or Oriental favorites at the Magic Wok.

You can shop to your heart's content every day except Christmas, New Year's Day and Thanksgiving.

Slate Belt

Majestic Athletic
636 Pen Argyl St., Pen Argyl
• (610) 863-6161

This warehouse outlet specializes in licensed sports apparel, including jackets, T-shirts, sweats and items such as the batting-practice jerseys and turtle neck shirts that Major League Baseball players use. Majestic also features clothing representing National Football League and National Hockey League professional teams as well as college teams such as Penn State and Notre Dame. It's the perfect place for sports lovers. This store stocks firsts and seconds.

Majestic Athletic is open Tuesday through Saturday.

Windjammer Factory Outlet
519 Penn St., Bangor • (610) 588-2137

This factory store is also a team athletic sportswear source. Clothing for the whole family includes sweats, hats, T-shirts and sports-related novelties featuring Penn State items —the hottest selling stock. Windjammer also carries replica helmets, key chains, and bumper stickers with professional-team logos. Crew-neck sweatshirts are available in hard-to-find sizes — up to 5XL; sweatpants, up to size 3XL. There are lots of irregulars and close-out bargains from which to choose. Custom printing is also available.

Windjammer is open Monday through Saturday year round. Saturday hours change in winter, so call ahead if Saturday is your shopping day.

Farmers Markets, Farmstands and Orchards

This area is known for its numerous little farms as well as large family gardens; there are also both major and small family orchards. And, lucky for us, these folks are always willing to sell their fresh, luscious, gem-colored treasures to the masses whose thumbs refuse to turn green! Summertime is a glorious time to buy fresh vegetables. Most stands also have a wide assortment of flowers and plants, including vegetable and herb plants.

As you drive along our many country roads (see our Getting Around chapter to get your bearings), you will spot little signs scrawled on oaktag, with arrows pointing to a cornucopia of tomatoes, sweet corn, peppers, summer squash, zucchinis, red potatoes, broccoli, cucumbers, pickle cucumbers, peaches and more. In fall, you'll see signs for apples — Macs, cortlands, red and golden delicious — by the basket, half-basket, peck, even pick-your-own (great fun and a cost-saver). In June you can pick your own strawberries; throughout summer, pick your own blueberries and peaches. Look in the *Pocono Record's* "Classified" section and throughout the paper for who's selling what, when and where.

We've included some well-known farmers markets for you, but it's also fun to discover your own special farmer or market. So don't forget to look for the signs as you drive along the country byways that criss-cross the Pocono Mountains. Fresh-grown delights await at stands along virtually every road. Even if you don't see anyone tending the stand, stop and see what's available. Many farmers operate on the honor system: Weigh your tomatoes, peppers or squash; count out your ears of corn; then drop what you owe into the money box. These folks trust you. It's quaint; it's a great reason to come here!

Delaware Water Gap

The Village Farmer & Bakery
13 Broad St., Delaware Water Gap
• 476-0075

This great little farm market specializes in locally grown, in-season fruits and vegetables, including strawberries, apples, blueberries, tomatoes, broccoli and our August delight — corn. But this delightful shop also sells wonderful baked items, including their famous pies — more than 40 different varieties, including blueberry, blackberry, pumpkin, strawberry, rhubarb, red raspberry and apple (a real drawing card). We suggest the "fruit of the forest" pie, which contains apples, strawberries, rhubarb, red raspberries and blackberries. You can buy any type of pie with a regular or a crumb crust. Other taste-teasers include apple walnut and pumpkin cream cheese — yum! And folks with special dietary needs can even buy pies made with Equal instead of sugar.

Breads are delicious too, including raisin, wheat, rye, vegetable, cheese and white. For a quick treat try the apple dumplings, old-fashioned donuts and fresh cider in the fall.

The Village Farmer & Bakery is open every day except Christmas.

Stroudsburg/ East Stroudsburg

A & J Vegetables
Chipperfield Dr., Stroudsburg • 424-2647
Pa. Hwy. 611, Stroudsburg • 424-2647

A&J Vegetables farmstand has two locations in Stroudsburg. Both stands are open from the end of July, when the first tomatoes and cucumbers and corn start to ripen on the Chipperfield Drive farm, until November, when the last of the apples, pumpkins and cider are gone. You can pick tomatoes and pumpkins at the Chipperfield Drive location; look for it near the Stroudsburg Middle School. The Pa. 611 stand is between Stroudsburg and Bartonsville.

The Farmer's Basket
764 N. Ninth St., Stroudsburg • 424-5333
1309 N. Fifth St., Stroudsburg • 421-6643

This market has two locations, both of which offer an abundance of fresh produce and specialty foods items such as Pennsylvania Dutch corn relish, locally collected honey and homemade jellies, jams and relishes.

The Ninth Street store is open every day year round and also features home baked items and local crafts, including carved nativities, ducks, baskets and more. The Fifth Street is open seven days a week from May to Thanksgiving.

Monroe Farmers Market
Main St., between Eighth and Ninth Sts., Stroudsburg • No central phone

Every Saturday morning from mid-June to Thanksgiving, you can discover the bounty of the Monroe Farmers Market. Farmers from Stroudsburg to Nazareth offer fresh-picked seasonal produce at this unique tailgate market. Others sell fresh-baked goods, jams, jellies, herbal vinegars, honey and other fresh homemade treats.

Pocono Bazaar Flea Market
U.S. Hwy. 209, Marshalls Creek
• 233-8640

This flea market has shops for clothing, shoes, crafts, health foods, housewares, wicker, antiques, collectibles — something for virtually any buyer. As for food, many farmers come for the day to sell whatever produce is in-season. In late spring, start looking for purveyors of locally grown vegetables and fruits as well as eggs, homemade pies, cakes, jellies, jams and relishes. R&J Flea World at the bazaar specializes in oak-furniture stripping and restoration. It also carries lots of antique jewelry, glass and other furniture, so it's a good starting point for exploring this large and busy flea market.

Mount Pocono Area

Pocono Farmstand and Nursery
Pa. Hwy. 611, Tannersville • 629-3344

This stand is open every day year round and features produce from local farmers such as corn, tomatoes, broccoli, strawberries, apples, beans, zucchini and more. It also has a great selection of bedding plants, annuals and perennials, shrubs and tress as well as lawn ornaments, pottery planters and other decorative garden items. While you are busy looking at the great buys, your children can enjoy the petting zoo. You'll also find a great country bake shop on the premises where fresh-baked pies and breads are sold; you can even order in advance, an especially helpful option around the holidays.

In Pocono Peddler's Village, about an eighth-mile from here, is the Old Country Store, a gourmet food shop specializing in some incredible tastes (see this chapter's "Shopping The Country Roads of the Poconos" section).

Milford Area

Heller's Farm Market
U.S. Hwy. 209 N., between Bushkill and Dingmans Ferry • No phone

You'll find Heller's Farm Market on U.S. Highway 209 N., in the Delaware Water Gap National Recreation Area, north of Milford between Bushkill and Dingmans Ferry. Heller's sells fresh vegetables all season long; you can pick your own berries and flowers too!

The federal government bought this property from the Heller family when acquiring land to build the Tocks Island Dam. Since the project was abandoned, the former owners lease the land from the government to farm it as their family had always done before. (See the History chapter for details about the Tocks Island farmers as well as the Close-up in our Native Americans chapter, which briefly discusses farms in the park area.)

West End

Heckman's Orchards
Pa. Hwy. 115 N., Effort • 629-1191

On Pa. Highway 115 N. in Effort, between Brodheadsville and Long Pond, is a large farm market with a great selection of fresh fruits and vegetables: beans, lettuce and strawberries in the early spring; great zucchini all summer long; tomatoes, corn and spaghetti squash in late summer; and apples, pumpkins and squash in fall. In June, Heckman's is a good spot for strawberry picking (for anyone 10 and older); in fall, pick your own apples (bring some cheese and have a picnic when you're through).

Lake Wallenpaupack Area

PJ's Farm Market and Garden Center
U.S. Hwy. 6, Hawley • 226-4121

PJ's Farm Market and Garden Center has plenty of fresh produce to fill summer vegetable and fruit baskets. Choose from locally grown corn, broccoli, tomatoes, apples, pumpkins, squash and other garden gems. You can also pick up bedding plants for your home garden.

Slate Belt

Elvern Farm Market
205 Blue Valley Dr. (Pa. Hwy. 512), Bangor • (610) 588-6335

This farm market sells produce (grown on its own 100-acre farm) and flowers from Easter until Christmas Eve Day. Staffers keep the stand stocked with whatever is in-season, including Easter flowers, bedding plants, scarlet summer strawberries and wreaths and poinsettias. Elvern's specialty is homemade apple cider, available once the apples are prime (usually around late September).

Valley View Orchards
Sunrise Blvd., Mount Bethel • 897-0591

True, the farm market here sells produce

grown on-site. But the real draw is the pick-your-own fruit — an especially popular family activity. The picking season starts late in June when the cherries are ready and ends the first week in November after the last of the pumpkins are gone. Pick-your-own fruits (as the season progresses) include cherries, nectarines, plums, apples, pumpkins — even tomatoes when the harvest is good. The orchard is open daily during the picking season; call ahead to find out what's ripe and ready.

Specialty Shops

Candle Shops

Candle shops are a real draw in the central Poconos. Some tour companies even bring busloads of shoppers here. Candle shops have mushroomed into emporiums that carry various styles and sizes of candles. They also specialize in custom-made candles for weddings, anniversaries and other commemorative events.

Most shops make candles on site — a curiosity draw and an integral part of the shopping experience. Candles are such a hot item, you'll find them in almost every gift and specialty shop in the Poconos. But the places we've included offer incredible selections, workmanship, quality and value.

Stroudsburg/East Stroudsburg

The American Candle Shop
Pa. Hwy. 611, Bartonsville • 629-3388

This is the Poconos' largest candle shop, encompassing more than 40,000 square feet. The company has its own manufacturing facility in Wind Gap to supply this store. Specialties include carved candles. And check out the huge wedding department, including favor supplies and unity candles.

Scheduled carving demonstrations are a big hit with bus tourists; drop-in shoppers are free to watch whatever candle-making activity is going on at the moment. This candle shop also houses a country candy store (customers love the chance to buy by the piece) and a gourmet coffee shop (enjoy a cappuccino while you browse). The American Candle Shop also stocks several collectibles series, including Armani, Dept. 56, Precious Moments, Hummel, Lladro and Heritage Snow Village. There is also a Christmas shop on the premises.

American Candle is open year round every day, except major holidays. Take Exit 46B off I-80.

Candle Towne USA
Ann and S. Ninth Sts., Stroudsburg • 424-8605

This small candle shop is in the Pocono Outlet Complex (see previous entry in "Outlets, Outlet Complexes and Malls"). It's an outlet for the larger Pocono Candle Shop in East Stroudsburg. Wedding candles and favors are made here, and this shop carries a wide variety of novelty candles — animals, birthday themes, psychedelic designs — and hand-carved candles by the grandmother who owns the main store.

House of Candles
Pa. Hwy. 715, Henryville • 629-1953

You are invited to watch the candle-making process as well as custom carving. House of Candles fills six rooms with its crafters' handmade specialties. This shop is known for its large selection of high-quality designs, including custom candles for weddings, anniversaries, commemoratives and other occasions.

House of Candles was started as a wholesale business in the 1960s and evolved to include its own retail shop — now its primary business. Currently it's owned by the original owner's son and grandsons. This third-generation business is known for high-quality candles sold at wholesale prices — approximately a third the price of an American-made candle of comparable quality. Wedding candles are specially carved to custom-fit a wedding picture provided by the customer. You'll find candles of more than 30 fragrances

— available in jars, pillars and votives — as well as other styles and types.

Decorative candles from other countries also are sold. Other items include rings, candle holders, Dickens Villages and other collectibles; but the main thing here is great candles, made here as they have been for more than 30 years.

While parents browse, children can visit with the pony, Chinese pheasants and ducks outside.

The shop is closed on Sundays and major holidays. Take Exit 45 off I-80; follow Pa. 715 north 4 miles.

Pocono Candle Shop
U.S. Hwy. 209 Bus., East Stroudsburg • 421-1832

The shop is filled with candles of all types, and demonstrations of ribbon candle making are a specialty. Collectibles for sale include Dept. 56, Precious Moments, Hummel, Norman Rockwell Figurines, Goebels and Salvinos. Other gift areas include the wedding candle gallery and the favors section, which features unity candles, a craft department, Pennsylvania Dutch souvenirs and a large selection of sports-related memorabilia. If you are hungry, try some homemade fudge. Bus tours are welcome.

Take Exit 52 off I-80, then go north on Pa. Highway 447. Make a right at the intersection of U.S. 209.

West End

Country Candle Shoppe
U.S. Hwy. 209 S., Kresgeville • (610) 681-5314

This candle shop isn't as large as some, but it specializes in candles with silk flower arrangements. All arrangements are made on the premises, so if you see a design you like but would prefer in different colors, one can be custom-made. This shop carries the top-of- the-line Yankee Candles in all types, in-

cluding tapers, jar candles and votives. This shop also stocks seasonal candles — for Christmas, Thanksgiving, even Halloween. Upstairs you'll find Christmas items and collectibles, such as the Dept. 56 houses and Christmas Villages, as well as Christmas candles, ornaments, centerpieces and wreaths. If you are hungry, buy some homemade fudge and eat while you browse.

Christmas Shops

Christmas items are sold in Poconos outlets and in specialty shops. Some candle shops (see previous section) stock extensive selections of Christmas collectibles; Mathews Hallmark and Littman Jewelers at the Stroud Mall (see "Outlets, Outlet Complexes and Malls") also carry a wide selection of quality-name collectibles, though generally at slightly higher prices than you'll find at outlets. Most gift and collectibles shops (see "Collectibles" in this chapter) also carry Christmas ornaments and decorations.

In this section we include shops that primarily sell theme trees, nativity scenes (wood, pewter, porcelain, ceramic, terra cotta), angels and scads of lacy, bright, tinkly, sparkly, romantic, heavenly, adorable, cute, gorgeous, wonderful, eye-popping Christmas-season decorations for home, hearth and tree.

Delaware Water Gap

The Christmas Factory
Broad St., Delaware Water Gap • 421-3607

This shop, like its sister store in Marshalls Creek (see subsequent entry), is open year round. The Christmas Factory stocks an extensive selection of collectibles from Dept. 56, Christmas ornaments such as Serephin Angels and theme Christmas trees (on display) that always sparkle with Christmas cheer.

To reach The Christmas Factory, take Exit 53 off I-80.

Stroudsburg/East Stroudsburg

The Christmas Factory
U.S. Hwy. 209 Bus., south of Marshalls Creek • 223-0717

This location of The Christmas Factory are open all yearand carries an extensive selection of collectibles, such as Dept. 56 snowbabies and carolers. There are Serephin Angels here to glamorize any tree. The famous Kurt Adler, Midwest and Roman ornaments sold here are displayed on the completely decorated trees that light up the store. The trees are decorated in themes, such as all angels, all reds, all village pieces and so on. The Christmas Factory also sells garlands, wreaths and bows that match and complement the trees and ornaments.

Other items for sale here include collectibles such as Annalee and Dynasty dolls and Melody in Motion figures (Coca-Cola, "I Love Lucy") and candles to brighten the holidays. Christmas ornaments and theme Christmas trees (on display) sparkle with Christmas cheer, even in July!

Take Exit 52 off I-80 to Pa. Highway 447 N. and proceed to U.S. Highway 209 Business.

Mount Pocono Area

Christmas Memories
Pa. Hwy. 390 S., Mountainhome • 595-2272

This small shop has a great collection of Christmas ornaments, including beautiful Serephin Angels and Victorian dolls. It also carries collectibles such as Hummel, Precious Moments, Cherished Teddies and Lladro. Christmas Memories offers specials on items that are going out of stock, so a trip there at any time of the year is sure to yield some bargains for the next year's Christmas decorating.

Collectibles

Collectibles are a major nationwide industry today, and they have quite a presence on shop shelves throughout the Poconos. Most stores carry collectibles of some type, including the candles shops, gift shops, food shops, Christmas shops and, of course, the major outlets mentioned earlier in this chapter. On your way to some of our favorite shops, which we note subsequently, you're bound to pass others we haven't visited yet, or ones that have just jumped onto the collectibles bandwagon.

Stroudsburg/East Stroudsburg

Old Engine Works Market Place
62 N. Third St., Stroudsburg • 421-4340

For antiques and collectibles, you have to stop at Olde Engine Works Market Place. You will find an incredible array, including old toys, dolls, books, spice boxes, sheet music, model trains and so on. It is a truly fascinating and fun place to browse. Fifties collectibles and comic books are big sellers here as well.

Mount Pocono Area

A&R's Crafts and More
Pa. Hwy. 390, Mountainhome • 595-6344

This stop sells craft supplies and giftware a well as collectibles. If you are looking for die-cast trucks for your collection, check out this place. It is also an authorized Anheuser-Busch dealer — a must-stop if you are shopping for steins.

Beary Best Friends
Peddlers Village, Pa. Hwy. 611 S., Tannersville • 620-2099

Don't limit your hunt. For a truly exclusive selection of teddy bears, seek out Beary Best Friends. The collection here, as at other places, includes the famous Boyds Bears. But this shop has the widest selection within a 50-mile radius. Also, these bears are well cared for by proprietor Susan Paul, who brushes their hair and irons their clothing before they are ready for your acquaintance. Paul's store is also an authorized Bearstone dealer and carries that entire line as well as the newly released Dollstone dolls by the same producer, Gary Lowenthal (catch him on cable television's QVC). A neat feature of Bearstone bears is their paw print to prove authenticity — you have to search for it though. Dollstone dolls also have both paw and shoe prints for authenticity — have fun searching for these too!

These delightful bears and dolls sell for between $5.99 and $50. Each is a limited-edition piece available only for one year — there are retired pieces too. This company also is famous for its posable, jointed beanbag bears; Beary Best Friends stocks a large selection.

You'll also find the Barbie of bears, Muffy Vander Bear, who has her own monogrammed towels, silver brush and mirror, beautiful furniture and, as Paul says, "enough clothes to make us all jealous!"

Beary Best Friends stocks exclusive handmade teddy bears from two local artists. The high-quality bears are unique collectibles made from the finest materials, with personality in their faces that immediately make you want to be friends. They sell for around $80.

Switzerland Old World Gifts
Pa. Hwy. 611, Tannersville • 620-2003

They carry all of the main collectibles including Boyds Bears and Bearstone teddies, but they also carry an extensive collection of Ulbricht and Steinbach nutcrackers and smokers and Anton Schneider cuckoo clocks from Germany's Black Forest. As part of their promotion of the Steinbach and Ulbricht items, the folks at Switzerland Old World Gifts invite these two masters to visit every summer and sign their work. Interested customers who can't make it in to meet these crafters can pre-order a signed piece by credit card; call in advance. This shop also carries Budweiser steins, Dept. 56, Swarovski and Harbor Lights as well as an extensive collection of Old World Christmas ornaments.

Lake Wallenpaupack Area

Ursula's Barn
Pa. Hwy. 191 S., Hamlin • 689-2649

You'll find a large collection of collectibles, folk art and antiques in this cow barn. Ursula's unique collection includes folk art of Vaillancourt and Leo Smith, Walnut Rich Primitives, Boyds Bears, Attic Babies, Lizzie High Dolls, All God's Children and June McKenna Collectibles to name a handful. Christmas ornaments and collectibles are abundant also, including Dept. 56, Heritage Village, Byer's Choice Carolers, Christopher Radko Ornaments, Old World Christmas Ornaments and lots of Santas. The selection here is enormous and includes many retired pieces and limited editions.

Kids Clothing and Toys

You'll find great deals on kids clothing in stores at most outlet complexes and malls. But we decided it would be nice to direct you to some of our favorite, unique spots. Be sure to check the previous "Collectibles" section for details about where to find teddy bears.

Stroudsburg/East Stroudsburg

Kid's Emporium
150 Washington St., East Stroudsburg • 421-4144

If you are looking for a truly exceptional children's outfit, stop at the elegant and upscale Kid's Emporium. Clothing for special occasions includes Christening outfits, flowergirl dresses and communion dresses. You'll also find everyday clothing from Osh Kosh B'Gosh and other name-brand manufacturers.

Pocono Bazaar
U.S. Hwy. 209, Marshalls Creek • 223-8640

This flea market (open weekends) is full of stalls with children's items. You'll find T-shirts, jeans, winter coats and brand-name sneakers for newborns to high schoolers, all at discount prices. Since this is a flea market, the players (and selection) change all the time — part of the fun of going there.

Totally Toys
Foxmoor Village Outlet Center, U.S. Hwy. 209 N., Marshalls Creek • 223-8706

Like Toy Liquidators, Totally Toys is a liquidator. What you'll find will be last year's models, generally, but the kids love them still. Board games such as Monopoly, Candyland, Yahtzee and Omni; children's books such as simple Golden Books, dictionaries and a mystery series for older kids; hand-held video games; and magic sets all are good finds here.

Mount Pocono Area

Toy Liquidators
Crossings Factory Stores, Pa. Hwy. 611, Tannersville • 629-4650

This is a good place to find toys of all sizes. The store is usually very crowded the month before Christmas, so shop early in the day to avoid the rush. Electronic games and video game cartridges such as SEGA and Nintendo are sold here at reduced rates — not the latest releases, necessarily, but many released in the past year. You also can find Mighty Morphin Power Rangers items, air-hockey games, in-line skates and Barbie and baby dolls.

Pottery and Glass

There are many potters in the Poconos. Shops crop up along the backroads between Bangor and Stroudsburg, Hawley and Mount Pocono, Jim Thorpe and Blakeslee and all around the mountain. Watch for them as you

What About Antiques?

Antiques? Did you say you are looking for antiques? Well, take a walk down one of our "main streets." Stop at one of the shopping villages on our Pennsylvania byways. Visit a flea market or bazaar. Drive any Pocono country road (see this chapter's "Shopping the Country Roads . . ." section or our Getting Around chapter). You will find antiques — more than you probably believed could exist and with more variety than you could hope for. Besides all the places we mentioned throughout this shopping chapter that sell antiques, there are many more, including a few huge places that are veritable antiques department stores. We point them out here. And we also note some places you'll find on roads we don't highlight in this Close-up. Always remember that shops come and go; don't think if you have shopped all those we mention, you've found them all. You haven't! Gas up and use the following touchstones to guide you as you embark on your antiquing voyage of discovery.

For the following destinations, it's best if not essential to call for hours; shop owners are often out buying, so hours vary. Happy hunting!

Stroudsburg/East Stroudsburg

First, the big ones. In Stroudsburg at 62 N. Third Street, you must see the **Olde Engine Works Market Place**, 421-4340, specializing in antiques and Collectibles (see Collectibles). More than 70 dealers take turns in this co-op, open seven days a week year round. This huge building is divided into the Flag Room, the Glass Case Room, the Welding Room and the Main Concourse. The Glass Case Room features antique jewelry, beaded purses, miniature porcelains and high-end toy collectibles from manufacturers such as Ephemera. The Flag Room features furniture of all types — especially primitives. The Welding Room is the place for pottery, with brands such as McCoy and Shawnee. The Main Concourse is a cornucopia of treasures, for aisle after aisle in this huge building. There is also a great selection of books about collectibles, including annual price lists.

Also in Stroudsburg is **Stroudsburg Antique Center**, 70 Storm Street, 421-4441. This multi-dealer mall of antiques and collectibles includes pottery, glassware, clocks, silver, quilts, lighting, glassware and advertising posters — all in 14,000 square feet of space. It is open Friday through Monday year round.

Collector's Cove, U.S. Highway 209 S. (exit from Pa. Highway 33), Sciota, 992-9161, has wholesale warehouses occupied by estate liquidators and dealers. This emporium (twice the size of the very large Olde Engine Works) is open to the public on Sundays only, year round. It's open the rest of the week for wholesalers exclusively. The prices are particularly competitive, because goods are sold by dealers and estate liquidators (who primarily sell to antiques shops and specialty stores) rather than collectors. There is an Antique Boutique Building, two Dealers Buildings, an Antique Warehouse and a Country Store in this complex. Other vendors set up outside the huge warehouses on Sundays, so there is always even more to see than what's inside. There's plenty of parking available in the 6-acre lot.

Also on-site is The Cafe, a great little restaurant for a homemade breakfast or lunch.

In the same area as Collectors Cove, take the Saylorsburg exit from Pa. Highway 33 to stop at **Apple Orchard Antiques**, 992-2988. This place is filled with Victorian and country antiques and primitives. This space is open Thursday, Friday and Monday; by appointment Tuesday and Wednesday; it's closed Sunday.

If you are already in the Sciota/Snydersville area, you might want to check out **Lea Z. Katz**, U.S. 209 Business, Snydersville (across from the famous Snydersville Diner), 992-5462, open everyday. You'll find collectibles from Belleek and Mary Gregory as well as Shirley Temple Dolls in their original boxes! Other treasures include Tiffany lamps and wondrous children's toys.

A few hundred yards north of Katz's is **Wakefield Antiques**, 992-7226, which specializes in bakers racks of every size, shape and form — mostly refinished oak, some metal, all delightful designs. Primitives are available too as well as gift items, such as tin boxes.

Farther south on U.S. Highway 209 in Sciota, you'll discover **Sciota Historic Crossing Antique Center**, featuring Yestertiques, 992-6576, Corner Antiques, 992-4893, and in a separate building, Raven Antiques, 992-9092. Yestertiques and Corner Antiques are in a beautiful old house at the intersection of U.S. 209 Bus. and Bossardville Road.

Yestertiques specializes in refinished oak and Victorian furniture, antique lighting and china. You'll also find refinished kitchen artifacts, Hoosiers, dry sinks, stepback cupboards and other country accessories. Check out the fine china from Limoge, Transferware and Flow Blue as well as the Depression glassware.

Corner Antiques is a cooperative of about 10 dealers who take turns in the shop on Saturdays, Sundays and holiday Mondays. Items include Victorian and primitive furniture; glassware, including green and pink Depression glass; kitchen collectibles such as those good old red and green handled utensils your mother used; and collectible toys including tin figures and windups.

Raven Antiques features an eclectic collection of everything — watches (American Waltham) and clocks, primitive local tools, local beer bottles and dairy bottles and costume jewelry. It's a fun place to dig around and discover something unexpected.

Farther south in Sciota, past King Arthur's restaurant on Center Avenue, you'll find **Halloran's Antiques**, 992-4651. This shop has been family-owned for two generations and includes two barns full of wonderful buys. One is devoted to furniture — primarily local primitives including blanket chests, rope beds and other unusual finds. "We specialize in the unusual" is Halloran's motto. The other barn is filled with country brass, copper and unique primitive metal work.

If you are in this area and need some restoration work done on an antique you've just bought or already own, **Heritage Crafts**, 992-CANE, on Cherry Valley Road at Camera Drive, Saylorsburg, specializes in restoring caning, rushing and splint in furniture and in baskets; it also sells supplies for these crafts. Owner John Skelton is a fourth-generation caner, and he and wife Pat do work for individuals, restaurants, resorts and antiques dealers. Heritage Crafts repairs cane, rush, seagrass, wicker, round reed and Shaker tape. The most fascinating repair work to date: a 300-year-old papier mâché chair from France, inlaid with mother-of-pearl.

West End

The West End is farther south along U.S. Highway 209. As you head toward Jim Thorpe, you'll find **Rinker's Antiques**, Village Edge Drive (next to the Century 21 building), Brodheadsville, 992-6957. This shop is only open weekends; look for the little cardboard sign at this intersection to direct you. Refinished oak furniture is the specialty here. Dressers, china closets, dining room sets, wash stands and other oak items are available here; you can schedule an appointment to check out these items during the week.

Jim Thorpe is the natural southern terminus for your U.S. Highway 209 antiquing discovery voyage. As we noted in "Main Streets" there are more than enough antiques shops in Jim Thorpe to discover at the end of the U.S. 209 rainbow. On Race Street, you'll find **Switchback Antiques**, 325-4088, for political and sports-related items, old advertising, antique bottles, 1950s and '60s "stuff" and local memorabilia relating to the heyday of Jim Thorpe when it was named Mauch Chunk. It is open weekends throughout the year. On W. Broadway, look for **Stone Row Antiques**, 325-4568, which carries wooden masks, old prints, etchings, old toys, silver, brass and furniture (open weekends May to December). Farther up W. Broadway, you'll find the **Selective Eye Gallery**, 325-8777, which specializes in vintage clothing, hats, purses, antique jewelry, glass and old prints. This store accept antiques on consignment (open weekends April to December).

Lake Wallenpaupack Area

In the Wallenpaupack Lake region you'll find the outstanding **Castle**, 226-8550 or (800) 345-1667, on U.S. Highway 6 at the top of the hill before you enter Hawley. This former silk factory really looks like a castle. When you walk in on the main floor, notice the exhibit of memorabilia depicting the growth of the area from the construction of the mill to the construction of the dam at Lake Wallenpaupack. Castle is filled with antiques and reproductions, all clearly identified by type. The first floor is the retail shop; the second floor is open to dealers with proper credentials only.

The antiques here have not been refinished. Available items change almost daily because of the huge volume of business. Most antiques are bought when a buyer calls and request an appraisal and sale; some furniture is imported. Besides furniture of every period and style, there are also collectibles such as Depression glass, tin toys and mechanical banks. Castle is open Monday through Saturday; it's closed on Sunday.

After a stop at the Castle, continue up the hill on U.S. Highway 6 to **Timely Treasures**, 226-2838. This shop specializes in Victorian and turn-of-the-century furniture. You can find a completely refinished piece or one that needs refinishing. If you don't want to refinish it yourself, you're in luck; the folks in the on-site refinishing shop do beautiful restoration work. Currently, there are three rooms of furniture, and three more are being completed by spring 1997. Furniture in the new rooms will be displayed as a room setting to help you envision how it would look in your home. Glassware is also sold. Local glass companies were once a thriving business in this area, and a large quantity of local glass from the turn-of-the-century is available at this shop.

Slate Belt

Pa. Highway 611 S. between Delaware Water Gap and Bangor has some fine antiques shops to discover. But before we get to them, we should mention a shop in Portland — not an antiques shop per se, but a wonderful furniture shop. **Frederick Duckloe and Brothers**, 897-6172, crafts exquisite wood furniture in the style of the best antiques. Leaving Portland and heading south, there are a number of destinations you might want to check out.

Richmond Antiques, (610) 588-0861, in the village of Richmond, specializes in sales and repairs of antique lighting from the 1870s to the 1930s, including brass and bronze fixtures, wall sconces and hanging lamps. It is open by chance or by appointment, so definitely call first.

You can reach Bangor by crossing over Bangor Mountain; Pa. Highway 191 will lead you past Stroudsmoor (see our Bed and Breakfasts and Country Inns chapter) and its shops. Here you will find quaint shops — **Godfrey's Ridge** (gift shop and garden center), **Victorian Treasures & Vintage Bridals** (trousseaus and crocheted ensembles) and **Wimbleton's Sellers of Fine Gifts, Art, Antiques** — surrounding the village commons that overlooks the town of Stroudsburg and the Delaware River. Stroudsmoor hosts an antiques and crafts fair.

drive. Many also are listed in the Monroe County Arts Council Directory, 476-4460. Call the council for the names of some potters or for a copy of the directory.

If you're interested in seeing some potters at work, you'll find them — and their pottery — at A Family of Artists, 420-9675 (see our Camps, Education and Arts and Culture chapters), Pa. Highway 447, East Stroudsburg. A number of fine artists in all media show and sell their work as well as teach in the little showroom at the front of this arts-directed center.

Lake Wallenpaupack Area

Holly Ross Pottery
Pa. Hwy. 191, La Anna (between Cresco and Newfoundland) • 595-3248

The sales room at this factory features pottery at outlet prices. There is a huge selection of pottery, fiesta glass and cranberry glass among the many types of wares. Free pottery-making demonstrations make this shopping stop a learning experience too. Outside, children can play in the free woodland park while you shop.

Reece Pottery
Crestmont Dr. (off Pa. Hwy. 191/507), Newfoundland • 676-9140

Functional and sculptural stoneware are the specialty of Thomas Reece. Reece has been making pottery for more than 30 years and has sold pieces in galleries all over the country, especially throughout New York and New Jersey. His functional, high-glaze pieces have even been bought by entertainment stars such as Rita Moreno, Bill Murray and Matt Le Blanc.

The Newfoundland shop (in a barn) has been expanding ever since it opened to the public in 1988. Reece's pieces are one-of-a-kind; special-order work includes vases, serving ware and sculptures, which he can even personalize with photographs.

Reece's Pottery is open from March through December. Hours vary seasonally; please call ahead.

Dorflinger-Suydam Sanctuary and Glass Museum
Long Ridge Rd., White Mills • 253-1185

This spot is a glassworks museum and gift shop, a wildlife sanctuary with nature trails and a concert center for the summer Wildflower Festival (see our Arts and Culture chapter).

The museum displays hundreds of pieces of cut, engraved and etched glass from Dorflinger glassworks. The gift shop sells fine contemporary glass pieces of every type — earrings, bowls, serving pieces, vases — as well as books about glass, wildlife and art. There is also an art exhibit in this shop that's only open Wednesday through Sunday from May to November.

Sweets and Eats

The following is a taster's choice of special places that create delectable goodies. Some offer tours and free tastes. Some will even ship their products all over the world. Check them out to your tummy's content.

Stroudsburg/East Stroudsburg

Country Kettle
U.S. Hwy. 209 Bus., Marshalls Creek • 421-8970

This delightful store is housed in a 150-year-old, white-columned country store/home that was expanded to match the shop's growth over the last 10 years. The store has two sections: the Country Kettle Candies section and the gift shop.

The Country Kettle's candy shop has barrel after barrel after barrel (more than 100) of candies, all at the same price, so you can mix and match to your heart's content. You'll also find barrels of sugar-free candies. But for folks who prefer their sweets with sugar, there are Pocono chocolates: dark cordial cherries; jumbo peanut butter patties; dark maple creams; and "Yum Yum Crunch" caramel corn — the house specialty.

Flavored sesame sticks include sour cream and onion, honey-roasted, mustard and honey, even Cajun. "Bagels 'n Bits" are another specialty — garlic, cinnamon raisin and Cajun. Coffee beans and flavored teas are popular items. Pennsylvania Dutch treats such as butter-toasted peanuts, peanut brittle and mixes for shoo-fly pie and funnel cake also are available.

The 15,000-square-foot gift shop carries brass, chimes, collectibles (Precious Moments, Precious Teddies, Disney Classics), music boxes and other items. Upstairs is a huge wicker shop, and the lowest level has a holiday shop that specializes in Christmas and other holiday candles, wreaths and decorations. You'll find bridal favors here too.

Mount Pocono Area

Callie's Candy Kitchen
Pa. Hwy. 390, Mountainhome • 595-2280

At Callie's you can watch candy being made in a room adjacent to the store. Mr. Callie will explain any phase of candy-making to you, and there are free samples for you to taste. The variety of candy is astounding. Pocono Mountain Bark is a favorite, with its varieties of chocolate and nuts. Another specialty in-season is chocolate-covered strawberries. You'll also find fudge, lollipops, hard candy, all kinds of chocolates, varieties of brittles and mints and . . . you get the picture.

This store is open daily (weekends only in January). Bus tours are welcome.

Callie's Pretzel Factory
Pa. Hwys. 390 and 191, Cresco • 595-3257

Handmade soft pretzels are made right before your eyes — fresh and hot. Onion, garlic, cinnamon, pizza, even hot dog pretzels are some specialties. Get a hot dog wrapped in a crisp pretzel (really good!) and a cinnamon pretzel for dessert, and you'll have a tasty, quick and inexpensive lunch while you shop your way down Pa. 390. The Pretzel Factory also carries more than 60 varieties of gourmet popcorn.

Callie's Pretzel Factory is open daily from April through December and on weekends only in January, February and March. (A side note: Callie's stocks more than 100 items for left-handers!)

Pocono Cheesecake Factory
Pa. Hwy. 611, Swiftwater • 839-6844

This constantly expanding slice of heaven began in the kitchen of owner Priscilla Moore. When the demand for her home-baked cheesecakes became too great to accommodate from her kitchen, she opened a small shop in Mountainhome, which she outgrew in five months. The current Pocono Cheesecake Factory has been expanded and renovated from a five-room house. Moore only sells 'em homemade, right on the premises in front of your eyes — huge, rich, creamy cheesecakes with a savory pastry crust. Amaretto, chocolate, chocolate chip, carrot cake, raspberry . . . the list goes as the combinations continue to evolve. Her latest sinfully delicious cheesecake is chocolate eclair, a layer of rich chocolate cheesecake and a layer of plain cheesecake topped with heavenly fudge frosting. You can also choose plain cheesecake and cap it with the fruit topping of your choice. Or, buy a slice of cheesecake to enjoy with a fresh cup of coffee. If a slice isn't enough, you can buy a whole cake, half or quarter. To please everyone, get a selection of different quarters; you won't be the first to indulge so shamelessly!

The Pocono Cheesecake Factory ships cakes all over the country. They're a great gift idea, and you can order them with your credit card. Pocono Cheesecake Factory is open every day except major holidays.

Truly Tasteful
Pa. Hwy. 390 S., Mountainhome
• 595-3363, (800) 938-4438

This shop stocks more than 40 gourmet food items under their own label. You can find

> **FYI**
> Unless otherwise noted, the area code for all phone numbers in this guide is 717.

Photo: Pocono Mountains Vacation Bureau, Inc.

Candle shops and outlets are plentiful in the Poconos.

gourmet pastas, sauces, hors d'oeuvres, jams, crackers, scone mixes, all types of teas, wonderful instant cappuccino and many varieties of gourmet coffees. All food items sold here, whether under the Truly Tasteful label or another, are personally taste-tested by all of the employees to determine if it is an item the store should carry.

The shop opened nine years ago as a 300-square-foot shop specializing in gourmet items; today the store encompasses 2,300 square feet not including a 1,200-square-foot assembly room where orders are prepared for shipping. Employees in the wholesale packaging section come from the Burnley Workshop, which trains handicapped workers and helps them find jobs in area businesses.

Ironically, this shop's huge growth came as a result of the terrible winter of 1994. When the weather prevented shoppers from getting to the store, the owner decided to try her hand at wholesaling — business boomed. The shop now sells wholesale to more than 2,300 stores both here and abroad. It ships gourmet gift baskets — choose a ready-made item from the basket menu or place a custom order — all over the world.

Upon entering the store, shoppers are offered one of the gourmet beverages on sale to taste while browsing. Every Saturday of a holiday weekend is an "Eat Your Way Through the Store Day," with free samples served all day long — steak in barbecue sauce, dips, pasta, muffins, jams, breads, mulled cider, Friendship teas. Thanksgiving weekend is a three-day "Eat Your Way" day.

Our Main Streets

Yes, the Poconos do have outlets and a

major mall as well as lots of minimalls and shops along our country roads. But we also have shopping opportunities on our "main streets." Each Main Street in the Poconos has a character all its own, reflecting the spirit of the community. Main streets are fun to shop; you can leisurely walk up and down, window shopping and enjoying the personality of the stores. Browse the shops or art galleries; you might even meet the owners, who likely will be glad to talk with you and answer questions. You can stop for a bite at a cozy little eatery and dine — maybe al fresco in nice weather — without feeling rushed or crowded. You can step back in time and shop like you or your parents did years ago, when everyone shopped on "Main Street." Some Poconos main streets even have museums — vestiges of their fascinating pasts. Please note that most main street shops close by dinnertime, except during holiday seasons and sometimes on Thursdays and Fridays; so, shop early.

Give yourself a treat. After you've hit the outlets and malls and surveyed the huge array of goods found at these complexes, take a break and go downtown to our main streets.

Delaware Water Gap

Main street here is Pa. Highway 611 as it meanders along the Delaware River toward points south. Amble through this mountainside town where you will find antiques stores, outdoor outfitters, museums, crafts stores and pottery shops. The Pack Shack, conveniently near the Appalachian Trail, provides mountaineering, camping, skiing, canoeing and other outdoor gear. The narrow, winding street climbs up to the Deer Head Inn, which overlooks the shops across the street such as the Shop at Delaware Water Gap, a draw for antiques hunters. At the Deer Head Inn you can grab a bite to eat; actually you can enjoy sumptuous food and listen to great jazz. Or, if you'd prefer, drop by one of the little pubs or spe-

cialty food shops scattered along Delaware Water Gap's main street and meandering side streets. As you enjoy your walk around this lovely town, head over to Delaware Street and look for The Studio and Art Workspace, for young and old. And don't forget to stop at the Dutot Museum (see our Arts and Culture and Attractions chapters) before ending your shopping day.

Stroudsburg/ East Stroudsburg

Stroudsburg

Stroudsburg's main street is Main Street — Upper Main and Lower Main. The old-fashioned gaslights that adorn the lampposts along this several-blocks-long street provide a sense of the past that's especially cozy and comforting. During the day the street bustles with activity as business people walk to and from meetings, to lunch or to the courthouse on Courthouse Square. Main Street is also our main business district.

Shoppers can find top-of-the-line children's shoes at George's Smart Footwear; a very elegant rare- and used-book store, Carroll & Carroll Booksellers; at least two retail art galleries including Bixler's, in a former hardware store from the early part of this century, and Artspace (see our Arts and Culture chapter); and antiques stores including Ibis (for one-of-kinds and no reproductions) and Eleanor's Antiques and Lavender and Lace. You'll also find clothing boutiques, smoke shops and newsstands, music stores, jewelry stores and the flagship J.J. Newberry store. Dunkelberger's is the shop for sporting goods and for women's classic clothes. There is the Best Western Pocono Inn (see our Accommodations chapter), at the corner of Seventh Street, and a number of eateries (formal and informal), pubs, ice cream shops (Sweet Creams, on Lower

INSIDERS' TIPS

Don't forget to look for the *Factory Outlet and Off-Price Guide* published by the *Pocono Record* every year. It is free and has valuable coupons. You'll find it in stores, diners and wherever there are racks filled with coupon books.

Main), delis and Weegee's for specialty coffees, gourmet food items and gift baskets. If you are an American Express cardholder, Anderson Travel, on Main Street, can help you obtain a temporary replacement card if yours is lost or stolen. This agency also sells American Express Travelers Cheques in six different currencies — available within two days of ordering for your shopping trips abroad.

Right off Main Street on N. Sixth Street is Wyckoff Travel, a pioneer in the travel business in the Poconos since 1928. This family-owned business started out booking trips for the employees and friends of Wyckoff's Department Store, a longtime Stroudsburg emporium. Since that time Wyckoff Travel has been arranging travel all over the world, including the 1934 World's Fair in New York City; this agency also was one of the first to charter for airlines in 1941. Today this five-agent firm arranges family vacations and group charters all over the United States and the world.

The Chamber of Commerce, the Monroe County Historical Association (in the restored Stroud Mansion) and the Monroe County Arts Council are also on Main Street.

Lower Main is also artsy and eclectic. The Holland Thread Mill Factory, a small shops and office building, is the touchstone of architectural excellence due to its restored brick front, small gardens and brick walkways as well as its use as modern apartments and office space.

The Wallace Building, a turn-of-the-century structure and another architectural gem, houses specialty shops such as the Bottom Line, which specializes in stationery and gift items including T-shirts. Across Lower Main is Children's Academic Learning Center (see Child Care), a day-care center for kids whose moms work at local businesses.

East Stroudsburg

Dansbury Depot is the centerpiece of Crystal Street — East Stroudsburg's "main street." A devastating fire in 1996 wiped out many of the stores on Crystal Street, but at press time it was well on its way to recovery. This restored train depot houses a great restaurant by the same name (see our Restaurants chapter). The Depot is enlarging its space and developing several specialty shops to complement its historic position in the town. Across the street at 65 Crystal Street is the nationally acclaimed LIZTECH Jewelry shop, which specializes in custom-made, chromium-mirrored jewelry. East Stroudsburg's main street continues around the corner to Courtland Street and the Pocono Cinema, an art film theater, art gallery and coffee shop (see Arts and Culture). Besides seeing great films you likely won't see at the mall theaters, you can enjoy tempting desserts and espresso, either before or after the movie. Also on Courtland Street is the famous Frazetta Museum (Frazetta is the illustrator of Conan the Barbarian, the famous comic book hero and film character played by Arnold Schwarzenegger). Housed along with the museum is Frazetta's Costume Shop.

Washington Street branches off from Crystal Street and leads you past Kid's Emporium clothing store (see previous "kids Clothing and Toys" section) to Rosen's huge furniture store and the Salvation Army Thrift Store. Plants and Design, on Lenox Avenue (off N. Courtyard Street), is a place to stop for trees, evergreens, shrubs and annuals. Its Christmas Shop is open every holiday season, with ornaments, garlands, wreaths and other seasonal items.

Mount Pocono Area

In Mount Pocono the main street is Pocono Boulevard (Pa. Highway 611). It is about three blocks long, and it is a nice little summer vacation town. The Casino Movie Theater and Ice Cream Shop in the center of town is quaint; it is not a cinema but a small-town movie house. Across the street is Candyland, a must-stop for gummy bears, chocolates and other candies. Also check out James Diamond's jewelry store and the impressive Joan Marie Gallery I, with an incredible assortment of Oriental rugs and antiques from Europe and Asia. If you're still hungry after feasting your eyes on the wonders of Jean Marie Gallery, you'll find pizza at Coffaro's Pizza and bagels at The Bagel Place.

West End

Jim Thorpe

The main street in Jim Thorpe is Broadway, which continues into W. Broadway. It starts at the railroad station (and tourist information center) beside the Lehigh River, passes Market Square and winds up the hill to W. Broadway. Race Street branches off it and forms a Y that leads down to U.S. Highway 209, which parallels the Lehigh River and is part of the street base of Jim Thorpe's shopping area. Take a walk up, down and around these narrow, winding streets with squares, courts and parks reminiscent of picturesque alpine villages of Europe. Shops line the streets as do galleries, museums, the Opera House (see our Arts and Culture chapter for extensive information), eateries, the Dimmick Memorial Library and the Old Jail (see our Attractions chapter).

Train rides leave from the historic station in town from May through October (see our Attractions chapter). Bed and breakfast inns such as Victoria Ann's, Alpine Inn and the Inn at Jim Thorpe are right in the middle of everything on Broadway (see our Bed and Breakfasts and Country Inns chapter).

If you start walking up Broadway from Asa Packer Park, across from the train station, you'll find gem shops, Irish imported linens at the Treasure Shop, antiques at Anne's Early Attic, hand-crafted jewelry at Chatelaine, wicker items at Wicker Works, designer apparel at 97 Broadway, original art and clay items at One White Flower and more antique stores, galleries, unique clothiers and gift shops. For those interested in knowing about positive magic, the Emporium of Curious Goods is a fascinating, floor-to-ceiling packed curiosity shop.

There are even more galleries as you wind onto W. Broadway past the Mauch Chunk Opera House. Race Street is a good place to amble through on your way back down to Susquehanna Street (U.S. 209). Here you'll find artist shops, hobby shops, Scott's Leather Works and Thunder Runners (equestrian items) tucked among the row houses that line this street. An excellent restaurant on Race Street is Black Bread Cafe (see Restaurants); you'll need reservations on weekends for this intimate dining spot.

On W. Broadway there are many little eateries to tempt and nourish you. Of course, the very Irish (direct from Ireland) Emerald Pub in the Inn at Jim Thorpe (see our Restaurants chapter) has excellent cuisine served with all the grace a Culinary Institute Chef would demand. Across the street is the adorable Chunker's, open for lunch and dinner, which serves soups, sandwiches and frozen yogurt in a Victorian dining room or al fresco on weekends in good weather. If pizza pleases your palate, you must stop at Two Brothers Pizza on Broadway. The stuffed vegetable pizza with broccoli, carrots, eggplant, tomatoes and olives is delicious, as are the strombolis.

Milford Area

Before we talk about the town of Milford, we'd like to direct you to a stop in the town of Bushkill, which is south of Milford along U.S. Highway 209. As you pass through Bushkill — part of the Delaware Water Gap National

Recreation Area — divert yourself off U.S. 209 to River Road, where you'll find the Delaware Water Gap National Recreation Area Bookstore.

Milford is a treat; there is an air of elegance. GreyTowers, home of Gov. Pinchot, sets the tone (see our Attractions and Arts and Culture chapters). Milford's main street is the junction of U.S. highways 6 and 209, a crossroads in the center of this bustling town amid museums (see our Arts and Culture chapter) and watersports opportunities (see our In, On and Around the Water chapter). The largest span of shops is at the corner, in the imposing, attached bluestone buildings that form a wall of antiques dealers and exclusive shops. Off this main street is Ann Street, with more antiques shops such as Dottie's Parlour, Paul Schmaltz Antiques and The East Ann Gallery. After you've shopped, revive yourself at Irene's Fudge Emporium (also on Ann Street), with great hot fudge and homemade chocolate; visit them for Easter candy if you can.

On Broad Street you'll find Hare Hollow, which specializes in gift items and collectibles, and Elizabeth Restucci Antiques. You'll also find the Dimmick Inn Steak House (see our Restaurants chapter), at the light, which is great for dining; eat on the porch in nice weather.

On W. Harford Street you'll find The Children's Learning Tree, a book shop specializing in kids literature.

If you venture to the shops at the Upper Mill (follow W. Harford Street from U.S. 6 and turn onto Sixth Street), you'll find Water Wheel Cafe and Bakery. The Upper Mill is a restored mill originally built in the 1800s that is working again today. You can take a self-guided tour through the three-story structure before shopping. Places here that might catch your fancy include Giffard & White for gifts and home accessories, Mill Run Booksellers, Le Monde et Vous for items from around the world, The Other Shoe Store for comfortable footwear and other shops catering to herb lovers, clothing lovers and music lovers.

From Milford, U.S. highways 6 and 209 continue as one route until Matamoras. Before these roads divide, look for Lazy River Booksellers, an offshoot of aforementioned Mill Run Booksellers in Milford.

Lake Wallenpaupack Area

Hawley

Our main street in Hawley is Main Avenue. It's part of a delightful district that starts at its intersection with U.S. Highway 6, runs through town and meanders down over the bridge at the bottom of the street where U.S. 6 continues on its way. There is an old Five-and-Dime specializing in toys, the excellent Gingerbread Gallery on the second floor of 309 Main Avenue (see Arts and Culture), Teeter's Furniture store, Cover to Cover book shop, gift shops and small galleries to discover on this small main street. See this chapter's "What About Antiques?" Close-up to find what awaits you on this main street (and others).

Shopping the Country Roads of the Poconos

In our Getting Around chapter we note the country roads of the Poconos — lovely, fascinating and part of the fabric of our lives. As you go from town to town, you will find many shops — so many and of such variety that we couldn't possibly list them all. We do, however, note a few of the shops you'll pass as you travel through the mountains. Remember, for every two we mention, you'll find two more that catch your eye. Keep looking, drive slowly and enjoy discovering new shopping opportunities.

Pa. Highway 611

From Stroudsburg to Mount Pocono you'll find lots of specialty shops, some minimalls, flea markets, antiques shops and clusters of little cottage shops. Some are noted in other sections throughout this chapter. Others you'll discover on your own.

In **Bartonsville**, look for L. Ion's Country Furnishings, a beautiful store carrying top-of-the-line furniture; about an eighth-mile north of this store is L. Ion's Younger Generation, a shop that opened this fall and specializes in high-end children's furniture. Next to Pocono Go-Karts (see Kidstuff), look for Imaginations, a delightful florist and custom decorating shop.

At Fountain Court you'll find a number of specialty shops, a florist, Chinese food and The World of Stamps and Coins. Teepee Town (see our Native Americans chapter) and Finishing Touches, a decorations and home accessories shop, are here too.

When you get to **Tannersville** (about a mile from Bartonsville), you'll come to Pocono Peddlers Village. There is a flea market here on weekends. You'll also find Beary Best Friends (see this chapter's "Collectibles" section); Ken-Bro Soccer, for soccer equipment, shoes and apparel; Heaven On Earth, a New Age emporium; and The Office Shoppe, practically a small department store of office supplies. There are other shops and a great place to eat, Matti's Deli. For gourmet food, including habañero and jalapeño pepper items, chocolate pasta and praline mustard glaze, check out the Old Country Store on the lower level. Farther along in Tannersville is The Cottages, a little village of shops where you'll find used furniture, collectibles, flowers and gift items. The focal point of The Cottages is Tie-Dye Dave's Hippie Gift Shop — a must for tie-dye T-shirts, sweatshirts, sweatsuits, bandanas and other psychedelia. Also on Pa. 611, you'll pass Stained Glass Creations, Gloria's Furniture, Deer Track Trading Post (see Native Americans) and Villager Card Shop. Merchants Plaza, on this stretch, includes a bank and the Tannersville Pharmacy, a friendly, family-owned establishment whose owner, Tony, is always glad to answer your questions.

Heading toward **Mount Pocono**, you'll pass Planet Earth Gallery, for furniture and home accessories made from natural elements such as wood, stone and sand. Lesh's Leather has a fine selection of leather goods, including moccasins, boots, handbags and jackets. A great stop for ice cream is Eats 'n Sweets (open April to October), and you'd hate yourself for missing Pocono Cheesecake Factory — trust us! If western is your thing, Skip's Western Wear and Boot Corral is a stop for you in **Swiftwater**. An upscale antiques shop on this road is Kelly's Antiques, also in Swiftwater. Watch for it carefully; it is near Connaught Laboratories. Just off Pa. 611 on Grange Road, about a mile past Connaught Laboratories, you'll find Memorytown shops, the Heritage Inn (see Restaurants) and the

charmingly rustic Tavern by the Lake, a great lunch spot if you're not in a hurry.

Pa. Highway 940

Leaving Mount Pocono, you have some choices to make. The road you choose will dictate what shops you pass. But since all the routes wind around into each other, you'll end up seeing everything eventually. So, if you take Pa. 940 eastward toward **Paradise Valley**, you'll find the Arts & Crafters Paradise Bazaar. If you head westward toward Pocono Pines and Blakeslee, you'll find The Booksmith book shop (in Mount Pocono Plaza), Hutton Metalcrafts, specializing in pewter, copper and brass lighting fixtures. You'll also find Christmas items including pewter angels, reindeer, snowmen, wreaths and more. Bendixen's "Bit of Country" is a country gift shop worth the stop. Lake Naomi is on the road to Blakeslee. In **Pocono Pines** you'll also find Gravesend Books, Van Gilder's Jubilee restaurant for breakfast, lunch or dinner, and the Pines Cafe, with a lakefront deck for dining. Outdoor Furniture & Gifts is across from the Jubilee. In **Pocono Lake**, you'll discover The Butcher Shoppe, which not only specializes in prime-cut beef, but also stocks exotic meats such as emu, elk, kangaroo and alligator. You'll also discover Pocono Gun Accessories before you reach Blakeslee. Right before Blakeslee is Timberline Sports Shop, which carries a wide assortment of sporting goods for skiing, fishing and hunting. When you reach **Blakeslee**, Pa. 940 toward Lake Harmony will lead you to Fisherman's Widow Gift Shop and the Evening Hatch Fly Shop.

Pa. Highway 191

This Pennsylvania byway traverses the entire Poconos region. In **Stroudsburg** it takes you to Stroudsmoor and its wonderful little village of shops — Godfrey's Ridge (gift shop and garden center), Victorian Treasures & Vintage Bridals (trousseaus and crocheted ensembles) and Wimbleton's Sellers of Fine Gifts, Art, Antiques. From Analomink, off Pa. 447, you can follow Pa. 191 to the Sterling and Hamlin areas. In **Cresco**, The Country Store is a stop for specialty furniture reproductions.

Holly Ross Pottery is in **La Anna** between Cresco and Newfoundland. Blueberry Hill, a delightful shopping village in **South Sterling**, features the Furniture Barn with two floors of furnishings, Uplander for hunting and fishing equipment, The Paperterie for children's books and party supplies, and both The Fudgery and the Corner Cupboard for tasty treats. All these shops surround the Blueberry Hill Family Restaurant. Farther down the road is the Linden Root Gallery (see our Arts and Culture chapter). U and Nancy's Barn, also in South Sterling, has a great selection of Victorian antiquities and some fine primitives.

Once you've passed though South Sterling, head toward **Hamlin** where you'll find Ursula's Barn (see this chapter's "Collectibles" section). In **Newfoundland** look for The Golden Egg for furniture, collectibles and antiques, and Growers' country store for garden supplies.

Pa. Highway 390

This route has some lovely shopping stops between Cresco and Skytop Resort (see our Accommodations chapter). In **Mountainhome** discover Cooks Tour Gourmet Shop and Cooking School, for every possible cooking need, including books, supplies, accessories and machines. This shop specializes in classes for international — Italian, Asian and others — and low-fat cooking.

Also look for The Other Woman to discover antiques — Victorian, country and primitives. In the Mountainhome area you'll also find Viva, with antiques, accessories and gift items, and Truly Tasteful and both Callie's shops — Candy Kitchen and Pretzel Factory (see this chapter's "Sweets and Eats" section). Also in this little village, you'll find Barron's Book Nook, a great resource for ordering hard-to-find titles. This shop is on-line with Books In Print, and staff can order any book currently in print directly from the publisher. You'll also find sheet music for piano, guitar and voice and can order any music on-line as well.

As you leave Mountainhome and head toward **Canadensis**, watch out for The Kitchen Garden, on Pa. Hwy. 447, in Canadensis. This shop specializes in Everlasting Spices, herbs, herbal products, gift baskets, teas, tea sets and garden accessories to help you plant your own kitchen herb garden.

U.S. Highway 209

This U.S. highway has main and business routes that intersect in **Marshalls Creek** at the junction of Pa. Highway 402. Just before this intersection is the Four Seasons Craft Show in Jay Park Plaza, next to Burgers & Co., which serves burgers (no surprise), fries, salads, milk shakes and tacos to quell your hunger. The Odd-Lot Outlet is in Jay Park Plaza too (see "Outlets, Outlet Complexes and Malls" in this chapter). One of the biggest shopping destinations on U.S. 209 is the indoor/outdoor Pocono Antique Bazaar and Flea Market, open Saturday and Sunday year round. You'll find virtually anything you need for yourself, your family and your home. Near Foxmoor (see "Outlets . . ."), Starting Gate Ski and Sport Shop can outfit you with anything you need for skiing or on-line skating; you'll also find an in-line skating park here (see Kidstuff).

Farther along U.S. 209 at **Bushkill**, next to the Bushkill General Store (groceries and sundries), you'll find the Bushkill Antique and Craft Market. This indoor market is open seven days a week — heated for winter and air-conditioned for summer. Across the road, you'll find Pennsylvania Crafts Gallery, which represents juried members of the Pennsylvania Guild of Craftsmen (see our Arts and Culture chapter).

Heller's Market is in the **Delaware Water Gap National Recreation Area**, north of Bushkill, is open spring through fall for fresh vegetables, fruit, flowers, honey, jellies and jams (see this chapter's "Farmers Markets, Farmstands and Orchards" section). Near the end of the park area in **Dingmans Ferry** is the Phoenix for antiques and gift items.

To supplement nature, the Poconos have a healthy variety of other attractions.

Attractions

The main attractions in the Poconos are the Poconos themselves. Most people come to these mountains for the scenery and a taste of life in the country.

While spending time in the woods is relaxing and enjoyable, some people want a little more activity. For them, after awhile the trees begin to look the same, and the antics of the cute squirrels, which successfully beg for peanuts while other less fortunate rodents lacking bushy tails are hunted by exterminators, become repetitive.

To supplement nature, the Poconos have a healthy variety of other attractions, such as museums, animal farms and play parks.

Many of the places mentioned in this chapter are featured in more detail elsewhere in the book. (For example, museums appear in the Arts and Culture chapter.) Consult our Shopping, Parks, Recreation and In, On and Around the Water chapters for more ideas about things to do.

Delaware Water Gap

Antoine Dutot School & Museum
Pa. Hwy. 611, Delaware Water Gap
• 421-5809

In 1793 Antoine Dutot purchased the land that is Delaware Water Gap. He designed the town, then called Dutotsburg, and in the early 19th century set aside land to be used for religious or educational purposes. Sometime later that century — no one knows exactly when — this school was built. Dutot would be happy to know that as a museum the building still serves an educational purpose, though its days as a school are over.

One classroom of the museum re-creates a school of the 1920s. A bell purchased by Dutot in 1821, which was used until 1969, is still in the building. Another room is filled with local memorabilia such as postcards and photos of the town during its glory days as a resort area. On the first floor, space is available for local artists to display their works.

Arts-and-crafts classes for both children and adults are offered regularly. (See our Arts and Culture chapter for more information.)

Museum hours are Saturday and Sunday, 1 to 5 PM. Donations are accepted.

Shawnee Place Play & Water Park
Exit 52 of I-80, Shawnee-on-Delaware
• 421-7231

Children love the variety of water slides and play areas at this park. They can splash around in the water or frolic in a large bin filled with small plastic balls. Magic shows and supervised hands-on workshops are held throughout the day. (See our Kidstuff chapter for more information.)

Shawnee Place is open daily June 17 to September 2, 10 AM to 5 PM. Adult spectators pay $5. General admission for children ages 2 through 12 is $10; Children less than 40 inches tall get in free.

Water Gap Trolley
Pa. Hwy. 611, Delaware Water Gap
• 476-0010

The trolley features the scenery and history of the Delaware Water Gap area. The three all-weather trolleys take visitors to the scenic overlooks and past such historic sites as the Cold Air Cave, Depuy Mansion, Castle Inn, the Dutot Museum and the famous "Indian Head" rock formation, all explained on the ride . You also will see some homes of the internationally famous jazz musicians who live in the town.

Guides explain the ways the area has changed from the time of Native Americans and early settlers to its emergence as a tourist attraction.

Tours are given every 1½ hours between 10 AM and 4 PM daily. The cost is $5 for adults and $3.50 for children.

Stroudsburg/ East Stroudsburg

Adventure Golf
U. S. Hwy. 209, Marshalls Creek
• 223-9227

A particularly artistic and challenging miniature golf course, Adventure Golf has sharks, bridges and castles among the hazards of its well-thought-out holes. During summer, children can enjoy a ride on the miniature train. A snack bar serves ice cream and sodas.

In spring and summer, Adventure Golf is open daily from 10 AM to 11 PM. Fall hours are noon to 6 PM Friday through Sunday. The train operates only in the summer.

Golf costs $5 for adults and $4 for children younger than 12. The train ride costs $3 per child.

Pocono Country Carriages Inc.
517 Hallet Rd., East Stroudsburg
• 424-6248

What better way to enjoy a ride in the country than in a horse-drawn carriage?

Pocono Country Carriages Inc. offers a 30-minute ride down country roads for $12.50 for adults and $5 for children. In winter, take a 20-minute sleigh ride, complete with bells and velvet blankets, for the same prices.

Other more expensive packages including dinner and/or accommodations are available. A personal favorite is the carriage ride that concludes with dinner at the wonderful Inn at Meadowbrook, a country inn whose atmosphere is exceeded only by its food. The trip and meal cost $95 per couple. For the ideal romantic surprise gift, turn the trip into an overnight stay at the inn, including champagne and a breakfast the next morning — $155 per couple.

Pocono Snake and Animal Farm
U.S. Hwy. 209, Marshalls Creek • 223-8653

Although Siberian tigers, cougars, monkeys and alligators are not native to the Poconos, they are just some of the more than 100 species to be found at the snake farm. Started more than 20 years ago as a glorified collection of about a dozen pets, the privately operated farm has expanded through donations and trades with zoos.

Exhibits explain details about the animals on display. For example, you will learn the death adder, a short, fat snake from Australia, kills half the people it bites, and that the basilisk lizard can run across water for short distances. The alligator snapping turtle, considered the world's largest species of freshwater turtle, lives in the southeastern United States and can grow to weigh as much as 220 pounds. Most of its life is spent immobile at the bottom of a pond.

FYI

Unless otherwise noted, the area code for all phone numbers in this guide is 717.

Many of the animals can be petted or fed. You can even feed the monkeys, bears and alligators! Particularly popular is a very hospitable potbellied pig.

. The snake farm is open 11 AM to 5:30 PM daily from April through November. Admission is $4 for adults and $3 for children ages 2 through 12.

Quiet Valley Living Historical Farm
1000 Turkey Hill Rd., Stroudsburg
• 992-6161

The farm presents the everyday lifestyle of a Pennsylvania Dutch family, several generations of whom lived here from 1765 to 1913.

Costumed in the traditional clothing of the Pennsylvania Dutch, guides and role players give you an idea of what life was like on the farm in the 18th and 19th centuries.

The complex contains 14 buildings, some original and some reconstructed.

Typical daily activities include spinning, weaving, meat smoking and vegetable drying. Depending on the time of the year, you might also witness broom making, butter churning and basket making. Children can pet the farm animals and play on the hay jump in the barn. (See our Arts and Culture chapter for more information. Also consult the Annual Events chapter for information about the Quiet Valley Harvest Festival held every October.)

The farm is open June 20 through Labor Day, Monday through Saturday 9:30 AM to 5:30 PM and Sunday 1 to 5:30 PM. The last tour

begins at 4 PM every day. Admission is $6 for adults; $3.50 for kids ages 3 through 12.

Stroud Community House
900 Main St., Stroudsburg • 421-7703

Stroud Community House is the newly restored home of town founder Jacob Stroud. It serves as the Monroe County Historical Society's museum repository for records, maps and memorabilia including early photos, tools and finished products highlighing area industries, presenting information on Native Americans in the region and showcasing early artifacts and fine art.

Like other county historical museums in the Poconos, this is a good place to go for information on your family history.

The society also operates two smaller museums: The Driebe Freight Station, with general store, Victorian parlor and children's hands-on area, is open noon to 4 PM Wednesday through Saturday from March through December; and the Bell School, a schoolhouse from the 1870s to 1953 that today includes exhibits on the history of Monroe County schools, is open 1 to 4 PM Sundays from June through August.

Stroud Community House is open 10 AM to 4 PM Tuesday through Friday and 1 to 4 PM on Sunday year round. Donations are accepted.

Mount Pocono Area

Camelback Ski Area
Pa. Hwy. 611, Tannersville • 629-1661

Do not mistakenly think this place is only exciting in winter.

The facility has bumper boats, miniature golf, go-carts, a swimming pool, a children's play area and a water slide. Guests can take a scenic chair-lift ride to the top of Camelback Mountain and enjoy the view. You can even get lunch at Cameltop.

For a quick trip down the mountain, try the Alpine Slide, a one-seat bobsled.

Hours of operation are 10 AM to 5:30 PM Monday through Friday and 10 AM to 6 PM

Saturday and Sunday from June 21 through September 2; 10 AM to 5:30 PM weekends only from May 18 through June 16; 11 AM to 5 PM weekends from September 7 through October 19; and 11 AM to 4 PM weekends from October 20 through November 3. Combination admission tickets, which allow unlimited use of all facilities except go-carts, are $19.95 for adults and $14.95 for juniors 33 to 48 inches tall. Individual tickets also are available for either $2 or $5, depending on the ride. Group rates are available. Call for more information.

> **FYI**
> Unless otherwise noted, the area code for all phone numbers in this guide is 717.

Colony Village
Pa. Hwy. 447, Canadensis • 595-0604

Among the gift shops and eating places at Colony Village are an outstanding mineral museum and mine replica. Also on the grounds are the 1867 McComas Church Chapel, a petrified forest and horseback riding.

The village is open 10 AM to 5 PM Friday through Monday, but call ahead because hours often vary. Admission is free to all the stores and attractions. A separate fee is charged for horseback riding (See our Recreation chapter for information on horseback riding and rates.)

Moyer Aviation Inc.
Pocono Mountains Municipal Airport • Pa. Highway 611, Mount Pocono • 839-7161

See the Poconos from the air on one of Moyer's air tours. The Mountain Tour lasts 10 minutes and circles Mount Pocono. The slightly longer Delaware Water Gap Tour ($15 per person) heads south over the Stroudsburgs and the famous Water Gap. The 25-minute Lake Harmony Tour ($25) flies over many lakes and Pocono Raceway (see this chapter's sidebar). The 30-minute Lake Wallenpaupack Tour ($32) offers views of the lake, Tobyhanna Army Depot, Skytop and Buck Hill Falls. You also can spend 30 minutes above the West End and see the Beltzville Lake area ($32).

Tours are available daily from 8 AM to sunset throughout the year. Call for reservations.

The Pennsylvania Dutch Farm Inc.
Grange Rd., Mount Pocono • 839-7680

Spend the day on an Amish farm and enjoy petting the farm animals, sampling fresh-baked cookies and pies and viewing exhibits that explain the Amish lifestyle and customs. Another unique treat are the Falabella (miniature) horses.

The farm is open April 15 through November 30 daily from 10 AM to 5 PM. The rest of the year it is open Saturdays and Sundays from 10 AM to 5 PM. Admission is $4 for adults and $3 for kids ages 2 through 12.

Pocono Historical Museum
Pa. Hwy. 611, Scotrun • 629-0700

Among the classic vehicles at this museum are a 1904 Horseless Carriage (top speed: 15 mph), a 1966 Lincoln convertible, a 1952 Vespa circus car that could hold 10 clowns and a 1920 Hudson Touring Car.

In addition to cars, the museum has vintage fire-fighting equipment, farm and construction equipment and an exhibit of old local postcards and period farmhouse furnishings. Other rooms house model ships up to 200 years old, toys, typewriters, old radios, ice-cream freezers and hundreds of antique household tools.

The museum is open June 15 through October 31 daily from 10 AM to 4 PM. Admission is $4 for adults, $3 for senior citizens, $2 for kids ages 6 through 12 and free for children 5 and younger.

West End

Cathedral Rock Climbing Gym
226 S. First St., Lehighton • (610) 377-8822

The inside of an 1842 church has been converted into a climber's paradise with more than 6,000 square feet of accessible area. Corners, cracks, slabs, overhangs, chimneys, mantels, roofs and caves will challenge climbers of all levels of experience.

Lessons are available. Admission is $11;

lessons cost $33. Call for group rates and private party options.

Cathedral Rock is open Wednesday through Friday, noon to 3 PM and 6 to 10 PM. It is also open Saturday from noon to 10 PM and Sunday from noon to 9 PM.

Hooven Building H.O. Model Train Display
41 Susquehanna St., Jim Thorpe
• 325-2248

On the second floor of the old Hooven Mercantile Company building, this two-level display boasts 13 separate trains pulling a total of 60 cars along nearly 1,100 feet of track. The elaborate re-creation contains more than 200 miniature buildings, 100 bridges, 1,000 street lights and 80 cars and trucks.

The display is open Monday through Friday from noon to 5 PM and Saturday and Sunday from 10 AM to 5 PM, July through October. It is open Saturday and Sunday from noon to 5 PM the rest of the year. Admission is $3 for adults, $2 for seniors 64 and older and $1 for children ages 6 through 14.

JEM Classic Car Museum
Pa. Hwy. 443, Andreas • 386-3554

OK, we concede this place is technically just outside the Poconos region, but if you're already in the West End, it's worth the trip.

Ranging from a 1902 Oldsmobile to a 1966 Plymouth Hemi, this collection has something for every car lover.

The most rare item is the 1929 Graham-Paige LeBaron Body Dual Cowl Phaeton, which is believed to be one of only two in existence. More familiar are such staples of the 1950s as a Corvette, T-Bird, Kaiser Darrin and Hudson Hornet.

In addition to cars, JEM has motorcycles dating from 1916 to 1968, 30 large-scale airplanes and juke box, antique doll and carousel horse displays.

INSIDERS' TIPS

If you can, please leave a donation, however modest, at the smaller museums and attractions that accept them. Most of them are staffed by volunteers and receive little outside funding. They need this money to remain open.

Pocono Raceway

It used to be a spinach farm.

Walking around Pocono Raceway these days, one has a hard time imagining the land being home to anything but racing. Excitement surrounds the track, even on non-race days. A stroll down the main straightaway, which you might expect would seem like wandering an abandoned parking lot, actually becomes a privileged experience — probably similar to a baseball fan standing at home plate in Yankee Stadium.

A ride around the track in an ordinary street truck is exhilarating. Trees fly by as the vehicle climbs the curves and accelerates coming out of them. Somehow, mere driving becomes racing — a glance at the speedometer indicates only 55 mph, though it feels closer to 200. (Makes you wonder what the real thing is like.)

Two weekends every summer stock-car racing's finest drivers return to the mountains to do battle on this strip of macadam. There are only four 2.5-mile tracks in the country, and the most unique is in the Poconos at Long Pond.

Almost as colorful as the races at Pocono is the track's history. A group of area businessmen, including Dr. Joseph Mattioli, purchased 1,025 acres of woods and spinach fields and began constructing the track in the early 1960s. By working through winters, the contractors had Pocono ready for the first event on its .75-mile oval in 1969; the initial 500-mile race on the 2.5-mile oval, the Schaefer 500, was run in 1971.

Today, of the original visionaries, only "Doc" Mattioli remains involved. His son, Joseph III, supervises the day-to-day operation of the track.

"Our first event was rained out, snowed out and fogged out," said Joseph Mattioli about the super-modified race that was rescheduled three times from October 1968 to May 1969. "We had a streak of the worst weather imaginable." The frequently uncooperative weather in the Poconos still occasionally plays havoc with the race schedule. Races have also been delayed by a stray deer or bear wandering onto the track, reminding everyone that, in spite of all the exhaust, they are still in the country.

The ultimate weather problem occurred during the track's second year of operation when Hurricane Agnes devastated the facility. After recovering from this, the Mattiolis went on to face financial difficulties that almost closed Pocono on two occasions. High mortgage rates and the energy crisis in the 1970s threatened the raceway. And while several other major tracks closed at that time, including Ontario, Trenton and Langhorne, Pocono managed to survive.

Part of the reason for the raceway's success is its easy accessibility for people from New York, Philadelphia and all of New Jersey. "We can draw from 60 million people who live within a 200-mile radius of the Poconos," Mattioli said.

While most people tend to associate stock-car racing with the South, many small ovals thrive in the Northeast. "Our area is a hotbed of racing activity," Mattioli said, while citing a long list of places that host weekend races. "Racing has long been established as a popular family activity here."

Given racing's longstanding popularity in the Poconos as early as the 1960s — and with thousands of fans waiting for someone to take the sport to the next level — the Mattiolis held on to their dream of hosting a 500-mile event.

That race ran on schedule in 1971. But, true to the edge-of-the-seat nature of the early days at Pocono Raceway, the Mattiolis cut things close.

Guiding You Through History.

The Lackawanna Heritage Valley Authority

(LHVA) is a partnership of government, business, community organizations and individuals. The LHVA mission is to convey the story of the Valley to residents and visitors through education and interpretation. Here are just a few of the many area attractions designed to link our past and present, through cultural, natural and recreational resources.

Steamtown National Historic Site ↗

Lackawanna Coal Mine Tour ↗

Anthracite Heritage Museum →

Lackawanna Heritage Valley Authority
1300 Old Plank Road Mayfield, PA 18433
Phone 717-876-6188   Fax 717-876-6199
e-mail - lhva@lydian.scranton.com

Steamtown National Historic Site

Discover the heritage of rail travel in the Eastern United States at Steamtown National Historic Site. Here, the National Park Service preserves the wonder of railroading at the Scranton Yard of the Delaware, Lackawanna & Western Railroad. A full history of transportation is presented through the exhibits, tours and aboard steam locomotive-powered excursions. The site also features a visitor center, theater, museum complex, special tours and performances. For more information call: **(717) 340-5200.**

Lackawanna Coal Mine Tour

Go down in history and explore 300-ft. beneath the earth in an actual mine. Learn from a real miner about life and hard coal times in the city that was once the anthracite capital of the world. Distinctive anthracite jewelry and convenient food service make this a terrific American history adventure for families or groups. Located in picturesque McDade Park, with outdoor activities available in every season. For more information call: **(717) 963-MINE.**

Pennsylvania Anthracite Heritage Museum

Explore the story of immigration and industry in the Anthracite Region. From the Paleo Indians to recent arrivals, experience the lives and labors of those who settled Northeastern Pennsylvania. Learn the history of the Hard Coal Region - at work, play and in the home through artifacts, images, sound and video. Visit the Museum Store for distinctive and educational gifts and books. For more information call: **(717) 963-4804.**

Everhart Museum

Since 1908, the Everhart Museum has been a center of arts and natural history in Northeastern Pennsylvania. Located within Nay Aug Park, the museum houses a variety of collections, including a bird gallery, dinosaur hall, fossils, rocks and minerals, mammals, American Folk Art, 19th and 20th Century American Art, Arts of the Oriental, African and Oceanic Societies and an ever changing exhibit gallery. $ for special exhibits. For special events and programs call **(717) 346-7186.**

LACKAWANNA COUNTY STADIUM

Take in all the excitement of professional minor league baseball at the beautiful Lackawanna County Stadium, the home of the **Scranton/Wilkes-Barre Red Barons,** Triple A Affiliate of the Philadelphia Phillies. And when the temperature falls, hit the ice on the Stadium's giant NHL-style ice rink, open from December 'til March. No matter what the season, you can enjoy terrific food and drink along with the great view at **The Stadium Club,** a stylish bar and restaurant overlooking the field action.

LACKAWANNA COUNTY STADIUM
Exit 51 Off I-81 Montage Mountain Road
(717) 963-2255
The Stadium Club Restaurant
(717) 963-6441

A Lackawanna County Facility   Joseph Corcoran, Ray Alberigi & John Senio, Commissioners

MONTAGE MOUNTAIN

Winter & Summer Resort

Ski Magazine consistently rates Montage as one of the premier ski facilities. From our friendly, wide open cruising terrain to the challenge of our newest Double Diamond slope "White Lightning," to the knee-knockin'est bump runs in the region — Montage means great, affordable skiing for the entire family. In June we convert the Mainline Trail near our base lodge into an outstanding outdoor concert spot, Montage Center for the Performing Arts. Crowds as large as 17,000 have enjoyed world class acts like: Sting, Hootie & the Blowfish, Rod Stewart, Bob Seger, Boyz II Men, Van Halen, Bon Jovi, Aerosmith, Reba McEntire, and Bob Dylan just to name a few.

MONTAGE MOUNTAIN
Exit 51 Off I-81
(717) 969-7669   1-800-468-7669

A Lackawanna County Facility   Joseph Corcoran, Ray Alberigi & John Senio, Commissioners

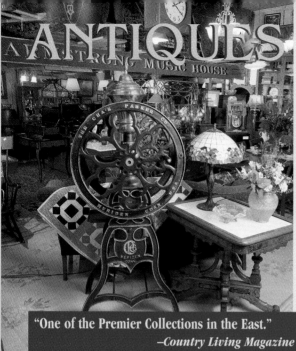

Photo: Brian Hineline

Mark Martin's pit crew changes tires and fills the gas tank during a pit stop.

Driver Wally Dallenbach visited the facility a month before the race and swore the track could not be ready in time. The finishing touches, such as painting seat numbers on the bleachers, were completed the night before race day. "We might have had some people walk out with 'N-22' on their backs," said Mattioli with a laugh that hinted of only slight exaggeration.

While Indy-car races, such as the Schaefer, were the main draw in the early days at Pocono, they ended in 1989 after becoming increasingly less profitable. Fortunately for the Mattiolis, the stock-car races have proven more popular than ever expected.

The track was constructed to accommodate both Indy and stock cars, and the two types shared the track for several years. Designed by two-time Indianapolis 500 winner Roger Ward, the raceway is a true tri-oval because it features only three curves instead of the usual four, each banked differently: a high-banked curve for stock cars, a flat one for Indy cars and a mid-banked curve with a pitch that falls between the other two.

Because of the nature of the countryside, Pocono Raceway lacks symmetry, making each turn an entirely different adventure. This poses many problems for drivers. Adding to drivers' headaches are three straightaways of varied lengths. The track's investors originally were hoping for a design similar to Daytona's or Indianapolis' Motor Speedway. That goal proved impossible, but they actually got a better track. Pocono provides an unmatched test of both equipment and driver skill because race cars cannot be set up for any one set of conditions; Pocono has them all. Many racers consider Pocono the toughest track in the country to successfully negotiate.

Racers at Pocono are the best the world of motor sports has to offer. Drivers such as Dale Earnhardt, Jeff Gordon, Bill Elliott and Ernie Irvan have hundreds of thousands of fans across the country. The main difference between auto racing and many other professional sports is that participants risk their lives every time they suit up. Mistakes are potentially deadly, and constant, quick thinking is essential. And although the drivers take the risks and receive the recognition, racing is a team sport that includes pit crews, car owners and families.

Stock-car racers, as much as any other professional athletes, inspire groups of loyal followers. Because the drivers are racing at speeds approaching 200 mph in cars that are actually modified versions of everyday street vehicles, fans often choose a favorite driver

Photo: Brian Hineline

Jeff Gordon is one of the NASCAR stars who races at Pocono Raceway.

based on the model of his car. Most drivers are ordinary guys without inflated egos, and many stop to pose for pictures and spend time with their admirers. To encourage the relationship between the fans and the drivers, Pocono Raceway created Autograph Alley, near the pits, where people go to get autographs, swap stories and ask questions.

The family atmosphere that characterizes stock-car races extends to the raceway staff as well. "There are people who have worked here for more than 20 years," Mattioli said. "Our staff swells to nearly 1,000 people on race day; and everyone, from firefighters to hot dog vendors, takes a degree of pride in their work. Many are executives who work at Pocono just to be a part of racing. They all know that, to some extent, the race could not happen without them.

"I have worked in nearly every department. I started at the track while going to high school and college," he said. "In addition to his duties as chief executive officer, my father still drives equipment and does all different kinds of repair work. Neither one of us is going to ask anyone to do something that we would not do. Often, we probably already have done the job ourselves at some time over the years. Once we had snow before a race; and everyone, from front office personnel on down, grabbed a shovel and helped clear the track."

While the Mattioli family and their staff essentially spend an entire year preparing for two weekends (on those days, Joseph III considers himself to be the mayor of a large city, because he supervises the safety of and the services for thousands of people), the track sees additional action. Motorcycle races and car tests are scheduled regularly.

All this activity brings thousands of people to the Pocono Mountains. Naturally, the money they leave behind gives the area's economy much-needed revenue and creates many jobs for residents. Based on an average annual attendance figure of more than 100,000, the Pocono Mountains Chamber of Commerce estimates Pocono Raceway's economic impact on Pennsylvania at more than $158,000,000 each year. The majority of race fans, more than 60 percent in fact, come from out of state and stay in the Poconos for several days, filling hotels, restaurants and most shops for the entire weekend.

The Mattiolis were recognized by Gov. Robert Casey, the Pennsylvania House of Representatives and the Pennsylvania State Senate for the raceway's economic contributions to the state. In addition to the financial benefits, Pocono races are televised nationally, giving the region millions of dollars worth of media exposure.

However, watching at home is not the proper way to experience a race. Like many other great sporting events, racing must be seen first-hand to be fully appreciated. Those who view a race on television miss the carnival-like atmosphere that precedes the nail-biting excitement. They miss the opportunity for a family picnic or a tail-gate party. At Pocono, both are possible within the huge infield (200 football fields could fit in it), which offers fans the chance to celebrate within the event rather than outside it. A thoughtful consideration: This space is separated into two distinct areas, allowing guests the opportunity to choose either the families' side or the partiers' side.

To understand that stock-car racing is more than a start, a finish and a couple of accidents in between, visit Pocono Raceway in June or in July. Watch the pit crews service cars in seconds. Develop an appreciation for the subtleties of driving strategy, such as when to pass and when to pit for fuel. Watch pit crews change four tires and fill a gas tank in approximately 20 seconds. See a burst of every imaginable color as cars roar by, only to be replaced by a completely different rainbow a few seconds later. Second-guess the drivers as they second-guess each other. Most importantly, pick a car and imagine yourself behind the wheel. Stock-car racing, more than anything else, offers spectators an opportunity to fantasize about driving in a way that defies traffic laws and common sense. We can't drive bumper-to-bumper at 200 mph on Interstate 80, but we can dream about it at Pocono Raceway.

You can view the collection daily from May 30 through October 31. Hours are 10 AM to 4 PM Monday through Friday and noon to 4 PM Saturday and Sunday. Admission is $4 for adults; $3.50 for senior citizens; $2.50 for kids ages 5 through 12; and free for children 4 and younger.

Mauch Chunk Museum and Cultural Center
41 W. Broadway, Jim Thorpe • 325-9190

The original stone structure, built in 1843, housed St. Paul's Methodist Church until 1978.

The museum tells the story of Mauch Chunk, including a 30-foot replica of its Switchback Railroad. (See our History chapter's Closeup for the story of this colorful mode of transportation.)

Other exhibits explain the importance of the region's early industries, teach visitors how a canal lock worked, discuss the presence of the Lenape Indians and reveal how the town came to be renamed for a legendary Olympic athlete. See our Arts and Culture chapter for more information.

The museum is open Thursday through Saturday from 10:30 AM to 5 PM and Sunday from noon to 5 PM. It is open by appointment only in January, February and March. Donations are accepted.

The Old Jail Museum
127 W. Broadway, Jim Thorpe • 325-5259

Built in 1871, the jail was where seven members of the Molly Maguires, a secret society founded in Ireland around 1843, were executed by hanging between 1877 and '79. These anthracite miners applied terrorist acts in an effort to force implementation of improved working conditions; as a result, they were hated by the mine owners and bosses. The Molly Maguires were accused of murder, though many considered the accusations unfounded. One of the men placed his hand against the wall of his cell prior to his execution and claimed that the handprint would remain there forever as a symbol of his innocence. It is still visible in Cell 17, although the wall has been washed and painted over.

The 72-room structure includes 29 cells, a warden's apartment and a 16-cell dungeon. It served as the county jail until 1995. Guided and self-guided tours are available. The last guided tour leaves at 4 PM daily.

The jail is open May 18 through October 31 from noon to 5 PM every day except Wednesday. Admission is $4 for adults, $3.50 for seniors and students with identification and $2.50 for children ages 6 to 12.

Asa Packer Mansion
Packer Hill, Jim Thorpe • 325-3229

Industrialist Asa Packer had interests in mining, canal boats and the Lehigh Railroad. He founded Lehigh University and ran for President of the United States in 1868. He lived a lavish existence in this mansion.

Built in 1860 by European craftsmen, the mansion and its contents are the same as they were in 1878 when Packer and his wife celebrated their golden wedding anniversary. In the library are a desk, chair and bookcase from Gen. Robert E. Lee. The crystal chandelier in the drawing room was used in the movie *Gone with the Wind*. Throughout the house you'll find hand-carved furniture, paintings, sculptures, china and gold-leaf walls.

The mansion is open 11 AM to 4:15 PM

daily from Memorial Day through October 31. It's open the same hours on weekends throughout April and May. Admission is $5 for folks 12 and older and $3 for kids 11 and younger.

Pocono Museum Unlimited
517 Ashtown Dr., Lehighton • 386-3117

Claiming to be one of the largest O-scale model train displays of its type in the country, this museum's layout contains 16 trains rolling down more than 2,000 feet of track. A highway contains moving vehicles; an amusement park has 16 operating rides. Did we mention the drive-in movie theater, the 40-foot-long lake with live fish and the zoo? Just don't get caught without an umbrella in the display's rain storm complete with thunder and lightning. Among the models are 105 structures, 705 vehicles, 10,800 trees, 4,043 lights and three waterfalls.

Hours of operation are 10 AM to 5 PM daily from January 1 through May 31; 10 AM to 5 PM Wednesday through Monday from June 1 through Labor Day; noon to 5 PM weekdays and 10 AM to 5 PM Saturday and Sunday from after Labor Day until December 31. Admission is $4 for adults; $3 for seniors 60 and older; $2 for kids ages 5 through 12; and free for children 4 and younger. Group rates are available.

St. Mark's Episcopal Church
Race St., Jim Thorpe • 325-2241

This ornate, Gothic Revival church, built in 1869 and still in use, features an altar of white Italian marble, Tiffany stained-glass windows and one of the older working elevators in the nation. The stone carving behind the altar is a replica of one in St. George Chapel in England's Windsor Castle.

The church is open for tours from Memorial Day through October 31; daily hours are 1 to 3:30 PM. It's open the same hours on weekends in April and May. Admission is $2.

FYI

Unless otherwise noted, the area code for all phone numbers in this guide is 717.

Yesterday's Train Today
Train Depot • U.S. Hwy. 209, Jim Thorpe • 325-4606

Relive the days when as many as nine trains per hour passed through Jim Thorpe. The steam engine pulls out of the town's train depot May 11 through September 2 on Saturdays, Sundays and holidays at noon, 1 PM and 2 PM for a 40-minute, 8-mile excursion through the Lehigh River Gorge and around the mountains. From September 7 through September 29, the train makes an additional run at 3 PM. The cost is $5 for anyone 3 and older. Children younger than 2 ride for free.

Longer outings also are available. The *Hometown Trestle Special* covers 32 miles in 2½ hours, and the *Lake Hauto Special* goes 20 miles in just less than two hours. The Hometown leaves every Saturday between May 25 and August 31 at 3 PM and costs $9 for folks 12 and older and $5 for children ages 2 through 11; children younger than 2 ride for free. The *Lake Hauto*, which travels on Sundays during the same period, also leaves at 3 PM. It costs $8 for anyone 12 and older, $4 for children ages 2 through 11 and is free for tots younger than 2.

Throughout October, Flaming Foliage Rambles are scheduled. The 34-mile trip takes just less than three hours and costs $14 for anyone 12 and older, $7 for children ages 2 through 11 and free for kids younger than 2. These trips often sell out prior to departure, so call ahead for schedule and reservation information.

Milford Area

Bushkill Falls
Bushkill Falls Road, Bushkill • 588-6682

Billed as the "Niagara of Pennsylvania," Bushkill certainly is one of the most impressive

Photo: Pocono Mountains Vacation Bureau, Inc.

The Poconos offers four season fun.

waterfalls in the region. Surrounded by moss, ferns and wild flowers, the Bushkill Creek plunges off a 100-foot cliff into a deep pool.

Four different trails wander through the woods. The green trail, the shortest and easiest, is a 15-minute walk to the main falls. The yellow and blue trails go farther into the woods — 45 minutes and 1½ hours respectively for a round trip — and take visitors to more falls and the beautiful Upper Canyon and Laurel Glen. If you like rugged hikes, take the orange trail. It's the longest, covering nearly 2 miles of slightly steep, wooded terrain; you will need at least two hours to complete it.

Also on the property are gift shops, miniature golf, fishing, paddle boats, ice cream and fudge shops and a Native American exhibit.

Bushkill Falls is open daily April through November from 9 AM to dusk. Admission is $7 for anyone 11 and older, $6.25 for seniors 62 and older and $1 for ages 4 through 10.

The Columns
608 Broad St., Milford • 296-8126

This distinctive building houses the museum of the Pike County Historical Society.

The museum recently received national attention when tests confirmed that the bloodstained flag in its collection was used to cradle President Abraham Lincoln's head after he was shot at Ford's Theater in 1865.

A significant exhibit is devoted to Charles S. Peirce — philosopher, logician, scientist and founder of pragmatism — who lived near Milford from 1887 until his death in 1914.

Museum hours are 1 to 4 PM Wednesday, Saturday and Sunday year round. Admission is $2 per person. See our Arts and Culture chapter for more information about The Columns.

Grey Towers
U.S. Hwy. 6, Milford • 296-6401

Grey Towers is the former home of two-term Pennsylvania governor Gifford Pinchot. He also founded the United States Department of Agriculture Forest Service. In 1963 President John F. Kennedy visited Milford to acknowledge Pinchot's conservation efforts.

His magnificent French-style château provides panoramic views of Milford and the Delaware River Valley. Its rooms are fully furnished, and memorabilia is exhibited throughout. Allow at least an hour to tour the building and the grounds. Guided tours are given every hour. The property is maintained by the USDA Forest Service.

Grey Towers is open Memorial Day through Labor Day from 10 AM to 4 PM daily. The suggested donation is $2. See our Arts and Culture chapter for more information.

The Pennsylvania Fishing Museum
Pecks Pond Store • Pa. Hwy. 402, Pecks Pond • 775-7237

This museum features exhibits of vintage fishing equipment including creels, rods, reels and lures. Also on display are early fly- and ice-fishing tools, motors, decoys and folk art. Anglers will enjoy comparing their equipment to that used decades ago.

The museum is in the Pecks Pond Store near Pecks Pond. Look for the large wooden fisherman outside.

Hours of operation are 9 AM to 6 PM daily, spring through fall; call for winter hours. Admission is $4 for anyone 13 and older and $2 for kids ages 6 through 12.

The Pocono Indian Museum
U.S. Hwy. 209, Bushkill • 588-9338

Artifacts and exhibits at this museum depict the history of Northeastern Pennsylvania from 10,500 B.C. until the arrival of European settlers just prior to the American Revolution. You can see examples of bark houses, pottery and weapons and learn how the Delaware Indians were nearly eliminated by whites over a period of roughly 100 years. (See our Native Americans chapter for more information.)

The 30-minute, self-guided tour is accompanied by an audio recording.

A gift shop sells Native American-related items, including clothing, toys, jewelry, pottery and literature.

The Pocono Indian Museum is open 9:30 AM to 5:30 PM daily. Admission is $3.50 for adults, $2.50 for seniors age 62 and older and $2 for children ages 6 through 16.

Zane Grey Museum
Scenic Dr., Lackawaxen • 685-4871

Regarded as the "Father of the Western Novel," Zane Grey lived in Lackawaxen from 1905 to 1918. The museum, operated by the National Park Service, is in Grey's former house.

The former office and study now house Grey's memorabilia, exhibits, photographs and books. Original artwork and manuscripts are among the collection.

While Grey lived in New York City around the turn of the century, he regularly visited the Lackawaxen area to fish. On one of these trips he met his future wife, Lina Elise Roth, while canoeing near the Delaware House. With her encouragement, he overcame early professional rejection and became a successful writer. Roth helped finance Grey's first novel, *Betty Zane*, which was published in 1903.

By 1905, Grey gave up his New York dental practice and the couple moved to Lackawaxen. Grey's first western novel, *The Heritage of the Desert* (1910), and his most famous, *Riders of the Purple Sage* (1912), both were published while he lived here.

The Park Service staff conducts guided tours, which take a minimum of 30 minutes. Souvenirs and copies of Grey's books still in print are available for sale.

The museum is open Memorial Day through Labor Day, noon to 5 PM daily; from mid-April until Memorial Day, and from after Labor Day to October 31, it's open Saturday and Sunday from noon to 4 PM. Admission is free. See our Arts and Culture chapter for more information.

Lake Wallenpaupack Area

Carousel Water & Fun Park
Pa. Hwy. 652, Beach Lake • 729-7532

This fun-park complex has water slides, bumper boats, go-carts, miniature golf, a batting cage, game room, Kiddie Kars, a snack bar and a picnic area.

The park is open Memorial Day through Labor Day, 11 AM to 10 PM daily; it's open the same hours on weekends in spring and fall. Admission is free; you pay for rides on an individual basis. A pay-one-price option, good from 11 AM to 6 PM, is available.

Cherrywood Fun Park
Pa. Hwy. 196, Sterling • 676-9920, (800) 624-1369

Cherrywood claims to have the largest indoor playland in the Poconos. Kids will enjoy the games, rides and outdoor miniature golf. The arcade boasts more than 80 games. Food, such as burgers, fries and pizza, is available.

The park is open daily year round from 10 AM to 10 PM. Admission is free; all rides are purchased with tokens, which cost 25 cents. Most games require one or two tokens.

Claws 'N' Paws Wild Animal Park
Pa. Hwy. 590, Hamlin • 698-6154

More than 100 species are featured in this wooded animal park. Rare animals include a white tiger and a snow leopard. Plus there are plenty of monkeys, wolves, bears, otters, parrots, snakes and an alligator. Special exhibits are devoted to farm animals, birds of prey and parrots. You will also have a chance to pet the alligator or the python.

Allow at least two hours to see everything.

Claws 'N' Paws is open May 1 through October 27 daily from 10 AM to 6 PM. Admission is $7.95 for anyone 12 and older; $7.25 for seniors 65 and older and $4.95 for kids ages 2 through 11. Call for discounted group rates.

Costa's Family Fun Park
U.S. Hwy. 6, Lords Valley • 226-8585, (800) 928-4386

Costa's specializes in finding something fun to do for every member of the family. Young children can peddle non-motorized go-carts or use the toys in a supervised climbing and slide area. Older kids can take a few swings in the batting cages or race the Indy-, IROC- and Jaguar-style go-carts. You'll find plenty of arcade favorites in the game room. Plus there's an 18-hole miniature golf course and a driving range. An air-conditioned restaurant and outdoor porch provide food.

The park is open 11 AM to midnight daily from Memorial Day through Labor Day and on weekends the rest of the year. Admission is free; you pay for each attraction individually. The children's play area is $3 per hour or $5 for the entire day. Other activities cost between $2.50 and $5.50 each.

Dorflinger Glass Museum
Long Ridge Rd., White Mills • 253-1185

More than 600 pieces of Dorflinger glass are displayed here. The company, established

---

INSIDERS' TIPS

When taking pictures outside at Poconos atttractions, remember to place the sun off to the side or over the shoulder of your subject to avoid the squinty-eye look. Also, to avoid stiff poses, have your subjects do something rather than just stand still. Candid shots look more relaxed.

Some of the top drivers in professional racing compete at Pocono International Raceway.

in White Mills in 1862, was known around the world as one of the best glass makers. Presidents Lincoln and Wilson both used Dorflinger glassware.

On a bright day, the sun shines through the museum windows, and the glassware is magically illuminated, taking on a colorful identity. The exhibit contains examples of cut, enameled, etched, gilded and engraved glass.

The museum is part of the Dorflinger-Suydam Wildlife Sanctuary, a 600-acre conservation area that hosts a variety of cultural activities during the summer (see our Parks, Annual Events, Shopping and Arts and Culture chapters for more information).

The on-site gift shop contains glass souvenirs, Christmas ornaments and an extensive collection of books on glassware.

The museum is open May 13 through October 29. Hours are 10 AM to 4 PM Wednesday through Saturday and 1 to 4 PM Sunday. Admission is $3 for adults, $2.50 for seniors 55 and older and $1.50 for children ages 6 through 18.

Golf Park Plus
Golf Park Dr., Lake Ariel • 689-4996

Two miniature golf courses contain unexpected hazards such as roughs, sand traps, water, islands and bridges. Other facilities include bumper boats, go-carts, a scenic train ride and a driving range. A snack bar and arcade also are available.

The park is open daily 10 AM to 10 PM from May through October. Admission is free; attractions are priced individually. Miniature golf is $5; bumper boats, $5.25 for 10 minutes; driving range, $4 for 40 balls; and go-carts, $5.

See our Golf chapter for information on the driving range.

Stourbridge Rail Excursion
742 Main St., Honesdale • 253-1960, (800) 433-9008

This steam engine train takes scenic excursions throughout the year. In spring, ride the rails on a two-hour trip with the Easter Bunny. Theme trips in summer include Great Train Robbery Runs, Dinner Theater and a Bavarian Festival. Fall brings a number of popular fall foliage outings, such as a 4½-hour trip along the Lackawaxen River with stops at the Zane Grey Museum and Roebling Bridge. Ghosts take over the train for Halloween. Santa and Mrs. Claus bring treats for children on the Santa Express held several times in early December.

The trips begin in downtown Honesdale.

The Dinner Theater costs $40 per person; the Bavarian Festival, $26; the Great Train Robbery Runs, $12; and the Fall Foliage, $17.50. All the other excursions cost $10. Call for the specific dates and reservations.

Photo: Pocono Mountains Vacation Bureau, Inc.

Wayne County Historical Society Museum
810 Main St., Honesdale • 253-3240

A replica of the *Stourbridge Lion*, the first steam engine train to run in the United States, is housed at the museum. The *Lion* made its historic trip near Honesdale. The original train is part of the collection at the Smithsonian Institution in Washington, D.C.

The museum has an outstanding collection of mining and canal photos, tools and other memorabilia. The city of Honesdale was founded as a port for trains hauling coal from the Lackawanna County anthracite regions to New York City. The coal was placed on canal boats in Honesdale.

The museum is open January and February on Saturday from 10 AM to 4 PM; March, April and May from 1 PM to 4 PM on Wednesday, Thursday and Friday and 10 AM to 4 PM on Saturday; June through September, 10 AM to 4 PM Monday and Wednesday through Saturday; and October through December 1 PM to 4 PM Monday and Wednesday through Friday and 10 AM to 4 PM on Saturday. Admission is $2.

Slate Belt

The Martin Guitar Company
510 Sycamore St., Nazareth
• (610) 759-2837

For more than 155 years, The Martin Guitar Company has been producing some of the world's finest acoustic guitars in Nazareth.

The list of famous musicians who have owned or played a Martin is a veritable who's who of industry giants. Although the company does not pay performers to endorse their products, notable guitarists/songwriters such as Eric Clapton, Bob Dylan, Johnny Cash, Elvis Presley, Hank Williams Sr. and all the Beatles except Ringo were/are avid Martin fans.

The company produces fewer than 10,000 guitars annually. Skilled luthiers on staff perform specialized tasks; roughly 25 people work to produce a single guitar.

Because of the extensive hand labor and expensive materials involved in production, Martin guitars are not cheap. The list price on the low-end models is around $1,500. Custom instruments can exceed $7,000. The company also produces lower-priced guitars that are assembled in Nazareth using imported parts.

On the guided tour, which lasts approximately an hour, you will see all aspects of guitar construction and string manufacturing. Also at the factory are a museum, which includes a guitar made in 1834 by C.F. Martin and a ukulele that accompanied Adm. Byrd to the North Pole, and a store offering Martin accessories and memorabilia.

The museum and store are open year round Monday through Friday from 9 AM to 5 PM. Tours are given Monday through Friday at 1:15 PM. The company is closed on holidays. Admission is free.

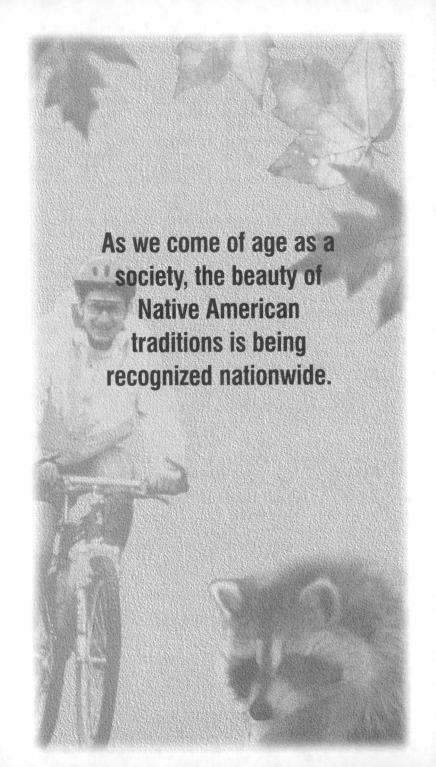

As we come of age as a society, the beauty of Native American traditions is being recognized nationwide.

Native Americans

The history of the Native Americans in the Poconos region fills volumes in museum research libraries, local libraries and bookstores. Archaeological digs under the direction of the National Park Service place Minisink peoples in this region during the prehistoric era (Paleo on the historic timeline). (Ed. note: As published in *The People of Minisink*, edited by David G. Orr and Douglas V. Campana, Minisink is derived from menesenk, meaning "island," according to Smithsonian linguist Ives Goddard, or "stony country" according to Jim Rementer, an Eastern Oklahoma Delaware.) "Faces in Clay," an exhibit of Native American artifacts in the Wayne County Historical Society Museum (see "Exhibits"), represents this timeline. The volumes in the research libraries focus primarily on what is called the Contact Period, which begins around 1638 when Swedish and Dutch explorers noted the existence of bands of Indians in the area north of Trenton, New Jersey. The period continues through the end of the 1700s, by which time virtually all Native American groups had either moved themselves or been removed by treaty or war to areas west and north of the Poconos.

In this chapter we concentrate on the disenfranchisement of the Delaware peoples through the infamous 1737 Walking Purchase, and the Delawares' retaliation in the Pennsylvania Indian Wars — part of the French and Indian War and even the Revolutionary War. The colonists' last response to the Delawares' attacks was Sullivan's March, which effectively ended the presence of Indians in the Pocono counties by 1783. A historical gap exists in Native American activities in this area until the 1900s because most of the Indians were gone.

Remnant groups and families still lived in the Poconos, but they didn't acknowledge their ancestry (until recently, to be Native American was considered a liability). As we come of age as a society, the beauty of Native American traditions (as with other traditions and nationalities that make up our nation) is being recognized nationwide. Today, we celebrate Native American traditions in the Poconos. And Native American people, working beside us as they have done for a long time, now acknowledge their rich heritage and share with us their understanding of life's mysteries.

History

The most clearly identified early Americans to inhabit this region were the Eastern Woodlands Indians. Recent discoveries date settlements as far back as 13,000 years ago. These prehistoric people were the predecessors of those who called themselves Lenape or Lenni Lenape (basically, "original people"; Delawares is another name ascribed to members of this group who lived near the present-day Delaware River). The Lenape the first European settlers met were of the Algonquin tradition. At the time of contact with whites, Lenapes were under the authority and protection of the more forceful Iroquois, leaders of the League of Six Nations, which governed the region. As time went on, the Lenape became known as Delawares along with the other groups in the region, including the Shawnee who came around the end of the 1600s. (Minsi and "Munsee" are also names given to the various people here; the name is derived from the dialect they spoke —minsi or munsee.)

Evidence suggests most of the Delaware bands were not warlike. Their weapons more resembled clubs than the hatchets that became common after European contact; most of the arrowheads found in early Woodland digs were for spears (hunting) rather than for bows and arrows (fighting). Contact Period (early to mid-1600s) observations indicate that if Indians and Europeans accidentally got in one another's way, the Indians would move, change their hunting trails or find another place to build their towns. Any warlike activity was confined to raids on villages to get more people for their tribes to replace lost relatives. Those captured became part of the family to which they had been delivered. Even later accounts of white prisoners show they generally were well treated and became family members. An interesting point: Indians were very respectful of women (societies even among the more warlike Iroquois were matriarchal) and never raped female prisoners.

The Delawares were farmers and hunters. They lived in small towns based around longhouses — long huts, sometimes 25 feet in length, constructed of bent saplings for support and covered by thick layers of bark. (See this chapter's "Exhibits" section to find out where to see reproductions.) Longhouses were usually shared by several related families who were under a matriarch. All land was considered open for everyone's use, though each band respected one another's tribal hunting grounds and farming land. This concept of the land belonging to all eventually brought the Indians into conflict with the European settlers who only understood the concept of personal ownership.

In 1682 William Penn had made an agreement with the Delawares for land that included Philadelphia, Chester and Bucks counties. It was said that in 1686 a further treaty was agreed to, which provided that Penn or his descendants could have as much land, going northward, as a man could walk in one and one-half days. This treaty was never found, though a supposed copy did show up in 1735 when Thomas Penn, son of William, decided he needed more land to sell.

Some of the language in this purported treaty conflicted with another Indian concept.

FYI

Unless otherwise noted, the area code for all phone numbers in this guide is 717.

The Delawares, who were forced to agree to the "purchase" made by their Iroquois protectors, had a different notion of the meaning of the phrase "walk in one and one-half days" than the European proprietors seeking land.

To the Delawares, "walk" meant amble along, stop for a smoke, hunt a little, walk some more and so on. To the Penns, "walk" meant cover the most distance possible in one and one-half days; they hired three professional walkers and rewarded the one who walked the farthest with a land bonus. Among the "walkers" was Edward Marshall (Marshalls Creek), who "ran" as reported by the Indians who could not keep up with him. (His two companions collapsed along the way.) He "walked" from Wrightstown in Bucks County to Mauch Chunk (now Jim Thorpe) — a distance of 65 miles.

From the time of the original treaty with William Penn, who acted honorably and respectfully to the Indians, the Delaware and Shawnee indians coexisted peacefully with the European settlers. With the Walking Purchase the trust that was the basis of that peaceful coexistence was destroyed.

The deal was further tarnished by the last concept involved in the treaty. The boundaries of the Walking Purchase were to be drawn in a straight line from the stopping point eastward to the Delaware River. To the Delawares, "east" meant due east. To Penn's men, "east" meant northeast. Based on the Delawares' understanding of the concept of "east" the line should have been drawn from Jim Thorpe to somewhere in the vicinity of the present-day town of Delaware Water Gap. Penn's proprietors' understanding of east allowed them to draw the line to the mouth of the Lackawaxen River where it meets the Delaware River — northeast. The territory included in the "purchase" encompassed what is today practically the entire Poconos region — roughly three times more land than the Delawares thought they agreed to in the Walking Purchase.

Not surprisingly, the Delawares were not happy; the Europeans had claimed all of the Indians' hunting, fishing and farming land. Feeling cheated, the Delawares appealed to their Iroquois protectors. Unfortunately, they

Photo: Pocono Mountains Vacation Bureau, Inc.

The Native American presence is alive and well in the Poconos, as evidenced by the handful of festivals and pow wows that celebrate the culture.

had complained to Penn's men and the governor first, who in turn also had complained to the Iroquois. Since the Iroquois had pledged to work with the settlers, they ordered the Delaware and Shawnee indians to vacate the land.

For five years the Delawares fought the expulsion through writings, meetings, even court hearings. For a while the Penns allowed them to stay on the land they actually (physically) occupied. A Christian chief, Tatami, specifically was allowed to remain. However, demands for land became great, and after a five-year transition period, the Penns told the Delawares at a meeting in Philadelphia on July 10, 1742, that they would have to leave. The Iroquois chief, Canassatego, was present at the meeting to represent his people, whose power was based on their status as leaders of the Six Nations (encompassing the entire region in Pennsylvania and New York). At the meeting Canassatego concurred with the Penns that the Delawares had to leave. Interestingly, in 1749 the Penns paid the Iroquois 500£ (English pounds) for a wide strip of land the Penns had already "purchased" from the Delawares.

Eighteen years after the infamous Walking

Purchase, the Delawares finally retaliated with all their might. Under the leadership of Delaware chief, Teedyuscung (converted to Christianity by the Moravians), and supported by the French who were fighting the British in the French and Indian War, they attacked. The irony of the revenge: The first attack, on November 24, 1755, was directed against the peaceful Moravians who had established a mission at Gnadenhuetten ("tents of mercy") and who supported the Indians entirely. (Teedyuscung, who had been baptized by the Moravians five years earlier, did not take part in that attack.) With Gnadenhuetten as their starting point, the Delawares waged a bloody assault against the settlers, killing them and burning settlement after settlement — but only in the area of the Walking Purchase.

Wars were waged by Indians and Europeans alike, and atrocities were committed on both sides. In 1756, '57 and '58, meetings were held to try and end the bloodshed. With some Quaker support Teedyuscung attended the meetings with the Colonists. In speech after speech, he defended his people and their position, pleading their cause to the governor in Philadelphia. Quakers urged Teedyuscung to have a scribe write down all proceedings to prevent another "agreement" like the one that precipitated the Walking Purchase problem — the never-found original 1686 treaty with William Penn. He pleaded to no avail, and the Delawares were ordered to remove themselves to Shamokin and Wyoming, Pennsylvania. Teedyuscung died in a house fire in 1763 during the years of tension-filled peace that followed the 1758 removal of the Delawares.

The peace was interrupted when the Iroquois joined forces with the British against the Colonists in the Revolutionary War. The Indians used the Revolutionary War to reopen their attack on the Colonists, and the Pennsylvania Indian Wars began again for a short time. The Colonial Army could not effectively help the settlers, who had crowded into Fort Penn, the fort controlled by Jacob Stroud in Stroudsburg. In 1778, Gen. George Washington sent the Continental Army, under the direction of Gen. John Sullivan, to march through the area and quell the Indians. The company of 2,500 men marched from Easton through the Susquehanna Valley into New York State, destroying every Indian village, sanctuary and means of livelihood they encountered. The army engaged few Indians in battle. Finally, the march complete, Sullivan's army was disbanded.

Indian attacks resumed and continued until the Peace of Paris treaty, which ended the Revolutionary War in 1783. At that time, the British ordered their frontiersmen to stop paying the Indians to attack the Colonists; Gen. Washington for his part banned all attacks on Indians in the area. The wars — all of them — ended. There was peace — but there were few Native Americans in the area.

Renewed Presence

There has been a resurgence of Native Americans in the Poconos. Over the past 10 years or so, more and more Native Americans

have made themselves known, establishing centers for their own enrichment and consciousness-raising as well as for others who would like to learn about Native American traditions. The members of these groups are intent on re-establishing the spirituality that once defined their heritage — the same spirituality that contributed to its downfall at the hands of the less spiritually directed Europeans. Conversations with any representative Native Americans include invitations to understand their spirituality, sense of family and love of the land, and a desire to be recognized for who they are not who they are perceived to be. They consistently speak of the oneness of all peoples of the Americas. They make no distinction among tribes with respect to status or value. They embrace peoples in both American hemispheres. As did the Native Americans who encountered early settlers, they seek not war but to share the land and their understanding of it in the circle of life.

The following two fledgling groups are very active in re-establishing the Native American presence in the Poconos.

Native American Spiritual and Cultural Center

U.S. Hwy. 209 Bus., Snydersville • 424-8449 (Grey Bear), 894-9880 (Pat Running Bear)

The Native American Spiritual and Cultural Center encompasses 10 acres owned by Grey Bear, a Comanche elder born in Pennsylvania. It has been his dream since World War II to develop a center for understanding and growth for the native peoples of the Americas. The group is open to all Native Americans and presently has among its members Comanche, Cherokee, Lakota, Taino, Mayan, Toltec, Winnebago, Cheyenne, Hopi and others.

The focus of the center is to show people the way of life as understood by the Native Americans — the "Great Mystery." The Great Mystery refers to the understanding of a higher power manifest in the four seasons, four direc-

Preserving Native American Archeology
of the Delaware Region

Archeologists at the Delaware Water Gap National Recreation Area have been very aggressive about protecting Native American interests in the park. They have spent many years discovering, cataloging and preserving sites of early Native American inhabitation. They note that the entire Delaware River region has been occupied for more than 13,000 years; 12,700 of those years were before Europeans arrived. Part of the Park Service's mission is to work with historical societies and Native Americans to protect and foster appreciation for the wealth of information and history still buried beneath the earth Native Americans walked and lived on for thousands and thousands of years.

One achievement in their mission was designating Minisink Island in the Delaware River as a historical landmark. Seventeen archeological sites on the island relate to the pre-European occupation of the area by the Minsi or Munsees and to early Colonial settlements. The last of the Munsees left in 1737 at the time of the Walking Purchase. Colonial buildings also have been preserved — the Bell House (from the mid-1700s) and the block house, which protected the settlers during the Pennsylvania Indian Wars.

Another Park Service achievement was realized in conjunction with professors from Seton Hall University and Franklin and Marshall University during the Tocks Island Dam excavations (see our History chapter). Professors Kraft and Kinsey, from Seton Hall and Franklin Marshall respectively, worked to remove, catalog and store whatever artifacts were unearthed while preparatory dam excavations were in progress. National Park Service archeologists were part of the team that managed the enormous task. The preserved artifacts are now on display in the Seton Hall museum and the New Jersey State Museum in Trenton. Other artifacts remain in storage with the Park Service until a facility can be financed and built on the Pennsylvania side of the park. An exhibit currently is being prepared for the visitors center in Bushkill and should be complete for the 1997 season.

National Park Service historians and archeologists are also active in restoring some of the land to its original state, as it was when Europeans first encountered the "original people" (Lenni Lenape). As Park Service archeologist John Wright notes, sitting by the river today is very much like seeing it from the eyes of the Native Americans who lived along its shores and farmed its flood plains for thousands of years. In fact, the Park Service is encouraging farmers to grow crops on the flood plains as Native American farmers and European settlers once did. Land has been put aside for farming as part of the restoration design.

Perhaps one of the Park Service's most exciting projects in support of Native Americans is currently in progress. During the Tocks Dam excavations, Native American burial sites were uncovered. Remains found at these sites as well as attendant funeral artifacts not found at the sites were assembled, cataloged and stored for preservation by the Park Service. For the past two years, the federal government has been negotiating with two Native American groups to repatriate the remains from these excavations. Representatives of the Delawares of Oklahoma and the Munsees in Wisconsin, displaced farther and farther west after the Walking Purchase, were contacted to discuss options for how to best repatriate their ancestors and their funeral belongings. Now arrangements are being made for repatriation burials at a site in the park that will not be disclosed to ensure that Delaware and Munsee ancestors rest undisturbed.

Visitors to the Delaware Water Gap National Recreation Area will not see the known burial sites. You can, however, walk where native peoples walked and see what they saw — a beautiful flowing river, eagles soaring overhead, trees and mountains reaching to the sky.

As you immerse yourself in the beauty, share in the knowledge that, in this place, respect is finally being paid the ancestors of those who walked the earth here for almost 13,000 years.

tions, four elements (earth, fire, sky and wind) and four auras (red, yellow, black and white).

Currently, the center, which includes a large teepee, conducts seminars on-site. Some vendors, who must only sell self-made wares, are on-site when programs are presented. They include basket and other weavers, pottery makers, silversmiths, jewelry artisans, painters and other Native American crafters.

As the center works toward its final plans, it concentrates on accepting speaking engagements for its speakers and lecturers, presenting small powwows (gatherings of all nations to feast and dance together and exchange wares; spectators are welcome), and holding seminars and programs on the property. Call to request a calendar of events.

Native American Pavilion of Pennsylvania
P.O. Box 1002, Saylorsburg 18353-1002
• 992-5647

The Pavilion welcomes all Native Americans and seeks to educate others in the Native American way of life. It holds monthly meetings (call for dates) at the Chestnuthill Township Park, Pa. Highway 715, Brodheadsville. The organization is represented by Don Wild Eagle who is certified through the Seneca Historical Society of Brant, New York, to impart his Wolf Clan's teachings.

The group hosts Native American Awareness Days, powwows and evening seminars and lectures throughout the year at various locations. Don Wild Eagle and other members participate in events for other organizations, offering their traditions and teachings. Other members deliver talks on nature, basket weaving, beading, pottery, herbs and more. They focus on demonstrating the art of their craftwork, their traditions and their means of survival. Storytelling and traditional dancing are other components of their events.

As with the Native American Cultural and Spiritual Center, many Native American groups are represented in the Native American Pavilion membership — Cree, Cherokee, Apache, Comanche, Pima and others. (Don Wild Eagle is Apache and Pima, originally from Arizona). Dancing is an integral part of most gatherings — The Round Dance, Women's Traditional Dance, The Sneakup Dance, The Crow Hop, Jingle Dress (Cree) and Men's Traditional Dance. Spectators sometimes are invited to join in. Seeing the dances for the first time is an enlightening experience. The beauty and grace of the women dancers is mesmerizing, and the men's ability to mix in with dancers from other tribes and immediately become one with the music and dance is fascinating.

One value Native Americans espouse, to which both Don Wild Eagle and Grey Bear attest, is the sense of family — their own, their clan's and their nation's. The value of elders — grandmothers and grandfathers (some of whom are still dancing into their 90s) — is emphasized. Don Wild Eagle teaches family values, leading interested learners in one-on-one personal searches and in seminars and lectures. For a calendar of events, or to arrange a seminar, lecture or demonstration, contact the Native American Pavilion.

Exhibits

Stroudsburg/ East Stroudsburg

Monroe County Historical Association
900 Main St., Stroudsburg • 421-7703

This museum has a small Native American exhibit housed in its cellar kitchen. There are three main collections of Lenni Lenape artifacts from the Delaware River region: the Brodhead Collection from the late 1800s; the Flagler Collection from the 1930s; and the Saylors Lake Collection from the 1930s. (Interestingly, even a century ago, the inherent value of the Brodhead Collection was recognized.)

The collections contain typical Stone Age tools, projectile points and pottery shards; and from the Contact Period, a few pipes, ornaments and a ceremonial mask. This museum also has a fine selection of books and vertical files on Native American history and traditions in the Poconos. (See our Arts and Culture and Worship chapters for related information about this museum.)

Hours are 10 AM to 4 PM Tuesday through Saturday and 1 to 4 PM Sundays. A donation is requested.

West End

Mauch Chunk Museum and Cultural Center
41 W. Broadway, Jim Thorpe • 325-9190

The Native American exhibit in this museum spotlights the Lenape Indians. Artifacts representing their daily life are the centerpiece. The main focus of this exhibit is Jim Thorpe, the Native American Olympian and professional football great. Rare photos of Thorpe's life are featured. The exhibit includes a photo display from his youth and late adulthood as well as a famous photo of Jim Thorpe and King Gustav of Sweden in 1912 after the Olympics. At that time the king told Thorpe, "Sir, you are the greatest athlete in the world," to which Thorpe replied, "Thanks, King!"

Other items in the Native American exhibit include artifacts of the Bear Clan as well as a reproduction of a painting of Lappawinzo, the first Native American to have his portrait painted, made in 1735 by Swedish artist Gustavus Hussielius.

The museum is open 10:30 AM to 5 PM Thursday, Friday and Saturday and noon to 5 PM Sunday from May through October. Admission is $2. See our Arts and Culture chapter for more information about Mauch Chunk Museum and Cultural Center.

Milford Area

Bushkill Falls Native American Exhibit
U.S. Hwy. 209, Bushkill • 588-6682

This exhibit presents aspects of a day in the life of the Lenni Lenape people of this region. Its centerpiece is an 18-foot-by-10-foot longhouse built expressly for the exhibit from the fallen trees on this Bushkill property. Builder Mark Nessa, who is also the main demonstrator and lecturer here, is part Sioux.

The exhibit has been here two seasons and continues to evolve. There are about 20 demonstrations, depending on the weather and visitors' interests. Nessa's objective is to keep the exhibit lively and fresh as he demonstrates how people went about their daily lives making arrowheads, tanning hides, building a fire and creating a dugout canoe. Lectures about the history and culture of the Lenape generally are given once a day. These are a mix of presentation, discussion and mutual sharing, with visitors volunteering what they know and Nessa providing further information, references and knowledge.

Besides the longhouse and demonstrations, visitors can check out display cases around the main exhibit room containing Indian artifacts and information about them. Gift shops outside the exhibit include an assortment of Native American crafts.

If you wish to eat here, there are picnic tables in the woods surrounding the parking lot and two covered pavilions. You'll find snack-food stands too.

Daily seasonal hours, April through October, are 9 AM until dusk for both the museum and the falls. The price of admission ($7 for adults, $2 for kids ages 4 through 10 and $6.25 for senior citizens) includes the exhibit and the falls. The rates are subject to change, and you are advised to call for them. The Native American Exhibit is handicapped-accessible; Bushkill Falls is not.

The Columns Museum of the Pike County Historical Society
608 Broad St., Milford • 296-8126

The Native American Exhibit on the second floor of this museum contains artifacts of the Lenni Lenape, including weapons and tools used in everyday life, such as scrapers, bowls, tomahawks and arrowheads. Documentation is provided for some items.

Hours are Wednesday, Saturday and Sunday, 1 to 4 PM; call to confirm. A donation is requested. (See our Arts and Culture chapter for more information about The Columns.)

The Pocono Indian Museum and Gift Shop
U.S. Hwy. 209 S., Bushkill • 588-9338

This museum is clearly a work of love. Housed in the annex of a huge, white-columned mansion, the museum is comprised of a carefully arranged series of six rooms. The rooms contain artifacts — many from Delaware River site excavations noted in this chapter's sidebar — and examples of Delaware (or Lenape) Indian lifestyles. Additional exhibits feature objects representative of other Indian nations and clans. Your tour includes a recorded narration explaining what is displayed. One room contains pictures of herbs used by Native Americans and includes clear explanations of how and why they were used. An article in one exhibit — innocently displayed, albeit shocking — is an Indian scalp.

The rest of the building is a gift shop with some very nice Native American crafts, tapes and CDs of traditional music and typical gift shop novelties. An important part of this annex is the upstairs bookstore/library, which features a large and interesting selection of reading material about different Native American tribes, including some from beyond the geographic scope of this region.

The museum opens seven days a week at 10 AM; it closes at 8 PM in summer, 6 PM weekdays and 7 PM weekends other times of the year. Admission is $3.50 for adults and teens and $2 for children 12 and younger.

Lake Wallenpaupack Area

The Wayne County Historical Society Museum & Research Library
810 Main St., Honesdale • 253-3240

This museum and research library has more than 4,600 Native American artifacts gathered from the Upper Delaware River and its environs. These pieces represent finds from the four major periods of inhabitation: Paleo, Archaic, Woodland and Contact. They are part of a much larger collection that was the lifetime work of late county historian Vernon Leslie, who willed them to the library with exact plans for how they should be displayed.

The exhibit is called "Faces in Clay," which is the name of one of nine books written by Leslie. A local high school teacher and amateur archaeologist, he began collecting artifacts at age 14 — a process he continued until his death at age 83 in 1994. The collection includes the very first artifact he found and the last one, which was left on his desk when he died. All artifacts are cataloged according to archaeological documentation standards. The catalog number identifies the state, county, site number and sequence found at the dig. They are documented on 3-by-5-inch index cards and are available for reference to the serious collector. These artifacts represent a third of Leslie's total collection.

The exhibit is housed a floor below the museum in a setting meant to represent the dark, quiet green of the forest primeval. The center of the space is filled with a dugout canoe, carbon-dated 1650 AD, which is backed by a lush forest scene. The clay-colored floor has bear prints to lead you around the exhibit; the walls are painted green; and lighted display cases lining the walls illuminate the room. As you walk through the exhibit and read the information provided, you are surrounded by the sounds of the forest and the river, including someone paddling a canoe. Along one side, artifacts are arranged in sites as you would have found them along the Delaware River from northern Wayne County through Monroe County. The sites are differentiated by green sticks. The artifacts on the opposite wall are arranged chronologically according to periods of habitation. The artifacts present important features of Native American lifestyles, including hunting and gathering techniques and social customs.

The museum also features an extensive research library of books and a vertical file of surnames (for genealogists) and history subjects. The museum also has newspapers on microfiche dating back to the 1840s, catalogs and maps. Library staff will assist with research for people who are unable to visit.

For the classroom teacher in Wayne County, the library has a "Traveling Trunk" loaded with materials for a Native American study unit. It contains everything about Native American history in the Poconos that a teacher needs — even a teacher who has no previous knowledge of the subject. It contains CDs, videos, a bear pelt, recipes, an illustrated book of children's toys, even an audio tape of the Lenape language for children to study. An exciting discovery tool is the mini-archaeological dig, with artifacts buried in dirt for children to excavate with the provided brush and trowel. Teachers can have the trunk for up to six weeks.

Hours vary according to the time of year, but the museum is generally open Monday and Wednesday through Saturday from June through December; Saturdays only in January and February; and Wednesday through Saturday in March, April and May. The Sunday schedule changes every year, so call for a brochure or information about Sunday and seasonal hours. Research library hours are the same as museum hours, but additional hours for research can be arranged. Guided tours are accommodated with advance reservations; fees are $3 for adults, $2 for kids ages 12 to 18 and free for children younger than 12.

Crafts

Stroudsburg/ East Stroudsburg

Teepee Town
Pa. Hwy. 611, in Fountain Court, Bartonsville • 620-2522

Teepee Town has a wide selection of silver and turquoise jewelry, additional jewelry and decorations from Canadian tribes, moccasins, clothing and other souvenir-type gifts.

Mount Pocono Area

Deer Track Trading Post
Pa. Hwy. 611, Tannersville • 629-4511

You'll find an interesting collection of crafted items for order. A large slab of a tree trunk, completely carved inside to display a woodlands environment, is particularly beautiful. You might gasp at the $4,000-plus price tag, but this piece is evidence of the one-of-a-kind workmanship you'll find here. Also check out the collection of beautiful women's dresses in rich, deep earth colors, with fine beadwork on buttery, soft suede. There are other items of note as well as souvenirs, but the clothing and special-order items are particularly appealing. Look for the huge teepee outside.

Suggested Reading

Some excellent reading material is available for anyone interested in learning more about Pennsylvania's Native American peoples. The following proved invaluable resources, especially in researching this chapter's "History" section: *History of Wayne, Pike and Monroe Counties*, Alfred Mathews, R.T. Peck & Co., Philadelphia, 1886; *Indians in Pennsylvania*, Paul A.W. Wallace, The Pennsylvania Historical and Museum Commission, Harrisburg, 1961; *The People of Minisink*, David. G. Orr & Douglas V. Campana, editors, National Park Service, Philadelphia, 1991; *The Story of Bushkill Falls*, Sally Walther, D. Hannan Associates, Stroudsburg, 1992.

Pennsylvania was
the birthplace of
commercial winemaking
in the United States.

Wineries

Never thought of the Poconos as a source of award-winning wine? While other parts of the country might have more wineries, the handful of winemakers in the Poconos produce some terrific products.

In fact, Pennsylvania was the birthplace of commercial winemaking in the United States. The Pennsylvania Vine Company was established in 1793 by Pierre Legaux and operated the first successful vineyard in Spring Mills, 13 miles northwest of Philadelphia. Today, approximately 50 wineries operate throughout the state, producing 700,000 gallons of Pennsylvania wine annually. Our state is the fifth-largest grape grower and wine producer in the United States. Although winemaking here began with native American grapes, growers have added many European varieties in recent years.

More than 40 types of wine are produced in Pennsylvania. Four white wines — Vidal, Seyval, Cayuga and Vignoles — are especially suited to the state's growing climate, which includes cold winters and unpredictable rainfall. Most Pennsylvania wineries are near Lake Erie or in the southeastern corner of the state. Many of our state's vintners claim Chambourcin, a dry red table wine, as their signature wine.

The native grape in the Poconos region — and most of the northeastern United States — is *vitis lambrusca*. In the Poconos it is most successfully blended with French hybrids, which are hearty enough to withstand early season frosts.

The passage of the 1967 Farm Winery Act, which allowed retail outlets and Sunday sales, resulted in explosive growth in Pennsylvania's winemaking industry during the past three decades. No wineries existed in the state prior to 1963, and only two were in business in 1969. This rapid increase in just more than 25 years is second only to Virginia in the southeastern part of the country.

By law, all wines made in Pennsylvania must be created with grapes grown in the state. And vintners must operate under a special license from the state that allows wineries to serve 2-ounce samples to adults 21 and older and sell bottles only for consumption off the premises.

Four wineries operate within the Pocono Mountains, all in the southern part of the region. Farther north, the often early and usually harsh winter weather conditions — particularly the frost — make growing grapes impossible. Unlike the great wine-producing areas of upstate New York, the Poconos region lacks extensive large bodies of water that help regulate the temperature of the surrounding countryside and prevent early frosts.

However, the proximity of Poconos wineries within the limited grape-growing region works to the advantage of wine aficionados, who can visit all area operations in a single day.

Each winery sells its own products and offers free tastings. Since alcohol sales in Pennsylvania are regulated by the state government, any other wine purchases must be made at the nearest state-operated Wine & Spirits Shop. Regional stores that have special sections devoted to Pennsylvania wines can be found at the following locations: Pocono Plaza, Lincoln Avenue, East Stroudsburg; 1060 N. Ninth Street and 761 Main Street, Stroudsburg; 551-553 Belmont Avenue, Mount Pocono; Blakeslee Village Center, Pa. Highway 940, Blakeslee; 106 W. Harford Street, Milford; 510 Church Street, Hawley; 34 S. Broad Street, Nazareth.

In fall, usually in September or October, Poconos wineries host special festivals to coincide with their annual harvests. These often include lunch, winetasting and some grape crushing. Many participants return the next year to purchase a bottle of the wine they helped make. Call the individual wineries for details on their planned events, as specific events and schedules vary from year to year.

At the end of June each year, Split Rock Resort in Lake Harmony hosts the Great Tastes of Pennsylvania Wine & Food Festival. More than 20 Pennsylvania wineries participate. See our Annual Events and Festivals chapter for details.

A rundown of wineries in the Poconos region follows. But before we look at each vineyard individually, we'd like to congratulate the local heroes who garnered honors at the 1996 Pennsylvania Commercial Wine Competition. The following wineries in the Poconos region received medals: Franklin Hill Vineyards, Cayuga White (gold); Big Creek Vineyards, Chambourcin (bronze); Slate Quarry Winery, Vidal-Brut Reserve (silver) and Quarry Stone White, Chardonel, Sauvignon Blanc and Chardonnay (all bronze).

West End

Big Creek Vineyard and Winery
Keller Rd., Kresgeville • (610) 681-3959

Fifty-five years ago, Dominic Strohlein's father had the foresight to purchase 80 acres of land in the then-rural West End. Dominic spent summers there as a child. Little did he realize then that he would later return to this same property to open a vineyard with his brother and mother. The 25 acres of grapes grown here eventually will produce 10,000 gallons of wine annually. The vineyard has yet to reach its peak growing productivity.

The land is perfectly suited to growing grapes. It has good slope, is well-drained and faces south, which helps insulate it from the cold winters.

The winery is housed in a magnificent building with white walls and a high wooden ceiling. Large windows provide panoramic views of much of the vineyard. A balcony in the tasting room overlooks the winemaking operation. The atmosphere resembles that of an art gallery. In fact, works from the nearby Faulty Beagle Gallery are on display.

In 1995 the business produced its first commercial wine, which probably will have sold out due to limited production by the time you read this. Prior to that, some uninvited area residents destroyed the previous crop, but Dominic developed a resourceful way to keep them away from his grapes.

Deer roam freely on the farms of the West End and quickly developed an appetite for grapes. To keep them away from his crops, Dominic installed 9,000 feet of nine-gauge copper wire underground, which created an invisible electric fence. He then got two dogs and put their food at one end of the property and their water at the other, forcing them to patrol the entire grounds. The dogs take the same clockwise course every day and instinctively chase any deer they see. The fence keeps the dogs in; the dogs keep the deer out. The orange flags indicating the boundary are enough to stop the dogs.

Big Creek grows varieties of grapes from France, Italy, Germany, Hungary and Russia. It produces five wines: Seyval, a dry white table wine that's an ideal accompaniment to spicy spring picnic favorites such as Buffalo wings; Dulcinea, a crisp German white wine that also goes well with picnics as well as Chinese food; Chambourcin, a dry red table wine that complements roast beef or pork; Chambourcin Riserva, a dessert-style red designed to be served with fruit, cheese or chocolate; and Vin Di Pasqualina, a dry red table wine named in honor of a great aunt whose personality matches the light, easygoing nature of the wine.

Big Creek Vineyard is open for free tours of the grounds Monday through Thursday from 1 to 5 PM, Friday and Saturday from 1 to 7 PM

INSIDERS' TIPS

With very few exceptions, all wines offered by Pocono wineries sell for between $5 and $10 per bottle. Look for discounts on case purchases; you usually can mix varieties in a single case.

BIG CREEK VINEYARD AND WINERY

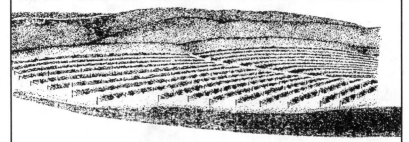

Located on Keller Road off of Beltzville Drive in Kresgeville. Follow signs.
Our tasting room is open each afternoon, 7 days a week.
Call 610 681-3959 for information.
www.pocono.com/vineyard.htm   bigcreek@prolog.com

and Sunday from 2 to 5 PM throughout the year.

Follow U.S. Highway 209 to Pa. Highway 534 W., go 0.1 mile to Beltzville Road, then 1.3 miles to Keller Road. Turn left onto Keller Road and go 0.3 mile to the second driveway on the left.

Cherry Valley Vineyards
Lower Cherry Valley Rd., Saylorsburg
• 992-2255

Upon arriving at Cherry Valley Vineyards, visitors usually are immediately impressed by the beautiful property. The farmhouse, which houses the tasting area and store, is fully restored and dates back more than 200 years. It once was owned by John Saylor, for whom Saylorsburg is named. A natural spring house, a charming little wood building, sits at the beginning of Cherry Creek, which is just outside the door. The Appalachian Trail traverses this property at the base of the Blue Mountains. Local legend claims Gen. John Sullivan and his troops stopped along the creek in this area during their famous Revolutionary War march. Another popular story claims the old one-room schoolhouse in the vineyard is haunted.

However, the focus of activity today is the wine made by the Sorrenti family.

Dominic Sorrenti is the chief winemaker and chemist, although he probably cringes at the latter title. At Cherry Valley, all operations are kept as organic as possible. Sorrenti uses a little chemistry and a lot of instinct. His is an Italian, old-school approach to winemaking. His wife, Mary, tends to the vineyard. The Sorrentis' four children also are involved in the business. Begun in 1981, the family operation's output is at least 12,000 gallons annually. The vineyards produce more than 12 varietals of grapes on 14 acres of land.

Cherry Valley Vineyards produces 25 varieties of wine. Regardless of your taste or degree of wine appreciation, you certainly will find something here that suits you.

Local favorites are the fruit wines — particularly apple and peach — made with fruits grown on the property. They are very refreshing, particularly on a warm summer day.

Cherry Valley's Champagne, made by the Champenoise process invented by Dom Perignon, has won gold medals in national and international competitions. It is created entirely by hand — a 2½-year process.

Unlike many small wineries, Cherry Valley does age some of its wine. In the near future, a 1994 Foch, a red French hybrid, will be released after spending 1½ years in oak barrels and 1½ years in bottles.

Other standouts are the Riesling, a sweet, German-style white; Niagara, a fruity white made with native American grapes; and Dominic's favorite, DeChaunac, a dry red French hybrid.

Enemies of the grapes at Cherry Valley are deer and frost. The Sorrentis are consider-

Photo: Pocono Mountains Vacation Bureau, Inc.

Discover the romantic side of the Poconos.

ing combating the latter with a computerized irrigation system that automatically mists the vines with warm water when the temperature dips to freezing. The grapes have begun to adapt to the region's climate by budding later in the year to avoid the frost.

The deer are even more problematic — and discriminating. They eat only the more expensive French hybrids and ignore the native grapes. The occasional warning gunshot is used to let them know they are not welcome.

The winery is open for tastings from 11 AM to 6 PM daily throughout the year. Free Tours are offered Saturdays and Sundays from noon to 4 PM. Cherry Valley also operates an outlet at 731 Main Street in Stroudsburg.

Personalized labels are available for all occasions.

Take Pa. Highway 33 south to the Saylorsburg exit. Turn left and proceed to Lower Cherry Valley Road. Turn right; the winery entrance will be on your right.

Slate Belt

Franklin Hill Vineyards
7833 Franklin Hill Rd., Bangor
• (610) 588-8708

Having begun as a vineyard 18 years ago, Franklin Hill has been producing wine since 1982. Owner Elaine Austen harvested 101 tons of grapes in 1995. The annual winemaking efforts total 13,000 to 15,000 gallons from 13 acres of grapes.

Austen discovered many Pennsylvania Dutch people, who comprise much of the population of the West End, do not prefer traditional red wine or dry wine. As a result, her best sellers are semi-sweet and sweet wines

INSIDERS' TIPS

The Poconos is home to one of the most highly regarded wine authors in the northeastern United States. John J. Baxevanis, a geography professor at East Stroudsburg University, edits the *Vinifera Wine Growers Journal* and writes extensively on viticulture and enology. In addition to his books on French wines, look for his outstanding *The Wine Regions of America*, published in 1992. Send any wine-related questions to Baxevanis at the magazine's address, 1947 Hillside Drive, Stroudsburg 18360.

— Country White, Country Red and Country Rose. Her personal favorite is Cayuga White, a medium-dry white wine that has been a gold-medal winner in the Pennsylvania Commercial Wine Competition. It has a fragrance reminiscent of Sauvignon Blanc and is perfect with cheese and crackers or Tex-Mex and other spicy foods. In addition to reds, whites and roses, the winery makes one fruit wine, the medium-sweet Country Apple.

Helping Austen with the winemaking is Head Winemaker Bonnie Pysher, a 12-year employee of Franklin Hill. Most other staff members are wives of nearby farmers.

The tasting room is amid the barrels and fermentation tanks. The winery is open for free tastings and sales from 11 AM to 4 PM Monday through Saturday year-round. Tours are available, but call ahead to make sure the staff is not in the field. If you like, bring a picnic lunch and eat on the grounds.

Franklin Hill offers custom labels for all occasions.

The winery's 16 varieties are available for sale at the vineyard in Bangor and at three outlet stores: The Grape Vine at Manayunk Farmers Market, 4120 Main Street, Philadelphia; The Grape Spot, 36-06 Nicholas Street, Easton; and The Wine Shop, Pocono Factory Outlets, Ninth and Ann streets, Stroudsburg.

If you visit the Stroudsburg location, you will likely meet Austen's father, Walter Pivinski. In addition to knowing a great deal about wine, he also can share a few tricks, such as how to remove a cork from the bottom of a bottle of wine.

Take Pa. Highway 611 south to Pulcini's Restaurant in Martins Creek. At the traffic light, proceed straight on Front Street. At the top of the hill, make a right onto Franklin Hill Road and proceed 1.7 miles; Franklin Hill Vineyards will be on your right.

Slate Quarry Winery
460 Gower Rd., Nazareth • (610) 759-0286

Sid and Ellie Butler started their business solely as a vineyard in 1981 after Sid decided to retire early from his career as a professor at Lehigh University. The Butler's winery has been open for seven years and produces 2,000 gallons annually from 13 acres of grapes.

All Slate Quarry wines are made with grapes from their property. Their land is mineral-rich and laced with slate. As the name implies, a quarry is nearby. Roughly 16 varieties of grapes grow in their vineyard at any given time. Experimenting with different grapes to see which grows most successfully is part of the appeal of the business for the couple. As of now, Vidal grapes appear to do best.

Among the most popular types of wine from Slate Quarry are the 1995 Quarry Stone White, a spicy blend of Gewurztraminer and the New York hybrid Traminette; Florental 1995, a medium-body Beaujolais-style red wine; Chardonel 1994, a dry traditional-style white wine that's a cross of Chardonnay and Seyval; and Sauvignon Blanc 1994, a classic French variety that's slightly astringent and is produced by very few wineries in this part of the country. The Butlers also produce such Pennsylvania wine staples as Vidal, Chambourcin and Vignoles. The best seller is Ellie's Rosé, a medium-sweet pink with muscat grape aroma.

The winery is open Friday through Sunday from 1 to 6 PM, February through December. Free tours must be arranged in advance; this is a small, family operation.

From Nazareth, take Pa. Highway 248 west to Pa. Highway 946 and turn right. Proceed .75 mile and veer right onto Knauss Road. After a half-mile, veer right onto Gower Road. The winery entrance is a quarter-mile up the road on the left.

You don't have to go to zoos or farms to see animals in the Poconos. Open your eyes as you drive our country roads and see all the animals that surround you — deer, wild turkeys, bears, hawks, herons and more.

Kidstuff

In days gone by, kids in the Poconos rode their bikes for miles, swam in swimming holes, joined 4-H Clubs or Scouts, went hunting, played under waterfalls, boated on lakes, went fishing, took part in church theatrical productions, went to the fairs, joined sports teams and generally just enjoyed life. Today, kids do all the same things — and a whole lot more!

We've included some kid-centered opportunities in this chapter. But other activities children might enjoy are detailed in other chapters, including Winter Sports; Recreation; Fishing and Hunting; Camps; Attractions; and In, On and Around the Water. Whatever your children's interests — or yours — you are sure to find activities kids will enjoy and you will enjoy sharing with them.

Thumb through this chapter. When the kids ask, "What is there to do," you'll be ready to respond, "I know, let's . . . "

Let's Play

There are several play parks in the central and northern Poconos that offer rides, picnic areas and various other action-oriented activities.

Delaware Water Gap

Shawnee Place Play & Water Park
Hollow Rd., Shawnee-on-Delaware
• 421-7231

Besides the many water attractions, this fun park has hands-on workshops, games and fun interactions. Also on the agenda are magic shows three times a day. It is a great place for summer birthday parties too. For families that have a mix of older kids and toddlers, there is a dry toddler area that is great for the little ones, while the bigger ones enjoy the more active rides. (See Attractions for more information.)

Stroudsburg/ East Stroudsburg

The Action Zone Party and Play Center
12 Fox Lane Rd., Marshalls Creek
• 223-7274

This is an indoor play area that's suitable for kids from toddler-age to 10 years. There is a play area with a castle, boat, piano and toddler-size rides.

Older children will be challenged by an 18-foot-long, 5-foot-high mountain-climb course, a foam-ball pit, the bolster bash foam obstacle course, a web climb and crawl unit, a tunnel and slide and an inflated bouncer room. There is also a room with arcade games and redemption games (winners receive tickets that are redeemable for prizes).

Kids can play here for as long as they want for a $5 admission charge. Hours are 10 AM to 8 PM Monday through Thursday, 10 AM to 9 PM Friday and Saturday and 10 AM to 6 PM Sunday. The last hour of the day, kids can play for $3 per person.

Parties are fun here too. The base party package for up to 12 kids is $99.95 weekends, $84.95 midweek; the ultimate party (with cake and 40 tokens for redemption games) is $129.95 weekends, $114.95 midweek. Parties include food, table decorations, all paper goods, goodie bags and more, depending on the party special you choose. This place has introduced a party package for as few as six kids; the norm is 12.

Big Wheel's Oasis
Pa. Hwy. 191, north of Stroudsburg
• 424-5499

Oasis offers a swim club (see our In, On and Around the Water chapter) and outdoor roller hockey in the summer season. The year-round game room and pizza snack bar is rapidly evolving into a pretty good fast-food restaurant. Oasis is a good place for birthday parties for as many as 10 kids.

Pocono Mountain Go-Karts
U.S. Hwy. 209 (off I-80 Exit 46B), Marshalls Creek • 223-6299

This go-cart fun park has two tracks, one for folks shorter than 54 inches and one for the bigger kids. It has miniature golf, batting cages, an indoor arcade and snack bar.

Go-carts and collision carts cost $3 a ride (four for $10). Rides in the junior area cost $1 to $2 per ride. The park is open Memorial Day to Labor Day, 10 AM to 6 PM Monday through Thursday and 10 AM to 10 PM Friday and Saturday. In spring and fall, the park is open Friday and Saturday 10 AM until 8 PM (until 6 PM Monday through Thursday). The park is closed in winter. Ask about family discounts.

FYI

Unless otherwise noted, the area code for all phone numbers in this guide is 717.

Mount Pocono Area

Camelback Ski Area
Camelback Rd., Tannersville • 639-1661

Camelback is renowned as a great ski area (see our Winter Sports chapter), but it's also a summertime play park. Kids love the Olympic-size outdoor pool, Alpine Slide (a one-seat bobsled on a fiberglass track), water slide, go-carts, bumper boats, carousel and miniature golf. Also enjoy a toddler and kiddie area and free outdoor entertainment on weekends. (See our Attractions chapter for details.)

Pocono Mountain Go-Karts
Pa. Hwy. 611, Bartonsville • 620-0820

You'll find two great go-cart tracks here, one for kids shorter than 54 inches and one for the bigger kids and their parents. It also has a mini Ferris wheel, miniature golf, batting cages, an indoor arcade, a skateboard shop and a snack bar.

The go-carts and collision carts are $3 a ride or four rides for $10. In the junior area, the rides are $1 to $2 per ride. The park is open Memorial Day to Labor Day, 10 AM to 10 PM, Friday and Saturday and 10 AM to 6 PM Monday through Thursday. In spring and fall,

the park is open Friday and Saturday 10 AM until 8 PM (until 6 PM Monday through Thursday). The park closes in winter. Family discounts are available.

Lake Wallenpaupack Area

Cherrywood Fun Park
Pa. Hwy. 196, Sterling • 676-9930, (800) 624-1369

This fun park has video games, kiddie rides, miniature golf, castles, a sea of balls and other kid activities. This park is new and expanding all the time, so call to see what's happening. There are two separate dance floors on two different levels. The top level is for adults; the lower level will be opening soon for teens. You can have birthday parties here too.

Admission to the park itself is free; rides require tokens. Please call for specific hours.

Costa's Family Fun Park
U.S. Hwy. 6, Lords Valley • 226-8585, (800) 928-4FUN

This park is east of Lake Wallenpaupack and features a game room, batting cage, miniature golf, go-carts, a driving range and a kiddie-land with tube mazes, crawling webs, a web ladder and a sea of balls. The restaurant has an outdoor porch for dining and offers Kids Meals.

Admission is free; you pay per ride. The park is open the first weekend in May through Labor Day; please call for specific hours.

Carousel Water & Fun Park
Pa. Hwy. 652, Beach Lake • 729-7532

This park has two giant water slides and bumper boats in its water area. There are also kiddie go-carts, adult go-carts, an arcade, batting cages and miniature golf. A snack bar is available for treats, or you can bring your own picnic and enjoy it in the free picnic area. See our Attractions chapter for details about Carousel.

Let's Make Something

Many area museums and arts organiza-

Photo: Pocono Mountains Vacation Bureau, Inc.

Cool off on a summer day at one of several Pocono area water slides.

tions offer classes for children throughout the year. These opportunities are generally for a few hours in the morning or afternoon. The *Pocono Record* is a good source to check for what kids can do at the local museums. The offerings change from month to month, but we will list a few of the places that provide opportunities throughout the year.

Delaware Water Gap

Antoine Dutot School & Museum
Pa. Hwy. 611, Delaware Water Gap • 421-5809

This museum offers arts and crafts classes at different times throughout the year. Fees are based on supplies needed and the length of the class. See our Attractions and Arts and Culture chapters for more information about the museum as a place to visit.

Stroudsburg/ East Stroudsburg

Stroud Community House
900 Main St., Stroudsburg • 421-7703

At various times of the year, this museum offers classes in different crafts, such as Victo-

rian Christmas decorations. At its smaller museum, Dreibe Freight Station (alongside an authentic caboose), 424-1776, they offer craft classes based on historical crafts and art forms from March to December. Downstairs in the small Dreibe museum, there is a hands-on children's museum displaying games and activities that entertained children before TV and video games became so popular.

West End

Marie Feliz Gallery and Sculpture Garden
60 W. Broadway, Jim Thorpe • 325-8969

This gallery cooperates with the Carbon County School system to put together a children's art show annually. In March (Youth Arts Month), teachers from the Carbon County public schools and Carbon County Vo-Tech enter 15 pieces from their kindergarten through 12th-grade classes' art portfolios in an exhibition at the gallery. There is an opening artists reception, and the children's works are on display weekends throughout the month. The same exhibit is then displayed at the Dimmick Memorial Library in Jim Thorpe during the Laurel Arts Festival.

Admission to the children's art exhibit is free. During the September Art Walk, in Jim

The Fine Arts Discovery Series (FADS): Concerts for Children

One of the most exciting programs for children (and their parents) in the Poconos is the Fine Arts Discovery Series (FADS).

This innovative program, which hosts performers from all over the country and the world, began as an idea among some parents and music teachers at the music studio of

Susan Stillo-Wilkins in Reeders (Stillo's Music Studio). This delightful music studio housed programs in Kindermusik and Kinder Beginnings as well as programs of study for piano, guitar, musical theater and voice. Susan was constantly looking for ways to enhance the programs offered at the studio: students were taken on field trips to recording studios and performances; they were encouraged to participate in the yearly Federation of Music Teachers competitions; and they were involved in performances themselves in semiannual recitals. But Susan felt a need for more.

Another teacher, Leesa Marks and a parent, Michele Royce, among others, also felt that need. They sensed that students need to see performances up close and interact with musicians willing to share their knowledge and love of music with students and their families. Discussions after classes and over coffee began to evolve a form and plan for a concert series for children. With the help of other active volunteer parents, the series took off. Its first season of performers had an audience of about 50 culled from the families that took music lessons at the studio. Today, the series attracts more than 300 audience members to the concerts, which are now open to the public.

The first concerts took place at a small country church, St. John's Evangelical Church, in Bartonsville. The performers were local professionals who had experience presenting programs for children. They were professionals who didn't mind holding question-and-answer sessions after performances or letting the children touch and try their instruments.

The first season began in the spring of 1990 and produced a concert a month for four months on Sunday afternoons. The children applauded vigorously, asked excellent questions based on their already extensive background from Kindermusik and instrumental music classes and had a wonderful time learning about the instruments up close. It was exciting to watch the children — from toddlers to teenagers — and their parents enjoy and participate in a 40- to 50-minute concert of classical and modern music on a Sunday afternoon.

Sunday afternoons have been a cornerstone of the program because of the Founders' intention to bring families together to share the musical experience. It has become a tradition for participating families over the years. Children get dressed up, as do their parents; lunches or dinners are planned around the outing; refreshments are enjoyed together at the program, and friends meet other friends from the studio for a cultural outing. And as the tradition has evolved, so has the scope of the performances and their backing.

The list of performers continues to include the local well-known professional musicians that Insiders in the area have come to rely on for good performances and dedication to the community. But performers from around the country and the world have also become part of the continuing seasons of the Fine Arts Discovery Series. Local performances have spotlighted the Pocono Youth Chamber Orchestra, the Poconos Saxophone Quartet, Janet Lawson and Trio, Ballet Guild of Lehigh Valley, Calliope with

Steve Mathieson, the Ballet Theatre of Scranton and others. National favorites performing have included the Mock Turtle Marionette Theatre, Jay Smar's History of Folk Music, the Touchstone Theatre, Rick Lyon and the Lyon Puppets, Ted Brown Productions (Masters and Maestros Series — Mozart), The Little Theatre of the Deaf, Marshall Izen ("Mozart, Monsters and Matisse"), David Holt's "Banjos, Bones and Hogaphones" and Spotlite on Opera. International programs have presented the Nai-Ni Chen Dance Company, the Ishangi Family Dancers (African dance, song and legends) and Soh Daiko (art of Japanese Drumming).

The 1996-97 season includes: "Animal Tales Concert" with Bill Shontz, a singer/ songwriter and virtuoso reedman (clarinet, saxophone, flute, pennywhistle and wind synthesizer) who presents his environmental message through music and animal tales; "Lakota Sioux Dance Theatre" an artistic collaboration between Henry Smith, artistic director of Solaris Dance Theatre, and the traditional artists of the Sioux Nation; and "The Monster" a story of bigotry and lessons learned when a king and his wizard disagree, performed by Rick Lyons Puppets. All of the performers in the Fine Arts Discovery Series season will participate in the question-and-answer session after the performance and demonstrate the use of their art to those who are interested — and believe us — all the kids and their parents are interested.

A fourth program will be offered in 1997 as a first-time fund-raiser — "The Cashore Marionettes," presented by Joseph Cashore in a program of short vignettes filled with emotion ranging from laughter to tears. This special program will be presented in a smaller, more intimate setting than the other performances.

Photo: FADS

A SOH DAIKO drummer demonstrates drumming technique to a Fine Arts Discovery Series audience member.

As the scope and size of the audience has grown, so has FADS. It now has an elected president, vice president, secretary, treasurer, nine-member board of directors and 15 committees to organize things such as workshops, fund-raising and study guides.

FADS has tried to maintain its policy of affordable fine arts programs for the family. The 1997 season fund-raiser is one way FADS is coping with the rising costs of producing high-quality concert programs for children. They also have developed a strong corporate-backing program that helps offset costs for the programs. In the past, grants from the Monroe County Arts Council have helped as well as grants from other state agencies. These efforts have helped to keep ticket prices an excellent bargain: Season reserved seat tickets are $20 per person; general admission seating prices are $15 for the first person and $10 for each additional family member. At the door, prices per show are $6 for adults and $5 for children and senior citizens.

As Susan Stillo-Wilkins reiterates in press releases and conversations, she and the people who now are the backbone of the Fine Arts Discovery Series for Children feel "that in these times when children are constantly bombarded with artificial stimulation from TV, video games, et cetera, there exists a need for family-oriented entertainment where young children can discover and experience the thrills and joys of live performances."

And they do, thanks to the founding members and the many volunteers of the continuing Fine Arts Discovery Series.

For more information about the Fine Arts Discovery Series (FADS) of Concerts for Children, call 476-FADS or write to P.O. Box 1126, Stroudsburg, PA 18360.

Thorpe, the gallery presents art workshops for children on the Sunday afternoon of Art Walk. The workshops are free, and the children are sent by the schools in groups of 10.

If your children are interested in participating, contact the gallery for information.

Let's Explore Our World

There is always something new to learn, and kids are excited by learning outside the classroom. Here is a potpourri of exploring opportunities in the area.

Delaware Water Gap

**Delaware Water Gap
National Recreation Area
River Rd. (off U.S. Hwy. 209), Bushkill
• 588-2451**

Two self-guiding programs are available for kids in the park area. The Junior Naturalist Discovery Pack, for ages 6 through 12, is for children to borrow to explore the world of nature. The backpack contains spades, bottles and other necessary implements to complete three of six suggested activities. The activities are meant to orient children to the park and its natural offerings. When a child completes the required activities, he or she receives a Junior Naturalist patch and is eligible to do the self-guided Junior Ranger Program.

The Junior Ranger Program involves a booklet of activities that kids 7 and older can complete at their own pace during a visit to the park. One activity requires the child to speak to a park ranger and attend a presentation about how rangers interpret the park for visitors. The emphasis is on understanding a ranger's daily responsibilities. Program packets are available at the Visitor Center in Bushkill or at the Kittatinny Center on I-80 in New Jersey, (908) 496-4458.

There are also programs that allow teachers to use the park as a classroom. Teacher-led geology classes, hikes on a portion of the Appalachian Trail and the Junior Naturalist Discovery Packs are classroom opportunities. The Pocono Environmental Education Center (PEEC), 828-2319, in Dingmans Ferry, is a wonderful place for teachers to take their classes for an overnight or two of exploring the environment (see the related Close-up in our Parks chapter). Workshops are offered to the students in nature studies, canoeing, problem-solving activities and other nature-related programs. The facilities here are excellent, and the experience is one that makes a deep impact on the children and their teachers. Many Poconos school systems take advantage of these programs with their students throughout the year. Weekend seminars and workshops are available to the public.

Stroudsburg/
East Stroudsburg

**Monroe County
Environmental Education Center
Running Valley Rd., Bartonsville
• 629-3061**

The Environmental Center offers programs

for children during the week and on weekends year round. Many homeschooling parents (see our Education chapter) take advantage of these programs to enhance the science portion of their home-based curriculum. Programs begin for children as young as 3 years old. There are summer opportunities here (see our Camps chapter for summer camps programs) for kids ages 3 through 18. Program topics include "Insects," "Animal Tracks," "Trees and Paper," "Worms," and many other subjects of interest to kids. Birthday parties are a specialty at the center for a $75 fee that includes a birthday cake, juice, pencils and erasers for all party-goers and a T-shirt for the birthday child. The party includes an activity on a chosen topic, which can be based on wildlife, predator/prey, trees, birds, a scavenger hunt and other fun, nature-oriented topics.

Mount Pocono Area

The Nature Conservancy in Northeastern Pennsylvania
Long Pond Rd. (near Pocono Raceway), Long Pond • 643-7922

This center is part of the Pennsylvania Chapter of The Nature Conservancy, a non-profit, land-conservation organization. The Poconos region has been named to the Conservancy's list of the world's "Last Great Places." Within its 12,000 acres it offers programs year round for adults and children. It's a great outlet for teenagers because it uses their help all summer to mark trails, keep the preserves clean and participate in any impromptu projects. The Conservancy also has the Kids' Conservation Corps for ages 8 through 12 on Thursday mornings in the summer. There is a new program each week, so kids can come to one or all. Preregistration is a must, but there is no fee. In the summer Monday Nights at the Movies are a hit with films about black bears, the reintroduction of the osprey, white-tailed deer and other learning-filled presentations. You can take classes in woodcarving, take blueberry-picking trips (ages 6 and older), study waterfowl at Lehigh Pond and watch for snowshoe hares, song-birds, coyotes and black bears at Darling Preserve. There are also lots of programs for adults and kids to do together. Most programs, if they are not specifically children's programs, are for ages 10 and older.

The Conservancy also sponsors walks in the Tannersville Cranberry Bog, 629-3061, that are open to children. The Cranberry Bog is a northern boreal bog, considered unique in this area. The schools take field trips here too.

Let's Go To The Fair

See our Annual Events chapter for some fair-type events that happen in the Poconos. Most fairs, carnivals and circuses are summertime kid-stops. Look in the local papers for schedules and discount coupons. The circuses are usually sponsored by local community service organizations such as Kiwanis or Lions clubs. The local carnivals are generally for the benefit of the local volunteer fire departments. The townspeople volunteer to run the booths, and the rides are brought in by a promoter. Ticket prices vary, but there are always family nights that offer a set price ticket for the whole night. If you have moved into the area, consider volunteering at one of the stands. It's hard work, but it's a great way to meet your neighbors.

Let's Go To The Park

We have noted the many opportunities available in our state parks in many other chapters of this guide. Check our Parks, Recreation, In, On and Around the Water, Winter Sports and Camps chapters. These activities include the many sports and outdoor learning experiences that abound in these state treasures. In particular, check out Beltzville State Park, in Leheighton, and Promised Land State Park. These two sites have an abundance of programs for children that are noted in the aforementioned chapters. Promised Land runs nature-based free programs all summer long. Beltzville offers day camps, day programs, weekend programs for families and other activities throughout the summer season, all based on nature.

If you want to just enjoy a day at the playground with your children, there are quite a few neighborhood parks open to the public. Many of our residents live in communities that have their own private playgrounds, recreation clubhouses and swimming pools. These parks are primarily in towns. For other fun options see our Parks chapter that points out the wonders of the national and state parks in the Poconos.

Delaware Water Gap

Shull Park (Town Park)
Oak St., Delaware Water Gap • 476-0331
This lovely, little park has a swimming pool (see our In, On and Around the Water chapter), a basketball court and a playground. There are also some tables for a picnic lunch with your friends while the toddlers play.

Stroudsburg/ East Stroudsburg

Dansbury Park
Day St., East Stroudsburg • 421-6591
This park has a great swimming pool and a swimming lessons program. (See our In, On and Around the Water chapter.) Also in this town park are a playground, basketball courts and picnic pavilion. There are lots of trees and benches to enjoy while the children play.

Stroudsburg Municipal Pool
W. Main St., Stroudsburg • 421-5444
Besides the pool (see our In, On and Around the Water chapter), this town park has a playground, tennis court, basketball courts, baseball field and other areas that are part of

the public recreation center in Stroudsburg. There are places to picnic after a hard game of ball.

West End

Mauch Chunk Lake Park
Lentz Trail Hwy., Jim Thorpe • 325-3669
This park is discussed in other chapters (Parks; Recreation; Winter Sports; and In, On and Around the Water). It is an especially nice family park in the summer, with swimming, boating and court games available. Biking trails make it a fun spot for family bike treks that can be centered at a campsite in the park or the destination for an exhilarating daytrip. See In, On and Around the Water and Parks for more camping information.

Slate Belt

Weona Park
Pa. Hwy. 512, Pen Argyl • (610) 863-9249
An Olympic-size pool for residents and nonresidents is a centerpiece of this well-used town park (see our In, On and Around the Water chapter). A picnic area is available, and there are playing fields for soccer and baseball, and basketball and tennis courts. Also check out the old-fashioned carousel in one of the buildings.

Let's Go Skating

If your kids like to skate, they have the options of ice-skating or roller-skating all year round at various facilities.

Stroudsburg/ East Stroudsburg

For ice-skating (see our Winter Sports chapter), Pocono Ice-A-Rama at Penn Hills, 421-6465, is open year round; Mountain Manor, 223-8098, is open for ice-skating in the winter and roller-skating or in-line skating in the spring, summer and fall. Other places to ice-skate are also noted in our Winter Sports chapter, including Mauch Chunk Lake Park and some of the state parks. Many of the resorts in our Accommodations chapter also have ice-skating and/or roller-skating, so be sure to check for these activities when you review our Accommodations chapter.

For roller-skating try the following places.

Big Wheel
Pa. Hwy. 191, Stroudsburg • 424-5499

Big Wheel has special nights for adults and teenagers, but Saturday afternoons are for the kids. The Hokey-Pokey and the Chicken Dance on skates are real highlights for kids. Sunday afternoons are for families. Sunday evenings and some weekday evenings are set aside for roller-hockey leagues to practice. Programs for toddlers are on Wednesday mornings. Children can use their kiddie skates or ride their big wheel trikes, and parents can skate with them. Admission and skate rental costs about $5. Some in-line skates are acceptable, but not those meant for street hockey. Check to see if your kids' skates are allowed; if not you can rent them for $1.

Parties are fun here in the party room. The $60 charge is for a minimum of 12 kids and includes a hot dog, drink, admission and skate rental. You bring your own cake and supplies. There is always lots of activity here on the weekends, but a separate smaller skating area in the party room makes the parties manageable. Party hours are 1 to 4 PM Saturday and Sunday.

The Starting Gate
U.S. Hwy. 209, Marshalls Creek • 223-6215

If your kids are heavily into in-line skating and skateboarding, take them to The Starting Gate, about a quarter-mile north of Foxmoor Village. Children younger than 18 must be accompanied by an adult, and a permission slip must be signed to use the facility. It has a 6-foot mini-ramp, fun box, pyramid, slant ramp, other ramps and neat things for kids to jump on and off of with their skates or skateboards.

There are no restrictions on types of in-line skates; however, pads and helmets must be worn. If you don't have them, you can rent them for 75¢ a set for pads and $1 for helmets for the day. You can rent skates and all protective gear for $10 for the day. The all-day admission charge is $5. The Starting Gate is open every day, generally from around 9 AM to 6 PM, but call ahead to check because hours do change.

Mount Pocono Area

Wheels In-Line Skate and Skateboard Park
Jack Frost Ski Area, Pa. Hwy. 940, Blakeslee • 443-8425, (800) 468-2442

For more high-speed fun, try this park in Blakeslee. You can in-line skate, roller-skate or skateboard here. There is a freestyle area, a one-quarter pipe, rail slides and a 120-foot-by-60-foot street-hockey arena. Children younger than 18 must have their parents sign a waiver to allow them to skate here. Skaters must wear protective gear and helmets. Rentals are available for the knee pads, wrist pads, elbow pads and helmets; the price depends on what you need to rent. For skates and all the protective gear, including the helmet, the fee is $10 for the day. The park is open April through October, depending on the weather conditions. Hours are 9 AM to 5 PM everyday. Admission is $7 for a half-day and $10 for a full day.

Milford Area

Big Wheel North
U.S. Hwy. 209, Matamoras (10 miles north of Milford) • 491-1117

This rink is owned by the same people that own the Big Wheel in Stroudsburg. It has the same programs, but toddler day is Tues-

INSIDERS' TIPS

Check out *The Miracle Shopper*, *The Poconos This Week* and *Yankee Clipper* for discount coupons to many of the places mentioned in this chapter, including skating rinks, animal parks and playlands.

day. Both Big Wheels have facilities for birthday parties, church parties or PTO events and special nights that can even include line-dancing. In-line skates are restricted to approved types, so if you have your own, be sure to check in advance to ensure yours are acceptable. It costs about $5 for admission and skate rental. Saturday and Sunday afternoons from 1 to 4 PM are set aside for children.

West End

La Rose Roller Rink
U.S. Hwy. 209, Lehighton • (610) 377-1859

This skating rink has been family owned for more than 70 years, so families are a big concentration here. Sunday afternoons are for the whole family; Saturday afternoons are reserved for kids 12 and younger; and Friday and Saturday nights are for the 12-and-older crowd, including adults. You can rent in-line skates at La Rose, but you cannot bring your own because the floor is real 70-year-old wood. This rink accepts private parties every day. General rink hours are 7:30 to 10:30 PM Friday and Saturday and 1 to 5 PM on Sunday.

Let's Go Skiing

You will find some very good programs for children in the Pocono area ski resorts. Refer to our Winter Sports chapter for information about skiing.

Blue Mountain, (610) 826-7700, has the excellent SKIWee program that teaches children ages 3 and older to ski. Shawnee, 421-7231, and Blue Mountain also have racing programs for juniors. Jack Frost, 443-8425, which has produced several Junior Olympic Ski Team participants, also has a racing program. Big Boulder, 722-0100, has its C'n Ski programs for children that are also very popular parents. At Camelback, 629-1661, children go to

Cameland for lessons once they are 3 years old. There is also a fine weekend ski camp at Mount Tone, (800) 747-2SKI (see our Camps chapter for more information about this program).

Camelback, Big Boulder, Jack Frost, Shawnee and Mount Tome ski areas also have facilities for snowboarding and snowtubing (see our Winter Sports chapter).

Many area schools sponsor ski programs as part of their physical education programs. For a fee, students can ski for a six-week period during the winter season. The base fee is for a lift ticket, but the fees go up depending on the child's needs for lessons or ski equipment. Whatever part of the package you need, the programs are very reasonable (less than $100). Some ski programs are offered by parents groups through the schools, but they are not technically school-sponsored activities. Parents are responsible for pick-up and delivery. These programs are also incredibly low-priced, and fees are based on the child's needs (lift ticket, lessons or equipment in any combination). The school-sponsored programs provide school transportation to and from the ski areas. In late October, start looking for ski information from your child's school in the bottom of your kid's schoolbag, under the crushed Twinkies.

Let's Go Trick-or-Treating

Trick-or-Treating is a time-honored, but regulated tradition in the Poconos. Each town decides which day is trick-or-treating day (not always on Halloween). Curfews are set for the designated day. Be sure to check in the newspaper for the locally assigned dates.

The schools in the Poconos also hold costume parades at the individual schools at the end of the day they designate as Halloween Party Day. The custom is for the children to dress up and parade around the school

Photo: Pocono Mountains Vacation Bureau, Inc.

Join in a day of fun at Shawnee Place.

grounds while the parents watch and applaud each class's efforts. Even the teachers get into the fun and dress up in some pretty outrageous outfits. Again, watch for the school notices in your kid's bookbag; it's the crumpled piece of paper with the jelly on it.

Stroudsburg/ East Stroudsburg

The Stroud Mall has a Mall Trick-or-Treating night, usually the night before the town-sponsored day. Merchants stand outside their stores and hand out goodies, sometimes coupons, to an endless stream of children who seem to do a Halloween dance around the Mall. Check the *Pocono Record* during Halloween week for particulars.

Also, haunted castles, houses and hayrides seem to pop up out of nowhere at this time of the year. You'll see signs for them everywhere along the roads and advertisements in the newspaper; generally, they are run by the local community service organizations.

The Jacob Stroud Organization also sponsors a Halloween Parade in Stroudsburg each year. Children and adults dress up and march down Main Street, where merchants give away candy. The costumes are judged for prizes.

Frazetta's, 421-9054, in East Stroudsburg has a large selection of costumes for sale and rent. Following a recent fire, it is in the process of restoring the damaged parts of the facility (see our Shopping chapter for details). It also has an intense museum of horror about serial killers (which includes a terribly graphic mock execution) that is advertised around Halloween. Please be advised that we DO NOT recommend it for children.

Mount Pocono Area

A child-style Halloween ride is at the Pennsylvania Dutch Farm on Grange Road in Mount Pocono, 839-7680. It is low key and offers a fun maze, a petting zoo, a haunted wagon ride and other Halloween-theme activities.

Halloween parades are another township-sponsored activity. In Barrett Township, near Mountainhome, the local businessfolk dress up and parade with costumed children down Pa. Highway 191, distributing candy to all the parade watchers who scramble headlong after the treats. The Pocono Mountain High School Marching Band dresses up and plays as the parade marches on. This parade is usually held the Sunday before Halloween. Check your *Pocono Record* for the actual date and time.

West End

In Jim Thorpe, the main street (Broadway and W. Broadway) gets dressed up for theatrically inspired events, spearheaded by the group at the Mauch Chunk Opera House. The Emporium of Curious Goods, 325-4038, on Broadway, is an interesting Halloween stop that has information on white magic and other curious subjects.

Let's Talk To the Animals

Animals, wild and domestic, are always a draw for kids (and grown ups), so here are a few places to find them in the Poconos.

By the way, zoos and animal parks are not the only place to see animals in our Poconos. A daily trip to the grocery store can provide lots of excitement when you spot a fawn and its mother waiting by the side of the road or chasing each other across the road. You can spot wild turkeys along roadsides and herons in the ponds that dot the countryside. If you slow down, you might see red-headed woodpeckers knocking on the trees alongside the road, hummingbirds hovering around the planters on someone's deck and hawks circling overhead. And, on some days, you just might be slowed down by bears — black bears — who think nothing of ambling down the road in front of your car. If you're an Insider, you may also see them tearing through your trash cans if you didn't put the lids on tightly. Our trash cans have big claw holes from the bears pulling the tops off!

Open your eyes as you drive our exciting country roads and see all the animals that surround you. Oh, and watch out for that possum! Did you ever hear the joke about possums? Why did the chicken cross the road? To show the possum it could be done.

Stroudsburg/ East Stroudsburg

Pocono Snake and Animal Farm
U.S. Hwy. 209, Marshalls Creek • 223-8653

This farm has more than 100 reptiles and live animals. Besides monkeys, alligators and really huge snakes, it has a petting zoo for the little ones. (See our Attractions chapter for more information.)

Quiet Valley Living Historical Farm
Turkey Hill Rd., Stroudsburg • 992-6161

Quiet Valley also has a petting zoo. In the spring the annual Farm Animal Frolic lets the children —and you — delight in seeing the newborn lambs and other baby animals interact with their parents and each other on a living farm. (See our Attractions, Arts and Culture and Annual Events chapters for more information about this museum for all seasons.)

Mount Pocono Area

Pocono Farmstand and Nursery
Pa. Hwy. 611, Tannersville • 629-3344

If you've already read our Shopping chapter, you probably noticed the Pocono Farmstand. It has a free petting zoo, so stop and let the kids talk to the animals while you buy some fresh corn, choose a few perennials or purchase some home-baked cookies to snack on as you wend your way home.

Milford Area

Malibu Ranch
Seventh St., Milford • 296-7281

For a real change of pace, you might want to consider this dude ranch, which features rodeos and other special horse events throughout the year. Stay overnight or make a day trip just for the rodeos. A day at the rodeo costs $40 per person and includes lunch and all events. If you want to participate in any of the rodeo competitions, the entrance fee is $5 per competition. This is a family fun place that also offers trail rides, tennis, fishing and a rifle range among other opportunities. (See our Accommodations chapter for information on staying here.)

Lake Wallenpaupack Area

Claws 'N' Paws Wild Animal Park
Pa. Hwy. 590, Hamlin • 698-6154

This is another great place to talk to the animals (see our Attractions chapter). For those who love tigers, this is the place to see a rare white Siberian tiger. For those interested in less exotic animals, there are also farm animal exhibits, petting zoos and birds of various types. So, there's an animal for each member of the family to bond with and enjoy watching.

What About Teens?

Teens in the Poconos have plenty of opportunities for activity. There are lots of programs for them at the schools — sports teams, bands, theatrical groups, activity clubs, yearbooks, literary magazines, school papers and so on. There are also youth groups for teens at churches. We have noted several opportunities for teens throughout the book: the Pocono Youth Orchestra (see our Arts and Culture chapter) is an excellent outlet for young musical talent; in our Winter Sports chapter, we note programs for teenage skiers; in our

Recreation chapter, we point out many different opportunities for your family's teenagers, especially if they are into biking, with a focus on great bike trips in Jim Thorpe and Mauch Chunk Lake Park. In this chapter we note the many area skating rinks and education-based programs that also offer teens some great choices for their leisure time. See our Camps chapter for specialized programs that cater to your teen's sports and arts interests.

The arcades at Cherrywood Fun Park in Sterling and Pocono Go-Carts in Bartonsville and Marshalls Creek (see the "Let's Play" section in this chapter) are places teens like to go. And teens like to meet at Stroud Mall's well-protected and well-maintained arcade.

Our Attractions chapter includes lots of places teens might enjoy, such as minigolf courses. One attraction your more adventurous teenagers might find fun is the Cathedral Rock Climbing Gym in Lehighton (West End). The interior of an old church has been converted into an indoor climbing area of more than 6,000 square feet. Lessons are available for those who want to learn. There are climbing places for all levels here.

If your teen is a budding guitarist, check out the Martin Guitar Company, in Nazareth, with him or her. The place is a guitar player's mecca. See our Attractions chapter for details.

If you're an Insider, don't forget volunteer opportunities to keep your teens happy. The Nature Conservancy (see the "Let's Go To the Parks" section in this chapter) and libraries are always looking for volunteers. Also, in Pennsylvania you can get your working papers at age 14. Many teenagers here start working as soon as they reach this golden age.

One day during the first week in January, folks who have never skied get the chance to learn for free.

Annual Events and Festivals

People in the Poconos love a good time as much as anyone. We throw parties and hold special events nearly every week all year long. Church groups hold craft shows and bake sales. Fire departments host carnivals in summer. Communities have flea markets. Agricultural fairs have provided fun family entertainment for decades.

The following list describes some of the larger annual activities held in the Poconos. They are arranged by geographic region and approximate chronological order by month. Admission fees cited are for 1996 events; while some might stay the same, please note that fees for 1997 events are subject to change. Call the numbers with each listing for exact date and cost.

January

Pennsylvnia Learn to Ski Free Day
Various locations throughout the Poconos • (800) 762-6667

One day during the first week in January, folks who have never skied get the chance to learn for free. Participating ski areas in the Poconos include Alpine Mountain, Camelback, Big Boulder, Blue Mountain, Jack Frost and Shawnee. Reservations are required. Call the individual ski areas (see our Winter Sports chapter for details) for restrictions and reservations. Or call the listed toll-free number to speak with a representative of the Pocono Mountains Vacation Bureau about this program.

Ski the Poconos College Week
Various locations throughout the Poconos • 424-6050

College students compete in such unusual activites as snow volleyball and snow golf. If you can't get to Florida for the winter, come to the Poconos for Frisbee and bikini contests. Also part of the week is a free one-hour introduction to snowboarding (reservations are required). Spectators and participants are welcome at all activities. Admission varies by site and activity. Call for information about individual events and locations.

Delaware Water Gap

Mid-Atlantic Snowboard Series
Shawnee Mountain Ski Area • Hollow Rd. (off I-80, Exit 52), Shawnee-on-Delaware • 421-7231 Ext. 249

More than 100 top snowboarders from across the East Coast compete in this United States Snowboarding Association-sanctioned event featuring half-pipe and free-style events. Held mid-month, the competition is free for spectators.

Stroudsburg/ East Stroudsburg

Cooking Class
Naturally Rite Restaurant • U.S. Hwy. 209, Marshalls Creek • 223-0140

At the end of January, a chef teaches you how to prepare healthy soups and stews. Best of all, you get to sample the finished products. This is truly a chance to immediately reap the benefits of education. Reservations are recommended; admission is $10.

Mount Pocono Area

WSBG's Northeast Pennsylvania Bridal Expo

Pocono Manor Inn• Pa. Hwy. 314, Pocono Manor • 421-2100

Anyone planning to "walk down the aisle" should not miss this expo—billed as "the largest bridal event in the Poconos." More than 40 vendors exhibit all the accessories needed for a perfect wedding, at Pocono Manor in late January. There's also a professional fashion show. Admission is free; call for tickets.

West End

Festival of Ice

The Mountain Laurel Resort Hotel and Golf Club • Pa. Hwy. 534 (off I-80, Exit 41), White Haven • (800) 458-5921

In mid-January, join the crowd to watch champion ice carvers compete to create the most magnificent sculpture. Crafts are displayed and sold, winter activities are offered and food and drinks are available. Admission is free for spectators.

Annual King of the Poconos Ice Fishing Contest

Pennsylvania Fishing Museum • Pa. Hwy. 402, Pecks Pond • 775-7237

Held at either Pecks Pond or Lake Wallenpaupack (depending on ice conditions) in late January, this contest attracts the best hard-water anglers in the Poconos. Participants cut holes in the ice and try to entice prize-winning fish. Admission is free for spectators.

February

Stroudsburg/ East Stroudsburg

A Snowy Mountain Craft Fair

Stroudsmoor Country Inn • Stroudsmoor Rd., Stroudsburg • 424-1199

Special crafts and antiques shows feature handmade and vintage gift items in addition to what's available in the 10 shops always open at Stroudsmoor. After shopping, enjoy a delicious brunch at the inn; there is a nominal charge. Admission to the shows is free. This fair takes place in late February.

Mount Pocono Area

Presidents Festival Celebration

Alpine Mountain Ski Area • Pa. Hwy. 447, Analomink • 595-2150

Skiers receive two lift tickets for the price of one in mid-February in honor of Valentine's Day. Enjoy ski and snowboard races and free clinics, giveaways, live entertainment and drink specials in the lounge.

West End

Presidents Weekend Celebration

Various locations throughout Jim Thorpe • 325-3673

This annual mid-February event features special sales at shops throughout this quaint Victorian town. Cross-country skiing, ice-climbing and snowboarding demonstrations are held at Blue Mountain Sports. Ice-carving demonstrations in Packer Park also are part of this mid-month tradition. Admission is free.

Lake Wallenpauapck Area

Ice Tee Golf Tournament

Lake Wallenpaupack, U.S. Hwy. 6, Hawley • 226-3191

Golfers play nine holes on frozen Lake Wallenpaupack in late February. The fairways are lined with Christmas trees. A driving contest awards prizes to the golfer who hits a ball closest to a replica of mascot Wally Paupack. Refreshments are available. Admission is free for spectators.

March

Delaware Water Gap

Annual Costume Carnival Day
Shawnee Mountain Ski Area • Hollow Rd. (off I-80 Exit 52), Shawnee-on-Delaware • 421-7231 Ext. 229

Folks in costume ski for free. Seeing ski slopes packed with folks in their Halloween best in mid-March is quite the late-winter horror show. There's a costume parade and prizes too. (See our Winter Sports chapter for more information.)

Stroudsburg/ East Stroudsburg

Maple Sugaring Program
Monroe County Environmental Education Center • 8050 Running Valley Rd., Bartonsville • 629-3061

In early March, this environmental center conducts tours that discuss the history of maple sugaring as well as early Native American and pioneer methods of collecting it. Observe demonstrations of the methods of collecting and cooking maple sugar. Admission is free for Education Center members; nonmember fees are $4 for adults and $2 for children.

St. Patrick's Day Celebration
Alpine Mountain Ski Area • Pa. Hwy. 447, Analomink • 595-2150

Here's another chance for leprechauns to ski for free (if dressed in green). Hidden shamrock tokens yield prizes for lucky finders. Even the beer is green on St. Patrick's Day weekend.

Mount Pocono Area

Annual Chili Cook-Off
Daniels Family Resort • Pa. Hwy. 447, Canadensis • 595-7531, (800) 755-0300

The Pocono region's finest inns, restaurants and chili enthusiasts serve up their best

for you to sample in early March. The East Stroudsburg University Hotel School Culinary Arts Department adjudicates. Prizes are awarded, and country bands perform. Admission is free.

Luck O' the Irish Weekend
Camelback Ski Area • Off I-80 Exit 45, Tannersville • 629-1661

That's right, in honor of St. Patrick's Day, anyone dressed in green skis for free. Shamrocks hidden throughout the mountain are worth a pot of gold (well, at least a prize). This event takes place during St. Patty's Day weekend.

Milford Area

Pike County Builders Show
Best Western at Hunt's Landing • U.S. Hwy. 209, Matamoras • 296-5500

This late March show attracts all the leading commercial and residential builders and the lending institutions. If you are looking to build or remodel your home, you will get a lot of ideas here. Admission is $4 for folks 12 and older; children younger than 12 are free.

Lake Wallenpaupack Area

Easter Craft Show
Hamlin Elementary School • Pa. Hwy. 191, Hamlin • 689-4199

More than 40 crafters from New York, New Jersey and Pennsylvania exhibit their wares at this late March show. Admission is $1 per person for folks 12 and older, and children younger than 12 are free.

April

Stroudsburg/ East Stroudsburg

WVPO Health and Fitness Fair
Plaza Hotel • 1200 W. Main St., Stroudsburg • 421-2100

This day-long, mid-April event is organized

to familiarize people with the health and fitness options available in the Poconos. Free screenings and blood pressure tests are offered. Admission is free.

West End

Old-Fashioned Horse-Drawn Hayrides
Split Rock Resort • Pa. Hwy. 903, Lake Harmony • 722-9111 Ext. 500

Every weekend in April, you can tour the grounds of Split Rock and Lake Harmony on an old-fashioned, 45-minute hayride. Admission is $8 per person for folks 13 and older and $5 for children ages 3 to 12; kids younger than 3 are free.

Easter Bunny Train Rides
Rail Tours Inc. • Train Depot • U.S. Hwy. 209, Jim Thorpe • 325-3673

The Easter Bunny hosts a 40-minute train ride in early April. There is an Easter egg hunt at the end of the trip for children 8 and younger. Proceeds benefit the Fairview and Diligent Ambulance Association. Admission is $7 for folks 12 and older and $4 for children ages 9 to 11; two children younger than 9 travel free with each adult ticket purchased.

Celebration – A Musical Salute to Easter
Mountain Laurel Resort • Pa. Hwy. 534 (off I-80 Exit 41), White Haven • 443-8411, (800) 458-5921

Reservations are required for this early April show presenting highlights from *Godspell*, *Joseph & the Amazing Technicolor Dreamcoat* and *Jesus Christ Superstar*. This joyous event is fun for the entire family. Admission is $12 per person.

April Showers Concert
Mauch Chunk Historical Society • 41 W. Broadway, Jim Thorpe • 325-4439

Local performers and members of Studio Kids, a group of young performers, collaborate in a variety show including classics, show tunes, ballads and popular music. On the same mid-April weekend, the same performers collaborate on another variety show called Festival of Young Artists. Proceeds benefit Studio Kids and Mauch Chunk Historical Society. Admission costs had not yet been determined at press time. For more information, call the listed number between noon and 5 PM Thursday through Sunday and ask for Marie.

Lake Wallenpaupack Area

Bunny Run
Stourbridge Line Rail Excursions • 742 Main St., Honesdale • 253-1960

Another stop on the Easter Bunny's busy early April schedule is this two-hour trip that includes an Easter egg hunt in Hawley's Bingham Park. He is joined by Mr. Mouse for a 26-mile train ride, complete with treats for the kids. Admission is $10 per person.

May

Stroudsburg/ East Stroudsburg

Country Sampler Fair
Stroudsmoor Country Inn • Stroudsmoor Rd., Stroudsburg • 424-1199

Crafts, antiques, food, pony rides and a petting zoo comprise this traditional country fair in early May. Admission is free.

Farm Animal Frolic
Quiet Valley Historical Farm • 1000 Turkey Hill Rd., Stroudsburg • 992-6161

This mid-May event presents a special chance for parents and grandparents to educate children about the animals on a farm. Costumed guides provide information about baby animals and egg hatching in an incubator. Children enjoy the petting zoo, pony rides and a hay jump. Admission is $3 for anyone 1 and older.

Greek Festival
Holy Cross Greek Orthodox Church • 135 Stokes Ave., Stroudsburg • 421-5734

There's no admission fee to listen to the Greek music, watch the dancing exhibitions or enjoy the exhibits and church tours, but we challenge you to leave without buying some outstanding homemade Greek cuisine. The pasteries are so good that you will be glad take-out packages are available. This event takes place in mid-May.

Pocono Train Show
Stroudsburg High School • W. Main St., Stroudsburg • 421-1990

The Pocono Mountains Chapter of the National Railway Historical Society sponsors this model-train exhibit. A running layout and test tracks are provided. You also may purchase trains at this event, which takes place in late May. Admission for folks 13 and older is $3 per person; children 12 and younger get in free.

Mount Pocono Area

Great Chefs on the Mountain
Skytop Lodge • Pa. Hwy. 390, Skytop • 595-6260, 595-7551, 595-7401

Some of the finest chefs and restaurant owners in the Poconos serve samples of their best creations in early May. Proceeds benefit Christian Awareness Ministries Ecumenical, which provides a food pantry, medic alert program, senior center and transportation. Admission is $8 per person in advance (call for tickets) and $10 at the door.

West End

Annual Shad Fest
Asa Packer Park • U.S. Hwy. 209, Jim Thorpe • 325-9399

This mid-May event features shad fishing tips and shad dinners cooked on open-pit grills. Admission is free; the only thing you pay for is dinner.

Milford Area

Upper Delaware Shad Fest
Along the Delaware River, Narrowsburg, N.Y. • (914) 685-2489

Celebrate the great outdoors at this early May event featuring fishing, archery and turkey-calling contests. Fly-tying and casting demonstrations are offered. Other entertainment includes country music and children's games. Admission is free.

June

Stroudsburg/ East Stroudsburg

Cranberry Bog Nature Walks
Monroe County Environmental Education Center • 8050 Running Valley Rd., Bartonsville • 629-3061

Held every Wednesday in June, these guided tours are the only way to experience the unique natural wonder of the Tannersville Cranberry Bog. You will see orchids and insect-eating plants among other rare flora. See our Natural World chapter for more information on bogs. Admission is $2 for Education Center members, $3 for nonmembers and $1.50 for children.

Mount Pocono Area

The UAW-GM Teamwork 500
Pocono International Raceway • Pa. Hwy. 115, Long Pond • 646-2300

Two times each year, in mid-June and mid-July, the stars of NASCAR come to the Poconos to compete at Pocono Raceway. More than 100,000 fans fill the raceway to watch stock-car racing's superstars battle on this 2.5-mile tri-oval. Every race sells out, so order tickets early. See our Attractions chapter for a Closeup on the colorful history of Pocono Raceway. Tickets range from $40 to $375.

Laurel Festival of the Arts
Split Rock Resort • I-80 Exit 43, Lake Harmony • 722-9111, (800) 255-7625

The Artists in Residence of the Laurel Festival of the Arts perform chamber music at this mid-June concert. Admission is $7.50 per person for the concert; a concert and dinner combination costs $30.

Pocono American Roots Music Festival

Big Boulder • Pa. Hwy. 903, Lake Harmony • 443-8425

Nationally famous folk, gospel, zydeco, rockabilly and Tex-Mex performers play outdoors on two stages. The 1996 concert featured Joe Ely, C.J. Chenier, Sleepy LaBeef and Big Sandy & His FlyRite Boys. This late June weekend also features food and other vendors, workshops, demonstrations and screenings of rare roots-music films. Admission is $12 per day for adults and $1 per day for kids ages 2 through 12.

Great Tastes of Pennsylvania Wine and Food Festival

The Resort at Split Rock • Pa. Hwy. 903, Lake Harmony • (800) 255-7625

Winemakers from throughout Pennsylvania offer their products for sampling. Food, music and more than 50 arts and crafts dealers provide other entertainment when you need to take a break from the wine at this late June festival. Admission is $15 at the door ($13 in advance), and tots younger than 2 are free; group rates are available.

West End

Laurel Blossom Festival & Craft Fair

Train Station • Pa. Hwy. 903, Jim Thorpe • 325-3673

Crafters and ethnic food vendors surround the station. Train rides (with an admission charge of $5 for adults and $3 for children) leave every hour each afternoon of this early June weekend. Other activities take place throughout town. There is an art show; mansion, old jail, church and museum tours; and live music. Admission is free.

Mountain Bike Weekend

Mauch Chunk Lake Park • 625 Lentz Trail Rd., Jim Thorpe • 325-3669

This mid-June event is the oldest and largest noncompetitive mountain bike gathering in the eastern United States. Thousands of biking enthusiasts enjoy the numerous trails surrounding Jim Thorpe. Clinics, organized rides, a fashion show and a beach party are included. There is no fee to participate.

Laurel Festival of the Arts

Various locations throughout Jim Thorpe • 325-4439

This two-week concert series in late June, sponsored by the Mauch Chunk Historical Society, is the premier classical music presentation in the Poconos. In addition to the performances by nationally famous musicans, children's programs, exhibitions at art galleries and poetry readings are scheduled. Admission is $45 per person for all concerts, $20 for the opening chamber music reception and concert and $10 for each concert individually.

Lake Wallenpaupack Area

Mountain Top Pow Wow & Western Festival

Triple W Riding Stables • U.S. Hwy. 6, Lake Wallenpaupack • 226-2620

Native American and Western events such as drum and dance competitions, storytelling, tepee-raising, native food, horseback rides, live country music and educational programs are featured. Admission to this mid-June event is $6 per person in advance and $8 per person at the gate.

Wildflower Art Festival/ Wildflower Music Festival

Dorflinger-Suydam Wildlife Sanctuary • Off U.S. Hwy. 6, White Mills • 253-1185

Beginning in late June and continuing into July and August, this festival presents art exhibits and open-air performances of classical, jazz, early American and popular music. Musicans who played at the festival in 1996 include folk singer Tom Chapin, the Philadelphia Renaissance Wind Band and jazz pianist Butch Thompson. Admission for adults is $12; students cost $6.

Slate Belt

Wind Gap Bluegrass Festival

Mountain View Park • Pa. Hwy. 512, Wind Gap • (610) 759-8116

Local and national bluegrass performers pick and grin throughout this early June festival in the Slate Belt. Spectators travel from

Octoberfest is alive and well in the Poconos.

across the eastern United States to hear these talented musicians. The 1996 included nationally known acts such as Robin and Linda Williams, Del McCoury, Ralph Stanley & the Clinch Mountain Boys and Country Current, a unit of the United States Navy Band. Admission is $35 per person for the three-day weekend, $10 for Friday, $16 for Saturday and $14 for Sunday.

July

Stroudsburg/ East Stroudsburg

Cranberry Bog Nature Walks
Monroe County Environmental Education Center • 8050 Running Valley Rd., Bartonsville • 629-3061

The weekly Wednesday walks through the Tannersville Cranberry Bog continue through July. See the previous entry in the "June" section for more information.

Pocono Drum and Bugle Spectacular
Stroudsburg High School Stadium • W. Main St., Stroudsburg • 992-2318

Six world-class drum and bugle corps perfom at this mid-July concert. Music includes '50s favorites, show tunes and jazz. Performances are judged by Drum Corps Association representatives, and awards are presented. The reigning world champions, the Caballeros, played at the 1996 show. Admission is $8 for reserved seating and $6 for general admission.

Mount Pocono Area

"Brewgrass" & Folk Festival
Barley Creek Brewing Company • Sullivan Tr. and Camelback Rd., Tannersville • 629-9399

This mid-July weekend attracts the area's finest bluegrass and folk bands. Fiddle players of all ages compete in the Old Tyme Fiddle Contest on Saturday. Food, the microbrewery's own creations and nonalcoholic beverages are available. Admission for adults is free on Friday and $5 on Saturday; children get in free both days.

Pocono Country Music Festival
Bid Boulder Ski Area • Pa. Hwy. 903, Lake Harmony • 443-8425

Another large outdoor concert weekend at Big Boulder, the Pocono Country Music Festival is held in mid-July and books nationally know country acts. Food vendors, chairlift rides, dance instruction and special exhibits are included. Performers who appeared in 1996 include Bryan White, Lari White and Rhett Akins. Admission for adults is $8 per day at the gate ($5 in advance); children ages 2 to 12 pay $1 per day.

FYI
Unless otherwise noted, the area code for all phone numbers in this guide is 717.

Annual Antique Show and Sale
Mountainhome United Methodist Church • Pa. Hwy. 191, Mountainhome • 595-7282

Each year a different theme is selected for this well-attended annual show. In 1996 it was "Politics in America." Dealers try to focus their offerings around the chosen theme. For example, the 1996 included plenty of campaign memorabilia and presidential items. A donation of $2.50 per person is requested.

Miller Genuine Draft 500
Pocono Raceway • Pa. Hwy. 115, Long Pond • 646-2300

In mid-July the best stock-car drivers in the world return to Pocono Raceway for another battle. See this chapter's June listing and our Attractions chapter Close-up for more information.

Annual Pocono Blues Festival
Big Boulder • Pa. Hwy. 903, Lake Harmony • 443-8425

Some of the biggest names in blues music perform on two stages at this outdoor weekend festival in late July. More than 50 food vendors, seminars and chairlift rides are available. The headliners in 1996 were KoKo Taylor, Lowell Fulson and Robert Lockwood Jr. Harmonica players, guitarists and singers are selected to present a broad spectrum of blues music. Admission is $18 per person per day at the gate ($13 in advance).

Milford Area

Great Delaware River Raft Race
U.S. Hwy. 209, Matamoras • 491-2400

This 2-mile race begins in Matamoras and ends at The Best Western Inn at Hunt's Landing. The entry fee is $40 per team of one to four people and includes raft rentals for the race. The short distance means that even inexperienced paddlers can compete and have fun. Cash prizes are awarded the first-place finisher and the best-decorated raft. Proceeds benefit the Center for Developmental Disabilities Auxiliary. Spectators watch this event (in late July) for free.

Lake Wallenpaupack Area

Audubon Arts & Crafts Festival
Wallenpaupack Elementary and Middle Schools • U.S. Hwy. 6, Hawley • 226-8847

More than 90 professional, juried crafters and nature artists from across the country exhibit and sell their work at this mid-July show. Demonstrations, nature films, free environmental materials and homemade refreshments are available. Admission is $3 for folks 14 and older; children 13 and younger are admitted free.

August

Delaware Water Gap

Pocono State Craft Festival
Sun Mountain Recreation Area • Hollow Rd., Shawnee-on-Delaware • 476-4460

More than 100 juried designer crafters from the Pennsylvania Guild of Craftsmen sell their work here in late August. Craft demonstrations, musical entertainment and an interactive children's play area are among the activities held under tents at this lakeside center. Admission is $5 per person for folks 13 and older; children 12 and younger are admitted free.

Stroudsburg/
East Stroudsburg

Clyde Beatty–Cole Brothers Circus
Stroudsburg Middle School • Chipperfield Dr., Stroudsburg • 421-1131

In mid-August the circus comes to town with its trapeze artists, acrobats, stilt walkers, elephants, tigers, aerialists and The Human Cannonball. Arrive early for an elephant ride. This two-hour show, sponsored by Stroud Township Volunteer Fire Department, has been a hit with local children for many years. Admission is $10 for folks ages 13 to 64 and $6 for children 12 and younger and seniors 65 and older.

Pocono Garlic Festival
St. Luke's Church • Ninth and Main Sts., Stroudsburg • (610) 381-3303

Sample garlic-laced foods to your heart's content for free. Garlic-eating tuba players provide music. If you love the spice, you will love this late August afternoon sidewalk fair sponsored by the Pocono Garlic Growers Association. Admission is free.

Mount Pocono Area

Annual Country Barbecue and Pocono SPAM Bake
Tannersville Inn • Pa. Hwy. 611, Tannersville • 629-3131

The fabled luncheon meat is celebrated in a mid-August day of SPAM juggling, SPAM arts and crafts, SPAM comedy routines and SPAM cooking. You can try some SPAMbalaya, SPAM casserole, SPAM skillet, potato SPAM or Hawaiian SPAM pizza. Country music is played (we believe without the aid of SPAM), and some non-SPAM foods are available too. Admission is $5 per person.

Poconos Musical Gathering on the Mountain
Big Boulder Ski Area • Off Pa. Hwy. 903, Lake Harmony • 722-0100, (800) 468-2442

This two-day, mid-August festival features music from the late 1960s. Fans of the Grateful Dead will love it. The 1996 lineup included Big Brother and the Holding Company, Jefferson Starship, Richie Havens, Matt Kelly's Kingfish and The Band. The Bizarre Bazaar contains an assortment of crafters and other vendors. Admission is $22 per person in advance and $27 at the gate.

Firefighter's Competition
Camelback Mountain • Camelback Rd., Tannersville • 629-1661

In late August, local fire departments compete in the keg on a wire (two teams armed with firehoses use a spray of water to push the keg over the opponents' marker), bucket brigade (firefighters heave buckets of water onto a roof, and the runoff flows into a single bucket), decathlon (a multiple-skills event including hose connections, wood splitting, ladder climbing, bucket brigade and transporting a contestant on a backboard) and drafting contest (hooking up a hose and spraying a cone off a barrel). Fire-safety demonstration, fire apparatus exhibits and equipment vendors also are featured. This is a fun day and an opportunity to acknowledge the work of our volunteer firefighters. Spectators watch for free.

Cajun Fest
Tannersville Inn • Pa. Hwy. 611, Tannersville • 629-3131

Originally scheduled to coincide with Mardi Gras, this festival was moved to late August because the Poconos' weather in February is not conducive to outdoor dancing, zydeco music or feasting on Cajun food. Traditional American foods are available for those who do not want to try Cajun catfish or jambalaya. The event benefits Women's Resources, a domestic violence and sexual-assault crisis center in Stroudsburg. Admission for folks 12 and older is $6 in advance and $8 at the gate; children younger than 12 cost $3.

Grand Emerald Fling
Jack Frost Mountain • Pa. Hwy. 940, Blakeslee • 722-0100, (800) 468-2442

At the end of August, folks who enjoy Irish bands, dancing, food and vendors visit Jack Frost for this two-day, all-day event. Mass is celebrated at 11 AM on Sunday. Admission is $6 per day for anyone 13 and older and $1 for children ages 2 through 12.

West End

West End Fair
West End Fairgrounds • U.S. Hwy. 209, Gilbert • (610) 681-4293

For 75 years, people from throughout northeastern Pennsylvania have been visiting the West End in late August for this agricultural fair. Antique farm machinery is displayed, and prizes are awarded in many craft and cooking categories. Local businesses set up booths to promote themselves. The food — everything from carnival snacks to full dinners homemade by representatives of local nonprofit organizations — is outstanding. Try the elephant ears (fried dough topped with apple, cherry or blueberry). In addition to the free music, nationally famous country stars (Joe Diffie and Tracy Byrd in 1996) perform at the grandstand for a separate charge. The demolition derbies are always packed with folks who enjoy watching their friends destroy unwanted automobiles. Admission is $3 for anyone 13 and older; children 12 and younger get in free. Ride tickets are sold individually for 75¢, 14 tickets cost $10, and 30 tickets cost $20.

Lake Wallenpaupack Area

Wayne County Fair
Wayne County Fairgrounds • Pa. Hwy. 191, Honesdale • 253-1108

During the first week of August, you can pay one price and enjoy all of the carnival rides, agricultural exhibits and shows. Tractor pulls, horse pulls and livestock shows are featured daily. Big-name country and polka singers perform in addition to professional wrestling and automobile thrill shows. Harness races and a demolition derby are scheduled throughout the week. The fair began more than 134 years ago and currently attracts nearly 100,000 people annually. You also can find some delicious food at this country fair. The $6 admission fee includes most shows except the demolition derby.

Greene-Dreher-Sterling Fair
Pa. Hwys. 191 and 507, Newfoundland • 646-4047

This agricultural fair, held from late August through early September, includes live farm animal exhibits, arts and crafts, diving mules, live music, great food, puppet shows, country music and demolition derbies. Admission is $3 per day during the week, $4 on weekends. Some events, such as rodeos, demolition derbies and motorcycle thrill shows, have a separate $5 admission charge.

Slate Belt

Blue Valley Farm Show
Blue Valley Farm Show Grounds • Pa. Hwy. 512, between Bangor and Pen Argyl • (610) 588-9026

One of the last free-admission farm shows in the state, Blue Valley presents live entertainment nightly in early August and has such fun competitions as Pet Parade, Mr. Legs, The Windy Woman Contest and Baby Photo Contest. The Eastern Regional 4-H Livestock Club presents a show and sale too.

September

Delaware Water Gap

Celebration of the Arts
Throughout Delaware Water Gap • 424-2210

This nationally known outdoor arts festival brings together talented artists, chefs and jazz musicians in early September. Food concessions and artist booths supplement the terrific music on stage. Big names such as Phil Woods, Bob Dorough and Kim Parker share the spotlight with promising students and other area performers. Admission is $5 on Friday and $15 per day on Saturday and Sunday ($20 for both days).

Scottish & Irish Festival
Shawnee Place & Shawnee Mountain • Hollow Rd., Shawnee-on-Delaware • 421-7231

Enjoy Highland athletics, the bagpipe bands and parade, working sheep dogs, fiddlers, Irish and Scottish bands, Irish step dancing, Scottish exhibitions, whiskey tastings and other vendors at this two-day mid-September festival. Admission is $10 per day for adults ($18 for both days) and $5 for children 12 and younger ($8 for both days).

Mount Pocono Area

Oktoberfest
The Edelweiss • Pa. Hwy. 940, Pocono Lake • 646-3938

Three large tents are filled each Labor Day weekend with German music, dancing, food and drinks. Children enjoy the clowns and the petting zoo. Arts and crafts are sold. However, the main attraction is the food — wiener schnitzel, bratwurst, knockwurst, pretzels, pastries and much more. See our Restaurants chapter for more information on dining at The Edelweiss during the festival.

West End

Palmerton Community Festival
Palmerton Borough Park, Palmerton • 826-2505

This weekend celebration in early September features live music (country, oldies and polka), rides, bingo, a crafts tent, art show, flea market, Chinese auction, plant sale, pig roast and assorted ethnic foods. Admission is free; you pay for food and rides. Call the Palmerton Borough Hall for more information.

Art Walks
Throughout Jim Thorpe • 325-8969, 325-4041

Self-guided tours of the galleries, craft shops and historic sites of Jim Thorpe are offered in late September. Studio visits, seminars and workshops also are scheduled. Stop by the Old Jersey Central Passenger Depot (U.S. Hwy. 209 and Broadway) for a free map. The Sacred Mountain Art Show, a juried show and sale at the Mauch Chunk Opera House, is part of the Art Walk program. Admission is free.

Milford Area

Pike County Agricultural Fair
Airport Park • 10th St., Matamoras • 296-8790

Agriculture contests, pet shows, Little Mr. and Miss Pike County, homemade foods, bands, cheerleaders, business exhibits, a watermelon seed spitting contest, fireworks, a diaper derby, music, demonstrations — everything you would expect at a local fair is here in early September. Admission is free.

Lake Wallenpaupack Area

Mountaintop Pow Wow & Western Festival
Triple W Riding Stable • U.S. Hwy. 6, Lake Wallenpaupack • 226-2620

Native American drum and dance competitions, storytelling, sign-language interpreters, hoop dancers, flute players, tepee raising, country music, horse and pony rides and hayrides are all part of this arts and crafts festival in early September. Admission is $8 for adults; children, senior citizens and physically challenged persons get in for $4.

October

Delaware Water Gap

Lumberjack Festival
Shawnee Place & Shawnee Mountain • Hollow Rd., Shawnee-on-Delaware • 421-7231

Competitions include log rolling, pole climbing, ax and chainsaw competitions, buck sawing and skunk racing. Arts, crafts, foods, chairlift rides and an all-you-can-eat buffet are available at this mid-October festival. Admission is $10 per person.

Shawnee Autumn Hot Air Balloon Festival
Shawnee Inn • River Rd., Shawnee-on-Delaware • 421-1500

In mid-October the skies over the Delaware River are filled by more than 25 hot air balloons. On Friday night, the balloons are inflated on the ground, and the glow of their burners creates a jack-o'-lantern effect. Launches are scheduled for morning and afternoon on Saturday and Sunday. On-the-ground activities include food and crafts vendors, live music, carnival rides, pony and mule rides, face painting, balloon sculptures, clowns and a puppet show. Admission on Friday is $5 for adults and teens and $3 for kids ages 5 through 12. Saturday and Sunday admission is $10 for adults and teens and $3 for the kids. Children 4 and younger get in free every day.

Octoberfest
Shawnee Place & Shawnee Mountain • Hollow Rd., Shawnee-on-Delaware • 421-7231

Celebrate the Bavarian spirit with food, pastries, bands, crafts, dancing and a German-style fest hall. Chairlift rides and a ski swap are part of the festivities. Admission is free to this late October event.

Stroudsburg/ East Stroudsburg

Harvest Festival
Quiet Valley Historical Farm • 1000 Turkey Hill Rd., Stroudsburg • 992-6161

Costumed guides carry out the typical routine of early Pennsylvania Dutch farm life, including demonstrations of beekeeping, needlecrafts, candle dipping, blacksmithing, wood carving, bread baking, spinning, dyeing, basketmaking, hewing, quilting, horse plowing and hearth cooking. You may sample foods, cider and breads and enjoy children's games, folk entertainment and pumpkin decorating contests. The Harvest Festival is held in mid-October. Admission is $5 per day for folks 13 and older; children ages 3 through 12 cost $2 per day.

Mount Pocono Area

Annual Arts & Crafts Festival
Jack Frost Mountain • Pa. Hwy. 940, Blakeslee • 443-8425

More than 60 artisans exhibit everything from fine art to country crafts including leather etchings, pottery, chair caning, tole painting, stained glass, quilting, photography, decorated eggs, porcelain dolls and metal sculpture. Other activities and entertainment include a ski swap, a Civil War encampment, a classic car display and chairlift rides through the fall foilage. Admission is $3 per day for anyone 13 and older; children 12 and younger get in free. This event is held in mid-October.

Octoberfest and Craft Fair
Camelback Ski Area • Camelback Rd., Tannersville • 629-1661

The German atmosphere at this late October festival is complemented with crafts, pumpkin painting, hay rides and authentic food and music. Admission is free.

West End

The Great Pocono Pumpkin Patch Festival
Country Junction • U.S. Hwy 209, Forest Inn • (610) 377-5050 Ext. 541

A month-long celebration of autumn, this festival features thousands of pumpkins, fall decorations, Halloween costumes, carnival rides, carnival food, hayrides, a haunted barn and a petting zoo. Admission is free, but there is a separate charge for some activities.

Pumpkin Patch and Homecoming Festival
Old Homestead Tree Farm • U.S. Hwy. 209, Kunkletown • (610) 381-3582

Every weekend in October, Old Homestead offers hayrides, a petting zoo, canoe rides and pumpkin picking. The farm is decorated for the season, and cider, jams and cookies are sold. Admission is free.

Lake Wallenpaupack Area

Hawley Harvest Hoedown
Main Ave. and Keystone St., Hawley • 226-3191

The fun at this community celebration in early October includes hayrides, square dancing, pumpkin decorating contests, country line dancing, a scavenger hunt and a flea market. Admission is free.

November

Mount Pocono Area

Great Brews of America Classic Beer Festival
Split Rock Resort • Pa. Hwy. 903, Lake Harmony • 722-9111, (800) 722-9111 Ext. 800

You must be at least 21 years old to sample the lagers, ales and stouts from more than 20 North American breweries. Two stages of music plus food and seminars are offered at this mid-November event. Admission is $15 per person in advance and $20 at the door.

December

Stroudsburg/ East Stroudsburg

Christmas in the Country Fair
Stroudsmoor Country Inn • Stroudsmoor Rd., Stroudsburg • 424-1199

The holiday season comes alive in early December at this old-fashioned celebration. Crafts, antiques, horse-drawn carriage rides, homemade foods, street vendors, baked goods and Victorian shops create a festive atmosphere. Admission is free.

An Old Time Christmas
Quiet Valley Living Historical Farm • 1000 Turkey Hill Rd., Stroudsburg • 992-6161

Christmas is celebrated here as it was in the 18th century. Costumed guides lead you past candlelit windows and a living barnyard Nativity. Homemade trees and gifts are available. The tours are offered weekends in early and mid-December and cost $5 for adults and teens and $2.50 for kids ages 3 through 12.

West End

Olde Time Christmas
Throughout Jim Thorpe • 325-3673

We think the most beautiful event in this charming Victorian town is its Christmas celebration, held weekends in early December. Santa arrives on a lighted, horse-drawn trolley. A tree lighting ceremony, children's theater productions, concerts, caroling, horse-drawn trolley rides and decorated shops fill the town with holiday cheer. Admission is free.

Santa Claus Train Rides
Rail Tours Inc. • Train Depot • U.S. Hwy. 209, Jim Thorpe • 325-3673

When not on the *Santa Express* in Honesdale in mid-December (see subsequent entry), Santa takes folks on an 8-mile train ride along the Lehigh River. Admission is $7 for folks 12 and older and $4 for kids ages 9 through 11; kids younger than 9 (up to two per adult) ride for free.

Lake Wallenpaupack Area

Santa Express
Stourbridge Rail Excursion • 742 Main St., Honesdale • 253-1960

Weekends in mid-December, Santa and Mrs. Claus host a 1½-hour holiday excursion. Children receive a special gift. Admission is $10.

Artists are delighted by the Poconos' combination of country air, mountains, water — and proximity to New York City.

Arts and Culture

As we have noted throughout this book, the Pocono counties are exhibiting growth in every aspect related to the mushrooming population. The increasing number of arts-related activities and cultural programs are further evidence of this trend.

A few umbrella organizations in different counties coordinate arts activities, usually by networking. The arts are well represented now: painting, sculpture, photography, dance, theater, poetry, writing, music (vocal and instrumental) and crafts. Local historical museums are also part of the cultural picture because they provide a backdrop of the region's past.

The Monroe County Arts Council is the most developed and organized of the county arts organizations. They produce an extensive directory of artists and groups from Pike County and even New Jersey. The organization is funded by the National Endowment for the Arts, the Pennsylvania Council for the Arts, the Pennsylvania Historical and Museum Commission, the Monroe County Commissioners, local businesses and memberships. Only through its help and cooperation have we been able to present much of the information about the Monroe County arts scene.

While the Monroe County Arts Council is the most centralized and far-reaching umbrella organization, other areas of the Poconos are developing arts organizations in response to incoming artists who want to make this area home, and city folks who are used to diverse arts scenes. Artists are delighted by the Poconos' combination of country air, mountains, water — and proximity to New York City. They are moving to places like Jim Thorpe, where building after building is occupied by galleries, artisan shops and studios of all types. (Jim Thorpe is also the home of the Laurel Festival of the Arts — featured in this chapter's sidebar.) They are moving into Pike County, where the galleries are opening up in little spots all along the winding roads. The arts are changing the tempo of the Poconos. Classical and country music have blended to create a new sound, and gallery openings have become as attractive a Saturday evening event as hanging out in local bars. The arts scene truly has arrived.

In the following section, we point out the major arts organizations and representatives from each genre of the arts in the Poconos. We strongly encourage you, however, to contact the locals arts organizations for directories or calendars of events because we can't possibly cover all the groups and individual artists out there — and there are treasures in every art form waiting to be found.

Opportunities abound in this area to see, participate, perform and get involved in any other way you can. Explore the options — and enjoy!

Arts Organizations

Stroudsburg/ East Stroudsburg

Monroe County Arts Council
556 Main St. • Stroudsburg • 476-4460

The Monroe County Arts Council is a non-profit organization formed in 1975 by area residents to develop, foster and support cultural awareness and artistic excellence in the Monroe County region. It publishes a monthly newsletter of cultural events and opportunities, a county-wide calendar of cultural events and a directory listing artists in all disciplines.

Through its relationship with the county government and the business community, the council sponsors rotating art exhibitions in regional banks and public buildings, awards Arts Community Support Grants to local artists and art organizations, awards Youth in Music Scholarships to local young musicians and provides conduit grants from the Pennsylvania Council on the Arts to emerging arts groups, including A Family of Artists, The Monroe County Film Society, Pocono Mountain Quilters' Guild and Mountain Jubilee of the Arts. It also sponsors Pocono Mountainfest, an annual event showcasing the work of more than 100 members of the Pennsylvania Guild of Craftsmen, and the Delaware Water Gap Jazz Festival and Celebration of the Arts, held every September in the historic town of Delaware Water Gap. (See our Annual Festivals and Events chapter for details.)

Music Study Club of the Poconos
R.R. 1, Box 257 • Effort • 629-0363

The music club had been around since 1912. Its mission is educational and performance-based. It provides concerts throughout the year showcasing established and up-and-coming young performers. It offers two scholarships to Monroe County students and sponsors Pocono Mountain young musicians, supporting them in the National Federation of Music Clubs Junior Festival held annually at East Stroudsburg University.

We've attended concerts spotlighting young musicians and were impressed by the caliber of performance we heard. The program contained vocalists, violinists and cellists — and all were very impressive. Adult members of the group play at music club concerts and other arts events.

Members do not have to be musicians; they can just love music and be interested in supporting it in the Poconos.

Mount Pocono Area

Arts on the Mountain
Trinity Church • Trinity Hill Rd. • Mount Pocono • 595-2424, 421-7309

This group started in 1988 with the objective of presenting area artists in a series of events combining visual and performing arts. It presents four events a year that always include an art gallery opening and a vocal or instrumental music concert or dramatic or poetry-based performance. In 1996 it sponsored an Art Studio tour that culminated in a jazz performance at the church followed by a strawberry festival. The group always comes up with interesting combinations and is supported by quite a few notable area artists, including painters Peter Salmon and Penny Ross and performers the Dixie Gents.

West End

Carbon County Art League
Eighth Ave., R.D. 1 • Nesquahoning • 645-9701

This is an emerging organization that is

INSIDERS' TIPS

Most historical societies offer classes in crafts that were practiced during bygone eras. For instance, the Stroud Mansion, in Stroudsburg, offers ornament-making classes around Christmas time; and Driebe Station, also in Stroudsburg, offers Victorian crafts-making classes (for children too) throughout the year. Call your local museum or historical society and inquire about planned learning experiences for the whole family. The cost is usually nominal — $1 to $5 for supplies — or it's free.

taking part in the incredible artistic growth of the Jim Thorpe area. Presently it sponsors exhibits of local artists — some quite famous, such as nationally known watercolorist David Price and internationally known Shozo Nagano, famous for his three-dimensional oil paintings. Exhibits are displayed in the Mauch Chunk Museum and Cultural Center, the Mauch Chunk Opera House and other locations in the community. Businesses and business organizations such as the Rotary Club usually co-sponsor events; some exhibits are displayed at the Palmerton Library. Exhibitions also have accompanied other events, such as the Concert Series or performances at the Mauch Chunk Opera House.

A key part of the group's mission is the support of young artists, including a three-day youth program presented every fall.

Milford Area

Sunflower Hill Productions Inc.
101 E. Harford St., Ste. 3 • Milford
• 296-2033

This nonprofit cultural arts organization has been around since 1993 and is dedicated to presenting top-quality performing arts events in the Pike County area. To date it has supported more than 35 events, including International Performing Arts Festivals and Music Theater Workshops.

Lake Wallenpaupack Area

Hawley Regional Performing Arts Council
227 Main Ave. • Hawley • 226-3602

This organization was formed in 1991 to support artistically gifted area students. To that end it sponsors exhibitions of local artists to raise money for scholarships.

Recently, the council presented a beautiful photographic exhibit of Wayne and Pike counties by photo-artist, Marilyn T. Pardine, M.D., at the Gingerbread Gallery in Hawley.

Contact the council for a list of events.

Cultural Societies and Museums

Here, we focus on cultural societies and museums that reflect the history of the Poconos — and often are part of it. Other museums, such as the Jem Classic Car Museum in Andreas, are included in our Attractions chapter. While we acknowledge that they also represent our culture, such operations are essentially businesses that survive on more than a nominal entrance fee and donations. The Pocono Indian Museum is discussed in detail in our Native Americans chapter.

If you are looking for volunteer opportunities, museums and historical societies are always looking for helping hands. There are quite a few of them, and keeping them open to the public requires a reservoir of helpers. Since most operate on relatively small budgets and donations from visitors, volunteers are eagerly sought and highly esteemed.

We've encountered a number of volunteers, mostly retired citizens; their knowledge about the exhibits is impressive and their excitement contagious. They, of course, know all the rumors and tales attached to the artifacts, and they sometimes share personal histories — often just as interesting — as they lead folks around on tours.

Hours vary, so be sure to check with the museum before you go.

Stroudsburg/ East Stroudsburg

Monroe County Historical Association
900 Main St. • Stroudsburg • 424-1776, 421-7703

This historical society is housed in the Stroud Mansion on Main Street in Stroudsburg. It promotes the preservation and protection of the county's history through exhibits, lectures, workshops, educational programs, outreach programs and special events. Within it are many artifacts relating to the history of this area. The mansion is used throughout the year as a place for meetings and exhibits. At a recent exhibition of local artists sponsored by the Monroe County Arts Council, we were delighted to find the exhibit displayed in one of the large second-story rooms of this fine home. Opening-night refreshments were served in an adjoining, high-ceilinged room with beautifully polished wood floors.

The Dreibe Freight Station, on Ann Street in Stroudsburg, and the Bell School, a one-room schoolhouse in Stormsville, also are part of the Monroe County Historical Society. The Dreibe Freight Station, originally a railway station, is full of items representing life in the Victorian era, including a general store and blacksmith shop. The Bell School is a restored structure representing the Golden Age of one-room schoolhouses (see our Education chapter for

a related sidebar). Both are open for tours. Admission is free.

Dreibe Freight Station is open noon to 4 PM Wednesday through Saturday. The Bell School is open 1 to 4 PM Sunday from Memorial Day through Labor Day.

Quiet Valley Living Historical Farm
1000 Turkey Hill Rd. • Stroudsburg • 992-6161, 992-2803

The farm is open June 20 until Labor Day for guided tours 9:30 AM to 5:30 PM Monday through Saturday and 1 to 5:30 PM Sunday. Admission is $6 for folks 13 and older, $3.50 for kids ages 3 through 12 and $5 for seniors 61 and older. But tours are only part of what this living museum has going for it. There is a great Harvest Festival every fall, with old-fashioned food, games and craft demonstrations, and tours of the buildings that are part of the original farm. Programs are provided for school children at different times of the year, allowing hands-on experience in arts and crafts, animal husbandry and early living. Kids really seem to enjoy field trips there — especially the chance to jump into a haystack!

Two other events are on everyone's list for a delightful step back into the past. The Farm Animal Frolic ($3 per person) is a major event on the last two weekends in May. The farm is open to visitors to see livestock born that spring. The Old Time Christmas is scheduled the first two weekends in December; admission is $5 for adults and $2.50 for kids ages 3 through 12. Besides seeing the lovely decorations and enjoying the farm's Christmas beauty, visitors are entertained by choirs from local churches that perform in the open courtyard afternoons and evenings. Since this event is held outdoors in winter, dress warmly. Warm cider also helps keep the chill at bay. (See Attractions for more information.)

West End

Mauch Chunk Museum and Cultural Center
41 W. Broadway • Jim Thorpe • 325-9190

This museum is housed in the former St. Paul's Methodist Church — itself an excellent example of Victorian Ecclesiastical architecture. It features artifacts and photos of the history of Jim Thorpe, which embraces coal mining, canals, Lenape Indians and the town's namesake, the famous Native American football hero and Olympian.

The museum features working models of a canal lock and the famous Switchback Gravity Railroad (see the related sidebar in our History chapter). The very large exhibit demonstrates how the railroad car ascended Mount Pisgah (in its earliest days, pulled by mules), then used the force of gravity to return cars laden with coal. An interesting side note to the switchback design: It became the basis for the staple of all modern amusement parks — the roller coaster. Donations are accepted.

The Old Jail Museum and Heritage Center
128 W. Broadway • Jim Thorpe • 325-8380

This jail housed the Molly Maguires — miners hanged for their alleged subversive activities in trying to improve working conditions — before their execution. (See the Old Jail Museum entry in our Attractions chapter for details.) Admission is $4 for adults, $3.50 for students and $2.50 for young children.

Milford Area

The Columns
608 Broad St. • Milford • 296-8126

This museum is at the hub of Pike County in Milford. It is full of artifacts from the grand to the simple. There are gowns and antique furniture, an original restored railway stage and Native American artifacts including tomahawks and arrowheads (the kids like this section best). It also is the repository of an item of recent national interest — a flag supposedly stained with Abraham Lincoln's blood. The flag was placed under Lincoln's head after he was shot; it was taken from the bunting on the presiden-

tial box. Many items were taken from the scene after Lincoln was removed, and a flag is listed as one of the items never found. The caretaker of the Ford Theater is believed to have taken the flag and handed it down to his descendants, who moved to the Milford area. Guide Torrie Cory tells that the flag's whereabouts was kept quiet by the family, who stored it in a trunk. On occasion, family members would take it out in hushed reverence and show it to guests, then immediately return it to its hidden resting place. Recent studies have determined that the flag very well could be what it has been whispered to be for more than 100 years. If the blood is really Lincoln's, pending DNA tests will tell. If it is proven that The Columns' flag was the flag placed under the president's head, you likely will have to see it in the Smithsonian.

The museum is open 1 to 4 PM Wednesday, Saturday and Sunday. Admission is $2 per person.

Grey Towers
Pa. Hwy. 206 N. • Milford • 296-9630

The former estate of the late governor and conservationist James Pinchot, Grey Towers is a museum operated by the U.S. Forestry Service. It's named for the towers that make up the facade of this French château-style mansion. It is filled with memorabilia from Pinchot's career in the Forestry Service under President Theodore Roosevelt and his lifelong dedication to conservation. The beautiful grounds currently are undergoing restoration, as is the outside of the château. Since the restoration, a multi-year project, affects the museum's hours of operation, it's best to call ahead.

One fun part of the grounds is the Finger Bowl, a huge carved-stone table on a terrace under an arbor. The stone's hollowed-out center creates a shelf all around, and a pool of water fills the middle. The pool was used by guests to pass food items to one another.

Laurel Festival
of the Arts

Jim Thorpe was once one of the richest towns in Pennsylvania due to its place at the center of the coal-mining industry. One of its most well-known citizens was railroad builder Asa Packer whose mansion overlooks this hamlet. It is a mansion filled with Victorian woodwork and artistry fashioned by artisans and crafters imported from Italy for their expertise. (Their homes make up the lovely brownstones that rise up on either side of Race Street.)

In this little town, reminiscent of mountain villages of Switzerland and France,

Packer built the Mauch Chunk Opera House as a place for theatricals and other performances to entertain the wealthy population. After the coal industry went bust and wealthy supporters left Jim Thorpe, the opera house fell into disrepair. A home for vaudeville performances, it was also at times a movie theater. It eventually became a has-been, but a historic artifact still. Finally, the Mauch Chunk Historical Society acquired it and began renovations, which are on-going. It is managed currently by event coordinator Reggie "Robert" Pompa. With the historical society's support, it now houses local theater groups and hosts visiting performers.

In 1989 Marc Mostovoy, founder and music director of the Concerto Soloists Chamber Orchestra of Philadelphia, came upon Jim Thorpe when he was looking for a place to start a summer music festival. He thought the town was lovely (it has been named "Little Switzerland" by a Swiss contingent, as noted on a marker in the center of town). It seemed the perfect spot for a music festival; there was already a growing

Photo: Marc Royce

The Laurel Trio — Amy Levine Tsang, cello; Sunghae Kin, violin; and Dana Levine, piano — performs at the Laurel Arts Festival.

contingent of New York and international artists in the area as well as several burgeoning galleries. Also in place was the Bach and Handel Chorale, evidence to Mostovoy that an audience was ready and waiting for the best in national and international talent. Convinced the people were ready for another artistic outlet, Mostovoy needed a place to perform. The Mauch Chunk Opera House was suggested to him by Joel and Helena Le Bow, local artists and supporters of the arts.

According to Herb Thompson, a volunteer who became the first festival publicist, Mostovoy brought one of his musicians from Philadelphia to test the house. They entered, then clapped their hands to test the acoustics. Their immediate response was "this is the place we want." The acoustics were excellent — a perfect theater for instrumental and vocal music.

There was going to be a summer music festival, and the townspeople of Jim Thorpe were going to be part of the adventure.

With the help of the Le Bows, the Mauch Chunk Historical Society of Carbon County (begun by Peter L. Kern and managed by Laura Thomas) and many, many volunteers, the effort to establish a top flight festival of the arts in Jim Thorpe was begun.

The first festival was in June 1990, barely a year after Mustovoy discovered Jim Thorpe. With the help of the people of Jim Thorpe, plans were made, performers were hired, publicity was generated, and details of housing and other needs were outlined.

The exciting part of the volunteer involvement is the townspeople take total responsibility for the care of the world-class performers who come to play at the Laurel Festival of the Arts. Meals are prepared and delivered each day to their quarters, families invite the performers for meals in their homes, area bed and breakfast inns play host to the performers, and local folks keep them occupied in their time off. Kevin Chain, president of the Mauch Chunk Historical Society, likes to tell about taking off for a day of fishing with one of the artists who has come back since to fish with him. The day we were there — the day before the festival opened — people were loading and unloading cars and station wagons with food and supplies for the performers. That this event is a community effort is quite apparent, right down to the festival's sponsorship by the Mauch Chunk Historical Society.

And why are all these people so excited? It's the music. Mostovoy wanted a festival to rival the top music festivals in the country where artists of the highest level of artistry would perform chamber music. The artists that perform at the Laurel Festival of Arts fit his vision. They are performers that might be playing in Jim Thorpe one week and in Carnegie Hall or Tokyo the next. They are performers who have performed at Wolf Trap, Tanglewood and Marlboro. They are artists who have recorded for Sony, Deutche Grammophon, Decca and Philips. They are artists who come to Jim Thorpe for the joy of playing in a lovely, Victorian town, surrounded by mountains and supportive townspeople.

Cellist Bion Tsang is also artistic director of the Laurel Arts Festival.

Photo: Laurel Arts Festival and Columbia Artists Management and Waring Abbott

Marc Mostovoy stepped down as artistic director in 1996 because his performance schedule in Philadelphia was so intense. The position has been assumed by cellist Bion Tsang, who has worked closely with the festival since its inception.

Artists at the 1996 Laurel Festival of the Arts include: violinists Lynn Chang, Michael Davis, Eric Grossman, Sunghae Anna Lim and Keng-Yuen Tseng; violists Xiao-Dong Wang, James Davis and Wayne Roden; cellists Amy Levine Tsang and Bion Tsang; pianists Jeffrey Cohen and Dena Levine; clarinetist Todd Palmer; and French hornist William Purves.

Compositions performed over the three-weekend schedule (including mini-concerts at Palmerton Library and Split Rock Resort) include works by Martinu, Greig, Brahms, Mendelssohn, Mozart, Beethoven, Dohnanyi, Hummel, Shostakovich and von Weber. The Bach and Handel Chorale perform every year. Children also are welcome at the festival and are invited to free open rehearsals with their parents.

Asa Packer's Mauch Chunk Opera House is doing well again, filled with the sounds of beautiful music. And it's home to the Laurel Festival of the Arts, the only festival of its kind in the central Northeast.

If you are planning to attend the 1997 Laurel Festival of the Arts, contact the committee at 325-3441 for information, or write Laurel Festival of the Arts, P.O. Box 206, Jim Thorpe, Pennsylvania 18229. Admission for each concert is $12.

There are many lovely bed and breakfast inns within walking distance of the Mauch Chunk Opera House (see our Bed and Breakfast Inns chapter); there are other facilities nearby in Lake Harmony (see our Accommodations chapter).

The Laurel Festival of the Arts is the perfect centerpiece of a totally rounded vacation. There are museums, art galleries, antiques shops and emporiums of every type to whet your historical and artistic appetites. For your sporting appetite, a multitude of outdoor activities await at Mauch Chunk Lake Park. See our In, On and Around the Water and Recreation chapters for related information.

It's hard to beat Jim Thorpe: a Victorian town, an outdoor playland — and, thanks to Marc Mustovoy and the townspeople, the Laurel Festival of the Arts. We're ready — are you?

Wooden bowls were used as little boats to ferry salt, pepper, marmalade and other condiments across the table at the request of a dinner partner. The bowls are still there for you to try. Not surprisingly, children consider this the best aspect of the mansion.

Grey Towers is open 10 AM to 4 PM daily from Memorial Day through Labor Day. A donation of $2 per person is suggested.

Zane Grey Museum
Scenic Dr. • Lackawaxen • 685-4871

This museum, overseen by the National Park Service, is the homestead of the western novelist Zane Grey. It is very small, containing only a vestibule and two rooms that are open to the public. The two rooms are filled with memorabilia relating to his trips out west, his respect for Native Americans, and his championship of their rights — and women's rights — long before it became fashionable. The walls are made of what seems to be old, brown paper bags, but they are decorated with hand-painted pictures of Native American symbols. The paintings were done by Grey's sister-in-law, and they are remarkable for their beauty and good condition. Zane Grey's home is right on the Delaware River — a place he loved and in view of which he wanted to be buried. And he is; his grave is on the grounds of St. Mark's Church, next door to his home.

For the 1996 season, the museum was open Friday through Sunday from Memorial Day through Labor Day and weekends only throughout September and October; 1997 hours are contingent upon federal funding for staff, so please call ahead. Admission is free, but donations are appreciated.

Lake Wallenpaupack Area

Wayne County Historical Society Museum
810 Main St. • Honesdale • 253-3240

The main attraction here is the replica of *Stourbridge Lion*, the first steam engine to run in the United States. Models of the *Eclipse* railcar, a 1920s passenger car that carried riders up the gravity railroad track used by mineworkers, and other items that link Wayne County to its place in history — between railroads and canals — are housed in this museum.

Admission is $2 per person. See our Attractions chapter for more information.

Dorflinger Glass Museum
Long Ridge Rd. • White Mills • 253-1185

Guided tours of the glass works are provided. This museum contains a collection of antique crystal glassware, a gift shop, a wildlife sanctuary and the Wayne Area Sports Hall of Fame. Besides these attractions, the Wild-flower Music Festival is held every summer in the open-air amphitheater. Past performers include Tom Chapin, Celtic Thunder and Linda Eder. Bring your own chairs and blankets for the performances; the rain site is the Wallenpaupack Area High School.

Admission to the museum is $3 for adults, $2.50 for seniors 55 and older and $1.50 for children ages 6 through 18. Concert tickets are $12 for general admission; students 18 and younger are $6.

Art Galleries and Art Organizations

Artists receptions are one of the fun events sponsored by many area galleries and arts organizations. Receptions and openings are listed in the cultural calendar of the *Pocono Record* each week. Also, all galleries and organizations maintain mailing lists, which they use to inform members of openings. They are always delighted to add your name to their mailing lists if you are interested in being notified of upcoming events. The Monroe County Arts Council also publishes a monthly newsletter for its members that lists all upcoming cultural events.

Art Walks and artist studio tours and shows are also delightful events sponsored by different artists, art galleries and organizations in the Poconos. Maps are provided, and viewers can move at their own pace along Main Street in Stroudsburg or up and down the delightfully crooked streets of Jim Thorpe. Artists also open their studios for tours and exhibits, especially in spring and fall. They have found these tours and exhibits very profitable, gaining commissions for future projects and selling exhibited works.

Delaware Water Gap

Antoine Dutot School and Museum
Pa. Hwy 611 • Delaware Water Gap • 421-5809

This museum is in the town's original school (c.1860). It features art exhibits presented in showcases throughout the year (with an opening-night reception). Upstairs is an exhibit of artifacts from the town's history back to its beginning in 1793. It also presents an audiovisual show of the development of the Gap from its earliest history to the present.

Dutot Museum is situated in the town of Delaware Water Gap, where winding streets and lanes climb up the mountainside from the river. There are some lovely little cafes in the area where you can stop after your visit to the museum and before heading on to other attractions in this quaint turn-of-the-century resort town.

Stroudsburg/ East Stroudsburg

Artspace 534
534 Main St. • Stroudsburg • 476-5880

This gallery is a cooperative. Its more than 20 members present shows a few times a year. Other shows based on themes are curated for exhibits as well. Openings occur every month, with an opening-night reception to meet the artists. This gallery has supported poets too, presenting poetry readings to accompany exhibits during the year, especially in April (National Poetry Month). The director/founder is Andrea Levergood, and her work is presented at this gallery, which focuses on contemporary and mixed-media art.

INSIDERS' TIPS

An easy route to Jim Thorpe from the north, east or west is from I-80 W. From I-80, take the Lake Harmony exit at Pa. Highway 903 and follow Pa. 903 south into Jim Thorpe (about 20 minutes from the Lake Harmony exit). If you are coming from the south, take the Northeast Extension of the Pennsylvania Turnpike to the Lehighton (Pa. 209) exit. Follow Pa. 209 S. into Jim Thorpe.

Bixler Art Gallery
633 Main St. • Stroudsburg • 476-7666

This gallery concentrates on contemporary art. It has ongoing exhibitions and works for sale. It curates shows that draw local and regional artists. It is in a beautiful building that used to be the home of Bixler Hardware, an early merchant in Stroudsburg; its presentation area is also a work of art, with tin ceilings and polished wood floors.

Pocono Mountain Art Group
1817 Wallace St. • Stroudsburg • 424-1764

This group has been in existence since 1935. Today it has more than 100 members and sponsors art shows, exhibitions and demonstrations. For almost 20 years it has sponsored the annual Courthouse Square Art Show at the Art Learning Center, 17 Williams Street, Stroudsburg. It is open to all visual artists.

Richard E. Phillips Gallery
300 Main St. • Stroudsburg • 421-7872

This gallery presents wood and bronze sculpture, mostly the work of Richard E. Phillips. Phillips is a local artist whose work has gained him a national reputation, including exhibitions in New York City.

Mount Pocono Area

Linden Root
Pa. Hwy. 191/507 • Newfoundland • 676-4898

Betty Lindroth is the local artist who operates this gallery in a 100-year-old farmhouse. The work is by fine area artists, including Rita Reamer, Sally Millspaugh and Lindroth herself. Linden Root contains beautiful watercolors of flowers and nature scenes, oils of nature and still-life, and hand-painted porcelains. The painting style is traditional.

West End

David Watkins Price, Artist Studio
29 Race St. • Jim Thorpe • 325-4544

This studio is operated by owner/artist David Price who is nationally known for his watercolors, prints and graphic designs. He is also involved in the evolution of Jim Thorpe's historic and artistic center.

The Josiah White Exhibition Center
20 W. Broadway • Jim Thorpe • 325-4856

This museum presents exhibitions of contemporary art and sculpture, sponsored by the Anita Shapolsky Gallery in Soho, New York. Josiah White Exhibition Center is housed in a former Presbyterian Church (built in 1849).

Hazard House Gallery
38 W. Broadway • Jim Thorpe • 325-8778

The gallery exclusively features the acrylics and watercolors of Joel Le Bow, whose studio also is here. Hours are by appointment only.

Maria Feliz Gallery and Sculpture Garden
60 W. Broadway • Jim Thorpe • 325-8969

This lovely little gallery presents contemporary work in various media. The find at this gallery is the sculpture garden in the rear of the gallery that is nestled against the mountainside of Jim Thorpe. Local and regional artists, including some from New York City, exhibit here. The sculpture exhibit is always based on a theme, and the works chosen by the curator must be durable because they are displayed from spring until fall.

Shozo Nagano, Open Studio
39 Race St. • Jim Thorpe • 325-3988

This gallery presents acrylic paintings on shaped canvas by internationally known artist Shozo. The works are three-dimensional and

Photo: Pocono Playhouse

Pocono Playhouse presented this cast in *Hello Dolly!* in 1996.

present painting in a way that stretches both the art form and the imagination.

Lake Wallenpaupack Area

Gingerbread Gallery and Framing Studio
309 Main St. • Hawley • 226-3455

This contemporary gallery is a walk-up on Main Street in Hawley. It presents a series of art exhibitions from May to October of national and local artists in mixed media, pastels, folk art, photography, oils, watercolors and so on. It always introduces its exhibitions with an opening reception. It is linked into galleries all over the country by a CD-ROM ordering system that provides customers with the best available art to suit their tastes. The gallery is also especially proud of its framing shop, staffed by a trained museum-quality framer.

Slate Belt

The Faulty Beagle
499A Lower Smith Gap Rd. • Kunkletown • (610) 381-2108

This gallery exhibits contemporary paintings and sculptures by recognized local, national and international artists. International artists represented include Tom Jones (French) and Alejandro Mazon (Cuban); national favorites include Gary L. Wolfe and Sarah Zimmerman; local artists include Jim Hannon, Beth Hanson and Terry Bono. Every year in May, the Faulty Beagle presents a juried exhibition of national and international artists. In August, it sponsors a young-people's exhibition. Art from students up to high school age is displayed; works from high schoolers are part of a juried exhibition, which includes a day of fun and feasting as part of the opening.

Crafts

The numerous Poconos crafters sell their wares in little shops, through galleries (too numerous and unique to single out a few) or at the annual Pocono Mountainfest, which showcases the work of members of the Pennsylvania Guild of Crafts. Most regional crafters are listed in the Monroe County Arts Council Directory. However, we could not pass up the opportunity to direct you to a suitable starting point in your quest for crafts.

The **Pennsylvania Crafts Gallery**, U.S. Highway 209 at Bushkill Falls Road, Bushkill Falls, 588-9156, is a major draw for anyone interested in crafts. This gallery showcases the 2,000 members of the Pennsylvania Guild of

Craftsmen as well as the guild's 900 juried members. The gallery is managed by members of the guild who contract to run the facility for a certain period of time, generally a few years. At presstime it is being managed by brass sculptor Hilton Byrd and his wife, Vicki Byrd, a stained-glass designer, jewelry maker and brass sculptor. The last managers, Rod Meyer and Karri Benedict, specialize in functional pottery. During their tenure at the gallery they created new works in Japanese Raku, a highly decorated, non-functional pottery form. Presently, Meyer and Benedict maintain a showcase for their work in the barn at the rear of the property.

The gallery is in a house built in 1746, which is the property of the National Park Service in the Delaware Water Gap National Recreation Area. The guild leases this property, listed on the National Register of historic Places, through the Historic Property Leasing Program, authorized by Section III of the National Historic Preservation Act of 1966. This act identifies guidelines for leasing such properties deemed endangered if not properly maintained.

The guild's objective here is to exhibit the best works from members of the Pennsylvania Guild of Craftsmen and to nurture artists as they grow in their field. *The Washington Post* noted that folks should "begin [a] trip to the Poconos at Pennsylvania Craft Gallery."

From May through December, the gallery is open 11 AM to 5 PM Thursday through Monday; January through April, it's open 11 AM to 5 PM Friday, Saturday and Sunday.

Theater

Theatrical performances in the Poconos include full-time professionals, part-time professionals and amateurs (but mostly of truly professional caliber).

Plays and performances happen all the time, so the chance to audition and perform is always available. Auditions are announced in the *Pocono Record* or the *Pike County Gazette*. Sometimes auditions are posted on community bulletin boards in supermarkets or post offices. Call if you are interested in joining any theater groups or finding out about audition

or performance schedules; troupes are always looking for new members.

Delaware Water Gap

Shawnee Playhouse
River Rd. • Shawnee-on-Delaware
• 421-5093, (800) 742-9633

The Shawnee Playhouse is a tradition in the area. It is housed in a renovated church in the very picturesque town of Shawnee-on-the-Delaware. Smallness is part of the charm of this summer theater. It produces high-quality musicals all season long with energetic young casts imported from New York. Children's theater is also a component of the Shawnee Playhouse. This playhouse is quite close to Mimi's Streamside Cafe, which has an outdoor eating terrace overlooking a lovely stream, so dinner theater packages between the two are a great way to spend an evening.

> **FYI**
> Unless otherwise noted, the area code for all phone numbers in this guide is 717.

Stroudsburg/ East Stroudsburg

Fine Arts Discovery Series
P.O. Box 1126 • Stroudsburg 18360
• 476-3237

This organization is dedicated to making live performances accessible to area children. Each year it presents three live performances of top artists from all over the country. Performances are chosen to represent a variety of musical and cultural forms. While they are geared to children, they provide very rich entertainment for adults too. The purpose of the series is to have families share live performance experiences together. See our Kidstuff chapter for a full picture of the Fine Arts Discovery Series.

Pocono Lively Arts Inc.
P.O. Box 11 • Stroudsburg 18360
• 421-0936

This nonprofit, volunteer theatrical group has been in operation for almost 20 years. It produces professional-level musicals in July and November with orchestra accompaniment. Children always take part in the November production. And the talent in the area is so good, performances are always sold out; getting tickets in advance is a good idea.

The fall 1995 production of *Annie* received rave reviews — all the more exciting considering the show used two Annies! The group has open auditions, to which all members of the community are invited.

Mount Pocono Area

Pocono Playhouse
Pa. Hwy. 390 • Mountainhome • 595-7456

During her World War II tour, USO show manager Rowena Stevens learned many young soldiers had never before seen live performers. So after the war, she found a suitable field in Mountainhome, constructed a 500-seat theater similar to the ones used by the army for the USO shows and opened Pocono Playhouse in 1947 as the Poconos' first summer theater.

Its opening production was *Dear Ruth*, starring Richard Kiley. Stars at the Playhouse have been a tradition for many years; some top performers who have played here include Larry Hagman, Hal Linden, Eddie Mekka and Gloria Vanderbilt. The group holds auditions and rehearsals for its productions in New York City and performs here and in its sister theater to the south, Bucks County Playhouse in New Hope.

Pocono Playhouse features a hefty season of eight musicals between June and October. The productions are Broadway-scale — suitable for the size of the theater — and you'll still find big-name performers on the program. It also sponsors children theater every Saturday.

If you want to have dinner before the show, Jagermeister, a German-style restaurant, is right across the road. Or try Cappuccino's, an Italian restaurant on Pa. Highway 191 in Cresco, just five minutes away.

West End

Mauch Chunk Opera House
41 W. Broadway, in Opera House Square • Jim Thorpe • 325-4439

The Opera House is home for its own resident troupe and many groups that produce plays in the area. While it is known for the Laurel Festival of the Arts (see this chapter's sidebar), troupes from Allentown and surrounding areas also use the theater for productions. If you are interested in getting involved in any local theatrical productions, call the Opera House for audition and performance information; the opera house has hired an artistic director and is eagerly promoting its theatrical troupe. You also can call for a schedule of what programs are being presented.

The Opera House serves as a base for many artistic and cultural events in Jim Thorpe: as an art gallery, a reception site for exhibitions and even children's art clinics. The Opera House has been through various stages of use and is now coming back to its place as the center of the arts in Jim Thorpe.

Music

Ensembles and Orchestras

There are a number of instrumental and orchestral groups in the Poconos. Some are open to new members, others are closed groups that perform in this area and around the world. For instance, the Phil Woods Quintet, led by renowned jazz alto saxophonist Phil Woods, performs all over the country and at area events, including the Delaware Water Gap Jazz Festival. The Dixie Gents is headed by nationally known trombonist Rick Chamberlain. And the Pocono Musicians Local 577, composed of professional area musicians, plays throughout the state and elsewhere and offers free concerts throughout the year, showcasing artists such as Charlie Cole and Nancy and Spencer Reed.

The Summer Concert Series is held every Sunday evening at the Delaware Water Gap Presbyterian Church of the Mountain, on Main Street. It features free concerts, both instrumental and vocal, by well-known area performers. Seats are not supplied — you have to bring your own chairs and blankets. Some fine internationally and nationally known performers such as Michele Bautier, and favorite local groups such as River and Calliope, can be found there every Sunday night, rain or shine (if it rains, the concerts are held inside the church). The concert schedule is listed in the Sunday *Pocono Record* and in the extensive cultural calendar published the last Sunday of each month.

Delaware Water Gap

Phil Woods Quintet
P.O. Box 278 • Delaware Water Gap 18327 • 421-8615

The Phil Woods Quintet is a renowned jazz band directed by alto saxophonist Phil Woods. He and his group are part of the core of what has grown into a very important national jazz center in Delaware Water Gap. The group performs at the almost legendary Deerhead Inn in town and is affiliated with the Delaware Water Gap Jazz Festival and Celebration of the Arts. This year they put out a CD entitled The Jazz Mass after the annual event of the same name. A side note to the mass: It started in the late '70s at the Delaware Water Gap Presbyterian Church of the mountain when William H. Cochea Jr. was pastor — and an enthusiastic supporter of the effort. Today Cochea is president of Columcille, the Megalith Park and Celtic Art Center; he is profiled in the *Jazz Mass* CD liner notes. (Also see the Columcille Close-up in our Worship chapter.)

Phil Woods Quintet performs quite a bit in the area. Performance dates are published in the *Pocono Record*.

Stroudsburg/East Stroudsburg

Christ Church Brass Ensemble
205 N. Seventh St. • Stroudsburg • 421-7642

This brass quintet performs classical compositions as well as popular marches and parade music in concerts throughout the area and has performed as part of the Fine Arts Discovery Series (see this chapter's previous entry in the "Theater" section). Contact the group for a performance schedule.

Dixie Gents
R.R. 6, Box 6114 • Stroudsburg 18360 • 992-2612

This Dixieland jazz band is comprised of area professionals. They play at events throughout the year as well as at different area clubs and restaurants. The group is led by trombonist Rick Chamberlain. Call or write for a performance schedule.

Pocono Youth Orchestra
P.O. Box 1101 • Stroudsburg 18360 • (610) 965-0268

This group is responsible for two youth orchestras, the Junior String Orchestra and the Senior High Symphonic Orchestra. The Pocono Youth Orchestra is the only symphonic orchestra in Monroe County. Students in senior high are accepted based on audition for string, woodwind, brass and percussion. The Junior String Orchestra is the associate group that serves as a training ground for young string players who have taken lessons.

The orchestra performed in the Fine Arts Discovery Series (see the previous "Theater" section) a few seasons back and kept youngsters and adults enthralled. Their seriousness and dedication were apparent in the quality of their performance. Two formal concerts a year, in winter and spring, are highlights for music lovers young and old.

The Water Gap Brass
1253 Kroucher Rd. • Stroudsburg • 629-5647

This brass group performs at different area events throughout the year, including the Fine Arts Discovery Series, Arts on the Mountain and the Church on the Mountain Concert Series. The schedule is available by contacting the group.

Mount Pocono Area

The Jolly Rhinelanders
R.R. 2, Box 69 • Cresco • 595-2547

This group of about 10 members is billed as an oompah band. It performs for all occasions and is always open to new players; a non-threatening audition is customary.

Pocono Brass Quintet
R.R. 2, Box 69 • Cresco • 595-2547

This brass quintet performs brass literature, including Sousa marches, and arrangements of other music for community organizations and special events.

Choruses

There are several choral societies available for those who are interested in voicing their best notes. The groups usually require an audition of some type but emphasize that it is not meant to be threatening. Further notes about these groups: They are talented, and their performances are generally well attended.

A highlight of the Monroe County vocal music scene is the annual Messiah Sing, held at Shawnee Resort. Members of local vocal music organizations and anyone else who likes to sing get together to dine and raise their collective voices in beautiful song. It is quite an event, and one that always draws a crowd.

Stroudsburg/East Stroudsburg

Pocono Vocal Arts Society
31 Pocono Heights • East Stroudsburg • 223-0793

This new group is composed of 25 singers chosen by audition. It is under the direction of Melissa Kmierim. The society puts on four concerts a year and also performs locally at different events. Concerts include light opera, art songs by composers such as Schubert and Purcell, and Broadway show tunes.

Many members are experienced and/or trained performers and must be able to sing in French and Italian. This group features solo performers.

Pocono Choral Society
P.O. Box 5 • Stroudsburg 18360 • 476-0550 ext. 261, (610) 377-2880

This group performs three major concerts a year in Stroudsburg. Besides those main events, the chorus performs 40 to 50 additional concerts a year at various sites including East Stroudsburg University (for a five-week summer series), New York, even Europe. In 1996 the group went on an 18-day tour of the British Isles where they sang in 10 concerts and participated in festivals, including one at Westminster Abbey and the Welsh Festival in Wales. Pocono Choral Society usually tours some other part of the globe every four years, with most of the members participating. The group has been singing for more than 16 years under the direction of conductor Jerrold Fisher, who also conducts the Pocono Pops, the ancillary orchestra that performs with the Choral Society on a need basis.

Pocono Choral Society is an audition-only group. Call to find out about auditions or to obtain schedule information.

Mount Pocono Area

Chorus of the Poconos
R.R. 2, Box 69 • Cresco • 595-2547

This group is dedicated to barbershop harmony and is a member of the Society For the Preservation and Encouragement of Barbershop Singing in America. This group is open to new members, and its current members range from young adults to senior citizens still in their prime. It performs several concerts a year and participates in national and international barbershop conventions.

We followed them around Stroud Mall at Christmastime last year as they stopped, took their "A" from director Russel Speicher's pitch pipe and began to sing. The crowd reaction was incredible; people, young and old, stopped to listen, smile fondly and hum.

Speicher is a moving force in many local music groups; so in the instrumental category, you're going to see the same address pop up again and again for different groups. He is a phenom, and the groups he works with are highly regarded. He always encourages people to "dust off their instruments and join them"; so if you are a music lover and want to

---

INSIDERS' TIPS

Many Pocono resorts provide weekend arts and culture events throughout the year. Weekends devoted to national music or dance are big draws. Showcases for Big Band or jazz concerts are presented. So, when considering a place to stay on your vacation or weekend getaway, ask if any such events are planned.

perform, don't hesitate to contact Speicher at the listed address or phone number.

West End

Pleasant Valley Choral Society
P.O. Box 238 • Effort 18330
• (610) 681-5386

This group has been singing since 1983 and presents two concerts a year at Pleasant Valley High School. The society is dedicated to having fun; the repertoire includes pop tunes, show tunes, operettas and light classics. A non-threatening audition is standard.

The Bach and Handel Chorale Inc.
810 Carbon St. • Jim Thorpe • 325-9440

This group has been in existence since 1984 when it was founded to celebrate the births of Bach an Handel. It's conducted by Randall D. Perry. The chorale has performed with orchestras in Philadelphia and performs annually with the Laurel Festival of the Arts in Jim Thorpe (see this chapter's sidebar). In fact its existence was one of the reasons Jim Thorpe was chosen as the site for the festival. It also presents three major concerts annually — a Palm Sunday Cantata and two Christmas Concerts.

Its intensive schedule doesn't seem to daunt its members who come from all over the area, even New Jersey, to perform.

Dance

A number of dancers and dance instructors in the Poconos, teach everything from Scottish Highland Dancing to Line Dancing. Area professionals perform as choreographers and at in-school programs. For a complete listing of artists and their specialities, call 476-4460 to obtain a copy of the *Monroe County Arts Directory*.

Stroudsburg/ East Stroudsburg

Notara Dance Theater
700 Phillips St. • Stroudsburg • 421-1718

The Notara Dance company specializes in classical ballet and presents other artistic dance/theater ventures. It produces two programs a year — in winter and spring. The winter holiday season is always set off by the Notara production of *The Nutcracker*. Students of the Notara studio perform with dance professionals for a weekend of sold-out performances.

The Jazz Works Dance Studio
393 King St. • East Stroudsburg
• 421-5075

This studio is the home of the newest theater group, the Northeast Theatrical Alliance, which presents musicals to support area organizations such as RSVP. Owner and operator Sue Raesley has extensive choreography experience all across the East Coast, working with top stars in dinner-theater productions. The theater group is based at her dance studio, and all are welcome to audition for the shows she produces. Dance lessons are available in jazz technique.

Pocono Dance Center
115 Seven Bridges Rd. • East Stroudsburg
• 643-1507, 424-6883

This studio has been operating for 20 years under the direction of owner Carrie Evers, a former Rockette and resort performer. The emphasis here is on performance dancing, both for students and members of the center's dance company, the Pocono Dance Ensemble.

Film

Stroudsburg/ East Stroudsburg

Pocono Cinema and Coffee Shop
88 S. Courtland St. (Pa. Hwy. 209 Bus.)
• East Stroudsburg • 421-FILM, 223-0300, 421-5220

This art theater opened in 1996 and has been exciting many folks. The films shown here are the ones that aren't going to make it to the mall theaters. It also plays some old classics that are best captured on a big screen. What makes this place even more fun is the coffee shop right inside that facilitates before-and-after treats and talk time. In the coffee shop, you can continue to enjoy your immersion in the arts because the walls provide a miniature art gallery for local artists to exhibit their work. You can join the supporting membership group, the Pocono Film Society, for a family membership fee of $20 a year. Membership entitles you to the monthly preview newsletter and discounted ticket prices for your family and as many friends as you want to bring along. Admission with membership is $5; without membership, $8. Membership benefits include reduced rates for tickets. If you're not a member you can still go to see the harder-to-find films you are dying to see.

Literary Arts

Stroudsburg/ East Stroudsburg

The Forward Papers
2132 Wallace St. • Stroudsburg • 424-9701

This literary publication has been publishing quarterly for the past year. It presents articles, short stories, poetry, essays, reviews, artwork and children's literary and artistic efforts. The writers are area professionals who have been published and newcomers who are delighted by the opportunity to be published. It welcomes submissions, and if the work isn't quite up to publication standards, editors offer authors comments and advice, allowing for revision and reconsideration. Editors work on a volunteer basis. Authors, poets and artists are not paid for their submissions but they retain copyright. It has a growing following and boasts a circulation of more than 5,000.

Hands In Art
98 Henry St. • East Stroudsburg
• 420-4525, 420-4527

In the Stroudsburgs, poets are receiving a big lift from the number of open poetry readings sponsored by local art galleries. (It's almost as if the '60s have returned.) This new art gallery is one of the main places featuring a coffee house atmosphere and sponsoring open readings on the second and fourth Wednesday of the month. Poets are invited to read their works aloud. No preregistration is required; just show up and read.

Mount Pocono Area

Pocono Writers
P.O. Box 248 • Pocono Summit 18346
• 839-7633

This group of writers meets the last Thursday of the month at the Tannersville Inn to read their work. They come from all fields and all levels of ability, from just starting out to published authors. They are essayists, short-story writers, poets, novelists and playwrights. Works are read aloud and passed around. It is open to anyone who is interested. No previous notification is required other than to show up and be prepared to enjoy the interaction and support.

Quite a few fun and exciting places are within a two- to three-hour drive from the center of the Poconos.

Daytrips

There is so much to do in the Poconos, it is difficult to imagine you having time to take any daytrips. In fact, the area covered in this book is so extensive, you can actually take daytrips from one part of the Poconos to another. In this chapter we point out some daytrip destinations within the Poconos and Northeastern Pennsylvania as well as opportunities in the Scranton/Wilkes-Barre and Allentown/Bethlehem areas. Don't forget Philadelphia, New York City and northern New Jersey — replete with too many options to even begin to scratch the surface — although we tempt you with a few hints.

Again, it might seem surprising that you can take daytrips and still stay within the scope of this book. If you are in the Delaware Water Gap, Stroudsburg/East Stroudsburg or Mount Pocono area, you might consider a daytrip to Jim Thorpe (in the West End) or the Lake Wallenpaupack area. Check out our chapters on Attractions; In, On and Around the Water; Arts and Culture; Recreation; Winter Sports; Parks; Kidstuff; and Golf for some fun Poconos-region opportunities.

Metro Destinations

Philadelphia is less than two hours away by car from the central Poconos region. In the City of Brotherly Love, you can see the Liberty Bell, visit the Franklin Institute, explore the easy-to-negotiate Philadelphia Zoo or drink in a true sense of history at Independence Hall.

The most direct and least congested way to Philadelphia is to take the Northeast Extension of the Pennsylvania Turnpike (a toll road) from Allentown off U.S. Highway 22, or from U.S. 209 in Lehighton or Pa. Highway 940 in the Blakeslee area. When you get to the outskirts of Philadelphia, take the Schuylkill Expressway exit. There are signs all along here to the major attractions.

Venture into **New Jersey** to find a handful of places that might interest you. Right over the Delaware Bridge on N.J. Highway 519 S., in the town of Harmony, you will find Have Balloon Will Travel, (800) 60-TO-FLY for a three-to four-hour balloon flight (actual flying time is an hour). The Statue of Liberty and Liberty Park are a not-to-be-missed duo in Jersey City (about a 1½-hour drive). Take I-80 E. to the New Jersey Turnpike and head south to Exit 14; proceed to Liberty Park. From the park, you can take a boat to the Statue of Liberty. The Meadowlands sports complex is another close-by drive (less than two hours). Here you will find concerts, pro and college basketball, the pro football Giants, horse racing and flea markets. Take I-80 east to U.S. Highway 3 in New Jersey. There are plenty of signs to keep you from getting lost.

Then there's **New York City**. Buses to the Big Apple, including Martz Trailways and Greyhound, leave from Mount Pocono and Stroudsburg (see our Getting Around chapter) every day and return every evening. Or, you can drive straight into New York City on I-80 E. (about two to 2½ hours). Take I-80 to the George Washington Bridge and proceed downtown on the West Side Highway, from which you can turn off at almost any street between 125th and the Fulton Fish Market. You can also take I-80 to the New Jersey Turnpike; if you continue south, the turnpike will take you to the Lincoln Tunnel for uptown and midtown locations, or you can get to the Holland Tunnel for downtown, Greenwich Village, Wall Street, Chinatown and Little Italy.

Scranton/Wilkes-Barre Area

Scranton and Wilkes-Barre are towns in the Lackawanna Valley, which played an important part in the American Industrial Revolution. At one time this region was responsible for supplying more than 80 percent of the nation's anthracite coal. Around the coal industry grew the manufacturing (silk for one) and rail-transportation industries — part of the historical basis for many daytrips in this region. These towns were built in the heyday of the Industrial Revolution, and the architecture as well as the ethnic make-up of the towns reflect this influence. Whether you are lunching in the art deco beauty of the Lackawanna Train Station (with burnished wood, brass and skylights), walking through one of the ethnic neighborhoods where Old World languages and traditions are still honored, or stopping at a beautiful Gothic-style church, there is much to enjoy and marvel at in this area.

> ## FYI
>
> Unless otherwise noted, the area code for all phone numbers in this guide is 717.

The region has been undergoing a major revival partially due to the Lackawanna Heritage Valley Authority (LHVA), which is a partnership of government, business and community organizations and some individuals. Through Lackawanna Heritage Valley, Pennsylvania's first Heritage Park (see this chapter's Close-up), the story of the region's part in the Industrial Revolution is told through the different museums, historic sites and tours that provide historic, educational and recreational opportunities for daytrippers.

The information clearinghouse for the Scranton/Wilkes-Barre area is the Pennsylvania Northeast Territory Visitors Bureau, which is responsible for the daily coordination of the region's tourism-related activities. For visitors information about Lackawanna County, call the bureau at (800) 22-WELCOME.

Both Scranton and Wilkes-Barre are best accessed from Interstate 81. To reach I-81 from the Poconos, take I-80 W. from the Stroudsburg/East Stroudsburg, West End or Slate Belt areas. If you are in the Milford or Lake Wallenpaupack areas, you can reach Scranton and Wilkes-Barre via I-84 W., access this interstate from U.S. Highway 209 N. or U.S. Highway 6 W.

Armed Forces Air Show
Wilkes-Barre International Airport, 100 Terminal Rd., Avoca • 655-3077, 346-0672

This annual air show draws crowds from throughout the region. The day usually includes Top Gun Fighter Demonstrations, World Class Civilian Power Aerobatics, parachuting and wing-walking exhibitions. Past shows have included the Canadian Snowbirds Air Demonstration Squadron. You'll also find aviation-history exhibits featuring static displays, warbirds, classic aircraft and much more.

Carriage Barn Antiques
1550 Fairview Rd. (take I-81 Exit 59, Waverly), Clark Summit • 587-5405

If you have shopped all the antiques places in the central Poconos, consider this daytrip to the Carriage Barn, with more than 6,000 square feet of shopping space housed in a 100-year-old Pennsylvania hill barn (built into the side of a hill so there are two ground-level entrances, one at the hill's bottom and one at its top). This particular shop was featured twice in *Country Living* magazine.

It has an extensive collection of antique furniture, memorabilia and collectibles. You can find furniture from the most elegant period mahogany (17th, 18th and 19th century) to primitives and more modern entertainment pieces such as pool tables, juke boxes and entertainment centers. The Carriage Barn also features a sign collection that has been acquired over 20 years, with original advertising signs for Sinclair Gasoline and Breyers Ice Cream.

Restoration is a major part of the services here too; there's a full-time staff to return furniture to its original condition. People come from across the United States to shop here, and

---

INSIDERS' TIPS

Monroe County Recreation Department sponsors daytrips throughout the year. For a list of trips or just to find out what's going on that week, call Monroe County Recreation at 992-4343 or 421-2871.

These bikers enjoy sun and scenery in the Poconos.

the Carriage Barn will ship anywhere in the country. Visitors from 35 foreign countries have also found their way here to buy antiques.

Everhart Museum of Natural History, Science and Art
Nay Aug Park, Scranton • 346-7186

This museum is in Nay Aug Park, a city facility popular with Scranton residents in summer and winter. It has 15 galleries, each devoted to a special arts group or historical exhibit. There is a gallery for 19th- and 20th-

century European and American art works and one for American Folk Art. There are ethnic galleries exhibiting Chinese, African and South Pacific Oceanic societies. Other galleries house exhibits of prehistoric fossils, Dorflinger glass (see Attractions, Arts and Culture and Shopping), mounted birds in dioramas of wilderness settings and minerals of the region.

From Memorial Day to Columbus Day, this museum is open Tuesday through Sunday from noon to 5 PM; the rest of the year it's open Wednesday through Sunday from noon

Lackawanna Heritage Valley — A Gift of Nature and Man

The Industrial Revolution was powered by coal, a great deal of which came from Pennsylvania's hard-coal region centered in Scranton and Wilkes-Barre.

With coal mining came other industries — and thousands of immigrant workers seeking employment with them.

While coal no longer drives the economy of this region, its heritage makes the Lackawanna Valley a major point of interest to tourists and historic-area preservationists. The Lackawanna Heritage Valley Authority (LHVA) is responsible for Lackawanna Heritage Valley, Pennsylvania's first Heritage Park.

Through the reclaimation of out-of-use mining areas, railroad tracks, stations and trains as well as deteriorating industrial sites, LHVA has fashioned a wondrous recreation of what life was like for the Anthracite People — folks whose lives centered around anthracite mining and the ancillary industries of manufacturing and rail transportation.

The history of the region during the 19th century is presented through various exhibits and attractions that highlight the numerous innovations that changed the American industrial landscape, technology, institutions and labor. The Pennsylvania Anthracite Heritage Museum, Steamtown, Lackawanna Coal Mine, Scranton Furnaces and McDade Park are all results of years of work to restore this area.

A fascinating example is beautiful McDade Park.

Once a barren strip-mine wasteland, a park was reclaimed here as a test project by the U.S. Department of the Interior. From land wasted by years of mining, followed by years of disuse and neglect, a 200-acre garden spot was borne — and presented to the people of Scranton. This greenspace features an outdoor Olympic-size swimming pool, fishing ponds, tennis courts, a baseball field, a children's playground, hiking and walking trails, and picnic and pavilion facilities. It is also the home of the Pennsylvania Summer Theatre Festival, and new plays have been presented here by the Scranton Public Theater. In summer 1996, Jason Miller (a Scranton resident and longtime supporter) presented the one-man play *Barrymore*.

From a wasteland to a green retreat of beauty and culture in a few short years. . . .

---

to 5 PM. A donation is appreciated: $2 for adults, $1 for children. This stop is a big school field-trip destination.

Greystone Gardens
829 Old State Rd., Clark Summit
• 586-5493

This nursery not only sells plants and flowers, but also features a cafe in the midst of its planted perennial gardens, ponds and fountains. Floor-to-ceiling windows allow you to immerse yourself in nature while you sip a cappuccino or a glass of wine with your light

lunch. Menu items include pasta, soup, salads or sandwiches; all herbs used are fresh from the garden. Lunch is served from 11 AM to 4 PM. Afternoon "Tea for Two" is also served from 2 to 4 PM daily, including tea for two and a three-tier tray of finger sandwiches, scones, miniature pastries and desserts.

Oh, you'll also find plants: annuals, perennials, shrubs, trees and houseplants. (Take the Clark Summit exit from I-84 W. to Pa. Highway 611 N. Go through the commercial section of Clark Summit, cross the concrete railroad bridge and turn onto Old State Road. It's worth the trip.)

Houdini Tour & Show
1433 N. Main Ave., Scranton • 342-5555

If you are a fan of Houdini and magic, come here to learn about his history and secrets. Take an hour-long tour to view his memorabilia and see films featuring some of his amazing feats. From Memorial Day Weekend to September 15, tours are available seven days a week from 10 AM to 7 PM. Other times of the year, the tour times change, so you are advised to call.

In October, a special "Halloween Spectacular" includes a tour, magic show and some special acts for the whole family. Admission is $6 for children, $7.50 for adults.

F.M. Kirby Center of the Performing Arts
71 Public Sq., Wilkes-Barre • 826-1100

This performing-arts center hosts performances by prominent entertainers such as Bill Cosby and Neil Sedaka as well as road company tours of Broadway shows that feature famous actors of TV and stage, including Jamie Farr of *M*A*S*H* and country singer Glen Yarborough. This is also the sister theater for the performances of the Northeastern Pennsylvania Philharmonic; the other location is the Scranton Cultural Center. For a list of events call the box office while you're in the Poconos and make an evening of it. Prices vary considerably based on the type of performance and performer, so when you call for the performance schedule, be sure to ask for available tickets and prices.

Lackawanna Coal Mine
51 McDade Park, Scranton • 963-MINE, (800) 238-7245

This exciting trip is in McDade Park, site of the Pennsylvania Anthracite Museum (see subsequent entry). You actually walk down 300 feet below the surface of the earth. Tour guides are either retired miners or specialists (teachers and guides familiar with the industry) who give details about what life was like for the miners of "black diamonds" back in the days when the coal industry was king. The tour is a neat history lesson for kids and adults.

The entrance is through the original "shifting shanty" where miners changed clothing when they were changing shifts. It now houses the Company Store Gift Shoppe. The museum is open daily April through November, 10 AM to 4:30 PM (be there by 4 PM for the last tour, which takes about an hour). Admission is $5 for adults and teens, $3.50 for children ages 3 through 12.

Montage Mountain
Montage Mountain Rd. (Exit 51 off I-81), Scranton • 969-7669

Montage is an all-season activity center. It includes Montage Mountain Ski Resort, 969-SNOW, which is open in winter for skiing and snowboarding and in summer for warm-weather outdoor entertainment and recreation. There are 21 trails and seven lifts for skiing the mountain's 1,000-foot vertical drop. When Mother Nature won't cooperate, there's 100 percent snowmaking; and when the sun goes down, the lights go on for night skiing. The base lodge, the Lodge at Montage, has food concessions and rental concessions for all your skiing needs. Snowboarding is also allowed here.

In summer the mountain becomes a playland and concert amphitheater. There are waterslide rides, batting cages, picnic groves, a children's play area and headline entertainment at the Montage Performing Arts Center. Past acts at the 15,000-seat amphitheater include Reba McEntire; Michael Bolton; Crosby, Stills & Nash; Aerosmith; Sting; Hootie and the Blowfish; Jethro Tull; Bob Seeger; the Allman Brothers; and Foreigner. Bring a picnic supper and enjoy it before the show, or stop at one of the concession stands and buy anything from hot dogs to sausage with peppers and onions. Beverages, including beer, are on sale to quench your thirst. For concert tickets, contact Ticketmaster, 693-4100, or the box office, 969-7669; prices range between $17 and $30 per ticket, depending on the performer's rate.

Pennsylvania Anthracite Heritage Museum
McDade Park, Scranton • 963-4804

Like the Lackawanna Coal Mine (see previous entry), this museum is part of the Heritage Valley complex. Through images, sounds and video, visitors learn how immigrant miners lived. Immigrants were of major importance to the coal industry, and this museum traces their influence on the area's coal industry, the silk industry and community life. There is a collection of miners certificates that were awarded when the workers passed a licensing exam following a two-year apprenticeship as a laborer. Once they passed the exam, laborers were allowed to work independently as miners. Some certificates show national origins from places such as Poland, Wales, Ireland, Lithuania, Italy, England and Czechoslovakia. Also on exhibit is a reproduction of a mining tunnel, an actual silk threading machine and reproductions of a kitchen, church and saloon from the immigrant era, which began around 1820 and hit its peak during the coal boom years from the late 1800s to the 1920s.

The museum is open Monday through Saturday from 9 AM to 5 PM and Sunday from noon to 5 PM. It is open Memorial Day, July 4th and Labor Day; it is closed all other national holidays. Expect a nominal admission charge.

Scranton/Wilkes-Barre Red Barons
Lackawanna County Stadium • 235 Montage Mountain Rd. (Exit 51 off I-81), Moosic • 969-BALL

The Red Barons are the Triple-A baseball affiliate of the Philadelphia Phillies. Going to see them in action is a great family activity, and the players you see here one week can be playing in the majors the next. Throughout the season there are all kinds of giveaway games and special events such as umbrella giveaway night, free Camera Day caps, fireworks and so on. Special family nights are also great bargains. This is a small stadium and being here is a real taste of the good old days of baseball.

The Red Barons season runs from April to September. Games may be played any day of the week and starting times vary, so call the box office at the number above or at 654-2224 to see if the team is in town. You can order tickets by phone Monday through Friday, 9 AM to 5 PM and 10 AM to 4 PM on Saturday, and they will be waiting for you at the box office. Prices range from $3.50 for the bleachers to $6.50 for the lower box seats; talk about a bargain! Group rates are available. There's a Stadium Club Restaurant, 963-6441, if you want to eat dinner here, but of course, you can always rely on the hot dog man for a real home town experience.

Scranton Cultural Center
Masonic Temple • 420 N. Washington St., Scranton • 346-7369

The center's home is in the Masonic Temple and Scottish Rite Cathedral — an excellent example of art deco architecture and part of the Lackawanna Heritage Valley Heritage Park. This center is another site for cultural programs, including excellent productions of Broadway shows and performances by the professional Northeastern Pennsylvania Philharmonic, The Broadway Theater of Northeast Pennsylvania and Scranton Community Concerts. Call for the latest performance schedule and ticket prices.

Scranton Iron Furnaces
159 Cedar Ave., Scranton • 963-3208

The remnants of four massive stone blast-furnace stacks from the old Scranton Steel Company, the second-largest iron producer in the United States in the late 1800s, are the basis for this historic site. They were built between 1848 and 1857. The exhibit tells the story of how this important industry grew — and how Scranton grew up around it. The Steamtown train runs to this site as part of its excursion (in season). This mill is also within walking distance to Steamtown in downtown Scranton. The furnaces are open daily from 10 AM to dusk. No admission is charged.

Steamtown
Cedar Ave., Scranton • 340-5200

This national historic site is the place to

INSIDERS' TIPS

A number of churches and senior citizen clubs sponsor daytrips to different locations in the New York, New Jersey and Pennsylvania areas. Check the *Pocono Record*, *DIGNITY* and other local newspapers for information on these trips.

This couple shares some peace and quiet with nature.

climb aboard historic train coaches and discover the joys of rail travel as experienced during the last century. The trains run from Scranton to Moosic and back (stopping at Scranton Iron Furnaces) from their home in the Scranton Yard of the Delaware, Lackawanna & Western Railroad (maintained by the National Park Service). The ride includes a program presented by a park ranger that explains the history of the area's railroad and the railyard. The site also includes the Steamtown Museum, open daily year round from 9 AM to 5 PM. Learn about the history of railroading in the History Museum, a restored roundhouse. Also check out the Technology Museum, with a program explaining how the trains operate.

Steam excursions run Friday through Sunday in July and August; Saturday and Sunday in September and October. Since seating on the train is limited, reservations are suggested; adult tickets are $7, children 12 and younger are $3, and seniors older than 62 are $6.

Allentown/ Bethlehem Area

This area south of the Poconos is in the corridor between Stroudsburg and Philadelphia. The Allentown/Bethlehem/Easton Airport is in Allentown, just off U.S. Highway 22 W. Bethlehem is known for its Moravian background; there are still Moravian churches here as well as well-known Moravian College. In fact, there are quite a few well-known colleges and universities between Allentown and Bethlehem, including Lehigh University, Lafayette College, Muhlenberg College, St. Francis de Sales and Northampton Community College. Bethlehem, in particular, is a very quaint town with historic districts on winding hillside streets that add a special touch to this spot on the Lehigh River. A lovely route to this general area is Pa. Highway 611 south from Stroudsburg. For most of the trip you follow the Delaware River and end up right near Lafayette College in the historic section of Easton.

Crystal Cave
Pa. Hwy. 222, Kutztown • (610) 683-6765

This is a great daytrip — exploring underground caverns (maybe not for the claustrophobic). A guide takes you on a 45-minute tour through the caves and explains the many formations. There are concrete walkways and railings to keep you safe. The tour ends where it began; since there is only one way in or out, you make a loop. Outside the caves are a gift shop, miniature golf course (so the claustrophobic members of the group can stay occupied outside), a nature trail and a museum about caves and their development. It's a cool alternative in the summer and still not too cool in the fall and spring. The cave is closed December, January and February. Hours are generally 9 AM to 5 PM the rest of the year, but are extended to 6 PM on summer weekdays and 7 PM on summer weekends. Admission is $8 for adults; $4.75 for ages 4 to 11.

Hugh Moore Historical Park & Museums
200 S. Delaware Dr. (Pa. Hwy. 611), Easton • (610) 250-6700

There are several interesting places here at Hugh Moore Park. Besides areas to picnic, hike and bike on park trails, you can rent a boat to paddle or canoe or just play here parallel to the Lehigh River. Visit the Canal Museum, the Locktender's House Museum, the Archives and Library or take a Canal Boat Ride. The Canal Boat Ride is mule-powered, just as trips down the canal were managed in days gone by. The rides last about 45 to 60 minutes and include a costumed interpreter to explain what you are experiencing. The museum is open year round from 10 AM to 4 PM Monday through Saturday; 1 to 5 PM Sunday. Admission is $1.50 for adults and 75¢ for children 5 to 12. The boat ride is open five days a week Memorial Day to Labor Day. Hours are 11 AM to 4 PM Wednesday through Saturday; 1 to 4 PM on Sunday. Weekend-only hours in May and September are 1 to 4 PM. Admission is $5 for adults, $3 for children 3 to 12 and $4.50 for seniors older than 65. You can also rent bikes and boats during the same hours the canal boat ride is open.

Hawk Mountain Sanctuary
Hawk Mountain Rd., Kempton
• (610) 756-6961

Actually, the sanctuary may be closer to Jim Thorpe and Lehighton than it is to Allentown. From Bartonsville, take Pa. Highway 33 to U.S. Highway 22 W. and proceed to I-78 W. You can also reach I-78 via I-80 or I-84 to the Northeast Extension of the Pennsylvania Turnpike south. Either way, be sure to visit if you're a nature lover.

This sanctuary is atop the Kittatinny Ridge overlooking the Appalachia Mountains. The views from the lookout areas are breathtaking, but the real draw is the annual migration of hawks, eagles, ospreys and more than 10 other species of birds of prey that begins in September. The greatest number of birds arrives in October and ends in November. There are three trails, one of which connects to the Appalachian Trail. The trails lead to a north and south lookout and the River of Rocks. These are not easy trails to hike. Even the shorter trail to the north lookout has some very rough spots to negotiate. The 3.5-mile loop trail from the south lookout to the River of Rocks is very, very steep — almost gorge-like. If you are not in good shape, avoid the longer trails and take the short, easy trail to the first lookout; it will still be worth the trip. Spotters at this lookout are college students studying the birds of prey for the Hawk Mountain sanctuary association and are very helpful in identifying the birds flying by or circling overhead. There is a wonderful gift shop and museum here.

Admission during peak-season weekends, September through October, is $6 for adults and $3 for children ages 6 through 12. During the rest of the year (it is open year round), rates are $4 for adults and $2 for children ages 6 through 12. You can also rent binoculars for the day (a helpful option).

With more than 35,000 acres of state park land preserved and protected from development (not even counting the 70,000-acre Delaware Water Gap National Recreation Area), there always will be plenty to do outdoors in the Poconos.

Parks

Imagine rushing down a raging river in a raft, picnicking among lush forests with bald eagles soaring overhead or hiking to the top of the mountains that form Delaware Water Gap to view the surrounding countryside and relax on a cliff among ferns, rhododendrons and assorted birds and animals.

All of this and more is possible in the state parks and recreation areas of the Poconos. So whether you want to dare the Delaware River or just picnic beside it, we have facilities for you. Best of all, they are usually free.

All state parks are open to the public throughout the year. The parks are equipped to accommodate handicapped visitors with special parking and picnicking facilities. Day-use areas, such as beaches and trails, are open from 8 AM to sunset. Swimming in the river and lakes is permitted from 11 AM to 7 PM from Memorial Day weekend to Labor Day weekend only where and when lifeguards are on duty. (See our In, On and Around the Water chapter for more about swimming.) Swimming and use of all beaches and trails is free in the state parks and the Delaware Water Gap National Recreation Area.

Camping fees at the parks range from $10 for a campsite to $85 for a modern cabin that sleeps as many as 12 people. Senior citizens and those with disabilities receive a $2 discount. Use of a shower costs $2. Many commercial campgrounds also are located near the parks and recreation areas. Information on these may be found in our Recreation chapter. Boat launching permits are $6 per season. Private businesses rent boats, rafts, tubes and canoes to those who want to be on the water. (See our In, On & Around the Water chapter for information on locations and rates.)

Alcoholic beverages are prohibited in the parks, and no glass containers are allowed at beaches or near swimming areas. Open fires are permitted only in designated areas. All litter should be placed in trash containers. Pets must be kept on a leash, and they are not allowed in swimming or camping areas. Hunting and fishing during state-authorized seasons is permitted (provided you have a license) in parts of the state parks and within the Delaware Water Gap National Recreation Area. Consult the park offices to obtain information on where to hunt or fish.

With more than 35,000 acres of state park land preserved and protected from development (not even counting the 70,000-acre Delaware Water Gap National Recreation Area), there always will be plenty to do outdoors in the Poconos. So, whether you want an exciting boat trip, a mountain bike ride, a day at the beach or a nature-appreciation stroll, there is a spot waiting for you in the Poconos. Any of the following parks are well-worth a visit for at least a day. No vacation in the Poconos would be complete without a stop in one of these well-maintained, modern facilities to obtain a true appreciation of what the region has to offer. After all, the Poconos region is most famous for its scenery. (See our Fishing and Hunting chapter and our Recreation chapter for more about recreation in the natural areas. Also see our chapter called Our Natural World for insights on the plants and animals you may see in our parks.)

National Parks and Recreation Areas

Delaware Water Gap National Recreation Area
Park Headquarters, off U.S. Hwy. 209 just south of Bushkill • 588-2451

The most recognizable of all the parks in the Poconos, this national recreation area has the advantage of the Delaware Water Gap as its calling card. It comprises 70,000 acres along a 40-mile stretch of the Delaware River from Interstate 84 to the Gap and includes land in both Pennsylvania and New Jersey.

To fully understand the park, guests should begin their day at one of the visitors centers. These are at Kittatinny Point off I-80 in Delaware Gap, New Jersey, (908) 496-4458; and Dingmans Falls off U.S. 209 in Dingmans Ferry, Pennsylvania, (717) 828-7802. The Kittatinny Point Visitor Center is open every day from April to October and weekends November through March. Hours are 9 AM until 4:30 PM. The Dingmans Falls Visitor Center is open every day from April to October 9 AM to 5 PM and weekends November and December 9 AM to 4:30 PM.

Sightseers can explore the many back roads throughout the park and be rewarded with waterfalls, lush woodlands and beautiful fauna. Also watch for hawks and bald eagles, which winter here during January and February.

U.S. Highway 209 follows a close path along the river from Bushkill to Milford. Be sure to stop at Childs Recreation Area near Dingmans Ferry to view the waterfalls; they are a short, easy hike from the parking lot. The trail winds through a gorge filled with varied vegetation, deer and birds. Being in a gorge surrounded by waterfalls and thick tree cover is a great way to beat the summer heat. Enjoy the scenic drive along the river. But be warned: The National Park Service enforces the 45 mph speed limit. So take your time and look around.

The Delaware is considered an easy river for boaters because it is broad and flows slowly, and thousands take to the water in canoes, inner tubes and rafts each season. Access points are located approximately every 8 to 10 miles to accommodate daytrippers. More than 20 independent companies are licensed to rent equipment to boaters. Information on them and a map of all the access points can be obtained at either visitors center or at the park headquarters. Also, see our In, On and Around the Water chapter for details about some of these companies.

Two beaches are recommended for swimming — Smithfield Beach at the south end of the park north of Shawnee-on-Delaware, and Milford Beach right before Milford at the northern end. Both have lifeguards on duty every day until 6 PM, picnic areas and plenty of parking. They are open from mid-June to Labor Day. All of this is free and open to the public.

A cozier spot for swimming is Hidden Lake, which is surrounded by trees and tucked away in the mountains near Smithfield Beach. To get there, take River Road through Shawnee and turn left on Hidden Lake Road.

Hunting and fishing are permitted in the recreation area (see our Fishing and Hunting chapter for details).

There are extensive trails for hikers; maps are available at visitors centers. Approximately 25 miles of the Appalachian Trail are within the recreation area, mostly on the New Jersey side. A trail originating at the Dunnfield parking area off Interstate 80 in New Jersey takes hikers to the top of Mount Tammany where they are rewarded with a breathtaking panorama of the Stroudsburgs and most of the Poconos. What better treat after a long walk than the opportunity to relax on cliffs at the top of the Delaware Water Gap!

Rock climbers will find plenty of challenges here. Stop by the Kittatinny Point Visitor Center in New Jersey to pick up a free hiking map of the recreation area. Be sure to register with the Park Service before and after your climb, or notify a family member or friend of your intention to climb so someone can contact the Park Service should you not return at your expected time. Never climb alone.

Other sites of note within the recreation area are Peters Valley Craft Village (New Jersey) where crafters live, teach their art and sell their wares; Millbrook Village (New Jersey), a re-creation of a late 19th-century rural community; Pocono Environmental Education Center (in Pennsylvania; see this chapter's close-up); and Wallpack Environmental Education Center, which caters to elementary and intermediate school students.

In winter, Smithfield Beach becomes the starting point for two snowmobile trails. Lakes and ponds are ideal for ice fishing. And several trails and many deserted roads are open to cross-country skiers. (See our Winter Sports chapter for details.)

FYI

Unless otherwise noted, the area code for all phone numbers in this guide is 717.

Photo: Pocono Mountains Vacation Bureau, Inc.

Come sail away on one of many Pocono lakes.

Upper Delaware Scenic and Recreational River

N.Y. Hwy. 97 to I-84, Hancock, N.Y., to Milford, Pa. • 685-4871

Beginning at the northern boundary of the Delaware Water Gap National Recreation Area, this stretch of the Delaware River runs north to Hancock, New York. It offers some of the best boating opportunities in the Poconos.

The river runs through more than 73 miles of widely changing scenery and past historic buildings, including the remains of the canal system that once was the main means of transporting goods.

The fishing is outstanding. The most popular game fish are brown trout, rainbow trout, smallmouth bass, walleyes, shad (in spring) and American eels. Large stone walls resembling ski jumps in the middle of the river are eel weirs used by residents to trap the snakelike fish that many consider a delicacy.

While most of the river is considered tame with very little whitewater, there are a few places where rapids present challenges to boaters. The most difficult is Skinners Falls just south of Milanville. This section of the river is classified Class 1 in terms of difficulty, meaning there are few riffles, small waves and few obstructions. However, be careful around Skinners Falls just south of Milanville. The rapids here can be very dangerous. The National Park Service recommends scouting them from land before attempting passage.

Lucky visitors who carefully watch the skies might catch a glimpse of a bald eagle, osprey, great blue heron or great egret. More common sights are hawks, owls and turkey buzzards.

On land, keep a sharp eye out for minks, muskrats, beavers, deer, bears, skunks, porcupines, snapping turtles and raccoons, the latter of which are notorious for sneaking food from napping campers or inattentive picnickers.

Two historic sites of note are Roebling's Aqueduct, the oldest existing wire suspension bridge in the United States, and Zane Grey Museum, housed in the celebrated Western novelist's former residence. Both are in Lackawaxen. See our Attractions chapter for more information about both sites.

Almost all the land along the river is private property. Permission from the owner is necessary before camping overnight. Several companies operate campgrounds and rent canoes, rafts and tubes.

The National Park Service headquarters for the Upper Delaware Scenic and Recreational River is at approximately the area's midpoint in Narrowsburg, New York. Other large towns in the Upper Delaware are Matamoras, Lackawaxen and Shohola in Pennsylvania and

Port Jervis, Barryville and Callicoon in New York.

Car travelers can best enjoy the views by driving on N.Y. Highway 97, which closely follows the river.

For daily updates on river conditions and weather forecasts, call (914) 252-7100.

State Parks

Mount Pocono Area

Big Pocono State Park
Camelback Rd., Tannersville • 894-8336

From the summit of 1,306-acre Big Pocono State Park you can see most of eastern Pennsylvania as well as parts of New Jersey and New York. On the top of Camelback Mountain, Big Pocono is accessible to both hikers who enjoy rugged terrain and passing motorists who simply want to enjoy the view. Ten miles of interconnecting trails, ranging from smooth and flat to rugged and steep, wind through the woods. The mountaintop is encircled by paved Rim Road, so you do not even need to leave your car to admire the countryside. Fifty picnic tables are available. The South Trail and the Old Railroad Grade Trail are open to horseback riders. Approximately 800 acres of the park may be used by hunters.

The land for the park was owned by Henry Cattell around the turn of the century. He so loved the view from his property that he wanted to share it. Cattell constructed a stone cabin at the summit that remained unlocked and open to anyone as shelter. In 1928, 12 years after Cattell's death, the Pennsylvania Game Commission purchased the land. It became a state park in 1954. Cattell might be satisfied to know that his land is now enjoyed by even more people than he could have imagined.

The road leading to the park is very steep and winding. Vehicles with trailers in tow should not attempt it. The park, which is open daily until sunset, is closed in December and reopens in spring as weather permits.

Gouldsboro State Park
Pa. Hwy. 507, 1.5 miles south of Gouldsboro • 894-8336

Most people visit Gouldsboro for the hunting and fishing. Its 2,800 acres of land and 250-acre lake are a sportsman's paradise. See the Fishing and Hunting chapter for more information.

However, those who choose not to challenge the wildlife can enjoy the park's 8.5-mile hiking trail (parts of which are physically demanding), swimming area with lifeguards (open Memorial Day weekend to Labor Day) and wooded picnic groves. Boating is permitted in non-powered and electric-powered craft. Facilities at Parking Area I are handicapped-accessible.

Promised Land State Park
Pa. Hwy. 390, 10 miles north of Canadensis • 676-3428

Two lakes add to the beauty of this 2,971-acre park. Four campgrounds provide more than 500 campsites for tents and trailers. In addition, 12 rustic cabins equipped with electricity and private bath are available for rent. All are near recreational opportunities.

Swimming and picnicking are popular ways to spend an afternoon at Promised Land. The guarded beach area is open days from Memorial Day weekend to Labor Day.

During summer, the park staff offers environmental education programs on topics such as plant and animal study. The park has a small museum containing artifacts, depictions of the natural features of the area and the history of the Civilian Conservation Corps, the organization responsible for building many of

---

INSIDERS' TIPS

Hikers on the Appalachian Trail in the Delaware Water Gap National Recreation Area can expect to see predominantly small trees, mostly chestnut oaks. The rocky landscape combined with the steep slopes causes most of the soil to wash away. Also, the ridge is exposed to all the extremes nature has to offer.

Pocono Environmental Education Center:
The 200,000-acre Classroom

The typical high school nature class takes place in a room with gray concrete walls covered with maps and pictures of assorted wildlife. If students are lucky, there may be a stuffed squirrel or a fish tank in one corner. Textbooks attempt to convey nature's wonders through pictures and drawings.

Then there's the Pocono Environmental Education Center.

At PEEC, students and the general public learn firsthand about natural systems
and develop a better appreciation for the
beauty that surrounds us every day.

Formerly a resort named Honeymoon
Haven, PEEC was created after the National Park Service acquired the land

through the Tocks Island project. Started as a joint venture between the Park Service and Keystone Junior College in 1972, the facility became privately owned and nonprofit in 1986.

PEEC covers 38 acres, including 12 miles of hiking trails. Classes and workshops are conducted on the 200,000 acres of public land controlled by the federal govern-ment.

During the week, students — usually grades 7 to 9 — come to PEEC on field trips lasting two to three days. Teachers receive a list of available activities to choose from. Scheduled events usually include pond study, plant and animal study, and canoeing. Efforts are made to keep classroom work to a minimum and let the kids have fun while they learn.

The students, most of whom come from New York City and urban New Jersey, sleep in the 45 guest cabins that, years ago, housed young newlyweds. Because of their past use, the cabins are much better equipped than might be expected and feature huge, tiled bathrooms that cry out for heart-shaped tubs.

Meals are served buffet-style in the cafeteria by a professional food-preparation staff. An average day's menu might include corned beef hash for breakfast, a grilled cheese sandwich for lunch and spaghetti at dinner.

More than 30 different activities are offered to school groups at PEEC. Some of the more unusual events are Action Socialization Experiences, which teach students how to work together to solve problems. For example, they might encounter a rare "egg" (represented by a ball) and have to devise a way to return it to its "nest" (a bucket) without breaking the egg, throwing it or leaning against its tree.

Another popular activity is the Sensory trail, a quarter-mile hiking trail that partici-pants must navigate blindfolded.

While PEEC instructors conduct half the classes, teachers are expected to do the rest.

On weekends year round, PEEC offers workshops for anyone interested in learning more about nature. Teachers also can earn credit for participating in programs at the center. Among the many workshops available are weekend programs devoted to nature study, photography, environmental issues, bird-watching and family camping.

PEEC's staff maintains the grounds and buildings, leads the workshops and runs the day-to-day operation of what is essentially a hotel devoted to nature. Guests register in the main building, which houses the library, bookstore, offices, a swimming pool, and classrooms (formerly the bowling alleys in the honeymoon days).

The countryside surrounding the buildings is perfect for nature study because so much flora, fauna and landscape is represented: farmland, forests, ponds, a river and waterfalls. Thirty-nine areas near PEEC have been designated suitable for preservation and study by The Nature Conservancy.

Few realize that the sign on U.S. Highway 209 near Dingmans Ferry, Pennsylvania, points toward the largest residential center for environmental education in the Western Hemisphere.

A beautiful resort that could easily have been destroyed or abandoned has been reclaimed as a unique center for nature study. Nearly 250,000 people have come to PEEC to learn more about their environment and how to protect it. PEEC has worked so well, the National Park Service is considering replicating the system in parks across the country.

For information, call PEEC at 828-2319.

the state park facilities, including Egypt Meadows Lake within the park. There's a mile-long self-guided nature trail on Conservation Island in Promised Land Lake.

Boating, hiking and fishing are permitted. There are more than 30 miles of hiking trails. Maps and descriptive information are available at the guard station at the entrance to the park. One of the more popular walks for those who prefer strolling to hiking is Egypt Meadows Road, a 1.5-mile loop which ends at Egypt Meadows Lake. Before the lake was built in 1935, the entire area was covered with hollow, soft meadow grass. The famed Dorflinger Glass Works in White Mills harvested the grass and used it to pack glass to be shipped.

Snowmobiles are permitted only on designated trails. Selected trails are open to visitors on horseback. No rentals are available. Bicyclists can enjoy a hardy 6.5-mile ride around the lake. No bikes are allowed on the trails. Special picnic facilities and parking are handicapped accessible. See our Winter Sports and Recreation chapters for details about these and other related activities.

Tobyhanna State Park
Pa. Hwy. 423, 2.1 miles north of Tobyhanna • 894-8336

From early April to December, this park's 140-site campground caters to outdoors lovers. There are no flush toilets or showers, so be prepared to rough it. There are playgrounds for the kids and a swimming area with lifeguards. A beach is open in summer. Dress for cold nights due to the high elevation — nearly 2,000 feet above sea level.

Four picnic areas — three wooded and one open — provide 300 tables. There is also a picnic pavilion.

A 5-mile hiking trail, the Lakeside Trail, offers a mostly gentle walk; however, there are a few rocky stretches. Far more demanding is the 3.3-mile Frank Ganz Trail, which connects this park's trails with those in Gouldsboro State Park. The Lakeside Trail is marked in blue, and the Frank Ganz Trail is marked in red.

Ice skating and snowmobiling are available in winter. See our Winter Sports chapter for details.

Fishing, hunting and boating are featured activities at Tobyhanna. Electric-powered boats are permitted on the 170-acre lake, and many of the park's 5,440 acres are open to hunters during all recognized hunting seasons. Hunting is not permitted in shaded areas on the park maps, generally those close to recreation facilities. Rowboats, canoes and sailboats can be rented on an hourly, half-day or full-day basis. See our Fishing and Hunting, and In, On and Around the Water chapters for more information.

FYI

Unless otherwise noted, the area code for all phone numbers in this guide is 717.

West End

Hickory Run State Park
Pa. Hwy. 534, near Hickory Run • 443-0400

In the southwestern corner of the Pocono Mountains, Hickory Run boasts 15,000 acres for hiking, camping, hunting, fishing and nearly every other outdoor-recreation activity imaginable. Picnic and parking are handicapped accessible.

The campground's 381 sites for tents and trailers are equipped with modern facilities such as toilets, showers and electricity. A camp store sells groceries and gear.

A guarded, sand beach is open to swimmers from Memorial Day to Labor Day. A concession stand provides sandwiches and snacks, which can be enjoyed in the large (475 tables) picnic area.

Thirty-seven miles of hiking trails are available to those who want to explore the surrounding countryside and view local wildlife such as deer, turkeys, squirrels, bears and snowshoe hares. Several trails lead to waterfalls. One, the Boulder Field Trail, ends at Boulder Field, a glacial deposit of large stones that has remained relatively unchanged for 20,000 years. The trail is 2.75 miles long and includes a steep, uphill walk. Expect to spend four to five hours completing the trip. Trail maps are available at the park office.

Along the trails, hikers will notice the remains of sawmills and the dams early residents relied upon for power. Lumbering was a major industry here in the 19th century. Prior to the Civil War, the area was known as "Shades of Death" because of the thick forests of hemlock and white pine. According to local history, many early settlers died in these woods attempting to flee Indians. They became disoriented in the trees and swamps and starved.

Many lumber camps and villages were created in the mid-1800s to handle the demand for wood from this area. The hemlock bark was used for tanning, the white pine for building materials. All of the original trees were cut down by 1880. The park office and chapel are buildings that were part of the village of Hickory Run in the lumbering days.

Most of the park is open to hunters and anglers, except for those areas which are close to swimming, hiking or other recreation areas.

Winter options are snowmobiling, cross-country skiing, ice-skating, sledding and tobogganing. (See our Winter Sports chapter for details.)

To access the park, take I-80 to Exit 41 and proceed 6 miles on Pa. Highway 534 toward Hickory Run.

Lehigh Gorge State Park
South Entrance, Exit 40 off I-80, White Haven • 427-5000

As the name implies, this park is filled with steep cliffs and rock outcrops as well as thick vegetation. Its northern end is accessible in White Haven; the southern point of entry is in Rockport, where you'll find the park administration office.

This park's major draw is whitewater rafting. This is the most challenging area in the Poconos for boaters, canoeists, rafters and kayakers because it contains the roughest water in the Poconos. Inexperienced rafters are discouraged from taking this section of the Lehigh River without expert guides. Entry to the river is mostly confined to designated areas — White Haven, Rockport and Jim Thorpe.

Mid-March through June is the best period for the whitewater experience because of scheduled dam releases. The flow of water into the river is controlled by the U.S. Army Corps of Engineers at Francis E. Walter Dam. Flow rates can be obtained by calling (215) 597-5091. They range from 250 cubic feet per second to 5,000; the higher the rate, the more dangerous the water.

Licensed commercial outfitters approved to operate in Lehigh Gorge State Park are: Whitewater Challengers, 443-9532; Pocono Whitewater Adventures, 325-3656; Jim Thorpe Adventures, 325-2570; and Whitewater Raft-

---

INSIDERS' TIPS

Fossil hunters should visit Beltzville State Park near Lehighton. The park provides a designated area for rock hounds.

ing Adventures, 722-0285. A typical rafting trip from White Haven to Jim Thorpe may take 10 to 12 hours, so allow enough time to complete it before dark. See our In, On and Around the Water chapter for additional watersports information.

Hunting and fishing are permitted throughout Lehigh Gorge's 4,548 acres. Whitewater rafting between the Francis E. Walter Dam and White Haven is discouraged in order to promote fishing here. This area is stocked with trout and is very popular with anglers. Check out our Fishing and Hunting chapter for details.

More than 30 miles of abandoned railroad grade are available for hiking, bicycling and sight-seeing; no motorized vehicles are allowed. The scenery is a memorable combination of steep cliffs, thick vegetation and the weathered remains of the region's extensive canal system.

In winter, these trails are ideal for cross-country skiing. A 15-mile stretch from White Haven to Penn Junction is open to snowmobiles. (See our Winter Sports chapter for details.)

Beltzville State Park
U.S. Hwy. 209, 5 miles east of Lehighton • (610) 377-0045

When the U.S. Army Corps of Engineers created a flood-control project in Carbon County called Beltzville Dam, it also gave birth to this huge recreation center that provides popular weekend getaways for residents and tourists alike (nearly 500,000 people visit annually).

The park is among farms, orchards and forested areas along Pohopoco Creek. Most recreation is centered around the lake, which is stocked for fishing and open to recreational boating. Water-skiing is permitted in designated areas. Docks and launch ramps are provided.

Hunters are allowed access to 1,707 acres of the park's land during authorized hunting seasons.

Most people visit Beltzville to swim near the 525-foot sand beach, open and guarded from 11 AM to 7 PM daily from Memorial Day weekend to Labor Day. Showers, food concessions and first aid are available.

The hiking trails total 15 miles. One of the most popular trails, the Saw Mill Trail, takes hikers past the remains of a grist mill and a slate quarry from the 1700s. Stop by the park office to pick up a copy of the *Beltzville Trail Guide*.

An interpreter leads environmental education programs from March to November at the visitor center and amphitheater. Other activities include cross-country skiing on fields within the park and on the 9-mile Trinity Gorge ski trail, sight-seeing from Overlook Rotunda off Pohopoco Drive and visiting the old covered bridge, which was relocated to the park and provides access to the beach from the picnic areas. Nearly all the park's facilities, except the trails, are handicapped-accessible.

Natural Areas and Environmental Centers

Mount Pocono Area

Monroe County Environmental Education Center
8050 Running Valley Rd., Bartonsville • 629-3061

Founded in 1976, the center presents a diverse group of nature programs and promotes environmental awareness through hands-on study of the natural environment of the Poconos. Programs include bird walks, school visits, maple sugaring, cross-country ski tours and nature walks. Nature study programs generally last less than two hours and cost less than $5. Call the center for information on upcoming events or become a mem-

---

INSIDERS' TIPS

The trip down River Road in the Delaware Water Gap National Recreation area is particularly scenic. You find many beautiful spots to view the river along this wooded, rural road. Just be careful of deer and wild turkeys crossing in front of you.

Photo: Pocono Mountains Vacation Bureau, Inc.

Nature is omnipresent in the Poconos.

ber of the organization. An individual membership costs $7.50, and you will receive a newsletter each month that gives details on the center's activities.

The facility's Education Center is open Monday through Saturday throughout the year and houses a library, bookstore, classroom, observation deck and numerous exhibits. The building is on the grounds of the Kettle Creek Sanctuary, a 120-acre preserve with 1.5 miles of well-marked trails that are open every day.

From Pa. Route 611 near Bartonsville, turn east onto Rim Rock Drive, right on N. Easton-Belmont Pike and bear right onto Running Valley Road.

Tannersville Cranberry Bog
Bog Rd., Tannersville • 629-3061

Tannersville Cranberry Bog is perhaps the most unique natural attraction in the Pocono Mountains. Visitors to the bog are struck by how different it is from the surrounding countryside. The flora more resembles the Canadian wilderness than northeastern Pennsylvania.

The Tannersville bog is the southernmost low-altitude boreal bog along the Eastern Seaboard. Some of the most rare plants in the state grow here. Two of these — the pitcher plant and the sundew plant — are insectivores; that's right, they feast on bugs. The bog's orchids are quite colorful, as are the dwarf mistletoe, yellow-eyed grass, yellow lady slipper and rose pogonia. The skunk cabbage lives up to its name, as you will quickly smell.

The Nature Conservancy maintains the bog. Several nature trails are open to the public for hiking and cross-country skiing throughout the year. The trailheads are located along Bog Road near Cranberry Creek. Maps may be obtained at the Monroe County Environmental Education Center.

However, to enter the bog itself, you must be part of a scheduled bog walk or obtain a tour guide and special permission. Guided walks, open to the public, are held weekly from June to Labor Day. The requested donation is $3 per person. During the two-hour tour, you will learn about the bog's formation, the unique plant and animal life here and some handy general environmental knowledge. Call for more information. Do not go expecting to pick or buy cranberries.

From the intersection of Pa. routes 611 and 715, take Pa. 611 south and turn left on Cherry Lane, then turn right on Bog Road.

West End

Mauch Chunk Lake Park
Lentz Trail Hwy. between Summit Hill and Jim Thorpe • 325-3669

The park's 2,300 acres offer campers and daily visitors all the expected activities — hiking, jogging, swimming, fishing, boating, softball, volleyball, horseshoes and cross-country skiing, to name a handful.

The campground here is open from late April through late October (see the "Camping" section of our Recreation chapter). Outside visitors are permitted from 10 AM to 10 PM, and campers must not make any disturbances after 10 PM. Site reservations are encouraged.

The park is near four outstanding hiking trails, and maps are available. The 1.5-mile Shoreline Trail is favored by school groups because of the varieties of plants and animals that can be seen on the trail.

Lake Wallenpaupack Area

Lacawac Sanctuary
Pa. Hwy. 507 N., north shore of Lake Wallenpaupack • 689-9494

Named after the Lenape Indian word for "fork" (Minisink Path, a significant Indian trail, passed through here), Lacawac Sanctuary is a nature preserve owned by The Nature Conservancy. Within its 400 acres alongside Lake Wallenpaupack are a unique 52-acre glacial lake, Lake Lacawac, and mixed forest ecosystem.

Among the programs offered here are cultural workshops, environmental education classes, bird-walk breakfasts and art classes for children.

A mile-long public hiking trail, the Maurice Braun Nature Trail, loops through the property to overlook Lake Wallenpaupack. This leisurely two-hour walk begins in the sanctuary parking lot.

The sanctuary is maintained as a wildlife refuge. Lacawac Sanctuary Foundation is a nonprofit corporation dedicated to protecting Lake Lacawac and promoting the property's use for research and education. It is funded largely by the annual contributions of members.

The sanctuary is available (by appointment) for field trips by school groups. Under adult supervision provided by the school, students study flora, fauna and geology.

From Interstate 84, take Exit 6 north toward Lake Wallenpaupack.

Lake Wallenpaupack
U.S. Hwy. 6 and Pa. Hwy. 507, southeast of Hawley • 226-3702

Created by Pennsylvania Power & Light Company in 1926, this 13-mile-long, 5,700-acre lake offers year-round recreational opportunities, including fishing, boating, water-skiing and swimming.

There are family camping sites along the lake, maintained by PP&L (see the "Camping" section of our Recreation chapter). Boat accesses are available. Three natural areas provide trails for hiking and snowmobiling. Four islands have picnic facilities. See our In, On and Around the Water chapter for information on boating, swimming and camping at Lake Wallenpaupack.

Slate Belt

Jacobsburg Environmental Education Center
835 Jacobsburg Road, off of Pa. Hwy. 33, Wind Gap • (610) 746-2801

The primary mission of this facility is to provide year-round educational activities for students and educators. Programs also are available for groups and individuals; call the center for details and schedules.

Within the park lies the Jacobsburg National Historic District that includes the remains of the Colonial village of Jacobsburg, founded in 1740. In 1792 the Henry family built a gun factory here, manufacturing small arms until the late 1800s. When the West was tamed, Henry firearms were the weapons of choice due to their durability, accuracy and low cost. Only foundations of buildings remain of early Jacobsburg. However, two of the Henry homesteads from the early 1800s have been restored and are open to the public from April to October.

In addition to history, scenery is featured at Jacobsburg. Hikers, mountain bikers, horseback riders and cross-country skiers can enjoy 12.5 miles of trails. Environmental education workshops are held in the center's amphitheater. A picnic area is open to the public. Bushkill Creek in the park offers excellent trout fishing, and hunters may roam 937 acres of the park's land. Check available maps to see which lands are open before hunting. Hunting and fishing are permitted during authorized seasons.

Perhaps the best spot to visit is Henry's Woods. The 1.9-mile trail loop here provides dramatic views of the Bushkill Creek, slate outcropping and hemlock and oak forests. You are sure to see a rich variety of wildflowers and birds. During winter, the trail is perfect for cross-country skiing.

Jim Thorpe's mountain-biking trails are considered among the best on the East Coast.

Recreation

If water activities, winter sports and park visits are not enough options, here are a few more.

Mountain biking, horseback riding and paintball are popular outdoor alternatives. Bowling is fun throughout the year, especially on rainy days.

Golf is covered in its own chapter. Separate chapters also are devoted to winter sports, water-related activities and hunting/fishing. Hiking trails are included in our Parks chapter. Ice skating and in-line skating are discussed in our Kidstuff chapter.

Mountain Biking

Beginning mountain bike riders are advised to stick to less demanding trails, such as converted rail beds and deserted roads. Single-track trails (only one way through) over rough terrain can be very dangerous.

Use maps to select a trail best suited to your abilities. Take with you a helmet, drinking water, snacks and an assortment of wrenches, screwdrivers and an air pump in case of a breakdown.

Sometimes bikers share trails with hikers and horseback riders. Always yield the right of way to these other trail visitors.

Two Victorian towns are the destinations of choice for mountain bikers. While other areas have trails and roadways that are suitable, Jim Thorpe and Milford offer the best combination of accommodations, trail diversity and scenery. If mountain biking is the primary purpose of your trip, these are good places to go.

Upon arriving in Jim Thorpe, visit **Blue Mountain Sports & Wear**, Susquehanna Street, 325-4421. The staff knows all the surrounding trails and can recommend some to suit your taste and ability. Tell them you want a three-hour, gentle ride with views of the valley, and they will point you in the right direc-

tion. You also can rent or buy any equipment you might need and find maps of any trail you might ride. Better still, we suggest you pick up a copy of *A Guide to Mountain Biking in Jim Thorpe & the Western Poconos* by David Matsinko.

Jim Thorpe's mountain biking trails are considered among the best on the East Coast. Dozens of Colorado-style trails are scattered around the town.

Blue Mountain Sports & Wear provides a shuttle to the trailhead of the popular **Lehigh Gorge Trail**. The shuttle costs $15 per person and takes 40 minutes to reach the beginning of the trail. From White Haven, the trail travels along the Lehigh River for 25 miles and concludes back in Jim Thorpe. The trail is rated suitable for beginners and intermediate riders and takes one to four hours to complete.

Another option for beginners is the **Switchback Trail**, which follows the route of the former coal-hauling railroad. More advanced riders may want to continue to the **Upper Track** and tackle its more rugged terrain and the challenging descent down Wagon Road.

Mauch Chunk Ridge and **Twin Peaks** are the most advanced trails in Jim Thorpe. Riders must negotiate very technical single-track stretches.

For the best overall view, **Flagstaff Mountain Trail** includes a stop on the top of the mountain for an unforgettable panorama of the surrounding countryside.

Stream-crossing skills are tested twice on **Broad Mountain Loop**. Avoid this trail during hunting season, as it is on Pennsylvania State Game Lands.

P.W. Mountain Bike Center, Pa. Highway 903, Jim Thorpe, 325-3655, offers guided four-hour biking tours for beginning and experienced riders. Shuttle service, rentals and clinics also are available. The shuttle costs $15 per person. Shuttle ride and bike rental are $35 per person. To attend the clinic, rent a bike and use the shuttle is $60 per person; $40 if you use your own bike. Reservations are required for the shuttle and the clinic.

The maple-lined streets of **Milford** are tailor-made for casual bikers. The historic town is filled with interesting architecture. Ride over to former Gov. Pinchot's estate or visit the waterfalls right outside of town. Many streets continue on into the countryside.

Mountain bikers will enjoy the ride near **Stairway Lake** in Mill Rift. Rural trails and woods roads lead to an isolated pond, a waterfall and the remains of the region's bluestone quarries.

There are two looping trails — a 15-miler and a 25-miler — that take riders through the woods along the Upper Delaware River. They begin in Mill Rift and extend to Pond Eddy. Parts of both have steep climbs and demanding terrain.

Shohola Falls Recreation Area, 12 miles west of Milford, and the area around Lackawaxen offer several trails of varying length. They are flexible and can be as long and challenging as desired. Our favorite stretch of the **Lackawaxen** trails follows the river along what was once the towpath for the Delaware & Hudson canal.

New York and New Jersey are close to this corner of the Poconos. Trails run along the New York shore of the Delaware River. **Mongaup Valley**, north of Port Jervis, boasts a fine short run that goes past an old cemetery and several swimming holes. There is a good chance of spotting an eagle here.

In New Jersey, **High Point State Park**, the highest spot in the state at 1,900 feet, gives riders fantastic views and the chance to take a dip in several lakes. **Stokes State Forest**, 12 miles from Milford on U.S. Highway 206 in New Jersey, includes low-use roads and good

FYI

Unless otherwise noted, the area code for all phone numbers in this guide is 717.

mountain and valley views. Lakes are accessible for swimming and fishing.

Horseback Riding

Horseback riding provides a leisurely trip into the woods without a lot of effort (on the rider's part, at least). It is particularly popular during the fall foliage season when riders receive plenty of scenery with very little perspiration.

Always wear long pants to protect your legs from pinching or rubbing on the saddle. Shoes that tie on (not sandals) are best. In winter, long underwear might be a good idea, but definitely bring a hat and gloves.

Delaware Water Gap

Windrose Riding Center
River Rd., Exit 53 off I-80, Minisink Hills • 420-1763

Near the Shawnee resort area, Windrose offers 45-minute guided trail rides every hour on the hour from 9 AM to 3 PM. Hours are often expanded during summer months.

Beginning riders are encouraged; private lessons are available with prior arrangement. From Memorial Day to Labor Day, evening rides at dusk show off the changing colors of the night sky. Trail rides cost $20 per person; groups of eight or more pay $18 per person. Pony rides cost $3. Reservations are strongly suggested.

Stroudsburg/ East Stroudsburg

Colony Horse Ranch
Pa. Hwy. 447 North, Analomink • 595-0604

Behind the Colony Village complex of

The Mountain Bikers' Home in Mill Rift

Anyone coming to the Milford area for a mountain-biking excursion should consider staying at a place owned by people who love and support the sport.

Doug and Linda Hay operate **Bonny Bank Bungalow Bed & Breakfast** in Mill Rift, population 150 (depending on who is at home at the time). It is perched on the banks of the Delaware River a short drive from Milford.

The Hayses provide information on mountain biking in the region to folks who respond to their ads in magazines devoted to the sport. Their "tip sheet" is filled with suggested trails, distances and sites of note.

Bikers who stay here are given even more detailed articles on the region's offerings. Both Doug and Linda are retired newspaper people who can't resist the urge to write. They provide a shuttle service for their guests.

Their cozy B&B is not the lavish country inn type. As they say, "any antiques found here are incidental."

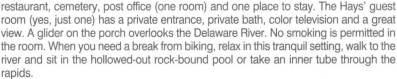

The town of Mill Rift has one of everything — a firehouse, general store, church, restaurant, cemetery, post office (one room) and one place to stay. The Hays' guest room (yes, just one) has a private entrance, private bath, color television and a great view. A glider on the porch overlooks the Delaware River. No smoking is permitted in the room. When you need a break from biking, relax in this tranquil setting, walk to the river and sit in the hollowed-out rock-bound pool or take an inner tube through the rapids.

Of course, there are plenty of other places to stay and sights to see in the Milford area (see our Accommodations and Attractions chapters for details), but mountain biking fans as well as outdoor lovers in general will be in their element at Bonny Bank Bungalow Bed & Breakfast, P.O. Box 481, Mill Rift, Pennsylvania 18340, 491-2250. As you might guess (given the number of guest rooms), reservations are recommended.

---

shops (see our Attractions chapter), Colony Horse Ranch offers 45-minute rides preceded by a 15-minute lesson. The trail is wooded, but it's an easy trip even for inexperienced riders. A guide is provided. Rates are $20 per person ($17 per person for groups of five or more). The stable is open every day from 10 AM to 5 PM. Reservations are suggested

Mount Pocono Area

Carson's Riding Stables Inc.
Pa. Hwy. 611, 1 mile south of Mount Pocono
• 839-9841

For more than 40 years, Carson's has thrilled riders year-round with guided trail rides. Cool off during summer with a ride down a shady lane. In spring, enjoy the aroma of the fresh flowers. The brilliantly colored foliage in fall and the peaceful, snow-laden hush in winter make for popular rides as well. Rides can be tailored to all abilities, and the staff always provides free instruction. Rides leave every hour on the hour from 10 AM to 5 PM. Summer hours may be extended, and reservations are appreciated. The guided rides cost $20 per person.

Fox Run Stables
Pa. Hwy. 715, south of Tannersville
• 629-9807

Wooded trails over rocky terrain mean the horses must be walked, rather than run, at Fox Run. A 45-minute ride costs $15. Rides depart daily at 10 and 11 AM, 1, 2 and 3 PM and occasionally at 4 PM. Call for reservations, especially on weekends.

Mountain Creek Stables
Pa. Hwy. 940, 3 miles east of Mt. Pocono
• 839-8725

Mountain Creek specializes in easy rides through wooded areas and streams. Guides equipped with radios accompany every trip. The rides last 45 to 50 minutes and cost $20 cash or $21 by credit card per person. Rides depart at 11 AM, 1 PM and 3 PM weekdays and every hour between 10 AM and 4 PM on weekends. Reservations are suggested. Pony rides are available, and there is a Western gift shop on the grounds.

Pocono Adventures
Pa. Route 611, 1 mile south of Mount Pocono
• 839-6333

Rides range from a gentle 45-minute ride along nature trails for $15 to a four-hour trek across varied terrain for $50. On the latter adventure, be prepared to walk, trot, canter and gallop — and bring lunch. There is also a condensed two-hour version of the same ride ($25). Trips are held rain or shine; rainwear is supplied. Guides and instruction before and during the ride are provided. Fishing trips are also an option. Call for reservations. Pocono Adventures is open every day at 8 AM, and the last ride departs at 4 PM.

Pocono Manor Stables
Just off Pa. Hwy. 314, Pocono Manor
• 839-0925

With more than 3,000 acres, Pocono Manor has enough trails to keep even serious riders occupied. Beginners enjoy leisurely rides through forests of white birch, rhododendron and mountain laurel. More advanced riders can canter along wooded trails to visit a stream or waterfall. Rides from one to three hours are available. A one-hour ride costs $17; two hours goes for $30. Both prices are per person, and group discounts are available.

The Pocono Clydesdales take groups on carriage rides throughout the year. Their sleigh

rides are winter traditions for many families. The group rate for sleigh rides is $7 per person. A smaller sleigh, suitable for couples or small families, costs $30 per person. Reservations are recommended.

West End

Deer Path Riding Stables Inc.
Pa. Hwy. 940, 6 miles west of Jack Frost Ski Area, White Haven • 443-7047

Deer Path specializes in teaching beginners. The staff can make even the most nervous rider feel at ease. Their rides stress a combination of lessons and actual riding. Once comfortable with the basic skills of handling a horse, guests are led along the nature trails. This is not the place for thrill-seekers looking for a wild ride. Instead, riders of all levels of experience are instructed on ways to improve their horse-handling abilities. Deer Path is open every day from 10:30 AM to 4:40 PM for rides. Reservations are advised. Rides last 45 to 50 minutes and cost $22 for adults and $21 for children 9 to 12.

Lake Wallenpaupack Area

Triple W Riding Stable Inc.
U.S. Hwy. 6, 4.5 miles north of Hawley
• 226-2620

Riders are interviewed about past experience, evaluated and assigned an appropriate horse from among the 50 or so at this 171-acre ranch. There are five trails graded by level of experience. Hay rides, sleigh rides and overnight camping trips, complete with cookout and country breakfast, are available. Basic rates range from $20 to $26 per hour depending on the length of the ride and the number of people involved. Overnight trips cost $105 per person plus tax and tips. Call for available dates and arrangements for groups.

INSIDERS' TIPS

Many mountain bike trails in the Delaware Water Gap National Recreation Area use the Old Mine Road in New Jersey, one of the oldest public thoroughfares in the country.

Photo: Pocono Mountains Vacation Bureau, Inc.

Many Pocono stables offer horseback riding tours to the public.

Paintball

Those who want more of a workout with their time in the woods should consider paintball. Dressed in camouflage, two teams attempt to capture each other's flag and return it to their base. Along the way, they "shoot" opponents with CO_2-powered guns loaded with paint pellets. The weapons and safety equipment have become hi-tech in recent years. As a result, serious injuries are rare, and the action is frantic.

Milford Area

Pike County Ambush
U. S. Hwy. 6, Blooming Grove • 226-8180

Conveniently situated near Lake Wallenpaupack and the Delaware River, Ambush's 250-acre field area has mature forests, rocky cliffs, streams, swamps and waterfalls. Play rates include the latest guns and goggles. Picnic areas are provided, and soda and snacks may be purchased.

Rates for one to nine people are $29 per

person. Groups of 10 to 19 people pay $27 per person. Groups of 20 or more also pay $27 per person, but the group leader plays for free. Half-day rates are $19 per person. Players receive 50 free paintballs. Reservations are requested. Call at least one week in advance for midweek play to make sure judges can be provided.

West End

Skirmish U.S.A.
Pa. Hwy. 903, Jim Thorpe • 325-8430

With 39 playing fields on 700 acres, Skirmish has a setting for every paintball taste. Thick vegetation, fieldstone walls and simulated villages provide cover. Fort Skirmish, Circle City, Baghdad U.S.A. and the 23-building village are alternatives to the conventional "run through the woods" game.

Groups of 20 or more may play on private fields. All equipment and "ammunition" is provided. Skirmish U.S.A. is open every day throughout the year. Rates are $29.50 for a full day and $19 for a half day per person. This includes field judges, gun rental and 50 paint pellets. Extra pellets cost 5 to 8 cents each depending on the number of pellets purchased. If you desire, you may rent camouflage clothing for $6. Skirmish opens at 9 AM and play ends between 3 and 6 PM.

Splatter
Interstate 80, Exit 43, Follow signs to Jack Frost Ski Area, Blakeslee • (800) 468-2442

Splatter features the first speedball arena in Pennsylvania. In "The Eliminator," shots fly by quickly as music pulsates all around the competitors. It is more intense than the conventional paintball game.

Other fields include Tunnel Town, a maze of trenches; Bunker Hill, filled with sandbag bun-

kers; Skid Row, with pallets stacked in various configurations; and the P.O.W. Game where teammates can rescue captured comrades.

All needed equipment is available for rent. Play rates, which include guns and all other needed equipment, are $27 for a full day and $15 for a half day per person. Full-day players receive 40 free paintballs. The field is open from 8:30 AM to 5 PM. The 2,500-acre complex is open all year, and the fields change with the seasons. Reservations are recommended.

Bowling

A family sport for generations, bowling appeals to everyone because it requires no particular physical abilities to participate. You do not have to be on a conditioning program to have a good time knocking down pins.

Bowling alleys have all the equipment you need. To choose the correct bowling ball from the house selection, pick a comfortable weight. Bowling balls generally weigh between 8 and 16 pounds. Your thumb should fit loosely in the thumb hole, enough to rotate freely. With your thumb in place, stretch your fingers over the finger holes. The big knuckle of each finger should be a quarter-inch past the near side of the holes. Always check for nicks in the holes that might cut your fingers.

The ideal bowling approach takes four steps. You should end leading with the foot opposite your throwing hand. If not, you stand a good chance of hitting your knee or foot with the ball, a potentially embarrassing and certainly painful accident.

Experienced bowlers use the marks on the lanes to determine where to throw the ball. It is much easier to aim for a mark closer to you than to just throw at the pins.

During the week, bowling alleys have leagues that use most of the lanes from ap-

> **FYI**
> Unless otherwise noted, the area code for all phone numbers in this guide is 717.

INSIDERS' TIPS

When walking or riding through the woods, remember to be wary of hunters. Many trails are in or near public game lands. Wear bright-colored clothes or avoid these trails during the fall hunting seasons.

proximately 6 to 9 PM. Call ahead to make sure a lane is available.

Stroudsburg/
East Stroudsburg

Colonial Lanes
N. Ninth St., across from Stroud Mall, Stroudsburg • 421-5941

Colonial features 33 lanes, a pro shop and a large snack bar. Pool tables and arcade games will occupy non-bowlers. Automated scoring computers keep track of your strikes and spares. Alcohol may be brought onto the premises. The Beef & Ale bar is just a few steps from the bowling alley's door.

Rates are $2.30 per game Monday through Friday from 9 AM to 5 PM; $2.50 per game Monday through Thursday after 5 PM; and $2.75 per game Friday after 5 PM and all day Saturday and Sunday. Shoe rental is $1.25 per pair.

Colonial Lanes is open daily 9 AM until midnight.

Skylanes
Pa. Hwy. 447 (Eagle Valley Mall), East Stroudsburg • 421-7680

With 24 lanes, several pool tables and arcade games, Skylanes has something to entertain everyone. Computers keep score for you, giving you more time to kick back with a beer, which is sold at the counter. A pro shop sells bowling accessories.

Rates are $2.75 per game, and shoe rental tacks on $1.25.

Skylanes is open weekdays from 9 AM to 11 PM. Leagues fill most of the lanes during the week until 9:30 PM. Call for reservations. Weekend hours are 1 to 11 PM on Saturday and noon to 11 PM on Sunday.

Photo: Pocono Mountains Vacation Bureau, Inc.

Snowmobiling — popular winter fun.

Mount Pocono Area

Pocono Lanes
Pa. Hwy. 390, Mountainhome • 595-2518

With a cozy eight lanes, Pocono Lanes is small yet perfect for families. The kids will not get out of sight. Arcade games and a small snack bar are available.

Pocono Lanes is open at widely varied hours Sunday through Thursday. Call ahead to make sure they are open. On Friday the lanes are open noon to 11 PM and 3 to 11 PM Saturday. The unusual hours are caused by leagues. With just eight lanes, they regularly fill the place.

The price per game is $2 until 5 PM and $2.25 thereafter. Juniors under 18 pay $1.50 and games for seniors older than 65 are $1.25. Shoe rental is $1 per pair. Alcohol is not served, but beer or wine may be brought in. Call ahead for group reservations for parties of more than 10.

West End

Haja Lanes
Delaware Ave., Palmerton
• (610) 826-2450

Automatic scoring is available on all 12 lanes at Haja. A small snack bar sells hot dogs, sodas and pizza. Other diversions include a few pinball machines, arcade games and a jukebox.

Alcohol is not sold and may not be consumed in the building. Lanes are open to the public at varied hours during weekdays, again due to league play, so call ahead. Weekend hours are 4 to 11 PM on Friday and 1 to 11 PM Saturday and Sunday. Rates are $2.25 per game, and shoe rental is $1. Call for reservations on weekends.

Ashley Lanes
Second and South Sts., Lehighton
• (610) 377-5022

Ashley Lanes offers computerized scoring, a snack bar, arcade games and a jukebox.

The lanes are open 3 to 11 PM Monday through Friday, 11 AM to 11 PM Saturday and 1 to 6:30 PM on Sunday. However, leagues occupy many lanes from approximately 6 to 9 PM every day during the week and on Saturday morning. Call for reservations.

Rates are $2 per game from 3 to 6 PM Monday through Thursday and $2.10 after 6 PM. Weekend bowling costs $2.25 per game. Senior citizens 60 and older pay $2 per game all the time. Shoe rental is $1.

Cypress Lanes
Fourth and Cypress Sts., Lehighton
• (610) 377-4570

A throwback to bowling's golden days, Cypress still uses the old-fashioned paper scoresheets to keep track of the action on its six lanes. You can bring beer with you. A snack bar sells refreshments, and a small game room has pinball and arcade machines.

Leagues fill the lanes on Monday, Tuesday and Friday. Lanes are open to the public Wednesday and Thursday from 9 PM to 11 PM, Saturday from 3 to 6 PM and 9 to 11 PM and Sunday from 1 to 6 PM. Cypress organizes children's birthday parties on weekends. For $5, each child receives two games of bowling, shoe rental, a hot dog and a soda.

Open bowling rates are $2 per game, and shoes are 85 cents to rent.

Milford Area

P. J. Bowl, Inc.
17 W. Main St., Port Jervis, N.Y.
• (914) 856-2113

Across the free bridge separating

INSIDERS' TIPS

A recent addition to the Jim Thorpe mountain biking trail selection is Psycho Betty's Revenge, which begins at the top of Flagstaff Mountain and boasts difficult, single-track stretches. It is named after a popular local rock band which performs regularly at the nightclub on Flagstaff Mountain.

Matamoras, Pennsylvania, and Port Jervis, New York, this establishment has 12 lanes, a large snack bar/coffee shop and a few arcade games. All New York State Lottery games are sold here.

Daytime hours and rates for open bowling vary, but prices for games and shoe rental are reduced on Tuesday and Thursday. Bowl on Friday from 10 AM to 1 AM for $1.25 per game, Saturday 1 PM to 1 AM for $2.25 per game and Sunday 1 to 5:30 PM for $2.25. Shoe rental is $1.25 except on Tuesday and Thursday when it's 75 cents.

Lake Wallenpaupack Area

Wallenpaupack Bowling Center
U.S. Hwy. 6, east of Hawley • 226-8499

Twelve lanes equipped with automatic scoring await bowlers at Wallenpaupack. An arcade and a snack bar are provided. Smoking and alcoholic beverages are not permitted.

Bowling is $2 per game from 11 AM to 6 PM Monday through Friday. Cost is $2.25 per game from 6 PM to midnight during the week and from 11 AM to midnight on weekends. Shoes are $1 per pair. Call for lane availability during the week due to league play.

Slate Belt

Blue Valley Lanes
Moorestown Rd., Wind Gap
• (610) 863-4621

Conveniently situated at the intersection of Pa. Highway 512 and Pa. Highway 33, Blue Valley has 24 lanes, computerized scoring, a snack bar, game room and a cocktail lounge.

Hours for open bowling are 10 AM to 6 PM and 9 PM to midnight Monday through Friday. Weekend hours are Saturday noon to midnight and Sunday 1 to 6 PM.

Bowling costs $2.50 per game. From 10 AM to 6 PM during the week, seniors age 65 and older pay $1.70 per game, children up to age 12 pay $1.85 and adults pay $2. Shoe rental is $1.50 per pair.

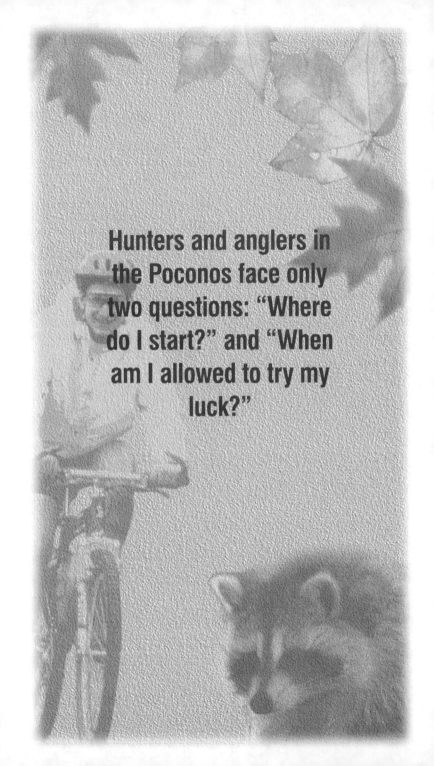

Hunters and anglers in the Poconos face only two questions: "Where do I start?" and "When am I allowed to try my luck?"

Fishing and Hunting

The diverse scenery attracts more than sightseers. Fishing and hunting enthusiasts visit the Poconos throughout the year to try their luck with our local fish and animals. With so much of the area's land and water controlled by the government, visitors do not have a problem finding excellent spots open to the public.

Our lakes, streams and ponds provide fishing opportunities for everything from casting from a boat launched on enormous Lake Wallenpaupack to standing in a famous trout stream and enjoying the romantic art of fly fishing. In addition, the Delaware River offers anglers plenty of challenges that can be enjoyed either by boat or on land.

State game lands and parks are home to animals of all sizes from bears to squirrels. The Poconos boast some of the best white-tailed deer hunting in Pennsylvania.

This chapter is separated into sections for hunting and fishing. Each presents descriptions of the most popular game and tips on how to successfully pursue them. At the end of each section, the best areas open to the public are identified, and the wildlife you can expect to find is discussed. Always obtain permission to hunt or fish on private property. Many private lakes, streams and woods are owned by rod and gun clubs whose members do not appreciate nonmembers using their treasured secret spots.

Licenses are required for both hunting and fishing. Information on where to purchase them and fees is presented in each section.

Fishing

Anglers can visit the Pocono Mountains and fish for several species, on more than one body of water, in the same day. In the four counties that comprise the majority of the Poconos, more than 12,000 surface acres of water and 300 miles of streams are open to public fishing. In addition, 140 miles of the Delaware River flows along the eastern edge of the region.

Fishing is a year-round activity in the Poconos.

In March shad begin their migration up the Delaware River; muskie and walleye fishing on the river is excellent as well. On large lakes such as Lake Wallenpaupack and Beltzville Lake, the striped bass start biting. The streams of the region become flanked by anglers in mid-April when trout season opens. Also, popular panfish such as sunfish and perch become active in shallower lakes. Trout, shad and panfish continue to be caught regularly through May. On the first Saturday of May, muskie, pickerel and walleye seasons open on inland lakes. Fishing for these species is allowed all year on most of the Delaware River. By June, shad start to spawn and die; walleye and muskie are harder to find. However, bass season opens in the middle of the month. Trout, bass and panfish are plentiful through the fall. In winter, ice-fishing enthusiasts can cut a hole in a frozen lake and try for perch and pickerel.

Anglers need a Pennsylvania license to try their luck on our waters. Licenses are available at more than 1,700 stores throughout the state. Annual prices are $17 for Pennsylvania residents between the ages of 16 and 64 and $4 for residents older than 65. Nonresidents 16 and older pay $35 for an annual license,

$30 for a seven-day tourist license and $15 for a three-day license. Licenses allow you to fish all public waters, including the Delaware River and the Pennsylvania, New York and New Jersey shores where the river separates the states. Minimum size requirements and daily limits are established for most species. Consult the fishing regulations you will receive with your license for information.

The most famous fish in the Poconos is the trout. In the late 1800s and early 1900s, resorts were opened to cater to the fly fishermen who came to ply Brodhead Creek. Flies such as the Artificial Fly, the Henryville Special, the Analomink, the Hamlin, The Paradise, The Swiftwater, The Cresco and The Canadens were created in the Poconos.

Standard flies such as Mayflies, Caddis Flys, Stone Flys, Drakes, Nymphs, Streamers, Wulff Flys and Compara Duns will attract trout in the Poconos. Rods should be 7 to 9 feet in length. You will need a strong reel and line that is between 4- and 8-pound test.

Brook trout are native to the Poconos. **Browns** and **rainbows** are stocked. In addition to artifical lures, trout will go after worms, flies and insect larvae. While they are smaller than rainbows and browns, brook trout are regarded as prize catches because they are far more rare. If that's what you're searching for, visit one of the small spring-fed brooks in the Poconos and use an ultra-light spinning rod and your lightest line with a very small lure or bait. Fly fishing for brook is difficult because the waters are usually very narrow and have overgrown banks.

Stream fishing for trout is easier because many waterways are stocked by the state with thousands of browns and rainbows each year. Larger rods and lures can be used on these bigger waters, and fly fishing is easier. Nymphs and streamers work best when fishing early in the season in cold water. Other than opening day, fall is the best time to land trout as they

FYI

Unless otherwise noted, the area code for all phone numbers in this guide is 717.

are more active when the temperature is below 50 degrees. The largest brown trout feed at night.

Even larger bodies of water such as the Lackawaxen River and the Brodhead Creek are considered to be among the best trout fishing spots in the country. Because they are so well-regarded and publicized, they are very crowded, particularly early in the season. You might be lucky to find a choice spot on the shoreline. Wading in these deeper, faster waters is not easy.

To catch the larger browns and rainbows, use a medium heavy 6.5-foot spinning rod with a ¼- to ½-ounce lure weight and 6- to 8-pound test line. Fly fishermen will want a 9-foot rod with 7- to 9-foot leaders to accommodate the longer casts required on the larger bodies of water.

Many local anglers enjoy trying for trout later in the season, when the fresh-stocked "easier" catches have been taken, and the more crafty, difficult fish are still around.

Smallmouth bass, which many fly fishermen consider to be just as fun as trout, are at their peak in fall. They are actively feeding to fatten up for winter and will attack lures, plugs and live bait such as earthworms, minnows, hellgrammites and leeches. In afternoons, bass can be found lurking in deep pools. Early mornings and late evenings they head for riffles in search of food. **Largemouth bass** prefer thick vegetation and submerged logs. They hide in these areas and wait to feast on passing frogs and bait fish. Cast into shallow areas with thick cover using weedless jigs.

Bass can be caught from a boat or by wading into shallow areas. On the Delaware River, smallmouth fishing is excellent after a summer shower. The rain lowers the temperature of the water and adds oxygen to it, which stimulates the fish to feed.

Equally fabled as sport fish are the **American shad**, which migrate up the Delaware River from the lower Delaware Bay to spawn.

INSIDERS' TIPS

Farmers love to see groundhogs hunted. They have a voracious appetite and dig tractor-catching burrows.

These silvery fish with deeply forked tails begin migration in mid-March and arrive near Bushkill by mid-April. At the same time, a small tree with white flowers blooms along the slopes of the river. Called serviceberry in other parts of the country, it is known as shad bush in these parts because its blooming coincides with the shad run.

This spring spawning run, estimated to include more than 1 million fish, is the only naturally spawning population in Pennsylvania.

Shad travel in schools and average 3 to 6 pounds. They may be caught from a boat or from land. Light equipment — 4- to 6-pound line and a lure known as a "shad dart" — is all you will need. Cast into slow-moving pools and use a slight jiggling motion to slowly reel the dart back. Also keep an eye on the anglers downstream from you. If they start catching shad, a school is headed toward you. Once you have caught one, you can look forward to a great meal. Shad fillets and smoked shad are some of the best local seafood.

Unlike shad, pike, pickerel, walleye and muskellunge travel alone, stalking other fish from beneath logs and protected areas. The best fishing for them is in still water in weed beds. Look for water about 5 feet deep with a lot of vegetation. **Pike** and **pickerel** action is strong in fall. **Walleyes** as large as 14 pounds are taken from Lake Wallenpaupack. Average fish are 18 to 22 inches and weigh 7 to 10 pounds. **Muskellunge** can grow to be more than 40 pounds and 50 inches long. They average 40 inches long and about 20 pounds. Pickerel more than two feet long are common in many lakes. Muskellunge must be at least 30 inches long to be legally kept, pickerel at least 15 inches, walleye at least 15 inches and pike at least 24 inches. These are the largest game fish in the Poconos. Their strikes are strong and dramatic, and they put up a great fight. You must use strong equipment to land them successfully. Spoon-shape lures work well because they move and glitter like living prey. Minnows also are effective as bait.

Pickerels, muskies and pike are popular with ice fishermen. In winter the water at the bottom of a lake is warmer than that on the surface. Early in the season, before snow covers the ice, is the best time to fish because more light filters through the ice and keeps the fish active.

Most ice fishermen use tip-ups, small wooden structures with a reel, line and hook attached. A flag on the pole is tripped by the reel to indicate a bite. Minnows make the best bait. Tip-ups are scattered across a lake approximately 15 to 50 feet apart. Placement is a matter of guesswork and depends on how many holes you are willing to carve in the ice. If you start getting strikes in one area, move some of your other tip-ups closer to the ones that are producing. Because your tip-ups may cover a large area, be prepared to get plenty of exercise checking them and take along an extra minnow bucket so bait is easily accessible. Use a dip net to get minnows out of the bucket to keep your hands dry. Wet hands chill quickly.

Your minnows should be set as close to the bottom as possible, ideally near underwater debris such as logs.

Since you will be outside on a cold day, dress warmly in layers and wear gloves. Make sure the ice is thick enough to support your weight. Bring extra clothes in case you do fall through the ice.

Perch, **bluegill**, **sunfish** and **crappie** — collectively known as panfish — are favorites of youngsters because they are plentiful and easy to catch. They enjoy quiet ponds, but also are found in larger bodies of water such as Lake Wallenpaupack and the Delaware River. Most are small, weighing less than a pound. You can fish for them throughout the year and keep as many as 50 of these combined species each day. There is no minimum size requirement.

INSIDERS' TIPS

If you fall while hunting and your shotgun dips into mud or snow, never continue hunting until you have checked the barrel for a possible blockage. Unload the gun and use a twig to make sure the barrel is clear. Serious injury can result from firing a gun with a blocked barrel.

Fishing and
Hunting Seasons

There is so much game in the Poconos, hunters and anglers are presented with only two problems: "Where do I start?" and "When am I allowed to try my luck?" The answer to the former question can be found throughout this chapter. To answer the latter . . . read on.

On the Delaware River, all species of fish, except sturgeon (which is endangered and can not be caught) and trout, are in season year round. Trout are in season from April 13 to September 30.

On all other waters, striped bass, sunfish, yellow perch, crappies, catfish, rock bass, suckers, eels, carp and white bass are open all year. Muskellunge, pickerel, pike and walleye are legal from May 4 through March 14. Bass can be caught from June 15 through April 12. Open season on trout and salmon is April 13 through September 2.

Hunting seasons for species common to the Poconos are as follows:

Squirrel and ruffed grouse, October 14 through November 25 and December 26 through January 27; cottontail rabbit, October 28 through November 25 and December 26 through February 10; pheasant, October 28 through November 25; snowshoe hare, December 26 through December 30; turkey, October 28 through November 11; black bear, November 20 through 22; antler-less deer, December 11 through 13; antlered deer (archery), September 30 through November 11 and December 26 through January 13; antlered deer (firearms), November 27 through December 9; and any deer (flintlock muzzleloader), December 26 through January 13.

Sometimes mistaken for a snake, the **American eel** is actually a long, slender fish. It is the only fish in North America to move downstream to the ocean to breed after living most of its life, usually around eight years, in fresh water. Females can be up to 48 inches long; males are usually about half that length. They leave our Delaware River to spawn in the subtropical waters of the Sargasso Sea southwest of Bermuda. Each female produces as many as 20 million eggs. After mating, the adults die. Only the females make the trek from the sea to inland rivers, streams and, by squirming through mud or wet grass, ponds. Males stay close to the sea.

Some residents along the Delaware River consider eels a delicacy. Traps, called weirs, are constructed to capture them. Anglers often catch them by accident while trying for other fish.

Channel catfish can weigh as much as 30 pounds. Typically, the ones you will catch will be of the 3- to 5-pound variety. They are most likely found in the deeper parts of the Delaware River. By the end of June they have spawned and want to feed to regain lost weight. The best baits are natural foods such as crayfish and minnows. One well-regarded local fisherman successfully uses fresh chicken livers. Fish for catfish in the evenings. They can easily be identified by their deeply forked tail and the four to eight whiskers, called barbels, around their mouths. The whiskers help the fish find food.

Following are some of the best public fishing waters in the Poconos and the fish you will find in them.

Delaware Water Gap

About 40 miles of the **Delaware River** are within the Delaware Water Gap National Recreation Area, which runs from Delaware Water Gap to Milford. Boat launches are off U.S. Hwy. 209. Beginning at the Kittatinny Point visitor center on the New Jersey side of the river opposite Delaware Water Gap and traveling north, the launches in Pennsylvania are Smithfield Beach Access, north of Shawnee; Bushkill Access, north of Bushkill; Eshback Access, south of the Pocono Environmental Education Center; Dingmans Ferry Access, at Dingmans Ferry; and Milford Beach Access, south of Milford.

Anglers can either take to the water or stay on dry ground. River game fish include American shad, smallmouth bass, muskellunge, sunfish, walleye, catfish, American eels, pickerel and walleye.

All other waters within the recreation area are open to sport fishing unless otherwise posted. Areas closed to fishing are the George W. Childs Recreation Site, Dingmans Falls during the day, and the pool at the bottom of Silver Thread Falls. Fishing from a boat is prohibited on Hidden Lake.

Stocked waters within the recreation area are **Hidden Lake**, **Bushkill Creek**, **Lower Blue Mountain Lake** and **Dingmans Creek**. They are the spots to try for trout, bass and sunfish. The National Park Service provides free maps showing the location of all of these bodies of water.

In winter do not try to ice fish on the river as the ice is rarely (if ever) thick enough to support a person's weight. Given the river's current, falling through its ice could be deadly.

Stroudsburg/ East Stroudsburg

While the big lakes and the rivers are in the mountain areas, you'll find some great fly fishing in the streams closer to these towns.

The best places for trout are the **Brodhead Creek** and **McMichaels Creek**. A 9-mile stretch of the Brodhead runs through the Stroudsburgs to the Delaware River. For the McMichaels, try the area of the creek near Sciota.

Northeast of East Stroudsburg on Pa. 447, **Gregory Pond** is a fun place to fish for bass, sunfish and perch.

Mount Pocono Area

North of Canadensis on Pa. Hwy. 390, Promised Land State Park's two lakes, the 422-acre **Promised Land Lake** and the 173-acre **Lower Lake**, are good places to try for bass, pickerel, muskellunge and panfish throughout the year. Boat launches are provided at both lakes.

The 250-acre **Gouldsboro Lake** at Gouldsboro State Park, on Pa. 507 in Gouldsboro, contains similar fish as the Promised Land lakes. A boat launch is available on the southwestern shore.

Tobyhanna State Park's 170-acre **Tobyhanna Lake** is considered by many locals the best fishing hole in the Mount Pocono area. Bass, brook trout, catfish, yellow perch and bluegill are common. In the winter try the lake for pickerel, perch and bass. Launch your boat from the eastern shore.

East of Blakeslee on Pa. 940, 229-acre **Brady's Lake** is popular for bass, muskellunge, panfish and pickerel.

For trout, try **Tobyhanna Creek** (Pa. Hwy. 611 near Tobyhanna), **Devil's Hole Creek** (Pa. 940 near Mount Pocono) and **Pocono Creek** (Pa. 611 near Tannersville).

West End

Beltzville Lake near Lehighton off U.S. 209 is stocked with trout. Panfish (sunfish, perch, etc.), pickerel, bass, muskellunge and walleye also may be found on this large manmade lake. Boat-launching ramps are at Pine Run East on the northern shore and Preacher's Camp on the south shore. Ice fishing is popular here.

The **Pohopoco Creek** below the dam is stocked with trout.

INSIDERS' TIPS

Boat docks are summertime hotspots for anglers to drop a line. They provide fish with comfortable shade and food.

Other popular trout spots in the region are **Aquashicola Creek** (Pa. 248, Palmertown), **Buckwa Creek** (Pa. 904, Little Gap), **Big Bear Creek** (Pa. 903, Jim Thorpe), **Lizzard Creek** (Pa. 248, Bowmanstown) and **Mahoning Creek** (Pa. 443, Lehighton).

Hickory Run State Park, off Pa. Rt. 534 near Hickory Run, has two stocked trout streams, the **Fourth Run** and the **Sand Spring**. Mud Run also is stocked with trout but is open only for fly fishing. The **Lehigh River** flows along the western edge of the park and contains some nice bass and trout. The 90-acre **Francis E. Walters Reservoir** is about 20 minutes away but is worth the trip for bass, panfish, trout and walleye. The area around Hickory Run State Park is easily accessible by taking Interstate 80 to Exit 41.

The largest lake in this area is the 330-acre **Mauch Chunk Lake**, near Jim Thorpe off U.S. Hwy. 209. Most of the game fish of the Poconos, bass, panfish, pickerel, trout and walleye, are found here. A boat launch is near the western end of the lake. Fishing is not permitted on the east end.

Milford Area

The most famous fishing here is at **Pecks Pond**, west of Milford on Pa. Hwy. 402 north of Marshalls Creek. It provides a 315-acre, very shallow home for bass, panfish and pickerel. The area around the lake is particularly scenic. Many trophy fish have been pulled from the thick vegetation in Pecks Pond. In winter, don't be afraid to bundle up and try some ice fishing; it's worth the effort. While here, visit the Pennsylvania Fishing Museum (see our Attractions chapter) in the Pecks Pond Store on the edge of the lake just off of Pa. 402.

Join the bald eagles and fish the 1,100-acre **Shohola Lake**, near Shohola Falls, which is renowned for its supply of bass, pickerel, trout and panfish. Avoid the posted restricted area where bald eagles nest.

Like the Delaware Water Gap National Recreation Area, the upper **Delaware River** is filled with bass, pickerel, eel and American shad. The best river access point for boats, and a great fishing spot as well, is in Lackawaxen. Western writer Zane Grey settled in this little town largely because of the great fishing nearby.

The **Lackawaxen River** is nationally celebrated as a trout lover's paradise. On opening day, its shores are jammed with anglers. However, the river is very large and abundantly stocked, so by all means make some room for yourself and enjoy. Savvy anglers pay attention to the water-release schedule of the dam at nearby Lake Wallenpaupack which empties into the Lackawaxen. The fishing is much better after rushing water from the dam enters the river and stirs up the fish.

Other less famous but productive trout waters are **Little Bushkill Creek** (near Bushkill), **Saw Creek** (near Dingmans Ferry), **Middle Branch Lake** (near Dingmans Ferry) and **Shohola Creek** (near Lords Valley).

Some lakes worth a look for bass, panfish and pickerel are **Billings Pond** (near Lords Valley), **Lake Minisink** (near Dingmans Ferry) and **Little Mud Pond** (near Dingmans Ferry).

Lake Wallenpaupack Area

Fishing is a year-round activity at **Lake Wallenpaupack**. While the peak seasons are spring and summer, ice fishing is prevalent throughout winter.

Anglers hope to catch bass, muskellunge, walleye, pike, trout, pickerel, perch, bluegill and crappies. In recent years the lake has developed large weedbeds that provide cover for young bass and panfish that sometimes grow to be trophy fish. The lake record for a brown trout is more than 17 pounds. The striped bass record is 34-plus pounds. The best places to look for trout around opening day are in shallow, rocky shoals. They like to hang out at the mouths of creeks that run warmer than the main lake. The best time to catch stripers at night is around the first full moon in June. By July the lake can become very crowded by pleasure boats, making finding a quiet spot more difficult. Labor Day signals the end of the main tourist season and anglers again dominate the lake. Fall is the best time to catch smallmouth bass. The best baits are spinner bait or crank bait. If you are looking for muskies, try fishing on a stormy day in November.

Encompassing 5,700 acres, the lake has plenty of room for everyone. Experienced anglers, as well as novices, will enjoy a day here.

Even if you go home empty-handed, the scenery is entertainment enough.

Boat launches are provided. (See our In, On and Around the Water Chapter for more information on the facilities at the lake.) The shoreline is filled with marinas, sports shops, boat rental stores, bait shops and supply stores. You can hire a guide to lead you to secret spots.

Other lakes of choice for bass and pickerel are **Belmont Lake** (Pa. Hwy. 371 in Pleasant Mount), **Prompton Reservoir** (Pa. 170 in Honesdale), **White Deer Lake** (Pa. 590 in Hawley) and **Fairview Lake** (Pa. 390 in Paupack).

Upper Woods Pond (Pa. 371 in Cold Springs) is one of the few glacial trout lakes in Pennsylvania. The waters stay cold and are 90-feet deep. The lake is stocked with trout and Kokanee salmon. It also is stocked in winter for ice fishing. The use of bait fish is prohibited.

Streams to try for trout are **Butternut Creek** (Newfoundland), **Dyberry Creek** (Honesdale), **Equinunk Creek** (Equinunk) and **Wallenpaupack Creek** (Newfoundland).

Slate Belt

The best fishing here is in the **Delaware River**. This section of the river is just below the Delaware Water Gap National Recreation Area. The fishing is generally considered to be better between Milford and Delaware Water Gap, but you might want to try your luck on this less crowded part of the river.

Hunting

The best time of the year for hunters to visit the Poconos is autumn. Hunters come from throughout the eastern United States each year to hunt here in the fall and winter. Our diverse public game lands include high

mountain meadows, thick wooded forests and flat farmlands. Habitats similar to those found in the midwestern United States, and even Canada, are found in the Poconos. Throughout Pennsylvania, more than 1.2 million acres of land have been set aside as state forests, parks and game lands. Both small and large game are plentiful.

All hunters are required to carry a Pennsylvania hunting license. Rates are $12.75 for resident adults between ages 17 and 64, $5.75 for resident adults between ages 12 and 16 and $10.75 for resident adults older than age 65. A nonresident hunting license is $80.75; $40.75 for nonresidents between ages 12 and 16. Muzzleloader and archery licenses cost $5.75 each. The fees for fur-taker licenses to trap are identical to the ones for hunters. To hunt waterfowl, residents older than 16 must purchase a special duck stamp that costs $5.50. Hunters between ages 12 and 16 pay 75¢.

The most popular animal to hunt is the **white-tailed deer**. The total deer population in Pennsylvania approaches 1 million. Hunters harvest more deer in Pennsylvania than in any other state except Texas, which has six times the land. Pennsylvania usually sells the most hunting licenses of any state.

Deer travel in small groups typically consisting of a doe, her fawns and young female offspring. Bucks tend to go their own way at an early age. They travel together from summer through fall. Leadership is determined by antler tests which sometimes become full-scale fights resulting in injury or death. Deer have been known to live as long as 18 years.

The average range for a deer is 500 to 3,000 acres. However, they might travel as many as 50 miles in winter to search for food. Deer, like cattle, are grazers. They eat grasses, herbs, leaves, buds, fruits and, to the frustration of many Pocono homeowners, landscaping.

INSIDERS' TIPS

More than 45,000 deer are killed on roadways in Pennsylvania annually. Always keep an eye out for them while traveling on back roads. This is especially true during November and December when icy roads combined with deer fleeing from hunters often cause traffic accidents.

Left uncontrolled, deer populations can overwhelm a forest, eating all vegetation within reach. Deer have few natural predators. Orchards, nurseries and farms suffer heavy losses due to deer who have nowhere else to feed. This affects the lives of both other wildlife species and human residents. In winter young deer can starve because of a lack of food. As a result, deer management through hunting is essential, but hunting is carefully monitored to maintain a stable deer population.

Deer have pupils that open much wider than those of humans, allowing up to nine times more light to enter their eyes. This gives deer much better night vision than us. Their antlers are among the fastest-growing living tissues; a buck's rack can become a quarter-inch longer each day.

Some common sense tips for hunters include not using scented shaving lotions, soaps, hair tonic or cologne before heading into the woods. Deer have a keen sense of smell and will quickly notice the unfamiliar odor. Hunters should start at first light when game is feeding. Deer move into the wind. You should find an appropriate hiding spot against the wind and let the game come to you. At dark and before sunrise deer move toward water.

If you spot tracks and want to tell if they are fresh, look for frost crystals. If they are there, the track was made the night before. When the sun dries the morning frost, the edges of the track tend to crumble. If the track is clean and there is no frost, then it probably is fresh.

Health-conscious hunters should know that deer meat, venison, is one of the most wholesome red meats. It has one-fifth the fat content of beef or pork. Venison also has fewer calories and more protein than lamb, veal, beef or pork.

After deer, the most popular target for hunters is Pennsylvania's largest game animal, the **black bear**. Pennsylvania bears tend to grow faster, obtain larger-than-average weights and breed earlier and more regularly than bears in other states. By age 3, Pennsylvania bears average 258 pounds. Adults range in size from 380 to 480 pounds. The larger sizes of Pennsylvania bears can be partially explained by the presence of many parks, campgrounds, picnic areas and landfills. They receive more contact with humans, and as a result more calorie-rich food, than bears in more isolated areas.

Pennsylvania litters average three bear cubs, but dens with four and five cubs are not uncommon. Many other states have never recorded a bear litter of four. Cubs are born during winter in the den the female has chosen for her period of hibernation.

Bears are much harder to take down than deer. They are also much harder to find. Pike County has the largest bear population in the state, estimated between 4,000 and 6,000. Should you find one, you better have a powerful gun. A bear's dense muscles, fat and bones can deflect shots from underpowered weapons. The average target area on a bear for a clean kill shot is less than one foot square.

Wounded bears head for the thickest cover available. If there is no snow on the ground, you must track the bear using a blood trail, so consider a bullet with enough power to pass through the animal and create a double blood trail.

Wild turkey season conveniently arrives just before Thanksgiving. Because there is danger of being accidently shot, hunters must wear florescent orange clothing when moving through the woods in search of turkey. Also, when stationary and calling, tie an orange band around the nearest tree so other hunters are not convinced enough by your call to begin shooting.

Proper clothing is essential. Wear good camouflage, a face mask and gloves. Also popular is a turkey vest which has a foam seat to make those calling positions more comfortable. The better vests have a pouch in the back to store your kill. Since turkeys can weigh more than 20 pounds, packing it there sure beats carrying it over your shoulder.

The other required accessory is convincing decoys. Make sure the turkey is in a comfortable shooting range, usually no more than 40 yards away.

FYI

Unless otherwise noted, the area code for all phone numbers in this guide is 717.

Photo: Pocono Mountains Vacation Bureau, Inc.

Enjoy some of the Pennsylvania's finest trout fishing.

Popular small game in the Poconos include **squirrels**, which are active just after sunrise and in late afternoon; **ruffed grouse**, which begin drinking and feeding just after sun-up; **pheasants**, which are found along roadsides in the morning and in farm fields later in the day; **rabbits**, which feed heavily at night; and **groundhogs**. Duck hunters can go after migrating **Canada geese, mallards, pintails, wood ducks** and several other species.

Trappers try to outwit **mink, muskrats, beavers, raccoons, foxes, coyotes, opossums, skunks** and **weasels**.

Following are some of the better public game lands in the Poconos.

Delaware Water Gap

The land of the **Delaware Water Gap National Recreation Area** is open to hunters except for areas within 450 feet of any structures or trails. Hunters also are asked to be wary of hikers and others using the park's fa-

cilities. No hunting is permitted in fields with unharvested crops. Artifical or natural bait is prohibited. No hunting is allowed from any motorized vehicle or on any public road. Tree stands must be free-standing and removable so they do not damage trees. No trapping is allowed.

Mount Pocono Area

Promised Land State Park, **Tobyhanna State Park**, **Gouldsboro State Park** and **Big Pocono State Park** all have public hunting areas and are good locations to pursue deer, black bear, turkey and small game. Trapping is permitted in designated areas.

This region is heavily forested with rugged mountain peaks and numerous glacial lakes. Many hunters consider these woods to be the most productive in the Poconos.

Two of the more popular state gamelands are the 8,600-acre **Delaware State Forest**, near Canadensis and Tannersville, and the

25,500-acre **SGL (State Game Land) #127** near Tannersville.

landowner of a choice site for permission to hunt.

West End

Hunting and trapping are permitted on 1,707 acres of land in **Beltzville State Park** near Lehighton. Game species include pheasants, rabbits, ruffed grouse, waterfowl and deer.

Hickory Run State Park, east of White Haven, is open to hunters from the end of September to March 31. Look for deer, turkey, black bear, squirrels and snowshoe hare, a rarity in the Poconos.

State game lands #141, #129 and #40 are near White Haven and north and west of Jim Thorpe.

Milford Area

This area is dominated by private residential communities and hunting/fishing clubs. Public lands are more scarce than in other parts of the Poconos. However, the wetlands and forests available hold many deer and black bear.

Northwest of Milford off U.S. 6 are **State Game Lands #209, #180, #116 and #183**. These game lands total 21,564 acres.

Lake Wallenpaupack Area

Hunters enjoy open stretches of land in northern Wayne County, near the New York border. **State Game Lands #70 and #299** are at the far northern edge of the county. Northeast of Honesdale is **Prompton State Park** with 850 acres of public land. It is the only state-owned park land in Wayne County. **State Game Land #159** is north of Honesdale on Pa. Highway 191 at Lookout. It covers 9,367 acres. Deer and small game are plentiful on these lands.

This region also is home to 14,000 acres of private farm lands which are great places to hunt pheasants and turkeys. Try talking to the

Slate Belt

The **Jacobsburg State Park**, off Pa. 33 near Belfast, provides 1,000 acres for hunting. **State Game Land #168** west of Wind Gap runs along the Blue Mountain for 5,173 acres. Both are good places to look for deer.

Outfitters

If you arrive in the Poconos with neither equipment nor a license, you can purchase both and be wetting a line or walking the woods the same day.

Bait and tackle shops stock live bait, such as worms and minnows, and an array of artificial lures. Most shops carry an assortment of line, hooks, swivels, bobbers, rods and reels. Some larger outfitters also stock fly-fishing gear. And don't forget bait and tackle boxes.

Hunters can find ammunition of all sizes and guns of all gauges in which to load it. Cleaning kits, oils, lubricants, scopes and grips are popular accessories usually in stock. Many outfitters also carry scents and calls as well as practice targets. And most sell an assortment of knives, binoculars and hunting apparel as well.

The following list includes some of the bait and tackle shops in the Poconos. Talk to the people who work at them for more tips and inside information on desirable spots.

Stroudsburg/East Stroudsburg: Family Bait & Tackle Shop, 624 N. Courtland Street, East Stroudsburg, 421-6918; Dunkelberger's Sports Outfitter, Sixth and Main streets, Stroudsburg, 421-7950; Windsor Fly Shop, 348 N. Ninth Street, Stroudsburg, 424-0938.

Mount Pocono Area: Blakeslee Sport Shop, Pa. Highway 115, Blakeslee, 646-2670; Canadensis Sporting Goods, Pa. Highway 390, Canadensis, 595-9296; JC's Fish & Game, Main Street, Tobyhanna, 894-1420; Pocono Gun Accessories, Pa. Highway 940, Pocono Lake, 643-1646.

INSIDERS' TIPS

Before becoming the first president of our country, George Washington earned his living netting shad on the Delaware River.

West End: Gary's Sport & Tackle, Barbara Court, Saylorsburg, 992-6837; Alpha Sporting 'N' Gun Shop, U.S. Highway 209, Sciota, 992-7026; Beltzville Pro Fishing, U.S. Highway 209, Beltzville, (610) 377-9115; West End Gun & Sport Inc., U.S. Highway 209, Kresgeville, 681-4117.

Milford Area: Inn Sport Shop, Pa. Highway 402, Pecks Pond, 775-0441; Angler's Roost & Hunter's Rest, Lackawaxen, 685-2010; Sportsman's Rendezvous, 113 W. Harford Street, Milford, 296-6113; Sisters Country Sports Shops, Pa. Highway 739, Dingmans Ferry, 828-2929; Dennis's Sport Shop, Shohola, 296-6283; Curt's Sporting Goods, Pa. Highway 97 Sparrow Bush, 856-5024.

Lake Wallenpaupack Area: Hunter's Gallery, Pa. Highway 590, Hamlin, 689-7898; Ironwood Point Sport Shop, Pa. Highway 507, Greentown, 857-0677; Northeast Flyfishers, 923 Main Street, Honesdale, 253-9780; Heberling Sport Shop, Prompton, 253-1801; Wallenpaupack Sport Shop, U.S. Highway 6, Hawley, 226-4797; Hemlock Gun Shop, Pa. Highway 590 and Crane Road, Lakeville, 226-9410.

Slate Belt: Quarry Sporting Goods & Lawn Equipment, 222 E. Main Street, Pen Argyl, (610) 863-5152.

With all the resorts and other types of accommodations vying for guests, many lodgings are adding more and more winter activities to their offerings.

Winter Sports

The Poconos are a vacation land in winter as well as a summer. The five major ski areas within an hour's ride from each other and the major resorts that include resort-size ski facilities make this an easy place to wallow in and whisk across the white stuff.

The Poconos are easily accessible from numerous major metropolitan areas and population centers. They are less than two hours from north, east and central New Jersey points; New York — Manhattan and Long Island — are from two to four hours away; Philadelphia is less than two hours away; southern Connecticut is between three and four hours away; and parts of Maryland and Delaware are only three to four hours away.

With all the resorts and other types of accommodations vying for guests, many lodgings are adding more and more winter activities to their offerings. Among the easiest to add are snowmobiling and cross-country skiing, which we discuss here. Ice skating, sledding and tobogganing, which are also available at many places that are close to the major ski areas, round out the available offerings.

Snowboarding and snow tubing are the newest entries on the Poconos winter sports menu. Snowboarding is not for the untutored, but snowtubing (sliding in an inner tube) is a winter activity the whole family can enjoy as they spill over one another down specially marked trails at the major ski resorts.

This section introduces you to main ski areas and resorts. It also offers information on the other available winter sports activities. New activities are opening at resorts all the time, so it is always to good to ask about winter sports activities for the upcoming season.

The major ski resorts usually offer special events throughout the season — races, carnivals, SKIwee Days, Torchlite Parades . . . the list goes on. Each ski area and resort puts out a brochure listing winter events, so calling in fall for a brochure will help you plan what ski area to visit and when.

Also, the major ski resorts usually offer preseason ticket packages at a large discount. Discounted fees also apply for different times of the day, midweek, weekend, six-days or five-days of your choice throughout the season. So, again, contacting an area of interest during the fall will ensure you'll know what preseason packages are available in time to take advantage of them.

Downhill Skiing

Major Ski Areas

Skiing has many variables when it comes to prices. The basic price is for a lift ticket, which is all most skiers who already have their own equipment need. Lift ticket prices are governed by factors such as time of day, day of the week and holidays. Age is a determining factor in prices also. Purchasing season passes or books of tickets in pre-season also affects the rates. Rates for lift tickets range from $18 to $40 for an adult midweek, depending on the time of day — morning, evening, twilight. The other option here is full-day versus half-day. Junior lift tickets rates midweek range from $16 to $40 depending on the time of day and whether the ticket is for a full-day, half-day, twilight or evening. The age of the juniors category varies from ski area to ski area. Basically children 12 and younger are considered juniors at most ski areas; however, there are exceptions. Youngsters participating in learn-to-ski programs for children, such as SKIwee, receive lift tickets as part of the packages. Senior citizens (age varies but starts between 60 and 65) discounts are available at all ski areas, though the amount of discount may vary by age and in some places is limited to midweek. Senior citizens older than 70 ski free anytime at Shawnee and free during midweek, non-holiday at Camelback.

Weekend and holiday rates are higher for all ages noted; the rates can run to $46 for a full-day lift ticket on the weekend. Note that prices are subject to change without notice. Package deals can offer inclusive rates for renting ski equipment, getting a lesson and using the lifts. Packages can also mean purchasing a lift ticket for a number of days at the ski areas or through a nearby accommodation. The packages are so many and so varied that providing rates and options here would be formidable.

You can rent equipment separate from lift tickets if you aren't taking a lesson package. Usually renting includes a complete set, skis, poles, and boots. Boot bindings are adjusted for you right in the ski shop. You can also rent just a piece of equipment that you may need — skis or boots or poles. Again, the ski shop will adjust boots or skis to fit your equipment, if necessary. Rental packages are also available for more than one day. Complete ski sets rent for about $20 depending on time of day or length of day, during the week or on weekends. Juniors rates are about $5 to $7 less at most ski areas. Each ski area has its own bargain days — Ladies Day, Tuesday, Monday, Civil Service Day (Shawnee has a Family Night on Sundays with 50 percent savings on lift tickets) and specialty days. While prices may seem high at first, there are many options for getting more skiing for your dollar. If you plan to ski regularly, there are season passes that also have variables. Season passes must be bought preseason, so if an area interests you, call or write for their rates and packages options before the season starts.

A word about amenities. All ski areas have lounges, restrooms, cafeterias and restaurants. You can bring your own food and eat on the decks at the base of the mountains or in the open dining areas. For a really special time, you can stop by the side of the trail and eat your own prepared picnic — just be sure to get far enough off the trail. You don't want to have a skier ski through your pasta salad!

Skilled technicians are in every ski shop. They can make repairs on your ski equipment for a fee, and they make sure that equipment you rent suits your needs. Lockers are available at all areas. They are of the same type that are in train stations, airports and bus stations. Parking is free at all ski areas. Of course the parking lots are large — we have a lot of skiers to accommodate; be prepared to walk a distance, carrying your gear.

Ski season opens depending on how cold the temperatures are on the mountains where the snow is made. Snowmaking generally begins around Thanksgiving (earlier if the weather cooperates). If temperatures stay below freezing at night, snowmaking can provide a solid base before Christmas. The season really is considered at its peak from Christmas through St. Patrick's Day, if cold conditions hold. Rates are not determined by factors such as high season or preseason, which only applies to buying your ticket before the season starts and receiving a discount); rather, they are regulated by the determiners noted for time of day, day of week and age.

FYI

Unless otherwise noted, the area code for all phone numbers in this guide is 717.

Delaware Water Gap

Shawnee Mountain
Hollow Rd., Shawnee-on-Delaware
• 421-7231, snow report (800) 233-4218

Shawnee has 23 slopes and trails served by eight double chairlifts and one triple chairlift. Its vertical is 700 feet. All trails are generally snow-covered from Christmas to St. Patrick's Day weekend due to its snowmaking system, which covers all of its slopes. Night skiing is one of its attractions.

Many ski packages are available, with special daily rates for Ladies Day, College Day or Civil Service Day. Several programs for beginners include equipment, and there are three lifts devoted to the beginners area. Seniors older than 70 receive free lift tickets, as do skiers age 7 and younger. Weekend training programs are also available for the whole family, including a developmental race program for juniors.

There are many programs for children

based on the nationally ranked SKIwee curriculum. It starts with Pre-SKIwee (ages 3 through 5) and continues up through Mountain Cruisers (ages 10 through 15). Baby-sitting service is also available for children 18 months and older. There is also a family-night package, so the whole clan can ski together.

Snowboarding is available at Shawnee on designated trails, in the snowboarding park and at the half-pipe area. Night snowboarding is also allowed.

There is a very large stock of high-quality rental equipment — everything you'll need. Rentals are included in beginner as well as other special ski packages. Complete snowboard outfits are also available for rental.

Many area hotels and motels also offer ski packages at Shawnee at discounted rates — in some cases free. See our Accommodations chapter for details.

Shawnee is the first ski area you pass as you come into the Poconos from points east on I-80, and as its name implies, it is on the west face of a mountain flanking the Delaware River (to the east).

Stroudsburg/East Stroudsburg

Alpine Mountain Ski Area
Pa. Hwy. 447 N., Analomink • 595-2150, snow report (800) 233-8340

Alpine Mountain has 18 trails, three lifts and a vertical of 500 feet. Its use of snowmaking equipment keeps snow on all of the trails. This is a small, family-oriented mountain. Lift lines are rare, and the slopes are scenic and range from gentle to challenging, depending on your bent.

There are a variety of learn-to-ski packages and season-pass rates.

A children's program, Just For Kids, is available for five Saturdays or Sundays; there is also a Kids Day Program that includes a lift ticket, equipment rental, a lesson and lunch. Just For Racing Kids is a five-time racing clinic; reservations are recommended. During the week, there is free child care to accommodate skiing parents. Baby-sitting is available on weekends.

Alpine offers snowboarding every day. Snowmobiling is offered on a special course kept ready by snowmaking.

Rental equipment is available for both skiing and snowboarding. Snowmobiles are rented for half-hour rides.

Nearby accommodations are available in Analomink, Canadensis, Mountainhome, Mt. Pocono and Cresco. Additional accommodations a half-hour to an hour away are in Bartonsville, East Stroudsburg, Stroudsburg, Newfoundland and Hamlin.

Mount Pocono Area

Big Boulder Ski Area
Pa. Hwy. 903 S., Blakeslee • 722-0100, snow report (800) 475-SNOW

This area has seven lifts, 14 trails from beginner to expert and a vertical of 475 feet. As with the other Pocono Mountains ski areas, snowmaking keeps Big Boulder's trails open throughout the winter.

Big Boulder's programs include beginner packages, and despite the range of challenging terrain, the entire feel is "easygoing." There are discounted rates for lift tickets, early-season specials, a Six-Timer Book and a Family

---

INSIDERS' TIPS

Pennsylvania Ski Area Operators Free Learn to Ski Day, usually during the first full week in January, gives folks who have never skied a chance to learn for free — completely free. Equipment, lesson and lift ticket are all free for the morning, afternoon or all day, depending on the ski area. To participate, call any ski area in this chapter to make reservations, which are necessary. For more information, contact the individual ski areas (the date is usually listed in their brochures; it's the same day for all ski areas) or check the *Pocono Record* the last Sunday in December and the first Sunday in January.

Dozen Booklet that lets family members transfer coupons. Lessons are available for skiing and snowboarding. Night skiing is available on all 14 trails, as is the half-pipe (for snowboarding) and even the snowtubing trails.

Family commitment is the watchword here, and to that end Big Boulder offers the Kids C'n Ski program for ages 3 through 10. (This package is also offered at night.) Youth tickets are available for ages 6 through 15, and children 5 and younger ski free with a paying adult. Competitive and noncompetitive Junior Racing programs (18 years running) are available for children ages 5 through 18. Baby-sitting is provided full-day, half-day and evenings.

An interesting program at Big Boulder is the Discovery Program, which allows beginning skiers to move at their own pace through a series of teaching stations that they can revisit as often as needed to learn a skill. It is available for one lesson or for a whole package, which includes lesson, equipment rental and a day or twilight lift ticket for limited terrain reserved for other "discoverers." Other learn-to-ski programs include group and private lessons.

Snowboarding, snowtubing, snowmobiling and cross-country skiing are also on the menu here. Lessons and trail guides complement the cross-country skiing options.

Snowboarders use the same trails as skiers at Big Boulder. The snowboarding experience is intensified, however, by the half-pipe off Trail 5, Big Boulder and by the Bonk Yard, which is the equivalent of a skateboarding park for snowboarders. There are ramps, barrels and slides to jump off, over and around. These areas are for snowboarders only. Snowboarders use the same lift tickets as skiers and pay the same lift rates. However, there is also a separate clubhouse at the base of the Bonk Yard for snowboarders. Snowtubing has its own trail and lift setup. For those who wish to try snowtubing, be aware that the lift ticket you buy for snowtubing does not provide you with access to the ski slope lifts. The

lifts are separate, and you pay separately to use them.

Equipment for adults and children can be rented for all activities: downhill and cross-country skiing, snowboarding and snowtubing. Group rates are available.

Accommodations nearby have package deals with Big Boulder, some of which provide lift tickets valid for as long as you are there. For lodging information, call (800) 468-2442, and see our Accommodations chapter.

Big Boulder is one part of The Big Two Resorts; Jack Frost (see subsequent entry) is the other. The same Big Boulder information — accommodations, ski packages, rentals and learn-to-ski programs — applies at Jack Frost. Jack Frost does have some differences, as you will note.

Camelback Ski Area
Camelback Rd., Tannersville • 629-1661, snow report (800) 233-8100

Camelback has 32 trails and 12 lifts, including two high-speed quad chairs. Its longest trail is a mile; its vertical is 800 feet. Camelback's snowmaking facility is the biggest in the Northeast and covers 100 percent of its area, ensuring plenty of snow throughout the season. Night skiing is available on 23 trails.

Camelback has many different ski programs and packages. Programs include: "introduce a friend to skiing"; "frequent skier"; value days, with bargain rates for ladies and students; treasure packs, with reduced rates at different times of the week or day; and other pass options. Seniors 65 and older ski at reduced rates, while those older than 70 may ski free midweek and non-holiday. Children shorter than 46 inches ski free when accompanied by a paying adult.

Kids' ski programs are based in Cameland where children receive three hours of instruction and continuous supervision as they try out their new-found skills. Child care is offered in the nursery for children 12 months and older.

Snowmobiling is a popular pastime at many Pocono resorts.

Recreational racing programs are available for juniors and adults. Season rates are available.

At Camelback there are a variety of sponsored seasonal events based on holiday weekends, special tribute days, festivals and races — all of which take place at the base lodge.

Snowboarding at Camelback is permitted on the slopes and in the very large, lighted snowboard park. In the park there are ramps, rails, platforms and other exciting formations for tricks and fun. Within the snowboard park there is also a half-pipe. Lighting allows use at night. Snowboarders use the same lifts and lift tickets as skiers. Once you buy the lift ticket, you can ski or snowboard as you choose. Snowboard equipment rentals and lessons are available. New in 1996-'97 is snowtubing exclusively on snowtubing trails.

Equipment rentals are included with some packages and are available for one or three days as a package.

Accommodations are available at the base of Camelback. You'll find other lodgings nearby in Tannersville, Swiftwater, Henryville, Bartonsville and Mount Pocono. See our Accommodations chapter for options in areas such as Cresco, Canadensis, East Stroudsburg, Stroudsburg and Lake Naomi — all less than an hour's drive from Camelback.

Jack Frost Ski Area

Pa. Hwy., 940, Blakeslee • 443-8425, snow report (800) 475-SNOW

Jack Frost has seven lifts, 21 trails and a vertical of 600 feet. Its terrain is much more challenging than Big Boulder's (see previous entry), which actually means skiers who want a challenge can be accommodated right next to those looking for an easier pace. You'll find all levels of terrain at Jack Frost. However, the ski schools and beginners packages are the same at both ski areas. Both have programs that provide solid beginner preparation, and both offer the Discovery Program. (See the previous Big Boulder entry for details.)

Because of the challenging terrain at Jack Frost, its racing programs (junior and adult) are renowned and have produced members of the U.S. Ski Team.

Night skiing is not available at Jack Frost. Snowtubing and snowmobiling are offered for nonskiers. Snowboarding is available. Lessons to get you off to a good start are available and suitable for every age level, as is the rental equipment.

As noted at Big Boulder, snowtubing has its own reserved trail and lift. The lift ticket you buy for snowtubing is not for use on the ski lifts or for snowboarding. Snowmobiling has its own course reserved exclusively for snowmobilers. You can rent a snowmobile by the half-hour or hour. Snowboarders use the same trails skiers use and the same lifts. If you buy a lift ticket for either skiing or snowboarding, you may change activities between the two and still use the same lift ticket. A half-pipe off Trail 13, Lehigh, adds to snowboarding fun at Jack Frost. Once you go onto the half-pipe, the area is exclusively for snowboarders. You can go up and down the pipe as many times as you like.

A program of particular note offered at Jack Frost is the exciting "Adaptive Ski Program" for the mentally and physically impaired. Skilled instructors make the experience of skiing available to everyone who wants to take part. Special Ski Olympics are held here for adaptive skiers, and local high school students act as helpers for the day.

West End

Blue Mountain Ski Area
Blue Mountain Dr., Palmerton
• (610) 826-7700, snow report
(800) 826-7700

Blue Mountain has seven lifts (including a high-speed quad), 20 trails and a vertical of 1,082 feet — the highest in Pennsylvania. There is also a mile-long beginners trail for those who want to take their time going down as they learn. The snowmaking equipment here keeps the trails covered day and night all winter long. There are learn-to-ski and improve-your-skiing packages. Women and seniors have workshops available to suit their particular skills. Beginners are eligible for a special First Day on Skis package, and there are daily specials, such as Ladies Day, College Students Day, High School Students Day, and Bargain Night. Senior citizens receive a 20 percent discount every day.

Children's lessons are provided through the SKIwee program for ages 4 through 12. Children younger than 6 ski free when accompanied by a paying adult. Baby-sitting is available for youngsters who don't want to ski; it's free during the week, and there is a $2 per hour fee on weekends and holidays.

The racing program at Blue Mountain is available for both youths and adults.

Snowboarding is not allowed at Blue Mountain. This area is dedicated to skiing only.

Equipment rentals — individual pieces or complete packages — are available for adults, juniors and children.

Accommodations for Blue Mountain are available as packages with area facilities. See our Accommodations chapter for details. Blue Mountain is also close to accommodations in the Allentown area; call the main number for information on Allentown area accommodations.

Blue Mountain, the Poconos southernmost ski area, is about 45 minutes south of the centralized major regional ski areas.

Lake Wallenpaupack Area

Mount Tone Ski Area
Lohikan Camps, Wallerville Rd., Lake Como • 842-2544

Mt. Tone has three lifts, 10 trails, a vertical of 450 feet and is in the northernmost part of the Poconos. It has a relaxed family atmosphere. This area is very different from the other areas we list here. It is basically a family-run operation and is open from the day after Christmas to the weekend of St. Patrick's Day. The slopes are considered perfect for beginners or intermediate skiers who want to learn to ski or practice their skills in a supportive environment. With this focus there are, of course, learn-to-ski packages and lessons available with skilled instructors. Snowboarding is available here on the same trails as the skiers and with the same lift ticket. Snowtubing is also an option on its own trail with a separate lift and lift ticket requirement. Equipment is available for all activities, including cross-country skiing on seven trails. A ski shop is there to perform any needed repairs or adjustments. While you may drop in for midweek skiing, Mt. Tone is predominantly a weekend ski area with very reasonable packages (a weekend will run you less than $100 for lodging, lift tickets, equipment, a lesson, special events and two meals). Mt. Tone has two types of ski camp programs during its season, one for groups and one for individuals in ski clinics. There are facilities for groups that include ski dorms, special events and meals. The format allows groups to bring along their own speakers and programs as adjuncts to the skiing activities. Scout groups and church groups find the format and the size of the ski area itself perfect for presenting their youth groups with a fun time in an environment that ensures maximum chaperoning options.

The trails and lifts are carefully maintained, and lift lines move quickly and safely. The second type of ski camp program is based on clinics — racing, freestyle and learn-to-ski. These are run on a camp basis; children can be brought up for the weekend by their parents and dropped off for a clinic. The children are fully supervised for all activities, ski dorm rooms are provided, as are all meals. For parents who want to drop the children for a ski weekend and wish to enjoy a winter retreat nearby, there are some bed and breakfast inns to explore, including: bed and breakfast inns: Black Walnut Country Inn, 296-6322 or (800) 866-9870; Pine Hill Farm in Milford, 276-7395; and Cliff Park Inn, 296-6491.

There are accommodations for families at Mt. Tone's country inn, but the rooms are few and must be reserved in advance. Mt. Tone is quite a distance from the major Pocono ski areas. It is in the northernmost part of the region and draws its clientele from Binghamton, New York, New Jersey, other parts of Pennsylvania and Maryland. It's able to draw from such distances because the rates are incredibly reasonable. Also Mt. Tone is of interest to youth groups directors because alcohol and cigarettes are not available, though adults may bring their own wine or beer for consumption in their rooms at the country inn.

Resort Ski Areas

Most Pocono resorts provide moderate skiing facilities as a recreational attraction for their guests. However, two resorts — Mt. Airy and Fernwood — have 100 percent snowmaking ability, and their facilities are geared to larger skiing experiences.

Mount Pocono Area

Mount Airy Lodge Ski Resort
Pa. Hwy. 611, Mount Pocono • 839-8811, (800) 441-4410

Mount Airy has two lifts serving nine trails, and the vertical at this resort is 250 feet. Snowmaking keeps the trails available for guests who want to do a little skiing. Ski instruction is available, and equipment can be rented here. Equipment is available for downhill and cross-country skiing. Snowmobiling and snowtubing round out the on-snow options.

Accommodations/skiing packages are available. And since this resort's accommodations are often the main reason for being here, meals, entertainment, indoor sports facilities and other amenities are available on site for your après-ski enjoyment. See our Accommodations chapter for details.

Another winter sport available here is ice skating — indoors and outdoors.

Milford Area

Fernwood Ski Resort
U.S. Hwy. 209 N., Bushkill • 588-9500

One lift, three trails and a vertical of 225 feet provide the skiing facilities at this resort. These trails are classified for beginners and advanced beginners.

Snowmaking keeps this resort's trails open for downhill skiing, snowmobiling, cross-country skiing and sledding. Cross-country skiing is available on 4 to 5 miles of trails on the golf course and is available weather permitting. Lift tickets and equipment rental is available for guests separately and in packages; nonguests can rent equipment and buy lift tickets for downhill skiing, cross-country skiing, snowboarding and snowmobiling. Guests only are allowed to use the sledding hill, which is also part of the snowmaking system and is groomed. Sleds are provided free, and sled-

---

INSIDERS' TIPS

Get to the slopes in the morning for less crowded, more relaxed runs. Also, night skiing is a good way to ski with fewer skiers. Just add more layers of clothing for night skiing — the sun isn't shining to warm you.

ding is free to the guests. Snowboarding is available also with the same lift ticket that skiers use. You can rent a snowboard, or you can bring your own as long as it is a regulation snowboard. Snowmobiling has its own groomed course next to the ski area and is maintained with snowmaking equipment. You can rent single and double snowmobiles by the half-hour.

Beginners lessons are available. This is a fun place to learn to ski, since there are other things to do to relax after a hard day on the slopes including swimming, playing indoor tennis, unwinding in a sauna or enjoying nightly entertainment in Weathervane's, Fernwood's on-site restaurant and lounge.

Equipment rentals and repairs are provided here.

Fernwood provides extensive accommodations. Included with a room are dining, entertainment, swimming, a sauna, indoor tennis and other activities. See Accommodations for more information.

Cross-country Skiing

Most Pocono resorts have some cross-country skiing trails and provide equipment rentals for anyone interested in adding some vigorous exercise to their vacation stay. In most cases, cross-country skiing packages are available with accommodations, including a number of bed and breakfast inns.

When tied to a resort stay, cross-country skiing is free except for rentals (see "Ski Resorts" in this section for specifics on their cross-country options and accommodations). Most resorts allow non-guests to cross-country ski for a fee; again, that information is noted in the "Ski Resorts" section of this chapter. Other cross-country areas are provided in state parks and state forests. One public area in Analomink is at the Evergreen Golf Course, 421-7721, which is part of the Penn Hills couples resort — 421-6464. This area has marked trails, not groomed, for beginners and advanced skiers. There is a trail fee of $6, and rental and trail fee packages are $11. These trails are open weather permitting because snowmaking is not part of the operation. Of course, many

folks have a lot of land around here, and they just ski off into their own woods on their own trails. Others have friends who have property they may use for fun. If you don't know anyone with available woods, and you don't want to cross-country on a golf course or at a resort, you still have some options for cross-country skiing au naturel!

Mount Pocono Area

Promised Land State Park
Pa. Hwy. 390, Promised Land Village • 676-3428

There are more than 30 miles of hiking trails in Promised Land Sate Park that crisscross between state park lands and the Delaware Forest lands. These trails are those used by cross-country skiers. Trails are weather dependent. They are not groomed or maintained. You do not need to register to use them or pay any fees. There aren't any rentals or amenities. The park office in Promised Land is open Monday through Friday during the winter from 8 AM to 4 PM. The office is not open on weekends, but a rack outside the door holds brochures. If you want to know if trails are snow-covered, you can call the park. The location of this park is right in the center of the Poconos, so it is accessible from the Milford-Lake Wallenpaupack areas and the Stroudsburg, East Stroudsburg and Mt. Pocono areas. The nearest town you can ski to is Promised Land Village, which abuts state lands.

West End

Mauch Chunk Lake Park
625 Lentz Tr., Jim Thorpe • 325-3669

The cross-country ski trail here is the switchback rail line. What this means to the cross-country skier is that this terrain gets very steep. There are flat areas, but once you start up the incline, the trail becomes very steep and difficult. As the History chapter notes, the switchback railroad was built based on its use of gravity to propel the train down the mountain. They used mules to get the train back up.

> **FYI**
> Unless otherwise noted, the area code for all phone numbers in this guide is 717.

But Is It Really Snow?

It's white and cold and looks like snow, but is man-made (manufactured) snow really snow?

Yes, Virginia, it really is snow. Snow is crystallized water that occurs when the air temperature drops below 32 degrees and any moisture in the air freezes into hexagonal crystals, which in aggregate form a snowflake. Manufactured snow is made when water is pumped from a reservoir and combined with compressed air that sprays the water into the atmosphere. The below-freezing air it encounters freezes the water into hexagonal crystals — snow!

The ingenious process of snowmaking requires a tremendous amount of equipment: huge air compressors; giant water pumps; miles and miles of piping for the air and water; enormous complicated, microprocessor-driven turbocharged generators; and hundreds of spray guns and nozzles to disperse the water into the air. All work together with Mother Nature and the snowmaking crew, to ensure that when you arrive to ski, snow is ready and waiting for you.

In an article "Snowmaking Is 40 Years Old" from *Ski Area Management* magazine, Arthur R. Hunt, one of the developers of the process, describes how snowmaking was invented in 1950 by three aeronautical engineers from Connecticut. Hunt and his partners, Wayne Pierce and Dave Richey, worked together to create a unique ski design, which they manufactured and sold. All was going well until a winter when the snowfall was negligible — and sales dropped drastically.

Pierce had an idea. In the backyard of the company, he set up a miniature snowmaker with a spray-gun nozzle, an air compressor and a garden hose. Pierce, with the help of his partners, put the equipment inside a box on a stand and started to spray the water into the cold air. The next morning they had a 20-inch-deep pile of snow covering an area 20 feet in diameter. The partners got a basic-process patent, and snowmaking began at Grossinger's in New York and Big Boulder (Split Rock Lodge at that time) in Pennsylvania. A new era in skiing had begun!

Photo: Camelback Ski Area

Giving nature a hand with snowmaking keeps Poconos ski areas open.

The partners sold the company and patents to Emhart and over the years have not made anything from the profits their invention has generated for others in the ski industry. But as the author Hunt remarked, he "still skis and [he is] glad the machine-made snow is there."

A great many other people are too. With the advent of snowmaking, ski enthusiasts no longer were dependent upon nature's bounty or whim; they could ski wherever there was a mountain with temperatures cold enough to manufacture snow. The industry boomed, and resorts that invested in the process flourished.

One of the first to take complete advantage of the snowmaking system was Camelback Ski Area in Tannersville. Camelback was built with the premise that it would exist entirely on man-made snow if necessary. As its trails were cut out of the landscape, manager Bill Toye explains, miles of pipelines for air and water were simultaneously laid out to ensure that every trail could be covered with man-made snow. Camelback has operated on that premise since it opened. In November, as soon as the temperatures start to cool down, the snow engineers begin the snowmaking process. The snowmakers provide a 3- to 5-foot base of snow with 2 to 10 inches of surface powder. Every night during the season (weather conditions permitting), the process is repeated to ensure maximum coverage, so all slopes can be open everyday.

But snowmaking has become a two-step procedure. Once producing snow was perfected, keeping it nice and neat became a concern. Thus, the procedure called "grooming" evolved. The idea of grooming is to smooth out the snow, eliminating the moguls that develop during the day as well as the ruts on the trails and the piles of snow alongside the trails. Grooming restores the powdery surface of the trails, eliminating most of the granularity that can occur due to weather conditions, excessive use or erratic snowmaking.

And grooming definitely evolved.

Bill Toye explained that in the beginning people tried everything to restore the surface of the snow. They used tractors to drag chains over the surface, Ski-doos to pull chain link fencing, tractors to pull harrows — ingenuity was the value of the moment.

Today, there are grooming machines. Crews of trained technicians use huge tractors, with 2-foot-wide treads running on tracks more than 3 feet high, to push, rake, smooth and crunch the snow into beautiful trails while skiers sleep.

But is it snow, you still ask? Will I ski well on it? Wouldn't it be better to go to a place where the snow is all real?

Yes, it is still snow, in its shape, density and basic creation. Yes, you will ski well on it — you may ski better, because manufactured snow stands up to skiers and weather conditions better than the natural stuff, is smoother and a little more slippery. Every ski area in America uses snowmaking to augment its seasonal snowfall, to get the season started sooner and extend it a little longer. From Mammoth in California to Vail and Aspen in Colorado to Killington in Vermont — no matter where you ski nowadays, some of the snow is "real" and some is manufactured.

So, if you are in the city and temperatures are in the 40s, don't think you've missed out on your ski weekend or midweek escape. Snowmaking takes place on mountains where it's always colder at night than at lower elevations. So, whether your destination is Camelback, Big Boulder, Jack Frost, Shawnee, Alpine, Blue Mountain, Mount Tome, Fernwood, Mount Airy or another snowmaker-based ski area, relax. While you are sleeping or making an after-work, late-night drive to the Poconos, the snowmakers are diligently working with Mother Nature, manufacturing snow and grooming the slopes for you and your family.

And it is real!

With this picture in mind, you can prepare yourself for what the trail will be like. Equipment rentals are available, either a whole set or just the pieces you need. The price for renting the set is $10 for skis, $7 for boots and $3 for poles; the prices are subject to change, so check with the office for up-to-the-minute prices. There is no fee to use the trail. This park is close to the Jim Thorpe, Lehighton and Blakeslee.

Milford Area

Delaware Water Gap National Recreation Area
U.S. Hwy. 209, Dingmans Ferry • 588-2451

There are two trails for cross-country skiing in the Gap national park area, one in New Jersey at the Kittatinny center, (908) 496-4458, and one at Slateford Farm, south of the town of Delaware Water Gap and part of the Appalachian Trail. The Slateford Farm trail is of varying degrees of difficulty (bear in mind it is the Appalachian trail). There are some nice flat areas and uphill areas. There aren't any fees to use the trail, nor are there any rental facilities or equipment. To get maps contact the parks offices. This area is close to the Stroudsburg, East Stroudsburg, Mt. Pocono and Bangor areas.

Snowboarding

Snowboarding is a relatively new phenomenon in the Poconos, but it is growing rapidly, and the ski areas are keeping up with the demand. Snowboarding is similar to surfing and skateboarding, except you do it on snow. The boards are larger than skate boards, but smaller than surfboards. The object is to move down the mountain in much the same way that you would surf a huge wave or skate down a very long hill. Snowboarders are allowed on the same ski trails as the skiers and use the same ski lifts and tickets at the same rates. There is controversy at times between snowboarders and the skiers because skiers feel invaded by the "shredders" who whiz by them. Snowboarders enjoy some amenities at most ski areas with what are called pipes or half-pipes and snowboard parks. Pipes and half-pipes are extensions off existing trails, reserved exclusively for snowboarders' use. The pipes provide an area where snowboarders can move up and down, jump, spin, slide and generally have a good time. Snowboard parks have equipment such as barrels, ramps, rails and slides where snowboarders can do tricks and practice their moves. At this time snowboarding is only available in the major ski areas: Alpine Mountain, Big Boulder, Camelback, Jack Frost and Shawnee. It is not available at Blue Mountain or the two resorts listed here.

For snowboarding facilities, check out the ski areas listings. Snowboarding is only allowed at those areas specifically designed for it.

A word of caution about snowboarding. While the sport looks easy, it requires a lot more skill than people expect. Since snowboarding has become so popular, accidents on snowboards have far outnumbered skiing accidents, and, unfortunately, they tend to be more severe. All of the major ski areas offer excellent packages for learning to snowboard, and some offer specially groomed snowboarding trails and parks. This is a really fun sport and one you and your family will want to take advantage of, but first invest in lessons. Learn from a pro before you go careening down those hills and sailing through those half-pipes.

Some resorts that have snowmobiling available are these couples resorts: Birchwood Resort in Tannersville, 629-0222 or (800) 233-8177; The three Caesar's resorts — Cove Haven in Lakeville, 226-2101 or (800) 233-4141, Paradise Stream in Mt. Pocono, 839-8881 or (800) 233- 4141, and Pocono Palace in Marshalls Creek, 588-6692 or (800) 233-4141; and The Summit Resort in Tannersville, 629-0203 or (800) 233-8250.

INSIDERS' TIPS

Pennsylvania State Tax (6 percent) is applicable on ski rentals; so, don't forget to add this figure into your budget.

Snowmobiling

Many Pocono resorts and ski areas offer snowmobiling as a winter attraction. Check the ski areas mentioned here for snowmobiling information. This sport is offered at an extra cost and on trails groomed for snowmobiling. The rental rates for snowmobiles are usually for a half-hour or hour for single and double snowmobiles. The section on "Resort Ski Areas" identifies the information you need to know about skiing there. Check our Accommodations chapter for more resorts-related information. Some resorts that do not offer skiing may offer snowmobiling. Another snowmobiling option is businesses that specialize in renting snowmobiles for a limited time (a half-hour to an hour) and take you to their own course, usually on-site. These are listed in the phone directory and the Easy-to-Read Phone Directory under the heading "Snowmobiles." Since operations offering this type of experience change focus many times, we won't list them here.

There are two parks areas that allow snowmobiling, Promised Land State Park and Delaware Water Gap National Recreation Area. In these areas you must use your own snowmobile, rentals are not available at these locations. However, there are qualifiers for using your snowmobile. If you use your own snowmobile, it must be registered for use on public land. Registration is through the Department of Conservation and Natural Resources Snowmobile/ATV Division, 783-1364. If you are from out-of-state and your snowmobile is registered in your state, you should check with the Department of Conservation/Snowmobile/ATV Division to see if the registration is reciprocal. It is not reciprocal with New York, but it is reciprocal with Maryland and New Jersey. To be sure, check. You do not need to register your snowmobile if you use the snowmobile only on your own private property. However, if you and others who may be driving it go beyond the boundaries and end up on land or roads that you do not own, you are driving an unregistered vehicle, and fines are applicable. The registration issue is not a concern when you're buying time at a ski area or renting from a snowmobile shop.

Mount Pocono Area

Promised Land State Park
Pa. Hwy. 390, Promised Land Village • 676-3428

There are 27 designated trails that traverse the state park and the Delaware State Forest lands. They are designated by orange diamond symbols. Maps are available at the park office in Promised Land and at the district office in Swiftwater, 424-3001. There aren't any facilities for your snowmobile, so make sure you bring what you need. The maps indicate the parking areas where you can park your cars and enter the trails. You can access the trails in the village of Promised Land behind Hall's Inn. As of this writing, there wasn't an open gas station here, so as we said, bring what you need.

Milford Area

Delaware Water Gap National Recreation Area
U.S. 209, Dingmans Ferry • 588-2451

This area is open weekends in November and December from 9 AM to 4:30 PM. The trails are not at this location, however. Loop 1 is at Smithfield Beach area, and Loop 2 is at another location off River Road that intersects the Smithfield Beach trail. Smithfield Beach is on River Road south of Bushkill, but you will need a map and directions to use these two trails that run along the Delaware River. The Smithfield Beach Loop 1 is on level terrain, so it is good for any type snowmobile. Loop 2 is very hilly and is not advisable for low-powered vehicles. There aren't any fees for use of this recreation area land. You must bring your own snowmobile; rentals are not available. Facilities for gas and food are limited on River Road, so you should gas up and get supplies before you go in. These are not groomed trails, and their availability is dependent upon the weather.

Ice Skating

Most resorts offer indoor and or outdoor ice skating on their grounds either in indoor or

Skiing is a popular wintersports activity for families.

outdoor rinks. It would be unusual to find a Poconos accommodation that didn't have ice skating available.

But you don't have to stay in a Poconos lodging to enjoy ice skating. Try one of the following rinks.

Stroudsburg/ East Stroudsburg

Mountain Manor
Creek Rd., Marshalls Creek • 223-8098

The rink is open from Thanksgiving to Easter. The times of operation are listed as all day, but count on 10 AM to 5 PM. Admission to the rink for non-guests of Mountain Manor is $6 for adults and $4 for children 12 and younger (guests skate free with complimentary skate rental) at all times, midweek and weekend. Skate rentals are $4. Hockey skates are allowed here as well as figure skates. Or-

ganized ice hockey is not available here, but pick-up games usually occur on Tuesday nights from 7 to 10 PM; the rink is reserved for these unorganized games. People come who want to play and form teams. If interest is high, sometimes Thursday nights become hockey pick-up nights too. Again, this activity is open to the public. Parties are an option at this rink. An overall price of $6 per person for a minimum of 15 people provides admission and food and drink (bring your own cake!); skates are $4 more to rent. Those who choose to party here do so among the other skaters. If you want to rent the rink for a private party, the base cost is $75. Private lessons are not offered here.

Pocono Ice-A-Rama
Pa. Hwy. 447 N., Analomink • 421-6465, 421-6464

This small, indoor rink is open all year, except for Christmas day, from 10 AM to 9 PM. It is part of the facilities at the Penn Hills couples resort, but it is open to the public at all times. For those staying at the resort, admission and rental equipment is free. For nonguests the price range for adults is $4.75 to $5.75 depending on whether it is midweek or weekend. For children the range is $4.25 to $4.75, again depending on whether it is weekend or midweek. Skate rental fee is $3.75, adult or child, midweek or weekend. This rink only allows figure skating and figure skates. It is a small rink, perfect for groups and parties but not large enough for hockey (hockey skates are not allowed or rented). Groups are accommodated at discount rates, but the rink is still open to the public when a group is there. The same proviso affects parties. Birthday parties and the like can be arranged through calling the main number listed here. Since this is a small rink, it does provide a controlled environment for groups and parties; it is rarely crowded, especially in the summer months. What a change of pace from a summer pool party! Private lessons only are available on a limited schedule. Call the main number to find when they are being offered.

Mount Pocono Area

Promised Land State Park
Pa. Hwy. 390, Promised Land • 676-3428
Ice skating is available on a reserved section of Promised Land Lake, weather permitting. The area here is maintained only in that the snow is pushed aside for skaters. Rentals are not available, nor are refreshments or accommodations of any kind other than a portapotty nearby. Since conditions change on a daily basis, call ahead for skating availability. (During winter months there aren't any running-water facilities available on park lands.)

Other Winter Activities

Sledding, tobogganing and sleigh rides are available at some resorts. In most cases, the larger the facility, the more activities it will offer. Checking the accommodations section and asking questions when you call those accommodations that interest you will tell you all the winter options that facility will have.

Sledding

Sledding is generally offered at resorts and other accommodations to guests only (see "Resort Ski Areas" in this section). These places usually have what they call their sledding hill, which is not groomed or maintained and is available as an activity weather permitting. Sleds are free for guests. Non-guests are not allowed. Some accommodations have toboggans, which are six-man sleds made of wood. Riding one requires coordination as you all move together to address the curves and slopes. Obviously, spills and tumbles are the order of the day when tobogganing, so be prepared. Dress warmly, and be sure to cushion all your tender areas.

Toboggans

At the ski resorts or accommodations that have toboggans available, they are provided free for guests. For those of us who live here, sledding is done on a favorite local hillside. There aren't any public sledding areas. If you want to sled, find out where your neighbors are going and tag along. Soon you'll know the good, private spots too. We've asked people who had hills on their property if we could let our children sled on them. Generally, the answer has been "yes," if we knew the people.

Horse-drawn Sleigh Rides

For a different and relaxing winter experience, consider a sleigh ride in a horse-drawn, antique sleigh from Pocono Country Carriages, 424-6248, in East Stroudsburg. The sleighs are drawn by two horses, Prince and Heidi, who are managed by their driver/owner Eileen Pasquin. The sleighs are beautiful antiques from the mid-1800s that she has lovingly restored. The sleighs are painted in shades of green or red, and the cushioned seats are color-coordinated as are the lush, crushed velvet sleigh blankets (Christmas green and mauve!) that keep you incredibly toasty warm. Attention to detail is obvious in the sleighs — Eileen has hand-painted the decorations on many of them herself. Her knowledge about the antique sleighs and carriages are part of the fun of the excursion. Eileen and her sleighs take you through the 20-acre mini-farm that is Pocono Country Carriages. The ride through snowy woods, cuddled in warm blankets take you into your own Currier& Ives print, with you as the focal point. To round out the experience, the antique sleigh bells jingle with the richness of sound that only antique sleigh bells seem to convey. As you whoosh through the countryside, you are sure to spot a few deer and pheasant who are enjoying the day with you. Rides are available during the day only. A package for a sleigh ride and lunch at Hallets Cozy Corner in Henryville (you drive there after your ride) make a lovely, winter's experience that you will treasure.

Ice Fishing

Another specialized winter activity is ice fishing. You can ice fish at Promised Land State Park, 676-3428, and Mauch Chunk Lake Park, 325-3669. These lakes are open to the public, but are not really maintained in any way. You must check with the park daily to find out if it is safe to ice fish, just as you must do to ice skate. If you want to ice fish, you must have a Pennsylvania State Fishing License (see our Hunting and Fishing chapter for where to obtain yours). The opening day for fishing licenses is April 1, and the license is good until March 31 of the next year; so, a license you buy in the spring will take you through the next winter's ice fishing season. Those who live in some of the four-season communities can ice fish on community lakes, weather permitting. Streams and ponds that are open to anglers, as noted in the Hunting and Fishing chapter, can be looked at as possibilities for ice fishing, provided you check with the authorities in charge for accessibility.

Water and mountains together — beautiful, peaceful, wild — characterize the Poconos.

In, On and Around the Water

As you might gather from our Parks, Natural World and History chapters, water is an important part of the Poconos' landscape, development and recreation.

The natural beauty of our rivers — the Lehigh and the Delaware — complemented by the remnants of the canal systems, the lakes formed in glacial depressions and the many man-made lakes created in communities and from rivers as a result of our dam system provide copious opportunities for fun. Fishing (see our Fishing and Hunting chapter), boating and rafting, water skiing, Jet Skiing and, of course, swimming are part of this fun.

In this chapter we focus on the opportunities that await you on our rivers and lakes through the national and state park systems and National Forest preserves. (See our Parks chapter for a detailed presentation of what facilities and recreational opportunities each park contains.) We also focus on municipal pools operated by towns for their residents. Still other focuses are private pools and beach clubs that are open to new members.

This chapter does not discuss the available options at the many lake communities that contain a large percentage of residential and vacation homes. (See our Accommodations chapter for information about vacation rentals.) It does, however, lead you to watersports havens in different regions of the Poconos (note each section's geographic subheaders). "National Parks and Recreation Areas" is not divided geographically, as both representative entries encompass more than one region.

Before you use park areas or any waterways with a boat or other watercraft, be sure to check with the respective park office or governing agency for a map and list of regulations (see our Parks chapter for contact numbers and other information about individual parks). There are always brochures available at the main national park offices in Bushkill and, in New Jersey, at Kittatinny Point Visitor Center on I-80.

Be aware that your motorized boat must be registered. Canoes, kayaks and tubes do not have to be, but if they are registered you don't have to pay launch fees at state parks. Registration for non-motorized watercraft is $10 for two years. In all crafts, you must have U.S. Coast Guard-approved, wearable, personal flotation devices (PFDs) or life jackets for each person on board. Be sure you know the Pennsylvania regulations for PFDs and boat (watercraft) registration; contact the **Pennsylvania Fish and Boating Commission**, Bureau of Boating, P.O. Box 67000, Harrisburg, Pennsylvania 17106-7000, 657-4518.

In general, alcohol and pets are not permitted in public park areas; alcohol is also prohibited on any boat trip booked through an outfitter, including whitewater trips. We point out areas and outfitters that allow pets.

Whether you are boating, water skiing or swimming, in most places you will be surrounded by the beauty of mountains rising around you, often encircling you in what seems to be a cradle of green leafy boughs, blanketed with clear, bright blue skies and rocked by sparkling, fresh water. Basking on a beach along the Delaware, whether one chosen for its lifeguard protection or one you discovered on your canoeing or boating sojourn, lounging by a pool nestled at the foot of a hill, watching your children play in a hidden lake near your campsite, or careening through the rapids at the bottom of the steep Lehigh River gorge, the mountains are always there — caressing, protecting, reaching, inspiring, invigorating, calming. And water rests contentedly — or courses wildly through gaps and gorges. Water and mountains together— beautiful, peaceful, wild — characterize the Poconos.

FYI

Unless otherwise noted, the area code for all phone numbers listed in this guide is 717.

National Parks and Recreation Areas

Renting a River Craft

You can rent a canoe, kayak, raft or tube for any number of on-the-water options, whether for a half-day of play, lessons on a new type of craft or overnight camping experiences. Rates depend on what you want to do, how many of you want to do it and how long you want to do it. Offers and coupon specials abound in this area, so keep an eye on local publications. Many concessionaires have family rates that allow a first child (usually younger than 12) to go free as a third or fourth person in a group. Seasons also affect the rates. Group rates are an option for your camp, church, school, office, reunion or even neighborhood outing, so don't be shy about asking.

Since rates are also subject to change, we only list a range for options here. To rent a canoe or raft, expect to pay at least $19 to $22 per person midweek and $25 to $30 per person weekends (based on two persons per canoe and four persons per raft) for a day. Self-transported canoes or rafts rent at a per-craft rate, generally about $35 per canoe and $70 per raft (again subject to change, days, outfitter, etc.). Overnight options are more expensive — they might include camping at a registered campsite — but often qualify for special discounts. Rates are also $1 to $2 higher without reservations.

Tubing is less expensive — between $14 and $17 per day. Kayaking and solo canoeing are more expensive because there's only one person per craft. The minimum cost is about $29. Besides craft rental and paddles, rates usually include life jackets; shuttle transportation for people, luggage and boats; river maps; and an orientation session. Again, group rates and specials are usually available. Credit cards and personal checks (restricted at some locations, so ask) generally are accepted.

Other costs include advance reservations and deposits (about $10 per person as a general rule), damage releases and security deposits (from $1.50 to $5, depending on options) and Pennsylvania sales tax (6 percent if you rent on the Pennsylvania side of the Delaware River, 7 percent if you rent on the New York side, where some upper Delaware companies are located). Guided trips are more expensive, and rates are subject to all the same considerations of day of week, number of persons, number of days and so on. Cancellations are penalized according to certain advance-notice guidelines, which usually consist of the per-person deposit. So, plan your event carefully to avoid cancellations.

Many provisioners also offer lessons and other specials along with rentals. Some of the outfitters licensed for use in the National Recreation Area by the National Park Service follow in the subsequent "Outfitters" sections.

Delaware Water Gap National Recreation Area

This 37-mile-long stretch along the Delaware River allows swimming and boating (gas- or electric-powered, canoeing, rafting, tubing and kayaking). The river is designated "wild and scenic," which means

Pennsylvania Power & Light Company

 ## Family Camping & Outdoor Recreation
Lake Wallenpaupack

13 Mile-Long, 5700 Acre Lake
Wooded Vacation Land in the Poconos

Ironwood Point	Ledgedale	Wilsonville
Thomas MacDonough, Dir.	Mark Pappas, Dir.	William Hopkins, Dir.
RD #2, Box 344	RD #2, Box 379C	HC6, Box 6114
Greentown, PA 18426	Greentown, PA 18426	Hawley, PA 18428
717 857-0880	**717 689-2181**	**717 226-4382**

there are no dams, and the shoreline and adjacent lands are maintained in their natural state. Smithfield Beach and Milford Beach are the two free, guarded sand beaches open to the public. Aside from swimming, these beaches also offer free boat launching areas. Hidden Lake, just off River Road and north of Smithfield Beach, within the park's confines, is open to swimmers but is *not* guarded.

With few exceptions, swimming is allowed almost anywhere in the park area where you can reach the river from a picnic area, boat launch or campsite. Swimming is not allowed at Dingmans Falls, George W. Childs Recreation Site, Van Campens Glen or within 50 feet of the top of any waterfall.

The Hialeah Picnic Area, on River Road, north of Shawnee-on-Delaware and south of Smithfield Beach, flanks the river though is high above the water at most spots. Picnickers do swim here, but the climb down to the river can be treacherous. Those who do climb down, sometimes with the aid of their own homemade rope guides, say the climb is worth it. You can walk out almost midway into the water, relax and talk with your friends as the river gently (unless we've just had a lot of rain) flows by. (Always be aware of weather conditions not only where you are but also at points upriver; heavy rains on the river or its tributaries can greatly increase the flow rate in a short period of time.)

There are no guarded beaches in this picnic area; in fact, the size and presence of a beach depends on the rainfall, which when heavy can raise the water level enough to cover any of the beaches — an unusual occurrence. You can also picnic at Toms Creek north of Bushkill.

Some words of caution are in order. The Delaware River in the park area is generally calm, with a lazy current and small, whirling eddies. But it is a river, and there are strong currents and sudden drop-offs at points. Always watch your step whether swimming or boating. Don't take the river for granted. And never try to swim across the river. You will only be putting yourself in great danger. At some points it seems narrow enough to swim across to the Jersey side, and it is tempting to take the risk. However, the currents change without warning, and there are deep areas that you might not see in the excitement of assessing whether you can make it. So, please don't try; people do drown here, including swimmers, boaters and anglers.

While swimmers can get into the river almost at whim, boaters should use the boat launches. There are several on the Pennsylvania side of the park, and all have parking areas for your vehicles. (See "More Boat Launch Areas" in this section.)

Note: Pets on leashes no longer than six feet are welcome at most locations. However, they are not allowed at Milford Beach,

Smithfield Beach, Hidden Lake Beach or on the mowed areas of the Hialeah Picnic Area.

The park headquarters are east of U.S. Highway 209, just south of Bushkill. Call 588-2451 for more information.

Smithfield Beach

To reach this beach take U.S. Highway 209 to River Road (at Bushkill if coming from the north; at Buttermilk Falls Road if coming from the south), north of Shawnee-on-Delaware, but at the southern end of the park.

Swimming

Swimming is allowed at this beach from 11:30 AM to 6 PM while a lifeguard is present. There are very clean restrooms and bathhouses (all of the park's facilities are well maintained), a large parking lot, picnic tables on the grassy slopes above the river and in the woods alongside, and a sandy beach. If you picnic here, you can bring a grill as long as it has legs; a fire box may not touch the ground. Alcoholic beverages and pets are not allowed. There isn't a snack bar here, but drinking water is available.

Boating, Rafting and Tubing

There are two boat launch areas at this site. The north end above the beach area is for personal boat and raft launching. The launch below the south end of the beach is for boat, raft and tube concessionaires to drop off and pick up rentals. You can use this beach area as the beginning, middle or end of a trip on the river, depending on where you start and where you want to go.

You can also water-ski or Jet Ski at this area, north of what is called the Smithfield Pool before the beach area. Gas and electric power boats are allowed.

Milford Beach

Just before Milford, at the north end of the park, you'll find signs on U.S. Highway 209 directing you to this area.

Swimming

Swimming is allowed at this beach from 11:30 AM to 6 PM while a lifeguard is present. There are very clean restrooms and bathhouses, a large parking lot, picnic tables on the grassy areas and in the woods alongside and a sandy beach. If you picnic here, you can bring in a grill as long as it is on legs; it cannot touch the ground. Pets are not allowed. There isn't a snack bar here, but there is drinking water available.

Boating, Rafting and Tubing

There are two boat launch areas at this site, one for personal boats and one for rentals picked up and dropped off by provisioners.

Hidden Lake

From U.S. 209 in Marshalls Creek, take River Road from either Shawnee-on-Delaware (at the south end of the park) or Fernwood (south of Bushkill) to Hidden Lake Drive. Proceed 3 miles to the parking area on the left.

Swimming, Picnicking and Fishing

Hidden Lake is nestled in a hollow in the Minisink Hills, hence its name. Swimmers will find an unguarded sandy beach. A grassy picnic area sloping toward this small area attracts families for casual swimming, picnicking and fishing. All activities can be done within about 20 yards of each other. The picnic area adjoins the beach and is close enough at points to hand treats from your table to a waiting child on the beach. For the anglers in your group, the area outside the mutually agreed-upon swimming area provides a fishing spot where you can keep an eye on your swimming companions. The only amenity at this area is a porta-potty.

Boating

You'll find a boating access area on the lake about an eighth-mile before the beach parking area, also on the left. Electric-motor boats are allowed here as well as any other non-motorized watercraft. This is a small lake (you can see both ends from the swimming beach), so large boats and open-water activities (water skiing or Jet Skiing) are not appropriate here.

Other River Options

You can canoe, kayak, power boat or raft down the Delaware River at points between Milford and Delaware Water Gap, putting in at park-owned campsites (these campsites and boat accesses are free) along the river. All campsites are clearly identified in the *Delaware Water Gap River Guide*, available at the Park Service offices, U.S. Highway 209, south of Bushkill, 588-2451. Campsites flank the shore from Milford south at Dingmans Campground, Hornbeck, north of Eshback Access, at Toms Creek (also a picnic site), Valley View, Bushkill and Smithfield Beach. You can also camp overnight on the following islands in the river: Mashipacong, Minisink, Namanock, Shapnack, Depew, Poxono, Tocks, Labar, Depue, Shawnee and Shellenberger. There are only a few campsites at each location (from single sites at Smithfield Beach and Bushkill to a maximum of five sites at Valley View and Minisink Island), and the rules are first come, first served with a maximum stay of one night. In fact, there are guidelines as to how many days it should take you to go from one location to another, governing how many nights you are allowed on the river; check with the Park Office for details.

Some campsite guidelines include: fires in the steel grates provided at each campsite must only be fueled with wood from dead, fallen trees (a camp stove is preferred); you must dig your own latrine; and water for washing must be used away from

the river. The Park Office provides guidelines for all needs, including quiet hours, so be sure to check with park staff before you begin any overnight river journey.

Outfitters

Kittatinny Canoes
Dingmans Ferry Base
Pa. Hwy. 739 S. , Dingmans Ferry • 828-7018, (800) FLOAT KC
Milford-River Beach Base
Off U.S. Hwy. 209, 3.5 miles north of Milford • 828-2338, (800) FLOAT KC
Matamoras Base
Delaware Dr., off U.S. 209, just before silver bridge, Matamoras • 491-2508, (800) FLOAT KC

Kittatinny offers canoes, tubes and kayaks. It has been around for more than 50 years (the grandmother, Ruth, is a legend on the river). Besides renting crafts, it also maintains two excellent campsites on the river for those who desire an overnight excursion. Children must be able to swim and must weigh more than 40 pounds to be properly fitted with a life vest.

Daily canoe trips and two-day trips for experienced canoeists and beginners are available, as are daily rafting and tubing trips. Whitewater trips depart from the Matamoras Base (about 8 miles north of Milford) and put in at an upper Delaware River location; trips range from 7 to 18 miles and last 3½ to 7½ hours. Easy, relaxed trips depart from Matamoras, River Beach and Dingmans Ferry southward. The best choice for novices, these trips last from 2½ to 5 hours and cover 5 to 12 miles. Daily tube trips run from the River Beach Base or a drop-off point in Barryville, New York, accessed from the Matamoras Base. Trip lengths vary according to water level, weather, wind, paddler's ability and type of craft. You can count on a canoe doing about 2.5 miles per hour; rafts, 2 miles per hour; and tubes, a mile per hour. Of course, you also should factor in time for swimming, picnicking, fishing and just enjoying the river and its environs.

Some specialty offerings are Learn to Canoe days, a two-day basic kayaking workshop, free mother or father paddlers on their special holidays, summer wildflower and wildlife tours (see eagles, ospreys and great blue heron) and a fall foliage tour (waterfowl and birds of prey often are spotted on this trip too). From the northern bases, a special introduction to whitewater rafting also is available.

The bases open at 8 AM weekends and 9 AM weekdays, Memorial Day to Labor Day. Bases might open mid-April and remain open through mid-October depending on weather conditions. Call for early- and late-season hours and to see which bases are staffed.

Adventure Sports
Canoe and Raft Trips
U.S. Hwy. 209, Marshalls Creek • 223,-0505, (800) 487-BOAT

This outfitter offers guided or self-guided canoe or raft trips for one, two or three days (consistent with park trip-length guidelines) beginning at any boat launch between Milford and Delaware Water Gap. This company will transport you, the canoes and rafts to a launch site and pick you up downriver at a predetermined destination. Those who rent and transport the canoes or rafts themselves pay a cheaper rate that includes paddles and life jackets. The minimum age is 2 years old; all participants must be able to swim.

For overnight camping trips this outfitter rents coolers, tents and anything else you'll need. Free campsites in the park are noted in the *Delaware Water Gap River Guide*, available at the national recreation area's park office, U.S. Highway 209, south of Bushkill, 588-2451. Remember, there are no reservations, even when going through a licensed outfitter.

Special arrangements can be made for groups of 10 or more for two-day trips. All necessary supplies can be rented too.

Shop hours are 9 AM to 6 PM midweek and 8 AM to 6 PM weekends from mid-April through mid-October. Take Exit 52 (Marshalls Creek) of I-80, then proceed 2 miles on U.S. 209 N.

Chamberlain Canoes
Minisink Hills Mall, River Rd., Shawnee-on-Delaware • 421-0180, (800) 422-6631

This outfitter has been on the Delaware 30 years. It offers canoes, rafts and tubes for day or overnight trips. Chamberlain Canoes offers

trips from Port Jervis, New York (north of Milford), southward to Slateford and Portland and any stops in between at any of the park's boat launches. Transportation to and from the river is provided.

The age minimums for this outfitter are 6 years old for canoes and tubes and 3 years old for rafts.

Specials are available for senior citizens, children and groups. An interesting option is the group eco-tour with a local resident biologist who offers a floating seminar on the ecology of the river.

Hours are 8 AM to 6 PM weekends and 9 AM to 6 PM weekdays, mid-May to mid-October depending on the weather. Take I-80 to Exit 53 (Delaware Water Gap). Follow River Road — accessible from this exit — for a mile to Minisink Hills Mall on the right.

Shawnee Canoe Trips
River Rd., Shawnee-on-Delaware • 421-1500, (800) SHAWNEE (ext. 1850 for both)

This outfitter is at Shawnee Inn, but is licensed to operate in the park and rents to the general public. It offers canoes, rafts and tubes for 3-, 6- or 9-mile unguided trips, beginning at Smithfield Beach and ending at Shawnee, Delaware Water Gap or Portland. Hours are 10 AM to 3 PM, and rentals are available every hour on the hour until closing. You must be off the water by 5 PM, however. Thus you have the opportunity to enjoy a water trip with less of a time commitment and morning scramble — perfect for those who like to rise later on their vacations.

The rate scale is a little different. While the base rate is per person (as with most outfitters), with two people per canoe or four per raft, an additional person costs $5 rather than full price (often $20 or more).

Age and height minimums to ride are: 42 inches tall for a canoe; 10 years old for a tube; and walking age for a raft.

Midweek specials — Tuesday, Wednesday and Thursday — are available. Call for details.

Take I-80 to Exit 52 (Marshalls Creek). Follow U.S. 209 N. to Buttermilk Falls Road and turn right, then proceed to River Road. Turn left onto River Road and proceed to Shawnee

Photo: Pocono Mountains Vacation Bureau, Inc.

Waterskiing on Lake Wallenpaupack.

Reception Center; staff will direct you to the canoe rentals.

Additional Boat Launches

Launching areas on the Delaware River in the recreation area are between Bushkill and Dingmans Ferry on U.S. 209. Sites other than at Milford Beach, Smithfield Beach or those managed by outfitters include Dingmans Ferry Access, Eshback Access and Bushkill Access.

All launching areas are clearly marked as you head north or south on U.S. 209. There are parking areas for your vehicles and trailers and direct access to the Delaware River. Neither fees nor registration is required to launch at these sites.

Upper Delaware Scenic and Recreational River

This section of the Delaware River, between N.Y. Hwy. 97 and I-84 from Hancock, New York, to Milford, provides moderate whitewater canoeing and rafting, manageable for beginners or the less experienced paddlers. While there are whitewater areas to challenge you on this stretch of the Delaware, there are also enough placid pools to allow you to relax and enjoy the landscape as you float or paddle. Along either side of the river from Skinners Falls in the north to River Beach at Milford, you might see — depending on the season — waterfowl, birds of prey, wildflowers and the beautiful colors of nature, especially in spring, summer and fall.

Land along the river is almost all privately owned, so check with the outfitter you use about spots on the New York side where it's permissible to stop, swim, picnic and rest. There are no places to picnic or camp on the Pennsylvania side of the river. Campsites for overnight trips can be arranged through the licensed outfitters listed in this section.

Trips on the river are arranged through the several licensed outfitters along the river, mostly on the New York side, except for Kittatinny Canoes (see the previous entry), which has three bases in Pennsylvania. Kittatinny's northernmost Pennsylvania base at Matamoras provides transportation to the northern access points upriver from Milford; its two New York bases are in Barryville (21 miles northwest of Port Jervis) and Pond Eddy (14 miles northwest of Port Jervis). Kittatinny also has campgrounds in the New York section of the Upper Delaware.

Rates for rentals, overnights, guides, groups and so on are the same as apply in the Delaware Water Gap park area. Reservations for these trips are always a good idea,

Headin' to the Swimming Hole

On a summertime blue-sky day in the Poconos, the locals are irresistibly drawn to the water. But for us the water isn't always a pristine, blue-painted pool at the park or the country club or a local lake. For most kids, young and old, the draw in the Poconos is the local swimming hole.

Swimming holes are pools of sparkling, gently rushing water formed in the numerous creeks and streams that criss-cross the mountainous landscape. Names like McMichaels and Brodhead and Red Rock and Pohopoco are whispered excitedly as soon as Memorial Day gives the annual signal to hit the water. Off our Insiders go, ready to plunge into the still-icy depths fed by the winter snow's spring melt.

Close-up

Usually, there are small, whitewater ruffles spanning the creeks at various points. With tubes or floats, the "kids" jump in and enjoy the rocky jostling as they tumble past bridges, trees, cliffs, outcroppings, use-worn beaches and the other sights a creek voyage presents.

At each swimming hole there is some traditional specialty. A rope hangs from a high tree limb to encourage would-be Tarzans to swing and jump, feet-first of course, into the welcome coolness. Wooden planks constructed between twin tree trunks are a place to climb up and jump from too — again, always feet-first for safety.

At another swimming hole, a specialty might be a deserted railway bridge. Here you graduate by jumping from the creekside cliffs, one higher than the other. When a neophyte has mastered the cliff jumps into the water below, the bridge is the next rite of passage.

There is trust at swimming holes among people who don't even know each other. Trust that you'll take turns. Trust that you'll help me climb the ladder if I'm too short. Trust

Photo: Leona Adamo Maxwell

A warm, sunny day brings kids, adults and even dogs to frolic in, on and around a Poconos swimming hole.

that you'll warn, "The water's rough today, better be careful." Trust you'll tell a newcomer "the rules." Trust that you will become part of the tradition.

Camaraderie develops quickly. A newcomer shows up, and you can't help but talk about the water level or the heat; can't help but gasp together at a child going higher on the ladders than adults feel comfortable with.

Kids at swimming holes take turns and help each other catch the rope, find the best spot to jump or catch a frolicking dog. Kids who are on different teams, in different grades, from different sides of town are swimming-hole comrades for the summer. Oldtimers help the kids with explanations — age differences are not part of the day, the friendship is.

Adults become swimming-hole friends. They talk about their kids, share concerns about the rope and maybe find out there's a committee they always wanted to join that's looking for help.

The water brings cleansing and peace. The swimming hole that carved its place along the creek beds carves its way into peoples' lives. They can sit back and believe they are in another time, when life was simpler.

There are no maps to our swimming holes. If you're lucky, maybe you'll drive past a bridge and notice the locals on the banks of the tantalizing creek below. If you're brave, stop and kind of hang out while you wait for someone to smile at you and let you know it's OK to be there. Maybe you'll discover one on your own. Whichever way you discover a swimming hole, don't be afraid to jump in — the water's fine!

---

but a spur-of-the-moment indulgence oftentimes can be accommodated. Remember sales tax: 7 percent in New York, 6 percent in Pennsylvania. Another expense sometimes associated with whitewater is wetsuits if the water is cold.

To obtain a list of available campsites and campgrounds not accessible through outfitters, contact the Park Service in Milford, 685-4871. Staff will advise that access to the river in this area be arranged through an outfitter who can transport you to one of its bases. There are no public access launches on the New York or Pennsylvania side as in the Water Gap recreation area.

The following are some of the major outfitters in the Upper Delaware Scenic and Recreational River area.

Outfitters

Lander's River Trips
N.Y. Hwy. 97, Narrowsburg, N.Y.
• (914) 252-3925, (800) 252-3925

This outfitter rents canoes, rafts, kayaks and tubes. Rates are based on two persons in a canoe and four persons in a raft; there is a discount for two-day rentals. Solo canoes or

kayaks rent for $29. Children 12 and younger go for half-price when accompanied by parent. Children must be 5 years old and weigh 50 pounds to fit into life jackets. Getaway Packages are available for four or more adults for one- or two-day overnights, which are spent either camping or at the Ten Mile River Motel. A $3 per person discount applies midweek, and group discounts apply for canoeing or rafting. There are also special rates for bus loads as well as scout, church, youth and other tax-exempt groups.

Unguided trips originate from as far north as Hankins, New York, and end at the base near Port Jervis. Tubing trips can cover as many as 5 miles, or you can stay at Skinner's Falls for the day. You can float around or through the falls, then portage your tube upriver along the path beside the falls. You can spend a whole day here — transportation to and from included.

Lander's has campgrounds along the river at Skinner's Falls, Narrowsburg, Minisink and Knight's Eddy for campers using Lander's or privately owned river craft. Campgrounds contain hot showers, snack bars and camp stores. Campsites and lean-tos are available. Rates vary from $10 to $12 per person; children ages 7 to 12 are half-price, and kids 6 and younger are free. Weekend stays include two nights; holiday weekends, three nights. Lander's also maintains the Ten Mile River Lodge, an aptly named motel 10 miles downriver from Skinner's Falls. Standard rooms for two people are $50 per night. Efficiencies for five people ($65 nightly) also are available.

Bases open at 8 AM weekends and 9 AM weekdays. Watercraft must be returned by 6 PM. Campers must be off the river by dark.

Tri-State Canoe & Boat Rentals
Shay Ln., Matamoras
• 491-4948, (800) 56-CANOE

This outfitter rents canoes, rafts, tubes and rowboats ($36 to $40) for self-guided trips on the Upper Delaware River. At its northernmost base at Pond Eddy, you can raft or canoe through whitewater down to the Matamoras base — about 10 miles; or take a leisurely trip from Matamoras south to Milford. Bases open at 9 AM weekdays, 8 AM weekends. All watercraft are due back at the base by 6 PM, unless the users are camping at a campground.

Reduced rates are offered for groups of 10 or more as well as for children ages 5 to 10. Reservations made 48 hours in advance get you a $2 per person discount. Weekend rates are approximately $2 more per person for each craft. Children must be 4 or older and able to swim (as must everyone) to go in a canoe; if you can't swim, you can rent a raft. All outfitters provide regulation life vests.

If you have your own craft, this outfitter will transport you to one of its bases for $25.

A special activity here is a guided moonlight raft trip during July and August on Saturday nights. Reservations are required, and the trip includes a barbecue. Adults pay $25 and children ages 7 to 12 pay $12.50 for this peaceful excursion. Note that children younger than 7 are not allowed.

Tri-State maintains its own campgrounds for overnighters, with sites for tents or RVs. It also rents travel trailers at the campgrounds. Rates vary by site; tent sites are charged a base rate for two people and more per additional person. "No Frills" RV sites are less expensive, and the base rate includes all occupants. A regular RV site includes a per-person

rate for up to four occupants. Generally costs run $20 per person; additional persons are $8. Group rates are available, and children 5 and younger stay free in campgrounds. (Please remember prices are subject to change at all these outfitters, so please check for up-to-date rates.)

From Milford take U.S. Highway 209 N. for 4.5 miles to the traffic light. Turn right at the light and the Tri-County sign. Follow the road to the river. Or, from points in New York and New England, take I-84 W. to Exit 11. At end of off-ramp turn left onto U.S. Highway 209 S. Turn left at the first traffic light, look for the Tri-County Canoe sign and proceed to the river.

> ## FYI
> Unless otherwise noted, the area code for all phone numbers listed in this guide is 717.

Wild and Scenic River Tours and Rentals
166 N.Y. Hwy. 97, Barryville, N.Y.
• (914) 557-8783, (800) 836-0366

This outfitter provides canoes, rafts, kayaks and tubes. Self-guided trips are available from one of three river-access sites. The rates here are $24 per person for adults; 10 cents per pound for children 5 to 12.

Discounts are provided for groups of 10 adults or more, Other group rates are offered depending on the size of the group; be sure to inquire.

Reservations are recommended. You can take a trip without a reservation if there's room, but a reservation insures a $2 per person discount. Trips can depart between 9 AM and 2 PM, but all watercraft must be back by 6 PM.

There is a small campsite available that caters to families. It includes shared bathhouses, a place near the water's edge to set up your tent, a picnic table and a fire ring.

From Pennsylvania take U.S. Highway 6 east from Hawley or west from Milford to Twin Lakes Road. Follow Twin Lakes Road across the Shohola Bridge into New York. Make a left onto N.Y. Highway 97 N. and proceed about .75 miles. Or, from points in New York, take N.Y. Highway 97 north from Port Jervis or south from Narrowsburg. The outfitter is .75 miles from the Shohola Bridge on N.Y Highway 97 N.

State Parks

Mount Pocono Area

Promised Land State Park

This state park on Pa. Highway 390, 10 miles north of Canadensis, offers a large lake for swimming, two lakes for fishing and boating, picnic areas and four campgrounds with facilities ranging from Class A to primitive. Access to all areas is free. Costs are only for rentals, supplies, campsites and launch fees for non-registered boats.

The park covers 3,000 acres. The upper lake is 450 acres; the lower lake 150 acres. Offices are on Pa. 390 past the Village of Promised Land, in the park. Hours are 8 AM to 4 PM Monday through Friday during winter; every day in summer. Handicapped-accessible areas including ramps and walkways are available; call the park office, 676-3428, or stop in for daily information. Improvements and additions are always being made.

Swimming

The main beach is on the north shore of Promised Land Lake. It's open 11 AM to 7 PM (weather permitting) from Memorial Day to Labor Day. The sandy beach includes roped-off areas for swimming, which is permitted only when lifeguards are on duty (see aforementioned hours). There is a snack bar at the main beach, tables and fire rings for your daily picnic and for guests at nearby campgrounds. Restrooms are available as is a bathhouse with a hot-water shower that you feed with quarters (50¢ to start). The shower is open for campers staying at the primitive sites as well as swimmers at the lake.

On weekends this lake is always crowded. If you want to come for the day, plan on arriving before the beach opens. The parking lot fills rapidly — remember campers are close by. By noon the parking lots usually are full, and you'll have to park on the access roads and walk in.

There is limited swimming on weekends (a lifeguard must be present, and the sched-

ule varies) at the beach at Pickeral Point Campground.

Boating

You can go boating or fishing on the upper and lower Promised Land lakes and on Bruce Lake (a natural glacier lake as is the park's very small Egypt Meadow Lake). Electric-powered motor boats — no gas-powered craft — are allowed on Promised Land Lake. Power boats must have a Pennsylvania registration. If your boat is registered out of state, you can buy a launch permit at the park office ($7). Manually powered boats (canoes, rowboats and such) require launch permits, which also can be purchased at the park office: $6 for Pennsylvania residents, $7 for non-residents. Launching sites are available from April 1 to November 1 (no boats permitted after November 1) at the docks. The cost for a season launch permit is $35 for Pennsylvania residents, $40 for non-residents. You can rent boats at the boat concession by the hour, day or several days. Rates vary according to the type of boat (paddleboat, canoe, rowboat) starting at $8 per hour, $5 for each additional hour.

Bruce Lake and Egypt Meadow Lake are not recreation areas; overnight camping and recreational vehicles are not allowed.

Bruce Lake is a 48-acre lake that is a 2.5-mile hike from the trail head originating on Pa. 390. If you bring your boat, you will have to carry it. It is part of the Delaware National Forest, and no motor vehicles are allowed; park at the trail head.

The hike to 60-acre Egypt Meadow Lake is only about a half-mile from the trail head on Pa. 390; this lake is very weedy, and the fishing here is not very good. Swimming is not allowed in Bruce Lake or Egypt Meadow Lake. Maps available at the park office show all the trails, lakes and campsites.

Camping

There are four camping areas with more than 500 sites for which you must register at the park office. Twenty-five percent of the sites are Class A — bathhouses, hot showers, flush toilet, open 24 hours a day. The others have a combination of flush toilets and outhouses, except the one primitive site that only has a camping space. The officials here suggest you call for what is available. Reservations are not usually taken; sites are available on a first-come, first-served basis. That might change, so check with the park office if you are interested in camping.

Hiking

There are more than 30 miles of hiking trails through the state park and the national forest area. Loops, short trails, long trails over moderate to gently rolling terrain all are marked on the maps available at the park office. If the office is closed, maps are kept in a rack outside the door.

Other Opportunities

Many events and educational opportunities are available during the summer season. There are naturalist walks and guided eco-tours by canoe and on foot. There are nature crafts and talks for the children. In the park you'll find a naturalist museum and a Civilian Conservation Corps Museum (CCC alumnae met here in 1995 for a reunion). The scheduled offerings vary, and most are free. Call the park for a definite schedule each week.

Tobyhanna State Park

Swimming, boating, picnicking, fishing and camping are options near the water at 5,440-acre Tobyhanna State Park, Pa. Hwy. 423, 2.1 miles north of Tobyhanna, 894-8336. The 175-acre lake is cradled on three sides by mountains; a sandy beach encircles the fourth. The lake is past the park entrance, and parking lots parallel the lake. The office and boat rentals are past the beach area on Pa. 423. The boat dock and beach are handicapped-accessible from any parking lot; the terrain is flat here, and there are paths to the water. There are restrooms and bathhouses but no showers. Bring your own picnic because a snack bar is not available.

Swimming

Beaches are open for swimming when lifeguards are on duty between 11 AM and 7 PM. There is no fee for swimming. Grassy picnic areas, wooded picnic areas and a small playground adjoin the beach. There are 300 picnic tables and grilling facilities (bring your own charcoal) throughout the lake area (the detailed map at the park office can help you find the one you prefer, other than those directly by the beach).

Boating

If you have your own boat you can use the docks to launch. The docks are past the park office, which is just past the beach area on the same road. Docks are open 24 hours a day. Night fishing is permitted. Your boat must be registered in Pennsylvania to use it on the lake. If your boat is not registered in Pennsylvania, you can purchase a permit — $6 for Pennsylvania residents and $7 for non-residents — from the park office.

You can rent canoes, rowboats, paddle boats and electric motor boats at the dock between 8 AM and 4 PM. The rates for non-powered boats are $7 for one hour, $5 to $6 each additional hour or $35 for the whole day. Electric motor boats rent for $14 an hour, $32 a half-day and $55 for the whole day (prices are subject to change). By law, boats must have approved life vests on board for all occupants; all rentals come equipped with approved life vests.

Camping

There are 140 campsites at Tobyhanna State Park. Register for a site at the park office. Reservations are not accepted; all sites are available on a first-come, first-served basis (hint: Be at the office early Friday afternoon to obtain a site for the weekend). Each site contains a fire ring and a picnic table. Rates for the site are $8 per night for Pennsylvania residents and $10 per night for non-residents.

Beltzville State Park

Swimming, boating, picnicking, fishing and hiking are available at Beltzville State Park, on U.S. Highway 209, 5 miles east of Lehighton, (610) 377-0045. The lake at Beltzville is the largest in this area of the Poconos (Lake Wallenpaupack has that distinction on the other side of the coverage area), so motorized boats are allowed here. The lake is 949 acres, a large chunk of the park's total 2,972 acres.

Camping is not permitted. Admission to the park is free. Boat launching is free for Pennsylvania residents; $7 for out-of-state visitors. Boat rentals range from $10 an hour for a canoe to $60 an hour for a motor boat or Jet Ski. The park office is open 8 AM to 4 PM daily from Memorial Day to Labor Day, and Monday through Friday the rest of the year. Beaches, boat launches and public areas are handicapped-accessible; call park for details.

Swimming

The beach here is the largest in any of the park areas. Lifeguards are on duty from 11 AM to 7 PM. There is a snack bar at the roped-off swimming area, picnic areas with grills, restrooms and bathhouses with showers. Pavilions for picnicking are available for free on a first-come, first-served basis; if you want to reserve one ($45), call the park office.

Boating

Unlimited horsepower is allowed on this lake. The speed limit is 45 mph. Water skiing and Jet Skiing are allowed here. (This is the only public lake beach to allow this activity besides Lake Wallenpaupack.) Boats must be registered in Pennsylvania, or you must purchase a launch permit ($6 for Pennsylvania residents, $7 for non-residents). Boat launches are open 24 hours a day, so fishing is allowed 24 hours a day as well. No fishing is allowed in the swimming area, but you can fish offshore.

More Opportunities

This park offers day camps for children throughout the summer. Crafts, nature hikes, swimming lessons, week-long programs, day-long programs, even family programs are available for free. Contact the park office in May to see what opportunities are planned for the summer season (local newspapers list them in summer-specials sections).

West End

Gouldsboro State Park

Swimming, boating, picnicking and fishing are water-related options here. The 250-acre lake is right past the park entrance on Pa. Highway 507, 1.5 miles south of Gouldsboro; signs for boat rentals and the dock follow — just past the swimming area. The boat dock and beach of this 2,800-acre park are handicapped-accessible from Parking Lot 1. There are restrooms and bathhouses but no showers. Bring your own picnic — there is no snack bar.

Beaches are open for swimming from 11 AM to 7 PM when lifeguards are on duty. There is no fee for swimming.

If you have your own boat, you can use the docks right past the beach 24 hours a day. Night fishing is permitted. Your boat must be registered in Pennsylvania to use it on the lake. You can rent canoes, rowboats, paddle boats and electric motor boats at the dock between 8 AM and 4 PM. The rates for non-powered boats are $7.50 for one hour, $5 each additional hour or $20 for the whole day. Electric motor boats are $15 for an hour, $5 each additional hour and $35 for the whole day (note that prices are subject to change). All boat users must have an approved life vest on board for each occupant; it is the law. Rentals come equipped with approved life vests.

Call the park office at 894-8336 for more information.

Hickory Run State Park

This 15,500-acre park on Pa. Highway 534 near Hickory Run has a small, 40-acre lake. Swimming, picnicking, fishing, camping and hiking are allowed at this state park. The office, also on Pa. 534, 443-0400, is open 8 AM to 4 PM. The campgrounds are 1.5 miles from the office. The beach area is a mile past the office along a service road. A handicapped-accessible ramp leads to the beaches and picnic areas; park personnel suggest you contact the office for details. There are no daily fees for fishing (you must have a valid Pennsylvania fishing license if you are older than 16) or swimming. Fishing is only available from the shore, since there is no boating on this lake.

Swimming

There is a small, sandy beach. Lifeguards are on duty 11 AM to 7 PM, Memorial Day to Labor Day. There are 475 picnic tables scattered around the sandy beach on the grass, under trees, along the grassy rim of the knoll behind the beach and in the woods further removed from the beach area. Grills are provided at some table sites. To reach the beach from the parking lot, you have to walk up a hill on paths. A snack bar, restrooms, bathhouses and showers are here.

Camping

Camping sites for 381 tents and trailers are available. They include modern facilities, electrical hookups, showers and restrooms. Sites are not near the swimming area; you must go to the beach area to swim or fish. Campsites cost $10 a night for one to four Pennsylvania residents and $12 for non-residents; additional campers pay $5 each.

Lehigh Gorge State Park

This park is primarily known for whitewater rafting. Hiking trails here become snowmobiling and cross-country skiing trails in winter (see our Winter Sports chapter). Camping and swimming are not allowed in this park, but Mauch Chunk Lake, a county-owned area, is adjacent to Lehigh Gorge at the Jim Thorpe end, and both activities are available there. (See our Parks and Hunting and Fishing chapters for information about other recreational opportunities.)

To tackle the whitewater in the turbulent Lehigh River and its canal, you must have an approved raft or canoe. Aluminum canoes are not recommended because they are easily dented. Regulation life vests or PFDs (we recommend Type II or V, designed for whitewater) are a must. Experienced paddlers can attempt this challenge without a guide; the inexperienced should not. Licensed con-

cessionaires are allowed to operate in the park (see the subsequent "Outfitters" section), and they can provide or suggest guide services.

There are no fees to enter the gorge area, but you should check with the park office before running the river. Water levels are controlled by dam releases in the spring and fall and at various times in summer. The releases greatly increase the flow, and thus have a marked effect on the danger of the river. The U.S. Army Corps of Engineers provides release information, (800) 431-4721, as does the park office, 427-5000. Also, very low water levels make for a different but similarly dangerous situation, so access to the river is controlled by the park rangers during low-flow periods; the inexperienced are not allowed on the river when the water is very low or turbulent. Also, the number of people allowed on the river is controlled to ensure safety. One way the numbers are monitored is through the licensed concessionaires; the other is through the park office.

Enter the park at the Rockport (south) entrance; take Exit 40 from I-80. Other access areas are in White Haven and Jim Thorpe. Pick up a map or call to park office to receive one if you are planning a trip here. Parking is only available at Rockport, so make arrangements to be picked up if you are paddling on your own. The water downriver from Jim Thorpe is not as difficult; by contrast, the upper waters are Class III (difficult) whitewater. Spring and fall are the most turbulent water times. If you want to try a whitewater adventure with your family, the summer is quieter, and local outfitters can turn you on to more low-key paddling opportunities.

One local outfitter, **Lehigh Rafting Rentals**, 242 Main Street, White Haven, 443-4441 or (800) 580-2847, rents rafts for self-guided tours only; call for reservations. Rates vary by season and day of the week, but you're looking at a minimum of $20 to $30 per person per raft (children are generally half-price) plus wetsuit ($10) , mittens ($3) and booties ($5) if necessary (depending on the weather).

Following are approved concessionaires that offer guided whitewater experiences as well as rentals for the experienced whitewater enthusiast.

Outfitters

Rates and methods of payment vary for trips coordinated through the following concessionaires (outfitters), depending on day of week, time of year, guided or unguided, dam-release specials, summer events and other options. For peak season (whitewater spring and fall), rates are from $40 to $46 per adult (children are about half-price or, with some specials, free with two paying adults). Wetsuit rentals ($10 to $18) also might be necessary and are mandatory between March 1 and May 1. Don't forget to add in Pennsylvania sales tax (6 percent) on trips. Each outfitter has its own specials, which change every year, so contact the ones that interest you for their latest brochure of offerings. Reservations are recommended. Trips usually run rain or shine. All trips include transportation to and from the river to your vehicle. All outfitters recommend you bring a change of clothing. Alcohol is not permitted!

Outfitters also offer picnics and barbecues, group rates, breakfast specials, kayaking opportunities and additional options too varied to list here. Contact any of the following for up-to-date offerings.

A little note to help save you money: The outfitters often have coupons in their brochures, so sending for one is a good idea. Also, they run coupon specials in the *Pocono Record*, especially on Sundays. In local grocery stores, diners, fast-food stands and tourist attractions, you'll find racks with local magazines that also might include outfitter coupons. If you are in the area, check out these publications before you pay full price.

Jim Thorpe River Adventures
1 Adventure Ln., Jim Thorpe • 325-2570, 325-4960

The season for this outfitter is March through October. For reservations only, call (800) 424-RAFT. Staff encourage early reservations with a deposit of $20 per person. They offer specials for dam releases and summer rafting, so call to confirm dates. This outfitter offers several family options (children must be 5 or older). You can also rent mountain bikes here for the non-whitewater enthusiasts in your party.

Pocono Whitewater Adventures
Pa. Hwy. 903, Jim Thorpe • 325-8430

Tubes, canoes and bikes are also available from this group, in case some of you want to whitewater raft and some of you don't. This outfitter offers a half-day biking adventure that ends with a half-day rafting adventure, family-style float trips and Skirmish, a paintball war game (see our Recreation chapter). There is a snack bar, sports shop and miniature golf at this facility. Call by 10 AM if you have a spur-of-the-moment urge; if there is space available, you can be headed for whitewater by 11 AM.

Whitewater Challenges
Stagecoach Rd., White Haven • 443-9532, (800) 443-8554

There are discounts and specials for youth groups — scouts, Kids Day, weekends, summerrafting and college days — as well as weekend trips, ice breakers, rafting/camping, rafting/hoteling and so on. Call for a brochure; the specials are always changing and growing. Age requirements vary based on the trip; the youngest age allowed is 5 for summerrafting. Biking also is offered as are kayaking clinics for groups.

Whitewater Rafting Adventures
Pa. Hwy. 534, Albrightsville • 722-0285, (800) 876-0285

Trips are offered at discounted prices in the summer when the water is less turbulent. Discounts apply to children and groups, scouts and families. Group specials also are available for whitewater high times (Class III+ experiences). Kayak clinics are available too. A complimentary cookout is part of this outfitter's package.

Natural Areas

West End

Mauch Chunk Lake Park

This park, on Lentz Trail Highway, between Summit Hill and Jim Thorpe, 325-3669, has an absolutely beautiful, clear, mountain-surrounded lake. It is part of the county system and is administered by the Carbon County Parks and Recreation Commission. Swimming is available on a guarded beach. Campsites are available within walking distance to the lake, picnic tables are on a pavilion area above the lake and in the wood around the lake, a snack bar adjoins the lake and pavilion area. Restrooms, bathhouses and showers are here too. Parking is directly in front of the lake. This facility is handicapped-accessible at all main areas.

Swimming

The sandy, guarded beach is open 11 AM to 7 PM daily from the close of school to Labor Day. Fees for beach use differ for Carbon County residents and non-residents (between $2 and $4 per person per day) and are subject to change. Physically disabled and senior citizens are admitted free. There is a tot-lot play area in the wooded picnic area near the beach. Across from the beach you'll find volleyball courts.

Boating

There is a camp store that rents boats by the hour and the day. Paddle boats, canoes, kayaks (single and two-person) and electric motor boats are available for rent. A valid driver's license and a major credit card are required to rent. Boat launches are open year round, 24 hours a day. Restrooms are available at the boat launch.

Camping

The two camp areas contain a shared bathhouse and restrooms. Reservations are necessary on weekends, and you must register at the park office upon arrival. The campground is open from the third Friday in April to the last Sunday in October. Pets and alcohol are not permitted in the campground. You can camp for up to 14 consecutive nights. Prices are subject to change, but for county residents they run about $8 a night per site for four campers, with additional campers tacking on $2 a person. Non-residents pay $14 per site for four persons and $4 per night for each additional camper.

Hiking

The Shoreline Trail is a 1.5-mile hike through deciduous woodlands, by open shoreline and along stands of laurel, rhododendron and hemlock. The park provides an interpretive guide.

Lake Wallenpaupack Area

Lake Wallenpaupack

The Lake Wallenpaupack area, southeast of Hawley at U.S. Highway 6 and Pa. Highway 507, 226-3702, has four Pennsylvania Power & Light-owned recreation centers that provide camping areas and boat launches managed by private concerns. There is a whopping 52 miles of shoreline in this natural area. PP&L also maintains two hiking trails around the lake, picnic areas on the four islands in the lake and a free public-access boat launch.

A public swimming beach is operated by Palmyra Township. Around the lake there are privately owned marinas and boat-rental concessionaires that use the lake. Water skiing, Jet Skiing, fishing, canoeing, rafting and rowing are all allowed on this large lake, whether from a campsite, a public launch area, the public beach or your own vacation home.

There are nature programs offered throughout the season at the individual recreation areas — Caffrey, Ironwood, Ledgedale and Wilsonville. Programs are free, about an hour long and include nature hikes, movies, lectures and the like.

Photo: Pocono Mountains Vacation Bureau, Inc.

These canoists find some quiet time on the water.

For information on specific offerings, call the lake superintendent's office, open Monday through Friday 8 AM to 4:30 PM from May to September. The number is 226-3702. Check out the writeups on these individual recreation areas following the upcoming sections on hiking, swimming, boating and picnicking.

Lake Wallenpaupack is a big boating lake. Large boats up to 20 feet are allowed here, so water skiing is a major attraction. For a special treat, take a cruise on the lake. The 48-foot-long *Spirit of Paupack* offers hour-long sightseeing cruises ($5 for adults; $2 for children) and sunset dinner cruises ($34.50 per person) from Pocono Action Sports at Tanglewood Lodge, 226-4556. Another scenic cruise, offered by Wallenpaupack Scenic Boat Tour, 226-6211, is a 30-minute trip on a patio boat. Trips run every day, 11 AM to 8 PM, from the end of June through September.

Hiking

Two hiking trails follow the lake —

Shuman Point and Ledgedale Natural Area. These are moderate-to-easy treks. Shuman Point, across from Caffrey Recreation Area on Lake Shore Drive, is densely wooded, and the lake is only visible at a few points. The Ledgedale hiking trail is about a quarter-mile inland from Ledgedale Recreation Area and is not in sight of the lake at all. You can get on the trails at the recreation areas. Trails are for daytime hiking only; trailside camping is not permitted.

Swimming

You can swim at the one public-access beach area on the lake, Palmyra Township Bathing Beach, 226-9290, managed by Palmyra Township. It is across from the Pocono Mountains Vacation Bureau on Pa. 590. The beach is open 9:30 AM to 6:30 PM daily; lifeguards go off duty at 6 PM. The beach area opens when schools close and closes when schools open. The cost is

$2 for adults, $1 for children. There is a picnic area with two grills, a snack bar, bathrooms, changing rooms and a shower. Pets and alcohol are not allowed.

Boating

The launching access at the four recreation areas are open to the public for a $5 fee. One other public access launch is available for free. Needless to say, it is very crowded on weekends, so we suggest paying the nominal charge at the fee areas for the convenience and elbow room. The free-access boat launch is run by the Pennsylvania Boat Commission, 477-5717, for the Lake Wallenpaupack area. It is at the north end of the lake near the dam off Pa. 590, a quarter-mile west of the U.S. 6 intersection. The launch is open 24 hours a day, every day, all year long. Parking is available. To launch from this site, your boat must have a valid registration. Pennsylvania registration is not required on this lake. Please note this is not the case at any lake in the state park system. Boating requirements for each lake area differ.

You can picnic at the four recreation areas on the grass around the docks for free or pay $2 for a table. The four islands in the lake — Epply, Kipp, Burns and Cairns — all have picnic areas with tables. Burns does not have restrooms, but the others do. You cannot camp on these islands and can only picnic during daylight hours; alcohol and pets are not permitted. These areas are accessible by boat only.

Boat Rentals

We recommend the following places to rent boats, Jet Skis, water skis and related watersports gear while in the Lake Wallenpaupack area.

Club Nautico of Lake Wallenpaupack at Shepard's Marina
Pa. Hwy. 507, Hawley • 226-0580

This is technically a members-only club, but non-members are welcome. Power boats and all the accouterments are available for rent here. The base price is $10 for two hours with a power boat. It is open for the summer season from 8 AM to 7:30 PM,

from May to mid-October and has a picnic area for renters.

Pocono Action Sports Marina and Boat Rentals
Pa. Hwy. 507, at Tanglewood Lodge, Lake Wallenpaupack • 226-4556

This shop has rentals for virtually everything you might need for your Wallenpaupack vacation. Rentals include power boats, sailboats, canoes, Jet Skis and WaveRunners Water-skiing instruction also is available. It is open from 9 AM to 7 PM daily from May to mid-October.

Pine Crest Yacht Club Inc.
Pa. Hwy. 507, on Lake Wallenpaupack, Greentown • 857-1136, 226-3077

This shop is part of the Pinecrest Resort. It is open to the public for power boats, water skis, Jet Skis and other rentals. Rates start at $35 per half-hour for boats and $5 for water skis. Hours are 9 AM to 7 PM daily from May to mid-October.

Recreation Areas

The recreation areas for Pennsylvania Power & Light all operate under the same basic guidelines. They provide camp areas with boat launch facilities for day- or short-term use, and slips that can be rented for a short stay or the season (April to October). Campsites are $14 per night for one to four persons and $2 per night for each additional person. Reservations are strongly suggested, and a deposit is required (credit-card deposits are not usually accepted). Campsites provide a tent site and electricity. Swimming is not allowed at the campsites or launch areas; however, there is a public swimming area, and swimming from a boat is allowed. Daily launch fees are $5, whether you are camping or just want to boat for the day. If you are camping, the $5 fee applies for the length of your stay. Seasonal slips are $850 (prices are subject to change).

Caffrey Recreation Area
Lake Shore Dr., Lakeville • 226-4608

Caffrey, the smallest of the PP&L camping areas, features 35 campsites that are open from April to October, weather permitting, and a camp store that is open daily during that period from 8 AM to 8 PM. The gate at the launch area is always open, and the owner is generally around from 5 AM on, so you can enter when you want. The honor system applies here, and there are instructions on site to tell you how to pay if no one is around. Gas is available at the docks, and you can pay for it with a gas credit card but not a major credit card.

Reservation deposits are required for campsites. If a reservation is made too close to the needed date, your credit card number will suffice to hold the site for you. Reservations require a two-night minimum stay and a three-night minimum on a holiday weekend. Write HC 1 Box 360, Lakeville 18438, or call 226-4608.

There is a picnic area available ($2) for launch users who aren't camping at the recreation area. There is also a small playground.

This site has boat slips available year round (rates are based on boat size and length of stay). You can also rent slips for the weekend ($15 per night) if you are camping here.

Rentals and repairs are available at Capri Marina, 226-2759, across the road. It has a lounge that's open on weekends.

Shuman Point is 3 miles long and takes about 1½ hours to walk. It climbs at its beginning and parallels the shoreline for most of its length. Besides the lake views, hikers will enjoy chestnut, red maple, white oak and white pine trees and a bounty of wildflowers.

Take Pa. Highway 590 from either Hawley or Hamlin toward Lakeville, next to Caesar's Cove Haven. Look for the blue signs to Caffrey's, on Lake Shore Drive.

Ironwood Recreation Area
Burns Hill Rd., Greentown • 857-0880

This area has 60 sites and is the only one

Photo: Pocono Mountains Vacation Bureau, Inc.

Boaters cruise on Wallenpaupack and other sizeable lakes throughout the Poconos.

of the four PP&L areas that has campsites right on the lake; so, it is very busy on weekends. Campers park in the provided lot and walk to the sites. Reservations are recommended for weekends, otherwise it is first-come, first-served; write RD 2, Box 344, Greentown, or call 857-0880, for details. The camp store is open from 8 AM to 9 PM; the launch access is open from 6 AM to 10 PM, whether you are overnighting at the site or using it for daily access.

There is a picnic area here for daily boaters. Tables, a pavilion and a small playground are also part of the amenities.

From I-84 take Exit 6. Take Pa. Highway 507 N. 2 miles to Burns Hill Road in Greentown. Ironwood is on this road.

Ledgedale Recreation Area
Ledgedale Rd., Ledgedale • 689-2181

This area at the southernmost tip of Lake Wallenpaupack has 69 campsites. It's remote and, therefore, very quiet — sought after by those who wish to boat away from the wakes of the thriving boating scene elsewhere on the lake. The campsites are across the road from the lake; the office, camp store and dock area are on the lake. Reservations are recommended for holiday weekends (please call), otherwise you can just show up and register on a first-come, first-served basis. There are seasonal campsites and boat slips that rent for $850 per season. The convenience store is open 8 AM to 9 PM, as is the boat launch. Daily boaters can picnic at the lakeside picnic area. This area is open Memorial Day to Labor Day.

For a side excursion, Ledgedale is near Claws 'N Paws animal park (see our Attractions and Kidstuff chapters). It's also only a quarter-mile from the Ledgedale hiking trail.

Take I-84 to Exit 6. Take Pa. Highway 507 N. a quarter-mile to Ledgedale Road and proceed to Ledgedale Recreation Area.

Wilsonville Recreation Area
U.S. Hwy. 6, Hawley • 226-4382

Wilsonville is the largest PP&L recreation area at Lake Wallenpaupack, with 170 campsites. Reservations are recommended two to three weeks in advance for holiday weekends; please call. The sites start a block from the dock area on the lake. Primitive campsites with no flush toilets also are available. This area's property adjoins the Palmyra Township Bathing Beach, a swimming area within walking distance for campers. A camp store is open 8 AM to 7 PM during the week and 8 AM to 10 PM weekends. If you get there before it opens, you can stop at the house next to the store to register; the owner is always up early. Boaters have no curfew here.

There is 500 feet of lakefront picnic area for campers and day boaters. Nearby restaurants include Ehrhardt's Lakeside, 226-2124, and Tanglewood Lodge, 226-4556.

Take U.S. Highway 6 to Hawley. The recreation area is at the upper end of Lake Wallenpaupack near the dam.

Public Swimming Pools

Four townships have public swimming pools that are open to residents and non-residents for the day or the season. Rates vary, and you should call in advance to inquire about them.

Delaware Water Gap

Shaw Park
Oak St., Delaware Water Gap • 476-0331

This lovely little community pool is plenty large for the size of the community. It opens for the season when schools close and closes when schools open. Lifeguards are on duty from noon to 6 PM. There is a small picnic area outside the fenced-in pool area. A small playground and tots wading pool also occupy the grassy area. This well-kept, unheated pool was recently renovated. Rates vary, but seniors (older than 55) and children younger than 4 get in free. Seasonal, resident and non-resident rates apply. Shaw Park has changing rooms and restrooms. It is a lovely family spot, and many folks who grew up swimming there now bring children of their own.

Stroudsburg/ East Stroudsburg

East Stroudsburg Pool
Dansbury Park, Day St., East Stroudsburg • 421-6591

This is a very busy pool. Free swimming lessons are offered 10:15 AM to 12:15 PM for residents and non-residents (any age) over six weeks. Resident and non-resident rates are available for daily and season passes. When lessons end in August, the pool is open for free swimming from 11 AM to noon. A diving area occupies a branch of this Olympic-sized L-shaped pool. A snack bar, changing rooms and restrooms are on site. Outside the fenced pool area is a toddler pool that is cleaned and filled every morning with chlorinated water, a playground and picnic pavilion. There is a director on hand at all times as well as nine lifeguards. This pool is well-maintained, and people from all around the county enjoy using it.

Stroudsburg Municipal Pool
W. Main St., Stroudsburg • 421-5444

Open to residents and non-residents alike, this pool opens for the season when school closes and closes the Sunday before Labor Day. Changing rooms, showers, restrooms, picnic tables and vending machines are by the pool. Outside the pool you'll find a playground, tennis court, basketball courts, a baseball field and other facilities that are part of the public recreation center in Stroudsburg. This pool is fully staffed and offers swimming lessons for 10 weeks in the summer. Two weeks of lessons are $25 per person for residents or non-residents. There are resident and non-resident rates for open swimming. Hours are noon to 6 PM Monday, Tuesday, Wednesday and Friday; noon to 7 PM Thursday; and 10 AM to 6 PM Saturday and Sunday.

Slate Belt

Pen Argyl Pool
Weona Park, Pen Argyl • (610) 863-9249

A lot of young people come here, and events geared toward them are sponsored throughout the summer; call for details. There is a snack bar, wading pool for toddlers, playground and all types of playing fields near the pool. There are picnic tables both inside and outside the pool area. Rates are based on residency and are subject to change. Hours are noon to 7 PM daily from when school closes until the Sunday before Labor Day.

If you tire of swimming, Weona Park has a 1896 Denzel carousel, the only complete Denzel with the original paint. Rides cost $1 per person.

Golf course architects
love to taunt Poconos
golfers with woods,
streams, lakes, hills,
cliffs, stone rows and
wetlands.

Golf

Some people who live in or visit the Poconos are not content to merely walk in the woods and admire the scenery. They insist upon chasing a small ball and trying to hit it into a hole. The odds are against them; the obstacles, seemingly insurmountable. Around here, we call these brave, crazy souls golfers.

Players of all abilities can find a suitable course in the Poconos. Families and beginners might try one of the many short, nine-hole facilities that have few hazards and generous greens and fairways. More serious golfers have their pick from many professional-caliber courses. Highly regarded designers such as A.W. Tillinghast, Robert Trent Jones, Donald Ross, Jack Nicklaus and Jim Fazio are represented.

The best courses utilize the existing natural features to create trouble spots. Golf course architects love to taunt Poconos golfers with woods, streams, lakes, hills, cliffs, stone rows and wetlands. Side-hill lies and undulating greens bordered by streams, woods and a few bunkers are common.

You'll find more than 35 courses in the Pocono Mountains. In this chapter, we've focused on some top choices among all types of courses.

In the July 1995 issue, *Golf Magazine* rated Shawnee Inn & Golf Resort, Tamiment Resort, Mount Airy Lodge Golf Course, Woodloch Springs and Skytop Lodge Golf Club as "must plays."

The *1996 Powers Golf Guide*, in its Northeast Region Readers Survey Top Picks, recognized Buck Hill, Hideaway Hills and Mountain Manor's Orange/Silver Course.

All yardage measurements are taken from the longest tees available — the professional, or back, tees.

Resort courses are accessible to guests of the facility, who usually receive preferred tee times. Through a cooperative effort among 10 of the resort courses, visitors staying at one of the accommodations may book tee times at any of the others as well. Private courses, which may be played only by club members or their guests, are not included.

Golf Courses

Delaware Water Gap

Cherry Valley Golf Course
Cherry Valley Rd., Stroudsburg • 421-1350

A typically hilly, wooded Poconos track with plenty of water, this 18-hole public course begins with its longest hole, a 470-yard par 5. However, most holes after it are in the 200- to 300-yard range for a total yardage of 5058 (par 71).

A pro shop, snack bar, restaurant and bar are on the grounds of the course. Weekday greens fees are $15 ($22 with cart), with a twilight special of $10 ($16 with cart) after 3 PM. On weekends, rates are $20 per person and $14 after 3 PM. Cart rental on weekends is $15 per person. A Thursday special includes greens fees, cart and lunch for $25 per person. Seniors also receive special discounts on Monday and Wednesday.

Shawnee Inn & Golf Resort
River Rd., Shawnee-on-Delaware
• 421-1500 ext. 1425, (800) SHAWNEE ext. 1413

The course here was designed by A.W. Tillinghast in 1907. Golfers will find 27 holes of championship golf at Shawnee, just 2 miles off Interstate 80 Exit 53.

On two holes, golfers must shoot across the Delaware River. The 177-yard 7th on the Blue Course goes from the island back to the inn. The green is nearly completely surrounded by woods. On the 159-yard 2nd hole of the Red Course, the destination is an elevated, heavily bunkered green on the island. Golfers hit their tee shots from the edge of the river, with the mountains in New Jersey as a backdrop. Both holes are par 3s.

The pretty par 5 No. 2 on the Blue Course runs parallel to the Delaware River.

The three nine-hole courses range in distance from 3438 yards (Blue Course) to 3227 yards (White Course); the Red Course is 3362 yards. Each course is par 36.

In addition to the bar and restaurant facilities at the inn, the course offers a driving range, lessons, a practice area, lockers, showers, a pro shop and a clubhouse.

Greens fees, including cart, are $46 per person Monday through Friday, $66 per person on weekends. Guests of the inn or timesharing facilities pay $33 and $43, respectively. After 4:30 PM, unlimited golf costs $20. See this chapter's callout for more information about this historic inn and golf resort.

Water Gap Country Club
Mountain Rd., off Pa. Hwy. 611, Delaware Water Gap • 476-0300

Built in 1922, this 18-hole par 72 roller coaster originally was called Wolf Hollow Country Club and was the birthplace of the Eastern Open.

Dramatic elevation changes produce tricky rolls and can turn seemingly great shots into nightmares. Bunkers are plentiful; fairways, narrow; and greens, small. First-time players, even scratch golfers, will have difficulty making par here.

Holes No. 5 and No. 14 present completely blind shots, and No. 12 is a tricky par 3 that travels 201 yards from an elevated tee, across a pond to an elevated green fronted by a 60-by-40-foot bunker. The total yardage of 6216 gives little indication of the difficulty of play at Water Gap.

The restaurant at this country club is a local favorite for both golfers and non-golfers and is reviewed in our Restaurants chapter. Also available are a pro shop, lessons, lockers, showers and a practice area.

Rates for nonmembers and guests are $18 on weekdays and $26 on holidays and weekends. The twilight special for play after 4 PM is $17 Mondays and Tuesdays and $20 on Saturdays and Sundays. Cart rentals are $32 for 18 holes and $16 for 9 holes. Carts are required for all players teeing off before 4 PM. Various membership programs are available.

Stroudsburg/
East Stroudsburg

Caesars Pocono Palace Golf Course
U.S. Hwy. 209 at Echo Lake, Marshalls Creek
• 588-6692 ext. 159

Trees lining the fairways make this a tougher-than-average nine-hole par 35. The course is relatively flat (especially by Pocono standards), and the greens are fast. At 2981 yards, Caesars is longer than most nine-hole courses in the Poconos.

Lessons, a practice area, a pro shop, a restaurant and bar and a driving range are among the amenities at this resort course.

Greens fees are $12 weekdays and $15 on weekends. Carts are $22 for two people. Guests of the resort receive preference for tee times.

Evergreen Park Golf Course
Cherry Ln., Analomink • 421-7721

Part of the Penn Hills resort complex, this par 35 is considered by local players as one of the Poconos' best nine-hole courses. Eight holes have sand traps, and four have water hazards. Irons receive a workout here. The greens are typically in very good condition, and pin placements change daily.

Evergreen offers lessons, a pro shop, a practice area, a clubhouse, a snack bar and a restaurant.

During the week, greens fees are $16; weekend and holiday fees are $19. Carts rent for $16 for nine holes and $24 for 18 holes. However, for golfers who enjoy the exercise, the course is relatively flat and easy to walk. Hand carts are available for rent for $3. After 2 PM, greens fees are $10. A discount package is offered on Friday, Saturday and Sunday after 2 PM: For $35, two people receive greens fees and cart rental for the entire day. Seniors receive discounts every day.

Glen Brook Country Club
Glenbrook Rd., Stroudsburg • 421-3680

An older (built in 1924) 18-hole par 72, Glen Brook is tucked away in the woods west of Stroudsburg.

It is a challenging 6536-yard scenic beauty, accessible to the public. Noteworthy holes include No. 7, referred to as the "airplane hole" because it plays from one plateau to another, and No. 5, which features a difficult confrontation with a creek.

Twelve guest suites on the property overlook a trout stream and are a two-minute walk from the first tee.

Facilities here include a driving range, showers, a practice area, a pro shop, clubhouse, lockers, a snack bar and a restaurant with a bar. Lessons are also available.

Greens fees are $18 on weekdays and $24 on weekends. Carts cost $16 per person. Senior discounts are offered Monday and Tuesday, and reduced twilight rates take effect at 3 PM.

Mountain Manor Inn & Golf Course
Golf Course Dr. off U.S. Hwy. 209, Marshalls Creek • 223-1290

Of the four nine-hole courses here, the Orange and the Silver provide the best 18-hole combination at 6427 yards. The views of the Delaware Water Gap from the Orange course are exceptionally picturesque. The Silver boasts a 670-yard par 6 monster.

Those looking for an easy walk over flat, open land should try the Blue and Yellow courses, which measure 6233 yards. They are shorter and easier to play.

Mountain Manor has both a PGA and a LPGA pro who offer lessons. Other facilities include a pro shop, practice area, showers, lockers, a snack bar, a clubhouse and a restaurant/bar. To best understand the subtleties of playing here, pick up a copy of a book written by the course pros that gives hole-by-hole tips on how to approach each shot. The book costs $5 and is available in the pro shop.

Weekday greens fees are $18; weekend fees are $28. Cart rentals are $18 for nine holes, $27 for 18 holes, $40.50 for 27 holes and $54 for 36 holes. Twilight rates (after 3 PM weekdays and after 4 PM weekends) are $10.

Terra Greens Golf Course
5006 Poole Rd., East Stroudsburg • 421-0120

A nine-hole par 36, Terra Greens has seven holes that are at least 350 yards long. (The total yardage is 3130.) This course is trickier than the average nine-holer. Greens are long and hard, and natural hazards such as trees and water that encase the greens and fairways are used effectively. Hole No. 2, a 480-yard par 5, runs parallel to a beautiful lake.

A small pro shop and a practice area are provided. Greens fees are $15 weekdays and $20 weekends. After 3 PM, fees are $10. Carts are $15 for nine holes and $20 for 18 holes. Club rentals ($5) and pull-cart rentals ($2) are available.

Mount Pocono Area

Buck Hill Golf Club
Golf Dr., Buck Hill Falls • 595-7730

Designer Donald Ross created the original 18 holes at Buck Hill, which were completed in 1906. Nine holes were added later.

The course was once part of a large resort that has since closed. However, the course remains in operation and is open to the public.

The Blue/White combination is the toughest, while the Blue and Red played together provide the best scenery. The course is heavily wooded, with rolling terrain and a creek providing natural hazards. The total yardage ranges from 6156 to 6496, depending on which combination is played.

No. 5 on the Red Course is considered by many locals to be the most difficult par 4 in the Poconos. It plays 470 yards. Shots must be

INSIDERS' TIPS

The Pocono Mountains Vacation Bureau publishes a golf brochure that provides a detailed map of locations and other information about 12 of the region's top courses. Call (800) 762-6667 to have a free copy mailed to you.

long and accurate. The green is frighteningly small.

On the Blue Course, No. 7 is a tough par 3 set on a hillside and featuring a significant gully between the tee and the green.

Lessons, a driving range, showers, a practice area, pro shop, lockers and a restaurant/bar are accessible to golfers. The semiprivate course costs $45 on weekdays and $65 on weekends. Discount rates apply after 3 PM on weekdays ($25) and after 4 PM weekends ($40). Cart fees are included and required. Memberships and group rates are available.

Mount Airy Lodge "The 18 Best"
Woodland Rd., off Pa. Hwy. 611, Mount Pocono • 839-8811

As the name implies, this course re-creates the best 18 holes in golf from around the world, including such fabled facilities as Pebble Beach and Augusta. Mount Airy is a public resort course designed for experienced players.

The 7123-yard par 72 course boasts 96 sand traps, and water comes into play on 10 holes. One of the best holes in the Poconos is the 350-yard, par 5 No. 16, which has bunkers on both sides of the fairway and a green surrounded by water and bunkers.

On the grounds of the course, golfers may utilize lessons, a driving range, a practice area, a pro shop, a clubhouse and a restaurant/bar.

Greens fees for the general public are

$55.90 Monday through Thursday and $65.90 Friday through Sunday. Guests of the resort pay $40.90 and $45.90 respectively. Carts are included. The twilight special is $20, including cart, after 3 PM every day. Advance tee times are required.

Mount Pocono Golf Course
Pa. Hwys. 940 and 611, Mount Pocono • 839-6061

This nine-hole course in the heart of the Poconos is perfect for young people and senior citizens. It is short (2400 yards) and easy to walk. Some holes are wooded; some have water.

Weekday greens fees are $9; on weekends, $10. Cart rental is $14 for nine holes and $20 for 18 holes. Club rentals are $4, and pull carts are $2. The facility has a pro shop. Discounts are available for senior citizens.

Mountain Laurel Resort & Conference Center
Pa. Hwy. 534 off I-80 Exit 41, White Haven • 443-7424, 443-8411

After an easy start, this 18-hole course gets very challenging. Holes No. 6 through No. 10 all have water, as does No. 13. Other than the first five holes, which are basically open, the course is wooded. At No. 10, a 360-yard par 4, golfers must navigate a narrow fairway and land on an island green. Par is 72, and the length is 6798 yards.

Amenities include a driving range, practice area, pro shop, clubhouse, snack bar, lockers, lessons and a restaurant/bar.

Greens fees, including cart, are $34 weekdays and $44 weekends. Seniors receive a discount every day. Reserved tee times are a must.

Pine Hollow Golf Center
Pa. Hwy. 390, Canadensis • 595-7202

Those just learning the game or experienced players looking for a good practice round will enjoy Pine Hollow. It is a beautifully landscaped, well-maintained nine-hole par 3 course. At 1400 yards (par 27), it is easy to walk and ideal for a family outing. Greens fees are always $5. Clubs are provided as are a practice area, pro shop and restaurant and bar. Senior citizens receive discounts.

Pocono Manor Inn & Golf Resort
Pa. Hwy. 314, Pocono Manor • 839-7111

Of the two par 72, 18-hole courses at this resort, the East is shorter (6480 yards) but more difficult — hilly, with small greens. Grass bunkers add a Scottish-links flavor. It is preferred by seasoned players. The West Course (6857 yards) is newer, flatter and more wide open. The Senior Pro Am was held on the East Course, which was built in 1902.

The par 3 No. 7 on the East Course runs 77 yards down over a cliff. The layout on No. 7 is typical of the physical characteristics of this course, which is set in the wooded mountains.

Pocono Manor offers golfers a driving range, practice area, lessons, pro shop, clubhouse, snack bar, lockers and a restaurant/bar.

Greens fees, including cart, are $33 weekdays and $43 weekends. Twilight play after 3 PM is $18. Advance tee times are necessary, except for twilight play.

Skytop Lodge
Pa. Hwy. 390, Skytop • 595-7401

Everything about this elegant resort is first-class, including the golf course. It is an 18-hole, par 71, 6256-yard excursion through a wooded mountain top. Shotmakers will enjoy playing here because placement is always crucial. The course is short, with tight fairways and small greens. Golfers face the toughest challenge on the last hole, a 352-yard par 4 with an elevated green bordered by a creek in front, a bunker on the right and a lake on the left. Many golf balls have tried to find the pin, never to be heard from again.

While at Skytop golfers have access to lessons, showers, a practice area, a pro shop, clubhouse lockers and a restaurant/bar.

Guests of the resort and club members receive preferred tee times. Greens fees are $35 per person weekdays and $49 on weekends. Carts rent for $35 and are required. Call ahead for information on non-guest play.

Split Rock Golf Course
Pa. Hwy. 903, Lake Harmony • 722-9111 ext. 774, (800) 255-7625

A nine-hole resort course open to the public, Split Rock is a par 35 that winds through the woods. It is scenic and well-maintained. The fairways are narrow. No. 6, a downhill par 3 that plays 200 yards, is a local favorite.

A driving range, lessons, a practice area, pro shop and a restaurant/bar are among the amenities.

Greens fees are $17 for nine holes and $25 for 18 holes during the week and $22 and $35 on weekends. All prices include a cart. The course is remote. To get here, take Interstate 80 to Pa. Highway 115 North. Go to the traffic light and turn left onto Pa. Highway 940. The course will be on the left two miles from the intersection.

West End

Hideaway Hills Golf Club
Carny Rd., off U.S. Hwy. 209, Kresgeville • (610) 681-6000

Completed in 1994, this public 18-hole, par 72 has become very popular with area golfers. The 6980-yard course is exceptionally well-kept.

Golfers encounter a little bit of everything here, including elevated greens, 84 bunkers and five lakes. After a comfortable start, holes No. 7 through No. 16 provide some interesting challenges.

The par 3 No. 7 is already a local legend. Its green sits 160 feet below the tee. For extra

Shawnee Inn & Golf Resort

Shawnee is probably the most famous course in the Poconos. It certainly has the most colorful history.

The course was designed by A.W. Tillinghast in 1907. This converted farm land along the Delaware River was the first project of Tillinghast, who became one of the top course designers in the United States.

The course's heyday began in 1912 when engineer and inventor C.C. Worthington built the Buckwood Inn, named for his 5,000-acre estate, Buckwood Park. His family owned the Worthington Pump and Machinery Corporation, which supplied the United States Navy with nearly 90 percent of its marine pumps between 1855 and 1944. Worthington retired from that business, founded the Worthington Automobile Company and introduced foreign cars into the American market. He then decided to settle permanently in Shawnee and made many improvements to the community, including building Worthington Hall, a meeting place for local residents. Property he owned on the New Jersey side of the Delaware River was ceded to that state and became Worthington State Park.

Close-up

From the beginning, the inn was destined to be different. Its floors and walls were concrete instead of wood, making it less likely to catch fire and safer than most other resorts of the day. The dining room featured the best produce from gardens on the property and nearby farms. An on-site creamery provided all of the dairy products. The drinking water was gravity-fed into each room from Sunfish Pond in New Jersey.

When maintaining the golf course became a concern, Worthington marshalled his creative skills. An experiment involving a Scotsman and his flock of sheep failed. So Worthington invented the first commercially successful gang mower. His device became popular; as a result, he founded the Shawnee Mower Company.

Being very proud of his course, Worthington invited a group of professional golfers to the Buckwood in 1912. Their meeting resulted in the creation of the Professional Golfers Association. The PGA championships were first played here, and the tournament returned in 1938, when course pro Sam Snead lost on the last hole.

The Buckwood prospered until the Great Depression changed the nature of travel. People no longer vacationed for several months. Since the resort was only open summers at the time, the number of guests fell greatly. Worthington sold it a year before he died at age 91.

Manwalamink Inc. purchased the Buckwood and renamed it Shawnee Inn. The head of that company was Fred Waring, who was internationally famous as the band leader of Fred Waring and the Pennsylvanians.

Surprisingly, Waring, like Worthington, had a flair for inventions and helped develop the Waring Blender, the first electric blender in the country.

To respond to growing demand for sheet music of his recordings, Waring formed Shawnee Press, which became a leading music-publishing house.

Because of Waring's tremendous popularity at the time, the resort became a prosperous, exclusive summer getaway. All his musical activities, including creating, rehearsing and broadcasting his radio show at Worthington Hall, were centered around Shawnee Inn.

Waring's celebrity status attracted many other important entertainers. His good friend Jackie Gleason played his first golf at Shawnee. He learned the game there while making the resort his summer home. Gleason's first round was a 143. Fifteen months later, he was consistently breaking 80.

Other celebrities who frequently stayed at Shawnee were Art Carney, George Gobel, Ed Sullivan, Eddie Fisher, Perry Como and Arnold Palmer, who met his wife at the inn's pro shop where she worked.

By 1974, Waring realized he could not devote enough time to the inn's operation and sold it to Karl Hope, who added timesharing and a ski area to make the resort a year-round destination. Olympic gold medal winner Jean-Claude Killy was hired as the first director of ski operations. He designed some of the trails still used today.

Hope sold the inn to Charles Kirkwood in 1977. He further expanded the recreational opportunities by adding an indoor pool, racquet club and a children's play area.

Still, the golf course is the star attraction. Tillinghast designed the layout by instinct, walking through the existing woods and deciding how to best utilize the scenery around him.

Most of the holes are on an island in the Delaware River. The original 18 holes (the Blue and Red courses) are rated higher than the newer nine holes (the White Course). A couple holes require shots across the river to an island. Others feature greens that are surrounded by woods or elevated and heavily bunkered. From some tees, the mountains across the river in New Jersey serve as a backdrop.

Shawnee Inn & Golf Resort is on River Road in Shawnee-on-Delaware. Call (800) SHAWNEE ext. 1413 or 421-1500 for information and see this chapter's entry for course details.

---

fun, the green is undulating; and a stream awaits those who hit short. No. 15 (a par 4) features an island green amid a 3-acre lake.

Complementing the course are a driving range, lockers, a practice area, pro shop, clubhouse, and restaurant and bar. Lessons are offered.

Greens fees and cart are $37 weekdays and $47 weekends.

Indian Mountain Golf Course
Pa. Hwy. 534, Kresgeville
• (610) 681-4534

The owners call their 3203-yard, par 36 nine-hole course the "longest in the Poconos." The fairways are open, and the greens are large. One of the toughest holes is the par 3 No. 8, which has an elevated tee.

Greens fees for unlimited play are $10 weekdays and $12 weekends. Carts are $12 for nine holes and $18 for 18 holes. You'll find a full pro shop, club rentals, a picnic area under roof, lessons and a luncheonette.

The facility also has a nine-hole, par 27 pitch-and-putt course, which is 971 yards long. The cost for it is $5 for 18 holes.

Mahoning Valley Golf Course
Pa. Hwy. 443, Tamaqua • 386-4515

Terrific greens are the star attraction at this 18-hole, par 70, 5785-yard public course. There are a few trees, but most of the course is open. The front nine holes are slightly hillier than the back.

Included at Mahoning Valley are a driving range, showers, a practice area, pro shop, clubhouse, snack bar, lockers and lessons.

Greens fees are $11 weekdays and $14 weekends. Carts are $20 weekdays and $22 weekends. Twilight rates after 3 PM are $7.50.

FYI
Unless otherwise noted, the area code for all phone numbers listed in this guide is 717.

Milford Area

Cliff Park Golf Course and Inn
S.R. 2001 (off U.S. Hwy. 6), Milford
• 296-6491

This nine-hole par 35 is a tough course. Good luck breaking par. The course pro likes the 198-yard par 3 No. 3, which travels from an elevated tee to an elevated green. Local seniors love to play here because the course provides short, scenic fairways. Many people choose to walk. At 3115 yards, the course plays long.

Jack Nicklaus' Great Bear Golf & Country Club

Fortunately for the Poconos, Jack Nicklaus enjoys designing golf courses more than playing on them these days. One of his recent projects is the Great Bear Golf & Country Club course north of Marshalls Creek off U.S. Highway 209.

Saying he "doesn't want to accept byes," the Golden Bear believes his days as a touring pro are nearly over. He has played in 147 consecutive major tournaments and plans to end the streak at 150. Acknowledging that his level of play has declined, Nicklaus does not want to take a seat in a tournament that could go to a talented young player. "I don't play golf as well as I used to. Lately, I haven't been playing much on the weekends," he says with a laugh, referring to his not making the cut for the final rounds at some events.

But do not feel sorry for Nicklaus. His Paragon Construction company currently has 30 courses under construction and 127 in use around the world. He began designing courses as a hobby in the mid-1960s when he saw owners putting great effort into poorly thought-out courses. By the 1970s that casual interest had become a major business venture.

"I just needed the money," Nicklaus says jokingly when asked why he pursued the occupation more seriously. "Heck, I wasn't making a living playing golf anymore. I believe that golfers can build better golf courses because they have a better feel for how a course should play. This allowed me to expand into other things and really build a business that was going to be here beyond my golf game.

"I love to put something on a piece of ground that is going to be here long beyond my lifetime. It also gives me the opportunity to develop a business my family can be involved in."

Photo: Brian Hineline

Jack Nicklaus has designed an 18-hole golf course that serves as the centerpiece of Great Bear Golf & Country Club.

In the mid-1980s, Nicklaus was asked to design courses that would be able to host professional tournaments. This gave him a reputation for building tough courses that featured long fairways and undulating greens. Today, he creates less-demanding courses intended to challenge, but not overwhelm, the typical country-club member.

When Nicklaus designs a course, he takes an active, hands-on approach; it does not earn his name as a mere marketing tool. During his numerous visits to Great Bear, Nicklaus regularly moved greens and added or removed bunkers as the work progressed.

This private country-club course is scheduled to be ready for play by the summer of 1997. Nicklaus says the course will be in peak playing condition by that fall.

Photo: Brian Hineline

Workers complete construction on one of the holes at Great Bear, a Jack Nicklaus-designed course north of Marshalls Creek.

Nicklaus claims the course is designed for "good, playable fun." On a difficulty scale of one to 10, he gives Great Bear a seven. Every hole is lined with trees. Other natural elements such as wetlands, lakes, streams and stone rows figure into the landscape.

The 18-hole course is 6754 yards from the pro tees, and par is 71. The views throughout are magnificent. Nicklaus' vote for most photogenic spot is the second shot on No. 18, with the clubhouse in the background on top of a hill. Asked which holes will give golfers the most headaches, Nicklaus listed No. 3, No. 5 and No. 18. Nicklaus does not envision a signature hole; instead, he expects golfers will gravitate to numerous holes based on personal preference.

The initiation fee as of October 1996 (it will increase with every 25 members) is $26,500, and annual dues for full golf membership are $2,400. In addition to the course, there will be a 15,000-square-foot clubhouse and restaurant, a full pro shop, tennis courts and an outdoor swimming pool. Lavish homes, some of the most expensive being built in the Poconos, are being constructed along the course. See our Real Estate chapter for more information.

Members at Great Bear will be permitted to join the Jack Nicklaus International Club. For a $250 annual fee, a golfer will be able to obtain tee times at more than 75 Nicklaus-designed courses around the world.

For further information on membership and available home sites at Great Bear Golf & Country Club, call 223-2000.

The course is on the grounds of the lovely Cliff Park Inn. Lessons, showers, a practice area, a pro shop, a snack bar and a restaurant/bar are provided at the course.

Rates are $12 weekdays and $23 weekends and holidays. After 5 PM, rates are $6 weekdays and $13 weekends. Carts are $12 for nine holes and $20 for 18 holes. Pull carts ($5) and club rentals ($11) are available. Season memberships are $370 per person with discounts for seniors and students.

Fernwood Resort & Country Club
U.S. Hwy. 209, Bushkill • 588-8500

This resort course is user-friendly but still holds a few surprises. It is 18 holes, par 72 and 6108 yards long. The most challenging hole is No. 13; woods encase the sloped fairway of this 348-yard par 4. The entire course is hillier than average for the Poconos.

Lessons, showers, a pro shop, clubhouse, snack bar, a practice area, lockers and a restaurant and bar are among the facilities at Fernwood.

Weekday greens fees are $25, and weekends are $35. Carts are $15 per person. The twilight discount begins at 4 PM and is $15, including cart.

Tamiment Resort & Conference Center
Bushkill Falls Rd., Tamiment • 588-6652

Robert Trent Jones designed this 18-hole, par 72 resort course, which was completed in 1958. A comfortable balance is achieved between long and short holes. That said, everything else about the course is big. The total yardage (6858) is filled out by huge bunkers, generous greens and football field-size fairways.

The prettiest hole is the 580-yard, par 5 No. 17, which provides golfers with panoramic views of the surrounding countryside. Perhaps the toughest hole is No. 6, which is walled in by trees, leaving a narrow path to a green guarded by four traps.

The course features lessons, showers, a practice area, a pro shop, clubhouse, snack bar, lockers and a restaurant and bar. Club rentals are available.

Greens fees are $40 weekdays and $45 weekends, including cart. Players must use carts.

Lake Wallenpaupack Area

Cricket Hill Golf Club
U.S. Hwy. 6, Hawley • 226-4366

A good short game helps at this 18-hole, par 70, 5603-yard course. This public course starts very open, but things get much tighter on the back nine. Eleven ponds are sprinkled throughout. A popular hole is the par 5, 455-yard No. 12, which starts with a quick dogleg then hops over a pond to a figure-8 green.

Among the amenities are a driving range, lessons, showers, a practice area, a pro shop, clubhouse, lockers and a restaurant/bar.

Greens fees are $20 weekdays and $22 on weekends. Carts are $18. After 4 PM, greens fees are reduced to $12 for all the golf you can play.

Red Maple Golf Course
Pa. Hwy. 296, South Canaan • 937-4543

This nine-hole, par 33 provides more tricks than the average short course. Its 2300 yards of rolling fairways, water and trees keep play interesting. You will need to be a skillful shotmaker to score well here. The natural hazards present a surprising number of potential problems. Do not let the short yardage fool you into thinking this is an easy course.

A pro shop and a snack bar are provided.

Greens fees are $10 weekdays and $12 weekends. Carts are $15.

The Country Club at Woodloch Springs
1 Woodloch Dr., Hawley • 685-2100

Many serious golfers in the Poconos regard this course as perhaps the most professional operation in the region as far as playability, staff and facilities. The 18-hole par 72 course is accessible to guests of Woodloch Pines resort, property owners or renters at Woodloch Springs and guests of other Pocono resorts as explained in this chapter's Insiders' Tip.

The course pro describes the course as challenging, offering "above average" difficulty. Rolling hills, trees and creeks are present throughout. As little of the surrounding countryside as possible was disturbed during construction of the course, which is just over five years old. The total yardage of 6579 gives an indication of the need for some long-driving ability.

The signature hole is No. 14, a par 5, 577-yard monster known as the Hell's Gate Gorge. To be successful here, golfers must carry a tee shot of more than 220 yards off a 200-foot drop through the gorge.

Three PGA pros are available for lessons. Amenities include a clubhouse, driving range, practice area, restaurant and bar, lockers and a swimming pool. In addition, the impressive facilities of the resort are explained in our Accommodations chapter.

Greens fees, including cart, are $46 weekdays and $60 on weekends. Reservations are strongly suggested.

Driving Ranges

Looking for a little practice before tackling those long Pocono fairways? Here are some driving ranges that will help you polish your skills:

Delaware Water Gap

Water Gap Driving Range
Pa. Hwy. 611, Delaware Water Gap
• 476-0130

This range has a very good pro shop that offers club repairs. Refreshments are available.

Rates for the range are $4 for approximately 35 to 45 balls and $6 for approximately 95 to 105 balls. Hours of operation are 9 AM to 9:15 PM on weekdays and 8 AM to 9:15 PM on weekends.

Stroudsburg/ East Stroudsburg

Golf Center Plus Driving Range
Pa. Hwy. 611, Bartonsville • 620-0820

As the name implies, there is more to do here than just visit a driving range. Added attractions include an 18-hole miniature golf course, a pro shop with club repair, batting cages, go-cart tracks for both adults and children, an arcade and a snack bar.

Fees for the driving range, which offers astro-turf tees, are $3 for a small bucket (25 to 30) of balls and $5 for a large bucket that holds about twice as many. Clubs may be rented for $1 with a $10 deposit.

Hours from Memorial Day to Labor Day are 10 AM to 10 PM every day. In spring and fall, the center is open the same hours but only Friday through Sunday.

Hamlen Golf Practice Range
Airport Rd., East Stroudsburg • 424-6376

Local golfers enjoy this range because it is rather secluded and has no other distractions. It's not part of a fun park, so it attracts only those interested in practicing their swings.

The operation isn't fancy — just a large open area and some chairs. The range covers roughly 265 yards before it hits woods. No clubs or artificial tees are provided. Snacks may be purchased in the small pro shop.

The range is adjacent to the airport and not visible from the road. Golfers must use the road leading into Stroudsburg-Pocono Airport.

Rates are $2.25 for 24 golf balls and $4 for 55. The range is open from 3:30 PM to sundown, perfect for after-work sessions, Tuesday through Friday. But do not arrive late on a Thursday and expect to stay for long; that's a mowing day. On Saturday and Sunday, hours are 10 AM to sundown, and the range is closed Monday. Hamlen closes for the season after Labor Day.

Mount Pocono Area

940 Golf N' Fun
Pa. Hwy. 940, Pocono Lake • 646-0700

When not on the 275-yard practice range, golfers may enjoy an 18-hole miniature golf course, an arcade and a snack bar. Group lessons may be arranged.

Since there are 20 tees, you should have no trouble finding a home on the range. Balls cost $4 per bucket of 40, and clubs rent for $1.

The park is open from 10 AM to 10 PM every day.

West End

Golf Plantation
U.S. Hwy. 209, Kresgeville
• (610) 681-5959

Regarded as one of the best driving ranges in the Poconos, Golf Plantation features covered tees, a putting green, a sand bunker and a complete pro shop capable of handling all types of club repair. Clubs may be custom-fitted with a Sportech swing-analyzing computer. Private lessons and a regularly scheduled golf school provide tips for those looking to improve their game.

In addition to the driving range, there is a tougher-than-average miniature golf course. Refreshments are available at the ice cream parlor/snack bar.

Photo: Pocono Mountains Vacation Bureau, Inc.

Enjoy more than a dozen fine golf courses throughout the Pocono region.

Rates for golf balls for the range are $4 for 40, $5.50 for 80 and $10 for 160.

Golf Plantation opens at 10 AM Monday through Friday and 9 AM on Saturday and Sunday. It remains open until 11 PM Wednesday through Sunday and 10 PM Monday and Tuesday.

Lake Wallenpaupack Area

Costa's Family Fun Park
U.S. Hwy. 6, 3 miles east of Lake Wallenpaupack, Lords Valley • 226-8585

Costa's provides plenty of entertainment for the entire family while the golfer practices. In addition to the driving range, facilities include batting cages, an 18-hole miniature golf course, two go-kart tracks, a children's play area and an arcade. A restaurant and ice cream parlor offer fast food.

The driving range has two target greens and 19 astro-turf tees. Baskets of balls are available in three sizes: 28 for $3.50, 42 for $4.50 and about 57 for $5.50. Clubs, including options for children and left-handed players, are provided free.

The facility is open every day from 11 AM to midnight.

Golf Park Plus

Golf Park Dr. (off Pa. Hwy. 590), Lake Ariel • 689-4996

In addition to a driving range, Golf Park Plus offers bumper boats, go-carts, two 18-hole miniature golf courses, a snack bar and an arcade.

Golf balls are purchased with tokens. Each $5 token is good for 40 balls. Golfers can take advantage of a special $20 rate for six tokens. Drivers and irons may be rented for $1.

The park is open every day from 9 AM to 10 PM.

Moss Hollow Creek Golf Park Plus
Golf Park Dr., Hamlin • 689-4996

The driving range at Moss Hollow is unique in the Poconos because it features eight over-water tees among its 20 astro-turf tees. It perhaps best simulates conditions encountered on a golf course. Plus even long-hitters will have trouble reaching the far end of the range some 450 yards away.

Non-golfers have plenty to do at Moss Hollow as well. The two miniature golf courses boast such obstacles as islands, waterfalls, bridges, bunkers, streams and lagoons. Also featured are go-karts, bumper boats, a train ride for children, an arcade and a snack bar.

Tokens must be purchased to obtain golf balls for the driving range. They cost $5 and are good for 40 balls. For $20 you receive a special rate of six tokens. Clubs may be rented for $1. Private and group lessons are available.

Open everyday at 9 AM, the park closes at 10 PM Sunday through Thursday and at 10:30 PM on Friday and Saturday.

Milford Area

Matamoras Golf Driving Range
U.S. Hwy. 6 and U.S. Hwy. 209, Matamoras • 491-4631

Next to the Best Western Inn at Hunt's Landing, this range has automatic tees and a grass tee area. In addition, there is an 18-hole miniature golf course.

Rates for the range are $3 for 25 balls, $5 for 50 and $7 for 75. Club rental is $1. Lessons are available.

The Matamoras range is open from 9 AM to 10 PM daily.

Golf Schools

The following schools offer extended lessons at three area courses.

In addition, single-day lessons may be arranged at most courses and driving ranges as indicated in the individual listings above. Call the course pro at the facility of your choice for cost and available times.

Delaware Water Gap

Swing's the Thing Golf School
Shawnee Inn, River Rd., Shawnee-on-Delaware • 421-1500 ext. 1704

The instructor here is PGA pro Dick Farley, recognized by *Golf Magazine* as one of the best teachers in the United States. Students receive a stop-action video and textbook as part of their instruction.

The three-day program includes all greens fees, 18 hours of instruction, three lunches and lodging.

Commuters pay $695 for three days without accommodations. Packages including lodging cost $875 per person. The schools are offered May through September.

PGA pro Gordon Neely also offers private lessons for those who want single-day instruction. A half-hour session is $35, and an hour is $60.

Mount Pocono Area

Professional Golf School of America
Mount Airy Lodge, Pa. hwys. 940 and 611, Mount Pocono • 839-8811

Each daily session at this school requires a minimum of five hours of instruction designed to improve your swing. The practice areas of the course and video analysis are used extensively. A student-teacher ratio of 4-to-1 is maintained to ensure maximum individual attention. After instruction, students try their new knowledge on the Mount Airy course, which is patterned after 18 of the best golf holes in the country.

An aerial view of the beautiful Shawnee Inn and golf course.

Schools run for one, two, three or five days. Commuter packages, which include lunch; are $150 per person. Those staying at the resort receive all meals and lodging in addition to the lessons for $225 per person based on double occupancy.

Milford Area

Bill Mackel's Golf School
Cliff Park Inn • S.R. 2001 (off U.S. Hwy. 6), Milford • 296-6491

Participants at this school stay at the inn for three days and two nights and receive 10 hours of instruction on a flexible schedule. Breakfasts and dinners are included.

Other options include less extensive, single-day lessons. The schools are offered from April to October.

Call the inn or Mackel directly at 296-7910 for current rates and availability.

The majority of the area loosely defined as the Poconos is on the Pocono Plateau, an uneven land mass ranging in height from 1,900 to 2,200 feet above sea level whose boundaries are the Appalachian Mountains in the south and the Moosic Mountains in the west.

Our Natural World

Whether appreciated on a leisurely drive or on a more rigorous hike, the Pocono Mountains provide enough natural attractions to keep people entertained for a weekend or a lifetime. Pristine lakes, gorgeous waterfalls and lush woodlands are features of the Pocono Mountains landscape. (Our Parks and Recreation chapters give more details about places to see plants and animals.) To contrast with gray rocks and evergreens, winter brings white, glistening snow, punctuated with cardinals and blue jays flying through the air. After the muddy runoff of melted snow, the mountains and valleys break out in spots of brilliant blossoms. The whites, pinks and yellows of spring are joined by brighter yellows, reds, blues, purples and oranges in fields of wildflowers and gardens. Then, for the grand finale, nature's paintbrush works overtime to give us flaming foliage in the fall. These darker earth tones are a noticeable contrast to the more pastel colors of spring and summer.

Geology

The majority of the area loosely defined as the Poconos is on the Pocono Plateau. This uneven land mass ranges in height from 1,900 to 2,200 feet above sea level. Its boundaries are the Appalachian Mountains in the south and the Moosic Mountains in the west. The gradual slope of the plateau toward the north in lower Wayne County is less noticeable than the more striking Pocono Escarpment, the dramatic descent of the plateau as it approaches the Delaware River in the east. There you find some of the region's best-loved scenic spots, such as the Delaware Water Gap National Rec-

reation Area and the towns surrounding Mount Pocono.

As streams run from the lakes on the plateau to the river, they carve gorges and create waterfalls. Of the 75 significant, named waterfalls in Pennsylvania, 30 are in the Poconos. Many of the most popular waterfalls are in two bands called fall lines, which correspond to the plateau's most obvious drops.

The first fall line is centered around Mount Pocono and includes Swiftwater, Paradise, Buck Hill and Indian Ladder falls. Closer to the Delaware River, the second fall line contains Winona, Resica, Fulmer, Dingmans, Silver Thread, Raymondskill, Saw Kill and the nationally famous Bushkill Falls. These are scattered between Bushkill and Milford; their locations and accessibility are discussed in our Parks, Recreation and Attractions chapters.

A continental glacier invaded this area 15,000 to 20,000 years ago. This huge mass of moving ice scarred the land and produced lakes, streams and a few geological quirks.

Glacial waters melting and mixing with rock fragments created one of the world's largest natural potholes — the 40-feet-by-40-feet Archbald Pothole in Archbald State Park. Standing on a platform near the edge of the pothole, visitors stare into a large black hole, which presents the illusion of going on forever, deep into the earth.

Also geologically unique are boulder fields where the glacier dumped huge rocks as it traveled across the land. Hickory Run State Park, a former valley, now contains thousands of stones, loosely packed 12 feet deep in an area about 400 feet by 1,800 feet. Hickory Run Boulder Field is registered as a natural landmark and is the largest field of its type in the Appalachian Mountains. A similar deposit called Devil's Potato Patch, a jumble of boulders strewn along the top of a ridge, sits at the top of Little Gap.

The glacier also created large bodies of water, such as Lake Harmony, Saylors Lake, Deep Lake and Bruce Lake.

Residue of the Ice Age can be found throughout the region in the form of fossils. Prior to the glacial activity, about 500 million years ago, all of northeastern Pennsylvania was under water. Shell fragments and fossils of dinosaur-era sea creatures, such as brachiopods, trilobites and crinoids, can be discovered by both serious paleontologists and weekend rock hounds. Ferns and other plants also have been preserved in the rocks, particularly near the coal regions.

Many of the rock cliffs and outcroppings in the Poconos contain fossils, which might be 310 million to 405 million years old, from the Mississippian and Devonian periods. Look for them in excavation debris and in the loose stones at the bottoms of cliffs, especially in shale and limestone. Handy tools to carry are a small hammer, chisels, newspapers for wrapping delicate fossils, safety glasses, gloves, a knapsack and a first-aid kit (to stave off injuries — you know that it never rains when you carry an umbrella). Look for ripple marks and mudcracks in shale, then gently tap with your hammer to separate the layers of stone. Be sure to turn over rock fragments in your search. Always make sure to ask permission to look for fossils when entering private property.

Popular fossil-hunting spots include Beltsville State Park, the cliffs along Pa. Route 209 between Raymondskill Creek and Milford, and just north of Weissport along the Lehigh Canal. Perhaps the most amazing fossil discovery was the mastodon skeleton found in John Leap's peat bog near Marshalls Creek in the 1980s. Archaeologists were shocked to discover this preserved beast, which roamed the earth almost a million years ago, in a region known primarily for small fossils of plants and shellfish. Although the Poconos have been explored extensively in the last few decades by archeologists looking for fossils and Indian artifacts, our land has not yet given up all of its treasures.

Bogs and Forests

That mastodon's final resting place, the peat bog, is also a rare product of glacial melting. Common in Canada and New England, bogs are wetlands that host an unparalleled bounty of wildlife.

Because of limited amounts of nitrogen and phosphorus salts, plants not found anywhere else in the region thrive in the peat bogs. Sphagnum moss, with its gray-green leaf color and pink or red tips, is the key indicator of a bog. Its specialized cell structure allows it to absorb as much as 18 times its own weight in water. While the exotic plants growing over the brown water produces an otherworldly environment, bogs are not nearly as scary as they are often rumored to be. Perhaps you have heard stories of large snakes, quicksand or poisonous plants. Words such as "boogyman" and "bogus" originated in discussions of bogs. The truth is far less dangerous, but still very interesting.

Bogs form when water becomes covered by a mat of vegetation, eventually including shrubs and trees. Common plants in a Pocono bog are black spruce, bog rosemary and poison sumac, which people should avoid. Poison sumac, found only in bogs and swamps, grows as a tall shrub or small tree and has white berries. Contact with its leaves can cause an itching rash or worse. Consult a park ranger or doctor immediately if you suspect you have handled poison sumac.

Of special note are the carnivorous pitcher plant and sundew that use their leaves to trap small insects. Few fish or animals live in bogs, however, you might occaisionally see an assortment of frogs, salamanders and turtles. Because there is little wildlife in a bog, they are usually remarkably quiet, almost to the point of eeriness.

In addition to their value as natural resources, bogs produce peat moss, an essential ingredient for gardens. Pennsylvania ranks second in the country in the production of peat moss.

The most famous bog in the region, the Tannersville Cranberry Bog, boasts a 1,450-foot-long boardwalk for visitor use. It is owned by The Nature Conservancy, a national organization that purchases land containing valu-

The Gap

For nearly 170 years, the Delaware Water Gap, often regarded as one of the most striking natural wonders of our country, has been a popular tourist destination. This breathtaking gorge in the Kittatinny Ridge separates Mount Tammany (1,527 feet) on the New Jersey side and Mount Minsi (1,463 feet) on the Pennsylvania side.

The most likely theory behind the Delaware Water Gap's formation is that moving water wore down and pushed through a weak spot in the ridge. The combination of the water cutting down and the rocks on either side pressing up created the Gap hundreds of millions of years ago.

The first resort opened near the Delaware Water Gap in 1829. By the end of the 19th century, there were more than 20 places around the Gap to accommodate the vacationers who arrived from surrounding cities to bask in scenic beauty.

In these years before extensive travel, the mountain peaks separated by the large river were the most wild environment many people from New York and Philadelphia had ever seen. The mountains were as green as the city skyscrapers were gray and bleak. Try to imagine sitting in a passenger train, meandering through the gap and seeing vast expanses of trees, rock cliffs and water as blue as the sky for the first time. While still magnificent today, the Delaware Water Gap must have been overwhelming to visitors in the 1800s.

Today, the Delaware Water Gap is a gateway as well as a destination. Many people enjoy the passing glance at it as they travel Interstate 80 toward Pennsylvania through the Gap.

Those who choose to spend more time at the Gap find the geological marvel easily accessible. On the Pennsylvania side, a 2.7-mile portion of the Appalachian Trail guides hikers to the summit of Mount Minsi. The trail is slightly steep but well-marked. A shorter walk on the New Jersey side leads to the summit of Mount Tammany. This portion of the Appalachian Trail offers the more spectacular views of the two summits but is also more dangerous — watch young children closely.

More than 25 hot-air balloons fill the air over Delaware Water Gap for the Shawnee Autumn Hot Air Balloon Festival held in mid-October.

Hikers can sit on rock outcrops and view the entire Gap, surrounding towns and such birds of prey as hawks, eagles and ospreys.

You also can appreciate the Delaware Water Gap by car — simply pull into one of several scenic overlooks. Locals on lunch break favor Resort Point on Pa. Route 611 just south of the town of Delaware Water Gap. Along the same highway, Point of Gap and Arrow Island are ideal picnicking spots.

During the tourist heyday, Point of Gap was filled with souvenir stands where visitors would pay to look through a telescope at a rock formation resembling an Indian head on the New Jersey cliffs. Time and erosion have not been kind to the Indian; he is barely recognizable today.

able natural resources, and is accessible only on guided tours. Another significant bog lies adjacent to Lake Wallenpaupack in the Lacawac Sanctuary. (See our Parks chapter for more about the bogs.)

The Poconos region also has plenty of forest. Fall foliage tours are common, and many vacationers plan their trips to coincide with the leaves changing colors.

Generally the brightest colors are produced after long, dry summers and cool, damp days in fall. Trees are tricked into ending photosynthesis more quickly, which means the trees no longer produce the sugar needed to keep the lush green color of chlorophyll. The underlying pigments emerge, producing the striking rainbow of color.

The best time to catch the spectacular reds, oranges and yellows is during the second week of October. The northern counties and higher elevations are first treated to this special show, which then continues southward.

From mid-September to the end of October, the foliage along our winding back roads becomes enveloped in the colors of fall. Some of the more popular roads to travel to view the fall foliage are Pa. Highway 507 near Lake Wallenpaupack; U.S. Highway 6 from Hawley/Honesdale to Matamoras; U.S. Highway 209 through the Delaware Water Gap National Recreation Area; U.S. Highway 209 from Stroudsburg to Jim Thorpe; Pa. Highway 402 from Marshalls Creek to Porters Lake; and Pa. Highway 390 from Mountainhome to Skytop. For the best panoramic view, take Pa. Highway 611 to Tannersville and drive to the top of the mountain at Big Pocono State Park. On a clear day, the leaves in three states will be visible. For updates on the changing colors, call the Pocono Mountains Vacation Bureau's Pocono Fall Foliage Hotline at 421-5565.

There are five major types of forests in the Poconos — northern hardwood (beech, birch and maple) to the north; mixed oak to the south and east; hemlock and white pine in scattered pockets, particularly in Monroe and Pike counties; chestnut oak to the south and along the Delaware River; and scrub oak in the south and west.

Most of the trees standing today are relatively young. Heavy cutting of virgin forests occurred in the late 19th and early 20th centuries when farmers cleared fields for farms. During this time, loggers harvested many other trees and tanneries used tree bark to change animal hides into leather. Mining and quarrying activities also scarred the land and destroyed many trees.

As a result, few trees are more than 100 years old. The best place to find the oldest trees is near the stone rows littered throughout the forests. Back when the farmers cleared their fields, they dumped the stones along the boundaries of their farms. The surrounding trees were spared because the land on which they stood was not used to grow crops.

While a variety of flowers add color to the fields and forests, the prevalence of mountain laurel, Pennsylvania's state flower, deserves special mention. Its white-pink flowers bloom from late May through early July. Did you know that mountain laurel is considered toxic? It is safe to touch but should not be eaten. Ingesting a small portion will cause flu-like symptoms and large quantities can be fatal. The leaves are poisonous to deer and livestock as well.

Mountains

Mountains are responsible for the Poconos' popularity as a scenic destination. The region would not be the tourist destination it is today without them. Their ridges and valleys create many of our natural wonders, such as waterfalls, streams and gorges. The Delaware Water Gap, our most famous natural landmark, would not exist if not for the Kittatinny Ridge and the river that cut into it. The scenery's diversity would be sorely lacking if not for the changes in altitude. These heights allow for driving, hiking, climbing and

Although also the name of a town and a resort, Split Rock originally referred to a 6-foot separation in a ridge of sandstone just west of its more famous namesakes.

Photo: Pocono Mountains Vacation Bureau, Inc.

Fall foliage peaks in October.

skiing in the mountains, all the while enjoying amazing vistas and wildlife. It's easy to forget the millions of years of geographic uplifts and erosions that created our landscape.

Weather

Mountains are also major factors in shaping the weather of the Poconos region. They act as physical barriers that affect the flow of air. As a result, an east wind, which usually brings mild temperatures and rain, may be forced to blow from the north and become a winter, snow-bearing monster. Elevation plays an important role in the weather as well. Areas located over 1,000 feet above sea level generally receive between 70 and 90 inches of snow annually. The valleys average 40 inches of snowfall. Towns may be separated by as little as 5 miles, yet one could receive a light drizzle and the other be covered with several inches of snow from the same storm.

Be prepared for sudden temperature changes, especially in fall and winter. When driving, be careful on wet roads that can suddenly become icy as the temperature drops. Spring is nicknamed by many locals as the Mud Season. Melting snow, thawing frost and heavy rains combine to saturate the ground and produce plenty of mud and small-stream flooding. During spring and summer, be wary

of flash-flood conditions. Our summer thunderstorms can drop rain at the rate of three or four inches per hour.

With thunderstorms come lightning, a deceptively dangerous natural phenomenon. In fact, more people are killed in the United States by lightning strikes than by tornadoes and hurricanes combined. In a thunderstorm stay inside, away from open doors and windows, and avoid using the telephone or electrical appliances. If you are outside, avoid isolated trees and hilltops. In an open field, crouch low to the ground. Do not lie flat on the ground as more of your body will be burned if lightning strikes the ground near you. Local television and radio stations provide updates should conditions warrant them.

Wildlife

The Poconos' vast assortment of other waters, such as ponds, streams, marshes, lakes and rivers, provide an abundance of fishing opportunities. Streams near Analomink are nationally famous as picture-perfect fly-fishing environments. Many early resorts in the area catered to anglers, and celebrities, including President Theodore Roosevelt, regularly visited to try their luck.

The waters of the Delaware Water Gap National Recreation Area, which stretches from

Delaware Water Gap to Milford, contain more than 55 species of fish. See our Fishing chapter for information on which fish are most popular with our anglers. Popular year-round river fish are bass, pickerel, walleyes, muskies, catfish and trout. Shad arrive in the river from the ocean each spring to spawn in numbers estimated at a half-million.

Often mistaken for a snake, the American eel, which can be as long as 48 inches, migrates from our fresh water to the ocean to spawn. Eels are the only catadromous (breeding in this fashion) species in North America.

The fish in the river attract other famous Pocono residents, raptors — birds of prey. Bald eagle and osprey populations have risen steadily since DDT (a pesticide used on farm fields and carried to the river in runoff) was banned, and successful reintroduction programs were started in the area.

Bald eagles and golden eagles are endangered species, and sightings are rare in the Poconos. The magnificent birds winter at sites along the upper Delaware River. A drive on River Road, beginning at Shawnee-on-Delaware, could give visitors a glimpse. Young birds of both species look very similar, as it takes bald eagles four to five years to acquire their distinctive plumage. Adult bald eagles, though, have white heads and tails, and golden eagles never become white-headed. Both the golden eagle and the bald eagle, the national bird of our country, are protected; severe penalties await anyone who attempts to hurt them. If you are lucky enough to spot one flying over the Poconos, you will agree that the majestic, broad-winged bald eagle is a perfect choice to symbolize our nation. Eagles fish the Delaware River and surrounding lakes, also looking for small mammals, frogs, snakes and lizards in the hills along the river.

If an eagle can't find its own meal, it is not above stealing a fish from one of our more common raptors — hawks and osprey. An osprey will hover over the Delaware River before making a dramatic plunge into the water to grab a fish with its talons. These birds, while still endangered, have been successfully reintroduced in the Poconos by a volunteer program that began in 1980. Again, enjoy looking at these fish hawks with their dark brown upper body and white underbelly; but do not even think of shooting at one.

Migrating hawks pass through the Poconos in autumn. They can be spotted from trails in the mountains and especially at Hawk Mountain Sanctuary just outside Allentown.

In addition to these raptors approximately 260 species inhabit the Poconos. Bird watchers keep busy looking for everything from herons to hummingbirds. The Delaware Water Gap National Recreation Area, Promised Land State Park, Hickory Run State Park and Tobyhanna State Park provide some of the best birding sites.

The state animal, the white-tailed deer, is even more noticeable. After nearly being eliminated by hunters around the end of the 19th century, the deer were saved by the creation of the Board of Game Commission in 1895. Today, approximately one million white-tailed deer live in Pennsylvania.

Drive down any rural road, particularly in the north, and deer sightings are almost guaranteed. Unfortunately, the deer often do not yield the right of way. So, while you're looking for deer in the woods, make sure there are none on the road in front of you.

The largest animal hunted in Pennsylvania, the black bear, keeps a lower profile. Generally nocturnal, bears sometimes are seen during the day, particularly in autumn when they feed heavily to prepare for their winter slumber. Because of their bulk, black bears are hard to miss. Typically 140 to 400 pounds, they can weigh as much as 650 pounds. They're often seen lumbering across the road, so watch out for them.

Rural residents often complain of too many visits from both deer and bear. The deer love

INSIDERS' TIPS

Those pink-purple flowers along most of the roads in the Poconos are crown vetch, planted by the Pennsylvania Department of Highways for aesthetic reasons, its ability to stabilize soil and its hardiness.

to dine on landscaping, and the bears are notorious for turning garbage into a buffet.

Some of the other animals you might encounter are raccoons, squirrels, rabbits, otters, chipmunks, groundhogs, coyotes, porcupines, foxes and mice. Squirrels, rabbits and raccoons roam most of the woods and suburban neighborhoods of the Poconos. Groundhogs are spotted eating grass along roadsides. Many unfortunate groundhogs decide that the grass is greener on the other side of the road and bravely make the trek across, only to be defeated by their inability to dodge fast cars. Foxes, otters, porcupines and coyotes are more private and are seldom seen on a typical nature walk.

Another animal's handiwork frequently is noticed. Remarkably ambitious beavers gnaw saplings and build large lodges out of branches and mud. Look for their construction efforts in small ponds and streams.

Those who choose to leave their cars and hit the trails might encounter one or more of the Poconos' snakes. The most common, the garter snake, is characterized by three yellow lengthwise stripes. It, like most of the region's reptiles, is harmless. However, there are two poisonous snakes that could be dangerous — the copperhead and the timber rattlesnake, whose names provide a good indication of their characteristics. The timber rattler has a flat head and is yellowish with dark, V-shaped bands and a dark tail. Its most distinguishing feature is its rattle. Located on its tail, the rattle gains a segment each time the snake sheds its skin. Nervous and aggressive by nature, the snakes use the rattle to produce a buzzing noise when they are alarmed. Copperheads are copper and orange with bold red-brown crossbands. Both snakes are usually seen on rocky outcroppings. While these snakes are non-aggressive by nature, they will attack if provoked.

Snakes are most active in spring when they sun themselves on exposed rocks after their winter hibernation. For sunning, snakes favor stone rows, the remains of old lumber mills and rock cliffs.

Hikers should avoid contact with snakes and other animals whenever possible. Also enjoy the plants and animals but avoid the temptation to remove anything from the parks.

Inexperienced hikers should not leave the established trails. In some cases hiking off the trails may damage natural resources by disturbing habitats, damaging plants and causing soil erosion. Do not attempt terrain beyond your ability. The equipment you should bring will vary depending on weather conditions, the length of your hike and the severity of the trail. Things you may need to bring along include hiking boots, insect repellent, rain gear, a notebook and pencil, a whistle, waterproof matches, a flashlight, food and water.

Poison ivy is common in the woods of the Poconos. It can be a trailing plant, a woody shrub or a climbing vine. In the spring the leaves appear dark red. They then turn to rust, green and back to red. Although poison ivy loses its leaves in the fall and winter, the plant is still poisonous. It contains an oil called urushoil that causes a rash and itching to those unfortunate enough to touch it. Indians named poison ivy "the stick that makes you sore." If you have been in an area with poison ivy, wash your skin with soap and water. Never use plain water because that will cause the rash to spread. In the wild, a plant called jewelweed has a juice inside of its stalk that can be applied before a rash develops and helps prevent it from starting.

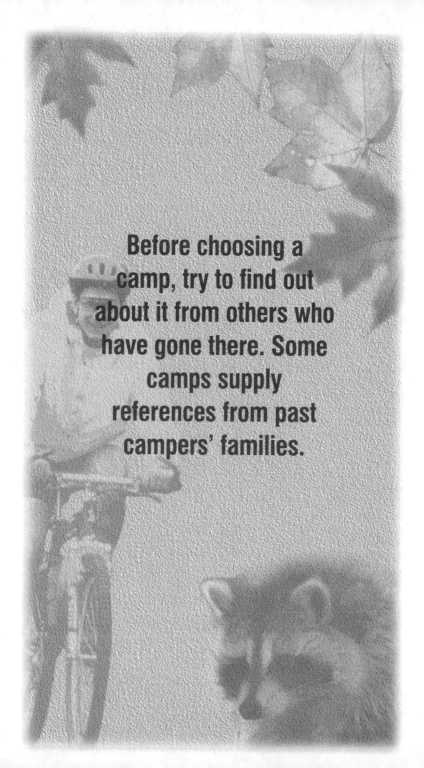

Before choosing a camp, try to find out about it from others who have gone there. Some camps supply references from past campers' families.

Camps and Conference Centers

Camps and conference centers are a combination we chose because they are specialties in this area that are worth pointing out in their own small chapter. Summer camps abound in our mountain woods, but this chapter will focus on those whose focus differentiates them from the coming-of-age kid camp movies à la *Meatballs*.

The Poconos region is home to camps based on science and the environment, art, religion (denominational and interdenominational) and sports. Scout camps are here, but they are managed and attended according to the councils to which they belong. For more information about scout camps, contact your local council for its camp and its location.

The Poconos is a great place for camps because of the mountains, hundreds of lakes and easy access from nearby states via I-80, I-84 and I-95. In fact, as we note in our chapter on Worship, this area has been a spot for camp-based activities for religious groups since before the turn of the century.

A word about facilities. Most camps are traditional in setup. Lodges or bungalows have from four to 28 bunks (the exception is the Pocono Soccer Camp held at East Stroudsburg University where campers stay in the college dorms). As a general rule bathroom and shower facilities are shared within a bunk unit. There is always a centralized recreation facility and eating hall. Most camps (excluding again the Pocono Soccer Camp that isn't in a traditional camp environment) have

the basic amenities covered in terms of swimming, hiking, sports activities, games, tennis, arts and crafts and some type of boating program. A swimming pool or lake is always available. All, of course, have the advantage of mountain-top, valley or lake-side views.

All of the particulars about a camp, from counselor to camper ratio to what kinds of food are served, are addressed in color brochures that each camp sends out to prospective campers. Wayne County provides a list of the camps in its area; contact the Wayne County Chamber of Commerce at 742 Main Street, Honesdale, 253-1960.

We won't list all the camps because there are so many, probably 20 for every one we do note, each with some trademark that differentiates it from others in the field. In this chapter we focus on camps that have programs of special interest or merit. We will give information related to programs offered, since if a camp interests you because of its programs, you will want to write or call for its brochures.

As for conference centers, the ones we mention here are small and more individualized, for the church group, the family or even for the single who just wishes to partake in a theme-oriented conference or a personal retreat. The major resorts in the area (covered in our Accommodations chapter) cater to large conferences for business needs, such as corporate executive retreats, team-building seminars as well as expos and other exhibition-type conferences.

Camps

The camp specialties we mention here are a sampling of the wide range of options and represent some fine choices and a variety of interests and price ranges. Christian camps and YMCA camps are a lot less expensive than the sports camps that feature guaranteed visits from the '76ers (as does the '76ers Basketball Camp), or coaching by Olympic-status coaches such as those at the International Gymnastics Training Camp.

Cost varies by type of camp, and prices change each year. A week at an overnight sports camp averages $350 for a Sunday to Saturday; the high end is around $450. Christian camps range between $160 and $250 for a week's stay (though Tuscarora does cost more); Jewish camps, usually set up for four- or eight-week sessions, average $625 per week. The specialized science camp, Camp Watonka, also offers four- or eight-week sessions at about $600 per week. YMCA camps cost about $350 for the week-long session.

Before choosing a camp in any category, check out what it offers and try to find out about it from others who have gone there; some camps supply references from past campers' families. Ask what the camp's philosophy is. Find out the qualifications of the director and staff. Ask about the camper-counselor ratio. Find out what type of transportation the camp provides and whether it has liability insurance. Inquire about safety procedures, medical procedures and first aid.

If it's a sports camp, make sure it separates campers by skill level and find out if it provides an assessment of the child's progress. Also, with sports camps, it might be important to know what other activities are offered. Some sports camps are totally dedicated to the one sport, and no other activities are included. Your child must really be dedicated to the sport because these camps do not offer other activities; two such camps are the Pocono Invitational Basketball Camp and the Pocono Cup Soccer Camp (though swimming pools are available at the facility).

Sports Camps

Stroudsburg/ East Stroudsburg

International Gymnastics Training Camp
Golden Slipper Rd., Bartonsville
• 629-0244

This camp celebrated its 25th anniversary in 1996. Operated by the International Gymnastics School and headed by All-American gymnast Bruno Klaus, the training camp is considered at the top in its facilities and coaching and training staff. The school operates during the school year, and the camp is its natural summer extension. Past and present coaching and training staffs have included many World Championship team members and American Olympians — Kurt Thomas, Brandy Johnson, Jim Hartung, Peter Kormann and Mitch Gaylord to name a few. Abie Grossfeld, a former U.S. Olympic Coach, has taught here, as have many international Olympians such as Romanians Constantin Petrescu, Mircea Badelescu and Lavinia Agache and Russian Olga Korbut.

The facilities are exceptional with four gymnasiums, circus performance facilities, bungee jumping apparatus, a lake for swimming, boating and Jet Skiing, and more after-gymnastics activities. The cabins are modern, the grounds, beach, trails and dining hall all are fine. The camp is completely international in flavor, from the decor to the coaches (did we mention

Ticks proliferate in the woods that surround all the camps. When packing those trunks for summer camp, be sure to throw in an insect repellent that repels ticks.

Christian Camps & Conference Centers

Member
Christian Camping International/USA

	A place "to play in and to pray in"	Scenic mountain setting with lake	Scenic river setting	Boating & swimming with lake	Variety of winter sports	Facilities for youth, adults & more	Year-round accommodations for groups	Adult & family programming	Summer children's camps	Christian Outdoor Education	Adventure Programs	Campground	Horses
PARADISE LAKE Retreat Center Bushkill – 717 588-6067	●	●		●	●	●	●	●		●			
POCONO PLATEAU Program Center Cresco – 717 676-3665	●	●		●	●	●	●	●	●		●	●	
SPRUCE LAKE Retreat Canadensis – 800 822-7505	●	●		●	●	●	●	●	●	●	●	●	
STREAMSIDE Camp & Conference Center, Stroudsburg – 717 629-1902	●	●		●	●	●	●	●	●	●	●	●	●
TUSCARORA INN & Conference Center Mt. Bethel – 717 897-6000	●		●	●	●	●	●	●	●	●			

Meng Kui Wang from China?) to the young gymnasts who attend.

Aspiring gymnasts, even beginners, are welcome — 50 percent of campers are new students to the sport. The staff is very helpful, and safety is a prime value. Staffers work at developing trust and showing respect for each student's individual abilities.

International Sports Training Camp
Golden Slipper Rd., Bartonsville
• 620-2267

This camp is a sister camp to International Gymnastic Training Camp. It too has excellent coaches, drawn from the surrounding university and high school coaching staffs, who specialize in each of the covered sports. There are camps for all sports and recreation including baseball, basketball, cheerleading, cross-country, field hockey, soccer, softball, volleyball and wrestling. While the camps are dedicated to a specific sport, there is free time each day to take part in some other activities, including horseback riding, Jet-Skiing, swimming, windsurfing, archery and so on.

The facilities include fields for each sport activity, a field house, a health center, a boathouse and canteen and cafeteria. Some facilities are shared with the gymnast camp, and all overlook the surrounding lake and the mountains. The sessions last a week and are scheduled from the very end of June to mid-August. All camps are open to boys and girls ages 8 to 17 (wrestling is 8 to 18) of all skill levels. If soccer is an interest for your child, but you do not think your child is ready for the Pocono Soccer Camp (see entry in this section), try this soccer camp for a beginner or intermediate experience.

Pocono Invitational Basketball Camp
R.D. 4, Box 4156 • Stroudsburg • 992-6343

This is the oldest, longest-running basketball camp in the country — the summer of 1996 was its 33rd season. At one time this family-pioneered and owned camp was by invitation only, hence the "invitational" in its name. Now, it is open to all boys and girls ages 9 to 17. This camp is considered a developmental camp, so there is a lot of teaching and evaluating. It is, however, entirely devoted to practice, lectures, drills and daily league competition. While there is an Olympic-sized pool to cool off in after activities, the stress here, that is reiterated by its director, is on basketball. Youngsters attending should know that playing basketball is what they will be doing the whole week! U.S. Women Olympians have trained and taught here, including medalists Nancy Lieberman, Anne Donovan and Vikki Bullett, and new Olympians Nikki McCray and Carla McGhee. Men players Terry Dehere of the L.A. Clippers, Kenny Anderson of the New Jersey Nets, Craig Ehlo of the Atlanta Hawks and Mark Jackson and Rik Smits of the Indiana Pacers have also coached here. The camp notes that its staffers and coaches range from "Margaret Wade to Rene Portland; from Carol Blazejowski to Nancy Liberman; from Dr. J. to Chris Mullin."

Pocono Soccer Camp
RR 5, Box 5640 • East Stroudsburg • 424-1157

Pocono Soccer Camp is totally dedicated to the serious soccer player. It is held at East Stroudsburg University and has overnight or day registration for the sessions, a women's camp with a special staff, and specialized Upper Ninety Goalkeeper Camp and Team Weeks camps. All coaches are top university and college performers including director Jerry Sheska, Head Men's Soccer Coach at East Stroudsburg University, Wayne Miller, Goalkeeper Coach at East Stroudsburg University, and Derek Arneaud, former National Team Player from Trinidad and Head Women's Soccer Coach at East Stroudsburg University. The program begins at 9 AM and ends at 10 PM, whether you attend as an overnight or as a daycamper. Many local soccer enthusiasts begin staying as daycampers, but as they progress year after year, they decide to stay for the full experience, which includes technical and fitness training all morning, tactics with games and teams in the afternoons, match play and assessment in the evening and a closing lecture and daily review each night, ending at 10 PM.

Programs here include the Upper Ninety Goalkeeper Camp and Team Weeks that run with the Advanced Weeks. There is also an Elite Week. Players must have reached an advanced skill level to benefit from this very focused program. The camps are for boys and girls ages 10 to 18.

Lake Wallenpaupack Area

Mount Tone Ski Camp
Pa. Hwy. 247, Lake Como • (800) 747-2SKI

This is a winter weekend camp. It specializes in theme weekends for skiers of any skill level. Weekends can focus on clinics in basics, freestyle and racing, for skiers interested in elevating their skill level with intensive, half-day coaching sessions at the Endless Mountain Ski Academy, the Mount Tone ski school. (See other Mount Tone ski information in our Winter Sports chapter.) The camp season is from Christmas week to St. Patrick's Day, and snow-making equipment on 90 percent of its trails makes every weekend a camp weekend.

The rate for the basic ski camp weekend package includes two nights' lodgings, two days of skiing, ski equipment for the entire weekend, two meals a day (continental breakfast and dinner), one beginner's group ski lesson (can be upgraded for additional nominal fee), special events (races, outdoor barbecues, volleyball, etc.), recreation center games and activities, a Saturday night DJ, and snow-tubing, ice-skating and cross-country skiing. Activities are coed. The weekend camp rates depend on the time of the season; opening weekends in mid-December and late-season weekends are approximately $89. High-season weekends are $102; if a weekend is a three-day weekend the rate is $122. The weekend ski camp is open to single campers, families of campers or groups of campers — church youth groups, school groups or scout troops. This camp is also open in the summer as a group recreational site and offers horseback riding, swimming, tennis, canoeing, hayrides, mountain biking and lots more. It has an Olympic-sized swimming pool and a lake as well as sports fields and a recreation center.

Slate Belt

'76ers Basketball Camp
Box 1073, Bala Cynwyd • (215) 542-2267

This is one of the few sports camps in the

United States affiliated with a professional basketball team. It is held locally in Bangor, although the main address is in Bala Cynwyd. Members of the '76ers and other NBA greats (including Derrick Coleman, John Lucas, Jerry Stackhouse, Clarence Witherspoon, Scott Williams and Derrick Alston) actually do participate in coaching. The camp considers itself a developmental camp and accepts interested campers from beginners through high school. Students come from more than 30 states and 20 countries to practice here. While basketball is the primary focus, the camp also offers a traditional summer-camp experience that includes swimming in the Olympic-size pool, Jet Skiing and other waterfront and sports activities. The May 1996 issue of *Sports Illustrated for Kids* listed this as one of the top-five sports camps.

The local camp in Bangor is an overnight program; however, if you live in southeastern Pennsylvania, there is a '76ers Basketball Camp in Bala Cynwyd that is a day camp.

Educational Camps

Stroudsburg/ East Stroudsburg

Monroe County Environmental Education Center
Running Valley Rd., Bartonsville • 629-3061

The center runs many programs, including day camps in the summer (see the Day Camps section in this chapter) and day classes (see our Kidstuff chapter) throughout the year. However, the center offers a residential Conservation Camp for county residents age 13 to graduating seniors, for one week during the summer. The week is usually in mid-July, and the program is held at Stony Acres Recreation Facility of East Stroudsburg University in Marshalls Creek. The program focuses on conservation-related topics, such as forestry, archery trapshooting, bee-keeping, fly fishing, water quality, taxidermy and many other related topics. Besides the activities at the center the camp sometimes includes a two-day canoe trip on the Delaware River. Kids can progress through

the experience by levels from beginner to advanced if they return every summer. They must have completed the previous levels to continue to the next; so, if this is a program your child might be interested in, contact the center in the winter that the child is 13 to participate in the full developmental program.

Lake Wallenpaupack

Science Camp Watonka
Wangom Rd., Hawley • 226-4779, 857-1401

This is a camp for "science-minded boys ages 7 through 15." It has a well-rounded program that includes all the regular camp activities, along with a daily science concentration, selected by the individual camper. The camp sessions are for four weeks or eight weeks. The camp fee is inclusive, there are no other costs for any activities, insurance or uniforms. Transportation is the only extra. It is not a summer school; it is an experience with science in well-equipped laboratories and computer labs. The daily lab instruction can be in astronomy, biology, botany, chemistry, computer science, electronics, ham radio, photography, physics, robotics, rocketry and more. The computer science lab was one of the first in the country and has programs for beginner, intermediate and advanced computer users. The arts and crafts are also explored in areas such as jewelry making, leather work, woodworking, dramatics and video production. Sports activities include swimming, sailing, windsurfing, canoeing and life-saving based around the camp's lake, and field and court sports such as soccer, baseball, badminton, tennis, basketball and volleyball. There are single-performer sports such as archery, riflery and trap and skeet shooting. There are many other activities here including trips to points of interest in the area, hikes, overnight campouts and orienteering. The camp uses the best equipment available, and the staff-to-camper ratio is about 1 to 2, which means a lot of close supervision and instruction.

Day Camps

Many of the area day-care centers provide

some type of day-camp experience. Also, some recreation departments sponsor programs, and, in some townships, day-camp type activities are held in the parks. Your best bet is to check with the township office or schools for possible leads. (See our Recreation chapter for a list of recreation departments.) There are a few day camps that have a particular difference that may be of interest to you, so we'll point those out here.

Stroudsburg/ East Stroudsburg

A Family of Artists, The Works
Pa. 447, E. Stroudsburg • 420-9675

This exciting group gets its name from its alliance of artists. The day camp emphasizes the interdisciplinary use of the arts based on cultural and arts-related themes. A week's theme might be Let's Sing or Circus or Native American or Renaissance. There are a number of fine artists on staff, and guest artists such as singer Janet Lawson, "School House Rock" composer Bob Dorough, Minas, Troy Richardson and others. The entrance has a wonderful gift shop that sells works of art created by the members of A Family of Artists and some of the kids.

The camp offers an array of arts-related equipment from potters wheels and sculpting tools to computers, keyboards and drums. The children are separated into different sections of the building by age, 8 to 11 and 12 to 18. The younger group members begin their day with a group sing-a-long time, then the members separate into smaller groups for each of the activities.

Mornings for both age levels are generally devoted to creating in the different art forms; those who stay the entire day go on an afternoon outing to the East Stroudsburg pool or another area swimming place. The camp also works with children who have mental or physical disabilities and provides an inclusive environment for them, with specially trained staff

to support them as they are mainstreamed with the other campers. This program has been running quite successfully for nine years. We know several children who have attended and all have enjoyed and benefited from the artistic experience.

International Day Camp
Golden Slipper Rd., Bartonsville
• 620-2267

International Day Camp is an affiliate of the International Gymnastics Camp and International Sports Camp. It shares the same beautiful mountain views and stresses fitness and sports- related activities in the kindercamp and sports camp. There are a multitude of activities including bungee jumping, gymnastics, swimming and trapezing.

Monroe County Environmental Education Center
8050 Running Valley Rd., Bartonsville
• 629-3061

This center offers two, one-week summer day-camp sessions each summer — one in July and one in August. The program for each week is the same, so children are only allowed to register for one session. The program is called Forests and Me Day Camp and is for children age 9 through 12. It is a hands-on experience and includes discovering nature in the forest, fields and wetlands that comprise the Environmental Center's domain. The camp is limited to 35 campers per session. Fees are based on member or nonmember, but are in line with area day camp fees. The camp day is 9:30 AM to 3:30 PM. The Center also offers a variety of day programs for children ages 3 though 9 that are for one morning or afternoon. These programs begin in late June and run through August.

A new program offered in 1996 is Kettle Creek Explorers for children 10 through 13. These programs are field trips for members and nonmembers (fee is based on membership category). Trips head to different places, and they can last from three to seven hours.

Trips have been run to find beavers, to hike at Mount Minsi and Devil's Hole, to bike through the mountains and to the Pocono Wildlife Rehabilitation Center and Hickory Run State Park. The *Pocono Record* publishes the offerings in its May publication, *Pocono Summer,* and the last Sunday of every month in its Community Calendar. If you miss the published dates, you can call the center for a schedule.

Monroe County Recreation Department
4221 Manor Dr., Kellersville • 992-4343

In Monroe County day-camp activities are sponsored in the schools in Pocono Mountain, Pleasant Valley and East Stroudsburg, from 9 AM to 3 PM June through August. The department also provides workshops and seminars at different locations throughout the county and swimming and tennis lessons at Pocono Mountain High School in conjunction with the Pocono Family YMCA. These programs are highly sought after, so attendees must attend for the entire session. The department also provides workshops in arts and crafts at different locations throughout the county. Summer programs are for students through 6th grade.

Stroud Township
1215 N. Fifth St., Stroudsburg • 421-3362

Stroud Township provides its own day-camp program at the Stroudsburg Middle School on Chipperfield Drive. It is open from 9 AM to 3 PM from late June to mid-August. The activities are based at the school and include arts and crafts and sports played on the school's playing fields or in the gym.

Mount Pocono Area

Camelback Day Camp
Camelback Rd., Tannersville • 629-1661

During the winter Camelback ski area has skiing activities for children, but during the summer it offers a day camp. The camp runs from 9 AM to 4 PM, but early drop-off and late pick up are available. The staff is made up of teachers and coaches from the area. The activities include the typical arts and crafts, nature studies, sports and swimming, and the atypical camp activities of the Camelback Al-

pine Slide, a waterslide, bumper boats and a miniature golf course. For those who are in the area for a summer vacation, it is good to note that you can send your children for two or three days; you don't have to register them for the whole week. In fact, moms who only need a two- or three-day camp experience can register their children here. Our children have been here and had a lot of fun.

West End

Beltzville State Park
Pohopoco Dr., Lehighton • (610) 377-0044

This park offers free, week-long day camp programs all summer for ages 4 through 11. Campers are grouped by age. Programs are based on nature, taking advantage of the lake and surrounding woods for nature walks and crafts (making things from natural materials), swimming and studies of fish, turtles or insects in the area. The camp lasts from 9 AM to 3 PM. Throughout the summer, daily programs are scheduled that last four hours. A program again would be based on a particular study, the rocks, the fish, the fauna or other areas of interest based on the park's environment. Every summer weekend at the park also offers nature-based family programs. The programs vary and the park staff suggests you call to find out what's going on when. The summer camp schedule and registration dates are published in the local newspapers (be sure to check the *Pocono Record*) in early May. The dates fill up fast, so if you don't see them in the paper call in May to find out the schedule. The programs begin when school closes and end before Labor Day.

YMCA Camps

Stroudsburg/ East Stroudsburg

Pocono Family YMCA
809 Main St., Stroudsburg • 421-2525

This day camp offers field trips to local attractions and swimming along with other camp activities. If there is an away day from the Y, the trip is planned for the whole day, and the parents drop off children at the other location and pick them up there too. The YMCA also offers a special-needs camp for children who would benefit from a one-on-one situation, and there is also a preschool camp.

Milford Area

Camp Speers-Eljabar
Pa. Hwy. 739, Dingmans Ferry • 828-2329

The Pike County YMCA has day and overnight camps at its 1,000 acre facility near Dingmans Ferry. All the traditional camp activities are here including archery, drama and swimming in the lake. The YMCA never turns anyone away because of inability to pay. This camp also offers family camp experiences on Memorial Day and Labor Day.

Conference Centers/Camps

The camps/conference centers included here generally operate as camps during the summer months and as conference and retreat centers during off months. Since these are all near ski areas, winter months provide some interesting retreat and conference options.

Stroudsburg/ East Stroudsburg

Mt. Gilead Camp and Conference Center
R.D. Box 8162, Stroudsburg • 629-0920

Mt. Gilead is a nondenominational, Christian girls camp during the summer and a conference and retreat center the rest of the year. The camp weeks are organized around a theme such a circus or holiday or "King Arthur's Court" or an activity such as canoeing, trekking the wilderness or horseback riding. There is not an on-site kitchen staff available throughout the year, so those who wish to set up a retreat or conference weekend must make plans with the center to have meals arranged

or bring their own supplies and cooks. Also, there aren't any programs planned; the center is available to those who have their own program in mind and bring the speakers and activities with them. This camp is built on very mountainous terrain. It is up the back of Camelback ski area, so it is for the hardy and those who enjoy rustic and woodsy surroundings.

Twin Pines Camp, Conference and Retreat Center
Twin Pines Rd., Bartonsville • 629-2411

An Evangelical Congregational Church Camp, Twin Pines has camp activities for boys and girls in senior high, junior high, juniors, special-needs students and family groups. There are sports and music camps, frontier and mountainside camping experiences at outpost camps and canoeing and hiking camps on the Delaware River and Appalachian Trail. The facilities are also available for retreats and conferences throughout the year. Twin Pines also operates an extensive retreat and conference center program each year, offering singles' retreats, women's retreats and more, and accepts groups who wish to be guided in their own experiences.

An interesting addition to this center is the Sweigert Nature Center that is managed by a staff naturalist and displays both mounted and live animals.

Mount Pocono Area

Camp Streamside
Rossinger Rd., Reeders • 629-1902

Camp Streamside offers Kids Kamp, Teen Camp and Pathfinders. This a Christian-based camp, but it does not represent any particular denomination. It offers all the usual camp activities but adds a 300-foot waterslide, giant mud pit and riflery and slingshot areas. There are fine conference facilities, and Streamside provides a host for each group during its stay along with other support through equipment and other options. It is near the base of Camelback ski area.

Pocono Plateau Program Center
Pa. Hwy. 191 N., Cresco • 676-3665

The 750 acres of forests, lakes, wildlife habi-

Photo: Pocono Mountains Vacation Bureau, Inc.

Deer are common and spotted often.

tats and hiking trails offer year-round facilities for Christian retreats, summer camps and outdoor education classes. Two lakes provide for swimming, boating and fishing. There are indoor and outdoor recreation pavilions for volleyball, basketball and other activities such as tetherball and ultimate Frisbee. A children's play area is also part of the complex.

In winter, weather permitting, there is ice skating on the lake and sledding. You can bring your own retreat here or you can take part in a Plateau-led retreat for children, young adults, junior and senior high students and families. On weekend retreats five family-style meals are served. Those who choose to camp at the Adventure Site in platform tents have the option of cooking their own meals at the tentsite or in the Adventure Lodge kitchen.

In summer several camps are offered — a day camp for children age 4 to 8, a resident camp, a specialty camp based on a special interests such as music, drama, ecology or adventure challenges, and off-site camps such

as backpack trips to New Hampshire and the Appalachian Trail, canoe trips or climbing/spelunking trips.

Accommodations include heated lodges, which are available for groups of 9 to 125, with one large bathroom/shower facility for each wing or floor; platform tents at the adventure site for groups of 8 to 72, with bathrooms and hot showers in the Adventure Lodge; and meeting rooms for 12 to 125.

Spruce Lake Retreat
Pa. Hwy. 447 N., Canadensis • 595-7505

This Mennonite owned and operated facility is a year-round adult and children's camp and retreat center. There are 320 acres with streams, waterfalls, wildlife, two small lakes and hiking trails. During the summer there are children's wilderness camps for ages 8 and older, a different age level each week (coed). There is even a mini-camp for youngsters ages 8 and 9 with a low camper-counselor ratio and seven kids to a tent to ensure a positive camping experience for new campers. Activities for all levels include swimming, paddle boats, mini-golf, tennis (two courts, one lighted), volleyball, sleep-outs, fireside activities, music, leather crafts, drama, survival games, soccer, basketball, rocketry, water sliding, rappelling and many more exciting activities. Besides children's summer camps, there are youth and adult programs for adventure activities such as wilderness expeditions, challenge course events, and cross-country ski weekends.

Family, special holiday and seasonal retreats are held. For schools, the Spruce Lake Outdoor School is an outdoor classroom education tool. There are programs for the day or three-day residence programs for grades 3 through 8. Programs include hikes, adventure activities and outdoor skills programs. The schools programs are centered around an outdoor education center that is specifically designed as a learning and display facility for nature subjects and outdoor class introductions.

This center has 51 private motel-type rooms with private baths, 8 conference rooms which accommodate from 20 to 200 (three have pianos), 60 wooded campsites with a heated bathhouse, a central dining room with buffet service and a multipurpose Lakeview Retreat Center Program. All meals are provided with the retreat and camping programs. An interesting option here is a midweek bed and breakfast program. Reservations are available any time of year. Nightly rates are from $27.90 to $32.90 for an adult; $9.45 for children age 6 and older.

Lake Wallenpaupack

Ramah in the Poconos
Lake Como • 798-2504

The conservative Jewish education programs at Ramah are for children in grades 3 through 10. Camp is divided into two four-week sessions or an eight-week session. The programs are sponsored by the Jewish Theological Seminary and offer Hebrew and Judaica programs. Activities include sports, arts, music, dance and drama. A lake provides for waterfront activities, and nature outings, camping and canoeing trips are sched-

uled. The camp offers three special programs: a one-week family camp, a four-day Elderhostel program and a family camp for the deaf and hard of hearing. Accommodations are in cabins that sleep 12 to 14, and the kitchen is kosher.

Milford Area

Paradise Lake Retreat Center
Sugar Mt. Rd., Bushkill • 588-6067

This lovely 500-acre center on top of Sugar Mountain in Bushkill accepts groups of any age with space for 25 to 200 persons. The facility is available for midweek retreats or even day-long retreats. Housing is in log cabins with bunk-style accommodations that can sleep between 20 and 56 people. There are also single rooms large enough for a whole group and special accommodations for group speakers. The accommodations, food and facilities are provided; you bring your own speakers and program.

A lake provides for boating and swimming, and there's also an outdoor pool. The large gymnasium is a great place for indoor basketball and volleyball. In winter, the mountain provides a fun spot for tubing and tobogganing, and the lake allows for ice-skating. There are numerous trails for hiking.

One of the most special features of the camp is a chapel of stone and glass that overlooks the lake. A supply store and gift shop, Fort Plenty, provides necessities. In the summer the center is used for a specialized summer camp.

Slate Belt

Tuscarora Inn and Retreat Center
3300 River Rd., Mount Bethel • 897-6000

This beautiful Lutheran Brethren Conference Center is right on the Delaware River south of Portland. It is primarily a year-round adult conference center, but it offers family weeks and weekends, young-adult retreats, a juniors camp week (3rd through 6th graders) and a teen week (7th through 11th graders). Capacity is 300. Summer Saturday night concerts and dinners are also an option here.

Throughout the year programs based on spiritual renewal and development are offered for men, women, singles, pastors and prime-timers.

Accommodations include decorated rooms in a main lodge, cottages with two double beds and private baths, deluxe, spacious rooms with private baths and dressing areas (and color TVs available) in the Riverside Manor, and dorms for youths in the Mountainview Dorms. Family-style meals are served in the main dining room at moderate prices (one fee for the duration of visit). Activities include swimming in the pool, water skiing, tennis on three tennis courts, soccer and softball on fields with bleachers and fishing on the river (with a license and your equipment). Winter activities include on-site tubing, sledding, cross-country skiing and ice skating. (Bring your own equipment.) There is a large gymnasium/auditorium for games and sports indoors and a grand piano and organ (the auditorium seats up to 900) for programs. You can bring in your own group and program at Tuscarora, and the center will provide services, meals, housekeeping, recreation and meeting facilities.

Kirkridge
2495 Fox Gap Rd., Bangor
• (610) 588-1793

Kirkridge sits on an absolutely beautiful vantage overlooking the Appalachian ridge valleys that roll below. Appalachian Trail hikers and those who happen to catch a glimpse of it as they drive to Bangor over Pa. 191 often stop just to see the view.

Kirkridge's history dates back to 1942. Its symbol is the Celtic cross, and its purpose is to be a blessing "for the soul-weary, those in need of healing, the discouraged." Kirkridge was founded by a Presbyterian minister, but it has a very ecumenical personality. It offers workshops, seminars and retreats that cross all belief lines. In 1996 Father Daniel Berrigan led a modern reflection time based on the ancient teachings of Jeremiah. Other workshops have included "Celtic Spirituality" and "Men and Their Fathers, Unfinished Business." Creative workshops on healing, drumming, sacred storytelling, play, movement and meditation have been presented. Today's issues are addressed in workshops and retreats — "Embodying Masculinity in Today's World," "Women Survivors of Sexual Abuse" and "Gay, Lesbian and Christian" are other programs that have been presented here. This facility is also available to those who wish to come alone and have a private retreat. The surroundings are truly conducive to spiritual healing. (Even two preadolescent boys we know were mesmerized by the view and wanted to stay at the end of a walk just to soak in the beauty around them.) Families often take advantage of the facility for reunions and weddings — arrangements can be made through the same number.

Accommodations are in four units with a minimum of 16 people required. Nelson Lodge houses 27 people and is at the very top of the grounds with wide windows and a large deck overlooking the mountains. It has two common rooms (one with a fireplace), a dining room and kitchen, wall-to-wall carpeting and twin beds. Turning Point is for 23 people and is made up of two buildings overlooking the valley. There is a large meeting room and a small meeting room, a large dining room, professional kitchen, wall-to-wall carpeting and twin beds. The Farmhouse holds 24 people. It sits in a glen, and the structure dates from 1815. There is a rafted dining room with a huge stone hearth, kitchen, meeting room, a separate quiet room with a fireplace and twin beds. The Hermitage, located on a wooded hillside, has the feel of a monastery and suits 16 guests. There are eight bedrooms and four baths, a raftered common room with large woodstove hearth, an adjacent kitchen and twin beds.

All accommodations allow you to do your own cooking, if you bring a group in. You can also enjoy a scheduled retreat and eat your meals buffet-style in the main dining room. Red meat is not served, though fish and fowl are.

There are also individual retreat accommodations that can accommodate up to six people. These range from small cabins for one or two to a house that contains two sets of quarters for up to six people. In the individual accommodations retreat guests are responsible for providing their own meals and linens.

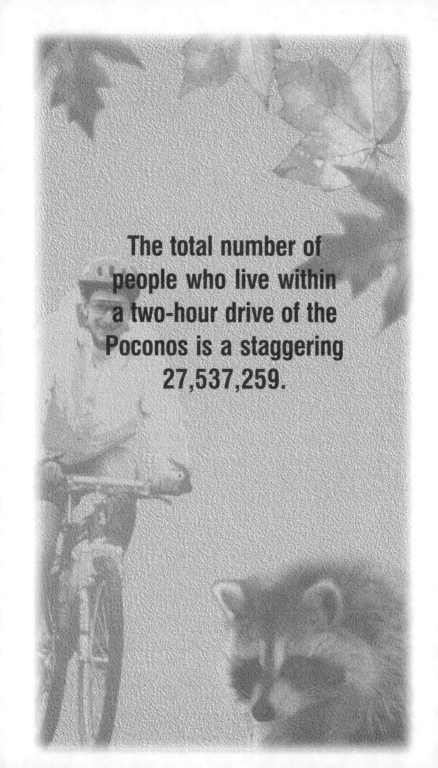

The total number of
people who live within
a two-hour drive of the
Poconos is a staggering
27,537,259.

Real Estate

For as little as $35,000 — or as much as $3.5 million — a piece of the Pocono Mountains could be yours. Many people have decided that the region is the perfect place to vacation, retire or raise a family. In fact, throughout the 1980s and '90s, Monroe and Pike counties, which most people consider the heart of the Poconos, have ranked first and second in percentage of population growth among Pennsylvania counties. Using 1994 U.S. Census Bureau figures, the population totals for the four counties that comprise the majority of the Poconos are as follows: Monroe County — 112,111; Carbon County — 58,869; Wayne County — 43,111; and Pike County — 35,489.

In additional, thousands of other folks have built second homes in the Poconos and are not counted on the permanent population figures. The total number of people who live within a two-hour drive of the Poconos — folks deemed most likely to consider a vacation home in this region — is a staggering 27,537,259.

People are attracted to the Poconos because of the quality of life. The air is clean. Brooks, ponds and waterfalls are sprinkled throughout. Wildlife is plentiful. Rivers offer boating and fishing opportunities. Thousands of acres of game lands lure hunters. And the scenery — from pastoral views of rolling farmlands to dramatic mountain cliffs and everything in between — is remarkably diverse. These are just some of the reasons people choose to vacation or live in the Poconos.

Other benefits of particular interest to home buyers include good schools, safe neighborhoods and lower taxes than in adjoining states. For instance, most property taxes are about half the rates charged for similar homes in New Jersey, the closet neighboring state. Homes are less expensive here than in New Jersey — an average of $25,000 to $50,000 less for comparable properties. Maintenance costs and the general cost of living also are lower in the Poconos.

Unfortunately, the market for high-paying jobs is not nearly as extensive as in New Jersey or New York City, slightly farther east. This leads many people to commute as many as two hours each direction to work so that their families might enjoy the benefits of living in the Poconos without suffering a dramatic loss in income.

Commuters have contributed to the rising value of real estate in the Poconos. In 1995, according to the Pocono Mountain Board of Realtors, 1,401 single-family homes were sold through the Multiple Listing Service at an average cost of $91,758. In 1985, the average cost was $64,702. Pike County had the fifth-highest housing cost out of 67 counties in Pennsylvania, according to a 1988 study by the local planning commission. That average — $105,027 — was exceeded only by the four counties surrounding Philadelphia.

More affluent commuters and second-home buyers have priced many locals out of the real estate market. Most residents who live and work in the Poconos earn roughly half the salary of those employed elsewhere. As a result, farmers have sold their parcels of land, which usually become residential developments. Former summer camps are also ideal for conversion to planned communities. Home buyers often look at property that was once part of the camp where they spent childhood summers.

Towns near the Interstate 80 toll bridge, the gateway to high incomes to the east, have seen the most dramatic increases. Homes in those areas not only are easily accessible for parents to commute to and from work but also are usually close to their children's schools.

The rush to buy second homes and permanent homes for commuters near Delaware Water Gap makes this one of the most active markets in the Poconos.

The real estate market currently is stable. Prices jumped severely in the late 1980s, then fell off in the early 1990s.

During the boom years, the housing market in the Poconos was corrupted by a number of unscrupulous opportunists who exploited the demand. Unbuildable land was sold to unsuspecting buyers. Builders completed inferior jobs — or never completed them at all. Real estate brokers took advantage of the rush to buy, selling homes at inflated prices. The corrupt businesses largely have been eliminated from the picture. However, buyers should still be careful.

Each county in the Poconos has a builders association. The association's members must guarantee to meet established quality standards and codes. They must provide a minimum one-year written warranty. Contractors must provide workers' compensation and general liability insurance in order to be affiliated with the association. Contact the **Pocono Builders Association**, 556 Main Street, Stroudsburg, 421-9009, for information on certified building companies. Also, for anyone considering building a new home, see this chapter's sidebar regarding suggestions from the Pennsylvania Builders Association to ensure you choose a reputable contractor.

Most Pocono builders offer home and land packages for $80,000 to $100,000. Be wary of exceptionally low prices — most likely, corners are being cut. Of course, higher prices for fancier styles are available, and builders also will customize a home to suit your needs.

The most popular areas for new home construction are the West End, Mount Pocono and Stroudsburg-East Stroudsburg. Models are on display along U.S. Highway 209 in the West End, Business Highway 209 from East Stroudsburg

to Marshalls Creek and Pa. Highway 611 from Stroudsburg to Mount Pocono.

When buying a lot for a new home, make sure the property can accommodate a septic system because most rural areas lack central water and sewer. If the property does not perk (the name of the test) you will not be allowed to build. Also, wetland regulations are strictly enforced and could prevent you from building on that dream lot with the wonderful view and surrounding water. If you have questions about these regulations and tests, contact the Department of Environmental Resources, 480 Clearview Lane, Stroudsburg, 424-3006.

If you are considering an existing house, hire an inspector to evaluate the current state of the structure and its internal systems. This inspector should not be affiliated with any contractors you might later use. Call an inspector after you have made an offer on a property and before you sign a contract.

The **Pocono Mountain Board of Realtors** monitors home sales in the region and maintains standards of ethics for its members. Their offices are on Business Highway 209 south of Stroudsburg, and they can be reached at 424-8846.

Many primary and secondary home buyers want to live in a private community. These subdivisions usually offer amenities such as lakes, pools, clubhouses, tennis courts and baseball and basketball facilities. Some even boast their own ski areas, golf courses, stables, archery ranges and hiking trails. They are designed for people who want to live in the country but also enjoy the benefits of the suburban lifestyle they might have enjoyed elsewhere. Roads are most often paved — a luxury in some of the more rural parts of the Poconos. Weekenders also enjoy living in these communities because they are frequently gated, requiring a key card or pass from a guard to gain entry; some have on-site, 24-hour security.

Dues in developments rarely exceed $500 annually, but make sure of the cost

> **FYI**
> Unless otherwise noted, the area code for all phone numbers in this guide is 717.

Hickory Lane Builders

Having recently celebrated its 30th Anniversary in the Poconos, Hickory Lane Builders has had more than $300 million in sales. In the three decades of home building, ickory Lane, has dedicated itself as a full service homebuilding rganization. "Our success has been the personal attention that e have given to each and every customer over the past 30 ears," explains Robert W. Boland, President of Hickory Lane.)ur widespread reputation for excellence in quality design and)nstruction has earned us the respect from countless home lyers," states Boland.

Located in the thriving Tannersville, Exit 46, region, it seems any miles away from the hustle and bustle of the urban reetscape, yet the Pocono area is remarkably close to the New ork Metropolitan Area and northern New Jersey. Commuting bus or car is easy, and rail service linking the Poconos with ew York is currently under discussion and nearing legislative proval.

nterstate 80, Exit 46B (Bartonsville) Route 611

717 894-4000   800 233-0355

before buying property. Also, developments often have restrictions designed to prevent owners from doing anything to depress surrounding property values. Some buyers might find these rules excessively strict, so make sure you understand the expectations of your community — again, before buying.

Some folks consider nearby neighbors and fancy facilities a drawback. They want privacy, which means a large parcel of land. Building lots in planned developments usually are a half-acre. As a result, you can expect to see your neighbors on all sides. If you want to see only wildlife from your doorstep, you'd be wise to look for larger spreads outside the private communities.

The primary market in the Poconos used to be for secondary homes. That is still true in much of Wayne and Pike counties. However, modern technology such as computers and fax machines allows many people to work from their homes. They do not need to go to the office every day and have the luxury of living far away from it. Primary home sales now dominate the scene in the Stroudsburgs and West End area. Commuters typically desire a home 20 minutes from Delaware Water Gap.

A glaring deficiency in local real estate is rental property; there is not enough of it. Families have a hard time finding an apartment complex, particularly one with rents below $750 per month. Private home rentals are in demand. When available, three-bedroom homes rent for $650 to $850 per month.

Students of East Stroudsburg University occupy most of the available rental homes near the campus. If your son or daughter plans to attend the university, be sure to investigate the borough ordinance against having more than two unrelated persons share a home. East Stroudsburg created this policy to prevent large numbers of students from overcrowding homes and apartments. Most of the apartments above stores on Main Street in Stroudsburg also are occupied by college students.

Three years ago, all homes for rent in the Mount Pocono area near Tannersville were snapped up by people moving to the region to work at Crossings Factory Stores, which employ more than 850. Brokers' rental listings that used to exceed 30 now are lucky to have a single available home.

Apartments also are scarce in the West End, Wayne County and Pike County. Developers make a greater profit using land for homesites than by building apartment complexes. Also, local residents, fearful of increasing the demand on overcrowded roads, usually oppose facilities that will bring large numbers of new neighbors.

We discuss vacation rentals, such as timeshares in our Accommodations chap-

LAKE NAOMI CLUB

Lake Naomi/Timber Trails was selected as one of the 99 Best Recreational Communities in America.

The most comprehensive recreational programming coupled with the meticulously groomed facilities make it so unique, you'll want to experience it for yourself.

- Clubhouse/ Restaurant
- Golf Course
- Adult Activity Programs
- 250 Acre Lake
- 2 Pools
- Boating, Fishing & Sailing

- 21 Har-Tru Tennis Courts
- Children's Camp Program
- Creative Teen Programs
- 7 Beaches

Located in the mountains of Northeastern Pennsylvania, just 2 hours from New York and Philadelphia.
Consider us your Backyard Playground.
For a free packet of information on how you can be a part of the Lake Naomi Club, call Greg at our Administrative Office at 1-800-NAOMI-EX (626-6439)

PROPERTY RENTALS & SALES

LAKE NAOMI
REAL ESTATE, Inc.

Continuing a tradition
since 1964.

Sales/Rentals

800-537-1479

At the traffic light ...
Corner Routes 940 & 423
POCONO PINES, PA 18350

Internet: www.lakenaomi.com

Pocono Lake
— Realty

20 Years of Integrity
IN REAL ESTATE
SALES & RENTALS

**Two Office Locations for
Your Convenience:**

Pocono Lake Realty
at Lake Naomi
1-800-588-1808

Pocono Lake Realty
at Locust Lake Village
in Pocono Lake
1-800-588-2808

Open 7 Days a Week for all
Your Real Estate Needs

MOUNTAINLIFE
REAL ESTATE, INC.

*Servicing
Lake Naomi,
Timber Trails, Pinecrest
& Other
Fine Communities*

717-646-6600

**Sales, Rentals &
New Construction**

P.O. Box M
Pocono Pines, PA 18350
Bob Kasper, Broker

FREE
Insider's Report
12 CRITICAL ITEMS TO KNOW
<u>BEFORE</u> YOU BUY OR RENT A
VACATION HOME!

The Poconos are dotted with many
recreational communities. Sorting
them out can be a real puzzle, but you
need not trust blind luck. If you call
for this free report you'll get advice
and counsel from those who have gone
before you. It is compiled from the
direct experiences of people who now
own or rent vacation homes in our
special part of the Poconos. Find out
why they chose this area over many
other Pocono locations. Be sure to get
this report <u>before</u> you make any other
real estate calls. If you don't, you may
wish you had.

1-800-962-7368

ter because they are designed for people visiting, as opposed to living, in the Poconos.

Delaware Water Gap

The "Holy Grail" for the average commuter is affordable property in this — the closest village to the toll bridge on Interstate 80 that leads to the higher-paying jobs in New Jersey and Manhattan. The area also is popular among artists and musicians. Unfortunately, few properties are available here, and most commuters are forced to look at nearby Stroudsburg and East Stroudsburg.

Because this was the original vacation destination in the Poconos, there are many beautiful older homes, usually large Victorians. However, they do not change hands very often. Newer three-bedroom homes outside Delaware Water Gap sell for an average of $100,000 to $150,000. Just north of the town along the Delaware River, two- and three-bedroom homes around Shawnee-on-Delaware sell in the $150,000-to-$200,000 range. To the south, the Cherry Valley region has similarly priced properties.

More affordable — less than $100,000 — are townhouses in Water Gap Village. Average townhome rentals range from $650 to $800 per month.

Stroudsburg/ East Stroudsburg

Essentially all aspects of Poconos real estate can be found in these towns and the surrounding area. Whether you are looking for an old-style home in a downtown setting, an affordable starter in a private community or a top-shelf estate on a private golf course, a broker can show you something near the Stroudsburgs.

East Stroudsburg has always had a reputation as a solid middle-class community. Homes are well-maintained, lawns are mowed and gardens are weeded. Most real estate prices fall in the $100,000-to-$150,000 range for three-bedroom homes built in the early to mid-1900s.

The town hosts East Stroudsburg University and Pocono Medical Center. A number of townhouse complexes were constructed that house many of the people who work at these institutions. Parktowne, Eaglesmere and Walnut Grove all offer two- and three-bedroom townhouses for around $100,000.

A newer subdivision for homes, probably the last one in East Stroudsburg as all available land has been utilized, College Hill Estates is bordered by East Stroudsburg University and Notre Dame High School. It boasts borough roads, sidewalks, central water and sewer. Three-bedroom homes start at $150,000.

Some of the most expensive homes in town, at least new homes, are at Stones Throw. Large three-bedroom homes in this upscale community start around $130,000; townhouses cost $118,000 to $160,000.

The shift from second homes to commuters can be seen at Penn Estates, which is between East Stroudsburg and Analomink. The community was designed for upscale getaway houses but recently has seen most of its buyers become permanent residents. Average home cost is just more than $100,000. The same change is evident at Saw Creek, west of U.S. Highway 209, just south of Bushkill. This large development, boasting six pools, tennis courts, skiing, a lake and assorted sporting opportunities, has seen an influx of year-round homeowners. One-half acre to one acre lots cost approximately $11,000; homes, $80,000 to $100,000.

Also on U.S. 209, two of the most expensive private golf communities have opened.

Homes in Great Bear Country Club surround an 18-hole golf course designed by Jack Nicklaus. The typical estate home is a stone and cedar, two-story Colonial with four bedrooms, a foyer, a library and mahogany decks overlooking the 12th hole — for $549,000. Homes range from $299,900 to $899,000; sites start at $79,000.

Country Club of the Poconos golf course was designed by Jim Fazio. Townhouses, golf villas, lakefront condos and cluster homes are offered. This project has won more design and building awards than any development in the Poconos. Low-end prices range from $130,000 to $160,000.

In Stroudsburg the most desirable addresses are in the Historic District — roughly Sarah, Thomas and Scott streets, and the streets around Glenbrook Country Club. The large, three-plus-bedroom homes here easily cost $250,000 to $500,000. They are the most historically and architecturally significant homes in the Stroudsburgs. Downtown homes start around $100,000. On the edge of Stroudsburg, a number of subdivisions have two- and three-bedroom homes in the $75,000-to-$100,000 range.

The most desirable townhouses are Knob Hill on Sarah Street in the Historic District. These are new buildings constructed to blend in with the surrounding older homes. They cost just less than $100,000.

LaBar Village, a retirement community for folks 55 and older, offers two-bedroom, two-bath homes for approximately $100,000.

Mount Pocono Area

Real estate in the Mount Pocono area ranges from two-bedroom homes in private communities costing as little as $50,000 to four- and five-bedroom estates in the $300,000 to $500,000 range.

The high end of the market is centered around the towns of Buck Hill Falls, Skytop, Mountainhome, Cresco and Canadensis — all along Pa. Highway 390, northeast of Mount Pocono. These were some of the earliest resort areas on the mountain and contain the most desirable older homes.

Many less-expensive homes in subdivisions with amenities are near Mount Pocono, Tobyhanna, Pocono Summit, Pocono Lake, Pocono Pines and Blakeslee. The market is a mix of primary and secondary homes, most of which are fewer than 15 years old. The majority of new home construction in the Poconos occurs here and in the West End. The population has increased dramatically in the last decade. The Pocono Mountain School District complex more resembles a university campus than the grounds of a high school.

Lake Naomi, near Pocono Pines, is a better-than-average development with waterfront homes of at least three bedrooms costing around $300,000. A large lot of more than one acre with a dock and boathouse can exceed $250,000. Homes not near the water can be found for less than $100,000. Lake Naomi Club has a restaurant, golf course, two pools, tennis courts, programs for kids and, of course, a 250-acre lake for boating, fishing, sailing or sitting at the beach. For information on the club or to arrange a tour, call (800) 626-6439. Realtors who handle property in Lake Naomi and the surrounding Lake Wallenpaupack area include Lake Naomi Real Estate Inc., (800) 537-1479; Pocono Lake Realty, (800) 588-2808; Mountainlife Real Estate Inc., 646-6600; and ERA Archer Commonwealth Realty, 676-3773. For a free report on Lake Naomi properties, call CR Baxter Rentals Unlimited, (800) 962-7368.

Other popular areas for home buyers looking for a planned community include Timber Trails, Pinecrest Lake, Lake View Estates and Locust Lake Village. Buyers should have no trouble finding a ranch- or chalet-style home in one of these communities for around $75,000.

On the western edge of the Poconos, Big Bass Lake, north of Gouldsboro, is a successful private community. Lakefront homes run from $147,500 to $275,000. Homesites away from the lake start at $15,000 for a half-acre and $26,000 for an acre.

INSIDERS' TIPS

Buyers looking for waterfront property should visit Wayne County. The high water table in the region has created an unusual amount of ponds, streams and lakes. More than 21 square miles of water are scattered throughout the county. Although Wayne County has more lakes than any other county in Pennsylvania, there are no lakes in Sterling Township.

Townhouses along the ski slopes at Big Boulder, Jack Frost and Camelback start at just less than $100,000.

West End

These farmlands have become the boom area for building in the last decade. Developers regularly solicit the remaining farmers to sell their land. Whenever an older farmhouse with at least 50 to 100 acres goes on the market, it is snapped up. Usually, the buyer sells the house to fund the development of the remaining land as a subdivision. Such projects are common from Sciota south to Jim Thorpe. Many are off U.S. Highway 209, which creates traffic delays on this road, particularly on weekends.

Some of the more popular developments are Indian Mountain Lakes, Pleasant Valley Estates, Birch Hollow Estates and Birch Brier Estates. Secondary homes in these subdivisions start at $50,000 to $75,000. Primary homes start at $75,000 and average $120,000. One-acre lots range from $18,000 to $30,000.

Two townships, Ross and Eldred, have no zoning regulations, making them ideal for those who want to run a small business at home or build their own residence at a leisurely pace.

To the northwest, Lake Harmony offers homes from $125,000 to $250,000.

The region is split evenly between primary and secondary residences. Most commuters to New York or New Jersey who buy homes put them back on the market in a year or two. The added distance from Delaware Water Gap — at least 30 minutes — makes the drive too far for most commuters. However, many residents work in the Lehigh Valley (Allentown, Bethlehem or Easton). Also, the Northeast Extension of the Pennsylvania Turnpike travels through the region near Lehighton, making job markets in Wilkes-Barre, Scranton and Philadelphia accessible.

Second-home owners are attracted by the recreational opportunities; several state parks, lakes, ski areas, golf courses and the Lehigh River are nearby.

As in most of the Poconos, homes for rent are rare. When available, a three-bedroom house typically costs $650 or more per month. No large apartment or townhouse complexes exist.

Some of the most affordable homes and rentals are at Saylors Lake in Saylorsburg. Cottages that were once weekend retreats can be purchased for around $50,000.

At the southern end of the region, Jim Thorpe has become a major tourist destination along the order of New Hope, Pennsylvania. The steep, narrow streets are lined with quaint boutiques, antiques shops and art galleries. Row houses and mansions built for the mine workers and executives, respectively, have been restored. The Greenwich Village flavor of the businesses, the Industrial Revolution-era architecture and the European landscape, as the Lehigh River makes a grand entrance through the sweeping Lehigh Gorge, create an intoxicating combination that strikes your senses like no other spot in Northeastern Pennsylvania. Understandably, many who visit want to live here; and the town has developed a reputation as an artists' community.

Older row houses just outside the main tourism areas around Broadway start at $50,000. Older Victorians in need of renovations can be bought for as little as $75,000. Typical rental cost for a one/two-bedroom apartment ranges from $350 to $550. Expect large rooms, big moldings, solid construction and perhaps less-than-modern wiring, plumbing and kitchen facilities.

Outside Jim Thorpe, homes in local subdivisions start at $80,000 and range upward to at least $225,000.

Nearby, the town of Lehighton presents a unique real estate situation. Few homes ever reach the open market. Most are passed from generation to generation. Like Bangor, the town's residents are loyal to the community and tend to stay in the area. The few homes that are available are priced too high to attract outside interest. The typical home here was built after World War II, needs some remodeling and would list for $80,000 to $100,000. Apartment rental prices here and in Palmerton are comparable to rents in Jim Thorpe.

Milford Area

Milford is a picture-perfect small town. Its streets are lined with old trees. Most of the homes are around 100 years old and are restored to closely resemble their original Victorian designs. Walking the streets in summer to admire architecture and gardens is a popular pastime. Residents and shop owners pride themselves on preserving the town's old-time character. As the county seat of Pike County, many legal offices and the courthouse

are located on Broad Street in Milford's main business district.

Outside Milford, along U.S. highways 6 and 209, commercial activity has increased significantly in the last five years. A Wal-Mart opened as well as another large shopping complex, the Westfall Towne Center. More major projects are planned in the next few years including another shopping center built around a large superstore. Commercial land fronting this well-traveled shopping route sells for $100,000 an acre.

Commuters can reach most of the major New Jersey job markets via Interstate 84, U.S. Highway 206 and Interstate 80. One-third of the entire population of the United States is within a six-hour drive of Pike County. The Victorian homes in downtown Milford sell for $125,000 to $300,000. A few townhouses are available for $90,000.

Hemlock Farms, the largest private community in the Poconos, is nearby. Its facilities, security, fire department and recreation, are so extensive that it functions almost as a self-contained town. Other well-regarded developments are Gold Key Lake and Pocono Mountain Woodland Lake. Homes in all three subdivisions generally range from $75,000 to $150,000. However, cottages with access to a lake can be found for around $35,000.

The most unique private subdivision is Twin Lakes, near Shohola. Centered around two lakes (one is the largest natural lake in the Poconos), all the homes are older — typically at least 100 years old — usually stone or log construction, and start at $350,000. An acre lot can cost as much as $175,000.

Land prices in other parts of the area are much lower. A typical acre lot starts at $8,000. If you want an acre along a lake, expect to pay at least $30,000. Keep in mind that almost three-quarters of the total land in Pike County is controlled by the government as state forests or recreation areas. This eliminates many prime residential and commercial sites from the market.

Rentals go quickly in Milford. When available, three-bedroom homes rent for $650 to $850 per month.

Some of the best deals on larger homes

Photo: Pocono Mountains Vacation Bureau, Inc.

Beautiful resort scenery is *de rigueur* in the Poconos.

are found near Dingmans Ferry, south of Milford off U.S. Highway 209. The town is just outside the Delaware Water Gap National Recreation Area — land controlled by the National Park Service. A fully renovated 1830s farmhouse on a scenic parcel adjacent to the park costs approximately $125,000. A 12-acre horse farm complete with barn, pasture, corral, garage, pool and four-bedroom Dutch Colonial home sells for less than $250,000.

Farther south, a number of private communities are just outside of Bushkill — Pine Ridge, Pocono Ranchlands and Pocono Mountain Lake Estates. Also, the Tamiment Resort sells townhouses with access to its golf course for around $80,000. That same price will get you a ranch-style home in any of the aforementioned Bushkill-area developments. The Bushkill area draws the most commuters in the Milford area because it is farthest south and closest to Interstate 80. However, the drive down U.S. Highway 209 to Delaware Water Gap can be a nightmare on weekends when thousands of cars jam the two-lane road.

Lake Wallenpaupack Area

Some of the most coveted real estate in the Poconos is lakefront property along

Lake Wallenpaupack's 52-mile shoreline. This 5,700-acre, man-made lake is the focus of recreational activity in the region. The cheapest homes on the shoreline start at $135,000 to $150,000 and can go as high as $1.2 million. Three-bedroom townhouses overlooking the lake and featuring a dock start at $139,000.

Prices drop dramatically as you get farther away from Lake Wallenpaupack. Homes in the region start at $50,000, and a three-bedroom ranch home can be purchased for $70,000 to $80,000. Homesites start at $5,000 to $7,000 for a half-acre parcel.

Two popular private communities near Lake Wallenpaupack are Hidden Lake Estates and Tanglewood Lake Estates.

Hidden Lake Estates is a quarter-mile from Lake Wallenpaupack and features its own 40-acre lake. Unlike many subdivisions, lots here are comparatively large, usually 2 to 12 acres, and start at $20,000. Lakefront property costs at least $90,000. Homes in this upscale community are priced at a minimum of $135,000.

Slightly farther away, approximately 5 miles from Lake Wallenpaupack, Tanglewood Lake Estates has a golf course, a small lake and recreation-oriented amenities. The lots here are much smaller, generally a half-acre. As a result, prices are lower than at Hidden Lake; and an above-average, three-bedroom mini-

How To Choose
A Reputable Contractor

The Pennsylvania Builders Association recommends buyers consider the following items when selecting a builder. For further information, call the Pennsylvania Builders Association at (800) 692-7339 ext. 3016.

•Call your local builders association for a list of members.

•Ask contractors if they belong to a builders association.

•Ask for an insurance certificate to verify workers' compensation and liability insurance.

•Ask for references. Talk to other people who have had work done by the contractor and find out if they are happy.

•Ask to see the contractor's work.

•Make sure the contractor has a permanent business location and a good reputation with local banks and suppliers.

•Make sure all warranties, guarantees and promises are incorporated into your written contract. All changes should be done in writing.

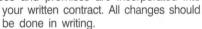

•Be specific about starting and completion dates, allowing for delays beyond the builder's control.

•Beware of unusually low bids and advertised prices.

•Choose a contractor who understands your tastes and needs and with whom you can communicate easily.

•Take your time. Never be pressured into signing a contract before you are ready.

The Pocono region has a handful of notable contactors with solid reputations, including but not limited to the following.

Hickory Lane Builders, Pa. Hwy. 611, Bartonsville, 894-4000 or (800) 233-0355), has more than 30 years in the business and more than $300 million in sales. The company also operates Hickory Mortgage Company and Pocono Hickory Lane, a land-development company.

J&S Custom Homes, 38 Learn Road, Tannersville, 629-5514, builds approximately 20 to 25 homes annually. With more than 10 years in the business, J&S prides itself on serving prospective homeowners of all income levels.

Liberty Homes Custom Builders, in Liberty Plaza, Pa. Highway 940, Pocono Lake, 646-4600 or (800) 326-9590, is a member of the Pocono Builders Association. This company has a reputation for building quality homes for 17 years and will work within any customer's budget.

LTS Builders, U.S. Highway 209, East Stroudsburg, 424-8867 or (800) 942-7450, is the Pocono region's largest custom builder and prides itself on providing professional service. In 1996, this company celebrated 20 years of producing quality homes.

Twin Builders, Pa Highway 903, Albrightsville, 722-9282 or (800) 836-4004), is a small, family operation that can accommodate construction jobs both large (new homes) and small (decks and additions).

estate primary or secondary home here could cost less than $100,000.

Many home buyers in this area are in their mid- to late 50s. They purchase homes to use for a vacation or weekend getaway until retirement, then become full-time residents.

Throughout the lake region, there is a huge demand for vacation rentals. Prices range from $600 to $1,400 per week for lakefront homes.

North of Lake Wallenpaupack, bargains on lovely Victorians can be found in Hawley and Honesdale, early industrial towns that are beginning to draw more tourists. Such houses, many suitable for conversion to bed and breakfast inns or small shops, are priced around $125,000. Honesdale's nickname is "Maple City." In 1847 borough officials had 1,500 maple trees planted to provide shade. Many of those same trees still decorate the downtown landscape. Hawley and Honesdale are too far away for most commuters, making real estate options less desirable than similar houses closer to the Stroudsburgs. The drive to most parts of the Scranton/Wilkes-Barre area takes about an hour.

Commuters who purchase property in Wayne County usually look to Damascus Township, the easternmost part of the county. From here, the drive to Manhattan takes two hours. In the southwestern part of the county, buyers sometimes travel to jobs in Scranton or Wilkes-Barre. They often look at homes in Waymart, Hamlin or Lake Ariel. Most desirable are "cottages," actually miniature mansions, which were built along the lake as weekend homes by the leaders of the coal industry. These lavish Victorians cost roughly $350,000 — when they become available. Less-expensive two- and three-bedroom houses, averaging $100,000 to $150,000, are available in The Hideout, a private community near Lake Ariel that boasts three lakes, beaches, golf, ice skating, pools and snowmobiling.

Another booming area is the southernmost part of Wayne County, in Lehigh Township. The greatest increase in housing construction between 1980 and 1990 in the county occurred in this 12.4-square-mile tract of prime real estate bordering Monroe County. During that decade, housing went from 479 units to 2,306 — a 440 percent increase.

Nearly 85 percent of the total land area of Wayne County is considered rural. More than 700 dairy and vegetable farms are currently in operation.

Perhaps the most luxurious community in the woods of the Poconos is Woodloch Springs, outside Hawley. Set on 400 acres of forests, streams, ponds, meadows, mountains and wetlands, the magnificent estates, usually costing more than $250,000, are anything but rustic. The 18-hole golf course here was selected in 1993 as one of the top 10 courses in the United States by Golf Magazine. Both the residential development and the adjoining Woodloch Pines resort are among the most professional operations of their kind in northeastern Pennsylvania.

In northern Wayne County, the most rural region in the Poconos, the market is almost exclusively secondary homes. Prices typically run from $70,000 to $400,000. The most requested features are privacy, view and water, such as a stream or pond. The hunting and fishing in this area are outstanding. The terrain often changes dramatically from rolling hills to heavily wooded mountains. Former farmhouses, often including a barn, pond and at least 10 acres of land, can be purchased for around $150,000, far less than in New York

Not every person who sells homes is a Realtor. That term is a registered trademark. Only members of a local association of Realtors, state association of Realtors and the National Association of Realtors are properly called Realtors. They operate under a specific code of ethics regarding professional conduct. The term "Realtor" is not synonymous with "broker" or "salesperson."

State or New England. Many residents own horses, and others earn a living boarding them for weekenders.

Slate Belt

The small towns in this region are popular with folks who want to belong to a close-knit community — the kind of place where neighbors help each other. Crime, traffic and pollution are not concerns here.

Tourism is less a factor in the local economy than in the rest of the Poconos. Most commercial activity is limited to small, often family-operated, businesses. The only part of the Slate Belt to experience a dramatic increase in commercial development is Wind Gap, particularly near Pa. Highway 33, where large shopping complexes and fast-food restaurants now dominate the landscape. Visible among the neighborhoods and commercial areas are mounds of scrap slate that gradually are being covered by vegetation. Another remnant of the slate industry are the huge pits, often several hundred feet deep, that were part of the old quarries. These have become filled with water and are quite dangerous; they should be avoided.

Most real estate activity in the Slate Belt is residential, almost always in the primary home market. Some people commute from here to the Lehigh Valley, and a few even travel as far as New Jersey to work. The region, while scenic and historic, lacks the easy access and rural privacy desired by most second-home owners.

Downtown Bangor resembles Lehighton — both were early industrial towns whose main source of income, the quarrying of slate in the Bangor area, is not as desired as it once was. Their business districts are dominated by large buildings constructed around the turn of the century. Today, these architectural marvels are occupied by small businesses that try to survive without the high volume of customers lured by tourist areas. Vacancies are common. Bangor has begun to court vacationing shoppers by adding antiques shops and eclectic boutiques to the mix of grocery and retail stores that serve residents.

Many families have lived in the Slate Belt for generations. Their loyalty to the region and each other is part of the appeal of living here. Folks looking for small-town unity will find it. Towns such as Bangor and Pen Argyl are the types of places where you might chat with about a dozen people on your walk from your house to the coffee shop to buy the morning newspaper.

The community spirit characteristic of the Slate Belt can be appreciated by looking at the creation of *Homefront*, a magazine published monthly during World War II from 1942 to 1946. J. Horace and Mona Strunk of Bangor organized volunteers and church groups to produce a glossy publication filled with news, photos and letters that was distributed free to soldiers fighting overseas. Perhaps no other neighborhood in the United States worked together so ambitiously to help the morale of our troops.

The largest community in the region is Bangor, with a population around 5,000. There — and in the slightly smaller town of Pen Argyl — older two- and three-bedroom homes cost $80,000 to $100,000. Most available land in these downtown areas is already developed; therefore, new home construction is rare.

However, developments in the Mount Bethel and Wind Gap areas have lots available, and a new two- or three-bedroom home can be built for around $150,000, including land.

Rural homesites are priced between $35,000 and $45,000 for a 1.5-acre parcel.

Retirement

It would be difficult to pick out the retirees or senior citizens around the Poconos and northeastern Pennsylvania if you based your judgments on a standard of activity. Seniors in the Poconos don't seem to sit still very long. You see them everywhere you go — volunteering as aides in the hospitals, as tutors in the schools, as ushers at the local playhouses, delivering meals on wheels, acting as friendly visitors, driving their neighbors to and from appointments, or counseling each other in senior centers or government-sponsored programs such as APPRISE, which helps with insurance claims. Seniors compete in Senior Olympic Games; marathons for different causes such as breast cancer and asthma; and walk-a-thons for wellness. They display their crafts at the State Craft Festival, at local flea markets and mall shows and at their own store, the Senior Craft Store at the Pocono Outlet Complex on Ann Street in Stroudsburg. They even perform in the local barbershop society (see our Arts and Culture chapter), the R.S.V.P. band, choral societies and brass quintets to name only a very few.

Senior citizens here are always in a process of beginning. You'll find them starting new businesses; developing new senior centers, such as the one opening in 1996 in Penn Forest Township; beginning clubs, such as the Pocono Singles Club and the Forever 50 Dance Club; supporting and managing arts organizations, such as Arts on the Mountain; introducing new programs to the community, such as the International Hearing Dog Association; and generally helping to ensure the quality of life for all residents in the Poconos. If you are looking for an active retirement life, you will find it in the Poconos where older adults comprise from 19 percent to 23 percent of the population in Monroe, Pike, Wayne and Northampton counties, and these figures increase every year.

Most seniors live on their own. They are helped by health organizations, such as the Visiting Nurses Association (VNA), hospice groups and other care-giver organizations. The area agencies on aging offer support of varying kinds depending on their charters. Some, such as the Pike County Area Agency on Aging, provide personal care through their own allocations, while others, Monroe County Area Agency on Aging for instance, work through outside groups. The focus in all the agencies is helping seniors remain independent for as long as possible — a goal most seniors have themselves.

When you come to the area, the first place you should call is your local area agency on aging (listed subsequently). Agencies provide brochures and pamphlets that outline all the opportunities and aid in the area, including how to volunteer, where to get hospice care, how to obtain identification cards for mass transit, and where to register for classes for driving, wellness or arts and crafts.

Area Agencies on Aging

The area agencies on aging, which follow state and federal guidelines for required services, are very active in Monroe, Pike, Wayne, Carbon and Northampton counties. They provide opportunities and assistance to meet medical and transportation needs. They also maintain senior centers in each county that serve as meeting places for seniors to play games, have socials, share meals, start clubs, sponsor trips and participate in agency-sponsored wellness programs, including exercise, health screenings and lectures. Monroe County even has a coalition of senior clubs, **Monroe County Senior Clubs Inc.**, 424-5290, which serves as a forum for all area senior-citizen clubs and sponsors inter-club events. Area agencies on aging provide identification cards for seniors that can be used for discount or reduced-rate programs. Call for application procedures.

Contact your area agencies for **American Association of Retired Persons** (AARP) information also. AARP offers 55/Alive Mature Driver courses at the different county centers.

Monroe County Area Agency on Aging, 62 Analomink Street, East Stroudsburg, 420-3735, maintains five senior centers: **Loder Senior Center**, 62 Analomink Street, East Stroudsburg, 420-3745; **Barrett Senior Center**, Pa. Highway 191, Barrett Township Ambulance Building, Mountainhome 595-9141 or 595-6004; **Chestnuthill Community Center**, Pa. Highway 715, Chestnuthill Township Park, Brodheadsville, 992-2916; and **Pocono Pines Friendship Center**, American Legion Building on Old Pa. Highway 940, Pocono Lake 646-9611.

Pike County Area Agency on Aging, 106 Broad Street in Milford, 296-7813, is responsible for two senior centers: **County Comers Center**, 10 Buist Road, Milford, 296-8730, and **Lackawaxen Senior Center** at the Lackawaxen Fire House, Pa. Highway 590, Lackawaxen, 685-2372.

Wayne County Area Agency on Aging, 323 10th Street, Honesdale, 253-4262, serves two senior centers: **Hawley Senior Citizen Center**, V.F.W. Building, Bingham Park, U.S. Highway 6, Hawley, 226-4831, and **Earl J. Simons Senior Citizen Center**, 323 10th Street, Honesdale, 253-4262.

Carbon County Office on Aging, 1121 North Street, Jim Thorpe, 325-2726, is responsible for five senior centers. These include **Lehighton Senior Center**, 243 S. Eighth Street, Lehighton, (610) 377-1530; **Weatherly Senior Center**, Zion Lutheran Church, Third and Fell streets, Weatherly, 427-8175; **Panther Valley Senior Center**, 353 W. Railroad Street, Nesquahoning, 669-9930; **Trescko Senior Center**, St. Bartholomew Founder's Hall, 49 E. Maple Street, 455-2511; and **Palmerton Senior Center**, Sokol Hall, 452 Lehigh Avenue, (610) 826-4505.

Northampton County Area Agency on Aging, (610) 559-3270, serves the Slate Belt section of the Poconos. The **Slate Belt Senior Center** is at 707 American-Bangor Road, Bangor, (610) 588-1224.

Transportation for Seniors

Specialized transportation for senior citizens is provided in each county through the area agencies on aging. Each agency provides transportation service a little differently, but all rely on a program called **Shared Ride**, which is partially funded by the Pennsylvania Department on Aging. The department's Harrisburg number is 783-8025. The revenue from the Pennsylvania Lottery underwrites the cost of Shared Ride in each county. Ride fees differ among area agencies, depending on the destination. Individuals must show identification to receive a reduced rate. Some drivers are retired senior citizens who work part time for Shared Ride. Please note that Shared Ride is not an emergency service.

Shared Ride is a major asset to Pocono counties because of limited public transportation, which only exists in Monroe County as **MC Transit**, 424-9500, in Carbon County as **Carbon County Community Transit**, and in the few privately owned taxi companies (see our Getting Around chapter for details). MC Transit provides transportation on the major arteries between Stroudsburg, Mount Pocono and Brodheadsville. It provides free transport to seniors during off-peak hours for folks with identification. MC Transit is also the carrier for the Shared Ride program in Monroe County.

Shared Ride requires advance notice, how much notice is needed depends on the particular agency. At minimum, it is 24 hours; Northampton requires three days' notice. Call the following agencies for more information:

> **FYI**
>
> Unless otherwise noted, the area code for all phone numbers in this guide is 717.

INSIDERS' TIPS

If you like to ski, note that area ski resorts offer senior-citizen discounts. At Shawnee and Camelback, seniors older than 70 ride lifts free.

Monroe County Shared Ride, 424-9500; **Pike County Shared Ride**, 296-9333; and **Wayne County Shared Ride**, 253-4280. Carbon County is in the process of changing its transportation program. Call the **Carbon County Office on Aging**, 325-2726, or **Carbon County Community Transit**, (800) 990-4287, for current transportation options. **Northampton County Area Agency on Aging** provides a Shared Ride program that operates based on need. To find out about transportation in the Slate Belt area, call the Northampton County agency, (610) 559-3270, or the **Slate Belt Senior Center** in Bangor, (610) 588-1224.

Job Opportunities

There are full-time and part-time jobs available for senior citizens who need to supplement their retirement income. The area agencies on aging work with seniors to place them in available employment opening. Opportunities vary widely and might surprise you. For information, call your area agency on aging.

Volunteer Opportunities

If you are interested in volunteering, you have many options. In Monroe County, contact the **Retired and Senior Volunteer Program (R.S.V.P.)**, which is affiliated with the national organization. R.S.V.P., 420-3747, is a clearinghouse for organizations that need volunteer help. If you are older than 55, R.S.V.P. will screen you to determine your likes and needs and will put you into their computerized volunteer file. In no time, you will be one of R.S.V.P.'s more than 1,200 volunteers who provide more than 200,000 volunteer hours a year in Monroe County alone.

Volunteers work in hospitals as dispatchers, porters and intra-office mail deliverers; in local community service organizations such as the American Cancer Society and American Red Cross; and in local arts organizations such as area historical societies. Local phone directories usually list individual organizations that need volunteer help. Look there if you are interested in contacting a particular group or organization. The possibilities are endless.

The Wayne County Volunteer Program, which evolved from R.S.V.P., offers volunteer opportunities in more than 50 organizations. Call 253-4262 for information about this volunteer program. To learn more about other volunteer programs, contact the area agency on aging near you.

In Pike County, volunteer efforts are coordinated through the Pike County Area Agency on Aging, 296-7813. Volunteers deliver and serve meals at local senior centers, provide transportation, act as telephone buddies and friendly visitors, shop for shut-ins and perform the myriad tasks that keep the aging citizens of the county serviced.

At the Slate Belt Senior Center in Bangor,

Northampton County volunteers help out at the center itself. They serve lunches, clean up, register riders for Shared Ride, sing at local nursing homes and perform whatever other odd jobs pop up. They are also active in the various local organizations and churches that depend on senior citizen volunteers.

Carbon County began an R.S.V.P. program, (610) 377-2021, in 1995. The office coordinates volunteers for community organizations, hospitals, community events, national groups such as the Red Cross and American Heart Association and numerous other programs sponsored by R.S.V.P. in the county.

Continuing Education

If you want to continue your education, courses toward degrees or just for enrichment are available at **East Stroudsburg University**, Storm Street, East Stroudsburg, 422-3542, and **Northampton Community College**, Old Mill Road in Tannersville, 620-9221 and Green Pond Road in Bethlehem, (610) 861-4551. The **Monroe County Vocational-Technical School** also offers a variety of courses from automotive technology to nursing. (See our Education chapter for details.) If transportation is an issue for you, the area agencies on aging can help. Often, seniors live far from the few mass transit options in the area, so transportation for those who don't drive might require planning. See this chapter's previous "Transportation" section for more information.

Wellness

Commitment to wellness is a cornerstone of the health programs in this area. Each of the agencies on aging offers free health screenings and exercise classes as part of the daily opportunities for seniors. The area hospitals also offer programs that promote wellness.

In Monroe County, Pocono Medical Center is well-known for its **Community Health Improvement Program** (CHIP) which has focused on senior wellness programs since 1980. Its Older Adult Exercise Program (OAEP) was cited in the 1996 report of the White House Conference on Aging for its recommendations on hospital-based senior wellness programs. Ongoing and short-term programs are avail-able, including the CHIP Health & Fitness Program. Besides low-impact aerobic exercise classes, this program offers classes on nutrition, stress reduction, coping with depression and others. Look for details in the hospital newsletter and in *Dignity*, the seniors newspaper published by the *Pocono Record.* Call 476-3332 for CHIP information.

Devereux Pocono Center in Newfoundland (see our Healthcare chapter) offers wellness clinics throughout the year. The public is offered free glaucoma exams, muscle testing, hearing and foot exams and other health tests. Mammograms and heart tests are available by appointment. For information, call 676-3237.

Gnaden Huetten Memorial Hospital in Lehighton offers the **New Seasons** program for folks older than 55. New Seasons features a free weekly exercise program, a care-givers support group, free or discounted health screenings, educational programs and a coordinator to help you decide what you need. Call (610) 377-7180 to speak with the New Seasons coordinator.

The **YMCA** is also an important source for wellness programs. The Pocono Family YMCA in Stroudsburg has a wide selection of exercise programs, including arthritis swims and health-specific classes for increasing aerobic capacity. Call 421-2525 for a list of the offerings. In Barrett Township (northwest of Stroudsburg in Mountainhome) older-adult exercise programs are available too. Call 595-2730 for information. In Pike County, the Pike County YMCA is an older-adult exercise-program source. To reach this YMCA in Dingmans Ferry, call 828-2329.

Monroe County Recreation, 992-4343 or 421-2871, sponsors some programs for older adults. It schedules lap swim times and other adult swim programs at the area high school pools. It is planning to start senior citizen walking clubs in the different communities by 1997. Along with the YMCA, CHIP and the Monroe County Area Agency on Aging, Monroe County Recreation sponsors the Senior Fitness Walk each May as a celebration of senior citizen physical fitness.

Retirement-living Options

As we've noted, independence is a key

Christmas in April

For those who lament that "Christmas comes but once a year," Monroe County has a surprise for you. Around here, it comes twice a year. Christmas in April – Monroe County, which debuted in Monroe County in April 1995, is a nonprofit, chartered organization and a member of the national, nonprofit group, Christmas in April – USA, begun in Midland, Texas.

The mission of Christmas in April is to keep low-income, elderly and disabled homeowners living in warmth, safety, independence, dignity and decency through home repair and rehabilitation volunteer services. In Monroe County, more than 25 homes have been rehabilitated through the financial and physical aid of local volunteers. One day each year, these folks devote their time, expertise, materials, money, support and spirit to help senior citizens continue to live in the dignity they deserve.

In Monroe County, the Christmas in April committee was especially lucky to have so many local building and architectural professionals offer their services to make plans and manage and teach the volunteer laborers. Of course, a large number of volunteers were senior citizens — their efforts focused with the help of the Monroe County Senior Clubs Inc. All work completed has to meet the National Home Safety Checklist guidelines developed by the national organization.

Members of the Monroe County Area Agency on Aging started the program and continue to run it on a volunteer basis. The Area Agency on Aging, the Advisory Council and County Commissioners support Christmas in April by allowing volunteers time to work on the project.

All materials are donated, so the repairs and renovations are absolutely free to the chosen seniors. Ramps are built, roofs are put on, bathrooms are repaired, trailer homes are made safe — whatever needs to be done is done through this program. In its first year of 1995, Christmas in April – USA rehabilitated 4,000 homes at an estimated cost of $24 million (donated) and through the efforts of 120,000 volunteers. Christmas in April – Monroe County was part of those statistics. It continues to be part of the group that has found a way to make Christmas come twice a year.

---

goal for senior citizens in the Pocono region. Consequently, there is not a wide range of options for assisted living, personal care or nursing homes, although there are some and their services vary. Many seniors live at home with the help of visiting nurse programs or homemaker aid provided through the area agencies on aging or other healthcare organizations.

Retirement Communities

The only retirement community in the area is **LaBar Village** on Village Circle in Stroudsburg, 476-3126. This housing development is on the outskirts of the city. Its residents live in townhouses on neatly winding lanes surrounding a community house with reception rooms and dining facilities. There is a community association, and transportation is provided by LaBar Village vans.

Senior Housing

Senior citizen housing is available at three Monroe County locations. The Shirley Futch Plaza is managed on-site, while the Monroe County Housing Authority manages the other two, Avon Court and Westgate Apartments. Eligibility for these senior housing options is

Photo: Pocono Mountains Vacation Bureau, Inc.

Who's having more fun — the ducks or this couple?

based on income guidelines (no more than $23,000, one person; $26,000, two persons) and age (must be older than 62). If you are interested in senior housing, realize that current waiting lists at each complex are approximately three years.

For seniors who have their own apartment or who have found a place to live but need financial assistance, look into a program administered by the U.S. Department of Housing and Urban Development referred to as Section 8 — Rental Certificate and Rental Voucher Programs. This program is processed through the housing authority in Monroe County, 421-7770, for families whose income does not exceed 50 percent of the median income for the area. There are other qualifications that give preference to those in displaced situations. Section 8 pays a landlord the difference between what you can afford and the amount of your housing.

Shirley Futch Plaza
4 S. Kistler St., East Stroudsburg • 421-1517

This is a lovely, well-maintained senior complex. It has five floors, elevators and all handicapped-accessible options. The units are one-bedroom apartments with a kitchenette, living room-dining room combination and bathroom. The grounds are nice, with tables for picnicking and relaxing, walkways and benches. The plaza is right across from the

Dansbury Depot and the Loder Senior Center. There is a bus stop out front, and it is within walking distance of East Stroudsburg University and a number of small stores.

Avon Court -
Monroe County Housing Authority
1055 W. Main St., Stroudsburg • 421-7770

Avon Court is actually in East Stroudsburg on Day Street across from Dansbury Park, but you must contact the housing authority at the above number or address for information. Housing is in cottages containing four units. Each unit has a kitchen, living room, bedroom and bathroom. Avon Court is convenient to the bus and to the small stores that make up the East Stroudsburg shopping area. It is also near the Loder Senior Center.

Westgate Apartments -
Monroe County Housing Authority
1055 W. Main St., Stroudsburg • 421-7770

Westgate is at 1055 W. Main Street across from Stroudsburg High School and the Stroudsburg Park. It has five floors of efficiency apartments with a few one-bedroom apartments. Upper-story apartments have balconies. There are well-maintained grounds with walkways and benches in this central downtown location. A bus stop is out front; a Wawa store is up the street. The center of town is about a five-block walk.

Personal-care and Nursing Homes

The two major types of institutional-based care for seniors are personal-care arrangements and institutions with skilled nursing care. Personal care is attended to in assisted living environments; skilled nursing in nursing homes. As the industry of providing care for the elderly has picked up and gained prestige, the difference between personal care and nursing home arrangements has clouded. Many nursing homes have expanded (or are planning to expand) their options to include assisted-living units. Many assisted-living complexes are evolving to provide nursing care units.

Assisted-living arrangements range from apartments in a complex to private or semiprivate rooms in neighborhood or countryside homes to cottages on the grounds of nursing homes. Nursing homes tend to offer fewer choices in living arrangements, as residents usually require full-time care and some rehabilitative services.

All the homes listed here as personal-care, or assisted-living, options provide services such as basic hygiene assistance (bathing, shaving, dressing and grooming), medication (storage and monitoring), housekeeping, laundry and other needs of ambulatory, healthy individuals as part of the living arrangement. It also means three meals a day with attention to special dietary needs and nutritious snacks.

Institutions noted as nursing homes provide complete 24-hour nursing care, rehabilitative and medical therapies, along with the "personal care" services that are part of assisted living. The following is a partial listing of area establishments licensed by the State of Pennsylvania. For more options, which are opening all the time due to the increase in the demand for elderly care, contact the local area agency on aging.

Stroudsburg/East Stroudsburg

Hillcrest Retirement Community
6000 Running Valley Rd., Bartonsville
• 629-2410

The name Hillcrest suits this retirement and personal-care community because it sits atop a hill overlooking the Monroe County Environmental Center and old farms that span the horizon. There are apartments with kitchenette facilities as well as private and semiprivate rooms. All rooms have controlled heat, air conditioning and cable TV outlets. Some private rooms have a bedroom and sitting room with large windows that provide lovely views.

Amenities include an indoor pool and covered walkways and patios (enhanced with colorful hanging plants and garden areas in the summer) that lead to apartment units. The buildings form a horseshoe around a protected outdoor recreation area for shuffleboard and other activities. Transportation can be arranged using the Hillcrest shuttle vans. The large common dining rooms overlook the grounds, and there are open rooms for socials and planned daily activities, including shopping and recreation trips.

Family visits are encouraged. Grandchildren are always welcome and even encouraged to visit in the advertisements for Hillcrest. The atmosphere is friendly and low-key. Costs are based upon room type. There is no entrance fee.

Joest's Boarding Home
Indian Way, Analomink • 424-6852

This is a very cozy, small personal-care boarding home for eight residents. Care is limited to Alzheimer and stroke patients. It is situated in the countryside on several acres of family-owned property. All rooms are singles. There are two double bathrooms and three half-baths. Activities are limited to monthly concerts. The operation is totally managed by the

Photo ID Cards for Non-Drivers

Senior citizens who do not have a driver's license can get a photo identification card that resembles a license and is accepted for ID purposes.

The Bureau of Driver Licensing in Harrisburg issues the photo identification cards for non-drivers. The IDs are the size of a credit card and include the individual's name, address, date of birth, signature and photograph. The non-driver identification card is

available to any Pennsylvania resident age 16 or older. It is a handy option for seniors who may have allowed their license to expire, failed a licensing test or surrendered their license due to suspension.

The cost of an ID card is $9, and they are valid for four years. A complimentary card may be issued by the Bureau of Licensing. If you formerly had a driver's license and a safe driving record or surrendered your license voluntarily for health reasons, you may be eligible for a complimentary card. For more information, write the Photo Identification Program, Bureau of Licensing, P.O. Box 68682, Harrisburg 17106, or call (800) 932-4600.

owners and a limited staff. Costs are based on individual requirements. Call for rate information.

Laurel Manor Nursing Home
1170 W. Main St., Stroudsburg • 421-1240

Laurel Manor is an intermediate-care nursing home, and it has a small personal-care complex. It is near the Westgate Apartments senior housing complex in Stroudsburg — a plus for keeping in touch with friends who want to stop — and it's convenient to many local stores.

There are currently 59 beds in the intermediate-care unit, five in the personal-care facility and four cottages. Rooms are private or semiprivate, based on specific needs, with baths in each. The major concentration here is nursing, so all nursing needs are provided on a 24-hour basis. Residents must be under the care of the facility physician. The daily rate includes meals, room, personal laundry and regular daily nursing. Medications, doctor visits, supplies and other apparatus are billed separately.

Private telephones, televisions, furniture and other amenities must be approved. Beauticians and barbers visit twice a week, and residents may have their account charged for the service. An activities director is on staff, and residents who are able attend outside events. Social activities and meetings are held in a lovely recreation room with a wood-burning fireplace. Pet therapy, movies, games, crafts and religious services are part of the social environment at Laurel Manor. The rooms are light and airy. The grounds cover 1½ acres and offer paths and outdoor sitting arrangements.

The personal-care program is designed to provide care when needed and to encourage seniors to live at their highest functioning level. Residents in the personal-care program live in a comfortable five-bed facility and in four cottages on the grounds.

Private rooms at Laurel Manor cost $150 per day; semiprivate rooms are $130 and personal-care arrangements are $90 a day.

Milford Manor
U.S. Hwy. 209 Bus., East Stroudsburg • 424-0343

Milford Manor is a 40-bed personal-care facility that provides supervision with independence. It is close to Stroudsburg and on the way to Milford and Dingmans Ferry, so it is convenient for visitors. There are three acres of property that provide natural views from all rooms. The decor is a blend of modern and period furnishings intended to create a friendly environment.

Nursing supervision is a major component here along with physical rehabilitation. There is a medical director, and attending physicians are available for emergencies and periodic examinations. Supervised activities stimulate social interaction and community involvement for residents. On holidays, fine china, elegant meals (the chef here has a great reputation) and entertainment for friends and family are offered. There is a lovely patio for seasonal picnics, exercise classes and other outdoor activities.

The grounds have grassy lawns dotted with benches and two ponds. Single and double rooms are air conditioned and decorated in bright, cheery colors. Matching comforters, dust ruffles and bouffant curtains make each unit a lovely, special place. There are pretty flowered prints and colors for the women and more subdued, tailored looks for the men. Plants fill the interiors, with fresh-cut flowers on sideboards, dining tables and in sitting areas.

Daily rates are based on room type and level of care needed.

Pleasant Valley Manor
4227 Manor Dr., Kellersville • 992-4172

Pleasant Valley Manor is a nursing home with 174 residents, all of whom have a significant medical need requiring 24-hour care. The home operates like a small village. There is a little gift shop and store run by a volunteer shopkeeper where you can buy treats or other items, and there is a beauty salon with a full-time beautician. There is a clean, happy air about the facility. Residents are identified in their rooms by mailboxes at their doors.

There is a lovely, awning-covered, screened porch where residents can watch the world go by or enjoy the cool breezes. Spacious halls lead to sitting or recreation rooms where residents may play games, watch TV, read or chat. There is a choice of where to eat — the dining room with its lovely view of the grounds through valance-topped windows; the outdoor, bricked terrace; or the rooms themselves for those inclined to dine alone.

Services at Pleasant Valley range from daily, personal care to laundry services and sewing. There is a large sewing room managed by the housekeeping unit where clothes are mended free as they come out of the laundry. There are skilled services to support hospital patients with rehabilitative needs. There are also rooms for physical therapy to treat lower-body needs and occupational therapy for personal, hygiene-related needs.

There are lots of things to do at Pleasant Valley — a full schedule of activities, including trips and socials, is available every day. A fun diversion for many, and one Pleasant Valley has become noted for, is making ceramics. Families find it an easy place to visit at any time; drop-in visits are encouraged.

Applicants must meet county and facility criteria for admittance to this nursing home, as it has been designated "county home" for Monroe County. To begin the assessment process, contact the Monroe County Area Agency on Aging, 420-3735. MCAAA has a booklet explaining the required steps and information needed to complete the medical and financial assessment process. Costs are based on all of the eligibility and needs criteria the different agencies apply. Some private-pay residents are also accepted, but the waiting list is a long one.

Mount Pocono Area

Brookmont Health Care Center
Brookmont Dr., Effort • (610) 681-4070

This nursing home provides long-term and interim care and is not for assisted-living residents. Programs address every level of need for rehabilitation, therapy, enrichment, exercise and skilled care, including care for Alzheimer patients. Brookmont is in the countryside near the thriving town of Brodheadsville.

Residents live in private or semiprivate rooms with baths. There are community rooms for social activities and events. Activities are offered daily, and residents may choose two or three from a list that includes exercise, sing-alongs, movies and videos, balloon volleyball, group discussions, bowling and off-site lunches for those who are ambulatory. A skilled staff provides an extensive program of rehabilitation services including physical and occupational therapy, rehabilitative nursing, respiratory therapy, speech pathology and audiology. Skilled care also includes basic personal care.

Wanderguard bracelets for Alzheimer residents are charged by the month. Costs are subject to change, but currently are $123 a day for semiprivate rooms and $133 for private rooms.

Getz Personal Care Home, Inc.
Pa. Hwy. 534, Jonas • 629-1334, 629-6111

This personal-care facility is in a lovely country setting near Kresgeville. The facility is family-owned and operated, and some family members are even residents. Children, grandchildren and great-grandchildren interact with residents to sustain the at-home feeling at Getz. The property is substantial and residents have access to ponds, a fish hatchery and hiking areas. Many residents take advantage of the setting to take long hikes in the woods. It is also close to a general store that provides a fun walking destination.

The residents here are generally ambulatory. They take part in senior center activities, go to concerts (transport provided via van), attend the annual West End Fair and participate in many community activities. For days at home there is a calendar of events and activities to keep residents busy.

The rooms are very homey with carpets, brightly colored curtains and matching borders helping complete the look of each room. Television and telephone hookups are available in each room for residents who want to enjoy these amenities privately. There are four wings, each with a sitting room or sun room; the most popular sitting room is the one in front where everyone comes and goes. There are private and semiprivate rooms with private

baths and shared baths. The dining room overlooks the grounds, and residents tend to cluster in neighborhood groups with others living in the same wing.

Costs are based on room type and are quoted on inquiry.

Sunset View Village
Pa. Hwy. 715, Reeders • 620-2330

The view from this personal-care facility is delightful. Sunset View is on a mountainside with vista views of the area between Brodheadsville and Camelback Ski Area. There are a total of 28 private and semiprivate rooms and small suites. The lodgings have a chalet look with a large patio that overlooks an outdoor pool and the 50 acres the village occupies.

Inside, there is a plant room and a country room with a large stone fireplace for cozy winter evenings or planned activities. The dining room is large and bright, and the TV room is quite spacious. Along with three meals a day, there are a fresh fruit and salad bar, nutritious snacks and juices offered daily. Standard personal care also includes local transportation and Bible study.

Special accommodations at Sunset View include security alarms to prevent Alzheimer residents from wandering. There are security guards and 24-hour nursing care. Other services include an on-site beauty and barber shop.

Costs are based upon room type and are available upon request by interested parties.

West End

Springfield Meadows
50 W. Broadway, Jim Thorpe • 325-2761

This 16-bed, personal-care facility provides two care levels — completely mobile and physically disabled. Springfield Meadows is in Jim Thorpe, a delightfully rich historic community surrounded by mountains. The building is a Victorian home on West Broadway,

> **FYI**
> Unless otherwise noted, the area code for all phone numbers in this guide is 717.

which puts it right in the middle of town. As with all properties on the main streets of Jim Thorpe, the grounds are behind the building.

This facility caters to Alzheimer patients and residents with dementia or confusion problems. The staff works very closely with families and provides a great deal of one-on-one support. The owners are nurses, and there is a facility doctor and podiatrist. All staff are CPR-certified and receive ongoing, in-service education, and there is 24-hour on-site, on-call care. Doors are alarmed for the protection of wandering residents.

There are private rooms on two floors, each with a full bath for the residents of that floor. There is a "stairchair" to the second floor. Monthly activities, including summer cookouts and holiday parties, are scheduled. The Christmas party — attended by residents and their families, and by the staff and their families — is always a special event.

Costs are based on room type and level of care and range from $1,250 to $1,800 per month. Many services are provided on a fee basis including cable TV, medications and hairdressing or barber services. There is another cost scale for immobile residents based on Pennsylvania codes. The base charges is $800 per month. Prices are subject to change and are negotiable for those with affordability constraints.

Lake Wallenpaupack Area

Devereux Pocono Center
Pa. hwys. 507 and 191, Newfoundland • 676-3237

Devereux offers several options for retirement and aging care. There is a residential section for those who need assistance with some daily living skills and for those requiring significant daily living assistance. Some residences are available for adults capable of semi-independent living.

Respite overnight care (care provided while family members are on vacation or dealing with other situations) and adult day-care programs are also available at Devereux, which

is part of a nationwide network of centers founded in 1912. The six residences in the village of Newfoundland blend in well with a community of the finest inns, resorts, shops, golf courses and park areas in the region. The residences have beautiful kitchens, comfortable living rooms and bedrooms. Pets are allowed, fireplaces and recreation rooms complement the facilities and a swimming pool adds the wellness factor important for adult physical health.

There are daily social, recreational and vocational activities at the Devereux Clubhouse. Fitness programs, discussion groups, woodworking and community involvement are also part of a Devereux day.

Costs for a basic program including room and board, assisted living, clinical supervision and nursing availability are approximately $110 per day for residential or respite care. Clothing, medical services and other specialized care is billed separately. Adult day care is $35 per day; $20 per half-day. This rate includes lunch and transportation within a 10-mile radius. All rates are subject to change.

This center offers an extraordinary vacation package for out-of-the-area families considering Devereux for a loved one. Call to arrange a visit.

Twin Cedars
2 Littlewalker Rd., Shohola • 296-7471

This lovely personal-care facility is just six years old and has room for 35 residents in private and semiprivate rooms. There is a cathedral ceiling in the ranch-style home, which is set among beautiful lawns with walkways and picnic tables dotting the landscape. A large deck with a suncovering overlooks a pond and waterfall fountain. The back grounds are surrounded by masses of blueberry bushes that provide residents with a year-round supply for pancakes, muffins, pies and other blueberry delicacies. Twin Cedars is on a quiet country road safe enough for residents to enjoy walks in the area.

All rooms are larger than state requirements, have private bathrooms and are cheerfully decorated. The main areas have cathedral ceilings, chandeliers, many doors opening onto the large deck areas and open, airy recreation rooms. "So very clean" is a phrase that often comes up when describing the accommodations. Families and residents love the attention to the beauty and cleanliness of the facility.

Regular activities are planned on a daily basis along with numerous field trips to exciting Pike County destinations such as the Zane Grey Museum, Grey Towers, the Pike County Historical Society, Shohola Falls and Roebling Bridge. There are also shopping excursions and trips termed "stay in the van," for those who cannot easily manage walking or getting in and out of the 15-passenger facility van but love to ride along the many scenic roads.

Costs for residents vary based on type of room and level of care needed. Please call for information.

Slate Belt

Blue Mountain Manor
Lower Smith Gap, Kunkletown
• **(610) 381-3116**

Blue Mountain Manor provides personal care as needed to help residents avoid institutionalization. It is in the small town of Kunkletown, which helps maintain a family-oriented atmosphere. The assisted-living facility is operated by the Pelczynski family. There are approximately 40 residents.

Included in personal-care attention here is financial management, transportation (for appointments, shopping, recreation) and help with insulin injections. There is a staff physician, and staff members are on duty 24 hours a day. Residents live in private and semiprivate rooms; some with private baths, some with shared baths. There is wall-to-wall carpeting, cable TV and outdoor recreation on the spacious grounds at the foot of Blue Mountain. Gardening, fishing and just walking are encouraged along with other outdoor hobbies

and activities. Three home-cooked meals are provided daily.

Costs are based on type of room and level of care needed. Call for information on rates.

Bush's Personal Care Homes Inc.
P.O. Box 327, Kunkletown
• **(610) 381-3713**

Bush's two personal care homes, Chestnut Ridge and Country View, allow seniors to live independently with some assistance. The homes are surrounded by lovely lawns and scenic views of the Blue Mountains, which can be seen from the rooms and patio. There are private and semiprivate rooms with private baths, shared baths, private bath/showers or shared bath/showers. The semiprivate rooms in the new Chestnut Ridge's new east annex are somewhat larger than the others in the facility. Also available is a two-bedroom, independent living unit.

There are lots of large windows and sliding glass doors; rooms are light-colored and cheery. Each room is equipped with an intercom, private telephone and TV hookups. Residents may bring their own furnishings and even maintain their own automobile. There are central socializing areas and lots of planned on-site activities such as weekly exercise programs, senior club meetings, games, education programs, day-care visits, gardening and movies. Field trips in Bush vans take residents to surrounding points of interest such as shopping outlets, country inns, seasonal sporting events, theaters and so on. Three meals a day are part of the care.

Personal-care assistance here also includes a weekly hair wash and set for ladies, transportation (for appointments, shopping, recreation) and other needs requiring assistance for ambulatory, healthy individuals. Immediate medical attention is available. For those recuperating from an illness or injury who only need short-term medical management, respite accommodations are available. Respite care is also offered for those who need

Photo: Pocono Mountains Vacation Bureau, Inc.

Memorytown, USA, is a popular attraction for young and old.

a place to stay, for as short a span as a week, while their caregivers are on vacation.

Costs are based on room type, shared or private bath and building or annex location. Rates range from $47.50 to $75 per day, with short-term stays costing an additional $5 per day.

The Chandler Estate IV
1569 Teels Rd., Pen Argyl • (610) 863-1569

This facility is on 12 acres in a residential area and looks like just another community. The Chandler Estate provides assisted living in garden apartments and personal care in private and semiprivate rooms. "A la Carte" services are available for folks living in the garden apartments who do not need a full complement of personal-care services. These include a beauty shop, housekeeping, bathing assistance, laundry, shopping, medication reminders, scheduling and appointment-keeping and other options on a per-service fee basis.

Each garden apartment contains a kitchen,

bedroom, living room/dining room combination, bath, large walk-in closet, patio and private outside and security entrances. Some two-bedroom apartments are available. Telephone and TV connections are included. Other apartments are in ranch-style buildings, four apartments to a building. There is staff on call 24 hours a day at the main complex if there is a need. Independent-living apartments and 30 personal-care private rooms are available in the main building. The objective is to keep residents living independently as long as possible.

At Chandler Estates the environment is set up to accommodate the stages that occur in the needs of the elderly. As more care is needed, residents can move from garden apartment to assisted-living apartment to personal-care private room, yet they can remain where they have made friends and established a support system.

Costs are based on type of accommodation and level of care needs. Call for a cost analysis.

Maple Run Manor
Pa. Hwy. 115, Saylorsburg • 992-5363

Residents at this comfortable personal-care home live in private or semiprivate rooms depending on choice and availability. In the hamlet of Saylorsburg, near Saylors Lake, it operates on a month-to-month plan that allows residents control of their assets. There is 24-hour monitoring by a nursing care staff.

Maple Run is small and homey and available for short- or long-term stays. There are three lovely porches overlooking the grounds, and common areas provide space for planned social and recreational activities. Private sitting areas are available for quieter times.

Private accommodations are $980 per month; semiprivate are $880. Cable TV tacks on an additional $10 per month, and there are per-trip fees for transportation to medical appointments.

Adult Day Care

Adult Day Care is available through Devereux at its **Devereux Pocono Center** in Newfoundland (see "Personal-Care and Nursing Homes" in this chapter) and its **Tri-State Adult Day Center**, U.S. 6, Milford, 296-4616. The $35 daily fee includes intergenerational activities such as pet therapy, music and cooking. A nutritious lunch and snacks are included as are all activity and craft supplies. Transportation is free within a 10-mile radius. For rates beyond 10 miles, contact the day services director.

The **Comfort of Home**, 745 Ann Street in Stroudsburg, 421-8447, also offers adult day care. The environment is a double-home with four living rooms, two dining rooms, a kitchen, two bathrooms and a large porch with swings. The furniture is comfortable, and the decor is Victorian. The intention is that clients feel like they're visiting a friend's home for the day, which lasts from 8 AM to 5 PM and includes lunch and snacks (breakfast too, if required).

Personal grooming (even bathing) is offered for those who need this personal-care assistance, and there is no extra charge for this service. Trips are planned along with other daily activities such as games, exercises classes and monthly musical entertainment provided by R.S.V.P. The fee is $37 for a full day or $5.50 per hour with a four-hour minimum.

The Comfort of Home is partially supported by the Monroe County Area Agency on Aging and is state licensed. Transportation may be arranged through Shared Ride. The facility offers a monthly Alzheimer's caregivers support group on the second Tuesday of the month at 7 PM. Care is provided for your loved one while you attend the meeting.

Home Health Services

The main services provided through home health service agencies are skilled nursing (blood work, catheter care, ostomy care, etc.), specialty care (wound care, IV therapy, EKGs, etc.), nutrition counseling, physical therapy, speech and occupational therapy and hospice care. All services are coordinated through healthcare benefits programs provided by private insurance companies, Medicare and Medicaid. Fees are based on insurance company guidelines for physician-ordered services. For those who need further assistance, some fees might qualify to be picked up by United Way or other charitable organizations.

For seniors who find they need help to continue living at home, we've listed just a few of the available services. You'll need to do some research to find the right one for you. The comprehensive list is extensive, so contact your area hospital, area agency on aging or phone directory for others that might interest you.

The **Visiting Nurse Association** (VNA), 421-5390, works with area hospitals and aging agencies as well as through **Home Care Services**, 421-5390. In Monroe County, the VNA also provides hospice services, as does **Lehigh Valley Hospice**, 420-0912. Some other home healthcare agencies are **Diamond Home Health Services**, 424-2557; and **Home Care of the Poconos**, 420-9917. Also note that the Monroe County Area Agency on Aging, 420-3735, has information on area home health service options.

Pocono Eldercare, Pa. Hwy. 390, Promised Land Village, 676-3359, offers nonmedical in-home assistance to anyone who needs daily or weekly care — five to 24 hours a day, seven days a week — for bathing, medication reminders, meals, light housekeeping, shopping or other nonmedical needs. Eldercare serves Monroe, Pike and Wayne counties. It also accepts those who are not yet elderly.

In Pike County, arrangements for home healthcare, including meals for the homebound, are coordinated through the Pike County Area Agency on Aging, 296-7813. The community health nurse arranges in-home assistance for the elderly.

In Wayne County, **Wayne Home Health Services** is the key provider for home health needs. Contact this service through Wayne County Area Agency on Aging, 253-4262.

In Carbon and Northampton counties, **Carbon County Home Health Care** provides personal service and healthcare to eligible clients as part of Gnaden Huetten Memorial Hospital's health system. Call (610) 377-7157 for service information. In Pen Argyl, you can also call **Slate Belt Visiting Nurses**, (610) 863-7281.

The emergency number to call in Monroe, Carbon and Pike counties is 911. Dial 0 for operator to reach emergency care in other locations.

Healthcare

There are four main not-for-profit hospitals in the Pocono region: Pocono Medical Center in the Stroudsburg/East Stroudsburg area, serving Monroe and Pike counties; Gnaden Huetten Hospital in the West End; Wayne Memorial Hospital in the Lake Wallenpaupack area; and Palmerton Hospital in the Slate Belt. Walk-in services are generally available through these hospitals' emergency rooms. While each of these hospitals offers extensive health services, many residents go to Scranton, Allentown/Bethlehem, Philadelphia or Danville for major health problems that require specialists who aren't available in these hospitals.

There are a few specialization centers, such as Gnaden Huetten's Open Forum for mental health and Winco Medical Center in East Stroudsburg for drug and alcohol problem treatment. Individualized home healthcare can be provided through the home-health and nursing agencies in the area, most of which work in connection with the area hospitals or through physicians' offices. These services are generally recommended by doctors. If you need them, your doctor, the hospital or the Area Agencies on Aging (if you are a senior citizen) will provide you with the needed referrals and information (also see our Retirement chapter).

Hospitals have limited ambulance service. Most ambulance service is provided by volunteer and privately owned ambulance corps. Volunteer ambulance services have been the backbone of the Pocono support system for a long time. All are run by the local responders who are trained EMTs. Trained First Responders are on call for each local ambulance corps.

When you move into an area, check with your local hospital or municipal clerk to find out which ambulance group serves your location. The emergency number to call in Monroe, Carbon and Pike counties is 911. Dialing 0 for operator will get you emergency care in other locations.

Hospitals

Stroudsburg/ East Stroudsburg

Pocono Medical Center
206 E. Brown St., East Stroudsburg
• 421-4000

Most Monroe and Pike county doctors are affiliated with Pocono Medical center. This 211-bed facility provides extensive services in every area of need from birth to life-threatening illness. It has been a leader in wellness services through the Community Health Improvement Programs (CHIP). It has a Women's Health Center and a Cancer Center. The mental health needs of the community are also met through this hospital's Mental Health Services and its coordination with Mental Health-Mental Retardation (MH-MR) for the Carbon, Monroe and Pike areas, a centralized mental health agency, 421-2901 or (800) 338-6467.

Outpatient and ambulatory services, including same-day surgery, are also provided through this hospital.

This year the hospital opened the **Pocono Community Health Center**, 476-3585, for prenatal and pediatric services. It is in a separate facility adjoining the hospital at 200 E. Brown Street. The center provides comprehensive preventive care and mother/child education services. All services and care are available to all families regardless of ability to pay. For those who need help with transportation to and from visits and classes, assistance is available. Childbirth classes are given; call 476-3584.

This center also maintains an immunization registry, the first of its kind in Pennsylvania.

The Pocono Medical center has a Physician Referral Service, (800) 851-0268.

West End

Gnaden Huetten Hospital
211 N. 12 St., Lehighton • (610) 377-1300

This 121-bed facility is the center for more than 30 medical specialties. It also has a 91-bed nursing and convalescent home and supports a mental health day treatment program in Stroudsburg called Open Forum, 424-1402.

It has recently opened the Gnaden Huetten outpatient center at Nesquehonning, 669-9240, where outpatient services and surgeries can be performed. Other resources are a cardiac rehabilitation unit, women's care offerings and a new older adults' program, "New Seasons," discussed in our Retirement chapter.

Palmerton Hospital
135 Lafayette Ave., Palmerton
• (610) 826-3141

This hospital is a 70-bed full-service acute-care facility. It provides emergency, medical/surgical, obstetrical, gynecological and pediatric care. It's a small, comfortable hospital that also supplies support services in vocational rehabilitation, speech pathology and patient education. Palmerton sponsors community outreach programs in cancer support groups, Meals on Wheels and a teen outreach program.

Outpatient facilities here include same day and outpatient surgery, a medical laboratory, radiology and nuclear medicine, ultrasound and mammography, echocardiography, oncology/chemotherapy, urology, physical therapy and more.

An interesting aspect at this hospital is the location of several physicians' offices right in the hospital. This arrangement allows patients to visit their physicians and have physician-ordered tests done without extra traveling. Internal medicine, OB/GYN, family practice, general surgery and orthopedics offices are all here and can be reached through the hospital's switchboard operator.

Palmerton has also established satellite physicians' offices staffed by Palmerton Hospital affiliated physicians in Franklin Township, Kresgeville and Gilbert; services include family practice, OB/GYN, internal medicine and nephrology. They can be reached by calling the hospital switchboard operator.

Lake Wallenpaupack Area

Wayne Memorial Hospital
601 Park St., Honesdale • 253-8100

This is a 98-bed, nonprofit, community-

INSIDERS' TIPS

Take your family on a hike in the woods along the trails in the national parks at Delaware Water Gap, or state parks at Hickory Run, Promised Land or Lehigh Gorge. Quietly walk through the woods, listen to the birds and observe the life around you. Or sit by the Delaware River — on a ledge overlooking it, or at its side in a clearing — and absorb the sound of flowing water. Allow your senses to transport you to an earlier time. Being open to the presence of those who walked the earth before you can provide as rich an understanding of Native Americans as any museum or exhibit.

We're Family.

 Wayne Memorial Hospital
Honesdale, Pennsylvania
(717) 253–8100

owned-and-operated acute-care hospital. Wayne Memorial operates four satellite locations for home-health services, rehabilitation services, lab and radiology: Lords Valley, 253-8100; Hamlin, 689-4670; Milford, 296-6358; and Stourbridge Mall in Honesdale, 253-7322. They are not walk-in healthcare facilities. All emergency care is handled at the 24-hour physician-staffed emergency room of the hospital.

Wayne Memorial is connected to HealthNet, Pennsylvania's Telemedicine Programs. This system allows local physicians and patients to consult with specialists in other hospitals via face-to-face teleconferencing all over the country for consultation.

The hospital provides a Health Resource Directory and a Medical Staff Directory, 253-8990, for those who would like information about available area doctors and services.

The hospital's Home Health Department provides home-health options for at-home care and a maternity program called New Beginnings for the latest in care from labor through delivery in one home-like room. Some other of its extensive services include: occupational therapy, cardiology, childbirth education, diabetes planning and support, a laboratory and regional blood bank, community health education, oncology and radiation consultation, social services, surgery, sibling education, a progressive care unit and volunteer ambulance transport. Its parent company, Wayne Memorial Health System, also operates a 121-bed Skilled Nursing Facility in Waymart, 10 miles from the hospital.

Mental Health Services/ Drug and Alcohol Rehabilitation

Most area hospitals provide mental health services. However, there are psychiatric facilities in the surrounding areas. Your physician or psychiatrist is the best source for this help and is required for referral and admission.

Drug and alcohol problems can be addressed through the Drug and Alcohol Commission, 421-1960, Greenway Behavioral Center and Open Forum (see below).

INSIDERS' TIPS

Weather in the Poconos varies. It is always a good idea to supply your summer campers with a supply of sweat shirts and pants or sweaters and slacks for those inevitable cold nights.

BROOKMONT
HEALTH CARE CENTER

- 119 Bed Rehabilitation & Skilled Nursing Facility
- Offering Outstanding Care, Exquisite Surroundings

For more information please complete the following:

I am interested in ❑ Long Term Care ❑ Interim Care

What rehabilitation services are needed?
❑ Physical Therapy ❑ Occupational Therapy ❑ Rehabilitative Nursing ❑ Speech Pathology ❑ Respiratory Therapy

Existing Diagnosis / Limitations
❑ Paralysis ❑ Multiple Sclerosis ❑ Fractures o Arthritis
❑ Heart Disease ❑ Cancer ❑ Other _____

Special Dietary / Nutritional Needs? ❑ Yes ❑ No

Recreational Interests:
❑ Exercise Groups ❑ Horticulture ❑ Sing-Alongs ❑ Arts & Crafts
❑ Movies & Videos ❑ Bingo/Table Games ❑ Bowling ❑ Balloon
Volleyball ❑ Parties ❑ Cooking/Serving Clubs ❑ Woodworking
❑ Off-Site Luncheon ❑ Trips ❑ Group Discussions ❑ Bible Study
& Current Events Groups

Name of Potential Resident _____

Phone _____

Name of Person Completing Reply Card_____

Address_____

City_____ State_____ Zip_____

Brookmont Health Care Center

P.O. Box 50, Brookmont Drive,

Effort, Pennsylvania 18330

Gnaden Huetten
MEMORIAL HOSPITAL

211 North 12th Street   Lehighton, PA 18235

(610)377-1300
Carbon County Home Health Care
Gnaden Huetten Nursing & Convalescent Center
Gnaden Huetten Memorial Hospital
Nesquehoning Outpatient Center
Women's Health Center (Lehighton & Tamaqua)
Inpatient/Outpatient Physical Therapy
New Seasons and *WomanCare*
24-Hour Emergency Department Service (610)377-7080

Stroudsburg/ East Stroudsburg

Gnaden Huetten Open Forum
912 Main St., Stroudsburg • 424-1402

This program is an outpatient program under the auspices of Gnaden Huetten in Leheighton. Patients participate based on doctor referral.

Mental Health-Mental Retardation Program, Carbon-Monroe-Pike Counties
804 Sarah St., Stroudsburg • 421-2901, (800) 338-6467

Mental Health-Mental Retardation Program, Carbon-Monroe-Pike Counties, is a county agency that operates in each of the counties. Counseling is available for children and adults. For MH-MR in Monroe and Pike counties call 421-2901. For its Family and Child Together program at 553 Main Street in Stroudsburg, call 421-5344; the outpatient Clinic is at 1 Crystal Street in East Stroudsburg, 420-8070. The Mental Retardation Department is at 136, N. Ninth Street in Stroudsburg, 420-8790. The Carbon County office can be reached at (610) 377-0773.

Pocono Medical Center, Mental Health Services
206 E. Brown St., E. Stroudsburg • 476-3393

An entire floor at this medical facility is dedicated to mental health patients. Patients can be admitted through the emergency room or an admitting doctor.

Greenway Behavioral
Pa. Hwy. 715, Henryville • 424-6233

This facility offers full drug and alcohol inpatient treatment programs for youths and adults. There are private counselors, Alcoholics Anonymous meetings, psychodrama

INSIDERS' TIPS

If you are traveling in our area, do not forget to bring your medical and hospitalization identification cards with you. All hospital facilities will accept your insurance cards, even Medicaid and Medicare. If you are elderly or on any type of ongoing medical care, bring all pertinent information (doctors names, prescriptions being taken, etc.) in case an emergency develops and coordination with your at home doctors is needed.

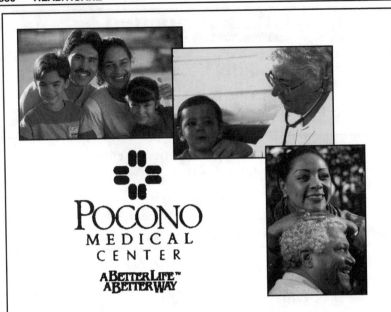

...*Serving the Medical Needs of a Great Community Since 1915*

206 E. Brown Street, East Stroudsburg, PA 18301 (717) 421-4000

groups, recreation therapy and a full line of insurance-accepted rehabilitation services.

Hospice/Hope Services

Stroudsburg/ East Stroudsburg

Lehigh Valley Hospice — Pocono
1273 N. Ninth St., Stroudsburg • 420-0912

Hospice provides a team of nurses, counselors and health workers to support the terminally ill patient in the comfort of the patient's home surrounded by family. It provides sup-port groups for the patient and family, 24-hour on-call service and is medicare certified.

Visiting Nurse Association/ Hospice of Monroe County
500 Independence Dr., East Stroudsburg • 421-5390

VNA offers a program called HOPE, an acronym that stands for "Hearts Offering Patients Encouragement." The program was conceived at an "I Can Cope" conference of the American Cancer Society and is now in operation. Its mission is to offer support to those who are fighting life-threatening illnesses. This program offers a team approach much like a hospice team but with the difference that the patient has elected to follow an aggressive response to his or her illness and wants help doing it at home.

INSIDERS' TIPS

Each of the hospitals listed here has a referral service. To reach physicians in other locations in eastern Pennsylvania, you can call Eastern Pennsylvania Health Network (EPHN) Physician Finder, 801 Ostrum Street, Bethlehem, (800) 422-7340.

The HOPE team consists of a nurse, social worker, chaplain, dietician and therapist, all of whom work together with the non-hospice patient to help with treatment and ensure that patients can be at home and as long as the treatment they undergo can be administered at home. The team works to develop a trusting working relationship with the patient. If a patient's illness progresses to a terminal stage, the same team that worked with the patient in the HOPE program will follow the patient into hospice, providing an easy transition. While its function may change, the team does not change.

Other Medical Care Options

Stroudsburg/ East Stroudsburg

Pocono Ambulatory Surgery Center
1 Veterans Pl., Stroudsburg • 421-4978
This facility is for outpatient ambulatory surgery. It specializes in those procedures that can be done safely outside a hospital setting. There are no facilities for overnight care.

Mount Pocono Area

Geisinger Medical Group – Mount Pocono
Mount Pocono Professional Centre • Pa. Hwy. 611, Mount Pocono • 839-3633
This facility staffs three physicians and a certified physician assistant and four healthcare providers who offer a full range of primary-care services. Offices are open Monday through Saturday year round.

Acupuncture

Stroudsburg/ East Stroudsburg

Eva Berend, L.Ac., NCCA Dipl, Acupuncture Treatment and Information Center
5187 E. Brown St., East Stroudsburg • 421-2209
This center specializes in acupuncture as its main concern.

INSIDERS' TIPS

In addition to the region's specialized psychiatric care facilities, most Poconos hospitals provide a range of mental health services.

Mount Pocono Area

Optimum Health Institute
Dr. P.J. Marceletti, Learn Plaza, Pa. 611 S., Tannersville • 629-5554

This is a multidisciplinary clinic specializing in electro acupuncture.

Important Numbers To Know

General

Adult Services Cooperative • 421-3050
AIDS/HIV Warmline • 688-9716
Hispanic Community • 420-8228

Children

Children and Youth Services of Monroe County • 420-3590
Children, Youth and Families Division, Northampton County • (610) 559-3290, (610) 252-9060
National Child Abuse Hotline • (800) 422-4453
CHADD (Children with Attention Deficit Disorder) of the Poconos • 421-0509
National Youth Crisis Hotline • (800) 442-4673

Mental Health/ Drug and Alcohol

Alcoholics Anonymous • 424-8532
Monroe County Drug and Alcohol Commission • 421-1960
Mental Health-Mental Retardation (MH-MR) - Monroe, Pike and Carbon Counties • 421-2901
MH-MR, Northampton County (Slatebelt) • (610) 974-7555
Al-Anon and Alateen • 424-1976
Narcotics Anonymous • Pocono Region 421-6618, Slate Belt (610) 439-1998

Monroe County State Health Center (referrals only) • 424-3020
Northampton County Drug and Alcohol Commission • (610) 559-3280
PA Substance Abuse Information Center • (800) 582-7746, 787-9761
Nar-Anon Hotline • (610) 778-2100
National Clearinghouse for Alcohol and Drug Information • (800) 729-6686
The Center for Substance Abuse Treatment Hotline • (800) 662-HELP

Women

Women's Health Center • 476-3581
Women's Resources of Monroe County • 421-4200
Planned Parenthood of Northeastern Pennsylvania • 424-8306
Crisis Pregnancy Center of the Poconos • 424-1113
Slate Belt Crisis and Pregnancy Center • (610)588-8400, (610)253-3373, 897-6060
Rape Crisis • 421-4200

Elderly

Monroe County Area Agency on Aging • 420-3735
Pike County area Agency on Aging • 296-7813
Elder Abuse, Carbon County • (800) 441-1315, Monroe County 420-3735, Northampton County (610) 252-9060, Pike County (800) 233-8911, Wayne County (800) 648-9620

Abuse

Child Abuse • Monroe County 420-3590
Childline PA Child Abuse Hotline • (800) 932-0313
Domestic Violence • 421-4200
ChildHelp USA (National Hotline for Child/Adult and Family Violence) • (800) 422-4453

INSIDERS' TIPS

Wayne County has more townships and villages named after places in the Bible than any other county in Pennsylvania.

Crisis Intervention/Suicide

Crisis Intervention Center • Carbon, Monroe and Pike counties 421-2901, after hours toll free (800) 338-6467, Northampton County (610) 252-9060

Suicide Prevention • 421-2901, after-hours hotline (800) 338-6467

Sexually Transmitted Diseases

C.D.C. National AIDS Hotline • (800) 342-2437

PA AIDS Factline • (800) 662-6080

STD Hotline • (800)227-8922

PA VD Hotline • (800) 462-4966

Planned Parenthood • 424-8306

There has been rapid student population growth, to put it mildly, in all Pocono public school districts over the past 10 years.

Education

Education is an often-discussed topic in the Poconos. Due to the incredible growth in the region, schools — their growth, philosophies and activities, in particular — are always in one spotlight or another. There are eight school districts in the Poconos and a few private schools that complement the public districts. Because Pennsylvania's state education philosophies have changed to an outcomes-based curriculum, public schools have gone through major changes in the past six years in their approaches to teaching methods and curriculae. Within the outcomes-based philosophy, discussed later in this chapter, there are further innovations, such as individual educational profiles for students with learning difficulties, and block scheduling, an innovation drawing a great deal of support (also discussed in this chapter).

While these innovations are of major interest to public school students and their parents, they have had little effect on the private schools. Private schools are not bound to follow state curriculum philosophies, thus they are free to pursue traditional education formats, Montessori or other specialized education philosophies, even open-classroom policies espousing teachers as supervisors to students who learn at their own pace within a guided curriculum.

There has been rapid student population growth, to put it mildly, in all Pocono public school districts over the past 10 years; the Pocono Mountain School District doubled its population from 1986 to 1996. Regionwide growth is due to the influx of homeowners who now use the Poconos as a bedroom community to commute to their jobs in New York, New Jersey and Philadelphia. Schools once catered to the children of local farmers, businessmen and service-based workers in the tourist industry, and most students went to the public schools. These were traditional schools that had evolved from one-room schoolhouses to consolidated schools. Eventually they became district schools that covered a wide geographic area. Their purpose: to provide better education for all in a centralized location. Then came the building explosion of the late '80s, and with it, the commuter population, the introduction of outcomes-based education from the state level and the innovations of inclusion for special students. In 1995-96, intensive or alternative scheduling was introduced in some district high schools, further changing the ways subjects are taught.

Philosophies and Methods

Outcomes-based Education

Outcomes-based instruction was mandated by the Pennsylvania Department of Education in 1990 as a way to address the needs of all students and to ensure that all received the required education. The premise: to establish outcomes or objectives for each grade level and work with students to achieve those outcomes. With this focus, it is understood that all students can achieve these outcomes; how and when they do so might vary. Ultimately, however, students must demonstrate they have achieved the outcomes or objectives.

Alternative methods of testing or demonstrating achieved outcomes are part of the process. For example, portfolios of work can be used to demonstrate competence and mastery, as can oral quizzes and tests.

Outcomes-based education is still evolving, and its name might change to stress performance as a keyword. Accordingly, outcomes-based may soon be called performance-based, as it is already in some districts. The name change emphasizes learning through performance and accentuates the system's performance-based objectives and standards.

Some educators have jumped on the outcomes-based bandwagon, happy about alternatives to the straight "you failed" or "you passed" options of yore. Not everyone, however, has been delighted, including some parents who seem more comfortable with the methods by which they themselves were taught — assessed for knowledge within a proscribed cirriculum and graded against a curve. Those parents usually move their children to the few existing church-affiliated private schools, which offer religious instruction along with a tradition-based education. Others have joined the ranks of the home-schooled (see this chapter's related sidebar).

Outcomes-based or performance-based education is here for now, and with it, many teachers and administrators have newfound opportunities and freedom in reaching students, providing them with alternative ways of learning that are at once more global and more individualized. For instance, students with reading disabilities can be tested orally. Co-operation among faculty in different subject areas has opened new ways of exploring topics. For instance, fine-arts teachers and science teachers might collaborate on a project, such that lessons become whole-school projects that decorate and dominate wall spaces and exhibition areas. Some faculty have even become involved in the environmental impact of the school facility (see the Pleasant Valley School District entry).

Inclusion is an integral part of the outcomes-based philosophy. Students that otherwise classified as "special education" are evaluated individually and presented with an outcomes-based, individual educational profile (IEP or IST depending upon the local acronym). This profile identifies areas in which a student needs special help. Then the child is assigned to work with the teacher assigned to that child's grade level for the subject areas in which she or he needs assistance. The rest of the day the child is included in regular class-

FYI

Unless otherwise noted, the area code for all phone numbers in this guide is 717.

room assignments and activities, including "specials" such as music, art and gym. There is justification and support for this approach because it has been proven that the higher the expectations for students, the more they will achieve. Those students who spend time in the classroom with their peers even part of the day are exposed to other ways of achieving and learning. They are not restricted to learning only what is taught to members of a small group all receiving special help.

Again, some educators and parents are advocates of inclusion; others are not, fearing that leaving the room for help singles the child out. Ostensibly, all students come to understand that everyone has gifts as well as problem areas that can and should be addressed. The emphasis is on acceptance and respect. At times, the special education teacher works with all the children who need help, even those who are not classified IEP students. The system has been in place for about five or six years in some districts and has proven itself highly effective.

Intensive Block Scheduling

Another exciting educational method currently practiced in the Pocono Mountain, Wallenpaupack and East Stroudsburg districts is intensive block scheduling or alternative scheduling. This innovation is being used in the high schools — seemingly much like what colleges have been doing for some time. Other school districts in the Poconos still use the traditional seven or eight periods a day of 40 to 50 minutes each.

With intensive scheduling, students have four 90-minute classes each day plus their specials, allowing more time to learn and perform in each subject. And with 90 minutes devoted to the learning process, the teacher has time to introduce a daily objective and immediately follow with a related activity, experiment or performance. Again, some traditionalists have been put off by the change, arguing that cirriculum blocks might not be chosen sequentially. For instance, a student might take French

Photo: Jen Yaneka

Track is a major event in the Pocono Mountain School District.

I in the fall of freshman year and French II as late as the winter of junior or senior year.

So far, most students are pleased with the block scheduling. The consensus opinion among students asked is that they are learning more and have less stress since fewer people are putting requirements on them throughout the day. Study halls have been eliminated because students spend more learning time in their classes.

Amid all evidence of growth and alternative methods of learning, intensive block scheduling is further proof that education is a priority in the school districts.

Public School Districts

Since so much goes on in each district, highlighting all parameters would be impossible. We'll touch on the main points that might be of interest to you beyond district size and philosophy and provide you with the numbers to call for more information. Most larger districts have extensive public relations packets, which they will gladly send you; some of the smaller schools only have pamphlet-like brochures. As you might expect, checking out the school facilities and grounds for yourself is the best way to get your questions answered. Another way is to speak with the person answering the phone or the secretary of different school officials. Your reaction to the gatekeepers might tell you something about what your reaction to the school districts will be.

Sports, music, art, academic and vocational-technical opportunities are the main categories we'll present in this overview.

Sports are a big draw for these school districts. Football, soccer and Little League begin at preschool age in most municipalities; by the time students are ready to enter high school, most of them already have some experience in the sports they want to play.

Interschool rivalries are prevalent: The Stroudsburg-East Stroudsburg Thanksgiving football game is an important, much anticipated annual event; and Pocono Mountain and Pleasant Valley fight over the "oak bucket" each year.

Girls and boys also compete in basketball, cross-country running and track. Varsity and intramural sports are strongly supported in most schools, and events are usually well-attended by parents and schoolmates.

Music resounds in most of the school districts too. Beyond the football-accompanying marching bands, you'll find concert, pep and jazz bands.

In 1996 four East Stroudsburg High School

The One-room Schoolhouse

On almost every country road where an early community once existed, you'll see a small, old building — usually white and generally in major disrepair. These buildings once provided the education for thousands of area residents who walked to school — rain or shine, snow or sleet — until well into the 1940s. About that time, several small schools consolidated, beginning the growth of what have become some incredibly large school districts.

Some restored schoolhouses are maintained by the local historical districts as museums — the Bell School in Cherry Valley and the Dutot School in Delaware Water Gap, among them. And on the grounds of the Pocono Mountain School District is a reproduction of a one-room schoolhouse, built by Monroe County Vo-Tech, that is open to the public the first Sunday of each month; its furnishings are all original.

But a particular one-room schoolhouse, built in 1836 and still used today, is Custard School, off Rimrock Road in Bartonsville. This schoolhouse still has its original blackboards and teachers desk. It no longer sits on a platform as it once did, according to graduate Keturah Hartman, a source for most related anecdotes and a second-generation (her father attended) Custard School student. It is still used every Sunday by the Sunday School teachers from St. John's Evangelical Church, which owns the building and whose Board of Trustees is responsible for its restoration and maintenance.

Attending Custard School was not like going to class today. For starters, all classes were taught in one room — grades 1 through 8 studied together. When it was time to give a lesson for specific grade, students went up to a big bench at the front of the room and sat together (still practiced at Sunday School). The other students sat at their desks and continued their work — reading, writing and arithmetic.

An interesting thing about one-room schoolhouses was the extent of the students' education. According to James Price, guardian of the reproduction at Pocono Mountain, students learned so much from each other. Since they were together all the time, younger students easily picked up knowledge and know-how from older ones, much as younger siblings do at home. The older students often taught younger classmates while the teacher worked with others. (An interesting corollary: Dr. Robert

Source: Keturah Hartman

Biggin, assistant superintendent in charge of curriculum at Pocono Mountain, notes that the late English educator Boyer advocated a return to the one-room schoolhouse approach for some of the same reasons cited by Price.)

Resources included books and a corner cabinet filled with nature items and pamphlets describing them. Hartman re-

members a large coconut shell filled with coconut that children would eat from when the teacher wasn't looking.

Recess included outdoor games, such as "ticleedy over." In this game, students would throw a ball to each other over the top of the very steep roof. In winter they hiked to the top of the meadow across the road from the school, taking along old boards to ride down the snow-crusted hills.

Classes weren't large; Hartman was the sole graduate in her 8th grade class. Graduations were sometimes held in local churches, such as the one in Kellersville. Each one-room school would send their graduating 8th graders to a general commencement ceremony.

Interestingly, when schools began consolidating in the late 1930s and early '40s, there was resistance. One teacher in Reeders refused to send her students, yet walked them down to the consolidated school in Tannersville every year to take the required state exams. This type of resistance mirrors present-day reactions from the growing population of homeschoolers in the area.

Holidays prompted simple celebrations. Halloween was always a time for mischief lead by the boys; as Hartman remembers, "every year the boys used to put the teacher's chair on the roof. Sometimes they'd turn over the outhouses." At Christmastime, students decorated a tree with colored paper chains and popcorn. There were also "box socials" attended by students and their families; young ladies brought lunches in fancy, decorated shoeboxes, and the young men would bid on the boxes to eat with the owner. There were also "shadow socials;" a sheet was hung, the girls had their shadows cast on the sheet by a lantern, and the boys would bid on the shadows to spend time with the girl. (Some women's lib groups could have a field day with these events today!)

Most schools in the Pocono region are getting larger every year. It's interesting to note that many are questioning if larger is better. Those with fond memories of their one-room schoolhouses might not agree.

---

band members were accepted to participate in the Honor Band of America at the National Concert Band Festival in Chicago. Other bands, notably Pocono Mountain, continue to compete and win awards all over the region for presentation, choreography and musicianship.

Vocal music is practiced in choruses, concert choirs, swing choirs, schoolwide musicals and show choirs. The caliber of performance from these groups from every school is exhilarating.

Most districts send students to district chorus and district band convocations and competitions. These lead to state choruses and bands also. Instrumental music starts in the 4th grade

in most districts as an elective class and continues through high school. Vocal music begins in kindergarten and also continues as an elective after the 5th grade. The influence of musical education is apparent in the number of students who continue to participate after graduation in community orchestras, bands, choral societies and musical productions.

Art as a discipline is taught in all the school systems and is supported locally. Every year student art work is exhibited in the Stroud Mall in Stroudsburg, judged in competitions sponsored by the Monroe County Council on the Arts, exhibited by Arts on the Mountain in student shows and presented at different open-house art shows in the school districts.

Each school district has gifted-and-talented programs and advanced placement classes as well as the previously mentioned special education accommodations. Also, as part of the outcomes-based requirements, all students must pass a writing assessment to demonstrate competence and adherence to the state performance standard. Students from the Pocono districts have been accepted into the top colleges and universities in the country.

Extracurricular activities support academic excellence: Scholastic Scrimmage teams (Pen Argyl won the regional competition in 1996 for the second consecutive year and placed second and third in the state), math scrimmage teams and forensic competitions in debate and speech, to name a few. (Six Pocono Mountain Senior High Speech and Debate Team students qualified to compete in the Catholic Forensic League's national competition in 1996.) There are also science fairs, math fairs — hosted by East Stroudsburg University — and a yearly science symposium held at the University of Scranton. Spelling bees, a Pennsylvania tradition since the days of the one-room schoolhouse, are held every year in the school districts, and for the past two years, Monroe County has sent a representative to Washington, D.C., as the regional entrant.

Vocational-technical schools are very strong in the Pocono region. There is a real commitment to preparing students to enter a career when they leave school. Preparation is such that many students go on to colleges such as Johnson and Wales culinary institute in Rhode Island to specialize in higher vocational training.

In Monroe County, for example, the Monroe County Vocational-Technical School supports the Pocono Mountain, East Stroudsburg, Stroudsburg and Pleasant Valley school districts. A major project at Monroe County VoTech for the past 20 years is the Student Built House Project, the sixth of was constructed in 1996. The homes are part of a development adjoining the school, and all of the homes have been sold (anxious buyers already are waiting to bid on the newest 2,500-square-foot, four-bedroom bi-level).

The school's Tech Prep Allied Health Program provides a health-related curriculum to prepare students for careers in healthcare services. In the adult education section, for instance, an Licensed Practical Nurse (LPN) degree program is offered.

In the Bangor and Pen Argyl school districts, vocational preparation is provided through the Career Institute of Technology and Tech Prep.

Obviously, all of the credits and honors for the various schools cannot be mentioned here, but this overview is meant to at least make you aware of the opportunities and strengths of the schools of the Pocono Mountain region. To receive further and more specific information about the school districts, contact them individually at the addresses and phone numbers that follow.

Stroudsburg/ East Stroudsburg

East Stroudsburg Area School District
321 N. Cortland St., East Stroudsburg
• 424-8500

Five elementary schools, an intermediate school and a senior high school comprise the East Stroudsburg district, which covers parts of Monroe and Pike counties, has a student population of more than 5,700 and incorporates a number of innovative learning projects. The Business Education Partnerships program matches representatives from local businesses, such as Patterson-Kelly, Connaught, Bustin, Weiler Brush, PP&L and Tobyhanna, with math or science classes to enhance instruction. Kids Around Town provides students experience with local government through the League of Women Voters. Art As A Way of

---

Learning has piloted a program in partnership with East Stroudsburg University, Northampton Community College and Binney & Smith to integrate the arts more fully in school curriculae. Students from the Delaware Water Gap area attend school in this district.

Stroudsburg Area School District
123 Linden St., Stroudsburg • 421-1990

Stroudsburg, the only city-type school district (students can walk to school and hang-out at candy stores nearby) has a population of approximately 4,000 students. It includes five elementary schools, a middle school and a high school. Since growth has been comparatively slow in Stroudsburg, schools in this district have maintained their neighborhood feel. The high school football and wrestling teams are very strong, and the music department produces consistently high-quality musicals.

Mount Pocono Area

Pleasant Valley School District
Pa. Hwy. 115, Brodheadsville • 992-5711

Four elementary schools, a middle school and a high school are part of Pleasant Valley School District, which includes approximately 5,000 students. This school system boasts an excellent instrumental music program, with six different bands and orchestras. With a strong reputation for active involvement, faculty recently participated in the development of an environmental center on the grounds of the new elementary center.

Pocono Mountain School District
Pocono Mountain School Rd., Swiftwater • 839-7121

The largest of all the school districts, Pocono Mountain has a student population of more than 8,800 and expects to add another 3,000 by the year 2000. This district includes seven elementary centers, an intermediate school, a junior high and a senior high school.

One principal was named Principal of the Year in Pennsylvania, and a counselor won Counselor of the Year as determined by the Pennsylvania School Counselor's Association. The district's newsletter consistently notes student and faculty honors in competitions and events throughout the region and state. The Pocono Mountain district is expanding continuously, and new programs, such as peer counseling and D.A.R.E., are introduced all the time to help students in all areas of their lives.

West End

Jim Thorpe Area School District
140 W. 10th St., Jim Thorpe • 325-3691

The Jim Thorpe Area School District includes an elementary school, a junior high school and a high school. It is the most technologically advanced of the districts in the Poconos. This district has had its own site on the World Wide Web for more than two years; visit its website (http:\\www.jtasd.k12.pa.us) for a virtual tour. Some Wilkes University professors utilize the state-of-the-art computers here to teach college courses. The district has its own satellite dish and is gearing up to offer distance learning — team teaching with teachers in other parts of the country and the world — in the near future. Every year, the district supports and participates in the student arts exhibit presented through the Maria Feliz Art Gallery in Jim Thorpe and the Carbon County Art League (see our Arts and Culture chapter).

Lehighton Area School District
200 Beaver Run Rd., Lehighton • (610) 377-4490

There are four elementary schools, a middle school and a high school in this school district. The Lehighton district, in Wayne County, has excellent sports programs; the football and track teams consistently compete for regional and state championships.

INSIDERS' TIPS

Students registering for school must be 5 years old by September 1 of their kindergarten year.

Pocono Mountain High School seniors volunteer for Special Olympics at Jack Frost ski area.

Photo: Nicloe Hammond

Palmerton Area School District
P.O. Box 350, Palmerton 18071
• (610) 826-7101

Palmerton Area School District, in Carbon County, has approximately 2,150 students between its two elementary schools, junior high and high school. Its vocational programs are supported through programs and classes at the Carbon County Vocational School. Strong football and track programs, a parent-supported marching band and club activities such as chess and astronomy round out extracurricular offerings. The growth in this community has been stable, so Palmerton schools have not seen the expansion evident in other Poconos districts.

Milford Area

Delaware Valley School District
HC 77, Box 379A, Milford • 296-6431

There are three elementary schools, two middle schools and a high school in this growing district in Pike County, which serves a student population of 4,080. Delaware Valley students are actively involved in their community. Week after week they volunteer on behalf of senior-citizen and church groups and other local organizations. The elementary school also has its own TV station (DVE-TV Channel 5), which actively pursues stories in Pike County as well as at places such as the United Nations in New York City. Academic scrimmages and science and math fairs also are strongly supported in this district.

Lake Wallenpaupack Area

Wallenpaupack School District
HC 6, Box 6075, Hawley • 226-4557

Wallenpaupack School District, which serves portions of Pike County and Wayne County, includes more than 3,000 students between its three elementary schools, middle school and high school. This district uses intensive scheduling blocks (see the related subsection in "Philosophies and Methods," earlier in this chapter). Beyond the academic track that prepares students for college, the district's vocational programs train students for building trades, power mechanics and food service.

Slate Belt

Bangor Area School District
44 S. Third St., Bangor • (610) 588-2105

There are three elementary schools, a junior high school and a senior high school in this district in Northampton County, which serves more than 3,000 students. Vocational-

Homeschooling

Homeschooling is strongly supported in the Poconos. Those who do homeschool their children are staunch advocates of the program and almost militant in their reactions to local school board regulation. Homeschooling has increased dramatically in the last 10 years, and more families seem intent on doing it. The numbers of homeschooled children seem to grow as school populations increase and course offerings begin to include nontraditional subjects and answers that go against parents' principles. Some do it, however, just because they want to be with their children and provide the guidance they feel appropriate and necessary for their kids' growth.

Homeschooling is accomplished in several ways, but all of them must meet the same basic requirements.

•The homeschooled child must be evaluated by an evaluator of the parents' choice who has been approved by the district.

•Parents must have high school diplomas and no criminal records.

•Parents must present curriculum plans each year by August 1, outlining their child's goals for the school year.

•The curriculum plan must be approved by the district.

•A log of each day's activities must be kept for each child and submitted to the evaluator.

•Students must receive a full 180 days of schooling.

Some families work together with a parent or parents from each family, teaching the students in their areas of specialization. This often works well and provides controlled socialization.

If the homeschooling parent is a certified teacher, all of the requirements for homeschooling are unimportant. The parent simply can register the child as being tutored at home. (Tutoring does not fall under homeschooling guidelines or requirements.) Since the 1988 approval of the Home School Bill, Senate Bill No. 154, homeschoolers at least have state's approval if minimum requirements are met and guidelines followed.

A new resource exists for those interested in homeschooling in Pennsylvania. Pennsylvania Homeschoolers, headed by Dr. Howard Richman, provides a newsletter and a free catalog of books about homeschooling. Send a self-addressed stamped envelope to this organization at RD 2, Box 117, Kittanning, Pennsylvania 16201, or call (412) 783-6512.

Other sources of homeschooling information are available. Often, you can seek out the source: Head to the library, and look for a parent with a group of kids who should be in school. Many churches have homeschooling families in their parishes or congregations — part of what almost seems like an underground network — so be sure to inquire.

Photo: Allan Clarkson

Home schooling can be as formal or as casual as the family requires.

The bottom line: The students do well. They score highly on the SATs and are sought by colleges. Nyack College in New York has recently begun sending letters to homeschoolers because they see them as motivated students.

A staunch advocate of homeschooling who, along with her husband, has homeschooled her own three children and others is Karen Clarkson of Henryville. According to Clarkson, "It's a way of life. We love it."

She doesn't seem to be alone; the ranks are swelling. And with some education experts coming out on the side of "smaller is better," homeschooling might be a wave of the future — or the past.

technical programs are provided through the Career Institute of Technology and Tech Prep. Of particular note is the district's Latchkey Program for students in grades 1 through 6 (see our Child Care chapter for details).

Pen Argyl Area School District
1620 Teels Rd., Pen Argyl • (610) 863-9093

Pen Argyl's district, in Northampton County, has 1,800 students and includes an elementary school, a middle school and a high school. Though relatively small, it sends 50 percent of its students to college, with generally two-thirds of its senior class taking SAT exams and consistently scoring above the state average. In 1995 and 1996, the scholastic scrimmage team won the regional competition and placed second and third, respectively, in the state finals held in Harrisburg.

Private Schools

As noted in this chapter's introduction, you'll find very few private schools in the Pocono region, and most are religiously affiliated. Two new schools include, A Family of Artists and the Evergreen School.

A new program developed at A Family of Artists, 420-9675, in East Stroudsburg, offers an alternative cirriculum to students who might benefit from a one-to-one learning. Curriculum modifications take advantage of the arts backgrounds of the faculty to help students achieve in an environment that is less structured than that of the average classroom. Students are referred by the area school districts. (See Arts and Culture, Kidstuff and Camps for other programs offered here.)

The Evergreen Community School, in Mountainhome, 595-6355, opened its doors in fall 1996. Currently it teaches 6th and 7th grades, with plans to add to the current classes

each year through high school. It emphasizes small classes, a hands-on learning environment and a continuation of philosophies somewhat based in Montessori teaching methods.

Stroudsburg/ East Stroudsburg

East Stroudsburg Christian Academy
9 Three Point Garden Rd., East Stroudsburg • 421-4087

This school is quite small (enrollment in 1996 was 42 students), especially considering it includes students from kindergarten through grade 12. In 1996 it graduated one student. It's been in existence for 20 years and is probably the closest you'll come to a one-room schoolhouse. The curriculum is Bible-based, with a traditional program taught in kindergarten through grades 6 and an independent, guided program for grades 7 through 12.

Notre Dame Elementary School
78 Ridgeway St., East Stroudsburg • 421-3651

This traditional Catholic elementary school has a preschool program and grades 1 through 6. The students from kindergarten through 6th grade wear uniforms. The local parishes send their students here, but unaffiliated students are welcome if there are openings. Students from here usually go to Notre Dame High School for grades 7 through 12.

Notre Dame High School
60 Spangenburg Ave., East Stroudsburg • 421-3651

This Catholic college-preparatory school is coeducational, with an enrollment of approximately 360 in grades 7 through 12. Its curriculum is strongly Catholic, although students of other denominations attend. Notre Dame's strong academic reputation means there is always a waiting list (90 percent of its students go on to college). One of the values of this school is its small size, which ensures faculty and administration get to know every student. Latin is one of the academic subjects taught here (three years of it), which attests to its traditional Catholic college-prep status. Activities include musicals and athletics, including boys and girls soccer (for which this school is known), baseball, basketball and field hockey.

St. Paul's Lutheran School
Craig's Meadow Rd., Marshalls Creek
• 223-7700

This Christian school does not teach any particular religious curriculum; it is open to all faiths. The grades here are pre-kindergarten through 5th. Students then go on to another local school.

Mount Pocono Area

The Growing Concern
Railroad Dr., Tannersville • 629-2754

This Montessori school has a preschool in addition to a kindergarten and elementary classes for grades 1 through 5. The classes are small, and parent involvement is encouraged.

Monsignor McHugh Elementary School
Pa. Hwy. 191, Cresco • 595-7463

This traditional Catholic elementary school includes kindergarteners through 8th graders; a preschool program starts at age 3. Students wear uniforms. Faculty is composed of laypersons, mostly, and a few religious sisters. Most students are from local parishes, but non-parish affiliated students are welcome too.

Slate Belt

Faith Christian School
122 Dante St., Roseto • (610) 588-3414

This Christ-centered school educates students from kindergarten through 12th grade. Its students consistently score above the national average on achievement tests and SATs. The programs cater not only to those interested in college, but also to those who are preparing for a vocational or business career. Music, art and drama classes are offered. In terms of athletics, secondary students participate in soccer, volleyball, basketball, track and cheerleading.

Immaculate Conception
Babbitt and Heller Ave., Pen Argyl
• (610) 863-4816

This is a traditional Catholic elementary school, grades 1 through 6. This regional school draws students from three Catholic parishes in the area. The students wear uniforms. Immaculate Conception is a feeder school for Pius X. Interestingly, this is the only Catholic school in the region with an entirely religious faculty, the Dominican Daughters of the Immaculate Mothers, a sisters order from the Philippines.

Our Lady of Mt. Carmel
80 Ridge St., Bangor • (610) 588-2629

This is a traditional Catholic school that teaches grades kindergarten through 6; the faculty is entirely lay people. This school also has a Catholic preschool — unusual for the area. Students wear uniforms and go on to Pius X (see our subsequent entry). Half the student body is parish members.

Pius X
580 Third Ave., Bangor • (610) 588-3291

Pius X is a Catholic college-preparatory school. It is coeducational, with an enrollment of 300 in grades 7 through 12. Most of its students come from the surrounding Catholic elementary schools, including Our Lady of Mt. Carmel in Roseto and Immaculate Conception in Pen Argyl. It has an intensive college-prep curriculum, including Latin. One-hundred percent of their graduates are placed in colleges, and more than 95 percent graduate from college. Extracurricular activities include music, sports (football is quite competitive), scholastic scrimmages and student senate.

Colleges and Universities

In the Pocono region proper, Northampton Community College – Monroe Center and East Stroudsburg University, both in the Stroudsburg/East Stroudsburg area, are the two main providers of higher education.

In the surrounding areas of Scranton-Wilkes Barre and the Lehigh Valley, colleges or universities include the University of Scranton, Lehigh University, Muhlenberg College and Moravian College.

East Stroudsburg University
Normal St., East Stroudsburg • 422-3311

East Stroudsburg is one of 14 institutions in the Pennsylvania State System of Higher Education. It was founded as a normal school (a.k.a. teachers college) in 1893, became a state college in 1927 and achieved university status in 1983. The university works closely with the community — cosponsoring math fairs, participating in experimental workshops and projects with different school districts, supporting local organizations' fairs and providing women's awareness programs. There are approximately 5,000 undergraduates students and 1,000 graduate students.

Undergraduate degrees offered are the Bachelor of Arts in most areas including special education, history, geography, physical education, music, secondary education, English, speech communication, psychology, early-childhood education and elementary education; the Bachelor of Science includes areas beyond the usual biology and chemis-

try, such as allied-health education, restaurant and tourism management and recreation and leisure services management. The Bachelor of Science degree is also offered in teacher-certification programs. Other programs — engineering, pharmacy and podiatry — are offered in conjunction with other universities in the state.

The graduate division offers Master of Arts degrees in history and political science; Master of Science degrees in biology, computer science, health education, general science, physical education and cardiac rehabilitation and exercise science; and Master of Education degrees in biology, elementary education, general science, health and physical education, history, secondary education, reading, political science and special education; and a Master of Public Health degree in community education. The university also offers certification degrees for principal, superintendent, reading specialist and special education supervisor.

Northampton Community College – Monroe Center
Old Mill Rd., Tannersville • 620-9221

This campus is a satellite to the main campus in Bethlehem. Students can begin and complete their general studies requirements at the Monroe Center. There are more than 50 associate degree programs and certifications available, including health science, education, restaurant management, computer science and library science.

The Monroe Center even has a truck-driving program that provides the various level certifications for tractor-trailer truck and school bus driving.

About 52 percent of students transfer to four-year colleges from Northampton CC. The small size of the Monroe Center makes it a particularly good place to start for students who need direction or are returning to college after a hiatus. Class sizes are small — in most cases a 17-to-1 student-to-faculty ratio — and

INSIDERS' TIPS

If you are transferring into a Poconos school district, have your immunization records available. Some immunizations, like the MMR, are now being required for a second time.

teacher accessibility is one of this school's hallmarks. Offerings include adult-education and community-outreach courses for individuals and groups trying to begin new lifestyles or careers.

Students participate in various community and college affairs including the Phi Beta Kappa honor society. The student body includes a large mix of high school graduates and returning adults. The college ensures its community affiliation by offering night courses in all area high schools with its regular and adjunct faculty.

Adult Education

Stroudsburg/ East Stroudsburg

Monroe County Vocational-Technical School
Laurel Lake Rd., Bartonsville • 629-2001

This vo-tech school offers extensive adult-education programs, including GED, enrichment courses and certification programs related to employment options in this area, such as healthcare assistant and technician. Maintenance certifications are available for working with refrigerants. The practical-nursing program, 629-6563, is a much sought-after educational option.

West End

Carbon County Vocational and Technical School
Pa. Hwy. 903, Jim Thorpe • 325-4140

This school offers continuing-education programs in enrichment and GED diplomas. It also has federally funded programs targeted to individuals with certain demographics; most notably, for the past 10 years this school been the county's site for the New Choices program, which assists displaced single-parent homemakers in the area of career planning.

Milford Area

Delaware Valley Community Education
RR 2, Box 2275, Shohola 18458 • 296-2778

Adult evening courses offered through this program are held in the elementary and middle schools. Options include personal-enrichment courses, academic courses including management skills workshops and Spanish, and Penn State courses for paralegal, real estate, child care (see our Child Care chapter for more information) and other undergraduate- and graduate-level courses.

Slate Belt

The Bangor School District
44 S. Third St., Bangor • (610) 588-2105

This school district offers tuition-free classes for adults seeking to improve basic skills or earn a general-education equivalency diploma (GED). Adult evening programs are offered in vocational and recreational skills. Additional courses are available through the Career Institute of Technology, (610) 258-2857.

Pen Argyl Area School District
1620 Teels Rd., Pen Argyl • (610) 863-9093

This district offers adults tuition-free GED and basic-skills classes. Programs in vocational and recreational skills are offered evenings; additional options are available through the Career Institute of Technology (610) 258-2857.

A designated preschool or nursery school requires a minimum two hours of planned instruction each day.

Child Care

Child care has become one of the fastest growing industries in the Poconos region due to the population influx over the last 10 years. In fact, most of the highly regarded day-care and preschool programs have waiting lists.

Day care is geared to the working family; it lasts all day and in most client-oriented centers or homes has early arrival and late pickup times. Many Poconos day-care centers take infants. Some centers also have kindergarten, 1st-grade and even 2nd-grade programs.

Preschool programs are usually half-day programs geared to the at-home parent who wants to expose his or her child to a dual educational and social environment. Some preschool programs center around specific interests such as music (at Kindermusik or Kinder Beginnings), gymnastics, swimming or art (see our Kidstuff chapter). These schools provide children's activities and programs guided by whatever private organization they are affiliated with. In many cases, such centers are not actually preschools according to state guidelines, because they only offer socialization opportunities. A designated preschool or nursery school requires a minimum two hours of planned instruction each day.

In this chapter we discuss the following child-care options: day care, group homes, family day-care homes and day-care centers as well as some of the standards by which they are measured. There are many existing centers, and more are opening all the time, so we suggest you check with the Pennsylvania State University Cooperative Extensions for lists of registered day-care facilities. Penn State, a land-grant university, has extensions in every county in Pennsylvania (all land-grant institutions are required to have extensions in each county of their respective states). Cooperative extensions in Pennsylvania offer courses for day-care providers and workers that prepare individuals to meet state requirements for continuing child-care education (12

hours annually). They also offer courses for those interested in setting up centers and obtaining licenses or certifications.

Most extensions maintain a list of day-care centers in their county that are registered with the Pennsylvania Department of Welfare, and can provide this list (sometimes for free, sometimes for a fee) to interested parties. Be aware that it's *not* a list of recommendations, rather state-licensed and certified homes and centers. Listings usually contain center names, addresses, phone numbers, contact persons, fees and hours as well as other general information. To obtain a list, call or write the cooperative extension in your area; be sure to send the appropriate fee where applicable.

The Pennsylvania State University Cooperative Extensions in the Pocono region include: Monroe County (fee $2), RR 7, Box 7391, Stroudsburg, 421-6430; Pike County (no fee), 506 Broad Street, Milford, 296-3400; Wayne County (no fee), Wayne County Courthouse, 925 Court Street, Honesdale, 253-5970 Ext. 239; Carbon County (no fee), P.O. Box 60, Jim Thorpe, 325-2788. Northampton County, Lehigh Valley, (610) 391-9840, does not maintain a list; contact the Pennsylvania Department of Welfare, (800) 222-2108, for information.

Each cooperative extension also publishes a newsletter on a regular basis. Call your county's cooperative extension to find out what's going on in area day care.

Another publication available through Penn State Cooperative Extensions is a pamphlet outlining what to look for in a child-care center. We highly recommend you have this resource when you begin your child-care search.

The information provided by each county's cooperative extension is also available in a comprehensive list from the Department of Public Welfare.

Since parents have their own standards and expectations about a day-care situation or nursery school/preschool, the cooperative extensions often serve as little more than a good starting place; often a parent's own investigation is the best way to determine an appropriate child-care center. When you visit a center, be sure to look for certifications by the Pennsylvania Board of Education (if its a preschool) and the National Association for Education of Young Children (NAEYC), and make sure teachers for early-childhood education or elementary education are certified.

Ask plenty of questions, such as:

• Do you have an open-door policy — can I visit at any time?

• Do you have a PTO or any other parents group?

• How do you communicate with the parents? Is it on a regular basis?

• How do you perform evaluations — social, developmental and educational?

• What is the ratio of children to staff? (The state age-appropriate guidelines range from 12-to-1 for 3-year-olds to 2-to-28 for a mixed-age group of 3-, 4- and 5-year-olds.)

• Is a schedule posted and visible, so I can check where my child will be and what he or she will be doing?

• Do you have a handbook that outlines the policies, structure and tuition schedule?

• Do you have accommodations for handicapped or physically challenged children?

For parents seeking an educational component, many larger day-care centers offer nursery school or preschool programs. So, when choosing a center, you might consider one where your child can grow into and through a preschool experience without changing centers.

A note about alternative types of day care is in order. Many women care for children of

friends or friends of friends in their homes. Other women advertise in the local papers and on bulletin boards in local supermarkets. Options exist but should be exercised with caution; remember that child-care providers are not regulated by the state if they are not registered with the state. While such options might meet your needs — and your pocketbook — you should exercise them with caution; at least check references and ask if care providers are certified in first aid and CPR for children.

FYI

Unless otherwise noted, the area code for all phone numbers in this guide is 717.

Most centers and homes prefer that sick children be kept at home. Some facilities provide a sick room for the occasional "feeling poorly" day. It is important to check with the center or home for specific sick-child guidelines.

There are certifications and licenses required by the Pennsylvania Department of Public Welfare that ensure all day-care programs meet state standards. Preschools or nursery schools are licensed by the Department of Education, Non-Public and Private Schools Division. Day-care facilities that include kindergarten and grade-school programs, or advertise preschool or nursery school (the terms are synonymous), also must be licensed by the Pennsylvania Department of Education, and therefore must have dual licensure. Some facilities are also members of a national organization, such as National Association for the Education of the Young Child (NAEYC), a children's-advocacy group that sets national standards and guidelines for quality education. Often the centers belong to local associations that identify affiliations or philosophies: child-care task forces or Montessori, for example. All licenses, certifications and association affiliations should be clearly visible to visitors.

INSIDERS' TIPS

Child-care centers are required to report suspected child abuse. To report abuse, call: Child Abuse Hotline (Monroe County), 420-3590; Childline (Pennsylvania Child Abuse Hotline), (800) 932-0313; Children, Youth and Families Division Northampton County, (610) 559-3290 or (610) 252-9060 (after hours); National Child Abuse Hotline, (800) 422-4453; ChildHelp USA, (800) 422-4453.

State Agencies

Pennsylvania Department of Public Welfare – Daycare Unit
339 S. Office Bldg. • 100 Lackawanna Ave., Scranton • 963-4525, (800) 222-2108

The Department of Public Welfare divides day-care facilities into three categories: group homes, family day-care homes and day-care centers.

A group home can accept no more than six children at a time. It must be registered with the Pennsylvania Department of Public Welfare to receive a license. It is inspected every two years to evaluate if it is in compliance with state standards. Homes with fewer than six children do not have to register with the state. While this option usually is cheaper, parents should be aware that such care providers and their facilities are not regulated by the state in any way; word of mouth is your only quality assurance.

A family day-care home can accept seven to 12 children. It must be registered with the Pennsylvania Department of Public Welfare to receive a license. It is also inspected every two years to evaluate its compliance with state standards — a comforting notion for many parents.

A day-care center can accept 13 or more children based on its physical capacity, determined through state requirements set by the Department of Public Welfare. To become a certified day-care center, applicants must undergo a precertification process not required of group homes and family day-care centers. This verifies that basic safety and health regulations have been met, thus the center can apply for certification by submitting appropriate paperwork and verifications of facility size, professional staff, equipment, course of study and health and safety specifications. Certification is evaluated every year to ensure compliance with state standards.

State standards ensure safety, health and quality of care and education in day-care settings. Safety standards require interior and exterior areas to be free of physical hazards and of adequate size for the number of children using the facility. Health standards require that someone certified in first aid and CPR for children be at the facility during all hours of operation. The standards for trained personnel require at least one certified early childhood or elementary teacher be on staff at all times. Also, all day-care workers must accumulate six to 12 hours of training annually in both first aid and early-childhood education.

The Department of Public Welfare has a pamphlet outlining all requirements for different day-care situations. Call or write the department to obtain a copy of this pamphlet or a list of all licensed and certified day-care facilities in the area.

This agency also provides information about the incidence and nature of violations at day-care centers. It can also let you know if any violations at the facility are being investigated.

Pennsylvania Department of Education – Non-public and Private Schools Division
333 Market St., Harrisburg • 783-5146

The Department of Education licenses pre-schools and nursery schools, which are defined as half-day programs focusing on education. The department has its own set of requirements and regulations separate from the Department of Welfare's. A list of licensed pre-schools and nursery schools is available from the Department of Education, as is a pamphlet outlining regulations and requirements. The department requires any day-care center offering a preschool or nursery school as a half-day adjunct to its day-care program have appropriate licensure from the Department of Education.

Extended Care

After-school care for children with working parents (a.k.a. latchkey kids) is a growing concern. Options exist, albeit few.

Many day-care facilities have expanded programs for latchkey kids. Program locations usually are recognized bus stops; children dropped off by their parents each morning are picked up at the centers before school and return there after school. Each center has its own age limit — in most cases between 10 and 12 years old.

Stroudsburg/ East Stroudsburg

A Family of Artists: The Works
Pa. Hwy. 447, East Stroudsburg
• 420-9675

This unique (for four reasons) latchkey program in Monroe County is not a day-care center but provides after-school programs for students as old as 18 (unique point No. 1) that are totally devoted to the arts (unique point No. 2). Programs include hands-on experiences in music, photography, computer art, painting, pottery, theater, dance, poetry, sculpture and more. It is open year round, and all disciplines are taught by top area artists (unique point No. 3). While students can be dropped off by district school buses, A Family of Artists also has six vans that pick up children at locations throughout the county and — the most unique point, No. 4 — take them home at day's end (6:30 PM). The cost is $14 per day.

Cherry Valley Methodist Day Care
U.S. Hwy. 209, Saylorsburg • 992-5292

This latchkey program accepts children from kindergarten through 7th grade. Students arrive by bus from the local schools. The program provides snacks, homework time and play time. The rate is $3 per hour.

Pocono Family YMCA
809 Main St., Stroudsburg • 421-2525

This YMCA has after-school programs, including help with homework, arts and crafts, gym activities and swimming, for children up to 4th grade. District school buses for Stroudsburg and East Stroudsburg drop off students at the Y, or the YMCA van picks up some students by prior arrangement. The cost depends on how many hours the child remains at the Y, but it ranges between $20 and $40 a week plus youth membership ($78 annually) and registration ($25) fees.

Mount Pocono Area

Magical Years
Pa. Hwy. 940, Blakeslee Corners
• 646-5604

This latchkey program takes students from

Parties are always a fun time at area day care centers.

kindergarten age to 12 years old. The children are bused here. The program provides snacks and offers supervised homework sessions (by request from parents) and free-choice activities such as arts and crafts, Nintendo, reading and outdoor play. The rate is between $25 and $65 a week, depending on how many hours the child attends.

West End

For Kids Sake Learning Center
Pa. Hwy. 715, Brodheadsville • 992-2420

This center is one of the fastest growing and most sought-after centers for day care and after-school care. School buses drop off children. The center provides snacks, supervised homework, crafts, computer activities, drama activities, reading time, discussion times and outdoor play. It is open on days when the public schools are closed, and it takes students for planned and emergency early dismissals as well as school holidays. If there is enough demand, it also opens on Saturday. The cost is $2.75 per hour.

Milford Area

Sunshine Station
U.S. Hwys. 6 and 209, Milford • 296-7241

This latchkey program takes children as young as kindergarten-age — students are welcome as long as they want to come. The buses pick up children here in the morning and drop them off in the afternoon. The program provides snacks, outdoor play, supervised homework and play-time activities. It is open during delayed school openings (due to snow) and early dismissals, both planned and unplanned (also because of snow). Sunshine Station also is open during snow days when schools are closed; parents are allowed five free snow days. The weekly rate is $30 for the morning session and $30 for the afternoon.

Lake Wallenpaupack Area

Discover the Rainbow
Pa. Hwy. 739 S., Lords Valley • 775-9000

Discover the Rainbow takes kindergarteners through 5th-graders. The students are bused here after school. The center provide snacks, supervised homework time and playtime. The rate is $5 per day.

Slate Belt

Bangor School District
44 S. Third St., Bangor • (610) 588-2165

This school district is the only one in the Poconos that provides a latchkey program. Children in grades 1 through 6 are bused from district schools to one centralized facility. Hours are from dismissal time to 5:30 PM. This center provides snacks, supervised homework time, outside play, board games, arts and crafts and other free-choice activities. The program accepts children on early-dismissal and in-service days but is closed on snow days when schools are closed. The cost for this preregistered program is $1.75 an hour.

Bangor Nursery School and Day Care Center
221 S. Fourth St., Bangor • (610) 588-1665

This latchkey program accepts children 13 and younger. It has before- and after-school programs. Buses from area schools pick up children at the center in the morning and drop them off here in the afternoon. The center provides snacks, supervised homework time, outside play time, a computer center, arts and crafts. This center is open on teacher in-service days and snow days at no additional cost. The weekly cost is $40 for either the morning or afternoon session, $65 for both.

Babysitting

It's a struggle to find babysitters in the Poconos. While smaller towns might retain the joys of babysitters (as in days gone by), Monroe County babysitters are like gold nuggets — hard to find and highly treasured.

However, if you are staying at a hotel, you probably can find sitters — services are provided at most resorts — but at a premium price (about $5 per hour, usually with a three-hour minimum). If you're staying at a ski area or resort, babysitting services are available in the lodge nurseries at reasonable rates ($3 to $5 per hour), and often during the week for free (see our Winter Sports chapter for details). Day-skiers also can leave their kids at the resort day-care facilities.

Also, the YMCA maintains a list of folks who have taken its babysitter course. Contact the Pocono Family YMCA (see previous entry in "Extended Care"), 421-2525, for a list of sitters who have consented to make their names available to interested parties. The YMCA in Pike County does not have such a course or service. Your best bet is to ask your neighbors or at your church about interested sitters with good recommendations.

Another Option

Head Start is a federally funded program that is responsive to community requirements and needs. Each Head Start program has locally designed options based on a community-needs assessment, which can change as the community changes. The program is reviewed by a county board of directors, a policy council, community representatives and parents participating in the program.

There are two basic types of programs: home-based and center-based. Home-based programs support the home as the learning environment and the parents as teachers within the environment. Usually the teacher spends part of a day each week in the home with the child and the parents — teaching, reviewing learning techniques and discussing age-appropriate development. One day a week is devoted to socialization; the child and parents attend a class at the center to bolster peer-interaction and developmental skills.

The center-based program is more child-centered. The child attends a class at a site for a certain number of days, depending on the community's needs assessment. There are also two home visits a year. This program is usually based on social skills as well as preschool learning skills and development.

Children ages 3 through 5 are eligible for

Toddlers enjoy a day at the sand table at For Kids' Sake Learning Center.

Head Start. It is free for families that meet locally defined income requirements.

To find out about the Head Start program and its space availability in a particular county, call the agency in your area: Monroe County, 421-2676; Carbon County, 645-7578 or 645-9376; Lackawanna, Pike and Wayne counties (Scranton-Lackawanna Human Development Agency), 963-6633 or 963-6836; Northampton County (Lehigh Valley Head Start), (610) 691-1819.

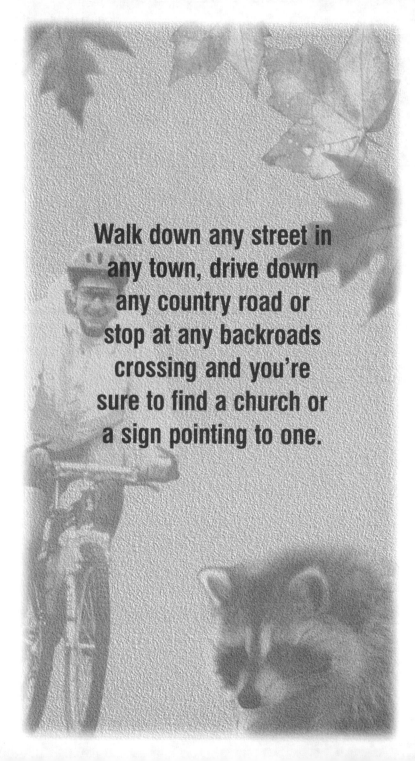

Walk down any street in
any town, drive down
any country road or
stop at any backroads
crossing and you're
sure to find a church or
a sign pointing to one.

Worship

William Penn established Pennsylvania to be a place of religious tolerance. The Poconos yesterday and today reflect and continue to foster that attitude.

Religious groups that settled in Pennsylvania in the 1700s included Puritans, Quakers, the Dutch Reformed, Moravians, Lutherans, Methodists, Amish, Labadists, Sabbathdayers and continually emerging splinter groups that found a home in our forests primeval. Among the first denominations represented in the Poconos region were Dutch Reformed, Lutheran, Methodist, Quaker and Moravian. As the 1800s came to the Poconos so did Presbyterians, Episcopalians, Wesleyans, more Methodists, African Methodists, Baptists, Shakers, Roman Catholics, Mennonites and the Salvation Army. The 1900s have seen the continuation and resurgence of earlier groups as well as the influx of even more diverse churches and faiths — Byzantine Catholics, Full Gospel Believers, Followers of Islam, Hindus, Jews, Jehovah Witnesses, Mormons and, again, the list goes on to include more than 200 churches representing the religious freedom of thousands of Poconos residents.

An interesting corollary to the foundation of faith-generated settlements was the force of the churches in the social and cultural lives of their members. The socials, holidays (holy days), suppers, picnics, musicales, seminars, speakers evenings, poetry readings, church sings, revivals, summer camps and outings were the cultural manna of early residents and later visitors. Today, churches remain an integral part of the social, cultural and artistic backbone of our communities.

As we noted, there are hundreds of churches and faith-related organizations in the Poconos. We do not intend to provide a directory here; you can find them all listed in the *Easy-To-Read Telephone Directory*. Also, the local newspapers, including the *Pocono Record*, provide listings of services in the Friday and Saturday editions. Walk down any street in any town, drive down any country road or stop at any backroads crossing and you're sure to find a church or a sign pointing to one. We mention a few churches of historical note in this chapter; their influence — past and present — is our focus.

In the Early Days . . .

Beginning in the early 1700s, congregations of Dutch Reformed, Lutherans, Quakers, Methodists and Moravians carved homesteads out of the wilderness surrounded by the friendly Native Americans they hoped to convert to Christianity. Their missionary zeal met with much success for at least the first 25 years of interaction with the native inhabitants. Then, as we discuss in our Native Americans chapter, the relationship between settlers and Native Americans, missionaries and converts, was seriously damaged in the mid-18th century by the repercussions of "The Walking Purchase" and the French and Indian War. (Native Americans were displaced from their homeland in both instances.)

INSIDERS' TIPS

From Camelback Mountain near Tannersville, you can see most of the Pocono Plateau beneath you to the south, Blue Mountain and even the Catskills to the northeast.

Dutch Reformed

Dutch Reformed churches were built as early as 1741 in Shawnee. The first church, called the Dutch Reformed Church, in Smithfield, was a log structure that in 1752 was rebuilt with native stone. An interesting design in the architecture of the meeting house was the placement of the windows above what was determined as head height to prevent the worshippers from being fired upon during the services by Indians. Today the site is still occupied by the Shawnee Presbyterian Church on Church Road, in Shawnee-on-Delaware.

Moravians

The Moravians exerted a strong presence in the 1740s. They came from settlements in the Bethlehem area to convert the natives. In 1743 they quickly established a mission at Gnadenhuetten ("tents of mercy"), near what is now Lehighton, and moved to the east side of the Lehigh River to Weissport in 1754. Believers started other missions in Stroudsburg, including the Dansbury Mission in 1747, and in surrounding townships — Gilbert and Polk (Wechequetank) and Eldred and Kunkletown (Meniolagomaka). Much of their movement was halted with the massacre at Gnadenhuetten, a mission that in 1755 became the first casualty of the French and Indian Wars (see our Native Americans chapter); some activity continued through 1760. However, most of the missions were destroyed during the French and Indian War.

Today, the only existing Moravian congregation in the Poconos is in **Canadensis** (Canadensis Moravian Church), though many exist in the Allentown-Bethlehem area. Their contributions are still evident in the presence of renowned Moravian College in

Bethlehem. North of Canadensis, on Pa. Highway 390 S., are the remains of the **Roemerville Moravian Church** (Wayside Gospel Chapel). If you are interested in the history of the Moravians in this area, the Monroe Historical Society, 421-7703, has two volumes of Moravian diaries: *The Dansbury Diaries, 1748-1755* and *The Moravian Travel Diaries.* Another volume in the Monroe Historical Society's collection, *Moravians in the Poconos*, was written by Rev. Warren D. Wenger, a former pastor of the Canadensis Church. This little book describes in homespun detail the various Moravian settlements and any remains of their sites, including cemeteries (the one in which the 10 victims of the Gnadenhuetten massacre are buried is off Union Street in Lehighton). Wenger gives detailed directions to monuments, cemeteries and church ruins, and shares interesting tidbits about his Moravian predecessors.

Methodists

Methodists also were a major missionary force in Monroe County. As early as 1788 they were established in the Stroudsburg area. In the 1800s the Stroudsburg Methodist Church, on Main Street, established in 1853 and still in existence today, became the nucleus of missionary outreaches to Cherry Valley, Paradise, Henryville/Oakland and Mountainhome. Other circuits included Dutotsburg (present-day Delaware Water Gap) and Mauch Chunk (Jim Thorpe). By 1860 there were 36 Methodist churches in the area. The expansion was stopped by the Civil War. After the war, in 1865, the first African Methodist Church opened in Stroudsburg on Third Street, where it remained until 1900. Today there are almost

---

INSIDERS' TIPS

Plan a weekend at Kirkridge Retreat Center, (610) 588-1793, and spend hours wandering through Columcille. Kirkridge is available for family events, so guests in the area for a wedding at Columcille can stay there.

50 Methodist churches in the area — some still standing from last century, such as **Cherry Valley Methodist** in Cherry Valley and **Cherry Lane United Methodist Church** in Tannersville (East Stroudsburg).

Presbyterians

Around 1814, Presbyterians began the Middle Smithfield Church in a barn near Marshalls Creek and shared a pastor and elders with the Shawnee Church. In 1823 they built the red brick church still in use in Middle Smithfield Township on U.S. Highway 209 near Marshalls Creek. Another notable Presbyterian church is Church of the Mountain, which is still in use in Delaware Water Gap (originally Dutotsburg). The Stroudsburg Presbyterian Church was built in 1830 on Sarah Street on land donated by Daniel and Mary Stroud. The Strouds, who were Quakers, gave land to both Quakers and Methodists. Time and again church records for various denominations reveal that land was donated by a Stroud family member even though the family was not part of that church. That the Strouds not only donated land to their church but also to many others demonstrates the tolerant nature of the people in this area at that time.

Quakers

In the 1800s the Quakers established two meeting houses in Stroudsburg — one on Ann Street and one in Quaker Alley. Originally one organization, they split over ideological differences. All that remains of their presence is two cemeteries, one on Eighth and Ann streets, the other in Quaker Alley between Fifth and Sixth streets. The best known vestiges of Quaker influence are Buck Hill Falls Manor, Pocono Manor and Skytop.

These summer resorts were opened by the Quakers from the Philadelphia area. They included not only beautifully appointed main hotels but gracious cottages (today we'd call them mansions), which surrounded the main grounds and were owned by members of their respective Society of Friends groups from Philadelphia. Pocono Lake Preserve was a very quiet camp facility that did not have a resort attached. It was strictly for members only and eschewed the more elegant trappings of the other three. Today Skytop and Pocono Manor remain prestigious resorts. For more information about them, we recommend *The Growth and Variety of Monroe County Resorts* by Roger A. Dunning; you can find a copy at the Monroe County Historical Society.

Catholics

Catholics started arriving in the Poconos in the late 1800s, and are now the largest religious denomination in the region. The first Catholic church, **St. Matthew's**, in East Stroudsburg, was established around 1850. Since then, several other Catholic churches have sprung up all over the Poconos. One of the largest and most active is **St. Luke's Church**, on Main Street in Stroudsburg, with a congregation of more than 2,000. Its members are involved in ecumenical activities, renewal liturgies, outreach programs for the homeless and otherwise needy, and church-sponsored events such as the annual Summer Festival and Flea Market, which lasts two days and provides a healthy dose of bargains and camaraderie. One of St. Luke's most inspiring outreach programs is its annual free Thanksgiving Dinner, served from noon until 2 PM to anyone who wants to attend; transportation can even be arranged if need be.

INSIDERS' TIPS

When vacationing in the Poconos, don't be afraid to stop at a local church-sponsored supper, feast or breakfast — advertised on banners across the roads, on grocery store bulletin boards, in the local newspapers and in church bulletins. Members want you to come. Not only are they fun and inexpensive, but you get to taste dishes and desserts from some of the best local cooks.

Columcille:
A Playground for the Spirit

The grounds of Columcille, south of the Stroudsburgs on the side of Blue Mountain, have been surveyed and catalogued by the Smithsonian National Museum of Art as a megalith park and Celtic art center. They include a round stone chapel, a bell tower and inner and outer megalith circles. The keeper of Columcille, Rev. William H. Cochea Jr., dean of the chapel and an ordained minister, refers to Columcille as a "sacred playground for the odyssey of the human spirit" and "a sacred earth space and place of myth and mystery."

Columcille is named in honor of Colum Cille, the 6th-century Irish monk who founded a monastic community on the island of Iona (which means Isle of the Druids) off the coast of Scotland. St. Columba traveled there in 536 A.D. with a group of monks, according to Cochea, to study and celebrate their Celtic Christianity. When Europe entered the Dark Ages, Iona remained a center of "culture, faith and hope; art flourished; nature was celebrated." The island has been called holy and sacred for centuries, as it was to the Celts and the Druids before the dawn of Christianity. Christians have called it the "cradle of Christianity in the Western Highlands"; modern-day pilgrims still find it a spiritual place.

At one time stones were set up on Iona similar to those erected throughout history in other parts of the world — Easter Island, Stonehenge, Brittany, Karnak. "From early times people have been setting stones. Our Celtic ancestors started setting stones 8,000 years ago. In Brittany and [throughout] France, stones were set. In France 5,000 were set in a straight line (2,300 are still standing). The stones were set in cairns and in various patterns. There is even evidence of stones being set in Wales 16,000 years ago by men living in caves," Cochea said.

This centuries-old impulse to set stones has been called "Megalith Mania." But Cochea believes that impulse comes and goes. Today, there are more than 50,000 stones still standing around the world. No one is quite sure why the impulse happens or what it portends, but many years ago on a trip to Iona, Cochea became aware that he needed to set up stones also. From that time on, he moved toward the vision he had at Iona of standing stones. In 1979, with his partner Fred Lindkvist, the first stone structure at Columcille was erected — the St. Columba Chapel in honor of Colum Cille.

The chapel is a round structure. Benches line the inside walls, and a stone altar stands at its center. There's no formality here. Cochea notes when people come here "the Spirit does its job. They go in with whatever they have. The Spirit works with them; then they leave. And I didn't get in the way." He says he avoids superimposing on people what they will see, or predisposing or conditioning them. Comments he has heard and read in the visitors book include "A healing place."

After the chapel was built, construction of the St. Oran Bell Tower followed. It is patterned on still existing 8th-century Irish bell towers. The Circle of Stones followed the bell tower, then a fresh water pond was added. The Megalith Park was the next and continuing stage of development for Columcille. It includes Thor's Gate, a trilithon (three stones making an arch) gateway, an enormous stone structure somewhat reminiscent of Stonehenge. You'll also find the Glen of the Temple, an arrangement of very large stones set in Celtic patterns — circles, trilathons — and several menhirs (tall upright megaliths). The park is still evolving and includes more than 60 stone settings. Two wooded sites are set aside for men and women who wish to meditate separately.

The word "stone" takes on a new meaning at Columcille. The huge stones are from Columcille and other sites — some nearby. Some weigh at least 30 tons and had to be lifted by cranes and backhoes, sometimes requiring the work of nine people to set. All are set in the ancient tradition: The foundations are dug very deeply and filled with many smaller stones. Then, the megaliths

Reverend William Cohea standing beside the altar in the chapel at Columcille.

are set on the base of smaller stones — the only thing that keep the megaliths erect.

Why did Cochea put these stones here? What motivated him?

"For me the energies of the stones are such that they seem to have their own energy, they draw energy from the land — healing energy," he explains.

He has found that some people respond to the stones, while others are frightened. He is drawn to them and has been since his visit to Iona 39 years ago.

Cochea says he feels the history of the world when he walks through Columcille. He is reminded how long stones have inhabited the earth compared to humankind — a thought he describes as "a very humbling experience."

Columcille is a place for quiet meditation. It draws people to sit and rest against the rocks warmed by the afternoon sun; to stand on the rocks to see as far as they can see;

One of the monoliths that are spaced throughout Columcille.

to inspect the rocks to see what fossils or truths lay hidden in their recesses. There is a feeling of peacefulness, of oneness with the earth. As you wander among the rocks, notice the hushed reverence people exhibit when they enter the circles. Conversations are whispered; wanderers search for places to sit in solitude.

Cochea believes most people today are on a personal and spiritual search. "They don't want to be told about upheaval. There is a new infusion of the Spirit," he explains. The stones of Columcille serve as a reminder of our place in the physical and spiritual world.

"We are not essential. Our role on earth is participatory with other energies. And we need balance. We need to get it back. It seems that something is going on out there.

There are no words for it. Maybe it is only to recognize our role. The role may be only to have compassion — compassion for all. But something good is going on."

Cochea thinks the spiritual search that drives some people to Columcille helps them develop their own inner spirit. "There is so much more than meets the eye. We think our universe is bound up in us, then we see the creative spirit continues to work. The divine spirit, however you want to define it, is still going on."

The St. Columba Chapel at Columcille is used for weddings, remembrance services and other events such as workshops, poetry readings and movies. It is open for free to people of all faiths and traditions. It is a work of art and a nurturing environment where people can derive the natural energy that helps them reach their spiritual potential.

Columcille, (610) 588-1174, is just off the Appalachian Trail. From the Stroudsburgs, take Pa. Highway 191 S. toward Bangor and look for Fox Gap Road. Columcille, right past Kirkridge Retreat Center (see Camps), is one of the beauties and joys you'll come upon driving the winding roads of the Poconos — looking for a camp, a place to eat or a place to rest.

Architectural Gems

Many Poconos churches have been here for more than a century, some even more than two centuries. Quite a few have some tie to our history that makes them an interesting side trip. In this section, we point out three churches of interest because of their architectural and historical significance.

Good Shepherd Church, on Pa. Highway 402 in Blooming Grove, was built in the mid-1800s. It's an exact replica of a Gothic country church in England. It is built of all native stones, with stained-glass windows imported from Italy. It is no longer in use.

The **Dutch Reform Church**, U.S. Highway 209, north of Dingman's Ferry, was built in Greek Revival style in 1850. It has four massive, wooden columns, heavily fluted in the style of ancient Greece. The church is now an antiques shop; it was acquired through a program called the Historic Property Leasing Program, authorized by Section III of the National Historic Preservation Act of 1966, which identifies guidelines for appropriate use of historic structures. The property is owned by the National Park Service, and the leaseholders must comply with park regulations for maintaining the integrity of the building and its setting and demonstrating its compatibility with recreation area activities.

St. Mark's Episcopal Church, in Jim Thorpe is at the bottom of Race Street, and its spires reach up to the mountains that encircle it. This Gothic Revival stone church was built in 1869. It features Tiffany windows, a wrought-iron passenger elevator and the original Minton tile floor made in England. The French Caen stone *reredos* (decorative screens above the rear altar) is a copy of St. George's Chapel, Windsor Castle, England. St. Mark's is still in use and is the site for concerts presented by The Bach and Handel Chorale Inc. (see our Arts and Culture chapter).

Sponsored Activities

The Poconos became a summer vacation spot in the late 1800s and with this designation became host to the many campgrounds, camp meetings and revivals sponsored by a variety of church groups. Methodists were the leaders in this field, and their camp meetings became huge events. The

Church meetings or worship services are sometimes held at Pocono schools or hotels. New churches are opening all the time, and many organizations and local properties are made available to them as they begin their growth.

Photo: Pocono Mountains Vacation Bureau, Inc.

The Poconos are renowned for many beautiful waterfalls.

most famous of the Methodist camp meeting grounds was at Lake Pauponomy — now Saylors Lake. In 1893 an estimated 5,000 people attended a summertime celebration of praying, singing and socializing. Camp meetings gave religious group members places to vacation together. Churches also sponsored musicales, band concerts, poetry readings, picnics, suppers and other social outings.

Today the churches in the Poconos still offer members — and anyone else who wants to come — a variety of social activities, and they continue to contribute to and support the arts. Every week in summer you'll find church-sponsored socials — tasting suppers, strawberry festivals, blueberry festivals, corn and doggie roasts and square dances. Throughout the year, you can enjoy concerts sponsored by church-related groups. Sunday

INSIDERS' TIPS

WVPO AM 850 offers church-sponsored programs on Sunday mornings. You will also find a range of national religious broadcasts on TV. The Blue Ridge cable network offers a religious channel too.

school classes perform plays, particularly during the holiday seasons and vacation Bible school sessions. (Vacation Bible school programs are further evidence of religious tolerance, as students bring friends from other churches and denominations.) Many churches sponsor art events too. And concerts by young artists are coordinated by music teacher associations and other musical groups within the churches. Some churches lend theatrical groups practice space, and some hold music school programs (open to the community) in their buildings.

Arts on the Mountain (see Arts and Culture) grew out of the Trinity Episcopal Church (1896) in Mount Pocono. Artists in all areas participate in dramatic productions as well as opera, art songs, violin concerts and other music events. To celebrate its centennial in 1996, church members organized the Centennial Orchestra, which performs its own summer concerts and even plays for other groups throughout the Poconos. Arts on the Mountain also presents shows featuring local artists such as Peter Salmon, Penny Ross, Andrea Levergood, Daisy Eiman, Gary Kresge and Tom Fish; it also sponsors a student exhibit each year to showcase new, young talent. Shows are free and open to the public.

The Presbyterian **Church of the Mountain**, in Delaware Water Gap, is a strong supporter of the arts and other activities. It was out of this church — particularly the work of Rev. William Cochea (see this chapter's Columcille sidebar) with local jazz greats Phil Woods, Eubie Green and others — that the Delaware Water Gap Jazz Festival was born. And from this popular festival comes the recently released *Jazz Mass* CD from the annual event of the same name that's part of the Delaware Water Gap Celebration of the Arts. Sunday evening concerts are presented all summer long in the outdoor gazebo on the church lawn (inside if it's raining). Church of the Mountain members built and maintain a shelter year round for Appalachian Trail hikers.

Historic **St. Mark's Episcopal Church** presents an annual concert series, aptly named "Music from Historic St. Mark's Episcopal Church," which consists of church recitals and concerts throughout the year. It's also a starting place for various art walks and other cultural activities that fill a full plate of cultural offerings in Jim Thorpe.

Recommended Reading

Many informative books about worship in the Poconos carry titles whose names do not specifically indicate them as books about churches. The Monroe County Historical Society has an 1886 edition of a massive volume (to which we are greatly indebted) entitled *History of Wayne, Pike and Monroe Counties, Pennsylvania,* by Alfred Mathews, that gives detailed accounts of the development of various churches, including who started them, who donated land for their buildings and so on. It's interesting not only because of its informal style but also because it was written in chronological proximity to the events it describes. The historical society also has history files of many different churches and many other volumes that touch on the influence of places of worship in Pocono history.

Another significant book in the Monroe County Historical Society's collection is the *Guide to Cemeteries and Burial Grounds of Monroe County, Pennsylvania,* compiled by Dale E. Berger. For those who enjoy reading about history and stories detailed on tombstones, or searching for long-lost records of dates and births, this book is a good find. It is well-researched, and much of its information about early church histories is culled from the aforementioned *History of Wayne, Pike and Monroe Counties, Pennsylvania*, condensed and described in the present-day context.

Whether you choose to worship in song, through art or through prayer and wherever you choose to do so — in churches, among rocks, in synagogues or temples — the Poconos have a place for you. The ideals of religious tolerance espoused by William Penn remain in practice by your hosts and neighbors.

The Poconos' primary media outlets are small regional newspapers.

Media

If you're looking for the lowdown on news and events in the Poconos, you'll find a smattering of local and regional information sources to consult. The daily *Pocono Record* newspaper, a handful of community papers and special-interest publications and a range of regional television and radio stations — from as nearby as the Scranton/Wilkes-Barre and Allentown/Bethlehem areas to as far-reaching as Philadelphia and New York City — keep residents abreast of local, regional, national and even international happenings.

Here is a rundown of some media choices you can access in the Poconos.

Newspapers and Magazines

Pocono Record
511 Lenox St., Stroudsburg • 421-3000

Acquired in 1946 by Ottaway Newspapers as the *Daily Record*, the *Pocono Record* is published every morning and is the only Poconos daily newspaper. It is the primary news and advertising publication in Monroe and Pike counties, and it keeps its finger on the pulse of the Poconos with circulation into Wayne, Carbon and Northampton counties — even Warren County, New Jersey. Local news coverage, particularly sports, is very comprehensive.

The *Pocono Record's* history can be traced back to April 2, 1894, when the *Stroudsburg Daily Times* began publication as a weekly. The earliest newspaper in Monroe County was the *Stroudsburg Gazette* from the early 1800s and its successor *The Monroe Democrat*, which was founded in 1836.

Called *Pocono Record* since 1965, the newspaper has grown and diversified in recent years. The advertising and editorial offices were completely renovated in 1996. A new printing facility was constructed in Tannersville in 1995. New media projects include this book; the annual *Factory Outlet and Off-Price Guide*; *Dignity*; InfoLink, a telephone information service that may be accessed by calling 476-5465; and a large-print, easy-to-use phone directory. The advertising in the *Pocono Record* gives a good indication of local stores and services. Look for restaurant and nightclub advertisements on Friday and Saturday to find out about specials and band schedules.

Circulation figures are 21,535 for Monday through Saturday editions and 25,842 on Sundays.

Pike County Dispatch
105 W. Catharine St., Milford • 296-6641

Another newspaper with a long history, the *Dispatch* began publishing in 1856. It is the primary source of news in Pike County. This weekly, published every Thursday morning, focuses on community events, church activities, school news and legal activities. Here is where you will see pictures of the star athletes and scholastic leaders. This is the only newspaper to offer timely news on issues within Pike County. The layout apparently has not changed much in the last 140 years. Pages are packed with columns of narrow type and few photos, like newspapers in the good old days.

The Gazette
84-88 Fowler St., Port Jervis, N.Y.
• (914) 856-5383

Another weekly owned by Ottaway Newspapers, *The Gazette* hits newsstands in the northern section of the Pocono region every Friday. Much of its coverage is devoted to New York State; however, Pike County information is provided.

The Pike County Courier
511 Broad St., Milford • 296-6397

One of the new kids on the newsstands

just celebrated its seventh anniversary in 1996. This monthly boasts a little bit of everything. Scoops on local issues share space with gardening, horoscopes, cooking, music and fitness columns. The emphasis is placed on Pike County stories written by local authors. Prominent and unique area residents are profiled regularly.

The Chronicle
RR 2, Box 132, Dingmans Ferry • 828-7782

This biweekly, printed on Fridays, comprehensively covers the township meetings of Pike County. It also contains *The Country Road Gazette*, devoted to stories about nature and pets.

Pocono Post
P.O. Box 100, Gilbert, Pa. 18331
• (610) 681-6499, (800) 526-7033

This weekly handles the West End, including Brodheadsville and surrounding communities, and is printed every Thursday. It contains schedules of upcoming events, police reports, school news and an excellent recipe column. Pleasant Valley School District sports activities are covered very well.

The River Reporter
No. 8 Main Street, Narrowsburg, N.Y. 12764 • (914) 252-7414

Southern New York state and northern Pike and Wayne counties are thoroughly documented in this weekly, printed every Thursday. Its tagline boasts that the paper "spans three states, five counties and over 60 communities and a river." Most of its pages are devoted to issues and news stories. The sports section and automotive column also are extensive.

The News Eagle
522 Spring St., Hawley • 226-4547

The largest-circulation newspaper in Pike and Wayne counties at 7,300 copies, *The News Eagle* is published every Tuesday, Thursday

and Saturday morning. Its content combines syndicated columnists, legal notices, local sports and regional news. Like the *Pike County Dispatch*, it packs a lot of information onto a few pages, usually 14.

Weekly Almanac
709 Church St., Honesdale • 253-9270

Published every Wednesday, the *Weekly Almanac* provides coverage of Hawley and Honesdale school activities, community events, local sports and church happenings. Several pages are devoted to editorials and letters to the editor, providing a good idea of where residents stand on local issues.

The Wayne Independent
220 Eighth St., Honesdale • 253-3055

National news and syndicated political columns diversify the content of this newspaper, which is published daily Monday through Friday and has a circulation of 6,198. It strikes a comfortable balance between world-event highlights and more extensive reporting on local concerns.

The Times News
First and Iron Sts., Lehighton
• (610) 377-2051

A 16,200-circulation newspaper published daily Monday through Saturday, *The Times News* combines national and international news with reporting from Carbon, Monroe, Lehigh, Schuykill and Northampton counties. Sports, both local and national, are thoroughly covered. The paper operates a telephone information service called TN Voicelink that may be accessed by calling either (610) 377-9133 or (717) 645-2222.

Northeastern Pennsylvania Employment Weekly
108 N. Washington Ave., Ste. 1105, Scranton • 344-2535

Although not based in the Pocono Moun-

For a free weekly local television guide, look for *Pocono TV Times* at the entrances to supermarkets and other stores.

Photo: Pocono Mountains Vacation Bureau, Inc.

The Poconos feature some of the East's finest fall foliage.

tains, this weekly is worth noting because it is filled with advertisements for professional jobs from throughout northeastern Pennsylvania. If you are looking for skilled employment in the region, you'll want to pick up a copy of this paper. Lower-paying jobs posted by regional job centers are listed in the back.

Freebies

In addition to the aforementioned newspapers, you can pick up many free publications at shop entrances in the Poconos.

This Week in the Poconos
Pa. Hwy. 940, Pocono Pines • 839-7103

This small magazine with a glossy, color cover is packed with information on area shops, restaurants and attractions and is one of the area's most popular tourist publications. A scan of its pages will provide visitors countless ideas for things to do. It focuses on Monroe County, Jim Thorpe and the Lake Wallenpaupack area.

The Pocono Where to Book
10 Wintergreen Ct., Stroudsburg • 992-8000

This is a slick, full-color advertising publication filled with coupons for restaurants and attractions, mostly in the Monroe County area.

The Blue Valley Times
411 S. Fourth St., Bangor • (610) 588-2310

The Slate Belt's largest weekly newspaper is this free publication. It is dominated by ads but also has stories on local events, church and school activities, a column for children, financial tips and regional sports.

The Press
1 Broadway, Bangor • (610) 588-6416

Its slogan, "serving the entire Slate Belt with happy news," accurately sums up the news offered in this free weekly. It is filled with pictures of smiling children who won school awards, star athletes and cute toddlers holding pets. Stories highlight local events.

News of the Poconos
Old Schoolhouse Rd., Swiftwater • 839-7967

Upcoming events and stories on local shops comprise the editorial content of this paper published 10 times each year. The owners, longtime Pocono residents, write an enjoyable column at the beginning of each issue. Some stories are saddled with humorous bylines such as an article on an Indian gift shop by Nate Eva Merikan and one on a seafood restaurant by Ivana Lobb Sturr.

Postscript
First and Iron Sts., Lehighton • (610) 681-6499

This is a weekly covering events, attractions and shops in the southern part of the Poconos. It is published by the owners of the *Pocono Post* and *The Times News*.

The Pocono Shopper
96 S. Courtland St., East Stroudburg • 421-4800

Other than a very interesting history column, horoscopes and press releases on local events, this weekly is designed as a vehicle for local businesses to promote themselves. It is hand-delivered to homes in most of Monroe County and readily available at the entrances of supermarkets. Other editions are distributed throughout the Poconos. If you want to compare prices at the local supermarkets, this paper is worth a look.

The Commuters' Express
P.O. Box 606, Reeders 18352 • 476-0601

Restaurant, movie and music reviews give those on their way to work something to pass the time on the bus. Nature, art and business articles also are included. The columnists are very good writers, making the paper a fun read any time. The paper is published monthly.

Focus
U.S. Hwy. 209 and Kevin Ln., Brodheadsville • 992-4949

Published weekly, *Focus* features event notices for the southern Poconos and the Slate Belt plus health, home improvement and real estate columns among its many advertisements.

Dignity
511 Lenox St., Stroudsburg • 421-3000

A product of the *Pocono Record*, *Dignity* is published monthly and caters to the 50-and-older population. It carries profiles on noteworthy older residents and covers events of interest to seniors. Essential phone numbers and activity calendars are featured.

The Forward Papers
2132 Wallace St., Stroudsburg • 629-8841

A quarterly literary magazine written by local authors, *The Forward Papers* mixes poetry, fiction, art, editorials and regular columns. It provides some thought-provoking reading and is available at stores throughout Monroe County.

Pocono Bride
RR 4 Box 4291, Bossardsville Rd., Stroudsburg 18360 • 992-5477

Everything a couple will need to plan a wedding in the Poconos can be found in this quarterly, glossy magazine. Articles offer tips on decorating, receptions, gowns and current trends. Advertisers include resorts suitable for

INSIDERS' TIPS

Many residents of extremely rural parts of the Poconos rely on satellite television dishes and video stores for entertainment because the cable company does not reach them.

receptions, videographers/photographers and limousine services.

Radio

Adult Contemporary
WSBG 93.5 FM
WDNH 95.3 FM
WTSX 96.7 FM

Classic Rock
WZZO 95.1 FM

College Radio
WESS 93.3 FM

Country
WWCC 1590 AM
WHCY 106.3 FM
WRNJ 107.1 FM
WDLC 1490 AM

Oldies
WYNS 1160 AM
WODE 99.9 FM

Talk, News, Weather
WVPO 840 AM

Television

ABC
WNEP-TV 16

CBS
WYOU-TV 22

Fox
WOLF-TV 38

Independent
WFMZ-TV 69

NBC
WBRE-TV 28

Public Television
WLVT Channel 39
WVIA Channel 44

Cable Television

Blue Ridge Cable Television Inc.
471 Delaware Ave., Palmerton
• (610) 826-2551

This is the cable television provider for the Pocono Mountains area. For information on rates for hookup, call the main office listed in the header. The company also has offices at 200 N. First Street, Lehighton, (610) 377-2250; 920 Ehler Street, Stroudsburg, 421-0780; 20 W. Ridge Street, Lansford, 645-5511; 204 Fourth Street, Milford, 296-8200; U.S. Highway 209, Gilbert, (610) 681-6100; P.O. Box 141 Tunkhannock, Pa. 18657, 836-5422; and P.O. Box 124, Hawley, Pa. 18428, 226-4914.

Blue Ridge Cable Television TV 13
936 Elm St., Lehighton • (610) 826-4060

The most comprehensive locally produced television station in the Poconos, channel 13 may be picked up by cable viewers in Monroe, Pike, Carbon, Schuylkill, Northampton, Lackawanna, Berks and Lehigh counties. At 5:30, 8:30 and 9:30 PM nightly, "Eyewatch News" provides complete coverage of local news, weather and sports. Other programs produced in-house discuss NASCAR racing, environmental issues and computers. A children's show called "Kids' Express" airs at 10 AM on Saturday and is rebroadcast at 9 AM Sunday, 3 PM Tuesday and 10:30 AM Thursday. Kim Bell hosts "Coffee Break," an informal talk show, Monday through Friday mornings at 10 AM with replays nightly at 9 PM. Local high school athletes and coaches are featured on "Monday Evening Quarterback" during fall and winter every Monday at 7:30 PM. Additional shows include talk shows devoted to education and entertainment (even one in Pennsylvania Dutch!) and a religious program with scripture readings. TV 13 also covers live local sports, political debates, television auctions, telethons and beauty pageants.

Index of Advertisers

Index